# AMERICA NOW

## AN INQUIRY INTO
## CIVILIZATION IN THE UNITED STATES

# AMERICA NOW

## AN INQUIRY INTO
## CIVILIZATION IN THE UNITED STATES

BY

THIRTY-SIX AMERICANS

EDITED, WITH AN INTRODUCTION, BY

HAROLD E. STEARNS

THE LITERARY GUILD OF AMERICA, INC.
NEW YORK          N. Y.

# CONTENTS

# CONTENTS

## EDUCATION

## TYPES OF LIVING

## HEALTH

## RACE

## RELIGION

## SUPPLEMENT

AMERICAN CIVILIZATION FROM THE FOREIGN POINT OF VIEW

*Translated from the Spanish by Henriette Romeike Van de Velde.

# INTRODUCTION

TODAY the fellowship of men with each other—out of which any true spirit of co-operation alone arises—is not to be found where most of us vainly and too often with passion look for it. Certainly it is not to be found in a narrow and inbred nationalism; and for civilized men, just as certainly, it is not to be found in race or in color. Aristocratic distinctions of caste, even the financial gradations of income which used to justify these distinctions but have now come to constitute a separate caste system in themselves—these aristocratic distinctions, just as inexorably as the more popular delusions of prestige, lead any perceptive and responsive friendships among men to the blind alley of barren exclusiveness. For the little islands of "clubs" and "sets" at which we laugh, within the local seas of humanity, are only ridiculous in the same way as are the larger continents of self-conscious races and self-conscious nations among the cosmopolitan oceans of the modern world.

Today, as always, the fellowship of men with each other is to be found in ideas, in a certain common point of view towards all problems. Though superficially the war-like mind appears to flourish stronger than ever, in reality it is waging a bitter losing battle—and it is trying desperately and futilely to impose its will upon a world which may not long, because it cannot long, support its philosophy of force, violence, and unreason. As we look towards Asia, and as we look towards Europe, we might be forgiven for believing that in our time men seem only to follow a single course with consistency and determination, and that course the one of self-destruction.

But happily there are other international forces at work besides the forces let loose by the war-mongers. These are the forces symbolized by science, by rapid communication and ease of travel, by commerce and productive industry. If the militarist were not too stupid to know it, these forces are not merely agents to give him new instruments for his old game, they are also powerful disinfectants against the whole game itself. If the militarist does not directly encourage, at least he thrives in a fetid atmosphere of international anarchy, and it is this atmosphere which these forces are helping to cleanse. The real prophylaxis, however, is something deeper and subtler and more difficult to combat: It is the prophylaxis of ideas. And these ideas are not the property of any one man, or any one group or any one nation. They are the common property of all men of good will; they constitute the communism beside which the shabby political doctrine of envy usually called by that name is as evanescent as steam—the communism of the spirit.

For the men and women who make up the list of contributors to this book are, many of them, personally not acquainted with each other. They live in different parts of the country; they are of different "racial" origins; their education and training and experience concerning American life are as variegated as our physical landscapes and our weather. But they are united in something which is stronger than mere chance neighborliness or mutual business and professional activities. They instinctively know the difference between interested propaganda and disinterested ideas; they have been disciplined by facts and reality rather than have they felt impelled to dress up fancy and desire into a pretty picture or a "perfect" system. In a word, they are united in that strongest fellowship of all, because it sets men free—the fellowship of the truth.

To enlist such a group in so complicated an enterprise as *America Now* inevitably demanded on my part time and patience, and—at least I can only hope it was so considered—a certain degree of tact and avoidance of the dogmatic temper. Nowadays, unfortunately, the hitherto laudatory adjective, tolerant, has a kind of hostile aura of vacillation and intellectual dubiety. Yet in the historic and truest sense of that adjective this is a tolerant book. And in that respect I believe it reflects our day and our time, at least here in the relatively calm oasis of America. Even Mr. Ernest Hemingway, for example, although he himself may not be fully aware of it and "hard-boiled" although he may pretend to be, is really, in his latest book, *To Have and Have Not,* attempting to make scallawags attractive—or at least to explain them. Indeed, the tones of mockery or of bitterness are singularly lacking in contemporary social criticism; even the communists have at least feigned to turn gentle and now—reflecting the temper of the day, practically in spite of themselves as it were—preach the revolution in almost honied words.

I think it noteworthy and indicative of our present tolerant attitude that in this book one of the most difficult and thorny topics—the topic of religion in the United States—is presented both from the Catholic and the

Protestant points of view. Without going into the question of how the horror of the present civil conflict in Spain may have galvanized the Catholic Church's defenders into a re-assessment of its true function and contribution to civilization, I question whether, even a generation ago, any editor could have obtained an article on Catholicism in the United States so dispassionate, simple, and American in the best sense of that adjective as Father Talbot's in this book. I am certain, too, that an analysis of the Protestant faiths, in the objective manner in which Mr. Douglas does it here, would likewise have been next to impossible to procure. From this a foreigner might conclude that we are more religiously-minded than we were previously. But the correct solution, it seems to me, is rather that our civilization, on one hand, has become less frivolous in tone, and religion itself, on the other, more directly concerned with immediate social problems. For many good souls this last means a loss of other-worldliness and a softening of doctrinal integrity; yet carried to its logical extreme this view implies the kind of sharp divorce between the concerns of this world and one's hopes for the next which is utterly alien to the American temperament.

It is noteworthy, also, that for four important subjects I found women contributors, as well as a woman translator from the Spanish for the article on the Mexican point of view towards the United States; and perhaps I should add that I myself have no particular feminist theories, one way or the other. It simply was the case that in these fields these particular writers were highly competent, and also, of course, willing to co-operate. Yet I very much doubt if a similar book in Germany or France or England or even Russia (except possibly *there,* self-consciously and for propaganda effect) would have included a like number of women writers. Whatever the facts may be abroad, however, certainly any book by many authors on civilization in the United States today which did not include among those authors at least a few women would be very likely to be one-sided and astigmatic. Certainly the present volume, whatever its faults, could hardly be called that. And if, for example, the specific topic of "Sex" is not included in this book, that is because women themselves have assured me the topic is "old hat" and *démodé.* As well, they say, have a specific article on cooking or nursing or the training of babies. Apparently sex, like philosophy, covers both too much ground—and too little. Besides, even for our children, any residual mystery about it appears to have vanished.

Perhaps I may be forgiven a somewhat personal final word. At bottom

I think it has been because I wanted a clarification of my own views, because, despite my thirteen years' French Sabbatical, I still have been more interested in my own country than in any other: Because of this I have gone ahead, sometimes when the difficulties seemed insuperable. Back of every book, however complicated it may seem in appearance and structure, is, or at least ought to be, a simple and direct human impulse. This book is no exception. Back of it is the desire to discover what civilization in this country is really like in this year of 1938, what, in brief, *America Now* is.

This book has furnished me with such a discovery, and it has also been an intellectual adventure in the doing. If it constitutes only a fraction of that discovery and that intellectual adventure for its readers, I think all of us who have contributed to it will feel amply repaid for our attempt.

HAROLD E. STEARNS.

*Locust Valley, Long Island.*
  *September, 1938.*

# THE ARTS

# AMUSEMENT: RADIO AND MOVIES

*[Louis R. Reid]*

## I. RADIO

IN THE production or mass entertainment, as exemplified in the last decade, by radio and motion pictures, America has achieved a position as startling and as significant as the rise of the industrial era following the Civil War. Upon these inexpensive, easily-accessible and closely-related amusements the public is so dependent that vast commercial, sociologic, technological and—not the least—artistic forces have been given new and powerful play in the nation.

As fantastic as it is incredible has been the development of these allied amusements with their billion-dollar investments, their properties employing hundreds of thousands of persons, their programs and pictures penetrating into the furthermost reaches of the globe. More than 85,000,000 persons are said to attend the film theatres in this country each week, while the national radio audience is reputed at more than 70,000,000 persons. Together, the radio and the screen dominate the American industrial world. Of the 90,000 motion picture theatres in existence, nearly one-fifth are in the United States. There are 600-odd broadcasting stations.

Obviously, radio's scope is the greater, because of the very limitlessness of the ether waves and because its mission is not solely to entertain but to educate and inform. The screen's purpose is only to divert, though as a patterner of human behavior, it too exerts an educational function; it shapes intelligence, emotions, concepts of life and character in spite of its wholly show-concerned producers.

Essentially, what the average film patron desires from the screen and the average listener expects—and selects—from his radio set is entertainment, such diverting matter as will provide escape from realities, furnish for a brief and welcome period the illusion of happiness and romance. The entertainment industry has assumed imposing force. So vast is the amusement spirit of today that the supershowmen of radio and the screen possess an economic and social power that is surpassed only by the government itself.

3

And yet broadcasters and film producers are at a disadvantage in offering entertainment. Their public has become so sated with impressive items on the airwaves and the screen that it no longer waits in keen anticipation of grandiose plans for its diversion. It demands the superlative in entertainment continuously, unmindful that the superlative is as hard to achieve in radio or the movies as it is in any field of endeavor. Added to their problems is the general economic distress with its accompanying decrease in theatre attendance and radio set purchases. The radio world gazes hopefully at the horizon for the sensational emergence of television upon a practical armchair basis, knowing that television, by revolutionizing electrical entertainment, will rehabilitate its finances. The motion picture world, as yet unconcerned over television because it does not believe film to be adaptable to it, seeks within itself, by charges and countercharges, to place the responsibility for the growing public indifference.

Light entertainment is the most popular part of radio programs. Based upon a tested vaudeville formula, the principal ingredient of which is sentimental song inspired chiefly under the sexual glamour and the luxuriant languor of Hollywood, it continues year after year as the backbone of American broadcasting. True, there is an audience, more respectable than respected, for the music of the masters, for discussions of every conceivable subject under the sun, but it is diversion that makes up the major portion of the broadcasting menu.

The radio showman, in particular, is handicapped in his entertainment mission. He cannot risk the displeasure of the Washington overlords and the possible loss of his operating license by drawing upon the often amusing vulgarity of the revue stage. He dare not now even risk competition with Hollywood in airing the insinuating persuasiveness of Miss Mae West lest he be accused of violating good taste. Indeed, his one misstep in this direction led to the hilarious official action of preserving for all time a recording of Miss West's reputedly tropical sentimentality within the appropriately chilled archives of Washington. He has yet to discover how he can convey sex appeal other than through the vicarious seductiveness of vocal cords.

Entertainment material is limited by the very consuming character of the microphone itself. A comedian, for example, is no better than his script, and the inexorable necessity of changing the program with each appearance at the microphone places a ruinous strain upon resourcefulness and originality. How can he freshen his material, change his act?

There is a limit to his invention and his energy. He may amuse his studio audience, the presence of which he deems essential as a barometer of his comic appeal, with bits of stage business, but if he is hopeful of making himself a household god, with all the gaudy glorification that accompanies such recognition, he soon realizes that the microphone is interested only in what he says and the way he says it.

Throughout the years it is those entertainers able to alter their styles of entertainment, even to discarding one type of role and assuming that of another, or who, if necessary, can present old jokes, old songs and situations in new dress, that succeed in remaining in the front rank of the radio parade. The microphone has no special welcome for art or beauty per se. The voice is primarily important, aided, of course, by such adroit uses of material of a calculatedly universal appeal as can be manifested.

It is this requirement of universality of appeal, together with the perverse blatancy of its commercial programs, which operates so effectively in hampering the progress of American radio entertainment. By striving to please all classes of people, radio all too often ends by satisfying none. In its efforts to sell its wares, it destroys, through the stridency and verbosity of its cries, the very good will it would create.

Satire, save occasionally in its broadest aspect, has no place at present on the broadcasting menu. There is no hospitality for the kind of sharp and swift wit which, on the stage, serves often to puncture social and political sham and stuffiness. Not so long ago, George M. Cohan appeared briefly as a master of ceremonies of a sponsored program, during the course of which he held up to kindly mockery radio's commercial circus. It was hailed enthusiastically by that small group who are impatient of the microphone's progress as a satiric force, but who are prone to forget that commercial radio in general will not tolerate any raillery at its expense. Cohan's broadcasting career was short-lived, and he retired to the friendlier shelter of the theatre, leaving the microphone to those entertainers who not only know the rules of the game but respect them.

The only acceptable approach radio has had in examining the foibles of contemporary civilization was in the observations of the late Will Rogers. His wide appeal, however, was not as a satirist but as a shrewd editorial cartoonist who, through a sly sense of humor and a native pungency of expression, was able to reduce the politically great to outlines of humanness recognizable to the average man. The broadcasters have held a vain search, since his passing, for one who can take his place, who can, by a felt-gloved spoofing of the current scene, open up an infinite supply of material to the comedian, the script writer and the tunesmith. Resigned, apparently, to the failure of their hunt, they have, with despairing impatience, given more and more time to those ubiquitous and highly-publicized commentators who pontificate upon the state of the nation to a lucrative benefit to themselves out of all proportion to the dogmatic cheerlessness of their observations.

Music continues as radio's principal field of endeavor, and to music radio gives its most skillful attention. Broadcasters have been enterprising in the development and cultivation of dance rhythms. Though they still are primly-squeamish about recognizing jazz as such, they have accomplished the astounding service of making the whole world jazz-conscious. Whatever its label by the broadcasters—at present "swing" is the cherished trademark—there is no question of the worldwide conquest of American dance music, and radio is responsible. To balance to some degree the stimulants of the rhythm-makers, the broadcasters pretentiously serve special blue plates of the music masters. The growth in popularity of symphony orchestras in America is due in large measure to radio's influence.

The listings of the symphony orchestras permit the radiomen to solace their artistic consciences, harried from prolonged occupation at the sales counters. Invariably entered in the red side of the ledgers, they give the broadcasters' bow to artistic idealism potent support of the principle of public service under which they are allowed by a benevolently censorious government to operate.

For several years their outstanding musical program has been the Sunday recital of the New York Philharmonic Orchestra. Its heavy cost to the Columbia Broadcasting System has been balanced by the enormous prestige it has brought its radio backers.

Now, one of the most healthy aspects of American broadcasting is the competitive system of its operation. Obviously, the public is the gainer, no matter how costly the effort on the part of one group of broadcasters to improve upon the ideas and standards of another. Thus, the CBS monopoly of the Philharmonic led to the organization by the rival National Broadcasting Company of a special symphony orchestra which derived its chief appeal and its sudden and solid prestige from its guidance by the now indisputably infallible Toscanini. Evidently, it was a simple matter for the NBC to bring Toscanini back to America, but unfortunately his concerts were scheduled on Saturday night and despite a bril-

liant and unceasing publicity campaign they failed to move the less zeal-
ous music lovers to sacrifice willingly, if temporarily, their customary
pursuits.

Mass America is still more concerned with Tin Pan Alley's cacophonic
absorption in moonlit romance than with Toscanini's bows to Beethoven
or Stokowski's brushes with Bach, though the growing generation is
showing an increasing interest in and appreciation of the masters. Without losing sight of the fact that America proudly takes credit for a
Gershwin, a Berlin, a Duke Ellington and a Benny Goodman, the younger
generation is today as familiar with Tschaikowsky as its parents were with
von Tilzer. But enjoying Tschaikowsky, it also delights in the current
rhythmic (and frequently melodious) expression of American gusto and
vitality.

Despite its incalculable value as a musical medium, radio has signally
failed to date to attract the foremost composers in writing expressly for the
microphone. Unquestionably, the arbitrary limitations of its time schedules are a leading obstacle to its appeal as a creative outlet. But, probably,
its sprawling novelty, the bewildering vastness of its power, its cold,
mechanical impersonableness and its lack of musical tradition play even a
larger part in the indifference of top-ranking composers. While it commands a vast audience, the microphone's appeal is wholly ephemeral.
There is no emotional éclat, no critical rhapsody or *danse de joie* to a
radio presentation of even the masters, save on those occasions when the
reappearances or farewells of Toscanini possess a news significance.

Radio will not come into its own as a creative musical force until it
attracts the talents of such men as Strauss, Sibelius, Respighi, Schoen-
berg, Shostakovitch, to say nothing of such noteworthy penmen of our
own panorama as Carpenter, Cadman, Delamarter, Taylor, Grofe, Still,
Bloom, Lane and others. A complete revolution in musical tradition, of
course, will be necessary for such a condition. It will be necessary, for
example, for broadcasters to set aside large portions of their own funds or
the funds of their yet-to-be-discovered endowments. It will mean also the
regular attention of music critics who will be forced to alter, on occasion,
their professional habits, substituting the simple disturbances of the sitting-
room for the manifold distractions of the concert hall. A new and proper
respectfulness will also be quite as necessary on the part of the listening
public.

Radio is still playing second fiddle in its musical presentation. It does
not inspire a Ravel to indite a "Bolero," but it can be omnipotently present

at the concert hall première of a "Bolero," and it can take the questionable satisfaction of being mainly responsible for the work's subsequent acclaim, albeit an acclaim achieved almost at the expense of national deafness.

Radio, thus, is an avid, if irresponsible, promoter of musical good will. There are times when it is also an effective pulmotor. It was radio which came to the rescue of the Metropolitan Opera Company, when, before the emergence of Flagstad and the resurgence of Wagner, it seemed that that organization was to be assigned a place in the American amusement limbo along with vaudeville and the minstrel show. The radio panjam-drums dipped again into their heaping treasuries, thumped their publicity drums, and, abandoning their custom of condensing everything to fit a time clock, brought grand opera in its full length to the firesides of the nation.

Everything is grist that comes to the microphone, from the newest agitation of the torso, the newest cogitation of the New Deal to the latest raucousness of the world's innumerable men of destiny. Between their output of jazz and comedy the radio mills grind out for the special diversion of the armchairs whatever news sensation is breaking, the turmoil along the Potomac, the tense reports of varied sports contests. Along with the excitement is a deadly parade of advisers to the household, maudlin story-tellers, inane domestic sketches.

It is chiefly women and children, who, during the daytime hours, can, if they choose, take or leave such excitement or ennui (it is a matter of personal opinion) as is available. The men of the house, on the other hand, must mostly be content with nighttime programs. For them, when the chores and the chase of the mocking dollar are done, come the sales messages of sponsors, and the accompanying routine of this clown and that orchestra. It is a strange paradox that the producers of radio put forth their greatest efforts to please their night audience though the entertainment offered has little of the spectacular appeal that frequently highlights the daytime hours.

Program repetition has become the curse of broadcast entertainment. The radio men still rely upon important news events to supply the necessary note of novelty to their schedules. The handicap of such a policy is that they never know when to expect the news events. There are frequently long stretches between the graphic description of a prison fire and the soothing accents of a President as a nation seemed headed for the financial, if not the social, equality of a nudist camp; between Byrd in Antarctica and a dirigible aflame at Lakehurst; between the broadcast of a wedding or even a funeral in Westminster Abbey and the unmajestic but immensely dramatic voice of a tired little man who, "at long last," could speak of the utter impossibility "of discharging my duties of King without the help and support of the woman I love."

So it is to their program producers—the showmen in the studios—they turn. The showmen are slow in responding. It is because they are too loyal to what has always proved popular. A bill comprising a band, a vocalist, a jester and a master of ceremonies has been successful. Therefore, the showman believes such a bill will always be successful, Thus results the repetition that has become the curse of radio entertainment. The program varies little. The treadmill goes on, and boredom creeps into those parlors whose inhabitants have neglected to turn the switch, only to be expelled when the broadcasters are up to their noses in news.

Radio broadcasting would seem to be marking time. The studios wait hopefully for something startling and spectacular—an around-the-world flight, for example—which will capture the nation, focus attention upon the microphone in something of the same degree that features a coronation or a Presidential campaign.

New ideas in programs? Where are they to be found? Where, indeed, are the radio men to turn next and avoid, thereby, the devastating blight of monotony? The music shelves have been ransacked and reransacked for material until today it is doubtful there is any music in the world that has not been poured into the radio hopper. The dance bands have had—are still having—their day; the crooner and torch-singer theirs. Every class of professional entertainer, save, happily, that of the female impersonator, has found in radio, at one time or another, the promised land. When it seemed, at last, that no professionals remained outside the radio gates, the bars were let down to a terrifying stampede of amateurs hopeful that ambition and persistence would make up for lack of talent and personality in gaining a foothold in the new El Dorado. The amateur craze, continuing over many months, was finally routed by the novel and sudden appearance of a ventriloquist's dummy who, under the magnetic name of Charlie McCarthy, has been —perhaps, still is—sitting astride the amusement world.

The Broadway comedian, the Hollywood star, now so abundant in all phases of amusement, the ever accessible "guest" artist from various pastures of entertainment, have, through the years, occupied the principal throne chairs in the radio realm, but as the rumble of impatience echoes from the firesides the broadcasters are wondering about the permanence of the throne chairs' occupation. Something new, something different —that is the eternal cry of the parlors. And the radio men are deeply perplexed as to how to satisfy it.

A broadcasting trend lasts ordinarily but a few months and then its popularity wanes. In keeping with what was known as "the Hollywood trend," programs were moved en masse to the West Coast as a means of fulfilling better the long-suppressed desire of the public to be on intimate armchair terms with the fabulous deities of the films. The Hollywood stars, already earning the largest salaries in the history of the world, found themselves scaling even higher economic heights as they took over the commanding positions on radio programs.

Like the broadcasting trends before them, the Hollywood programs also could not escape the curse of monotony and repetition. And the radio rulers were soon sighting their vision to new horizons, seeking an answer to the harassing question: "What next?" They are answering it in part by reoccupying their old and reliable Hindenburg line of New York, the while they wait for the garrulous gunners of politics to resume their blasting of the parlors in the deafening battle for the White House.

Meanwhile, the radio men have an opportunity. They can demonstrate their efficiency and enterprise during their spare moments by evolving new uses for their unsponsored hours. They can experiment in the still much-untilled field of drama. They can work out new ideas in musical instrumentation. They can summon more world leaders of thought to the microphone. They can evolve plans for easing the nation's earache of too-aggressive sales talk. Perhaps, also, they can give some study to the preparation of a formula by which commercial sponsors would not duplicate the entertainment styles of each other so insistently through a pathetic conviction that what was once successful is always so.

They have a reputation to maintain—the reputation that the American radio system is the most progressive on earth, presenting its programs, as it does, without prejudice and with a minimum of restriction. At least, in America all points of view are given access. At least, in America there is some effort to give listeners what they want rather than, as is the case in Europe, what the government decides it wants the listeners to hear. The American broadcasters cannot rest on their oars, satisfied that they have omitted from the microphone no phase of the bewildering variety of American life. Assuredly, they cannot be content if they are to fulfill their destiny as the supershowmen, along with their fellows in film production, of modern America.

Radio's world-wide scope has provided the broadcasters with the zest to hook up the Vatican one minute and Moscow the next, of following the serenity of Scandinavia with the confusion of Spain, of switching from a celebration of Bach to a celebration of Bacchus, of passing with ridiculous ease from hosannas to hi-de-hos. In their mad competition for new worlds to conquer they have overreached themselves. They have tapped every part of the globe, save Mt. Everest and the African jungle. They have penetrated the stratosphere and the ocean's depths. Presidents, premiers, publicists, priests, politicians, professors, poltroons, all have lifted their voices; some, as was the case of the late Ramsay MacDonald, with a surpassing poetic fervor; some, as was the case of Mussolini, with a surprising lack of dictatorial arrogance; some, as was the case of Bernard Shaw, with a caustic examination of our politico-economic bewilderment, delivered with a mellowed winsomeness that softened its sting; some, as was the case of the late Huey Long, offering incredible economic panaceas with an ear-tickling blend of the street corner vendor, the itinerant evangelist and the old-fashioned stump speaker.

While the raucous radio voices of the post-depression era, which so disturbed H. G. Wells during a visit to us, have become somewhat subdued, the politicians, as well as leaders in all walks of life, march regularly to the microphones. Strangely, practically all of them are indifferent to the immensely successful speaking style of Roosevelt, namely, of seeming to talk not only extemporaneously, but of addressing intimately each individual listener. Political oratory in America achieved a new triumph in Roosevelt's radio manner. But it can be called a one-man triumph. Old-style buncombe may have disappeared, but old-style windiness and pompousness are still with us. One explanation for the low estate of the Republican Party at the polls in recent years is its unintelligent disregard of effective radio speaking, its seeming indifference to finding candidates for high office who, in addition to other qualifications, can talk over the radio.

Politics, during the past decade, have been vitally affected by the radio. If, today, the electorate manifests a familiarity with the workings of government as well as with the personalities behind the wheels; if it reveals a growing independence of thought and action baffling, if not frightening, to old school political leaders, it is radio that is largely responsible. The microphone's ready accessibility has sharpened the innate inquisitiveness of the American people. Radio has stripped the politician of his mask. It shows him in campaigns and conventions in his true colors, whether he is a sincere and sympathetic toiler for the people, whether he is a tireless and tiresome tub-thumper of age-old bombast, or a straddler, deft or clumsy, of political issues.

Strangely, the average political speaker is persistently inept in the art of effective radio expression. It is because of his lack of naturalness and simplicity as well as the inexplicable casualness and indifference with which he regards his assignment.

As it has brought politics closer to the people, given the citizen a more intimate contact with the government, so radio has also proved invaluable in interpreting sports. Such experts in mass psychology as the late Tex Rickard and Knute Rockne were keenly aware of the power of the microphone in promoting interest in sports—an interest reflected, ultimately, at the turnstiles, though there are sportsmen, mostly of the baseball kingdom, who persist in believing radio a menace to the box office.

No sports event, which promised a fairly even contest, has ever suffered financially because of radio's presence. On the contrary, the microphone, ballyhooing the event for days in advance of its date, has aided materially in stimulating that instinct of gregariousness which urges the individual to attendance at great spectacles.

Sports events still take precedence over any other items that can be scheduled in appealing to the radio public. The largest microphone audiences are those that listen to the descriptions of heavyweight championships. And for the first time in our history women are manifesting a vivid interest in all classes of sports. It is radio that is mainly responsible—the presence of expert commentators at the microphone who possess the knack of giving not only a thrilling, but a clear and authoritative picture of the event.

The broadcasting studio is today a vast combination of circus and counting house, presided over by fabulous supershowmen who combine something of the amusement resourcefulness of a Barnum with the financial responsibilities of a Rothschild.

About the microphone there is something of the haphazard, hectic atmosphere of the days when the screen suddenly found itself articulate.

Commercial sponsors, alert to the armchair appeal of a celebrated name, scour the musical, dramatic, cinematic marts for talent. Impressed with their new and startling roles of showmen, they sit in a solemn judgment upon auditions, piped into their board rooms from distant studios, of this band and that comedian, this vocalist and that commentator. Nothing comparable to such activity has been seen before in industrial America. If soap or soup or cereal or cigarettes must be hymned into the empyrean there are hundreds of performers ready and eager for the job. In this fantastic amusement world many performers, indeed, have boldly, unashamedly, become criers of commercial wares.

Broadcasting, becoming a commercial giant, has opened up tremendous channels of propaganda to the business world that have not been overlooked, as usual, by the politicians. In the process it has acquired a pretense of stability quite in keeping with its magnitude.

The annual revenue of the network broadcasters alone has amounted in recent years to more than $30,000,000. A large part of this sum reached the pockets of entertainers. So vast has become the financial sweep of the microphone that radio has now engulfed all the leading concert artist agencies in the country. The loudspeakers have become the gold fields of the amusement realm, promising vast rewards for a minimum of time and labor.

There is, inexplicably, scant hospitality in the radio salons for the varied and picturesque flavors of American speech. The overlords of the microphone frown upon any attempt of their announcers to deviate from a standardized policy of unctuous pronunciation which they choose to call "cosmopolitan English." The policy may be a good one if it means the use of English generally understood by the people in the land. But it has its drawbacks. Particularly, it has its drawbacks if radio, like the theatre, is to be a true reflection of America and the American language. American announcers have been called more English than the English (oddly, many Britishers heard on the air—the late King George V was a notable example—sounded more like Americans than Britishers).

The masters of the microphone have long cherished the belief that radio has stimulated American civilization by converting every Main Street into a Broadway. Yet, the broadcasters' ideal of radio as a super variety show cannot be realized until the microphone men distribute their acts more reasonably, when they convince the abler orchestras and artists to regard radio as their primary activity rather than as a sideline to fabulously easy money, when they can persuade one out of every ten of their commentators to substitute sweet reasonableness for the pompous omniscience now so prevalent, when—and if—they can induce the songwriters of the nation to greater ingenuity in their amorous arias.

Aware that they must be all things to all people, the broadcasters aim to please the majority while still shuffling their specialized programs about in a manner calculated to appeal to the minority. The job really calls for supermen as familiar with music as with politics, as versed in sports as they are in economics, who have as wide a knowledge of show business as they have of world affairs, who are as authoritative upon the subjects of religion and education as with the japeries of comedians and the rhymes of moonstruck melody men.

It is questionable the broadcasters would avail themselves of the services of such men could they find them. The fees would be considered too high. It is an unfortunate condition that in radio the salaries of those who design and produce the programs are paltry in comparison with the fees of those who air them at the microphone.

Drama continues to hold an insignificant place on the broadcasting schedules. Its appeal is dependent chiefly upon the listener's development of his sense of hearing. It is necessary for an author to say what he has to say briefly, but to say it arrestingly. The actor must be intimate. It is difficult to be intimate and arresting at the same time. If he tries to play a highly dramatic scene in the key of ordinary speech, he is false to his role, fails to convince, and the impression grows in the listener that here is not an effective illusion of life, but a collection of words written on pieces of paper which actors are holding up to microphones at so much per minute.

Hearing a play on the radio demands concentrated attention, a quality not yet possessed by American listeners except that small group of earnest music lovers. It is doubtful they will ever acquire it. It is difficult to conceive of Americans minimizing the distractions to eye and ear about them to listen in silence and darkness—and silence and darkness are essential—to the broadcast of drama. The radio men making no effort toward darkened rooms, seek to heighten dramatic appeal by introducing a varied assortment of sound effects, until today sound effects have become the backbone of radio drama. Even though they engage noted Broadway stars, make use of material specially written by noted playwrights, their chief success has been in a technical direction and in experimental impressionism.

The most consistent failure on the airwaves, despite the large audience which it draws, is the average children's program. The radio lords do not expect to capture the rare spirit of Lewis Carroll or Edward Lear or Mark Twain or Louisa M. Alcott, but it would seem that they could approach their children's program task with less condescension, less of the adult viewpoint.

In plotting such presentations the broadcasters not only invariably fail to project childish imagination, but what is equally unfortunate, childish naturalness. As a result, the quality of genuineness is missing and in its place are an attitude of condescension, an adult viewpoint.

What has radio achieved with the child actor? Where are radio's Shirley Temples and Jackie Coopers? For that matter, where are radio's Walt Disneys? The great screen characters, Mickey Mouse and Donald Duck, which have made the whole world kin, have no counterparts on the radio.

Do children's hours on the air appeal only to children—and to them only occasionally? Can future productions be broadened to reach mature attention also, as is the case of Disney's fundamentally childish creations? These are some of the problems now before the broadcasters. To solve them means hard work for the radio men. It means cutting away from their present stupid conventions of Tin Pan Alley songs, Broadwayish conversation and patronizing program conductors, supplemented by insistently unctuous promotion of those staples related to childish diets. It means they will have to keep everlastingly on the hunt not only for sympathetic writers and producers but for authentic delineators, once the material is found.

Education is and has been consistently a difficult hurdle for the broadcasters. The matter of effective presentation has yet to be overcome. The late Elihu Root once said that "eye-minded people must become ear-minded before broadcasting would become really important other than in the field of music." In education there has been no progress in the ear-mindedness of America except in those instances when it has been coated with the sugar of entertainment. That the broadcasters are acutely sensitive to their shortcomings in this fertile territory—a failure which they are aware is becoming more and more disturbing to Washington— is evident in their recent affecting embrace of former President Angell of Yale, with a blanket commission to set up a system which will give education its deserved place in the radio scheme. However, any system devised by Doctor Angell which would effectively attract—and hold— the listener must entertain while it instructs.

Most successful of all educational programs because of its skillful showmanship is America's Town Meeting of the Air. The enormous appeal of this weekly broadcast, with prominent men and women engaged in frank and spirited debate upon the vital topics of the day, has given new life to controversial discussion in this country. If the instruction comes from the candid and comprehensive arguments of the speakers on the rostrum, the entertainment, dramatic, frequently amusing, is derived from the pertinent inquiries of relentless hecklers in the audience.

The program, the happy idea of its moderator, George V. Denny, Jr., stems directly from the old-fashioned New England town meeting. Throughout, it has been kept resolutely to the ideal of free speech, thereby giving new heart to those who have been despairing of radio as a medium for full and free discussion of public affairs, uncensored, unhampered by arrogant or timid officialdom. Yet, its immediate and significant success was due not so much to its useful and honest approach to a solution of our national problems, as to the vivid show presented.

For several years broadcasters have attempted to meet some of the criticism directed at the scanty representation of educational programs by establishing so-called "schools of the air," scheduling numerous talks by members of college faculties, by setting aside certain periods for the broadcast of information concerning the arts and sciences.

Some progress has been made, notably in the gradual increase of the schoolroom audience they were definitely seeking to reach, but the simple fact remains that the dissemination of culture and education languishes on the radio, chiefly because of the very nature of the broadcasting status in America. The radio, a commercial enterprise, is designed chiefly for entertainment, and the majority of listeners not only do not want education but resent any effort to present it on the air unless, perchance, it bears the guise of entertainment, as in the manner of the prevalent Professor Quiz type of program.

Obviously, then, the radio has definite limitations as a cultural outlet. Broadcasters, nationally, are dealing with mass distribution and the message aired must be suitable for mass consumption. What is meat to New York must not be spinach to Arkansas. With their eyes on the average man, whose intelligence the advertising agencies all too casually rate as adolescent, the radio chiefs seek to concentrate upon those subjects which have universal appeal and which admit broad treatment, such as music appreciation.

In their commercial relations with the listener the broadcasters are guided principally by the well-established concept of truth. The advertising that goes into the home through the loudspeaker, they state with the ecstatic glow of a great discovery, must tell the truth or confidence in the whole structure of American business is threatened. As to how the "truth" should be told they remain as reticent as ever. How the truth should be told is the crux of the whole problem of advertising as it affects the armchairs of patient America.

The true purpose of radio advertising is the creation and maintenance of good will. Yet, only in rare instances is it upheld. In general, commercial radio is not advanced over its position of five years ago—a mad scramble for time, circus adjectives voiced in strident tones, all kinds of dodges and contests, the response to which by listeners is erroneously believed by the sponsors, if not the broadcasters, to be a gauge of the program's value; the interrupton of continuity and the consequent breaking of a mood in order to introduce a snappy sales talk, the repetition of outworn, outmoded phrases of merchandising.

Here and there are advertisers who, with little or no encouragement from the radio men, have seen the light, have decided there is no profit in underestimating longer the tolerance of listeners, who have reached the conclusion that the briefer, and, if possible, the more amusing their sales talk, the more likely it is to register with the public. Sending out good will, it is reasonable to believe they are getting it back in increased measure.

It is the sales talk that contributes so mightily to the 800,000 words estimated as used on a radio station in the course of a week. At this rate nearly 500,000,000 words are given to the air by the 600-odd stations of the country in a single week. A Niagara of talk! And the end is not in sight. Some day it will have to be controlled as the production of cotton is controlled. A law compelling the radio stations to leave uncultivated over three-quarters of their crop of superlatives would be a big start toward humanity's goal—the peace that passeth all understanding.

Perhaps, people are not listening. Perhaps, the more uncomplaining people in the great stretches of the hinterland have become as oblivious to radio's noisy bazaars as to the rumble of motor trucks along the highways. Perhaps, while keeping their radios tuned to one barker after another, they wait the occasional accents of jazz bands and jesters as a means of furthering their escape from the reality of economic scarcity.

In their more careless moments the microphone men like to refer to radio as show business, but in their hearts they know it far transcends that concept. They have only to consider the tremendous potentialities of television and short-wave broadcasting to make sure.

Television, with its most-cherished prospect of bringing great public spectacles directly to the armchairs, is gradually emerging from the experimental stage. Many problems, however, must be solved before image broadcasting is established upon a practical basis. There are the prices and simplification of receiving apparatus to be considered, the allotment of channels, theatre competition, the matter of subsidizing the tremendous investments necessary to pioneer the new art and industry, the readjusting of the financial relationships of the electrical, motion picture and radio industry. Manifestly, television's appearance will be largely conditioned by the current economic state. If times become good television may be indefinitely postponed, since radio manufacturers will not wish to disturb the new inflow of revenue from the sale of improved receivers. Should the depression continue television may suddenly be introduced —it is essentially ready now—as a dramatic and promising means of reviving industry.

Experts of all research organizations are in accord that television, when at hand, will supplement rather than supersede sound-broadcasting. At present extensive experimentation is going on both here and in England. Prize fights, grand opera, football games as well as ordinary vaudeville entertainment have entered the televisionary state abroad with varying degrees of success. Here the images have been confined to specially designed skits, newsreels, classroom exercises, and simple forms of music and speech.

Back of the American scenes a great struggle is being waged. Huge corporations are fighting for control of the new industry as broadcasting becomes a new and more powerful means of mass appeal. Against the struggle for control with its tangle of some 15,000 patents, contracts, government decisions and corporation reports, there is the dramatic story of the inventive genius of two men, Philo Farnsworth, native of Idaho, and Vladimir Zworykin, a Russian émigré, who formulated similar ideas of enabling man to see by electricity. As great corporations have proceeded to work out their principles set down by these inventors, such important matters have arisen as the potential threat of television to the motion picture theatre, the possible development of a perpetual radio and television monopoly through the great pools of patents.

Whether television will be conducted along the lines of sound broadcasting with revenue derived from advertising sponsors or whether the government will control it as a public utility comparable to the telephone, in which event limited and guaranteed income in return for guaranteed public service will take the place of radio's free competition and free profits is yet to be determined. That there will be governmental regulation of some sort, however, seems assured.

At any event, television will mean a readjustment of human and economic values. Its sociological, educational, amusement entertainment, political implications stagger the imagination. Its effect upon mankind is in the laps of the gods. We can only wait. Conjecture is as fruitless as it is foolish.

With the development of short-wave broadcasting, radio has become the principal medium of international propaganda. Potentially the supreme bearer of understanding between nations, radio in its promotion of good will looms, despite the lofty enthusiasm of broadcasters at their banquet tables, no larger than a pinch of Gandhi's salt, as strident—and essentially fearful—voices of officialdom seek simultaneously to explain or justify their policies, win new spheres or influence and undermine the policies of their neighbors. Europe, in the past few years, has been arming itself with radio with a zeal and industry rivalled only by the race in shipyard and munition plant. Radio in America is still designed primarily for entertainment and not as an adjunct to the State Department. And yet America has begun to show symptons of joining in the international cannonading of the eardrums.

The concentration upon radio propaganda shows to what lengths ambition, suspicion and the loss of a sense of perspective have driven the heads of nations. Apparently, they do not appreciate that a receptive ear is quite as essential to their plans as a willing voice. Save for a questionable success in catching the attention of backward peoples there is no assurance their efforts meet anything but a complete wall of otic insensibility. Nor can they be sure of a welcome by the backward peoples. Even were the latter equipped with the necessary radio facilities, is it not possible they are as intangible, as vaguely realized an audience as that which prevails in supposedly superior countries?

It is essentially a comic opera war—this international gunfire of the short waves. It demands first and foremost a ready and attentive audience. Secondly, it demands voices of irresistible force and charm. Lastly, it demands messages of compelling appeal. Such imponderables make the whole scheme one of sheer lunacy. The more radio propaganda is studied the more idiotic and futile it appears. It could only be conceived by megalomaniacs who, in their frenzy to win sympathy and support, ridiculously overlook the obvious fact that the same behavior is open to their rivals.

Nationalism is too inbred a racial trait to be conquered by a voice across a frontier. True, Italy is not trying to make Italians out of Englishmen when she rushes to the short waves. She is trying to win adherents in

Islam by broadcasting in Arabic. Whereupon, England, finally suppressing her calm bewilderment at such didoes, believes she must counteract Italy by broadcasting to Islam likewise in Arabic. But is Islam listening? And if so, is it giving serious consideration to such elaborate alien heigh-ho? The competition was reduced to its more properly absurd proportions as England pitted a Piccadilly dance band and various Moslem voice-lifters against Italy's crooner, a gentleman called, not inconveniently, Abdul Wahab and acclaimed the "Bing Crosby of the Near East."

Germany uses a cultured Oxford accent to get its point of view over to English-speaking countries. But the stratagem fools nobody. Englishmen, as W. S. Gilbert took such pains to reveal, persist in being Englishmen. Similarly, it is not likely Americans would be swayed by a foreign tongue, trying, through imitation Americanese, to harness us to an alien point of view. We would be apt to be amused at the effort, even though the persistent American spirit of doubtfulness were not impregnable to the special pleading. They could not hope, of course, to compete with us in that propaganda disguised as entertainment, for the simple reason that we have practically a monopoly of entertainers.

Radio as a medium for political or military propaganda is most effective when one group within a country captures the government from another group, as was the case when Spanish revolutionists seized the throne and Alfonso's wireless at the same time. The latter kept the radio going day and night to hold the people, to hold the country. However, when General Franco's radio stentor has sought to convince the loyalists of the futility of their cause he has been greeted by stiffened resistance at the barricades, providing fresh proof that while radio propaganda may make considerable noise, it leads nowhere, and that Napoleon is still right: Heaven is on the side of the heaviest artillery.

Short-wave broadcasts, however, do exert novel appeal when the effect is one of eavesdropping upon the world, of making transoceanic cities instantly accessible. Listeners satisfy their curiosity by tuning in music and entertainment and news comment in distant lands.

More international influence and interest are exerted through broadcast song and symphony, through the motion pictures, than in all the special pleaders and obvious amusement ambassadors on the payrolls of the foreign offices.

Every section of the earth has been tapped by the tireless radio men. Short of Valhalla, itself, there is no longer any thrill available. What might have been startling a few years ago is accepted today as a matter of course. And yet, and yet, something new may happen to startle the consciousness of the air-conditioned public. Though short of contact with the spirit world it is difficult to imagine the public not receiving that something in any but its now accustomed matter-of-fact stride.

Casualness has become the prevailing mood before the microphone as well as in the rocking-chair. The chief fault lies with the listeners themselves. Their demands for first-class service, for want of a better term, have only to be insistent enough, or heavy enough, and the broadcasters are bound to pay heed. One trouble is that in the majority of homes radio has become a willy-nilly medium of entertainment, sought only when the listener is in a mood for it.

The radio lords naturally seek to keep to the great middle ground, feeling that in so doing they are striking an average, are satisfying the greatest number of eardrums. In keeping to this plane—and it is a plane that often leads to mediocrity in programs—the radio men are handicapped not only by their sponsors, but by the excess of radio time at their disposal. They were on their way to becoming independent in the control and operation of their own business when the depression overtook them. They had to trim sail, had to scrap their ideals, had to make room for indiscriminate trash because of the welcome tinkle of cash in the till.

Despite the growing cynicism and weariness of the public toward radio routine and ballyhoo, the microphone is a permanent medium of entertainment and information in millions of homes. Were it abolished, the wearied and the cynical would be the first to shout their protests to high heaven. The listener—even the indifferent listener—wants what he wants when he wants it.

He may keep his radio silent for days on end, tired of the repetitious hotchas of Broadway, tired of the ceaseless old gags, tired of the parade of economic panaceas from a thousand throats, tired of the windy superlatives of the salesman. But when a Windsor or a Kai-shek or a Philharmonic concert, or a Flagstad or a Heifetz or a Kentucky Derby or an Army-Navy game or a World Series or a heavyweight bout or a political convention is announced, he welcomes the assurance that his radio is within reach.

He may not glow with the enthusiasm that once was his when these items were new to his ears, but he is glad of the opportunity to enjoy them in their original glamour and appeal.

Meanwhile, he waits for something sensationally new, sensationally novel. Marconi might have provided it had he lived. Perhaps, the broadcasters, to whom anything is possible, are still banking upon Marconi—in Valhalla.

## II. THE MOVIES

Unchallenged is Hollywood's technical supremacy. In such details as photography, sound recording, set and costume designing, the California producers lead the world. Their artistic progress is still hampered by the seemingly inescapable necessity of making their dominant appeal to childish intelligence. Of secondary importance is that production based upon a maturity of story and treatment. Upon those occasions when progressive and imaginative directors break away from trite and childish formulæ to make pictures of mature intelligence, the result, in many instances, has been astonishingly profitable. Such films have been received with rejoicing among that portion of the public to whom movie-going means something more than a time-passing habit or an escape from realities.

So responsive are the West Coast artisans to this acclaim that they have fallen into the grievous error of copying their newly-found formulæ to tiresome lengths. Thus has come a succession of films, built upon the themes which had proved refreshingly adult. So impressed is Hollywood by what seems sure-fire that variety and change of pace, the mainstays of all genuinely successful amusement, are neglected.

The result of such pretentious self-plagiarism, even measured commercially, is obvious. The public, tired of the imitations, avoids the theatre, and the exhibitors taking their cue from the public, voice protests against the studios and their systems, call for new action, new ideas, and, above all, new faces. The theatre men depend chiefly upon the drawing power of the stars. Closer to the public, they are quick to sense the decline of a star's popularity. But the mighty competitive star system prevailing in Hollywood impels producers to sign their players to long-term contracts at fabulous salaries, which are paid long after the players have passed the peak of their box-office allure.

The regular program picture, the major portion of Hollywood's product, has during the period of the depression met a serious and growing loss of public patronage. Exhibitors, to attract audiences, have resorted to various devices and games of chance—bank nights, bingo, screeno; luring patrons with the possibility of winning quick and easy money or its equivalent in household staples. With the continuance of economic distress, the producers themselves have been forced to retrench in their policies, reduce their film costs, curtail their extravagance. Their retrench-ments, like the songwriters' clouds, disclose, however, a silver lining. Opulence, often unjustified, is giving way here and there to simplicity, super-splendor to imagination, though it is too early to say whether the depression will inspire that greatly-hoped-for ideal of the more sincere admirers and critics of the industry—fewer but better pictures.

Until reduced receipts at the box-office demanded an urgent reshaping of their policies, Hollywood's producers were all too content to follow well-worn formulæ of plot and characterization. Cycles have succeeded cycles, exemplified most conspicuously in the star-studded revue, the gangster film, the Cinderella play, the extravagant comedy of manners with its studied avoidance of reasonableness in theme and treatment. The insistent call of schedule fulfillment has urged Hollywood to wasteful repetition, and while the productions attained a high polish of technical proficiency, imagination and the audacity born of pioneering experi-mentation have lagged in direction, story creation, and projection of character.

Hollywood is so bound by its rigid fetish of entertainment that it im-pedes its own progress in superior film drama. Its common denominator of entertainment is, like that of its big brother of radio, the twelve-year-old mind. It refuses to concede the evidence published in its own trade papers, reflecting the opinions of patrons through the reports of exhibitors in all parts of the country, that the film-going public is becoming more and more resentful of the monotony of the fare, the seeming unwilling-ness or inability of producers to work out new patterns or, failing that, to fit new styles to old patterns. Even pretentiousness, Hollywood's too-long-revered criterion of merit, no longer exerts its former potency with the public, despite the ingenious advertising often employed to attract patronage.

The American film fan, like the over-indulged armchair listener, is today more exacting than ever before. Superlatives no longer sway him. He has been treated to such an endless array of spectacle, of glamorous personality, that he is spoiled for anything short of sensational. He takes for granted the expert skill, the lavish care given to the externals of production; he is reasonably sure the climax of his entertainment will competently disclose misfortune thwarted and love triumphant. He attends the movies, as he listens to the radio, either out of sheer habit or to pass the time or, as is most likely, out of a desire to escape monoto-nous, graceless reality.

He seeks the illusion of romance, of adventure, of idealism. He is most often satisfied in his search when his credulity has not been strained too greatly, or his intelligence insulted too outrageously. He demands authenticity, or the semblance of authenticity, in the unfolding of the story before him. He is generally captivated by dramatic projections of famous figures of the past. He is particularly partial to the natural charm of children and animals. Indeed, he achieves his truest escape from reality, finds his heart most cheered, his imagination most stirred by the glowing figures of Mickey Mouse, Donald Duck, the Three Pigs, Dopey and his dwarfish comrades, who have come to life under the faultless imprint and inspiration of Walt Disney. Mickey Mouse and Donald Duck have the universal appeal of all true great creative art. They, and more recently, "Snow White and the Seven Dwarfs," have been the greatest boon to the movies since sound.

"Snow White" appeared when the movies seemed to be marking time, when the producer was beginning to sense an atmosphere of indifference in the marketing of such pictures as were not of a surpassing excellence in story theme and treatment, in direction and acting. The growing sophistication of the American audience, the overpowering fear of offending the sensibilities of foreign patrons have made his production problem difficult. By trying not to displease any group, any nationality, he all too often finds that he has pleased none, that for all his vast expenditure of time and money and energy and apprehensive care he has a production on his hands that is as lacking in vividness as it is in vitality. The foreign taboos weigh him down unnecessarily. Were he to give less regard to the increasingly precarious markets abroad, he might discover at home a new commercial stimulation that would compensate for his inability to find a new technical medium, as a decade ago he discovered sound and a few years back came upon, all too disturbingly, technicolor.

The mass production of the screen schedule occupies the paradoxical position of hampering artistic progress the while it develops commercialism. Forced, under its highly competitive system, to turn out five or six hundred pictures a year, Hollywood faces the continuous problem of presenting its material in terms of the widest appeal. Superficially, it accomplishes its purpose. Its tricks are often spectacular and exciting. It can alter a work of subtlety and imagination beyond recognition and yet afford through its effects enlivening entertainment. Also it often invigorates a hopelessly banal script by the dexterity of its technical treatment and the skill of its direction and performance.

Thus, showmanship is employed to heighten excitement. The spectator, it is expected, will be so engrossed by the compelling externals as to fail to detect the fundamental weaknesses of the story. Many costly productions regularly give spectators the conviction of significant entertainment through their adroit use of showmanship in technical effects. Later, advertising specialists add new emphasis. In novel dressings of hackneyed superlatives, in ornate and striking electrical displays, in all the deft practices of ballyhoo they seek to create public interest which will reimburse the producers for their extravagant investments.

Significantly, new and contrasting competition has encroached of late upon the domains of the West Coast studios. From Europe has come a large number of film plays which stress simplicity rather than spectaculariness, in which fresh and vivid treatment make up for conventionality of structural outline of plot, in which characters move in correct relationship to their lives and their environment. There is understatement, a quality of artful suggestion that makes all the more moving the drama depicted. Moreover, the result has been obtained at comparatively meager costs. With small budgets at their disposal, the European producers have to persuade their audiences with the lucidity and honesty of their story, the genuineness of their characters, the subtle overtones to familiar situations.

The European films are having an effect upon Hollywood. West Coast producers are bestirring themselves with forthright plans to return to what they call the fundamentals of picture making, by which they probably mean not only an emphasis upon action but the re-creation of such honest situations and honest characters and honest talk as are encompassed in human experience.

Hollywood has a number of actors who, when equipped with a shrewd script and understanding direction, can bring warmth and intensity to whatever roles they are assigned. It possesses directors, likewise, who, supplied with a first-rate story and skillful players, can impart intriguing suspense and vividness to their drama, depth and glow to their comedy, authentic sweep and richness to their pageantry. Its weakness lies in its overproduction, in its overcrowded schedule, in its stultifying policy of counterbalancing its worthwhile and frequently costly product with wholly mediocre films. Hollywood has been geared so long to a scale of extravagance that it measures its art in terms of money expenditure. It takes rewrite men from newspapers and pays them fabulous salaries as scenarists that far exceed the annual income of best-selling novelists.

Its fees to players have practically denuded the American stage not only of the majority of its established stars, but of young women who, in addition to the eye-filling charms of face and figure, are pleasantly-spoken and winsome of personality. It pays the magnates themselves, their producers, directors, composers, technical experts and costume designers truly staggering salaries, depending, in part, upon the quality of salesmanship employed in the slick art of contract-dickering, in part upon their most recent success in production and such potent ties of blood relationship as intrude themselves upon the economic background.

So accustomed is Hollywood to costly budgets that any attempt at financial retrenchment affects, seemingly, the quality of the product. The ambitious producer-distributor is beset by a multitude of problems. In addition to the risk that his picture will lack the entertainment appeal which means profit at the box-office, he is confronted by the increased demands of his players, the rapid spread of union organization, the difficulties of world sales as a result of wars and economic barriers, heavy taxation at home, statewide censorship restrictions, chain restriction laws, the constant threat of governmental interference.

Also, he is harassed by growing radio competition, the pressure to show a healthy financial accounting to Wall Street overlords, ever-changing public taste, the rising spirit of independence on the part of his stars, the constant and widespread political intrigue within the studios. Added to these problems is the public's steadily increasing resentment against the double feature, which, designed as a feast of cinema riches, is all too regularly a famine of entertainment.

Hollywood, itself, does not attempt to dodge the responsibility for the censure. In the spectaculariness, the very extravagance of its super-productions, it is aware it has set a criterion by which all subsequent merchandise is measured. During the boom season of 1936–37 more than forty pictures costing in excess of $1,000,000 were made, most of the expensive productions being representations of dramatic episodes of history or grandiose elaborations of great adventure stories. Occasionally, a politico-sociological aspect is introduced. In the last analysis the emphasis, however, is not upon the story but upon the star. The exhibitor demands names because he has found it is names which attract the larger part of his theatre audiences.

Nevertheless, despite the development of technical skill, the motion-picture public, like the public of the radio, is exercising greater fastidiousness in its selection of entertainment. It has even revealed at times an astonishing failure to be attracted by either potency of personality or lavishness of scene. Such an attitude is not accepted in Hollywood supinely. With a characteristic resort to showmanship it is taking steps to combat the sudden critical manifestation of the public. The more visionary would depend upon extensive drum-beating under the curious misapprehension that such a device would be a fitting substitute for superior screen fare. The more realistic would institute that long-bruited policy of fewer but better pictures, capitalizing upon the scarcely-tilled field of the nation's schools, making honesty of plot and character the chief desideratum of theatre fare, tapping the inexhaustible reservoirs of history and biography, of social and political science.

Obviously, there are too many poor pictures just as there are too many poor radio programs. The production system is determined largely by the extent of its outlet. Just as the broadcasters' program schedules must embrace a continuous stretch of sixteen or more hours, so the picture producers are confronted by the necessity of supplying 90,000 theatres throughout the world.

Long a tradition of motion pictures is the hero worship of the public for its favorite actors and actresses. Their association in the popular mind with romantic glamour, the fantastically-luxurious lives they lead, the voluminous and persistent publicity showered upon them have served to set up for the film stars a mass obsequiousness comparable only to that given to sports champions and the sombre-shirted dictators.

The adoration endures, however, only so long as the stars have the good fortune to be presented in superior plays. Let them be assigned to mediocre films over a definite period and their decline of popularity is at once apparent at the box-office. Producers, misled by the hero worship or, perhaps, wishing to take advantage of it, seek an occasion to win back the great sums they pay the stars, for whose services they often compete with reckless disregard of cost, by presenting them in inferior entertainments. The scheme in the long run proves disastrous to producer, exhibitor, player and patron alike. Diminishing returns at the theatre prove the inadequacy of robbing Peter to pay Paul.

This short-sighted production policy has led many exhibitors, resentful of the increasing loss of theatre patronage, to place the blame upon the stars, affirming with a bluntness more picturesque than positive that many of the highest-salaried players are "poison" at the box-office.

In a further effort to compensate for the falling revenues at the box-offices, independent exhibitors have availed themselves of a practice, distasteful to Hollywood, of showing advertising films on their screens. Such undisguised commercial propaganda is undoubtedly injurious to the institution of the screen, but exhibitors justify themselves upon the plea that it is only through such films they can recover part of the rental prices they pay for entertainment pictures.

It is not the star system which is primarily at fault for the decline in public interest, for the exhibitors frankly acknowledge many stars are riding the crest of popular favor, though omitting to state that the latter have the benefit of better pictures. It is the subject matter provided that is responsible for Hollywood's distress. Emphasis is placed upon vehicles when, obviously, it should be upon good plays. An actor is no better than his material whether he is on the stage or the screen or the radio. If the economic disorder has the effect of giving new force to the old, but neglected truth of the theatre that it is the play that really matters, it will place the art, as well as the business of the movies, upon a firmer and more progressive basis.

It is not that Hollywood rejects first-rate material. Indeed, the producers entice leading playwrights and novelists with lavish fees to the studios. The trouble is that the film men often do not know definitely what they want of their writers once they have them under contract.

Again, Broadway hits, obtained at fabulous prices under sharply-competitive bidding, are frequently so changed in their transference to the screen as to have little resemblance to the original manuscripts. The scramble for the plays in the face of their subsequent transformation seems all the more questionable as producers proceed to discard even the titles by which they are established in the public consciousness. Names are substituted which, though alien to the original subject matter, are believed to possess that necessary blend of sex and sentimentality which has been called the secret of box-office allure.

Supplementing the dearth of suitable fare for the big names of the screen, the producers, to meet the demands of their schedules, reel off from their assembly lines numerous "class B" pictures as well as pictures ranking even well below that category. The "B" pictures, supplying theatres operating upon a double-feature and block-booking policy, costing between $150,000 and $250,000 a production, are made to meet Hollywood distribution requirements, and they will continue to have an important place in the production scheme, serving as they do as a proving ground of new acting and directorial talent, and since manifestly the studios cannot afford continuously high budget pictures. Many "B" pictures are enormously popular; especially is this true of those films which, presenting various stars in a series of adventures, become favorites of neighborhood audiences throughout the country.

Occasionally a "B" picture offers such a fortunate combination of appealing story and effective direction and performance as to jump into the "A" class as exhibitors of first-run houses buy it on a percentage basis. The "B" picture is not necessarily an inferior product. Here again the peculiar psychology which measures the artistic standards of a film by the cost of production places the Hollywood system upon a false premise. It may well be that the wide and growing popularity in America for comparatively low-cost European pictures in which emphasis is made upon novelty and effectiveness of story and performance will lead American producers to give less attention to classification of their films according to financial costs and more to the determination to make good films, letting the box-office chips fall where they may.

If the producers have come to rely more and more upon the profits of the "B" pictures to tide them over for their splurges upon "A" pictures, it might be well for them to consider the freedom from such dependence that would be theirs were they to substitute merit as a criterion in place of the dollar mark. If a certain production plan calls for elaborateness of scene and character there should not, of course, be any unreasonable financial restriction which would hamper the effective presentation of the spectacle. On the other hand, the needlessness of heavy financial outlay upon a simple but well-told story, confined within a small but vivid canvas, should not automatically stamp a film as unworthy of serious consideration. The former may turn out to be a dud, the latter a stunning success. Under the present misplaced standard of values, the public is led to anticipate the "A" picture as something superlatively good because it cost a million dollars and the "B" film as mediocre because it was produced for one-quarter the expense.

Happiest is Hollywood when, employing a straight photoplay idiom, it projects its characters against a background of panoramic action and excitement. Mass movements, large-scale pageantry, melodramatic excitement enable producers to create their most effective illusions. But to be entirely appealing their vast scenes must be accompanied by eloquent stories, authentic characters. Even toward such sheer spectacles as battles, conflagrations, tremendous storms, modern audiences are unresponsive if the personal narrative upon which film production is based is failing in dramatic power or genuineness of characterization.

Current headline sensations, provided they are not controversial in subject, serve often as material for the screen. Meanwhile, the creation of great illusion has become largely process work wherein miniature models are put through their thrill-designed paces. Through process work Hollywood, thus, films a schooner race in a tank, utilizes cartoon animation, coffee shots and telephoto glimpses of grasshoppers for its make-believe of a locust plague in China, employs wind machines and water sluices for its projection of a devastating hurricane. Expert technicians have made it possible to re-create stupendous adventures of the human spirit with little of the expense and inconvenience of location work that formerly were involved.

Incidental music plays an important part in modern screen production, whether it takes the form of songs expressly written by the experienced tunesmiths of Tin Pan Alley, or a special score, with motifs for the principal scenes and characters, prepared by composers who have toiled for the major portion of their lives in the classical vineyards. The so-called super-films invariably have special scores, the tradition stemming from "The Birth of a Nation."

The foremost contribution of sound to the movies is the musical film. Musical movies have taxed ingenuity in songwriting, in gag writing, in piling one spectacular scene upon another, in out-colossalling Hollywood's peculiar devotion to the colossal. With astounding regularity these films emerge from the studios, the majority of them a series of vaudeville and night club turns, strung upon a fragile thread of plot. Rarely is one offered which, combining cleverness of idea and brilliant music, offers a new and adult sophistication. In some of the early musicals, designed to lampoon various banalities of radio and the movies, there was indicated a welcome superiority to the stage revue. But the early promise was not fulfilled. Fertility in ideas has been lacking and recourse has been chiefly upon the patter of comedians, upon dancers trained in the tap and singers skillful with the torch.

Amid this welter of imitative, over-elaborated floor show, Hollywood has enterprisingly shown, however, it can break away from the monotonous and superficially glittering. In "100 Men and a Girl" it found a new use for the musical screen in the employment of a symphony orchestra. The picture made its appeal not through its adroit merging of sprightly and sentimental comedy, but through its dramatic dependence upon great music expertly played.

If sound revolutionized the screen, color can be called a step in its evolution. The technicians have achieved some remarkable beauty, have succeeded at times in the true purpose of making their color heighten emotional effect, but generally its dramatic potentialities have been subordinated, so proud are the producers of the lingering charm of their pastels. Color is thus given an importance out of all proportion to its value. By dominating a scene it tends to arrest action—the very mainspring of the motion picture. With few exceptions, color has not been employed to step up emotions.

Though garishly handled in "Becky Sharp," color in that film was effectively synchronized with dramatic situations, employed most compellingly in the splashes of crimson of officers' cloaks as the word of cannonading interrupted the ball and soldiers rushed to battle. Since then Hollywood has attempted to subdue not only the clash of color but chromatic excitement in general, with the result that it has overlooked, except in the most obvious cases, its dramatic promise, while over-emphasizing its æsthetic appeal. Whether mobile color may turn out to be, as Robert Edmund Jones confidently believes, the new art form of tomorrow will depend upon the harmonious interdependence of the dramatic and graphic arts.

In making its feature pictures Hollywood spends annually in excess of $150,000,000. Of this sum more than 20 per cent, it is estimated, is sacrificed to the inability of studio heads to decide upon details of script and production. A director may be engaged and never used or he may be dismissed after working two weeks and a fresh start is made. Writers and actors and producers may be idle for months without assignments. Stories and plays may be bought and stored away never to be filmed. Thus is force given to Hollywood's legend of incredible topsy-turvydom.

Sometimes an expense of $1,000,000 is incurred by the time a picture is completed, though it does not follow that such a picture will be exploited as a $1,000,000 picture. The latter term is customarily utilized when the studio has determined at the outset that a picture will have a $1,000,000 budget. A picture in this class, to be profitable, must pile up a gross of $5,000,000 at the box-office. It requires 20,000,000 patrons at an average admission price of 25 cents to turn a $5,000,000 gross.

Paradoxically, the purely dramatic offering, contrary to the general impression, is less expensive to produce than the film designed to amuse. It is because the demands of comedy make necessary the employment of more skillful performers, require greater, more painstaking time and effort. The chief artistic development of West Coast producers in recent years has been in the presentation of comedy.

The primary function of the motion picture, of course, is to entertain. Praiseworthy are the recent efforts of Hollywood to provide entertainment through the depiction of stirring events and characters of history. Secondarily, a phase of education is going on, for public opinion is being taught not only through significant episodes of history and world progress, but with the accuracy of thorough research that is not sacrificed to the element of showmanship. A powerful instrumentality for the molding of public opinion is thus set into effect, ranking far above radio, because the eye is added to the ear.

Since world opinion today is more important and authoritative than ever before, the public must be informed and stimulated. Great events must be interpreted in understandable terms. Through its primary expression as entertainment, the screen is providing an expansive door to knowledge.

Fulfilling its high promise of enlightenment the while it entertains, Hollywood has demonstrated it can also achieve a brilliant financial triumph. Specifically, in "The Life of Emile Zola," Hollywood showed it could be engrossed with the sociological, philosophic and political implications of a great struggle for justice amid powerful military intrigue without the sacrifice of any of the episode's dramatic import. The penetrating insight into human motivation, the logical and simple exposition of cause and effect in the various sequences, the careful observance of historical accuracy coupled with a compelling sincerity in the telling of the story gave to the picture an educational value which, obviously, enhanced the universal appeal of its entertainment.

The insistence upon diversion as the sole object of all motion picture production has its roots in the long-cherished notion that the box-office must not only be the depository of the movie patron's cash but of his intelligence as well. Producers, harking too much to those who are believed to be the practical showmen of the industry, overlook the mental and spiritual acquisitiveness of humanity, forget that people are ever seeking satisfaction for the inner urgings of their consciousness in their plays and stories, are ever seeking to personalize themselves in the romances unfolded. The picture which, along with its prime mission to entertain, makes an appeal to intelligence, to imagination, to man's ceaseless quest for truth and knowledge is the film that invariably reflects the greatest triumph at the box-office whether it takes the form of a

"Zola," a "Pasteur," a "Captains Courageous," a "David Copperfield," a "Good Earth," a "Robin Hood," a "Thin Man," a "She Met Him in Paris" or a "Carnival in Flanders."

While they scour the world's literature for stories, assign their more adroit scenarists to devising original photoplays, the West Coast producers inexplicably neglect the vast and significantly dramatic panorama of contemporary America. Whatever attention they have given to the American scene has invariably been focussed upon the colorful and teeming pageantry of pioneer life, of the development of the West, the first surgings of the industrial era, the dramatic political rise of picturesque and forceful figures.

These efforts have been entertaining as well as helpful in cultivating in Americans a deeper awareness of our historical significance. Current civilization, however, is passed over either because of a fear of controversial implications or because of a feeling that sufficient perspective is not yet available to portray contemporary life accurately. Rarely, too, does an American photoplay interpret the essence of the country in those universally vivid terms with which the better foreign films evaluate life and character of the particular country from which they emanate. A French picture is curiously French in manner. A Russian or German film is essentially Slavic or Teutonic in theme and treatment. An American picture is only superficially American. It penetrates only episodically to the core of American life. In its overwhelming aim to divert it all too often stresses wholly fictitious types and action.

It would seem opportunity and inspiration are at hand whereby the producers might advantageously foster a spirit of progressive, but unblatant, nationalism through pictures dealing with the tremendous aspects of our social and industrial life. The great film of vast, vivid, fantastic New York, for example, has yet to be made. Likewise, the great story of modern Washington, with its immense social and political implications, has not been told. Modern Detroit and Chicago and Pittsburgh are unsung. What of the new South? That, too, is overlooked. And where are the pictures concerned with our own youth movements— in music, in athletics, in scholarship, in a renewed appreciation of the democratic tradition? Where, indeed, is the picture which would show the inherent substantiality of the American character, the fundamental soundness of the American system amid the noisy storms of totalitarianism?

For every feature picture there are three or four short films produced yearly, the majority of which, until recently, were devoted to monotonous slapstick comedy, uninspired two-reelers exhibiting dance bands and night club stars, travelogues and cartoons. Hollywood is becoming aware of the artistic potentialities of the short subject with which to supplement its major product. Though the two-reel film, ideal for the purpose, is rarely used to tell a short story, such material as biographical and historical episode, scientific research, in which human interest is paramount, expositions of stories-behind-the-news, sport topics are receiving attention. The short film, it is being recognized, can stand on its own legs as an artistic entity, assuming the same relation to the feature picture that the magazine and newspaper do to the novel and the comprehensive history and biography. The two-reelers, whether fictional or factual, are, when painstakingly produced, the most desirable complement to the single long feature.

Unfortunately, they are still regarded by many exhibitors as fillers rather than as attractions in their own right. Designed to round out a theatre program, they are often so hacked to fit a performance's specified time limit that much of their entertainment and educational value is lost to the patron. Large portions of the public in various polls have manifested a decided preference for one or more short subjects in place of the double feature. But precedent and tradition are as hard to break in film presentation as in film producing and the short subject continues to be a stopgap in the general exhibition scheme.

Likewise, the newsreels which have made significant strides in the enterprise, the impartiality, the fine freedom, the speed with which they tap the world for their material are often subjected to harsh treatment by those exhibitors bound to the schedules of their double-feature showings. Newsreel-making is a highly specialized field, for the cameramen concern themselves not only with the big news of the day as it is happening, but with those matters of universal appeal which come under the head of human interest. They must concentrate in the brief time at their disposal—an average of ten minutes twice a week—upon what constitutes the spectacular and the exciting. Today, the newsreels are enjoying a prestige as extensive as it is deserved, for in them is seen not only swift and accurate representation of news but the closest approach to the ideal of genuine freedom of the press. They present the news as they see it without fear or favor, keeping ever to the mission that they must entertain the while they inform. So vital are the newsreels as adjuncts to the movie industry that many theatres are devoted exclusively to their presentation.

If political partisanship occasionally finds its way into the newsreels, it is invariably counterbalanced by opposing views and comment. The newsreels have made it possible for the public to have first-hand glimpses of modern warfare in the making, of close-ups of the principal personalities in the international political parade, of the gaudy regimentation that is going on in Europe; of enjoying vicarious thrills of great sports events unfolding before their eyes. If Americans today have a clearer understanding of what is happening in China and Spain, in the armament-racing nations of the world as well as in the varied and exciting life of their own country, it is because of the newsreel.

Hollywood, it can reasonably be expected, can look for fewer and fewer profits from European markets, once so impressive as to comprise 35 per cent of the total gross of its pictures. Various trade barriers, the complexities of foreign exchange, the diversion of a large part of public interest to war and preparation for war have made the lot of the American photoplay abroad hazardous and uncertain.

The curtailment of these markets may be a blessing in disguise, spurring producers to win new and regular audiences at home by the same daring and imagination in the discovery and treatment of their themes as they continually display in their external details. Relieved of the pressure of appealing to all nationalities, they will be free to seek greater artistic progress through the abandonment of overworked patterns and cycles, and the substitution of new material or striking handling of old material, keeping to the fore the reconstruction of life in a manner fascinatingly and peculiarly American.

It will mean a readaptation of present values, but out of the confusion and economic storm may come a saner, more wholesome production system; a purpose, perhaps, resolutely held of rising above mere eye-and-ear appeal.

The screen has made stupendous strides in the past decade in technical proficiency. It is not too much to hope that by reason of its forced economic readjustments it will achieve in the more intangible creative field of the human spirit the dignity, the virility, the inspiration and significance of all great art.

# LITERATURE

## [John Chamberlain]

BACK in 1921, writing for Mr. Stearns' earlier *Civilization,* Van Wyck Brooks lamented that the sustained career in American letters was a rarity; "the blighted career, the arrested career, the diverted career"—these were the rule. There was considerable excuse at the time for Mr. Brooks's gloomy pronouncement, even though the 'teens, with their *Spoon River Anthology* and their *Winesburg, Ohio,* their *Chicago Poems* and their *Jennie Gerhardt,* had been a time of literary vitality and promise. The undigested war, the idiotic peace, the Palmer Red hunts, the Harding reaction, the 1921 depression—these set the lugubrious tone of the period, and Mr. Brooks was bound to reflect his mental climate. But the darkness soon proved to be temporary; the renaissance of the '20's—if it was indeed a renaissance—was just over the horizon. Even as Mr. Brooks was poeticizing his sense of woe, the scoffing Sinclair Lewis and the young F. Scott Fitzgerald and the intransigeant Eugene O'Neill were beginning their careers—and as time went on these new men seemed to have staying qualities.

All through the '20's American literature was chronically promising. Lewis wrote better novels than *Main Street,* Dreiser wrote *An American Tragedy,* Willa Cather did her best work in *A Lost Lady* and *The Professor's House.* Scott Fitzgerald spoke of the sad young men, but sad or not the young writers seemed both ready and able to continue a deepening tradition of critical honesty; they wrote books as Socrates asked questions. One could confidently predict great things, or at least interesting things, from the author of *The Great Gatsby,* or from the young expatriate Mr. Hemingway whose short stories were collected in 1925 in a volume called *In Our Time.* The promise that inhered in such books as Glenway Wescott's *The Apple of the Eye,* or Elizabeth Madox Roberts's *The Time of Man,* or Thornton Wilder's *The Cabala,* or John Dos Passos' *Manhattan Transfer,* or Edmund Wilson's *I Thought of Daisy,* or Ludwig Lewisohn's *The Island Within* seemed immeasurably bright—or maybe we were merely young and unselective at the time. In any event American literature was exciting and provoked argument,

36

and the argument seemed important to those who fought over Hemingway's muscular sentences or Dreiser's sense of doom.

But it didn't seem important for very long, and perhaps that is a measure of the shallowness of the literature of the '20's. With the coming of the depression this literature suddenly seemed to lack an appreciation of central issues. For example, it side-stepped the Class Struggle, or it lacked Social Consciousness, or it tended to be Escapist, as in Sherwood Anderson's *Dark Laughter* or Floyd Dell's novels. Adventurous young critics, feeling their first flush of interest in a reviving labor movement, called for a proletarian renaissance, and some fair-to-middling or even good strike novels—William Rollins's *The Shadow Before,* Leane Zugsmith's *A Time to Remember,* Robert Cantwell's *Land of Plenty*—were produced. But the books of the '30's that had selling qualities were mostly historical novels, and the American Civil War began to come into its own. The "great writers" whose absence Van Wyck Brooks had deplored seemed more absent than ever. Why? What had happened to the promise of the '20's? We had had good realism then; why couldn't this realism be made the basis of a literature that would come to grips with the great issues of contemporary life that had been obscured in the fat decade of 1921–29? No one knows why, but there are various tentative suggestions that may be offered.

One of these is that a moral crisis underlies the paralysis of American fiction. The doctrine, so popular on the Left, that the end justifies the means (whether the means is absolutely essential to the attainment of the end or not) has robbed the young—and necessarily radical—writer of all moral perspective. Lacking personal touchstones of character, the young writer is powerless to create heroes or villains, or even to satirize shortcomings in those who are neither heroic nor villainous. The result is a feeble literature in which the issues are purely provisional, subject to change when the "line" changes. I am not arguing that the young novelist should not be vividly aware of the topsy-turvy and wholly unstable nature of his world. But he should not be compelled to shift his values overnight; it is impossible to deepen and develop and mature when one is constantly waiting for a new command on the morrow.

The dilemma of the socially conscious writer is illustrated by a young novelist of my acquaintance who has been trying for years to finish a book about the San Francisco waterfront strike of 1934. He cannot finish the book because he is all at sea concerning the motivating philosophy behind it. From month to month and year to year his attitude toward the personal values of his protagonist keeps fluctuating with the movement of radical values, of radical morality, in a world of Moscow trials, undeclared wars, "Trojan-horse" tactics, and political "timing" that frequently works out into two-timing. Are the communists right? Are they really democratic? Is opportunism justified, and if so, when? —and under what conditions? Should one be a direct-actionist, or is the Fabian attitude the proper attitude for a young writer of good will? Or should one be an ironist, ready to apply the perfectionist measuring-rod to all human beings and institutions?

Until history on one hand, or a deeply felt personal philosophy on the other, has told this young novelist what to think about ultimate issues he cannot successfully create a hero. The historical novelists have the better of him here, for in turning to the past they can let history substitute for the individual conscience. Drama must finally come to rest —it must result in a purgation of the emotions—to be effective. Where a theme already has a proven historical destination (as in the case of the American Civil War), the novelist can pick his side with a full knowledge of the implications of his choice. He can be "with history" (which may be the supreme opportunism), or he may be against history, but whether he regards the trend of past events as tragic or hopeful he can be firm about his values. The philosophical firmness of Margaret Mitchell's *Gone With the Wind* and Stark Young's *So Red the Rose* may seem reactionary to a Connecticut Yankee such as myself, but at least it gives backbone to character and integration to chapters. Books like *So Red the Rose* move, even though they may move in the wrong direction.

The central problem of the '30's is the relation of the individual to the mass in a period when industrial techniques necessarily underwrite the large—and therefore collective—institution. But the answers to the questions posed by the problem are not apparent, even though the Marxists think they have them all written down in the book. Simply because the future is more opaque now than it was a generation ago it takes a very courageous novelist to grapple with the central problem. He must not only create his characters, he must invent the answers which alone can give their activities meaning. Some novelists duck the issue entirely by writing of parochial things—Ellen Glasgow in her last novel, *Vein of Iron,* is a case in point. Some novelists cease to write novels—as witness Theodore Dreiser in the upper age brackets and Glenway Wescott in the lower. But some pound ahead, even though they have not actually settled for communism, fascism, distributivism, democratic syndicalism, or the kind of society that has been created by the Swedes. Most of the hardy sloggers are young people; our established writers are fearful of rushing in where the ideological angels dance on the head of a pin. But three of our established novelists—Ernest Hemingway, Sinclair Lewis, and John Dos Passos—have come to grips with the central issue. Their courage is commendable, even though all three of them fail in the final analysis. Hemingway's failure comes from an inability to handle ideas; Lewis's from a perverse unwillingness to let himself feel as he is able to feel. And Dos Passos, widely ranging traveller and sympathetic observer though he is, has failed to make his *U. S. A.* trilogy great or even adequately meaningful simply because he has travelled and observed in the wrong places. His tragic example of modern frustration is the engineer—but the engineer is the one human being Dos Passos does not know.

I do not wish, here, to treat of Hemingway (or Lewis or Dos Passos, for that matter) in the round: that job has been done in Malcolm Cowley's symposium, *After the Genteel Tradition*. But since the time John Peale Bishop paid homage to Hemingway for Mr. Cowley the author of *The Sun Also Rises* and *A Farewell to Arms* has changed, a little. His *To Have and Have Not* has all the virtues of the earlier books: the singing movement of speech, the glory in the precise recording of action, the delight in the good things of the senses, the fearful fascination of death and annihilation. But in *To Have and Have Not* Hemingway is trying to become philosophical; he is trying to make a simple and exciting action story carry with it a commentary on the central problem of the '30's. If he does not succeed, it is not for lack of will; it is simply because his "own material" is not of a nature to support his conclusions, which seem tacked on. It is as if Hemingway had written a rippling, fast-moving, wonderfully readable novelette for Arnold Gingrich's *Esquire* and then decided to make it suitable for *The New Masses*.

The protagonist of *To Have and Have Not* is a thirty-minute egg named Harry Morgan who makes his meager living by running rum, guns, Chinamen, and fishing parties in the waters of the Florida Keys. Harry had no money, but he did have his masculinity—his biceps, his colossal nerve, his boasted *cojones*—and he could and did succeed in pitting himself against the whole of organized society for the first part of his life. In the end, of course, he got his, as most people do when they single-handedly flout the laws and customs of the tribe. Pursued to this rather platitudinous conclusion, there is nothing wrong with the philosophical implications of *To Have and Have Not*. Hemingway is writing his own gangster morality yarn, a vastly superior version of Jack Black's *You Can't Win*.

And the proud slayer of the great Kudu should have left his jungle story at that. For Harry is no more a commentary on the failure of individualism under democratic law and modern industrialism than was John Dillinger. Harry is in love with his wife, but aside from his sense of honor as a husband he has only the faintest rudiments of a moral code; he is willing to kill if he can get money for it, and the fact that he does it for the wife and kiddies doesn't make the picture any prettier. It is perfectly true that Harry has often been wronged, and since the law of the jungle is "My life or yours" he has some justification for his own willingness to double-cross the double-crossers, cheat the cheaters, and murder the murderers. But when Harry kills the suave Chinaman, Mr. Sing, after taking a thousand or so dollars from him on condition that he will smuggle twelve Chinese from Cuba to the United States mainland, the scene makes Hemingway's hero a repellent person at the start. And when Harry, with the money in his pants, puts the twelve Chinese ashore in Cuba, even the "honor among thieves" axiom fades away; Harry is no one to keep a bargain with a dirty Chink. It is perfectly obvious to the reader that Harry is a bum, yet Hemingway would have you believe that he is a great symbol of wronged humanity.

Presumably Hemingway's idea is to make Harry Morgan seem a good man gone to waste because of the organization of a society that permits poor human stuff to get to the top by trickery within the law. Hemingway is scornful about the world of successful cheaters, and to show his scorn he takes the reader from yacht to yacht in the harbor of Key West. We see rich homosexuals and drunken grain brokers, smug patent-medicine kings and Hollywood nymphomaniacs. These, says Hemingway, are the successes of this world, and they are, by implication, to blame for an unequal division of things that puts Harry Morgan at the other end of the scale. But the joke is on Hemingway, for actually the yacht owners are cut from the same cloth as Harry Morgan. The great difference between the grain broker and Harry is a difference in intelligence, not in worth or morality. Is Harry somehow better than the grain broker because he has stronger muscles? Or because he has a good time with his wife and consequently remains faithful to her? Possibly he is a more admirable character because of his biceps and his *cojones,* but these can hardly be made the basis of a social morality; people can get along badly in catch-as-catch-can wrestling or with their wives and still refuse to steal. Conversely, men can live like saints at home or be as muscular as Joe Louis and still play the devil with society by gambling in Wall Street or La Salle Street.

Because of his inability to make even the most elementary moral distinctions it is difficult to make out what Hemingway is trying to show. Is he trying to prove that a collective way of life would release people like Harry Morgan for constructive building of the new order? If he is attempting to demonstrate this (and what else can Harry Morgan's sudden last-minute insight about the hopelessness of being a lone wolf mean?), then he hasn't made it clear, in dramatic terms, just why this is a valid inference to be drawn from *To Have and Have Not.* Inasmuch as Harry is presented as one who will murder to make a living, what assurance have we that, under communism, he wouldn't stoop to Ogpu cruelties of the worst sort—for the wife and kiddies and Lenin, of course, but cruelties, nevertheless? What assurance have we that Harry Morgan wouldn't turn his gangster proclivities to the most horrifying sort of work for a Yagoda? With his biceps and his sluggish moral sense, Harry Morgan might be even more of a menace if directed by a dictator than when directed by himself. And as for Mr. Hemingway's fine collection of literary wastrels who wander from bar to bar in Key West, they might thrive in the new world as party propagandists and palace-politicos.

If there is a lesson in *To Have and Have Not,* it is not the one Mr. Hemingway intended. The real lesson is an old one: that means frequently determine ends. If you develop claws you also create a vested interest in those claws; they will itch to rip even though the occasion has passed. The old doctrine of the Jesuits was that any means was justified that could be proved absolutely essential to reach the end. But the doctrine is not to be trusted. For since human beings can't read the future they can't ever know what means are absolutely necessary to the end. You may begin killing and robbing with the most noble intentions, but the game does something to you. And that is precisely what Hemingway proves. As a *deus ex machina* to blot out Harry Morgan at the proper moment, Hemingway introduces three Cuban revolutionaries who stoop to rob a bank for the "cause." One of these Cubans is a blood-weltering fool who has come to like the taste of human gore. Thus, on the other side of the barricades, we discover people behaving as Harry Morgan has sometimes behaved—and where is your better world? It is right here that we come upon the only valid meaning of *To Have and Have Not*—that people who stoop to ignoble means must become ignoble people, whether they do it for the wife and kiddies or for *Cuba libre* or for the world revolution. But Hemingway, a victim of the moral crisis that underlies the paralysis of our fiction, can't see the lesson of his own *dénouement*. His reportorial sense, always acute, completely contradicts the drift of his thinking. But he thinks on, and a good book is thereby spoiled.

Sinclair Lewis, who is as sensitive as litmus to changes in the ideological climate, has, in *The Prodigal Parents,* tried to say what Hemingway failed to say in *To Have and Have Not.* Lewis is aware of the central problem of the '30's; he knows the world is in the grip of change. But he knows it only imperfectly, and he has let his disgust for some of the tactics of change pull a veil over his eyes. Not so many years ago, before disgust seized him, Lewis thought to do a labor novel. He gave it up presumably because he couldn't find a dedicated Martin Arrowsmith of unionism among the bureaucracy of the American Federation of Labor. Since Lewis made his decision the labor movement has grown, and some of its new or reborn leaders are of a type which would have appealed to the creator of Arrowsmith or Sam Dodsworth. But Lewis has backtracked for subject matter, and has made his separate peace with George F. Babbitt.

He sees Babbitt, now, as a bewildered but honest creature who should be praised for his solid virtues instead of ridiculed for lack of grace and cultivation. The recreated Babbitt of 1938 is Frederick William Cornplow, who sells automobiles in an up-State New York city. Fred is a "bourjoyce," a kindly, self-respecting, hard-working husband and father who treats his children too well for their own good and even gives jobs to his leech-like country cousins. Fred's son and daughter, and the country cousins, are of the new generation that annoys Mr. Lewis because of the flavor, rather than the aim, of its revolt. The daughter, Sara, is a snob and a prig; she becomes a Communist sympathizer merely because it is the fashionable thing to do. Her mentor is a black-eyed agitator named Gene Silga, who believes the end can justify any means.

Now, with Mr. Lewis's schematization I have no desire to quibble; Lewis has a firm hold on his values and is thus in a position to create recognizable, consistent character. Lewis realizes, as any novelist should, that duplicity, smugness, vengefulness and tosh are no more palatable on the Left than they are on the Right; he realizes that the doctrine that honesty is a "bourgeois" virtue is an insidious one that leads directly to the Reign of Terror. And in realizing all this he is simply remaining true to the Lewis of *Main Street* and *Arrowsmith*. But the moral revulsion has not resulted in a good novel; in his rush to write a tract Lewis has lost his will to understand the whole inwardness of the situation. It is true that communists have frequently countenanced dirty political tricks. It is also true that many in the middle class are people of good will, sober, long-suffering, kind. But men can be knaves and still represent the lunatic fringe of a movement whose aspirations toward a decent life are understandable and noble. And middle class Americans can be sober, industrious and kind and still be sadly deficient in brains and political imagination.

In brief, Lewis succeeds where Hemingway fails, and fails where Hemingway succeeds. He used to succeed on all counts, in comprehension, in sympathy, in tact—and in thinking. Like his Sara Cornplow, Lewis's Carol Milford was pretty much of a snob and a prig. But Carol had an aspiration that made her wistful and appealing in spite of her talk about Maeterlinck and continental manners. Presumably Sara has her appealing side, but Lewis plays this down. Doc Kennicott of *Main Street* was very much like Fred Cornplow of *The Prodigal Parents*. But the young Sinclair Lewis knew that Doc was circumscribed and dull as boiled cod, whereas he can't see that Fred Cornplow is ignorant about the economic aspects of his business and provincial about all other things. Granted that Frederick William is honest. It still remains true that Fred Cornplow is dumb about the world of 1938 and hence is undeserving of the adulation which Lewis heaps upon him by a novelist's inference. Lewis makes Fred Cornplow wistful and that is supposed to excuse him for refusal to think. But a younger, more resilient Mr. Lewis made Babbitt wistful and appealing without excusing him at all. The difference between *Babbitt* and *The Prodigal Parents* is the difference between the wise surgeon who would cut and heal and the sentimentalist who would cure by saying "Oh, the poor thing!"

When he comes to create his radical agitator, Gene Silga of the black-enamel eyes, Lewis appears at his shoddiest. I share Mr. Lewis's disgust for political monolithism and for the sort of intellectual who is willing to let the politician do his thinking about social matters for him. I share his disgust for the tactics of jesuitry, for the doctrine that the end justifies the means. Nevertheless it is true that many communists are honestly convinced that devious tricks must be countered by devious tricks, that one good hypocrisy deserves another. Mr. Lewis portrays his organizer, Gene Silga, as cheap and cynical. But cheap and cynical people don't willingly risk blows from a nightstick for an ideal. The matter is more complex than that. Silga is a subject for high tragedy, not for cackling jeers. Lewis has come forward with the right answer. But he has come forward in a spirit of levity, and the people who would profit most by listening to him can hardly be expected to take him seriously.

Hemingway and Lewis have hit upon the central problem of the '30's, the relation of the individual to the mass, almost as an afterthought; apparently instinct had more to do with it than conscious planning. Sometimes it is better that way; certainly *To Have and Have Not* and *The Prodigal Parents,* disappointing though they may be, are better novels than some of those worked up by proletarian slide-rule. But where feeling and thinking coalesce, as in Dos Passos' *U. S. A.* trilogy, we have the most satisfactory fiction of the '30's.

When Dos Passos was writing *Three Soldiers* and the now forgotten *Streets of Night* the world was something to be kept at a distance; only the artist and his problems were real. But Dos Passos had too much fundamental curiosity to remain a precious analyst of the emotions of musicians, poets and æsthetic young men. As the remembered horrors of the World War became less painfully acute he began to look about him, to write of the sweep and color and meaning of events. *The 42nd Parallel, 1919* and *The Big Money,* a "collective" trilogy that tries to measure a variety of men and women against the drift of history from 1900 to 1929, is for the most part a magnificent job. Granted that its narrative is sometimes spare to the point of dryness, and that its intruding technical devices of Newsreel and Camera Eye are frequently confusing to the reader who wants to get on with the story. These points may be made again and again, but it is the very spareness of the prose and the staccato interruptions of the news headlines and the novelist's own stream of consciousness that carry the emotional tone of a disappointing epoch. And the rich rhythms of the interspersed Whitmanesque biographies of actual people—of Big Bill Haywood, Randolph Bourne, Thorstein Veblen, Sam Insull, Thomas Edison—all have their contrapuntal meaning. For these rhythms point by lush contrast the flat emotional life of Margo Dowling, the Irish girl who became a movie actress, or J. Ward Moorehouse, the dreary public relations counsellor, or Richard Ellsworth Savage, the Harvard æsthete. By his juxtapositions Dos Passos is trying to say that our common life is unable to make use of the brains of our exceptional men. The result of this social compartmentalization is a tragedy both for the Bournes and the Veblens and the Richard Ellsworth Savages and Margo Dowlings.

But in his crucial juxtaposition—that of Thorstein Veblen, author of *The Engineers and the Price System,* and Charlie Anderson, the drink-loving, woman-chasing aviator and inventor who goes up and down like a rocket in *The Big Money*—Dos Passos fails to draw the correct inferences. Like Hemingway, Dos Passos is all too willing to put the blame for personal disintegration on Society even in the most questionable cases. Charlie fails, we are given to understand, because the social system of the '20's encouraged all that was weak in him; it caused him to put money ahead of the technical problems of aviation engine design, and it made him into a drunken stock promoter instead of a serious contributor to the community's welfare. Charlie, the engineer, is the personal goat of the price system.

But that is not at all what Veblen has said. The truth of the matter is that the engineer, as a class, goes on working; very few inventors become lost by the wayside as stock promoters or climbers. As a type the engineer is far closer to Sinclair Lewis's Young Arrowsmith than to Dos Passos' Charlie Anderson. Take Thomas Midgeley, the chemist who synthesized the non-toxic, non-inflammable gas that is used in all good refrigerators. Take Leslie Middleton, the exuberant young engineer of Toledo's Electric Auto-Lite Company. Take Frank Conrad and Harvey Rentschler of the Westinghouse Electric Company. Take General Motors's Charles Franklin Kettering. The list might be extended from Schenectady to San Diego, but the same picture would emerge: engineers are not like Charlie Anderson. Patience, the will to qualify and refine, the sheer absorption in the technical problem at hand—these do not make for unstable characters.

But sheer absorption in the technical problem at hand does make for something else: it makes for a sort of engineer group-mind that is oblivious to social considerations. The real tragedy of the engineer is that the product of his brain and institutional background cannot be made available to more people under the price system. That is the meaning of Veblen, but it is a meaning that has eluded Dos Passos. In trying to personalize his feelings about the social system of the '20's Dos Passos has fallen victim to easy melodrama; he has let the Marxians, who unlike the Veblenians specialize in unsubtle distinctions, betray him as a social analyst. The result is that the *U. S. A.* trilogy ends on a false note of sentimentality. Like Charlie, we are invited to excuse our troubles on the theory that "Society done me wrong." But that is the way we lose our will to alter society by patient day-by-day work; self-pity leads to nothing but sterility. If Charlie Anderson were a valid character there would be no condemning Dos Passos as a novelist on the score that he inculcates a sense of frustration. But since Charlie is not valid, Dos Passos can be condemned in this instance as a bad realist and therefore a bad symbolist. The sense of frustration is not necessarily integral to a realistic consideration of the engineer. Indeed, the spectacle of the engineer working on in spite of social catastrophe all about him can be taken as one of the more hopeful auguries.

In painting my lugubrious picture of American fiction in the '30's I have slighted the work of Thomas Wolfe and James T. Farrell. Both Wolfe and Farrell can project live-and-kicking character on to the printed page; both have shown that they can sustain their work (although unevenly) through more than one book. But neither one of them has, as yet, shown what he can do with material that does not derive from experiences in boyhood and adolescence. Thomas Wolfe's Old Gant is wonderful, and young Gant (although frequently unable to distinguish between great and small adventures) is pretty good. But can Thomas Wolfe people a whole world, as Balzac and James and Howells peopled their worlds? Similarly with Farrell: can he go on from the world of the Chicago Irish of the 'teens and the '20's and write of the New York Irish of the '30's and '40's? The problem of continued immersion is important here; our writers have a habit of cutting themselves off from the life of our society as soon as they become writers, and the insulation results in desiccation once boyhood and youth are fully written about.

As for the lesser ornaments of our literature, such as John Steinbeck, I have no wish to decry them by omission. Steinbeck's versatility in encompassing both the lovable simplicity of *Tortilla Flat* and the stormily electric *In Dubious Battle* is fit cause for wonder. But I am one who thinks *Of Mice and Men* a phony, and I still want to be shown that this book is a mere interlude in a career. An author can stand one *Of Mice and Men,* but if Steinbeck continues to make tragedy out of involuntary knee jerks he will be lost.

Beyond Hemingway, Lewis and Dos Passos, beyond Farrell and Wolfe, the fiction of the '30's that one remembers is sparse indeed. There is Clyde Brion Davis, who can be both amusing and heart-wrenching, and there is William Saroyan, on his more inspired occasions, who can expand the living moment. Erskine Caldwell and William Faulkner have their points, but they have not developed into major artists. The proletarian school of Michael Gold, Edward Dahlberg, Edwin Seaver, Louis Colman, Edward Newhouse, Grace Lumpkin and the latter-day Sherwood Anderson has failed to keep up with events; they have followed good books with mediocre books, or they have written nothing at all. Fielding Burke and Leane Zugsmith have shown signs of growth within the dimensions of proletarianism, but Josephine Johnson has lost edge and finesse by embracing the Class Struggle before learning some elementary facts about the structure and movement of society. Albert Halper is good in precisely the proportions that he is warmly Dickensian about his factory hands; he would be the same if he wrote about the middle classes. The one real accomplishment of the proletarian drive is Thomas Bell's perfect little *All Brides Are Beautiful,* a sympathetic story of young love in the cluttered Bronx. But in general the proletarian revolution in literature has aborted, and we have had no other movement to take its place. Why has the drive fizzled? Can it be that the ideological panjandrums of the '30's have effectively held that life is too cheap to bother with fictional dignifying? Inasmuch as both the communists and the fascists are willing to wipe out human beings when they get in the way of ideology, perhaps we need a real resurgence of the democratic idea against the claims of each extreme before we can get an enduring American fiction. For when the popular philosophy holds that the human being is made for the State, the corollary will be cheap and timid citizens and novelists too fearful of the consequences to write honestly of the debased personalities they find around them.

# POETRY

*[Louise Bogan]*

The age demanded an image
Of its accelerated grimace,
Something for the modern stage,
Not, at any rate, an Attic grace.

Not, not certainly, the obscure reveries
Of the inward gaze;
Better mendacities
Than classics in paraphrase!

The "age demanded" chiefly a mould in plaster,
Made with no loss of time,
A prose kinema, not, not assuredly alabaster
Or the "sculpture' of rhyme.
E. Pound, H. S. Mauberly (London, 1920).

After such knowledge, what forgiveness?
T. S. Eliot, Gerontion (1920).

## I

AMERICAN poetry in 1912 had not even sighed or turned in the sleep that fell upon it late in the 90's. During the twenty-five years from 1912 to 1937 it was not only awakened, but kept awake through a series of shocks both real and artificial. Exotic and unforeseen example was dinned into its ears, and phantasmagoria of all kinds paraded before its eyes. Also, it was brutally confronted with some thorough glimpses of hard reality. That it has now lapsed back into a kind of exhausted coma is not surprising.

Coma is, perhaps, too hard a word. Magazines in America still publish poetry, and American newspapers and magazines still review it. Books of verse are brought out by publishers year after year; one or two prizes are still awarded; and the Guggenheim Foundation annually includes two or three poets in its list of Fellows. But from any point of view the present situation is in no way comparable to the situation which existed in the years 1912–1918, when, as if at a given signal, American poetry burst into unprecedented activity. The dead hand of the bearded masters of the school-books—Longfellow, Whittier, Bryant—which had still been felt, hard upon the poetry written earlier in the young century, now was thoroughly shaken off. The expansive Whitman technique, which had earlier experienced some modified revival in the poems of Stephen Crane, again came to life, at the touch of the *vers libre* forms so agitating to formal French verse in the '80's. From 1912 up to the time of America's entrance into the War, American poetry stiffly competed with American fiction in popularity: books of poetry became best-sellers; the country's lecture-halls filled with audiences eager for the voice and works of lecturing poets. Controversy raged over the hitherto, to the general populace, inactive issues of poetic content and form. And not only was poetry read, bought, and listened to; it was written in quantity by, it sometimes seemed, every third literate person on the North American continent.

This "poetic renaissance" might easily be explained if the poets who appeared in its forefront had been drawn exclusively from racial groups newly introduced into the American scene: from the children of Scandinavian, Italian, German, Irish, Polish and Jewish immigrants who, after having had the advantages of American compulsory schooling, the use of free American libraries, and so on, came to maturity in 1912. This explanation does not entirely fit the case, since several of the most spectacular talents of the poetic awakening stemmed from native American stock. Robert Frost, Edwin Arlington Robinson, Vachel Lindsay, Wallace Stevens, Sara Teasdale, Marianne Moore, and Amy Lowell shared a native Yankee heritage. A student of the period, casting about for explanations, is soon struck by the fact that the leadership of the new movement was from the first almost exclusively in the hands of cultured and more or less affluent women. The influence of American patronesses on the American arts has never been gone into thoroughly. Henry James, who scrutinized American and European society (and all combinations of the two) during the '80's and '90's, has repeatedly depicted the sometimes touching, sometimes crass, but always persistently eager American girl and woman set free by the business success of husband or father, and enabled to roam Europe in quest of "better things." This type, by 1912, had become poised and sophisticated. In Western cities, as well as in Boston and New York, the tentative gropings toward culture of women of a previous generation came out in courageous and serviceable form, in the characters of certain cultivated bourgeois women.

In the field of poetry, the patroness type emerged as a real fighter for a cause. Harriet Monroe founded, in Chicago in 1912, *Poetry: A Magazine of Verse*. Amy Lowell, in Boston, from a small start as a member of the Imagist group, advanced into practical generalship of the entire poetic revival. These women enlarged the rôle of patroness. They did not merely coddle and encourage; they fought, developed, and irritated.

The flood of *vers libre* was in part checked by the War. The poetic revival, according to one pleased professor of the old school, had "petered out, ending in a complete debâcle." The exact contrary was true. The real fight against Victorian sentimentality, academic timidity, provincial ignorance, and lack of taste—the real exploration of new, and exhumation of forgotten or overlooked, reputations, had just begun. Emily Dickinson, for example, was brought forward from almost complete oblivion, after 1920; her genius became so much a contemporary one that she was nearly always referred to by (in her own affectionate fashion) her first name.

In 1910, two years before Miss Monroe established *Poetry,* an American living and studying in Europe published in London a book of essays entitled *The Spirit of Romance*. The author, in his preface, said:

This book is not a philological work. Only by courtesy can it be said to be a study in comparative literature.

I am interested in poetry. I have attempted to examine certain forces, elements or qualities which were potent in the mediæval literature of the Latin tongues, and are, as I believe, still potent in our own.

I have floundered somewhat ineffectually through the slough of philology, but I look forward to the time when it will be possible for the lover of poetry to study poetry—even the poetry of recondite times and places—without burdening himself with the rags of morphology, epigraphy, *privatleben,* and the kindred delights of the archæological or "scholarly" mind. I make no plea for superficiality. But I consider it quite as justifiable that a man should wish to study the poetry and nothing but the poetry of a certain period, as that he should study its antiquities, phonetics or paleography and be, at the end of his labours, incapable of discerning a refinement of style or a banality of diction.

These convictions Ezra Pound (for the American was indeed he) was soon to elucidate both to Amy Lowell and Harriet Monroe. Pound became the foreign correspondent of *Poetry* soon after the magazine came into being. Amy Lowell met Pound in London and carried back to America her own kind of enthusiasm for his theories, and her own interpretation of the exotic literature he had brought to her attention. She translated, imitated, prosecuted, and proselytized.

But it was not until ten years later that a truly remarkable, a completely successful and integrated, illustration of Pound's theories came into view. Granting the excellent work written, and the unflagging courage displayed by American poets, before and just after the War, the triumph of the American Poetic Renaissance was indubitably *The Waste Land,* by T. S. Eliot, Pound's self-confessed pupil. This poem first appeared in America in *The Dial,* in November, 1922.

## II

It is evident, then, that the more cursory the survey of the present state of American poetry, the more important it is to give Ezra Pound his just due as fore-runner, instigator, and innovator. His self-imposed exile from America is now of thirty years duration. Since his voyage away, due both to his own efforts and his influence upon his gifted pupil, T. S. Eliot, English poetic expression has been released from the muted tone which had fallen upon it during the early years of the present century. After taking his Master's degree at the University of Pennsylvania, which he had entered at the age of fifteen, he published his first book of poetry in Venice, in 1908 (*A Lume Spento*) at the age of twenty-three. He soon took up residence in London and had already launched, before the War, in that city, the first of his invigorating "movements": the Imagist. The Imagist program laid down for the first time the main tenets in Pound's artistic creed. His main insistence, after he had emerged from youthful enthusiasms for Browning and Villon, was placed "on clarity and precision, upon the prose tradition: in brief, upon efficient writing, even in verse." The Imagist manifesto (1913) read, in part: "To use the language of common expression, but to employ always the *exact* words, not the merely decorative word. . . . To create new rhythm, as the expression of new moods. . . . To allow absolute freedom in the choice of subject. . . . To produce poetry that is hard and clear, never blurred or indefinite." Pound also insisted on texture, sincerity and concentration.

These rules, as we have seen, were distorted and popularized in America by the proselytizing efforts of Amy Lowell. Pound, meanwhile, had found a new disciple, a man whose intellectual equipment exceeded that of any one who had come under his influence up to that time, and a man whose own poetic style was already to some degree formed. T. S. Eliot had already practised in his early poems, written at Harvard and thereafter, an eclecticism of differing styles (Laforgue and the Elizabethans). Pound's own practice, of ranging freely through the literary styles of periods widely separated in time and countries widely separated in space, reinforced and enlarged Eliot's. The range of Pound's enthusiasms, now fairly familiar to readers, may here partially be listed: "The Seafarer," the pre-Dante Italian lyricists, Dante, Propertius, the Alexandrian Callimachus and the classical Homer, Chinese poets and Japanese Noh dramatists. The two poets deliberately set about the task of disinterring concrete and passionate talents, chiefly English, French and Italian, over which a cloud of indifference had passed. They began to incorporate into their writing elliptical effects taken over from the French Symbolists, and broader ones derived from Dante, Baudelaire, the Jacobean playwrights and the English metaphysical poets. John Donne in particular was singled out as a man whose work closely coincided with the modern temper. (A definitive edition of Donne, edited by Professor Grierson, had appeared in 1912.) Donne's power, expressed in simple and intense statement, or in the elaborate conceit, made a particular appeal to modern complicated, realistic but disoriented sensibilities. The malicious remark of a conservative critic: "It is one of the illusions of our age that Donne was invented by T. S. Eliot," is in some ways well taken.

Pound's critical writing after the rather conventionally written *Spirit of Romance* had been of an eccentric kind—more in the nature of fulminations than ordered precepts. His insights had been projected with insolence, his major intuitions announced with sarcasm. Always against the complacency and slickness and shallowness of the academic mind, he had permitted himself only an anecdotal and disjointed style.

Critically, his habit was to turn even on his own convictions; to change constantly; continually to turn up and discover. Eliot, on the other hand, with more patience, was capable of molding the critical theories he shared with Pound into form. His volume of essays, *The Sacred Wood,* published in 1920, became the critical Bible of the younger generation of American poets.

Pound's poetry, although vivid and accomplished, was as fragmentary as his prose. It was also equally bad-tempered. He was liable to combine, even in a brief lyric, abuse with delicate taste and illumination. Sometime before 1920 he turned away from *vers libre* and produced *Hugh Selwyn Mauberly* (London 1920). According to his characteristically expressed version of the matter, he and Eliot made the decision for form in collaboration.

At a particular date in a particular room, two authors, neither engaged in picking the other's pockets, decided that the dilution of *vers libre,* Amygism, Lee Masterism, general floppiness, had gone too far and that some counter-current must be set going. Parallel situation centuries ago in China. Remedy prescribed *Emaux et Camées* (or the Bay State Hymn Book). Rhyme and regular strophes. Results: Poems in Mr. Eliot's *second* volume, not contained in his first *Prufrock* (Egoist, 1917), also *H. S. Mauberly.* Divergence later.[1]

Eliot's second volume of poetry, *Poems,* was published in America in 1920. Its effect, at first slight, was soon to become the strongest shock that his young contemporaries received. It was Eliot's *Poems* and his *The Waste Land* which were to bear fruit in very nearly every poetic talent functioning in America from 1920 on. Their influence has not been entirely dissipated up to the present moment, although the peculiar post-war disillusion into which they were first projected has largely disappeared, or at least given way to disillusions of a different order.

Pound's *Mauberly* was not published in an American edition until 1926 (*Personæ*). By that time American poetry had become thoroughly saturated with Eliot. But it is important that the initial efforts of Pound should not be overlooked or underestimated. If it is true that culture rolls up to a certain point and unexpectedly explodes through the highly charged individuals which punctuate its course, Pound was certainly the person who, in the barren 1907 American literary scene, received the spark from the invisible current. Though it is now the fashion to speak of him with condescension, no one interested in American poetry should for one moment forget his importance, however much he has been surpassed in entirely successful achievement by his pupils, or belittled by the academic minds he has spent his life in insulting.

## III

*The Waste Land* bore the dedication: "To Ezra Pound, *il miglior fabbro.*" Its effect was immediate. The poem at first infuriated all but a small section of the Americans who read poetry, critics and laymen alike. Its emotional power, which fused into Eliot's own tone a *pastiche* of lines and phrases drawn from other poets, its extraordinary range of reference, its complexity and great technical ease—all these elements at first baffled readers unused to the shock of true originality. Later, Eliot's imitators, by their more ordinary efforts, padded the impact of Eliot's emotion and softened his manner to such an extent that at fourth or

[1]Essay on Harold Monro, *Polite Essays,* by Ezra Pound. Faber and Faber, 1937.

fifth remove they became not only acceptable but even popular with the general public. The theme of "spiritual drought" coincided with the general post-war let-down, so that *The Waste Land* came to be a kind of spiritual *vade mecum* to the intelligentsia of the '20's. Eliot himself published little during the ten years after *The Waste Land*. *The Hollow Men* (1925) indicated, in the concentrated beauty of its final pages, the change in Eliot's beliefs. He became a British subject in 1927, and announced in 1929 his conversion to Anglican religion and Tory politics. *Ash Wednesday* (1930) celebrated his conversion, but with a note of technical weariness and spiritual depletion. Eliot did not, however, stop his technical experimentations. The *Collected Poems* published in America in 1936 gathered together the frequently beautiful and consistently original experiments with which he continued to concern himself. This volume contained, as well, the choruses from *The Rock,* the pageant written by Eliot in 1934 for a charitable purpose of the Anglican church, to a fellow-Anglican's scenario. These choruses show the unimpeded spirit working in full strength in new channels. This later phase of Eliot's development did not draw disciples into its orbit. It was the Eliot of *The Waste Land* and the *Poems* who continued to set his accent upon the younger writers of the time.

Although Eliot's influence was pervasive, it was not all inclusive during the decade from 1922 to 1932. The revulsion from *vers libre* brought into popularity certain talents which would have come into being in any case, if Eliot had never existed. Running parallel with the schools of experimentation, an unexpectedly pure and completely traditional lyric movement began. This showed almost simultaneously in the work of two women, Edna St. Vincent Millay and Elinor Wylie. Edna Millay had been writing since 1912, when her first book, *Renascence,* appeared, and had achieved some minor reputation as the mouthpiece of emancipated youth. But her first completely integrated book, *Second April* (1922), followed Mrs. Wylie's *Nets to Catch the Wind* (1921). *Second April* brought out clearly Miss Millay's great endowment, a talent both direct and poignant, which, although expressed in conventional meters, was not stiffened into awkwardness or led into mawkishness by them. She depended, in her best work, hardly at all upon literary ornament (her ornament, when used, was, to be sure, rather threadbarely "classic"). Her lines carried the weight of their emotion on the whole with unambiguous simplicity. Unlike Miss Millay, Mrs. Wylie tended toward color, imagery used for its own sake and elaborate rhymes. She later came strongly under the influence of Eliot and of Donne. Both women instinctively rejected the humanitarian sentimentality of an Elizabeth Barrett Browning, coming closer, in spite of their modern attitudes, to the anguished clarity of Christina Rossetti.

This lyric impulse had, for a time, a great influence on the whole body of American poetry. Men came under its dominance as well as women. Critics and the reading public succumbed to Miss Millay completely. Her sonnets were compared to those of Shakespeare; phrases from her lyrics passed into current speech. Mrs. Wylie's posthumous volume, *Angels and Earthly Creatures,* published after her untimely death in 1928, contained her finest work, including an extraordinary sonnet sequence. Miss Millay published in 1931 a book of sonnets dedicated to Elinor Wylie, with a title again drawn from Donne (*Fatal Interview*). Here her technical virtuosity outran emotional impulse, and Miss Millay's vein for the first time seemed forced. These two sonnet sequences closed the possibilities of this form, so far as it could be further exploited by women, for some time to come. The whole lyrical school, in fact, now began to suffer an eclipse. It was a school which could too easily be enfeebled by the functioning of feeble gifts within it. Its virtues of simple directness, if not kept absolutely clear, faded into inanity. Its high tension was difficult to sustain. When unmixed with new hardness and vigor, its forms dropped into limpness or its emotion receded into bathos. Female lyric grief soon came in for some ridicule, and not a little contempt. In 1937, a member of the Poets' Session of the League of American Writers decided that "the lyric is dead." His remark met with little skepticism.

## IV

Poetry, during what has recently been called "the mediæval '20's," was diffused throughout America by means of little magazines, the number of which was unexampled. *The Dial* continued to be, throughout the decade, the main æsthetic organ. Its period of publication coincided almost exactly with the opening and closing of the ten years: it began in January 1920 and ceased publication in July 1929. During that era it presented for examination examples of literary experimentation in prose, poetry and criticism, drawn from the work of writers of many nations. Its first editor was Scofield Thayer, its second an experimental poet of the first rank, Marianne Moore. For a time *The Dial* awarded the annual sum of $1000 to the writer who produced, in its editor's opinion, the year's most distinguished writing. It overlooked very little new talent: Hart Crane, for example, was published in *The Dial* as early as 1922. *The Little Review,* a magazine originating in Chicago, which brought out sections of James Joyce's *Ulysses* in 1918, also kept itself open to new writers and new forms, both American and European, up to the spring of 1929 when it, too, perished. *Poetry: A Magazine of Verse,* although hospitable to all schools, was more kindly to the native lyric than its sister publications. *The Hound and Horn* (designated, in its first numbers, "A Harvard Miscellany") functioned as an æsthetic outlet later than most others (1927–34). The lesser monthlies or quarterlies were legion. They appeared all over America—in Peoria, Illinois; Chapel Hill, N. C.; Davenport, Iowa; Madison, Wis.; Athens, Ohio; Baton Rouge, Louisiana; Providence, Rhode Island, as well as in New York, Boston, and Cambridge, Mass.

Following the exodus, in Pound's and Eliot's footsteps of writers to Europe, which occurred as the '20's began, the unheard of phenomenon of magazines published in Europe under American editors came into being. These were often polyglot, with contributions in several languages appearing in the same issue. Poetry of all kinds (although the poem written with rhyme and "regular strophes" was rather rare), written by Americans expatriated and otherwise, flooded their pages. Typographical effects, ranging from no punctuation, no capital letters, through wrenched punctuation and occultly used capital letters; Poundian effects of foreign tags and quotations; Joycean effects of elided and distorted English; infusions of *argot* and obscenities; approximation of "jazz" rhythms; oblique references to people and things real, recondite or mythological—all these means were used to strike not only the entire gamut of actual emotions in the reader, but also to express an abstruse range of feeling supposititiously existing in, over, and around the reader.[2] *Transition,* founded in 1927, at a time when the new fields of expression were being most diligently explored, soon became the official vehicle for the publication of Joyce's "Work in Progress." Joyce's experiments in language had a strong influence on poetical form. As Edmund Wilson has remarked, prose, before this, had begun to draw poetry into its province. Poetry then took back effects from this poetically infiltrated prose. From the base line of Gertrude Stein, James Joyce, and the Dadaists, experimental poetry flew off into surprising and aerial tangents. *Transition*

[2]That poetry was plumbing the Freudian subconscious, the Jungian "racial memory" was sometimes, but not always, admitted by the poets.

(the initital T wavered from lower to upper case) stated its beliefs from time to time:

*Transition* believes in the occult hypnosis of language. *Transition* demands an insurrection against the rationalist metaphor. . . .

and later, in 1932, when enthusiasm was waning and the economic crisis thinning the ranks of enthusiasts, *Transition* began to link up the economic crisis with a passionately announced crisis in art—the "World-Revolution" with the "Revolution of the Word." It called itself, at this time: "An International Workshop for Orphic Creation."

While the general crisis is being liquidated, the new *Transition* proposes the revision of all values that no longer answer our deepest needs. The new *Transition* (publication had lapsed in 1930) proposes to defend the hallucinative forces now trodden underfoot, and to maintain their primacy under any social system that may come. . . . The new *Transition,* having little faith in Reason or Science as ultimate methods, proposes to establish a mantic laboratory that will examine the new personality, particularly with relation to the irrational forces dominating it. The new *Transition* proposes to encourage all attempts towards a subliminal ethos through mediumistic experiments in life and language.

Desertion from the ranks, in spite of this call to arms, went on steadily. A former member of the army of æsthetes definitely stated his position when, in 1935, *The New Transition: An International Workshop for Vertigralist Transmutation* sent out a questionnaire, designed to sound out writers' reactions to the crisis through which, it was convinced, language was passing. Malcolm Cowley answered, briefly, that he thought a revolution in language was "useless."

As for creating new words, Lenin and Stalin did that by helping to create new conditions that would call for them. . . .

A full stop in the energy released by Pound in Venice, Italy, in 1908, had evidently been reached.

## V

Before describing the consequences of the almost complete ingestion, after 1930, of the æsthetic by the political Left, we must look briefly at one or two original talents and one or two schools which came into being before 1930. Expatriate poets and critics who had come back to America, in 1928 or thereabouts, in the short interval between their return and the onset of the financial depression, went through a period of seeking a poet who could sum up in his work their taste for force and unconventionel form, and express in his life their determination to keep the bourgeoisie continually and thoroughly struck with astonishment. They unanimously decided that Hart Crane was the man. His genius was incontestable and of the *poète maudit* order. He strove to define, in his poetry, some symbolical meaning drawn from the disorder he experienced both in the outer world and in his own complicated nature. Several self-appointed John the Baptists tendered the robes of a poetic Messiah to Crane, and hailed his long poem *The Bridge* (1930) as a prophetic book.[3] Crane, coming to a tragic creative and spiritual *impasse* which he could not resolve, committed suicide in 1932. By that time most of his disciples had decided against an isolated æsthetic Messiah and had gone toward a complete economic religion.

Several "regional" schools of poetry sprang up. The most vigorous of these was the Fugitive Group of Nashville, Tennessee, whose members combined, to some degree, both experimental and "reactionary" forms. Allen Tate and John Crowe Ransom, the group's most gifted members, drew nourishment from the Valéry-Mallarmé school directly, as well as from French Symbolism already filtered through the talents of Eliot and Pound. Another "regional" phenomenon was Robinson Jeffers, a Californian who produced a series of extraordinary Gothic-Greek tragedies enacted against a California back-drop.

The principal popularizer of the Pound-Eliot formula was Archibald MacLeish. MacLeish went to Europe in 1923, and soon afterward began producing poems which were built directly on the *Gerontion* and *Wasteland* framework. MacLeish's popularity reached its high point in 1932, with *Conquistador*. Stendhal's axiom: that it takes eighty years for a work of art to reach the public, has been proved more often than it has been refuted. The public will, however, appreciate skillful dilution of such a work immediately. Once Mr. MacLeish had smoothed the rough edges, harmonized the dissonances and knitted together the discontinuity of the Pound-Eliot manner, the public took it to its heart. *Conquistador* (Pulitzer Prize, 1932) leaned heavily not only upon the expatriate Masters themselves, but upon Eliot's translation of St. J. Perse's *Anabase*.[4] The influence of the Great Exiles had at last returned to native

---

[3]Waldo Frank's introduction to *The Bridge* exposes this pseudo-religious feeling in a remarkable way.

[4]*Anabase* by St. John Perse, translated by T. S. Eliot, London, 1930.

shores, insinuated into a poem with a native American theme. *Con-quistador* did not enjoy the popularity of Stephen Vincent Benét's *John Brown's Body* (Pulitzer Prize, 1929), a long narrative which owed nothing to European coloring, either in subject or form. MacLeish's poem enjoyed a great *succes d'estime,* however, and later cast its composite shadow on the work of many younger poets, Stephen Benét, oddly enough, among them.

## VI

The movement of the poets toward the Left, from 1930 on, was so complete as to be almost symptomatic. The former "expatriates" and "æsthetes," now somewhat middle-aged and disabused with the non-paying school of *l'art pour l'art,* went over to Belinsky and Stalin[5] in a body. Only those poets whose reputations, established before the war, were mellowed by time stood free of the general alteration in belief. Their ranks were somewhat thinned. Amy Lowell had died in 1925; Lindsay had committed suicide in 1929. Frost, Sandburg, Wallace Stevens, Marianne Moore (whose *Collected Poems* received a critical accolade from Eliot in 1935) and Robinson, up to the time of his death in 1935, continued to produce work dictated by their talents and not by ideological formulæ. MacLeish, too, for a short time stood out for art, as opposed to politics, and treated the Marxian dialectic and the foreign accents of its adherents to some gentlemanly ridicule (*Frescoes for Mr. Rockefeller's City, 1933*). But in a remarkably short time he, too, was swept away to a Leftish position—to the point, at least, of recommending that "love harden into hate," and of advising scholars to come out of their studies and go into action. His manner still irrevocably colored by private pathos, he came out for "public speech." The result was a curious one.

The persistence of pathos, nostalgia and non-cheering irony (all of which were explained, by the converted, as results of a dying bourgeois culture) in poetry springing from the fresh impulses of political faith, produced some strange results. The new political verse was infused with a kind of gloom. Its hopeful tendencies were accompanied by no clear clarion voice. When it tried to be ambitious it became turgid and dull; when it strove to be vigorous and heartening it often gave off a shrill hysterical sound.

Meanwhile, in England, a group of young men with Oxford educations

[5]The first whole-hearted allegiance has suffered several severe splits. Writers with Left convictions have divided into Stalinist and Trotskyite groups. The Stalinists now claim to be the voice of American democracy; the Trotskyites claim a purer revolutionary passion.

and, in some cases, high poetical endowments, had espoused the cause of the proletariat. The poems of W. H. Auden, C. Day Lewis and Stephen Spender, published in American editions in 1934, at once gained warm disciples. When these latest influences were added to the ones already existing, the confusion grew. For Auden and Spender, one a satirist and the other a romantic lyricist, were heavily indebted, stylistically, to several obscure and complicated fore-runners, Gerard Manley Hopkins and Wilfred Owen in particular. When Hopkins's violent concentration and "sprung rhythms," and Owen's off-rhymes were added to Eliot's oblique reference, the result was stupefying. In place of the prosodic clarity and emotional force desiderated for the expression of new and sincerely held beliefs, a kind of spiritual paralysis and enveloping turgidity fell upon young American poets. Auden soon cleared himself up, through continual experiment and a growing capacity for detachment and light-heartedness. His admirers remained, however, for the most part, stuck in his earlier manner, being unable to surmount it through any individual growth of their own.

## VII

Perhaps the most dreadful human situation conceivable would be an age of dogmatic faith unenlightened by the use of the spiritual side of man. Although a major achievement of our time has been the clinical proof that the letter killeth, while the spirit giveth life; that it is healthier to love than to hate; that maturity means responsibility; that the closed nature is the nature in which mania takes root; that if one refuses to go forward, one immediately starts to go back, this discovery has not been generally absorbed. Nostalgia, cruelty and gloom are not so much the signs of the death of a culture as they are of individual regression. The artist, as one Marxian critic has pointed out, does not function in a vacuum. Neither does he function out of a vacuum. Poetry is an activity of the spirit; its roots lie deep in the subconscious nature, and it withers if that nature is denied, neglected or negated. No amount of heroic action, no adherence to noble beliefs can release poetic expression to order. The dialectical play of the mind or the aggressive action of the body effect its functioning not at all. Its battles are fought in secret and, perhaps, "are never lost or won." The certain method of stilling poetic talent is to substitute an outer battle for an inner one. A poet emerges from a spiritual crisis strengthened and refreshed, only if he has been strong enough to fight it through at all levels, and at the deepest first. One refusal to take up the gage thrown down by his own nature leaves the artist confused and maimed. And it is not one confrontation, but many, which must be dealt with and resolved. The first evasion throws the poet back into a lesser state of development which no show of bravado can conceal. "A change of heart" is the result of slow and difficult inner adjustments. A mere shift in allegiance, if it is not backed up by conflict genuinely resolved, produces, in the artist, as it produces in any one, confusion and insincerity. The two great poets of our time, Rilke and Yeats, because they fought their own battles on their own ground, became, first, mature men, and then mature artists. They drew to themselves more and more experience; their work never dried up at the source or bloated into empty orotundity. The later poetry of both is work based on simple expression, deep insight and deep joy.

At present, the signs of spiritual health in American poetry are few. Elaboration of method has been accompanied by impoverishment of matter. Forms built out from inner intensity are in disrepute. And strong flavors are avoided; one rarely comes upon, for example, "the strychnine and capsicum of irony." Taste is damned as precious; small effects, though well-observed and deeply felt, as "futile." The clarity, complexity and vigor which Pound and Eliot endeavored to define critically and use creatively have been so weakened and sweetened that they are now indistinguishable from the Victorian insipidity which went before them.

But the current is invisible, and even now, as we deplore its absence, it may again be ready to discharge its spark.

# MUSIC

## [*Deems Taylor*]

SEVENTEEN years ago I wrote the chapter on Music in the earlier version of *Civilization in the United States*. After re-reading that chapter, which I did the other night, I begin to realize what people mean when they talk about age bringing tolerance. How crystal clear was the vision of that young man in his early thirties; how keen his analyses; how irrefutable his logic, and how merciless his conclusions! "Mellow" is hardly the word that I would apply to his point of view. Boiled down, his conclusions were that American composers had some talent, but were musical illiterates, and suffered from an inferiority complex. The latter, largely, because Americans as a whole thought musicians were sissies and didn't give a damn about music anyhow. I can say only this for him: That he thought he was right.

As a matter of fact, I am not at all sure that he wasn't right—then. He might be now, but for a phenomenon that has changed our entire attitude toward music in the incredibly little space of less than twenty years. As a preamble to discussing that phenomenon, let me quote a paragraph from the earlier chapter. It runs as follows:

The American is by no means as unmusical as he thinks he is. His indifference to art is only the result of his purely industrial civilization, and his tendency to mix morals with æsthetics is a habit of thought engendered by his ancestry. The Puritan tradition makes him fearful and suspicious of any sort of sensuous or emotional response, but it has not rendered him incapable of it. Catch him off his guard, get him away from the fear of being bored, and he is far from insensitive to music. He buys Victrola records because he wants to hear the expensive Caruso and Kreisler and McCormack; but inevitably he is bound to take some notice of what they play and sing, and to recognize it when he hears it again. In spite of himself he begins to acquire a rudimentary sort of musical background. He begins by buying jazz rolls for his player-piano, and is likely in the long run, if only out of curiosity, to progress from "blues" to Chopin, via Moszkowski and Grainger.

I am secretly proud of that paragraph, for subsequent events have proved its author to be absolutely right in his estimate of the average American's potentialities as a music-lover. On the other hand—and I offer this sentence free of charge to proponents of a planned economy—it is a striking illustration of the fact that one can be quite right in his elucidation of a desirable objective and quite wrong in one's guess as to how it is to be brought about. The Victrola that my younger self mentions is still in existence as a pleasant adjunct to other methods of hearing music, but it has not, I think, proved to be a particularly valuable educational force in this country, so far as concerns the average American. As for the player-piano, while it is not quite one with Nineveh and Tyre, it has been too expensive to be useful in spreading music except among a handful of the highly solvent.

Our author makes no mention whatsoever of the medium that has brought about the miracle for which he hoped—for the simple reason that it did not then exist. It was in 1922, at the offices of the old *New York World,* that I was led up to a weird accumulation of batteries, coils, and miscellaneous evil-looking gadgets that covered most of the top of a largish table. Some one handed me a pair of earphones, and through them, faint and far, I heard something that approximated the voice of a woman singing.

How was I, or any one else, to know what a fabulous future lay ahead of that piece of laboratory apparatus? The earliest radio receiving sets were home-made, and what rudimentary entertainment they transmitted was offered, as a stimulus to trade, by the manufacturers of parts. The trade flourished, and other manufacturers began to subsidize radio programs as publicity for their particular wares. Then enterprising manufacturers began to make and market completely assembled receiving sets. These were far better, if not cheaper, than the home-made variety, so much so that their owners began to take good reception for granted, and began to listen critically to the quality of the programs. And programs began to improve.

The depression was a godsend to radio, although it seemed far otherwise at the time. Up to 1929, the average radio set was a bulky affair, about the size and weight of an old-fashioned cabinet Victrola, and expensive. With the crash, the market for these heavy and costly affairs vanished almost overnight. In order to keep their heads above water, the radio manufacturers had to develop lightweight, portable sets, which could be sold cheaply enough to fit the average depleted pocketbook. Simultaneously, as people found themselves with no spending money for theatres, night clubs, and vaudeville, they stayed home, perforce, and bought those portable sets in order to have something to listen to during the lean winter evenings. Wide distribution made mass production possible, with improved quality and lowered prices. No one knows exactly how many radio sets are in use in this country today, but the number is probably not less than 20,000,000. Counting two listeners to a set, 40,000,000 Americans listen to radio programs today, using apparatus that is the best and cheapest in the world.

And what do those radio programs bring them? Let me quote another author, a high-school girl in Santa Rosa, California. This is part of a letter she wrote me concerning the Philharmonic-Symphony broadcasts:

About five months ago I got the idea that it might prove rather interesting to keep a record of all the symphonic music that I heard on the radio. And so, ever since, I have written down in a little black book the name and composer of every number I have heard, also the orchestra performing it, and the date it was played. I think the result is rather an accurate account of what an average listener who is really interested in good music can hear. I have not included in my list any of the operas, performances by chamber ensembles, or recitals by concert artists that I have also heard—nothing but strictly symphonic music. Also, nothing that I have included was a recorded performance. Here are a few of the results of my five months of radio listening:

I have heard fifty-two complete symphonies. Included in that number, the following were played three times each: the Brahms First and Second, the César Franck D minor, and the Sibelius Fourth. I have heard twice, the following: Mozart's Haffner and G minor symphonies, the Beethoven Fifth, the Brahms Fourth, the Tschaikovsky Fifth, the Sibelius Second, and Mendelssohn's "Italian" symphony. The others, which I heard once, included all of Beethoven's except the Fourth, and all seven of the Sibelius symphonies. Among some of the symphonic works played less frequently, I heard symphonies by Borodin, Bruckner, Quincy Porter, and Shostakovitch; also, of course, single movements of many other symphonies. I have heard a total of 582 overtures, suites, symphonic poems, and ballets, played by practically all of the leading orchestras of the country, including those of Philadelphia, San Francisco, Cleveland, Chicago, Rochester, Seattle, Portland, Los Angeles, Detroit, and New York. Needless to say, I have heard as many fine conductors as I have orchestras. I listened to six all-Wagner programs, two all-Strauss, and two all-Ravel.

Now that letter can be construed as a vivid and effective testimonial to the virtues of American broadcasting; but its implications are wider than that. If there is available on the air such a quantity of good music as my correspondent describes, there must be an audience for it. American broadcasting, unlike any other system in the world, is on a highly competitive basis. The three big networks and the countless small local stations have one main objective in common: to gauge public taste and cater to it. Like the newspapers, they not only mould public opinion, but reflect it. If they devote a respectable percentage of their hours on the air to broadcasts of serious music, it is because they have discovered that a respectable percentage of their hearers want serious music.

How was this revolution in our attitude toward music brought about? By the simple process of exposure. The average man is suspicious of all "art," as expounded by the experts. He is afraid that it will bore him; and he dreads, too, I fancy, the humiliation of discovering that it is beyond his comprehension. He will not readily visit an art gallery or a symphony concert. But radio banished his fears. It offered him serious music, free of charge, in his home, under conditions whereby, if it happened to bore him, he could simply shut it off. So he tried it. For some time it made little impression on him. The early radio "symphony" concerts were so by courtesy only, rarely rising above the level of the "William Tell" overture, and they brought little response. Gradually the response grew. In 1931, not without misgivings, the National Broadcasting Company began broadcasting the Saturday matinee performances of the Metropolitan Opera Association, and the Columbia Broadcasting System did the same with the Sunday afternoon concerts of the New York Philharmonic-Symphony Orchestra. Both ventures were instantly successful and have continued ever since. Today, many of the commercial sponsors, corporations whose radio programs have no other aim than to appeal to potential buyers of their wares, find it profitable to engage concert and opera stars and the country's finest orchestras to entertain their listeners.

Before radio, the American musical public, such as it was, was restricted to the comparatively few who could afford to pay for their music and who lived in or about our urban centers. Now, for the first time in our history, our entire people has been given access to music, regardless of financial or geographical conditions. Its response has been hearteningly cordial.

There was a time, roughly from 1930 to 1934, when it began to look as if radio, arousing our interest in music on the one hand, might destroy all forms of public musical entertainment on the other. People had little money to spend. The radio was free, and moreover could be heard without the exertion of going to a concert hall or opera house. Our symphony orchestras and opera companies suffered accordingly. The concert business became practically non-existent. But the pendulum has swung, and not simply because money has become a little more plentiful. As a matter of fact, at this writing we are in the midst of a recession, a polite term for a depression nearly as bad as that of 1933. But the music field holds its own surprisingly. Our orchestras still play to deficits, as they always have and always will; but the deficits are met, and met, significantly enough, much more by small contributions by the many, than by heavy subsidies from the few. The Metropolitan and Chicago opera associations are not exactly flourishing, but they survive. Singers and instrumentalists still find audiences vastly greater than those they faced five years ago.

The fact is that radio has passed out of its craze stage. It is still our most popular form of entertainment, but we are beginning to recognize it for what it is: not a source of music, but an immensely cheap and convenient medium for the *reproduction* of music. Having developed a taste for serious music, as a nation, we are becoming increasingly interested in hearing first-hand performances by singers and instrumentalists, orchestras, chamber ensembles, and opera companies. Almost any high school of any pretensions now has its own band or orchestra; some of our college glee clubs, particularly those of the coeducational colleges of the Middle West, are choral organizations deserving of serious consideration, both as regards repertoire and performance.

One curious result of the crash of 1929 was that it set even the reluctant feet of the American government upon the path of æsthetic civilization. Our official attitude toward the arts has always been completely agnostic, as compared with that of the Continental countries. The encouragement of theatres and opera houses in the form of governmental subsidies, taken so much for granted on the Continent, has never been dreamed of here. Nor has our Federal government ever taken the slightest interest in the graphic and plastic arts. But when, as an aftermath of the depression, the Works Progress Administration, confronted with the task of making work for some millions of unemployed Americans, began classifying them according to their various trades and professions, it discovered, with a start of surprise, that it had to deal with some thousands of actors, painters, writers, composers, singers, and orchestral musicians. Almost overnight, the Federal government took official cognizance of the existence of the arts in America. Today, thousands of square feet of wall space are being covered with mural paintings, and plays, operas, and concerts are being produced and managed, at the expense of the government. The Coffee Bill, introduced in the House in January, 1938, even calls for the establishment of a permanent Bureau of Fine Arts.

Up to now, these practitioners of the arts are allowed to enjoy governmental patronage only on condition that they take the pauper's oath, *i.e.* go on relief. While it is quite true that in these times a fine artist may starve for want of employment, it is unfortunately equally true that a starving artist is not necessarily a fine one; and so far our WPA musical and dramatic productions have been more successful in keeping artists alive than in carrying forward the banner of art. Furthermore, the proposed Bureau of Fine Arts, as outlined in the Coffee Bill when last I had a look at it, is little more than a permanent relief bureau for artists, making no attempt to establish and maintain any standards of artistic production. These shortcomings, however, are not the main point, which is that the Federal government has at last been induced, no matter under what circumstances, to take an interest in painting, sculpture, literature, the drama, and music. I am optimist enough to believe that having got the bear by the tail, it will be unable to let go; that eventually we shall have government subsidies for music, administered by a genuine Department of Fine Arts, backed—as such a department must be in any country—by public interest in its activities.

The growing intensity of that interest is unmistakable. Take one simple illustration, the phonograph-record business. At the outset of this chapter I quoted myself, writing in 1921, as saying: "The American . . . buys Victrola records because he is a hero-worshipper, because he wants to hear the expensive Caruso and Kreisler and McCormack." In those days that was strictly true. There was a brisk market for recordings of dance music and popular songs; but the only way by which a recording of a piece of serious music could be sold was by offering it as a performance by a famous singer or instrumentalist. Caruso records sold as high as six dollars apiece; but the music that he sang, offered without his name, would not have taken in enough money to pay for the recording. For orchestral music there was virtually no market at all.

Today there is still the market for dance records—very little, significantly enough, for popular songs as such. People still want to dance; but if they want to listen to the *singing* of a popular song they would rather hear it over the radio, at no expense. Recordings of serious music do not, as a rule, sell on names alone. The few names that are still potent are those of famous orchestras and famous conductors. It is no longer such names as Caruso and McCormack and Farrar that sell records, but Toscanini, Stokowski, and Koussevitzky. And the staple money-makers of the record dealer today, outside of his dance records, are albums—recordings of entire symphonies, suites, string quartets, even entire operas—a condition that was unthinkable fifteen years ago.

So much for the audience. What of the American composer? First of all, he is infinitely better trained than he used to be. Fifteen years ago, he found it necessary—or at least thought it necessary—to find the time and money to study in Paris, Berlin, Leipzig, or Vienna if he aspired to be a thoroughly trained musician. Today, such conservatories as the Eastman School in Rochester, the Curtis Institute in Philadelphia, and the Juilliard School in New York—to name only three—with their magnificent teaching personnel and heavy endowments, offer him a chance to become a technical master of his craft without leaving his native country. Most of the larger conservatories maintain student orchestras, and some of them are amazingly good. Thanks to them, he not only studies how to write music, he has an opportunity to hear it played after he has written it, a practical aid whose value it is difficult to overestimate.

Not only has he a chance to acquire the tools of his trade; he has an ever-increasing chance to be heard in public. The WPA, being a government institution, is naturally inclined to be prejudiced in favor of works by native composers; and it is safe to say that during the past two years the WPA orchestras alone have probably performed more American music than our other symphony orchestras, combined, during the past ten. Those same symphony orchestras, by the way, are immeasurably more hospitable to American music than they used to be, thanks to the increased interest of their audiences and boards of directors in native composers.

His economic status is nothing to boast of—it never has been, in any country, and never will be. Just the same, he is, on the whole, better off, financially, than he was fifteen years ago, thanks to the American Society of Authors, Composers, and Publishers. This organization, familiarly known as ASCAP, was founded in 1914, in an effort to protect composers from unauthorized performances of their copyrighted works. It was bitterly opposed from the start, particularly by the hotels and motion-picture houses. After six years of litigation ASCAP emerged victorious, the United States Supreme Court ruling that composers and authors have the right to collect royalties on performances of their words and music given *for profit*. In 1921 the society collected its first royalties, and its fees now form a substantial part of the income of its members. Like the European performing rights societies, it is an association whose members assign to it the "small" performing rights of their works for a term of years. Acting in their name it collects royalties and, when necessary, brings suits for infringement of copyright. It differs from the European societies in that it does not collect on performances by cultural institutions such as churches, symphony orchestras, and recitals. It differs also in that in Europe collections are made on a "usage" basis. Every performance is a separate item, subject to a specific royalty. In a country of this size (we have over 400 radio stations, as against England's three) the amount of policing necessary to collect on such a basis would involve an army of scouts and clerks whose salaries would far exceed any possible collections. ASCAP, therefore, issues a blanket license to every commercial user of music (its principal licensees are radio stations, dance halls, hotel orchestras, and motion-picture houses) giving that user unlimited use of the ASCAP catalogue of copyrighted material in return for a percentage of the user's receipts.

Its members are grouped in classes, classification being based on availability (*i.e.,* the number of works a given member has assigned to the society), popularity, prestige value, and other considerations, every class receiving a proportionate share of the fees collected. Inevitably, the largest share of the money goes to the composers of popular songs and musical comedies, because their work is the society's largest revenue-producer. Even so, the so-called "standard" (serious) composer receives a small income from performances of his music, whereas fifteen years ago he received nothing.

In one other respect ASCAP differs from the European rights societies. They have the complete support of their governments, who not only admit but insist upon the right of copyright owners to organize in any way they see fit in order to collect performance royalties to which they are entitled. Here the situation is far different. Almost simultaneously with the beginning of the WPA's solicitude over the welfare of American singers and instrumentalists, the Department of Justice was bringing suit against American composers, in an effort to dissolve ASCAP as a monopoly in restraint of trade! In other words, we have the curious spectacle of the United States Government, which grants copyrights to authors and composers, undertaking to destroy the only means those authors and composers have of enforcing their copyrights. The suit was postponed, by the way, shortly after the beginning of the trial, at the request of the government, but it has not, up to the present, been dropped.

With an audience for his art infinitely larger than anything he could have imagined twenty years ago, with orchestras and choral societies ready to play and sing anything of merit that he may write, with his own government smiling benevolently, if not on him, at least on those who perform his music, what is the American composer doing?

He is doing more than he used to, but still not enough. There is something wrong with him. In an effort to see what that something is, suppose we go back to Bad Ischl, in Austria, in the year 1880, when Johannes Brahms wrote out the first bars of the Blue Danube waltz on the autograph-fan of Fräulein Alice Strauss, and signed it, "Unfortunately not by Johannes Brahms." Here was one of the great serious composers of his time expressing his admiration for what we may call the most popular song-writer of his time. Johann Strauss was not less an admirer of Brahms' genius. And why? Because both men inhabited the same world, musically speaking. Both spoke the same language, however different might be the things they employed it to express. Now try to imagine any one of a score of modern serious-minded American composers writing the opening bars of "Smoke Gets in Your Eyes" on a lady's fan and adding, "Unfortunately not by Blank." There are a few who might; but they are very few. The American composer of popular music, admittedly the best in the world today, employs an idiom that includes genuine, if sometimes undistinguished, melody, intelligible harmonization, and vigorous rhythms. His "serious" confrère writes music that might be from another planet, so far as any kinship between the two is concerned. The popular composer, however superficial his output may be, at least knows exactly what he is doing. From a great deal of American symphonic music, on the other hand, I get the impression that its composers do not at all know what they are doing, have not made up their minds what they *want* to do. They are employing an idiom that is little more than a continuation of the experiments that began in Europe about the beginning of the century, experiments whose results, so far, have possessed little more than laboratory value. If Oscar Wilde wrote "Salome" in French, successfully, it was because he had mastered French when he sat down to write "Salome." A great many American composers strike me as having failed, so far, to master the language in which they undertake to write. The result is feeble, tentative, and even when interesting, certainly not moving.

If you tell me that I don't know what I am talking about, that my younger confrères decidedly *have* mastered their idiom, and that if I don't like their music it is because my ears are prejudiced against the sort of music they write, I cannot prove you wrong. I can, however, offer a negative defense. One of the most uncompromising exponents of the modern atonal musical idiom was Schönberg's greatest pupil, the late Alban Berg. Yet little as I may "like" the score of his opera, "Wozzeck," I found it powerful and tremendously stirring music, because while I might not always know what he was talking about, his music left me with the inescapable conviction that he, at least, did know. He wrote the kind of music he did because he thought music that way. So many of the younger Americans leave me only with the impression that they meant it to go that way—which is far from the same thing.

The result of this tinkering with idiom instead of worrying about subject-matter is that the average American composer is painfully out of touch with his audience, and moves farther away from it every day. The radio has created for him listeners literally by the millions (the Sunday afternoon Philharmonic-Symphony broadcasts are heard by approximately 9,000,000 persons, according to reliable engineering estimates), a potential audience such as no composer has ever before enjoyed. But this vast audience, so eager and hopeful, is incredibly ignorant and innocent. A large proportion of it is comprised of adult Americans who, before radio, never heard a symphony orchestra or a string quartet, men and women approaching middle age to whom Mozart's G-minor symphony is an exciting novelty, the Beethoven Ninth a discovery, the Tschaikovsky Sixth a revelation—grown-up persons for whom the standard orchestral repertoire is a mine of hitherto unsuspected treasure. They are people to whom Wagner is a modern, to whom *L'Après-midi d'un Faune* is the work of a daring and rather puzzling innovator. In short, the American composer of today must, if he is to gain any real hold on the affections of his countrymen, conquer an audience, not of 1938, but of 1898.

Which is not to say that he should write down to his public. After all, the opening movement of the Beethoven Fifth is not exactly "writing down." But what he must do is find an idiom that is intelligible to the people around him, worry more about what a Kansas masonry contractor thinks of him (and I can assure him, take it from my correspondence, that the Kansas masonry contractor is no fool about music), and worry less about whether or not Belà Bartók would approve. If he can do this, if he can write with the vigor and honesty that, to millions of his countrymen, are synonymous with great music, he will have an audience that any composer, anywhere, might envy. If he cannot, Mozart and Kern and Gershwin will leave him hopelessly outdistanced.

# THE THEATRE

## [*Joseph Wood Krutch*]

AT THE present moment the American drama is an integral part of American literature. To say that is not to repeat a truism but to cite a fact of considerable importance. No similar statement could have been made thirty years ago because thirty years ago the American drama was, as the drama of all countries so often is, almost sub-literary. The purely popular dramatists were at least not above the level of popular novelists or poets and the best or most respected dramatic writers which the nation had produced were very far from equalling in literary merit a Melville, a Hawthorne, a Mark Twain, or a Henry James. Today, whatever the absolute value of his work may be, the American playwright is as much a part of contemporary American literature as the writer in any other form. The best play of the year is likely to be quite as good as the best novel.

The American theatre has, to put the fact in a different way, achieved the rather remarkable feat of escaping from the deadening limitations usually imposed upon the stage. The serious dramatist meets no resistance greater than that which the serious writer in any other form has to overcome and it is assumed that he enjoys a freedom of expression very nearly as great as that which the novelist or the essayist can claim. The result of this fact is that the writer with something to say no longer feels that he is imposing upon himself unnecessary difficulties if he happens to choose the theatre as the place for saying it. The English and American drama of the 19th century was, until the very end of the century, an artistic and intellectual backwater. The strong currents of thought and imagination which flowed through poetry and the novel left its stagnation undisturbed. Today, whatever we think or feel finds its way into the drama almost as readily as it does into any other form of literature. Whatever else the contemporary theatre may be it is not behind the times. It is as profound and serious, or as superficial and trivial, as our literature as a whole.

Since the War many American plays have been produced with success in England, in Germany and, to a somewhat less extent, in various other countries. Nevertheless no American playwright except O'Neill has achieved as an individual any large European reputation, and the fact is perhaps of some significance. We have produced a large body of work intellectually respectable but no single playwright whose impact is even remotely comparable to that of Shaw or Ibsen. Any list of our leading dramatists changes radically almost year by year and this means, perhaps, that the outstanding achievement is rather the creation of a flexible and living theatre than any large body of dramatic literature destined to be of permanent interest. Certainly no individual genius has overshadowed it and neither has it been remarkable for the creation of any school of playwriting. Even the self-conscious rebels who launched the Theatre Guild and the Provincetown Theatre two decades ago were not committed to anything more definite than hospitality to literary as opposed to non-literary dramas, and the playwrights whom they and, after them, the more adventurous commercial managers encouraged, were alike only in a determination to vivify the theatre by the introduction of themes already making their way in the novel and short story. Thus the drama has been not only as good as other contemporary literature but also as varied and changeable. It is lively, competent, honest, and adventurous. It has produced few playwrights who, on sober second consideration, seem to tower far enough above their fellows to be singled out as permanently memorable.

Of the theatre as an institution one may ask two things: First, that it should keep alive some portion at least of the world's dramatic literature and, second, that it should find a place for the best that the contemporary dramatist has to offer. The American theatre had ceased during the latter part of the 19th century to make any pretense at satisfying the first of these demands and showed, until very recently, no disposition whatsoever to undertake the task. It has, however, for nearly two decades, been remarkably hospitable to the best contemporary playwrights it can find and if it has exhibited during that time much lively and interesting work without revealing more than one or two dramatists who seem even possible candidates for permanent fame, the fact calls for some comment.

One may say of course merely that genius is unpredictable and that the muse does not always respond even when a theatrical producer invites; but it is also reasonable to ask to what extent circumstances were favorable, and it appears that in this case they were favorable to exactly the sort of work which has been produced. An age as interested as

ours in new facts, new theories, and new observations encourages a
literature whose virtues are reportorial and journalistic whereas the drama
at its best is conspicuous for the extent to which its virtues are formal.
The modern American drama has succeeded admirably both in presenting certain aspects of modern life upon the stage and, even more
conspicuously perhaps, in expressing changing attitudes towards traits
of human character and recurring situations. But it has only in rare
instances succeeded in so thoroughly mastering its material as to achieve
the peculiar finality characteristic of drama at its best.

That this is true is indicated by the fact that though the most admired
play of a given year is frequently topical or journalistic it is also often
almost entirely forgotten two years later, while the three or four playwrights who most persistently reappear in any discussion of the possibly
permanent achievements of the contemporary drama are men in whose
work the formal element is conspicuous. Eugene O'Neill, S. N. Behrman, and Maxwell Anderson have all, to be sure, treated current topics
and could not have the kind of importance they have if they were not,
among other things, a part of their age. But one does not think of them
as primarily belonging to a school of thought. One thinks of them primarily as, respectively, a tragic writer, a comic writer, and a dramatist
who uses verse in the theatre. They stand out because each has thought
his way through his material with sufficient thoroughness to enable him
to give it a form recognizable as one of those eternally appropriate to
the drama. The re-emergence of these forms is the most encouraging
sign that an American drama more than merely respectable and temporarily significant may be on the point of developing.

The case of O'Neill is especially interesting, not only because his is
the largest and the most solidly founded fame, but also because his career
reveals so plainly the struggle of the first-rate dramatist to discover the
relation between what is peculiar to his age and what is permanent,
not only in drama, but in human nature as well. No one has responded
more readily to current interests or even current fashions. He has been
social critic, Freudian psychologist, and even protagonist in what is
known vaguely as the anti-Puritan revolt. His plays at one time came
so close upon one another's heels and seemed to represent experiments
in so many different directions that one might possibly have wondered
whether his work had any center at all. Indeed, a man less energetic and
more stable would doubtless never have needed to experiment so widely.
But to look back now upon a career more than twenty years old is to

see that his effort was always to find the core of tragic emotion in situations or experiences as varied as a restless modern mind could suggest, and that what he wanted to do was to write tragic drama, modern in the sense that its premises were the premises of the modern man, timeless both in the sense that it revealed the tragic predicament of man as a timeless thing and in the sense that its purpose was to purge the soul as the great tragedies of Greece or of Elizabethan England had purged it. *Mourning Becomes Electra* is perhaps the finest American play in part because it is at once unmistakably of our day and yet unmistakably in the tragic tradition. No anachronism of thought or feeling suggests the *pastiche* or the academic exercise. Yet it attains to a formal perfection and, accordingly, produces an effect of completeness and finality possible only in a play which has achieved one of the classic patterns.

S. N. Behrman is the most substantial—not necessarily the funniest—of our comic writers for a similar reason. His plays are comedies rather than squibs or sketches, extravaganzas, or farces because they are illuminated throughout by the steady light of a comic intelligence. His themes are as timely as the newspaper, his characters men and women to be met in any drawing room, but he is not merely topical or journalistic. Portraiture is carried on from the point where it is merely a recognizable likeness to the point where it becomes a generalization, and the conflicts of the moment are revealed as part of that persisting conflict between passion or enthusiasm on one hand and good sense on the other which is the essence of comedy. Form in the drama is not something artificially imposed from without. It is the shape which material inevitably takes when it has been thought through to the end and its pattern revealed. Mr. Behrman's plays are real comedies because Mr. Behrman has more than shrewdness and wit. He has a comic philosophy as clearly defined as the tragic philosophy of O'Neill.

One of the great boasts of our playwrights has been that their dialogue is realistic, that their personages talk as real people really do. This is, of course, an exaggeration since the most literally realistic dialogue which can possibly be tolerated is a good deal more economical and pointed than actual conversation ever is. In so far, moreover, as their dialogue really is relatively close to every-day speech, the virtue implied is a mediocre one at best. In so far as "realistic dialogue" means that the playwright has discarded conventional rhetoric and the *clichés* of a worn-out tradition it means that he has achieved a freshness which befits the journalistic fidelity of his most typical plays. In so far as it means, on the other hand, that he cannot make his characters talk very much better than their immediate prototypes would, it indicates a failure analogous to his failure to achieve finality of form.

Mr. Behrman makes his characters masters of a phraseology neat enough to satisfy the demands of comedy where the convention requires only that all the characters should be endowed with wit equal to that of their creator, but the outstanding defect of O'Neill is just that his characters are seldom if ever as eloquent as they ought to be. Probably no prose would be good enough for them; they ought to speak verse; and it is Maxwell Anderson's attempt to naturalize verse in our theatre which gives him an important position despite the fact that, so far at least, the force of his tragic imagination seems far less than that of O'Neill.

Here it should be observed that verse is not something which can be successfully imposed upon a play from without; that a poetic drama is not a prose drama translated into verse. When, however, any play reaches a certain degree of intensity it tends to rise naturally, to leave the ground as an aeroplane leaves the ground when it has attained a certain speed. One feels suddenly that it should, not that it should not, fly; and if for any reason it fails to do so, as O'Neill's plays commonly do, one suffers from an expectation disappointed, from a sense of heaviness impossible to shake off. If, however, it does take to the wings of verse, one rises with it into what seems the natural element of the imagination.

Mr. Anderson has a facility in versification greater than is perhaps good for him and a merely romantic fancy which sometimes tempts him to put into verse scenes for which prose might do as well. He has also had a tendency in plays like *Mary of Scotland* or *The Masque of Kings* to choose subjects which are traditionally poetic, to which the imagination of others has already given literary form. The almost inevitable result of this is that they have about them that air of *pastiche* which it is one of the great virtues of O'Neill never to suggest. They are tragedies because that is what they have been for a very long time, not because the author has revealed the tragic pattern underlying the facts or situations observed for himself. But once at least, in *Winterset,* Mr. Anderson did just that. He took a situation obviously suggested by the Sacco-Vanzetti case, discovered in it a universal theme concerning the nature of justice, gave it the form of true tragedy, and invented a suitable language, rhythmical and elevated even if not usually arranged in regular verses. The play stands as one of the most striking achievements in the recent theatre.

Mr. Anderson had previously written a play called *Gods of the Lightning* in which he transferred directly to the stage the events of the same *cause célèbre* which furnished the suggestion for *Winterset,* but the two plays present in violent contrast the difference between the journalist and the tragic writer. The first, however honest and important it may have been, was honest and important in the fashion of an editorial or a "feature story." It saw no deeper into the events that any one might see, revealed no implication that had not already been revealed, discovered no form different from that into which the incidents themselves had fallen. It represented merely what Mr. Anderson, as a citizen had to say about the Sacco-Vanzetti case. *Winterset,* on the other hand, represents what Mr. Anderson as a poet had to say, and the fact that some of its principal characters are gangsters does not, as some seemed to feel, make the elevation of their language ridiculous or inappropriate. It is true that gangsters do not speak verse. Neither for that matter does anybody else. The fact that it can be made to seem suitable even to them is the best possible proof that an imagination has been at work. Unfortunately the play also reveals touches of Mr. Anderson's most conspicuous weakness. The love story is at times tainted with mere romantic sentimentality and the end purely fortuitous. The fact remains nevertheless that *Winterset* is the best example outside the works of O'Neill of the manner in which a modern American tragedy might be written.

This same play also suggests the problem of the relation of "social significance" to the drama and suggests also at least one solution of that problem. Ever since the War most of our outstanding dramatists have been to some degree what used to be called "advanced." They have, that is to say, tended on the whole to be critical of conventional judgments on moral or social questions and to speak for the intellectual rather than for the man in the street. At least until near the end of the 20's, however, they were usually not definitely political; they were sceptical rather than dogmatic, and more concerned with social than with economic phenomena. But after 1929 sharper lines began to be drawn. Dissenters ceased to feel that they were united by their common differences from the man in the street and that to call a man "advanced" was to define him as far as was necessary for practical purposes. On the contrary, newly emerged communists began to hate wavering socialists more ardently than they hated the bourgeoisie and to demand that the author of a play should unequivocally declare his political faith. They wanted the drama to deal with specific social problems and to present a specific solution. Such, they began to say, was the business of the playwright who must regard art primarily as "a weapon."

Out of these convictions a number of plays were written, usually from a point of view near that of the communist if not avowedly identical with it, and many created a considerable furore in the public press even though comparatively few attracted any considerable audience other than that outside of the special group to which they were in the first instance addressed. Most suffered under the limitations usual to a play written exclusively for the sake of a predetermined moral and most failed to reveal any unusual dramatic gifts in their authors. One playwright of conspicuous merit did, however, emerge, and Clifford Odets has come, not without reason, to be regarded as one of the most promising young writers for our theatre. But far from indicating that the success of a playwright depends upon the correctness of his political creed the fact tends, on the contrary, to confirm the opinion that imagination and a sense of character and of dramatic form are much more important. Odets' gifts as a playwright are far more conspicuous in his plays than his gifts as a political thinker.

He has himself, to be sure, stressed the importance of his creed and posed as a Jeremiah crying woe upon the modern world and all its works. But the didactic conclusion to his first full-length play, *Awake and Sing,* was so little an integral part of what went before it that it seemed merely an afterthought and *Golden Boy,* his most successful work to date, would be perfectly capable of holding the interest of a spectator who had never so much as heard of the economic interpretation of human character. Mr. Odets has, in addition to an actor's instinct for the purely theatrical, a remarkable gift for portraying the agonies of frustration and his two best plays present two remarkable studies of lower middle-class groups whose members cannot understand one another because each is cherishing some symbol of material success or spiritual fulfilment which the others are incapable of understanding. Both suggest in theme the plays of Checkov and *Golden Boy,* especially, may be very readily though not inevitably interpreted in the Marxian terms which Mr. Odets would no doubt insist upon. But both owe their excellence to a warmth of imagination rather than to an intellectual creed and their author is by far the most interesting of the revolutionary group, not because he is the best revolutionist, but because he is the best playwright.

Whatever future the Marxian drama may have, will depend, like the future of the American drama as a whole, upon the extent to which the playwright discovers how to make drama out of the material which interests him. So far Mr. Odets is the only one of the group who has achieved a success even remotely comparable with that of O'Neill, Behrman, and Anderson in writing plays more interesting, more moving, and impressive, than a mere abstract statement of the author's creed would be.

There are, of course, those who see the future of the American theatre as lying wholly in the hands of the various insurgent groups or, perhaps, with the Federal Theatre which has, indeed, been responsible for at least four or five remarkable productions. They point also to the astonishing success of the Mercury Theatre which discovered that Shakespeare could still be a popular playwright and that there was an audience unsuspected by commercial managers for a rowdy Elizabethan comedy. They forget, however, that the history of the recent past reveals a remarkable power on the part of the "commercial theatre" to learn from the little groups and that these little groups tend either to disappear or, like the Theatre Guild, to become transformed, while the commercial theatre absorbs the playwrights and the audiences which they may have helped to discover. Probably the process will continue and the "commercial theatre" survive all the ills from which both its enemies and its workers are continually predicting its death.

It is true that the moving picture has robbed it of an enormous audience and that Hollywood is perpetually drawing away the most promising playwrights and the most successful performers. It is true also that the annual number of new productions is not half what it was before 1929.

But New York is still the most active theatre in the world and, despite the wails of managers, still very profitable indeed to those who know its ways. That the American theatre hardly exists outside a few big cities is a distressing fact, but there is no indication that it is on the point of disappearing from them. On the whole it appears that the best plays being written get a production in New York and that a sufficient number of them prosper to suggest that, for the immediate future at least, the playwright will find a market for his best wares.

What will his plays be like? I have already suggested that those of the recent past which continue to be interesting are those which achieved a certain formal excellence, which tended to become comedies or tragedies rather than merely presentations or discussions of topics of current interest. It might be interesting to look at the season of 1937–38 to see if the outlines of any tendency emerges from it. At least half a dozen plays of more than passing interest were produced and if one adds several revivals well worth the doing as well as rather more than the usual number of pleasant diversions, the total is very respectable indeed considered merely as evidence that the theatre is a going concern. To those who bestow the Pulitzer Prize the best play was Thornton Wilder's *Our Town;* to the Critics Circle it was John Steinbeck's *Of Mice and Men;* to those interested in the progress of Marxism in the theatre either Clifford Odets' *Golden Boy* or Marc Blitzstein's satiric cantata *The Cradle Will Rock*. But perhaps the enthusiasm provoked by Mr. Orson Welles and his Mercury Theatre, devoted wholly to revivals, is as significant a symptom as analysis could discover in a season rather more remarkable for diversity of aims and manners among the most successful playwrights than for any obvious trend. Despite *Golden Boy, The Cradle Will Rock* and the Federal Theatre's remarkable editorial in tableaux called *One Third of a Nation* there was no indication that the proponents of left-wing agitation were actually on the point of capturing the theatre and it would require a great deal of ingenuity to discover a common denominator between the elegiac fantasy *Our Town* and the sentimentally tough melodrama *Of Mice and Men*. Something might be made of the fact that at least six new plays dealt with the supernatural in some form or other, but if that is more than an accident it is, like the success of the Mercury Theatre, only another indication that the public has grown rather less literal-minded than it was a few years ago.

That, indeed, seems to me a phenomenon worth considering. I doubt whether this public knows exactly what it is that it wants, but audiences are no longer complacently superior to whatever is not realistically prosy in matter and manner. Two of the most popular plays of the year, *On Borrowed Time* and *The Star Wagon,* seemed to me rather silly, but fantasy is merely imagination not powerful enough to convince itself, and an audience which acclaimed them is an audience which would like to be convinced if it could. Much has been made of Maxwell Anderson's recent experiments in poetic drama, and at least one of his plays is as good as anything the theatre has recently produced, but they are no more important as symptoms than the rediscovery of Shakespeare as a popular dramatist or the success of a play so unconventional in form and theme as *Our Town*. Perhaps there was a touch of mere preciosity in both the bare walls of Mr. Welles's *Julius Cæsar* and the obstreperous informality of Mr. Blitzstein's skeletonized opera, *The Cradle Will Rock,* but the fact remains that both paid audiences the compliment of assuming that they were capable of imagination.

The contemporary drama may not be going anywhere. The very fact that no two playwrights seem to be aiming at quite the same thing may possibly mean that it is frittering itself away, since as my friend Mark Van Doren once maintained, the very best plays seem to be written when everybody is trying to write the same one—when a Congreve finally achieves, in *The Way of the World,* the work a whole generation had been laboring at, or when a Shakespeare manages to stand on the shoulders of a race of poets whose similarities are at least more significant than their differences. But if the modern drama is going anywhere at all, I venture to predict that it is going away from simple realism in the direction of something more intense. Mr. Welles, Mr. Wilder, and Mr. Blitzstein have discovered that the shortest distance between two points may often be by way of an artificial convention. Mr. Anderson is trying to take advantage of the fact that men may most truly reveal themselves in language better than any they have ever actually spoken.

# ART IN THE UNITED STATES, 1938

## [*Sheldon Cheney*]

I T WOULD be absurd to maintain that art claims the attention and devotion of the mass of American people as do such major interests as crime, sports, Hollywood romance, society, and war. But this is, no doubt, a criticism applicable to all the so-called civilized peoples. We are to take "civilization" in a comparative sense. By tacit understanding art everywhere is, to all intents and purposes, a class affair, limited; terms such as "popular art" and "democratic culture" are, strictly speaking, overstatements.

To study the general absence of art in the United States one need not go into the cultural desert-areas of the nation: the garment district of New York City, the factory towns of New England and the South, the Pennsylvania mining districts, or the remote plains belt of the West. The division is not territorial. One might better examine the minds of the hundreds of thousands of readers on the commuting trains into, say, New York, Chicago and Boston,—clerks, executives, lawyers, dentists, printers, salesmen. One would find first devotion, probably, to sports, then to scandals and the current crime trials and criminal-hunts, to politics, the comics, wars. Art would in any case be near the end of the list. But so it is, if one be realistic in one's overseas observation, in London or Paris, in Berlin or Prague. Or—at home again—turn to any chosen university campus: A survey of the minds of students and professors alike would indicate a scarcely greater knowledge of or attachment to painting and sculpture (our particular art-subjects in this article).

Perhaps this is a price the modern world has paid for "progress." The struggle to establish what is called 20th-century civilization has left to the minds of the mass of working people, of even highly educated people, only the catchiest of excitements and interests, aside from work. Organized education has been driven to a central concern with science and commerce. We all have been made job-conscious, success-conscious, engineering-conscious, war-conscious, but very, very few of us art-conscious. Even religion, although it has been sliding downhill badly, occupies a place higher in public esteem, bulks larger in news, claims more of man's "off" hours.

And yet, small as is the place permitted to the arts by the present form of civilization, no one ever questions their importance. It is a truism: Without art we are less than civilized. A nation's standing, moreover, will be judged ultimately almost solely upon the evidence of surviving works in the field of the arts.

We are faced, then, by the paradoxical fact that art is a thing considered to afford civilized complexion to civilizations, but civilization in general, in order to get to where it has got, has consistently subordinated the artist's activities to those of such immediately revered figures as the warrior, the banker, the politician, and the priest; and latterly to those of the business-man, the educator, and the scientist. Our whole inquiry is a compara-tive one.

What we are concerned with is the question whether American civi-lization has arrived, not at some absolute saturation-point of art, but at something like the average degree of culture illustrated in "leading" European countries, where also the current of art has very little to do with the surface aspect of life—as that is shown, for instance, in news-paper headlines, or in the curricula at colleges, or in conversation at men's clubs. Especially, how would the works of our native artists hold up if shown on the walls of international galleries?

To say that in the past the United States has commanded the interest of the rest of the world less for its art than for certain aspects of its state-craft, its economy, and its scientific-inventive achievements is vastly to understate the case. The nation has demonstrated a fairly peaceable and an unparalleled union of States; has conducted a capital experiment in heterogeneous, if not promiscuous, mixing of racial blocs; has marked a milepost in the march from autocracy to democracy (or from autocracy to plutocracy, which is at least on the way); and has achieved amazing material advance by technological invention. In these matters the older countries have shown an interest. But again we return to the truth that ultimately the American nation and the American people will be judged, by historians and sages, for their poetry and their painting, their archi-tecture and their sculpture, their designed utensils and their dancing.

Scrutiny of the earlier records of the nation, as regards painting and sculpture, leaves one less than reassured. The Colonial American branch stemmed from the least solid limb of the European art tree, the English.

It is true that a sort of inventive honesty redeemed part of the output of the Colonies and of the early Republic from the category of mere provincial imitativeness. In a small way we may take pleasure in our "American Primitives," and a certain satisfaction in finding Benjamin West cutting a handsome figure overseas (even to the extent of presidency of the Royal Academy), and Copley and Stuart recognized as foremost portraitists of their era. But the overseas significance hardly concerned other than the British galleries, and Copley's and Stuart's are not widely international reputations.

It was, let us say, a promising beginning on the road to a civilized art, for a newly created nation concerned with a multitude of more pressing problems. An excellent school of portraiture (often a sign of a prosperous and elegant, but not necessarily of a thoroughly cultured society) survived until the decade of the Civil War. But for a full half-century thereafter, the record is read most clearly in the essays of critics who successively pointed out that America had no appreciable art and was at best keeping up as an accomplished imitator of European fashions.

The most astute of American art critics wrote, at the beginning of that half-century, that "whatever feeling for beauty the coming American may possess, that of the present one is the most obtuse or wanting of any people, except the English." He spoke of "the reproach now cast on it [the United States] by learned Europeans, of being a great nation destitute of any art." The most promising sign he could see was in a certain susceptibility and, given opportunity, a freer range of interest, on this side of the Atlantic—so that "I sometimes think that there is more æsthetic bottom to the half-fledged American people than to any of the older races at this moment." Thus James Jackson Jarves in 1869.

Through the following fifty years, there was the eloquent example of the art students and artists who deliberately expatriated themselves. In Jarves's own time there had been a colony of American sculptors in Rome, and another in Florence. The Paris and the Munich and the Düsseldorf schools of "American" art are well known (it hardly matters that some students stayed in the foreign cities and others returned home, to be little local Parisians or Romans or Düsseldorfians). The supreme example, and the one most to be regretted, was that of Whistler, if—as seems to be true—it was a case of a sensitive artist not able to contend with the "obtuseness and want of art" in his native land, as shown on the one hand in the lack of a national tradition or an enlightened patronage, and on the other in a Chauvinism that elevated the "juvenile efforts" of the academicians and illustrators to a pinnacle.

In 1905 Samuel Isham opened his *The History of American Painting* thus: "The fundamental and mastering fact about American painting is that it is in no way native to America, but is European painting imported, or rather transplanted, to America, and there cultivated and developed; and even that not independently, but with constant reference to the older countries, first one nation or school having a preponderating influence, then another."

Well into the decade of the 'twenties, discriminating criticism similarly continued to put the rank of American painting and sculpture at something less than civilized. As a sort of summary, or clinching confirmation, one may go to the chapter on art in the counterpart of this book, *Civilization in United States,* published in 1921. There, only seventeen years ago, a leading American painter-critic, Walter Pach, published an article in which the general tone is one of unbelief, and impeachment of the American output as still provincial. He could mention Winslow Homer and Albert P. Ryder, only to add, "It must be men of such a breed who will make real American art when we are ready to produce it." He was deferential to the "great" or French tradition; and he found only Maurice B. Prendergast worthy of individual mention, among contemporary American workers.

Here then is a record of a national art definitely—one cannot deny the evidence and the overwhelming weight of opinion—inferior to that of the older nations, up to the early 1920's. Looking back from the 1930's, having learned, in what we believe to be a civilized way, to value creative plastic invention, along with what other qualities art must purvey, we have discovered nevertheless that there were American solitaries, two or three lonely creative geniuses, who were overlooked by the apologists (and equally by the nationalists who continued to celebrate anæmic academic painting and other conventional or fashionable art as if it were of world eminence: the sculpture of Hiram Powers, J. Q. A. Ward, and Daniel Chester French, and the painting of Johnson, Wyant, Weir, Dewing, Thayer, Tarbell, Chase, and Sargent).

Since 1920 two painters in particular, Albert P. Ryder and John H. Twachtman, have been recognized as geniuses largely overlooked in their time, but today measuring up as creators whose canvases any world gallery would be wise to seek out—in other words, universal rather than merely national figures. If one add to these the expatriate Whistler, there is the nucleus, even before 1900, of a tradition of originality—a heart or center needed to make really important the body of art that had long been marked by all the secondary virtues of competence, honesty, vigor, dignity, and adaptiveness, in, say, the canvases of Inness, Homer, Eakins, Duveneck, Cassatt, Fuller, and Hassam, and, in sculpture, the monuments of St. Gaudens.

Whistler is hardly to be urged as prop to any claims of a national tradition whether American, British, or French; we are left with Ryder and Twachtman. Ryder, despite his retirement from the common life and his detachment from the native scene (except as the sea may be considered a native interest to a child of the New England coast), is the more American figure of the two—in his vigor, his simplicity, and his Whitmanlike disconcern with European influences and modes. He is at last firmly placed as America's first great creative painter, civilized in something more than a national or immediate sense. The recognition of Twachtman for an equally original, if more delicate, contribution has come slowly, and even yet the critics and historians are not fully agreed regarding his claim to second place in the 19th-century American roster. But wherever form-organization, or plastic order, is accepted as a prime test of picture-making, Twachtman's reputation grows, for it is seen that his canvases, at first fragilely Impressionistic in aspect, are enriched with subtlest abstract rhythms. This distinguishing plastic aliveness, so far beyond any quality in Impressionism as such, yet so different from any achievement to be found in the foreign leaders of Post-Impressionism, is easily overlooked if the observer has come to appreciation of Modernism by way of the French or the German masters. Understanding follows rather appreciation of Oriental art.

The elevation of two or three painters to the list of masters is only one part of the revolutionary change accomplished in the history of American art in the past fifteen years. Events and occasions as well as men have been re-assessed. In the perspective that has levelled so much, two events of the new century, both formerly opposed or ridiculed as serious influences, rather than praised, are now found outstanding. One is the exhibition of international Post-Impressionist art in 1913, known as the Armory Show. The other is the series of exhibitions presented under the direction of Alfred Stieglitz at the 291 Gallery between 1907 and 1917.

The Armory Show was a single, sudden, and explosive incident, serving to focus attention upon revolutionary tendencies, spotlighting the European "radicals" who, as was believed by a very few people then, and by a great many people after another twenty years, had epochally turned the current of creative art; and it was an incident that gave valuable publicity and a sense of solidarity to American creative workers. The

Stieglitz series of exhibitions, numbering almost a half-hundred in the ten years, served a more intimate and a continuing purpose, establishing a known center of essentially original and vital art in New York. Aside from the special things like Negro sculpture and children's drawings (the first shows of the sorts anywhere), the exhibitions introduced Cézanne, Picasso, Braque, Matisse, and other foreign masters to American audiences; but the majority of showings were from the brushes of the leading native creators.

Other facts that come clear, in the latest historical perspective, bearing directly upon the appearance of a civilized art in the country, are these: First, a group organized as early as 1908 had paved the way for the coming of an original and a dynamic art paralleling other national movements, when "The Eight," originally of Philadelphia but soon centered in New York, rebelled against the currently popular Impressionism, and went far to kill out a pervading sentimentalism, æstheticism, and effeminacy; although in their own contribution, substantially realistic, the members turned out neo-traditionalists—Sloan, Luks, Glackens most notably, with George Bellows a late adherent to the group and its most accomplished artist.

Second, the deeper lessons of French Post-Impressionism had been thoroughly learned by a number of Americans by the time of the Armory Show, as proven there and in many of the exhibition-shows: Max Weber, Walt Kuhn, Bernard Karfiol, John Marin, and Abraham Walkowitz particularly demonstrating a mastery of technical equipment second only to that of the leading Frenchmen—and it was seen that the tide of native invention need no longer be retarded for lack of knowledge "how to paint, and in the contemporary significant way."

Third, the widespread agitation for an art of the native scene, between 1920 and 1935, as a revolt against too much emphasis on technique and formal experimentation, and against excessive French influence, brought in a healthful return to immediate and human subject matter, and restored a needed balance; though the American Scene art as such proved to possess in the end little more than the interest of picturesque regionalism and satiric amusement.

In any case, out of these several currents came in the 1930's— or so it seems to this observer—a body of art that is sufficiently original and distinctive to be called American, at the same time sufficiently endowed with plastic vitality or formal creativeness to stand with the major civilized cultures in other lands. Most important of all there is today a new pervasive *spirit* of art: a felt confidence, a self-sufficiency, and an artist-solidarity, at a score of centers of activity—a vibrancy and vigor of the art-life not before sensed.

It is no new thing for the larger American cities to provide the finest artistic fare from other countries and other times. We are extraordinarily served by permanent historical museums, and with occasional comprehensive shows organized by the older museums, by special museums of Modern art, and by expositions. But it has been true only within a very few years that we have been able to look forward to each new season as certain to bring a cycle of native art deeply pleasure-giving, exciting, even splendid. Nor had we any right to expect five years ago that today we should be seeing native mural painting excellent in quality, and spread to the four corners of the country, to an extent beyond the dreams of any idealist. By a curious chance the opportunity came two years ago for scores of talented and eager artists to express themselves in wall-painting. It came by the back-door opening of emergency relief; and thus the painting that is most a community affair flourishes—with, at the moment of writing, nearly one hundred mural projects going forward in public buildings in New York City, and hundreds more in cities and towns elsewhere in the land.

For those who are less impressed with advances on the "fine arts" front, who feel, perhaps, that the purer arts are alien to the American genius, which has been supposed to have a special pragmatic bent—for a certain type of intellectual materialist, in short—there is evidence on a wholly different front: That of the arts of use. And indeed the most sudden, most striking display of American originality has been signalized in the development of a machine-age industrial design. As the native architects, most notably Sullivan and Wright, pioneered in creating an architecture which is sweeping the Western world, a type of building accepted now as the first authentic *style* in post-Renaissance times, they also laid the foundation for a new machine-age craft, destined to replace in innumerable fields the manual crafts. By abandonment of the "arts and crafts" and "revival" approaches, by returning to basic engineering procedure, by advocating acceptance of the machine as (in Wright's words) a peerless creative tool, they paved the way for the present generation of industrial designers, who are at last transforming the face of our visual environment, in accordance with an æsthetic of the machine.

We have before us daily the evidences of this revolutionary substitution, this transition from a world manually implemented to one machine-implemented: in the design of automobiles and streamline trains, refrigerators and bathtubs, silverware and flatirons, compacts and clocks. The artist has stepped in at the point where the modern industrial designer must begin, before the model for mass-produced articles is approved. With full consideration of mechanical factors and use values, he brings to bear the knowledge of abstract composition, of plastic organization, inherited from the Post-Impressionist painters and sculptors. He has destroyed the old artificial conception of machine products as necessarily inartistic, and has convinced many that a new epochal method and a new epochal style have been brought into currency.

This is one point at which exception must be noted to this article's initial generalization, that the visual arts really are not popular, that they do not serve more than a class. The new mass-production design touches into the lives of all. But in the end—however important industrial design may seem to the rationalist and the functionalist—it is not eminence in the arts of use which will gain the United States a place among the leading nations. It is a civilized thing, no doubt, that we have created a craftsmanship in keeping with our mechanized ways of locomotion, communication, and manufacture. But "art in civilization" implies advance rather in the fields of the pure or expressional arts. (These too have experienced the impact of forces out of the new functionalism, have developed a special soundness of craftsmanship and a directness of statement, relevant to "machine-mindedness." The ways are not to be explored in an article so brief; but one gains perspective on the whole of modern art by seeing the industrial designer as blood-brother to the Expressionist painter or sculptor, as having arrived with him, not against him.)

Original creative works of painting and sculpture do not go into the homes (or even the schools and other common meeting-places) of the average citizen. We do not live intimately with art at its intensest. But this, again, is a condition, a limitation, which obtains throughout the European-American world: Due to the prevailing economy—which, to secure to the artist any market at all, must create about his product an atmosphere of scarcity and rarity, with the price of each picture enormously swollen through the artificial system of dealing, advertising, criticism, etc. The business of art-merchandizing is notoriously speculative, if not unscrupulous and unethical. Its methods are contrary to all idealistic notions of a civilized relationship between those who produce art works and those who desire them. However rosy may be one's account of American art production, this reservation must be made regarding distribution.

There is one exception, in connection with a minor graphic art which, like painting, has within a decade come to flower: print-making. By co-operative understanding and effort a large number of artists practising in the field have brought prices for the finest prints to amazingly low levels, establishing direct contact between an artist-owned depot and the consumer: and this at a time when the American lithographer and engraver have arrived at a mastery worthy of the world-tradition of creative print-making. The print-makers have learned the lesson that formal excellence is of first importance in the lithograph or engraving, as in painting. The advance is so marked that it is difficult to believe that the soundly creative and natively original contents of the American portfolios of today follow so closely upon the poorer ones of five years ago—when American work was markedly inferior to the French, to the German, even to the English.

It is easy for any art lover or observer to test or check the present writer's judgments—what may be considered his enthusiasm—as regards prints. Unfortunately a report upon the state of painting and sculpture in the Union demands exceptional study—and exceptional travel. New York City remains the creative and the show center; and certainly the readiest estimate is formed on the basis of works that are hung upon the metropolitan gallery walls. But when one has found, for instance, the New York showings of the season 1937–38 extraordinarily rich and full, one should confirm or enlarge the impression by going to Chicago and Philadelphia, Detroit and Iowa City, Santa Fé and Los Angeles, San Francisco and Seattle. In each city one will find the spirit at work, and a surprising actual output of inventive painting.

But most convincing of all, one should visit the national capital, that was for so long a capital of every other thing before art; for at Washington—where, the infrequent visitor must remind himself, are the variously excellent art museums known as the Phillips Memorial Gallery, the Freer Gallery, and the Corcoran Gallery, and the rich but dismally exhibited collections of the Smithsonian Institution and the National Gallery—at Washington is a collection of immediately contemporary painting and sculpture which, better than any other single exhibit, affords the measure of American art production today. It is in the improvised storehouse of the WPA Federal Art Project. To this depot are sent chosen works of government-paid artists from all parts of the Union; and there the investigator may read the breadth and the quality, the originality and the proficiency, of the *mass* of national artists—in a single showing enormously encouraging and even impressive.

Certainly no one should presume to speak of American art, of its civilized or uncivilized status, without having thus gained a sense of the current, both broad and deep, of art produced by scattered and largely unrecognized individuals; for this background, this mass demonstration, is more eloquent of the livingness of the national art than are the works of the outstanding individuals whom we know and enjoy familiarly through routine exhibitions. For one thing, knowledge of so wide a cross-section of the country's output saves one from the danger of judging by New York's activities alone. The habitual New Yorker has his own sort of provincialism. Fortunately the United States escapes the dangerous over-centralization, even monopoly, of the national art-life exemplified in Paris (or London), but our story is only fractionally told by reference to the works of metropolitan "successes."

Taking the country as a whole, one may pertinently ask what is the peculiar character or bent, the constitution or timbre of its art. Especially, what are its racial affinities? If we are a racial hodge-podge, can any special strains of heritage be marked as dominating our emerging art-production?

In the beginning we were a colony of England; and the British domination continued, in our art, long after the country gained its independence politically. But today there is no slightest fealty to England in any art outside literature—and may one say "Thank God!" for that? We have, in the visual arts, outgrown the English love of the sentimental, the literary, and the photographically true. This does not mean that our "colonial stock" is unrepresented among foremost creative painters. But of the influences that flowed into our national tradition, the English has been most weakened—liquidated. On the other hand there was gain from all those devoted bands who went to other European centers to study, and came back to demonstrate the methods of Rome or Düsseldorf or Munich, or, in successive generations, Paris.

It is of course to the school of Paris that our artists as a body—like those of Germany or Russia or Mexico—are primarily indebted. But the finally important question is: Have we built the gains of French training and French understanding firmly and inventively into our own native work, departing confidently at last from French modes?

There are, no doubt, imitation Frenchmen among us. But in general the gains have been absorbed and overlaid with our own idioms. Is there any one in France whose work can account for Marin, or Mattson, or

Carroll, or O'Keeffe, or Gropper, or Hirsch? One may as easily find reminders of China or Japan or Mexico—but no strain is dominant.

The link with France is most strongly apparent, it may be added, through the exceptionally large and exceptionally gifted group of Jewish painters in New York. Leaders among them—Weber and Sterne most notably—might, by the evidence of their canvases, be described as within the French current as quickly as the American: Weber remaining as insistently Jewish as his racial brothers Soutine and Chagall in Paris; Sterne taking place as one of the world's most accomplished followers of Cézanne, whose canvases are at home on walls in Paris or Berlin or London as easily as in New York or Boston or San Diego.

It is a mark, no doubt, of the breadth and cosmopolitanism of American civilization that its front rank of artists should include these great internationalists. But when the subject is the fusion of elements into a national tradition, few commentators would care to contend that either a master whose work might have evolved wholly in France, or a world leader who leans habitually to Jewish idioms of expression, can be paraded as central to the national achievement. Even though we believe, almost fanatically, that great art must rise above nationalism, we can hardly expect to trace the growth of a civilized art in these United States—flatly our subject here—without making the concession that environment and the flow of the life of the times will be reflected to a certain extent in the subject-matter, and, in a subtler and indescribable way, in the painter's *grasp* upon his art.

At the very center of the current are other painters who, while not accepting the blinders decreed by the American-scene people, have an American quality, in this other sense. To take three figures, John Marin, Henry Mattson, and John Carroll (they would not be every one's choice as *the* ranking painters, but probable entries on every progressive critic's list of the leading ten), they may be considered central in the American achievement because all three have absorbed the influences of international modernism, even while each one has displayed a native originality more American than foreign. Indeed, no one of the three could be mistaken as a French or a German or an Italian painter. So distinctive is the work of each, moreover, that no picture from the brush of any one could be mistaken as the work of any other painter. It is out of such originality—seen, however, as conditioned farther back by the forces of change that have swept all Western countries—that the American tradition has been forged.

Marin, indebted at first to Cézanne, early turned his back upon Europe, literally and metaphorically. Treading at times close to abstraction, and putting formal excellence above documentation, he took his subjects, insofar as they survive, from solidly native sources: rocky Maine, teeming downtown New York, the valleys and ranges of the Southwest. Of these subjects he has made paintings that are distinguished in any company—vital, sensitive, often breath-taking.

Henry Mattson, who came late rather than early to the group of form-conscious artists, is likewise an individual genius and the product of world modernism. Lately there has been in his work a still beauty, not to say a splendor, of a sort unparalleled in the pictures of any living European master, most suggestive, indeed, of the American Ryder. As the third example, Carroll veers away from any habitual reference to local or national environment or life, to be in the truest sense an independent. Like the other two, he is in the international current, in accepting the philosophy of art and the methods of painting that have been developed in the way marked out by Cézanne, but he is as far from current French practice as are such Central European leaders as Klee and Kokoschka.

One feels the necessity to press a little the point of a dual achievement: That the artist shall have found his place in relation to a tradition both universal and modern, and at the same time be intensely original—differing in achievement from artists within the other national branches of the universal stream. This over-emphasis is necessary because the failure to achieve a civilized art of our own during that more-than-half-a-century was largely due to a dichotomy at this point: One-half of our painters overlooking or resisting the current of change flowing from the European centers of art, and so continuing to paint in the conventions of the eras preceding; the other half so absorbed in European modernism that they cut all links with America as such.

One should mention Marin, Mattson, and Carroll only to add immediately that they are representative of a large group of established artists who are both natively original and, shall one say, "universally formed." At one end of the list, over where the international current is strong, would be found Walt Kuhn and Bernard Karfiol, and Marsden Hartley, all veterans in the struggle to bring the United States abreast of the international tide of Modernism, as it was, and all at last considered respectable and masterly, even by the museums. With them one might name Abraham Walkowitz, Morris Kantor, Henry Lee McFee, and Peppino Mangravite.

At the other end of the list, hardly less influenced, at first, by the Post-Impressionist proceedings, but branching thereafter to separate and personal destinations, are Georgia O'Keeffe with her exquisite, musical, feminine harmonies, which are formal magic to a special audience, but unexciting if not obscure to others; and Charles Sheeler, who purifies his painting almost to the point of abstraction; and Louis Eilshemius, who would be in danger of being labelled a romantic if it were not for a naïveté of conception and an intuitive grasp of formal design that carry many a canvas over into the field of delightful "modern-primitive." There are others of these native "independents" who are less known—for instance, Arnold Friedman and Matthew Barnes—and there were Arthur B. Davies and Preston Dickinson and Maurice Prendergast.

It touches upon a quality of American civilization, no doubt, and is indicative of a tolerance and a receptiveness, that two of the ablest figures of the sometime Modernist movement in Germany have come to live and paint among us. This is in line with the old national ideal of offering asylum to the persecuted. (The ideal is as likely to be popularly condemned today, at least by those who, so to speak, have been called upon to run the asylum.) But when the immigrant is so great an artist as George Grosz, once a leader of the celebrated *Neue Sachlichkeit* school, of "Verists," he is unreservedly welcomed. Known in Germany as the ablest living painter-satirist, a master who lifted caricature and social documentation to new heights, he has, since coming to the United States, made over his philosophy of art and his painting methods. Lionel Feininger, famous as one of the three great experimental painters of the Bauhaus group, though coming ostensibly as a radical expatriated with other Modernists, is really returned thus unexpectedly to the country of his birth—having gone from America to Germany originally as a student of music.

Grosz and Feininger cannot be said as yet to have been absorbed into the current of American tradition. Where they already are helping shape it is in their teaching. This is true of another painter whose name would adorn any national roster: Jean Charlot. His work still has the distinctive appeal that can be traced to his double heritage, French and Mexican; it speaks very little as yet of the United States. But slowly the gifts and the example of such a creator are bound to affect fellow artists.

The cases of these three imported leaders afford occasion to mention one other racial strain that flows persistently and creatively in our exhibition halls, the Japanese. One is likely to find some of the most enjoyable bits of formal composition in any comprehensive American show signed by Japanese artists resident here; and Yasuo Kuniyoshi may be considered one of the ablest painters of the time. The output of such a man, since it fits into no other national tradition, goes to the credit of the American. Yet it cannot be considered a resultant of the strictly native environment or life. (Kuniyoshi, though, did some early studies of Western farm life which are as charming as anything within the body of American "modern-primitive" painting.) It is this sort of thing that makes exceptionally difficult the measuring or bounding of art life in the United States.

The artists so far named might be said to afford the evidence of an *established* American body of creative painters. They have had recognition, they have enjoyed honors, they are "standbys" in representative exhibitions (as are such less modern but widely respected favorites as Leon Kroll and Eugene Speicher, or—nearer the modern mode—Alexander Brook and Ernest Lawson). But the more exciting sign of the maturing of the national art is the sudden emergence, as already noted, of a younger generation with an amazing, if not consistently masterly, grasp of Post-Impressionist methods, and with individuality, power, and vision. Some of these men have had one or two exhibitions in recognized centers—or it may be, have yet to know their first solo shows—and most of them are obviously too young to be considered as other than on the way to creative leadership. Such are—one observer's list, compiled out of personal if not casual contacts—Elliot Orr, John Gernand, Howard Cook, Philip Evergood, Millard Sheets, Joseph Sheridan, Jon Corbino, Louis Schanker, Kenneth Callahan, Robert Philipp, Joseph de Martini, David McCosh, Mervin Jules, Robert Franklin Gates, Joe Jones, Jacob Burck, Lee Gatch, Marion Greenwood, Carlos Dyer, William S. Schwartz, Herman Maril, James Sterling. Better known but not yet at the height of their powers, and seemingly in line for definite leadership, are Franklin Watkins, Karl Knaths, Arnold Blanch, and Paul Sample.

The members of this group seem destined to prove in the decade to come that among the less recognized people there are talents that will be the equals of Marin's or Mattson's, of Sterne's or Weber's.

The people of the United States are not likely to have, for many generations, an art so *distinctively* national as, for instance, the Mexican. The extraordinary school of painters in Mexico today affords the outstanding example in the Western world of a powerfully creative, exclusive, racial style. The only comparable, easily marked national movement was the German Expressionism of 1915-30, now officially outlawed and denied.

The United States cannot expect to develop a style or school in that limited sense. It is rather in process of welding a tradition out of many influences and trials—as happened in France, where the Dutch Van Gogh, the Spaniards Picasso and Gris, the Italian Modigliani, the Russian Soutine, and many other "alien" artists have been welcomed and absorbed.

The cry that we must above all be American led, after the World War, to the wide exploitation of regional illustrational painting. "American scene" art became the most popular and most publicized form—as if devotion to localisms of environment, and sly, if not cruel, observation of the foibles of character in the back-eddies of our civilization, were sufficient to make an art. But the phenomenon that threw up Wood and Benton, Burchfield and Curry, Marsh and Hopper, passed into history as a phase of the process of finding the *double* basis necessary to expressive painting. It is seen that Curry and Marsh and Burchfield are creative artists not by reason of the cornfields and cyclones, the night-clubs and burlesque shows, and the dilapidated General-Grant-period houses which are their subject-staples, but only as they bring to the treatment of these undoubtedly American things the quality of mastery that Marin and the others have shown without over-insisting upon native picturesqueness or strangenesses of character.

The important thing about the American-scene phenomenon, in other words, is that it finds place at one end of a very wide range of accomplishment; it has demonstrated that even in illustrational painting (generally with a sentimental or nostalgic tinge) or in social satire a mastery of plastic organization *can* be implicit—as especially in Curry's most successful Western pieces, Marsh's metropolitan studies, and Paul Sample's least barber-shoppy compositions. At the other extreme of the range, equally eloquent of the breadth of our recent gains, but equally to be understood as a "special" phase, is the school of abstractionists, surprisingly numerous, and recently very vocal in the halls where art theories are discussed.

Internationally considered, abstract art has not claimed a large number of leading painters; but the key to the modern movement lies in new knowledge of the abstract elements underlying the art. It may well be, too, that the next great release will come after further purification, further progress toward the non-representational estate of music. In any case the American painters have been constant experimenters in that direction. Agnes Pelton exhibited at the Armory Show; Charles Sheeler, the late Charles Demuth, and Raymond Jonson have found enthusiastic if limited recognition through many years; and today the increasing interest is symbolized, in New York, in two museums of abstract art, and in the existence of a flourishing society, the American Abstract Artists. The group has turned up no Kandinsky or Klee; but among the native artists who consider objective painting materialistic and old-fashioned there is a very high level of plastic inventiveness, and occasionally in the abstract galleries there is a flash of genius that opens new vistas upon the possible future of "pictures."

One other school is sufficiently defined in principle, and sufficiently successful, to demand mention also as a separate creative unit in the mosaic which is our American art: the "socially conscious" painters. Politically far to the left, the school is the only one that deals frankly in "message" art and yet transcends the limitations of mere illustration and caricature. The better men in the field—perhaps William Gropper, one of our greatest painters, is foremost, and Benjamin Kopman, a high-ranking member—have been more successful than the American-scene people in bringing formal excellence to their statements of fact and opinion. Some of the leaders, Gropper and Maurice Becker in particular, were known as caricaturists for such radical journals as *The Masses* before they came into the ranks of masterly painters.

Largely out of the struggles and convictions of the group—frankly communistic at first—came, in 1936, the organization known as the American Artists Congress, which is the most dynamic and articulate art society in the country. It started with a militant program which included action "against war and Fascism," but at present it is content to label its 800 members as artists "of growing social awareness," banded in defense of democratic institutions, aiming to assure the artist the right of free expression, and to counteract the tendencies, shown by some conservative elements, toward isolation of art as a decorative or aristocratic phenomenon or as a precious cultural indulgence.

It is certain that with such an alert and aggressive socially-conscious agency in the field, American art-life is not going to be too quickly centered in the pastures, supposedly remote from the common life, now under cultivation by the abstractionists. No American artist will take up residence in the perhaps mythical Ivory Tower without having been made aware of the dangers he thereby incurs. By contrast with the

American Abstract Artists and the Guggenheim Foundation for the promotion of non-objective art, the American Artists Congress points up the thesis underlying this whole analysis of our civilization: That our tradition cannot comprise a compact or "pure" style; that it is rather characterized by breadth and contrast and freedom.

Since we have been more or less listing the organized or like-minded groups, it may be added that the National Academy still exists, and holds exhibitions. This too has to do, no doubt, with civilization, since all civilized nations have academies.

Socially conscious artists have found a medium especially congenial and effective in murals. The close link of the famous Mexican muralists to revolutionary activities in their country proved a stimulus and an example to the left-wing painters here, and on both coasts there were, some five years ago, sporadic ventures into the field. But two things occurred which served to broaden beyond class lines the impulse toward mural art. One was the entrance of the United States Government into the almost vanished list of patrons of the art. The other was the formation of relief projects for unemployed artists, at first under State administrations, then in a unified program under the Federal Government's Works Progress Administration (with the PWAP a link between).

The Government, lacking still, after decades of agitation and balked effort, a Bureau of Fine Arts, had until five years ago a very uncivilized record in relation to creative artistry. But in 1933 a sort of bureau of decorative arts turned up within the Treasury Department, and was put under the able direction of Edward Bruce. Then it was decreed that one per cent of government money spent on new buildings should be diverted to the fine arts incidental to architecture. A number of artists—mostly from along the conservative fringe of modernism—were called in; and now the administrative palaces at Washington are adorned, in still unfrequent spots, with native wall-paintings. The achievement under Treasury Department auspices has been satisfactory rather than thrilling; but the panels by Boardman Robinson and George Biddle in the Department of Justice Building, and those by Reginald Marsh in the Post Office Department Building, may be singled out as exceptionally fine; and the standard is bettered as the administrators liberalize their attitude toward modernism. The Treasury Department work has spread also to post office buildings scattered over the country.

It was rather in the activities of the WPA Art Project that mural art really came to flower. Originally taken over by the Government under Edward Bruce's direction in the winter of 1933–34, the Project found its continuing and present form in 1935 under the direction of Holger Cahill. With, at the peak of the Depression in 1936, more than 5000 artists under Government pay, Cahill and his associates saw the opportunity to bring almost unlimited numbers of murals to public buildings, and at the same time to afford mural artists a place for fulfillment of their fondest dreams.

To say that the more than a thousand placed panels are, as a whole, great mural art would be more than hazardous. But one cannot fail to see that wall-painting has been firmly established here, perhaps as in no other country in modern times; that in giving opportunity to hundreds of painters, the Project has turned up hitherto unknown muralists who are competent to produce creative work beyond any standards believable five years ago. More heartening than the success of a dozen already recognized artists (who nevertheless were thrown on "relief" projects during the Depression), is the emergence of unknown masters in the field. Sometime left-wing radicals like Mitchell Siporin have made their marks beside Hester Miller Murray, who has a genius for animal and children studies, for schools, and Joseph Sheridan, sometime abstractionist.

Thought of the WPA Art Project leads necessarily to consideration of the general economic situation of the artist in American civilization. Before abandoning the question of art achievement, however, for that of artist security, it may be as well to say what little needs to be said about sculpture.

If civilization hangs upon the sculptors, mankind is in something of a dark age—in America as elsewhere. Even France has failed of leadership here. Germany scores with a group of artists pleasingly creative but hardly exciting (since Lehmbruck's death); and England has more good modern sculptors than painters, but there is no great new world-release in the practice there. The United States claims similar progress, very promiseful, obviously on the first courses of a new post-realistic slope, but certainly without men who are giants in the eyes of the world.

It is a relevant fact that there is hardly a first-class sculptor in the country who goes back to "old American stock." (Indeed it may seriously be questioned whether the English-speaking peoples ever in history have produced a truly great sculptor.) The greatest of American modernists in the art was Gaston Lachaise (who died in 1936), a true genius—but born and largely schooled in France. Of those who might be listed as

the top twenty practitioners—judged for creative ability and originality—
the following can be mentioned as indicating the polyglot nature of our
sculptural studios: Polygnotos Vagis, José de Creeft, Oronzio Maldarelli,
Isamu Noguchi, Ahron Ben-Schmuel, Alfeo Faggi, Heinz Warneke,
Simone Brangier Boas, and José Ruiz de Rivera. Although the names fail
to indicate clearly, five others of the leaders were born elsewhere: Zorach,
Sterne, and Cashwan, all from Russia; Robert Laurent, born in France;
and Hunt Diederich, born in Hungary. To these can be added a very few
names more standard in the national life: most notably John B. Flanna-
gan and Marion Walton. Curiously enough the sculptor who seemed
fifteen years ago most likely to enlarge the range of the national achievement, Paul Manship, appears in this later day a neo-classicist, without
American accent. Hardly more related to the national environment,
although certainly one of the greatest creative figures among us, is
Alexander Archipenko, who had shown himself one of the foremost
trail-blazers in Central Europe before coming to America in the mid-
Twenties.

Here, then, is a prime trying-ground for the thesis that mixed blood
gives rise to a people's finest art. But when—and whether—these many
strains may flow together and give rise to a national tradition, is any one's
guess. At present the observer can only say that sculpture seems to be
entering into the civilization on this side of the Atlantic to about the same
extent, and in the same uncertain way, as in Europe. Fine talents are to
be detected in all parts of the country; but the brutal truth is that there
doesn't seem to be much place for sculpture in our contemporary
environment.

Again it is the WPA Art Project more than any other factor that seems
likely to bring renewed life to the art. Probably two-thirds of the really
important sculptors are on the government rolls. While an attempt is
being made to bring them to the service of public architecture (and thus,
by example, to lead to increased use of sculpture in privately financed
building), the results are not yet to be hailed with that enthusiasm
warranted in speaking of mural-painting or easel projects.

Just how far the artist-government relationship will affect the next cycle
of art life in the United States no reporter or prophet may venture to say.
It is evident, however, that official subsidy given to thousands of artists—
for reasons that had nothing to do with cultural idealism—immensely
increased the number of young painters and sculptors bringing creative

work into the exhibition galleries, put art works into circulation in literally thousands of places—public buildings, schools, remote libraries and museums, newly created art centers—where these things had not been known before, and in countless ways served to revivify art interest, art education, and art showing.

In short, when artists were at the point of starvation, the Government stepped in, decided on the only logical and dignified sort of relief—pay for work in the recipients' own field. It soon found itself administering the greatest art project in history. Since it cannot, apparently, withdraw from its rôle of supporter and director for many years to come (until the problem of general unemployment is substantially solved), it would seem wise to look at the other half of the picture, the undoubted great gain for both artist and art-loving public, and see if the advantages so unexpectedly accruing cannot be perpetuated.

Even in good times it was no new experience for the professional artist to be close to starvation. Painters and sculptors have been the step-children of society ever since specialized competitive organization of society put the artist at the mercy of what is politely termed "public demand"; and the Anglo-Saxon nations have been exceptionally negligent of artistic talent. In America, outside acceptance of a few favored con-formists and panderers to fashion, we have been pretty insensitive and even cruel to our makers of pictures and statues. A few, of course, have been born to sufficient money to tide them along, if not to give them full independence. A very few have found individual patrons. A somewhat larger group have "got along somehow" on the scantiest of sales. A few have committed suicide, and the great majority have been diverted into illustration, commercial designing, teaching, and writing about art—or have carried these as side-lines to afford a slim margin for creative effort.

When the Depression came, the market for side-lines disappeared as quickly as the picture-market. Moreover, the more remote refuges—jobs in groceries, filling-stations, restaurants, washrooms and the like, all known to have been filled by artists on occasion—disappeared. When the WPA tardily arrived to co-ordinate work-relief, a wise administrator saw the opportunity at once to do an emergency work that had to be done and to conserve a great part of the artistic resources of the nation (theatre artists, dancers, and a certain number of writers were put on projects also). It is hardly too much to say that the great catastrophe that we call the Depression gave the mass-profession of American painters and sculptors its first opportunity to show fully its capabilities—its great ability, and its occasional flashes of genius.

That is where the United States stands in regard to the fine arts today. The most relevant fact in this year 1938 is that the Government—in the past incomparably the most innocent of any interest in art, among the great nations—finds itself actually supporting and directing the majority of the producing artists in the forty-eight States. Art as such has unmistakably flowered under the arrangement. We all have been shown that if for a long period art seems to have no significant place in a nation's life, it is likely to be some narrowing influence in the form of its civilization and not a failure of the artists that is to be blamed.

The artist as an entity has somehow persisted through an extended period when he seemed not to be greatly needed or wanted by society. Given, suddenly and in a fantastically irrelevant way, the barest of holds upon economic security, he has responded constructively, even splendidly. Together with those few hardy ones who had independently survived the stress of "making a living" by art, he has demonstrated the existence of a body of art that would seem to make our cultural future, as regards this one commodity, certain and civilized.

And the immediate aspect of that future? Only some method of continuing the mass security which has given us the present benefits seems reasonable or possible. The far-reaching question is how to transform the rather hastily contrived "relief" organization into a mechanism designed to give, on a discriminating and ordered basis, security to artists, even while (so long as competitive economy continues to control our life) the burden is shifted to private patronage or the open market whenever and wherever conditions permit. That question unfortunately is beclouded by a more immediate controversy, between two extremist parties, who want the government projects either designated as *permanent* support-agencies, or scrapped without more ado. On one hand the more short-sighted project artists, seeing the question as flatly one of job-or-no-job, have organized to propagandize the WPA into permanency. On the other hand outraged taxpayers, realizing that they are carrying the bulk of the artists of the country—and believing, possibly, that they have proven that they can get along well enough without art anyway—clamor for the liquidation of the projects willy-nilly.

This article being a statement and an analysis of conditions in 1938, not a prophecy, we may leave the matter there, in clouds of controversy, obscured by not a little political heat. It is enough that we have detected the existence of a rich and rewarding body of American work—sufficient for the claim that the nation is now served with a vital native art—and that the experiment of extending government security has seemed a major factor in that gain. The artists, perhaps, have no more right to demand permanent security than any other group in society. At the moment it is obviously all civilization that is perilously insecure, not a nation within it, or the art within a nation.

Another way of putting the conclusion is this: Civilization is shaky, therefore the United States is shaky, therefore American art is shaky. But among the component parts or forces of American civilization, art is at last well up as an accomplishment. The *production* of art is on a civilized basis.

# ARCHITECTURE

## [*Douglas Haskell*]

### THE PEOPLE READY TO CHANGE

RUSKIN voiced the accepted attitude toward architecture when, speaking of the "Lamp of Memory," he plead for utmost permanence. "Therefore, when we build, let us think that we build forever. Let it not be for present delight, nor for present use alone; let it be such work as our descendants shall thank us for, and let us think . . . that a time will come when these stones will be held sacred because our hands have touched them. . . . For, indeed, the greatest glory of a building is not in its stones, nor in its gold. Its glory is in its Age. . . ."

If such was the belief of Ruskin, age was venerated ten times as much in that notorious stratum of Americans ready if necessary to secure antiquity by purchase, on occasion buying and transplanting shrines and ancient castles stone by stone.

A people that has explored, exploited, and half wrecked a continent in the span of a century is accustomed in its daily life to a condition of constant change; no monument is sacred. Hence, in every moment that the American had free for "culture," he felt dastardly about the improvisatory nature of his daily life; but once having done penance at some shrine of accepted art, he has always been found back again among his accustomed vices.

What we have suffered from this recklessness we have already found out to our sorrow. Scarcely is it necessary to repeat the account of appalling loss to agriculture of fertility through loss of soil; the loss to architecture through the destruction not only of masterpieces but of whole areas of decent older buildings.

On the other hand: all this is already lost, and the habit of change is unlikely to diminish. Meanwhile we possess no systematic record, no appreciation, of what the habit of rapid change has brought or could bring to architecture as a positive gain. For, against the testimony of Ruskin, there stands another opinion, voiced by Hawthorne's young photographer in the House of Seven Gables, that "houses should be built fresh for every generation instead of lingering on in dingy security, never really fitting the needs of any family but that which originally achieved and built it." Such, at least, has been the American view: and the sentiment, as compared to Ruskin's, is rather more unselfish.

To build freshly has meant chiefly, so far as the American contribution was concerned, to install those "modern improvements" which superior European culture affected to despise. But we possess no coherent cultural history of what was done. The architecture books are all in terms of the Greek Revival as beauty and Victorian Gothic or General Grant as ugliness, where they should be tracing the unparalleled American contributions to modern culture through the American bathroom, central heating, and Edison's electric light. As for more liberated books, they have been so intent upon denouncing the mechanical *panacea* as to have taken mistakenly for granted the fruits of the mechanical advance.

It required Adolf Loos, the fine Austrian architect, to discern that no carver, no decorator, but the American plumber was the possessor in the 19th century of the spirit of craftsmanship; that he was the modern craftsman *par excellence*. This is true not only because the plumber followed the great central tradition of craftsmanship, which was to do what was needed in the most efficient way, but because his creation opened the approach to an entirely new concept of the house. It had been a shell. The palaces of Florence, for example, were beautiful shells: beautifully proportioned and finished but still essentially shells, capable of holding people and wardrobes, jewelry and wash-basins. Now it was through plumbing, heating, and lighting that the house became more than a shell. A "machine" the Frenchman Le Corbusier now calls it, because, through plumbing, heating, lighting, and subsequent equipment, the house has become a modern instrument planned to take an active, not a passive part in giving us a shelter service. So grateful were we to Le Corbusier that we forgot we had furnished the basis for his concepts. But Le Corbusier still lacked the American background. And that was why he felt he had done his job when he related the new machinery to a geometry of space that should permit linking the new architecture to the great tradition including the Parthenon, Byzantium, and Michael Angelo.

But American experience with instruments tells us that such redesigning only meets the beginning of the problem. An instrument, as we all know through our cars, is a vastly livelier organism to handle than a shell. It brings forth a whole series of new factors. They are chiefly related to Time. Though it would be inaccurate to say that architecture had acquired a new dimension, it is true that the time factor, which had lain almost dormant, had suddenly jumped into control.

To begin with, instruments have a shorter life. Four walls of stone under a tile roof can maintain a low-grade existence for many centuries; but a structure that provides conditioned air, controlled temperature and light, all kinds of power outlets, devices for cooking or refrigeration, elevators, and the like, wears out or goes obsolete without even wearing out. Buildings are used up the more rapidly, the more specialized they are to individual needs, the more articulated in plan for a close fit, the better equipped in operating services. Not only do all buildings go faster but there is a different pace among different kinds, and among the different parts of the same one.

According to the attitude taken toward these problems raised by change, the building community can be divided into three groups: the reactionaries, the progressives, and the sluggards. The sluggards embraced almost the whole real estate and financial community who, as the Depression has revealed, simply expected to offset losses through obsolescence by means of automatic increases in value brought about by increasing population. As their tenements, for example, grew older, they expected a greater pressure from new applicants to save them in use. Now that this naïve procedure has failed, the financial community holds on still more wilfully, refusing aid to new enterprises for fear of revealing the weakness of its outworn "investments." Reactionary, too, is that mistaken if well-meant attitude that prevails in some "housing" circles, which would forestall "obsolescence" by keeping the houses of the poor simple and unequipped and thus capable of a long survival: but survival on a low plane, and with a hopelessness of improvement not worthy of the dignity of an American.

Specifically, what has the time factor, the factor of rapid change, brought as conscious innovation in design? First of all, it has humbled the designer. No longer a lordly architect fashioning a "monument" once for all, he is responsible, like the anonymous designers of a ship, for proved operation. Two writers in the *Architectural Record,* Holm and Larsen, have contributed the keenest analysis of the problem. They have shown that every building has a life-cycle. It begins with design and erection, continues through use and consumption, to end always in final demolition. To foresee this cycle, to cope with it in the very first concept of the building, so that not only erection and use but even the final demolition is envisaged and calculated for in the very first design: that is a difficult new piece of work; but it is also an art nobler than fashioning the old arches, more fascinating than relating only masses, surfaces, and details.

It is in order to cope with change that our buildings grow flexible. The center of a building used often to be a big space. Now it tends to be a service core. In the center of the skyscraper is the elevator stack; apartment houses pivot on stair halls and plumbing stacks. However cunningly the spaces branch forth, they keep their relationship to this trunk. It is in order to stay flexible that our rooms are subdivided as little as possible; not just to give the thrill of new shapes and flowing spaces. Thus skeleton construction has made possible floors independent of walls, so that walls and partitions may be shifted at will. The house must stand ready to meet change with change.

In community relationships, the fact that time rules buildings has led to a new proposal, by the same authors, for community control. No longer can a single building, once erected, have the right to linger indefinitely in a neighborhood seeking to change, blighting the whole neighborhood or reducing it to chaos. We forbid a new industrial plant in a residential district; we should also be able to forbid an old one. To achieve this, buildings can be not only zoned but licensed. At the end of a reasonable period the license expires, allowing the community to reconsider what use is to be made of the land. The community will have time-control.

That design for the needs of a day need not be inferior to design meant to last a century is supported by more than the scriptural reference to the lilies of the field. There exists in recent history a first-rate architectural example. Throughout a period of subtle civilization in Japan, an architecture grew up that used bamboo, paper, and grass mats, the most ephemeral of materials, to effect consummately dignified and charming combinations in the creation of houses that were permanent only in the sense that the human race is permanent: by constant renewal, not by posthumous domination. And among the architectural products of the last decade in the United States, some of the most delightful were a small set of canvas and redwood cabins, "desert schooners" set by Frank Lloyd Wright in the Arizona desert. Once the occupants departed, the cabins were forthwith quietly taken away, at night, by the Indians.

### THE DEFEATED SKYSCRAPER

Now that Rockefeller Center has been with us for nearly a decade, it seems surprising that its forms should have been so savagely attacked by critics. The center has the New Yorker's affection. For it is not only the largest skyscraper aggregation of all, but it gives a good show.

Even architecturally it gives a good show. The vast cliff of the R. C. A. Building, rising among the lower buildings, is still astonishing and exciting. Of classical proportions it has none. It rises precariously on edge, a sight far more spectacular than the Empire State Building. The narrowness of the slab accents its height; the restlessness corresponds to the city's mood. Even viewed broadside, the R. C. A. Building seems endowed with movement, through the progressive rhythm of the narrow setbacks. The pattern of the walls in many of the Rockefeller Center buildings is uncalculated and ugly; but this strikes us as a mere incident, as if the designers had been out for more important things. The disparity in proportion between the Fifth Avenue buildings and the taller ones behind serves, like a deliberate musical discord, to accentuate the contrast. Rockefeller Center is an imposing modern group.

Why, then, does Rockefeller Center still strike as the last output of a defeated day? Because the city goes with it. Like a dictator, Rockefeller Center is magnificent only when attention is focused on itself alone. But like dictators, such structures exist by sucking life out of those around them. Finally the skyscrapers overreached themselves. The congestion they created; the expense of subways and other services; the municipal debt; all the results of overcrowding: skyscraper construction is at a standstill.

It may revive again, as dictatorships do. But there will never again be the same naïve enthusiasm for it. It has dawned on too many people that the cost is "on them."

### THE MAN WHO FLIES

The man who can fly has acquired a new eye for the way in which people have settled the earth. From his station high up in the clouds, the airplane passenger cannot help but see how insignificant have been the claims for space of even the most magnificent of buildings, as compared to the vast empty space that floats across the gigantic continent. A speck by day or a few pin-pricks by night account for the structures of the most ambitious: tiny cubicles of air bounded against the infinite, for purposes of safety, sociability, and domestication.

Flight humbles us as individuals while it gives a grand new sense of the human community as a whole. The ground below is seen in terms of Plan. By day we note the great checkerboard of fields, the threads of rivers and railroads, the location of deserts, oil fields, mines that make up the environment. By night we are more aware of Man, who proclaims himself through the abstract pattern of his lights. Scattered here, clustered there, these lights appear as spots of existence suspended in the vast dark space; the little headlights stabbing back and forth to establish the paths of connection.

That is the pattern of architecture drawn to twentieth-century scale. For, just as the draftsman learns to treat any single door or window in itself as a mere "detail" once he has learned the greater importance of the general scheme of openings and fenestration, so the shape and peculiarities of individual houses are mere details compared to the pattern of human habitation.

On the American continent this pattern in one respect is highly peculiar: namely in its distribution. Huge blaring ganglia of lights alternate with areas of black vacancy. When every human being, to begin with, gets so tiny an allotment of space, why should he decrease it by huddling up to his neighbor, and letting these vast areas of space go unused? Of what is he afraid? The map gives no satisfactory answer.

### THE PEOPLE WHO COULD SPREAD

Daniel Boone was already worried about congestion:
"I first removed to the woods of Kentucky. I fought and repelled the savages, and hoped for peace. Game was abundant and our path was prosperous, but soon I was molested by interlopers from every quarter. Again I retreated to the region of the Mississippi; but again these speculators and settlers followed me. Once more I withdrew to the Licks of the Missouri—and here at length I hoped to find rest. But still I was pursued—for I had not been two years at the Licks before a damned Yankee came and settled down within a hundred miles of me."

Daniel Boone's requirements for elbow room may have been uncommonly generous, but there is at least a distinctly American flavor in the scope of his complaint. Being American then meant having more of everything than was needed. It showed up even in American humor; for if the English on their small island cultivated the art of understatement, the pioneer delighted in cosmic exaggeration.

The continent still gives us a generous allowance, as civilized countries go, for space to move in. We are still only forty to the square mile against England's seven hundred and fifty. On the face of it, the American should have nineteen times as much land as the Englishman, nineteen times as much road, and a house nineteen times as large if he should want it so.

Struck by this opulence, an Englishman, Sir Raymond Unwin, made the calculation that every family in America could be housed within a gross area no larger than the State of Connecticut, at only twenty families to the acre; there would still remain free for public buildings and for recreation an area larger than Manhattan. Then why do we crowd, why is New York more congested than London?

The worst of it is that even our "reformers," even the humanitarian "housing" experts, are infected with pinchbeck standards of space. They are happy when they achieve openness and space on terms comparable to Europe, whereas Europe should be considered a mere beginning compared to us.

Here, for example, as a New York dwelling complex: not a slum but a well-known 1933 example of "slum-clearance," namely Knickerbocker Village. Now if the whole population of the United States were to be packed as tightly as the occupants of Knickerbocker Village, who live a thousand to the acre, then all 130 million of us could be humped together on an area not more than fourteen miles square. At touring speed a passenger car could be driven around the loop encompassing us all, within an hour. Are not Daniel Boone's successors a humble folk?

The result is the more peculiar, since the United States was settled largely by homesteading, which put every man on his hundred and sixty acres. But the whole country was used only for rapid exploitation, rather than permanent occupation; hence when the cities seemed to offer the best chance, all moved into the cities. Now the cities have been thoroughly exploited, and the best exploiters are on top; vested ownership and institutions center in the cities; the cities also present the biggest snarls; and few are the large-minded architects or "city planners" who can divert attention long enough from the city (even from criticism of the city) to observe the enormous resources of useful dwelling space that lie outside. We are still a people who can spread.

## THE HIGHWAY

There exists, nevertheless, the American road. And what a change has come over it in the past ten years, through popular action alone! The roads are no longer mere connecting links from town to town. They are lined with structures. These are of a new class. At night, in thickly settled areas such as northern New Jersey, they make driving one continuous battle against blare. Gas stations, Socony, Gulf, Sunoco, Texas, or name your own favorite brand. Gas stations with "lubritoriums," and announcements of "inspected" rest rooms. Gas stations with lunch rooms and tourist cabins. Harry's diner, surrounded by huge Diesel-powered trucks and trailers whose drivers are inside exchanging information on the whereabouts of the different inspectors. Paradise Dance Hall, whose parking lot explains itself. But the majority of the groups are straight "cabin camps" ministering to the ubiquitous transient called the "tourist."

Unexpectedly, these hit-or-miss cabin camps have begun to expand and improve. In the middle States, for example around St. Louis, such camps have become really ambitious. Some are decked out with every Hollywood gee-gaw but others are downright handsome. Here is one: straight rows of trim stucco cottages, so cleanly executed that only the red tile roofs and the fake chimneys betray the hand of a professional architect. Neatly painted benches face the common court. At the entrance a neat washrack for the car; at the rear a neat laundry for clothes. Inside, the American finds everything that he likes. His car is right beside him, accessible through a single door. He has his bathroom, telephone, radio, "Beautyrest" mattress, candy-tuft bedspread, sanitary steel wardrobe; there is plenty of air though small windows admit not much sun or view.

Small wonder that tourist camps are begining to come into demand as year-round apartments. They produce a fine community life in terms acceptable to the wide range of people who visit them. Indeed, in a very modest way they begin to approach the layout and atmosphere of the new Greenbelt towns on which have been put forth the best efforts of professional architects and planners. What the tourist camp has, at its best, is cheapness and popular support, in a great movement of decentralization. What it lacks, that the Greenbelt town has, is control over a large area of land and a coherent plan for future industry and expansion.

Our planners might well pay more attention to these indigenous developments along the road. That they have not done so comes partly out of an accident in our architectural history. This history has never been kind to the pioneer and has not noticed the nomad. Our architectural history began, and received its guiding ideas, in the Colonial period. This period was distinctly *not* a period of the great Open Road. It was one hundred and fifty years of concentration on a coastal strip not more than one hundred and fifty miles wide. In its early phase, the Colonial period in New England had produced its splendid democratic community forms: the village common, the unpretentious meeting house, the group of trim dwellings under spreading trees. Leaving all this, the pioneers of the West must have seemed like cultural ingrates. But the emigrants had not been the people to enjoy it! They were mostly Scotch-Irish and Moravians who were landless and overcrowded. These were the people who lived for years in th Appalachians exposed to Indian attack and waiting for the big opportunity. These were the builders of the log cabin which the people have always loved and architectural writers unjustly despised. And, as humble folk, they ended by laying the groundwork for an American architecture no longer colonial but Continental, with potentialities that have only begun to be tapped. So too the new humble re-explorers can help recapture the country which had somehow drained into the city, and re-establish our pattern of settlement on a far more dispersed and grander scale.

### GREENBELTS

Not many would have dreamt in 1920 that within two decades the largest builder of shelter in the United States would be the Government! Yet at the moment of writing, more than fifty large projects have been completed under Government control, and sixty-six are earmarked for the immediate future.

The sociological aspect of Government entry into housing does not here concern us. What strikes us is the pattern the Government is setting as an example to all private building. For already the Metropolitan Life is planning to beat the Government at its own game, with a $50,000,000 private project.

This Government architecture is *par excellence* an architecture of correlation. The details are often not remarkable. The buildings are usually plain, if not blocky; the materials are inexpensive. Yet the result is often distinguished to a degree.

It comes from being able to attack the problem as a whole. Since the builder owns the whole plot, he need adjust to no neighbors. He need build no unnecessary streets, and is therefore able to strike cross lots with his houses, as if the ground were a park. Rid of the streets, he has gained additional space at no expense; his coverage of the ground is low, leaving an impression of great open areas covered by green. And these fundamental amenities: the wide spacing, the good orientation, the air of harmony, are enough to give almost any decent architecture a powerful effect.

The Greenbelt towns are a special type of government project, done by the Resettlement Administration. Here the new town is set not in the midst of an old one, but in the midst of its own surrounding, protective belt of open farmland. It rents to its own stores, has its own community center, has its own provisions for future industry. Our Greenbelt towns are adapted from England and Germany. From England comes the concept as a whole, of "garden cities." From Germany comes the simpler placing, in the case of Greenbelt, Maryland, of the houserows. And it all does very well in America, since green foliage and sunlight have the same value all the world around.

### HOUSES ON WHEELS

From America came the impulse to make architecture the child of time; to render it flexible in the face of change. In America is developing another new impulse, with an aim no less radical than that of making architecture mobile.

The trailer sprang into being as a vacation adjunct to the automobile. Only later did it attempt to open up and blossom out into a full-blown mobile house. The trailerite is an idealist and a bug.

Indeed, the trailerite is an escapist and a romantic. He is fleeing from the ground rents of congested cities. He is trying to run from the type of home ownership, so cleverly exploited by employers, that ties you to one mill, one job, one boss. The trailerite workman driving from job to job follows a century-old dictate of Engels, that labor to avoid slavery must remain mobile.

But, like Boone, the trailerite has met limited success. The speculators catch up to him. He had planned to escape real estate taxation by means of his unattached "chattel"; but the assessors find judges willing to snare him with new interpretations. Even "housing" officials fear for his "responsibility" and help to frame him in regulations sanitary and other.

The trailer towns are of course the most innocent and law-abiding of communities. They take such pride in themselves, and they are laid out as straight and tight as Flatbush! Those seeking permanent homes in trailers are people who could think of owning no other permanent home; and their conveyances take them where they could otherwise never live, in the open, with elbow-room. The thought of such modest home-ownership is not to be sneered at, even though the trend today is toward renting and the efficiency of large-scale management. Even Socialism might vastly profit, when bureaucracy grows sluggish, by giving people the pride of their own private homes.

Of course the real perfection of a mobile trailer home waits on a civilization not more primitive, not more "nomadic" in the accepted sense, but more advanced, technically more skilled than ours, and socially better controlled. We have said that American improvements laid a new demand on modern architecture: flexibility to time. Mobility adds a still more difficult demand: flexibility to place.

Just because this ideal is so difficult, the idealists pursuing it have been obliged to penetrate much farther than the practising architects in their analysis, and have brought up some highly useful ideas along the way. Thus Buckminster Fuller, perhaps the chief proponent of the mobile house, has furnished the advance guard of existing industry with numerous guiding concepts that are filtering through. These include the idea of radical pre-fabrication, making the house in the factory; the idea of radical innovations in structure; of radical reduction in weight; the incorporation of previously unheard-of efficiencies in service; even the idea of streamlining. Streamlining, for example, has a faddish sound, until we ask an engineer about the cost of "wind-resistance" in existing frames, and until, with Fuller, we examine the highly developed mechanism for streamlining that exists in every tree.

Even before achieving full success in their ultimate aim, these investigations must greatly aid the industry which, next to average farming, is the most glaringly inefficient of all. Indeed, the greatest service performed by the proponents of mobility has been their insistence that building is by no means an industry, but an outmoded and awkward half-handicraft, with an impossible employment system, a feudal or less than feudal concept of the land, an ignorance of service, a complete dependence on speculation and the hit-and-run sale. The determined effort to make building an industry should go hand in hand with the effort at humane planning. Indeed, the advocates of mobility, pre-fabrication, industrialization, should act as a corrective to the one big mistake being made by the fine regional planning school of thought known chiefly through the writings of Mr. Lewis Mumford. This mistake consists in bad timing; for this school of thought has become intensely aware of the deficiencies in "merely mechanical" thinking and "merely mechanical" solutions to our dwelling problems at just the moment when the building game, which is *pre*-mechanical, needs every bit of mechanization it can get, every ounce of industrial organization and scientific control, in order to enter into coherent relations with the modern world at all. The undercurrent of hope for a new community that runs through even the periodical literature of the trailerites shows that they would be a class more open than most to the finest ideas in planning.

### THE ARCHITECT

Architecture is a long art, constantly growing longer. New capacities, new forms, do not replace old ones entirely but range themselves alongside, as greater diversification. Thus, despite increasing mobility, there will always remain structures by nature attached to one place, just as the law of motion itself permits a condition known as rest. New virtues do not displace old ones. In a civilization addicted to change, it becomes all the more important that we can retreat into repose, that we have ways of feeling ourselves secure. The more our opportunities branch out, the easier it is to forget the sense of the whole, and to divide architecture into one of its parts.

This brings to mind the great resource that America possesses at this time, in the personality and powers of its one world-famous architect, Frank Lloyd Wright. His virtue is that, possessing the most remarkable powers of innovation, he still preserves, uniquely, age-old sources of strength.

A lifetime of seventy years, all active, is a long span as generations go, and enough to serve as a connecting link. Within that lifetime, architecture has developed its new flexibilities. Wright had a strong part in most of them. Thus, for example, his hands opened up the box that houses had been, converting it eventually into a series of screens, some opaque, some transparent, some open, some closed, letting space flow through and guiding it to serve human purpose and human mood. Europe has taken hold of this idea more fully than America, so that never before has architecture had so great a space-freedom.

Wright helped devise the more modern, fluid structures. One of the spectacular devices was the cantilever, reaching far out beyond supporting posts, giving at the same time a new type of sheltered but open space, and a sense of acrobatic strength and *dance* in the construction. This cantilever as a liberating device was a forerunner to others, such as the stamped-sheet forms new being experimented with, dependent on machine production, which strengthen themselves, without a frame, through curvature or corrugation in their own shape. Wright has not worked with all these forms but in compensation his work with such elements as the cantilever has reached unprecedented daring. Himself the son of a pioneering family, accustomed to generous American scale, he has not been afraid to lay hold of all the material and money needed to perform such feats as the Kaufmann House, a veritable counterpoint of cantilever upon cantilever, suspending long rooms and balconies out over a waterfall, with a daring unreached in Europe. Unfortunately not America but Europe has given the greatest study to structures such as Wright's, and it is there not here that builders are now able, through the new fluid means, to dispense altogether with the more elementary symmetrical geometric shapes that have hitherto dominated architecture even in the free baroque. They are now able to draw the boundaries of irregular spaces, irregular because responding to all influences, such as contours on the outside and use areas inside, with a freedom almost freehand.

Wright's wealth of forms parallels the great wealth of our country, and derives from Nature. As a child of farmers one generation removed —a species so different from the peasant as to be American only—Wright had the sense of natural, organic structure to serve as guide through all changes of means and methods. Since the machine which was meanwhile the ideal in Europe is an organism at second hand, Wright's source was the more reliable and fundamental.

As we study the work of any one man, the human errors, deviations, unsuccessful experiments, cannot be sidestepped. There are some "lallapaloosas" of overemphasis or exaggeration in some direction or other obscurely hidden in the past record. In some of Wright's efforts there is too much weight (only with maturity did he become the consistent apostle of lightness), in others too much ornament; in others an intricacy too unmanageable, in still others a virtuosity lifting the geometric framework of his plans from a liberating means to a restrictive end. In his autobiography Wright on occasion hints that he knows what his temptations are. Yet even in the shortcomings, or shall we say his longcomings, Wright's example is instructive for us as children of this continent. He never takes, and we should never take, too little. If we err, let it be that we have tried not less but more. The great temptation is to wait for our forms on Europe; to content ourselves with the space achievements and the tight scale of Europe; to take as room only what the city speculator allows; to build modestly for the "poor"; to center on "economy" as pinching. Our own past achievements, of a more exhaustive sort, are what Europe, without too many thanks, is living on now, as "Americanization": on the whole, beneficent. We have been the people ready to change; we have been the people free to move; we are the ones to develop architecture from its old work of embellishing fixtures to the new work of devising a continuously improving, continent-wide, shelter service.

BUSINESS
AND
LABOR

# BUSINESS

## [*John T. Flynn*]

THE FERMENT in modern society which fills more than half this anxious planet with the menace of war arises out of the struggle for the conscious control of the economic mechanisms in all communities. We are no longer presented with a battle between socialism on one side to subject society to deliberate economic controls and capitalism on the other to keep it free from such controls. The true meaning of all that goes on around us is found in the definitive adoption by the ruling capitalist groups of the socialist theory of the controlled and directed economic state and the consequent clash between three principles of action—government of the economic society by the workers, government of that society by the owners of capital and government of it by the whole democratic citizenship.

It is of no importance that the organized groups of enterprisers still mutter the ancient shibboleths of laissez-faire, form themselves into Liberty Leagues to preserve the forms of the democratic state, angrily denounce the modernists who would forge chains for business and the individual. Behind these tattered banners they advance for the greatest assault upon the democratic state the world has seen since the rise of democracy in the modern age. The disturbing element of this is found in the fact that few of them realize what they are doing or whither they are marching.

The thing we call business now takes on a shape it has not assumed for three or four centuries; has not, indeed, ever assumed upon so large a scale. It is a vague shape and the ominous character of it grows out of the world-wide struggle of business to divest itself of its quality of vagueness.

For what is business? We know what *a* business is. It is an enterprise of some sort, set up to produce goods or services and to earn a profit. But it is a mere unit in the economic world. It is one enterprise or a cluster of enterprises under a single ownership. That is what we understand by *a* business. But what do we understand by *business*? Almost daily one is told what business ought to do; what powers business has for the regeneration of society if it will but act. Ordinarily we understand by the word business that area of human activity in which enterprisers operate—the sum total of the community's energies applied to the production and distribution of services and goods. As such it might include nearly the whole adult community, since almost all grown men and women perform some service in providing for the community's needs. It might include the master and his craftsmen, the banker, the lawyer and their several clerks. Yet when we say that business ought to be permitted to do this or that, we obviously do not mean that the adult population, organized as business men rather than as citizens, should be permitted to act as a unit in pursuit of some objective. There is a vague meaning here that what we loosely call "business men," which clearly means enterprisers and their chief administrative agents, ought to be allowed, acting as an integrated unit, to perform certain social acts.

But if you will turn this idea over a little you will see that while there are business men, there is no such thing as business in the sense of an organized, integrated, recognizable unit, capable of acting as such. Groups of business men have associations, lodges, combinations, institutes of all sorts for research, for propaganda, for pressure. But they are far from being united into a confederacy of any sort capable of acting with a central intelligence for all the enterprisers in the society. Indeed the trade association itself is usually far from being qualified to speak even for the whole trade or to act for it. Therefore when we say that business ought to do this or that, that business ought to enjoy the privilege of self-rule, that business ought to co-operate with the government, we are talking about something that does not exist. There is no such thing as business in this sense. There is no defined and integrated unit, qualified and empowered to decide upon a settled policy, to pursue it and to enforce compliance with such policy.

Business is a vague economic area, comprising a great variety of conflicting and even hostile units, but without government of any sort.

It is of the first importance to fully grasp this. Because everywhere there is a clamor for business to act, for business to defy the very government itself, for business to look upon itself as some sovereign personality which can treat with the government almost as an equal and make peace or war with it. This clamor represents the wishes, the devout and even resolute intentions of great numbers of people who have the intelligence and the resources to make their wishes corporate and endow them with energy and power. And if it means anything at all it means that to give effect to this drift we shall presently have to recognize this political vagueness of business; we shall have to organize it, erect it into a political unit or division of some sort and confer upon it some fragments of sovereign power.

Such a thing we had in the period of the guilds, when the state itself relinquished or delegated certain of its powers over portions of the economic system to the merchants or craftsmen formed in guilds. The guilds made laws which were binding on the community. They proclaimed ordinances which regulated trade, prices, production, methods of competition and terms of employment. They regulated trade between one city and another. And presently we saw, as in the case of the great Hanseatic League, more than a hundred cities united through their merchant guilds, which maintained police, operated fleets of war, even made war and concluded peace and treaties with rival city guilds.

But the rise of modern capitalism in the 15th and 16th centuries, the development of the great merchant companies of England and Germany and Italy and France and Holland, the emergence of the Italian and German bankers and the advance of modern deposit banking put an end to the dominion of the guilds and paved the way for the dawn of the era of laissez-faire which was to begin its development at the end of the 18th century.

The last hundred years have seen in America a great laboratory and proving ground for a group of devices which have revolutionized modern life. These devices are commercial banking, the corporation and the machine. It will, perhaps, surprise some readers to be told that these things, along with some of their most baleful supplementary apparatus, made their appearance in this country a hundred years ago, and that they were not invented by the modern promoter. In Lowell, Massachusetts, as early as 1837, promoters had begun to experiment with the rudiments of most of those dangerous weapons which have played such havoc with our modern society. There were to be found the holding company, the interlocking directorate, the watering of stock, the exploitation of banking and insurance reserves, the first vertical industrial structures, the wide dispersion of stock ownership, the introduction of machinery and its inevitable social corollaries, female labor, company housing, company towns, house organs, the beginnings of industrial welfare experiments and the first signs of the great industrial struggle.

Through those last ten decades, and particularly the last six, the inventor and engineer, the banker and promoter, the corporation lawyer have brought credit, machinery and the corporation to an amazing degree of development. And it was the rise and expansion and perfection of these three powerful engines which produced that glittering structure which so tragically deceived its builders and in 1929 plunged headlong into what many supposed was that capitalist catastrophe of which the Marxists had talked so long.

Rooted deeply in selfishness and greed, in the hopes, the credulity and the yearning of men for individual freedom, this system did indeed offer a wide free market for pragmatic intelligence. It has displayed a robust durability which has been the surprise of its critics. It is a singular evidence of the vitality of the capitalist economy that when the long-awaited catastrophe arrived in this country, the first victim of its fury was the break-up not of capitalism, but of the Socialist party. It would, however, be a very superficial estimate of this episode in social disintegration if we permitted it to rest upon this observation. For while the Socialist party mechanisms did indeed practically disappear, socialist ideas took on new vigor, asserted themselves in the programs of the old parties and got themselves mixed up more or less vaguely in the capitalistic dialectic.

Under no conditions and with no implements can the capitalist money economy be managed to produce continuous abundance for all or to avoid occasional intervals of depression. But during the last one hundred years and, more especially, during the last seventy years, as these powerful engines—commercial banking, machinery, corporations—have gotten under full steam the dislocations in the economy have been more violent and more prolonged. And these dislocations have steadily set business men and labor leaders and statesmen off upon all sorts of adventures in the management and control of the system. This has led to that complicated maze of regulatory implements with which the government has undertaken to protect society from the undisciplined forces of economic law.

These efforts at regulation arose out of two urges. One was the demand of citizens to be protected against abuses at the hands of powerful corporate groups. The other was the effort of business men to protect themselves by combination and association from the effects of competition and over-production.

The first halting experiments in railroad regulation were to save farmers along the roadways from the damages resulting from fires from

the spark-throwing locomotives. It was some time before this spread
out into protecting merchants and shippers and the public from discrimi-
natory rate-making and finally from the financial jugglery of the stock-
throwing promoters.

But always business itself has been deeply infected with the desire to
protect itself from what it feelingly calls the losses inflicted by unrestrained competition. The business man is primarily interested in profit,
and necessarily with prices out of which profits must come. He sees his
rival underselling him and cutting his profits. He finds himself betrayed
into heavy production schedules by the promise of continuing prosperity,
only to be caught with shelves groaning under the weight of merchandise
he cannot sell. Then the unsaleable goods clutter up the market and he
and his competitors proceed to cut each other's throats in an effort to
recoup part of their outlays. This pattern is found everywhere—in
industry, in power, on the farm, in the store. And so over-production
has come to be the great ogre of modern business.

Soon the government, which started out to regulate the capitalist
economy by restraining enterprisers from committing abuses against the
helpless public, is importuned to protect the enterprisers from one another. The history of the last seventy years is marked by one stream
of desperate demands by business organizations for protection by the
government against the unscrupulous competitor and the ruthless monopolist, and an equally vigorous stream of indignant protests by business
organizations as a whole against government interference in business.
Almost any trade magazine will afford instances of angry outcries against
government interfering in business and further suggestions by the editor
or the trade association he serves for new forms of government interference in business which the trade would like to see for its own benefit.

Thus we see all this began with an appeal to the government to help
business. Its next phase was a demand that the government restrain
business from the commission of certain abuses. The next phase is the
slowly forming conviction of business men that the trouble does not lie
wholly in abuses—acts tainted with the ingredient of dishonesty or fraud.
It is marked rather by the feeling that there is something the matter
with the economic system, that the idea of *laissez-faire* which has claimed
the lip service of the business man must be subjected to certain modifications, that, in short, altogether aside from the ethical elements involved,
the economic system must be controlled, must be directed to avoid
certain purely economic maladjustments.

One of these maladjustments is, of course, the recurrence of depressions. Behind this is the tendency of the system to run into periods of over-production, all of which is accentuated by the savage lengths to which otherwise good and sound business men will go in the struggle to survive. And it is this conviction which gives to us the most significant and probably the most serious peril of the coming years. This conviction now enters its most serious stage of development and may, indeed, decide the form and character of the next stage of capitalistic business evolution. When we have looked at this a little more fully we shall be able to form a clearer estimate of the meaning of certain drifts in this troubled world.

The central idea, therefore, is not merely that business must be regulated or controlled, but that the economic system must be governed. But by whom? The settled principle of Anglo-Saxon law for centuries has been and still is that this is the function of the sovereign power only. The individual business man may be a monarch within the four walls of his own shop, but he has no right either singly or in concert with his fellow business men to make laws governing the economic system in which his own plant is but a small unit. Neither he nor all his colleagues together have the right to fix prices, to determine how much goods shall be produced, to arrange the terms upon which others may enter this trade, to make ordinances establishing the nature and extent of credit or the persons to whom it may be extended, settling standards of quality or methods of selling. These things must be determined by the sovereign or must remain undetermined. Remaining undetermined satisfied the business man for several centuries. But now he has changed his mind about this. Now he thinks that some power should be entrusted with the regulation of all these disturbing forces. But what power? If they must be regulated, then under existing standards, there is but one regulatory agency in society and that is the state. But he does not want the state in the equation at all. He now speaks with unrestrained scorn and even hatred of the state's intrusion into business. Who then is the proper agent to perform this great function in modern society? Who but business itself? And here he falls instantly upon one of those deceptive slogans behind which an idea can be so handily advanced. In a democratic society who should control business but business? This is self-rule. And therefore "self-rule in business" becomes the great concept with which this new reform is sold to the public.

In other words, the business man thinks the steel industry, which comprises stockholders or owners, bondholders, managers, workers, jobbers and thousands of fabricators who use steel and are as much in the steel business as Mr. Eugene Grace or Mr. Tom Girdler, should be governed under the beneficent principle of "self-rule" not by all these people, but by the handful of men who manage the great steel-producing corporations. Nothing, of course, could be further from "self-rule" than this. For under our established traditions of government, the steel industry, while looked upon as an economic province in which innumerable private enterprisers may apply the technique of private property, nevertheless as a social province is an area which, so far as it is governed, may be governed only by the sovereign power, represented by the state.

The idea of self-rule in business there, as understood, becomes a revolutionary one—a negation of accepted and lawful standards, an abandonment of the democratic doctrine and a reversion to the idea of the oligarch. It may be wise, it may be best for society, which we do not pretend to examine here, but, whatever it is or isn't, it is not democracy.

However, the full significance of this movement arises out of the processes essential to making this new doctrine effective. After a fashion it may be justly observed that business has always controlled government. In the cities real-estate men, merchants, rings of contractors, chambers of commerce and boards of trade have exercised a powerful influence upon the government. And in the nation, rich and powerful corporations have managed to get laws passed and to determine the course of administration as suited their interests. But this is very far from the kind of government of and by business which is now being proposed.

Business men have attained their ends in the state by virtue of the use of their money power, their contributions to campaign funds, their many means of conferring favors, fees and opportunities upon political leaders and their dependents and by means of outright bribery. But here again the ends have been achieved by various groups of business men pursuing a wide variety of objectives, often contradictory objectives. These groups have had to treat with the politicians. They had to get what they could. And what they wanted was as a rule some special favor for their own industry or trade or enterprise.

What business seeks now is something very different from this. It seeks not the opportunity through a friendly government of putting over this or that objective or preventing unfriendly acts. It seeks now the right to install itself as a governing unit where, in its own right, it will have the power to enact laws and administer them. It wishes to have the economic life of society distinguished from its other social and political functions. It wants that function detached from the political organisms and recognized as a separate area of government. In short, it wishes to have the economic and the political state divided into two distinct states. The political state will, of course, be under the dominion of the political machinery, whatever form that takes. The economic state will be governed by "business."

Now, of course, "business," as we have seen, is a vague thing. There is no such thing as business. But if business is organized and defined by law, implemented with officials, administrators and a constituency, then business will be no longer a vague thing. It will be a very definite, integrated, recognizable entity in society, armed with the powers of government over the economic life of the people. It will have the right to make laws, to administer them, enforce them and, in some respect, submit them to judicial interpretation.

Nothing is wanting in this outline save to define the constituency of this new arm of the state. Who will be included among the effective citizens of this governmental unit? After all, as we look this over, we will see that business is not a simple thing. The nation as a whole is always divided for obvious reasons into provinces. And so the great economic territory called Business is divided naturally into provinces— economic provinces as distinguished from the geographic units of the political state. Instead of the province of New York and Georgia, there will be the province of Steel and Coal and Automobiles. And, of course, these provinces will be organized as integral units in the economic state. More specifically all business will be divided into trades or industries or professions and organized as such, with geographical divisions within the trades for administrative purposes.

Here we may return to the question of the constituency of Business, with the observation that what follows is not a fantastic dream but a plan which is already in operation in some European states and which, upon a large scale, has already been attempted here. In the geographic political state the whole adult population are the citizens; and where that is a democratic state, the whole population exercises the right of suffrage. The extent to which they enjoy it determines the extent and character of the democracy. One might logically conclude that the economic state is nothing more than the citizens of the political state grouped according to trades rather than neighborhoods. It is a reasonable proposition that certainly those who are ruled by the economic state are the same persons who are ruled by the political state merely arranged in different categories. If the economic state is to be governed on the democratic pattern then all who are subject to that government will participate in the selection of the government and its personnel. And therefore if this economic state is to be governed on the democratic pattern all those subject to its statutes and decrees will be its citizens.

If the great province of Steel is to be organized as an economic unit and governed on the democratic pattern then all who are subject to the laws and administration of the province will be its citizens and will select its rulers. Intelligent men might well differ on the question of who belongs in this province of steel when the argument reaches the periphery of its citizenship; where its frontiers become dim. But we need not here concern ourselves with these marginal problems. Certainly no man in his senses will say that the workers in steel form no part of the province and no man who understands the language he uses will say that in a democratic organization of the province of steel the workers will be excluded. And, hence, there can be no validity to the term which describes as "self-government" a government of the province of Steel which excludes the workers. And what of those who must pay all the bills of the steel industry, who will be taxed to support its prosperity—the buyers of steel? And who are the buyers of steel? How far will they participate in a government of the great steel-producing function of the nation which can determine for them how much steel will be produced and what the prices will be and who shall be permitted to sell steel and on what terms, and, more fundamentally, whether they shall get along upon an abundance or scarcity of steel?

The importance of this discussion lies in the fact that the protagonists of this new theory of economic government and the inventors of the phrase "self-rule in business" intend no such democratic form in the government of that industry. On the contrary they propose to limit suffrage to the owners of the industry, a mere handful of persons governing a vast citizenship. To the extent, therefore, that the government of the Steel province is limited to a handful of owners, with all the hundreds of thousands of workers excluded, the democratic principle is completely abandoned. And to the extent that this new idea of a separate economic state under the rule of the owners is introduced into society democratic government in the nation is destroyed. And as, in the highly complicated corporate and machine society of this age, the economic affairs of the people occupy the major concern of government and the number of enterprisers becomes proportionately less, we are actually confronted with the eclipse of the democratic state.

What is pictured here is no finespun tale of some remote peril. Organized business groups have campaigned for it with great intensity for two decades. It has actually come to pass in several European countries and it has been tried here. Of course business men do not put forward this theory of government with the frankness employed in this outline, nor do they use the same terms or face seriously the full implications of what they are aiming at.

But to illustrate how imminent is this danger look for a moment at the steel industry in the United States in 1934. Under the National Recovery Act the government of the steel industry was placed under what was called a code. The members of this code were the producers of steel. The code authority for the industry was the Board of Directors of the American Iron and Steel Institute. About forty corporations were members of the code. Each member had a number of votes based on the dollar production of steel in the preceding year. Thus arranged all the members had 1428 votes. But the United States Steel, the Bethlehem Steel and the Republic Steel together had 757 votes. Thus these three companies could dominate the code membership. The code authority or managing directors of the industry were, as stated, directors of the American Iron and Steel Institute who were elected by the Institute. The members of the Institute are the officers, directors, managers and employees of various steel companies, plus some independent consultants, experts who get their business from the big steel companies. Half a dozen large steel corporations had enough of their employees with membership in the Institute to control the vote of that body.

This code authority was empowered by law to govern the steel industry of the United States. It was empowered to regulate what are euphemistically called "unfair trade practices" under cover of which it could enact a wide variety of ordinances. It could under certain circumstances control production, punish violators, impose fines and damages, regulate prices and act as enforcing officer and judicial interpreter of the code and its regulations.

All this was done under the authority of the law of the land. And behind the laws enacted by the code authority were federal civil and criminal penalties. In the management of the industry labor had no voice whatever; neither did consumers, even consumers whose sole business was the fabrication of iron and steel products. Of course the consumer had no authority whatever. Labor had the right of collective bargaining, but this applied only to wages and, of course, was a right which labor could enjoy if it was strong enough to enforce it by violence.

This is what the United States Supreme Court declared to be unconstitutional on the ground that it was an abandonment of the sovereign power of Congress. And this is of the very first importance—for here is a unanimous decision of the Supreme Court on the very point I have been laboring—that these powers over trade which business has coveted and which it actually exercised during a brief time are sovereign powers of government. It must be remembered that this steel code was one of about 700 such codes formed under the NRA.

Of course all these proposals for business control over economic areas are accompanied with the admission that the President should have supervision over them. The President could veto the acts of the code authorities. He could veto the codes. But, after all, no one questions that Congress exercises sovereign governmental powers of the highest order merely because the acts of Congress are also subject to veto by the President.

The NRA was, of course, a mere phase of this development. Business returns to the attack again and again. There is in existence now a thing called the Bituminous Coal Commission, under whose supervision the owners of the soft-coal mines are highly organized, with the backing of the government, to regulate the bituminous coal industry. The commission itself consists of seven members, two representing labor, two the producers and three the public. But as always happens—and it happens now under a so-called progressive Democratic administration—two of the alleged "public" representatives team up with the producers' representatives to dominate the commission.

But as the economic system totters and as confusion thickens, the fatal plausibility of the idea that business ought to be allowed to "work out its own salvation," to "govern itself," to "assume its responsibility of providing jobs and prosperity" will assail the public mind. And as that economic system seems to crumble utterly a desperate middle class supported by large sections of labor will be ready to take whatever measures are necessary to give business its chance. Let it not be forgotten that it was John L. Lewis who forced through Congress the Coal Commission and that Lewis, Sidney Hillman and David Dubinsky were the most effective supporters of the NRA policy.

It is difficult for Americans to understand the apparent paradox of business being at once the chief instigator of the NRA and its most violent foe. There is no paradox. Business was not the foe of the NRA. It was the foe of those troublesome consequences which flowed from the labor difficulties which the NRA ran into. Business men were naive enough to suppose that they could set up this government of theirs and that labor would offer little more than that futile kind of resistance to which they had been accustomed under the enfeebled Federation of Labor. They were not prepared for the wave of labor organization which swept over industry. And as the NRA itself made little effective provision for labor, labor took to the field and used the only weapon it has ever found effective—the weapon of force. In the end the whole structure became so unmanageable partly because it was reared too rapidly, partly because of its shockingly inept management and partly because of the insolubility of the labor element in the problem that many industrialists became disgusted and eager for the repeal of the whole effort. But they have not abandoned their ideal of business organized and endowed by the government with sovereign powers over the economic life of the nation.

After all this is the very heart of the thing we have beheld in Italy under the name of fascism and in Germany under the name of Naziism. The public eye has been caught by the purely accidental characteristics of these two fascist experiments. The militaristic adventures, the marching black-shirts and brown-shirts, the gaudy and posturing dictators, the appeals to the prejudices and emotions of the people, the barbaric suppressions and displays—these have become the marks of fascism to the casual newspaper reader. But the heart of these strange national enterprises is found in the effort to save the hard-pressed capitalist systems of Italy and Germany from ruin by a conscious effort to control the national economy. And this has been attempted by this division of the state into the political and economic state with the business groups exercising through corporatives, which is their way of saying codes, the powers of the sovereign over their several economic provinces.

It is true that the corporative state itself now flounders and that the great industrial and financial leaders, the Thyssens in Germany and the Toplitzes in Italy, have seen the dictators move in on the domain they had hoped to pre-empt for themselves in the business of government. But this is probably an inevitable phase in the development of this idea. The control of the economy by organized trade associations formed and implemented under the law is impossible in a democratic state. It is impossible first because it is a negation of democracy. But it is impossible for a more practical reason. No government set up to regulate the economic lives of the people as minutely as this system entails can enforce compliance with the regulations without the power of a ruthless dictator behind it. Wherever the system is installed, the successive and spreading revolt of people against the regimentation which it implies calls for greater and greater assumptions of power in the hands of the compliance agent. And that compliance agent can be nothing less than a despot if the system is to continue.

How long it will last, in what form it will finally visit these shores and fasten itself upon our social organisms, what course it will run— these belong in the domain of guesswork. But it is in this direction that our highly complicated machine and corporate civilization drifts.

# THE NEW LABOR MOVEMENT

## [*Louis Stark*]

AMERICA in transition is a nation in labor. Not without pain are new concepts born. Out of the clash of opinion and of warring interests come new attitudes towards old problems, the problem of the individual wage-earner in a corporate-controlled society, his job tenure, his old age, his health.

The fight of the individual wage-earner for status is making comparatively rapid progress. Discrimination against his collective action has not ceased, but it has lessened and has tended to take on more subtle forms.

The story of labor's progress towards status is inextricably bound up with the years 1933–1938 which mark a turning point in American labor history. It was the advent of the New Deal that released barriers that had previously held fast against successful organization in the nation's basic industries.

Repeated thrusts by labor against steel, citadel of the open shop, had been defeated by that powerfully entrenched industry.

The automobile industry, second only to steel, had successfully set its face like granite against the human battering ram represented by organized labor. Likewise, the rubber industry, aluminum, lumber, cement and many others. Up to 1933, time, money and effort, to bring them within the fold of organized labor, had collapsed, not merely because of the resistance of the industries themselves, bitter and unrelenting as that was. Labor itself had had no efficient plan of organization. It also lacked that governmental "lift" which was required to neutralize, partially at least, the weapons of discrimination, espionage, favoritism and company unionism that had kept these industries free from independent unions.

Half a century of the American Federation of Labor had achieved organization of less than 2,500,000 by 1933. The unions existed mainly in the building and metal trades, printing trades, transportation and amusement trades. Little effective organization had been achieved among the professional and white-collar groups, and in the basic and mass-production industries.

The reasons for these failures lie in the structure and policy of the American Federation of Labor. Created as a revolt against the Knights of Labor which had mingled all crafts in so-called Assemblies, erroneously referred to sometimes as industrial unions, the A. F. of L. preached craft separatism and did so successfully. It was true that the Knights of Labor had failed to help the skilled workers as they had hoped but that failure was inherent in the Knights' political aims and not in its organizational base. As a matter of fact the political panaceas sought after by the Knights had turned from that organization the skilled craftsmen who saw in their skill a basis of bargaining power which they did not have in their alliance with other elements.

The result was that under Samuel Gompers and his associates the A. F. of L. formed and strengthened tight craft unions which in time grew to considerable stature. Correspondingly, the Knights declined and eventually went out of existence.

From its inception, the A. F. of L. passed through many vicissitudes that are somewhat reflected in the ups and downs of its membership charts.

It is significant that during the nation's greatest period of prosperity, 1923–1929, the A. F. of L. did not increase its power and prestige. This was the period of welfare work among the large corporations, of the rise of company unions, of the rapid merging of corporations into super-corporations.

Labor, as exemplified by the A. F. of L., merely retained some of its gains of previous decades but made no progress in the new industries like automobiles, rubber, aluminum, electrical manufacturing, radio.

The depression of 1930 and the following years hit labor hard. From 1930 to 1933, labor took one direction and that was down.

Lack of employment caused a falling off of dues, members dropped out of the unions, some organizations depleted their treasuries in paying unemployment benefits, organizers were laid off and many unions were reduced to a skeleton basis, barely able to keep alive.

The advent of the New Deal found many unions practically bankrupt and almost ready to give up the ghost. It is no exaggeration to say that the National Industrial Recovery Act was the beginning of labor's revival. Section 7A, which assured employees that they had a right to organize without interference by their employers, gave the workers their first ray of hope in several years.

Immediately a wave of organizational activity began that was quite unprecedented. The moribund unions began to revive, their hopes fastened on the new legislation. Not only did the existing unions benefit from the Act but new unions sprang up like mushrooms. It should be said here, however, that the unions which benefited the most and very rapidly, indeed, were those which had prepared themselves for the passage of the National Industrial Recovery Act. I refer particularly to the United Mine Workers of America whose organizational plan was completed early and in anticipation of the N.I.R.A.'s enactment. Organizers of the miner's union almost "jumped the gun" as the Congress expressed its approval of the measure.

Also in the forefront of unions which, by intelligent leadership and direction, profited immediately by passage of the Recovery Act were the Amalgamated Clothing Workers, the International Ladies' Garment Workers' Union, some of the marine workers' unions, the International Brotherhood of Electrical Workers and a few others. Strangely enough, many unions were caught unawares and lagged behind in taking advantage of their opportunities under the Act.

By the formation of a Labor Advisory Committee under the N.I.R.A., labor gained another advantage. Coincidentally the rise in the incidence of labor disputes led President Roosevelt to create the first National Labor Board with Senator Robert F. Wagner of New York as chairman. This board, comprising representatives of labor, industry, and the public, was the forerunner of the two national labor boards consisting solely of public representatives.

In the hurly-burly of labor disputes, strikes and threats of strikes, that filled the air during the early NRA period of 1933 and 1934, labor and industry came to grips with some of the problems on which they could not agree. These tugs of war were generally settled between the parties but frequently the outcome resulted from pressure by General Hugh Johnson, the NRA administrator.

This period was exceedingly important to labor for it showed, as never before, the organizational and structural defects of the A. F. of L. and pointed directly to the remedy: industrial organization of workers in certain industries.

As early as October, 1933, General Johnson, addressing the Washington convention of the A. F. of L., pointed to the need for what he termed a vertical organization of trade unions to parallel that of industry.

In fact, industrialists were, in some cases, agreeable to that form of organization, for they reasoned that inasmuch as collective bargaining was the law of the land, they would be better off if they dealt with industrial unions and were assured of freedom from jurisdictional disputes between the craft unions. One large manufacturing executive made a proposal to A. F. of L. executives, expressing willingness to permit unionization of his various plants on condition that they be taken into one organization and not be divided among twenty. The leaders of the international unions discussed the problem and arrived at no conclusion and for the time being the matter was dropped but was later revived by another labor group at odds with the A. F. of L.

As the months went by and the wave of organization continued it swept into the A. F. of L. a large number of automobile, steel, aluminum, cement, lumber and rubber workers, properly classed as employees of basic and mass-production industries. Hundreds of thousands of workers, believing they were freed from the fear of employer retaliation, spontaneously organized themselves into groups and begged the international unions and the A. F. of L. to send organizers. The Federation itself increased the number of organizers on its pay roll.

In the steel industry nearly 100,000 employees joined local lodges of the Amalgamated Association of Iron, Steel and Tin Workers. This moribund association, comprising perhaps 6000 to 8000 workers, with extremely conservative leadership, was unable to assimilate the new membership. The old leaders, brought up in a craft tradition steeped in the traditions of the skilled steel workers, found themselves overwhelmed with problems relating to mass organization and were unable to solve them. The newly organized, revolting from the company unions, handed themselves over to the old leaders, "on a platter," demanding the workers in the various plants be permitted to join the local lodges. They wanted to get out from under the "paper" jurisdictional claims of the craft unions which had a scanty membership in the steel mills and which had vainly sought to organize steel workers from time to time on the basis of ultimate craft separation.

The problem of organization was one which neither the Amalgamated Association nor the A. F. of L. were prepared definitely to handle. A strike was threatened in June, 1934, and merely resulted in the creation of a National Steel Labor Board which held prolonged hearings while employers "stalled" or refused to abide by their decisions.

In the automobile industry there was a similar fiasco. Literally tens of thousands of automobile workers, responding to the stimulus of section

7A of the N.I.R.A., had organized themselves with the assistance of A. F. of L. organizers. They, too, threatened a strike in May of '34 and on their behalf President Green of the A. F. of L. and his associates negotiated an agreement that created the Automobile Labor Board, headed by Doctor Leo Wolman of Columbia. This Board foundered in a few months. The workers, clamoring for strong unions, joined together on an industrial basis, were put off by the A. F. of L. from month to month. The men became discouraged. An automobile Workers Council, comprising delegates from the various locals, was formed, presumably as forerunner to an industrial set-up, and Mr. Green placed in charge Francis J. Dillon, a member of the highly skilled pattern makers' union whose task it was to keep the members in line so that ultimately the craft unions might harvest their members out of the crop. Previously a member of the street car men's organization who longed ardently to return to his home in the "Hudson Valley"—he had lived in Yonkers—had been placed in charge of the auto workers' union by the A. F. of L. Both men had been criticized by the auto workers as being craft-minded men, unaware of the problems of mass-production industries and particularly of the automobile industry.

Belatedly, in 1935, the Executive Council of the A. F. of L. gave the automobile workers a national union charter which it claimed was the most "liberal" ever granted in satisfying any group's demands for industrial union recognition. This did not, however, satisfy the auto workers because of certain exceptions favoring the craft unions. What they wanted was an industrial union charter modelled after that of the United Mine Workers, who were entitled to take into their organization all workers "in and about" the mines.

In the rubber industry there was a more or less similar evolution. The wave of enthusiasm that had accompanied the "revolt" against the company union in this industry in 1933–1934 broke on the rock of distrust respecting the future of their organization, then under the A. F. of L. tutelage. The question was the same as that of workers in other mass-production industries—"Will we be divided up among the craft unions later on?" Their anxiety was not allayed by the craft union Federation organizer designated to guide their destinies.

These then were the sort of problems that had to be faced by the A. F. of L. in its conventions from 1933 onward. Nothing was done at the 1933 convention on industrial unionism.

At the 1934 convention in San Francisco the entire problem of industrial unionism broke, but it was confined mainly to the resolutions committee. There for five days John L. Lewis, Charles P. Howard of the International Typographical Union and their industrial-union-minded associates fought for recognition of the fact that in the basic and mass-production industries only the industrial type of union which eliminated jurisdictional disputes could succeed. The opposition was led by Vice-President Matthew Woll of the Photo-Engravers' Union, John P. Frey of the Metal Trades Department, Arthur O. Wharton of the Machinists' Union. Finally a compromise was effected and adopted by the convention.

This compromise recited the need for a change of organizational policy and agreed that national union charters, presumably on an industrial union basis, were to be granted the automobile, cement and aluminum workers, and that an organization campaign be started in the steel industry under direction of the Executive Council. In addition the resolution also stated that the jurisdictional claims of the craft unions were to be respected. This last "saving clause" led to the adoption of the resolution on the convention floor, for otherwise the craft unionists would surely have defeated it.

That this "compromise" bore the seeds of misunderstanding was apparent in the next year, but to Lewis and Howard it was something necessary at that time to "save the face" of the craft union leaders.

The following January a special meeting of international union leaders was held in Washington, in order to activate the San Francisco resolution. This meeting accomplished nothing, for it merely drew up another "face saving" declaration which got nowhere.

Nothing was done during 1935 to give effect to the proposed campaign in the steel industry though the time was ripe for an organization drive. The internal squabbles of the steel workers' union became interminable, lodges were expelled or stopped paying dues and memberships lapsed by the thousands.

By the time the October, 1935, Atlantic City convention rolled around the industrial unionists in the A. F. of L. felt they had been tricked. Lewis told the delegates he had been "seduced with fair words" at San Francisco and felt like rending his seducers limb from limb.

This convention was the high-water mark of the discussion of industrial unionism in the A. F. of L. There were several "full dress" debates participated in by the principal leaders on both sides—besides Lewis and Howard the industrial union advocates included David Dubinsky of the International Ladies' Garment Workers' Union, Sidney Hillman of the

Amalgamated Clothing Workers of America, Philip Murray and Thomas Kennedy of the Mine Workers and many of the young leaders of the new unions. On the craft union side were Daniel J. Tobin of the Teamsters, Dan Tracy, Electrical Workers, and Messrs. Frey, Wharton and Woll.

A test vote showed that the industrial unionists had close to 40 per cent of the roll-call votes. This was like an electric shock to the craft-union group which dominated the Executive Council. The vote was significant, for it was the first ballot ever taken at an A. F. of L. convention on the straight issue of industrial unionism. It proved to both groups that the principle of industrial unionism in the basic and mass-production industries was near to acceptance by a majority of the A. F. of L.

Elated by this advance John L. Lewis, of the miners, and representatives of seven other unions met directly the Atlantic City convention was over and formed the Committee for Industrial Organization. Their stated objective was to carry on a campaign of education among the organized and to aid in organizing the unorganized within the confines of the A. F. of L.

Immediately the tug-of-war began between the C. I. O. and the A. F. of L. Barely three months passed before the Federation's Executive Council was denouncing the C. I. O. as a "dual" or rival organization, calling upon it to disband. From the beginning the attitude of the A. F. of L. leaders was: "This is a dual movement. It is like the I. W. W. in its desire for One Big Union in each industry. No dual movement has ever succeeded in this country and the C. I. O. will collapse."

As the C. I. O. in the next two years went on from success to success, achieving what seemed to be miracles of organization in an incredibly short time, the Federation reiterated its comment, "It is bound to fail."

Before the C. I. O.'s campaign began in steel the cry of Federation leaders was, "They will never organize steel. We tried it and failed."

After several hundred thousand steel workers had been won over by the well-planned strategy of Philip Murray, Chairman of the Steel Workers' Organizing Committee, the Federation leaders changed their tune. "They cannot consolidate their gains."

It was the same in whatever field the C. I. O. ventured—in textiles, shoes, retail office employees, laundry workers, marine, lumber. Of course there were setbacks for the C. I. O. The most important was that of "Little Steel," which successfully fought off a strike during the summer of 1937.

The intransigent attitude of A. F. of L. leaders during the early months of the C. I. O., the delay between February and May of 1936 before the Federation peace committee conferred with John L. Lewis, and the conviction of the "die-hards" on the Executive Council that the C. I. O. was bound to fail, set their imprint on the relations between the organizations.

As late as the Tampa convention of the A. F. of L. in October, 1936, the Executive Council was still refusing to agree that the steel industry was one in which the industrial form was desirable and that the craft unions should adopt a "hands off" policy and not make jurisdictional claims once organization was effected in that industry. Such a concession would actually have meant a split in the C. I. O. and the defection of at least the International Ladies' Garment Workers' Union and the millinery workers who pressed for it behind the scenes. These unions were ready to leave the C. I. O. had this single concession been granted. Again the craft union leaders reiterated their cry: "This is a dual movement and will fail."

It was this convention at Tampa from which the C. I. O. unions had been excluded. They were suspended after refusing to appear for trial, two months before the convention was held. The circumstances of that suspension will be dealt with later.

In the meantime what was happening in the C. I. O.? During the spring and summer of 1936 there was a wave of union organization similar to that inaugurated in the early NRA days. By an agreement with the Amalgamated Association of Iron, Steel and Tin Workers, the C. I. O. formed the Steel Workers' Organizing Committee and put into the "kitty" its first $500,000 fund toward organizing steel workers. (To date more than $2,000,000 has been spent in steel alone.) The union at this time had been torn to pieces by internal strife and dissension and it was hardly more than a hollow shell.

In a few short months, following a campaign laid out by Mr. Murray and his associates, the company unions, set up by Arthur Young, master-mind on company unions in the service of the U. S. Steel Corporation during the NRA days, began to revolt.

This chapter is one of the highlights of the C. I. O.'s campaign and deserves more extended treatment than is possible in this brief account. Suffice it to say that in seven or eight months the company union barriers to independent unionism went down like ninepins and by February, 1937, the U. S. Steel Corporation had capitulated by signing a one-year contract. The effect of this trade-union advance on the citadel of the open shop cannot be exaggerated, for it stimulated the entire organized labor movement to hope for the achievement of new goals.

Soon other contracts were made and in a few months the S. W. O. C. had contracts with a large number of employers. The contracts were not for a closed shop, for they were made with the union as agent for its members only. They were, however, regarded as a great advance and were extended in February, 1938, on a twenty-day "escape clause" basis, either side being permitted to call for changes on ten days' notice with a twenty-day period to allow for agreement.

Concurrently with the steel campaign the United Automobile Workers' Union carried on a strong offensive in the automobile industry, culminating in the sit-down strikes against General Motors Corporation which began in the closing days of 1936 and ended with a signed agreement on February 12, 1937.

This was another historic milestone in the C. I. O. campaign. The A. F. of L. sought to prevail upon General Motors to withhold recognition of the United Automobile Workers in so far as the skilled craftsmen were concerned. The proposal was taken up at the joint conferences. John L. Lewis offered to leave the conference and permit negotiations with the A. F. of L. if General Motors executives felt that the A. F. of L. could call off the strikers. That ended the argument.

In the South the C. I. O. fought to organize the textile workers who have been beaten back again and again in their attempts to join the United Textile Workers of America, an A. F. of L. affiliate. By an arrangement similar to that between the old A. F. of L. steel union and the C. I. O. the latter organization practically took over as bankrupt the unsuccessful U. T. W. of A. The campaign that followed was largely financed by the Amalgamated Clothing Workers of America, led by Sidney Hillman. A new organization, the Textile Workers' Organizing Committee, was formed and into this committee's coffers the Amalgamated poured an initial expenditure of $500,000 for the work, augmented by contributions made by several other unions.

Several hundred organizers carried the T. W. O. C. appeal into the South and despite the bitter opposition of mill managements and local authorities they made considerable headway. The depression caught the textile drive in the middle, but it seemed evident that this was merely a temporary setback. At the very peak of the depression, in the spring of 1938, the T. W. O. C. was still winning many elections for collective bargaining representatives held under National Labor Relations Board auspices; this despite the unprecedentedly low state of employment, the hostility of the manufacturers and of the A. F. of L.

Collective bargaining contracts were actually signed for the first time by leading manufacturers of rayon, silk, woollen and worsted and cotton textiles.

At the same time virile elements among the maritime workers overthrew their moribund leadership among the east coast sailors, and the militant west coast longshoremen adhered to the C. I. O.

Into the terra incognita of public utilities, department stores, insurance companies and other hitherto unexplored fields marched the C. I. O. hosts. Mistakes were made, of course, partly in an excess of enthusiasm and partly due to inexperienced leadership.

In some quarters it had been felt that the C. I. O. should legally contest its suspension by the A. F. of L. Executive Council in September, 1935, two months before the annual convention at Tampa. It was decided not to do so for fear that the legal hullabaloo would distract attention and energy from the organization campaign which by that time was well under way.

It may be apropos here to recount briefly the circumstances of the suspension of eight unions comprising approximately one-third of the Federation's membership. The unions refused to obey a summons for trial in August, 1936, because they held that the Executive Council, under the constitution, did not have authority to try them even though the Council had drawn up a resolution investing itself with that authority. But the trials were held nevertheless and the C. I. O. unions were found guilty in absentia. When they refused to leave the C. I. O. in thirty days, they were suspended. The Council claimed that under the resolution it had adopted it was permitted to suspend the C. I. O. unions. Privately some of the Council members frankly admitted that they lacked this power but they felt they had no other recourse.

Why did they feel they had no other recourse? Warned by the tremendous voting strength of the C. I. O. unions at the Atlantic City convention the Council feared that by the next annual meeting the C. I. O. would have made enough headway to have a majority of votes. Then the C. I. O. leaders would have taken control of the Federation out of the hands of the craft-union group which had dominated it for so many years and made a clean sweep of the Council itself, reorganizing the Federation from top to bottom. There is no doubt this danger was a real one for the "machine" leaders.

Particularly important was the fact that the Council was egged on by W. L. Hutcheson, President of the United Brotherhood of Carpenters and Joiners, whose 3000 votes out of a total of 26,000 at the convention were very necessary to the Council group. Hutcheson threatened to leave the Federation if the Council failed to suspend the C. I. O. unions. A defection of 3000 votes would have made the fight in the Tampa convention so close that the C. I. O. group might well have carried the day. Faced with the Hutcheson ultimatum, the Council suspended the C. I. O. unions.

The suspension made no difference to the C. I. O. in so far as its organization work was concerned. In a dozen industries it went forward, intent on its drive to organize the unorganized.

By October, 1937, when it held its conference at Atlantic City coincidental with the A. F. of L. convention in Denver, the C. I. O. was able to make these claims:

Membership, 4,000,000.

Adherence of 32 national unions.

The first union contracts ever signed in the automobile and rubber industries.

Some 430 steel companies with 500,000 employees under union agreements.

At the April, 1938, meeting of the C. I. O. Director John Brophy reported 39 national unions in membership; the newcomers included unions of furniture workers, quarry workers, the Inland Boatmen's Union of the Pacific and the Marine Cooks and Stewards of the Pacific.

Making allowance for possible exaggerations, the record nevertheless was an unusual one. In the short space of two years a new labor movement had been launched. True, there was no central, general staff of officers, no constitution or by-laws, but nevertheless, in everything but name the C. I. O. was a rival to the A. F. of L. that was seriously threatening to undermine the latter's prestige.

On the political side the C. I. O. leaders had organized Labor's Non-Partisan League which had been of notable assistance to President Roosevelt in the 1936 campaign. Back of the formation of this League was the idea that in the 1940 campaign it might play an important part in throwing the weight of labor towards candidates sympathetic with labor's aims. At the same time the local and state chapters of the League were handy instruments that might be used by the C. I. O. if the A. F. of L.

cast out all C. I. O. affiliates from city central labor bodies and state Federations. And the A. F. of L. did exactly that, purging its affiliated groups of all dissident C. I. O. elements. Whereupon the C. I. O. promptly began the organization of rival city and state central bodies, using in some places the members of the local sections of Labor's Non-Partisan League as the nuclei for the Industrial Councils.

The economic recession of the fall and winter of 1937–1938 affected all organized labor but particularly the C. I. O. As the new unions were caught by the economic undertow before they could consolidate their gains, the C. I. O. found itself facing the problem of retrenchment and survival. The A. F. of L. unions, accustomed to such recessions, have a long-standing technique for maintaining themselves during periods of stress provided they are not too long. The C. I. O. unions, with meager treasuries, faced the immediate future with some anxiety. It is noteworthy however that despite the obvious weakening, for example, of the Steel Workers' Organizing Committee, the U. S. Steel Corporation subsidiaries renewed their union contracts in February, 1938. Other C. I. O. affiliates did not fare so well and here and there the early winter saw the inauguration of wage cuts, but not many.

Faced by the economic recession, the C. I. O., despite its curtailed staff, continued its effort to hold the line so as to be ready for the next swing of the business cycle.

Does anything on the C. I. O.'s broadening horizon give any hopes for peace with the A. F. of L.? It should be recalled that a major peace effort failed in December, 1937. Nevertheless, the will to peace in the rank and file persisted and still persists. It is one of the many anomalies of the dispute that despite the will to peace among the workers in the ranks peace has not been attained. The Federation's limited concessions have apparently not approached the C. I. O.'s "asking price" and a bargain acceptable to both has not been arranged.

The split in the labor movement was made all but irrevocable when, in the spring of 1938, the C. I. O. heads met in Washington and decided to call a convention in the fall in order to set up a permanent organization.

Shortly afterward the A. F. of L. Executive Council revoked the charters of the C. I. O. unions which had been suspended in September, 1936, but omitted the International Ladies' Garment Workers' Union from its "purge" in the hope that within a reasonable time the Dubinsky organization would renew its allegiance to the Federation and cut loose from the C. I. O. By this move the A. F. of L. hoped to capitalize Mr. Dubinsky's differences with John L. Lewis over the collapse of the peace conferences in December, 1937.

Reunion with the A. F. of L. had definitely failed. No formula had been evolved which could bridge the gap of conflict. For nearly two years the C. I. O.'s dizzy rate of success had left the Federation leaders far behind in their calculations and their concessions were limited accordingly. Now a depression had set in and the Federation argument was that the C. I. O. "would go the way of all dual movements."

But the C. I. O. did not show signs of giving up the ghost despite the depression setbacks. It went forward into new fields, breaking the ground that had scarcely been touched by its rivals in industries such as the utilities, insurance companies, banks, and department stores.

Hand in hand with the industrial form of organization went the struggle for civil liberties. Company-dominated steel towns, hitherto closed to the unions, were "opened" and union meetings were held for the first time in years. Municipal elections, in some cases, swung labor leaders into office, ushering in a new era of freedom from company rule. The new unions banded in a co-operative effort to put down anti-union vigilantes and there were many militant struggles in the rubber, automobile and steel industries not only between the C. I. O. unionists and the self-styled "citizens" groups but also between the new unionists and the police. The latter clashes were marked with violence on both sides revolving usually about the problems arising from mass picketing.

The C. I. O. is also breaking new ground in its relationship to the unemployed. Realizing that the overhanging millions of idle threaten hard-won standards, the C. I. O. has worked out plans to organize WPA workers into auxiliaries of their own crafts and into unions exclusively consisting of WPA workers. The latter would eventually be allocated to the C. I. O. unions of their calling. To these workers will go a double appeal calculated to impress them with the need for organization along political as well as industrial lines. This new sortie by the C. I. O. is freighted with the utmost importance for workers' solidarity.

Peace or a truce between the rival labor groups may come in time but the date is unpredictable. If it comes it will be on the basis of industrial unionism in the basic and mass-production industries, the C. I. O. goal from the beginning.

Speculation on the future is dangerous. Nevertheless I would hazard the guess that it is not without the bounds of possibility that the two rival organizations may go on for years side by side, dividing the field roughly between them, not by agreement, but by rule of thumb. This does not mean that the internecine war will be a sham battle. It will be marked by attacks, reprisals, jurisdictional "raids" and the usual concomitants of such a struggle. In the end that organization will become the most powerful which will give the workers in American industry the form of organization they demand. If the A. F. of L., despite its craft basis, continues to "go industrial" it will undoubtedly make important gains. But by the very nature of the case, this reaching out for membership in allied fields will bring the A. F. of L. unions to new internal crises, springing from absorption of members attracted by the principle of industrial unionism.

Thus, whether the A. F. of L. makes its peace with the C. I. O. or not, the principle of industrial unionism has won out. This victory has brought with it possibilities for the future that are boundless. Not only may it well stimulate organization on a scale hitherto undreamt of even by the most optimistic but it may also sow the seed for the formation of a new political orientation of labor and agriculture.

# ECONOMICS

## [*Walton H. Hamilton*]

IN THE DRAMA of America, industry must be cast in a cultural role. Its regular occupation is to make the wheels of the economic order go round; if it keeps the zig-zags that spell depression or prosperity in an approximation to a straight line, it does about all that ought to be expected from it. But its hours on duty fall far short of its full-time office. It helps the language on its way; formulates the problems with which politics must deal; supplies the material which artists turn to account; creates the common sense which lies at the base of all belief; and touches with its inescapable incidence literature, education, religion, the liberties of men and their pursuit of an elusive happiness.

Industry has been no conscious creation of man. Its omnipotence and omniscience have not been passed down from everlasting to everlasting. Its untrim lines, blurred pattern and pervasive control tell of no design gone somewhat wrong in execution. Instead it is an intricate pattern which has been many centuries in the making; it has emerged from the past, reveals for the moment its changing shape and runs forever on. The economist crowds its wealth of concretion into a term and makes it "a result of cumulative causation." The jurist, with an eye to the folk-lore of the law, refers to it as "a work of communal authorship." To "the reasonable man" of the world "it just grew."

A polite play might have taken its gentle course down the decades; but in the revolutionary drama, "The Coming of Industry," lusty actors had to be found for the parts. At the stage door appeared the sign, "None but radicals need apply"—and fate did the casting and enforced the rule. The trio of creative roles were assigned to the technician, the business man and the lawyer. The technician, the mildest soul in an unorthodox trinity, was a queer fellow, intent upon his tinkering, and inclined to scant respect for established industrial procedure. His eye was always alert to novelty—a new ware of trade, an improved process, a novelty in shortcut or the clipping of a corner. The business man was the man of action; his judgment always reached out towards a competitive advantage in the game of money-making. He was quite forgetful that in respect to the Fathers he was Posterity; and he turned reverence for the good old ways into irrelevance. The lawyer was the High Priest in the piece. It was his task to harness the art of logomachy to a subversive cause, to dress up novelties in venerable verbiage, and circumlocutiously to show that nothing wanton had happened and that all that had was according to the law.

The man of business had the strategic place. As the technician proffered his innovations—an invention, a process, a corporate device, a factory lay-out, a market method—he sat in judgment. His sole requirement for admission to the shop, to the industry, to the culture was that the novelty should promise to serve with diligence the pursuit of gain. In his radical role the captain of industry was dedicated to the service of God and Mammon and the price of survival was obedience to two masters. If Mammon was not appeased, his profits would dry up and he would be compelled to yield his place to a less scrupulous adventurer. But if God was not served—at least with such a due as the law commands—trouble waited in the offing. In such a situation he turned for guidance and consolation to the lawyer, whose ethical problem became that of the industrialist whose retainer he took. As an attorney his duty was to the interest of his client; as an officer of the court his respect went out to the law. He must cut channels for the pursuit of gain which kept technically clear of statute and ordinance. The resulting web of industrial and corporate usage, in which for most matters business and the law are as one, is among the greatest of the creations of man. As a work of art it towers far above our drama, our science, or our statesmanship. In subtle touch and flexible device, in everyday utility and architectural grandeur, only the American language is its equal.

It is odd that a trio of radicals should have been allowed to have their way with a culture. But among them the lawyer alone saw the social implications in what to the other conspirators seemed to be a mere domestic matter. In defense he will plead that mighty matters came to pass with hardly a dent upon the corpus of the law, that the biggest of all revolutions was brought off without violence, and that a one-way ticket to the everlasting bonfire is no fit reward for such arduous work. Moreover, things were in the saddle; and, amid the seething course of change, there was no power of god or man to bend human behavior to a national purpose. The government was weak, divided and viewed with suspicion;

its usages had been contrived to serve purposes other than domesticating an unruly business system to the common good. The legislation of old for the regulation of industry had rusted into repeal. Ancillary agencies of control—education, religion, public opinion—had been suited to the discipline of the individual within a society taken for granted. In business the leaders held office by self-election; and captains of industry were far too intent upon raids upon the public, forays against each other, conquest of corporate domains and accumulation of accumulations to create a structure for industry or even to ponder much the way of industrial order.

The result was that public welfare had to wait upon individual enterprise. The major decisions through which so much of a constitution as we possess was fastened upon industry emerged of themselves from between the lines of a myriad of petty judgments. Questions were answered before ever they were asked and many parties at interest were excluded from the mercantile scene where a culture was shaped. As issues were shifted from the political to the economic arena, the people were admitted to a larger and larger share in government. The final touch of irony came when—just as one after another the barriers of property, color and sex fell and suffrage came to be universal—the judgments upon which the lives and destinies of men depend came to be vested elsewhere. In politics we became a democracy just as power passed on to industry where for the time at least it is safely out of popular reach.

## II

To assert that industry blundered into being is not to condemn. It serves merely to identify its quality and to assign it place among man's creations. The American language had no origin in design; nor did law, or etiquette, or the dietary, or any other of a hundred institutions with which man every day makes merry or miserable. And if a government, or a church, or a corporation seems to be an expression of documented purpose, it is only make-believe. For a constitution, a creed or a charter is at best an enabling act which permits a group of usages to be called into existence. The great fountain of creation is the response of the multitude to the impact of events; any work of man which is not constantly refreshed by contact with its source quickly grows sterile. To find out the manner of thing an authority would make of industry, one has only to peruse in drab gray the austerities in a book on economics. But the actuality—the color, the drama, the survivals from the past, the life that pulses towards the future, the living pattern that defies diagram—do not emerge as the fulfillment of a plan.

The principle of growth is catch as catch can. As a process of accommodation goes its endless way, a stream of immediate judgments leaves its deposit in usage; and, as the game is played, the rules emerge. The mark of its multiple origin is upon industry. If it had been a conscious creation, the economic order might be resolved into industries and industries broken down into separate establishments. But, as advent by chance decrees, enterprises are only loosely bound together into industries and only by a heroic feat of the mind are industries aggregated into a "system." As growth would have it, an infinitude of detail marks the pattern; a color, drama and variety abound which line and symmetry could never impart; and industries are as distinct in their identities as persons in a play. Accordingly reality is to be found—not in "the economic order" or an abstract industry—but in the concrete pictures presented by anthracite and cement; steel, lumber and sugar; shoe machinery, motion pictures and retail merchandise. For industry, as for any creative work of man, meaning lies in the particular, in the instance, in the case.

As an initial picture for an industrial gallery, one subject is as good as another; for, where growth creates, there is no logical order. Ask the bystander for a distinctive American industry, and he will name the automobile; or, if inclined to precise ways of speech, come across with the automobile, the tire and gasoline. If pressed he will admit that the matter is not as simple as all that; for automobiles are assembled and not made; a number of other industries, from rubber plantations to electrical appliances, contribute to the product; and servile provinces stretch away from Akron to the Orient. As fuel for the engine, gasoline is only the first among the products of petroleum, in its own right a lordly industrial province. The motor-car is useful only on the go; the concrete highway is its necessary complement. A man, playing at being a capitalist, may own and operate his own car; or as a mere member of the proletariat, lay out a part of his wage for a ride when he needs one; and he may have chattels to haul as well as person or family. So the subject runs out through the taxicab to the motor bus and truck, and skirts the frontiers of trolley-car and railway. The purchaser of the automobile usually lacks the price; so the finance industry has to be drawn upon for funds to give an appearance of substance to ownership. The lender, whether the Good Samaritan or Shylock, will eventually claim his legal due; and

attention reaches out to the multiple sources of earnings where installments must be found. A depression appears; the motorist is too deeply
in to back out; the protection of the investment demands that payments
be kept up; income is withdrawn from other purchases; and the whole
industrial order comes into the picture. The automobile is still the focus;
but many other subjects appear as the scene falls away into background.

By no other norm than its own performance is the automobile industry
typical. Its process of fabrication is a rather formidable "concatenation
of mechanistic processes"; the tag "Made in America" is stamped all over
the industry and its product. But even in America the pattern of the industry could have been created at no other time than the decade and
a half following the turn of the century. The horseless carriage was a
luxury which required time, patience and money to keep going. The
bankers had no faith in the contraption; and without funds giant factories could not be set up for its manufacture. So reckless adventurers had
to contrive their shifty expediencies. Lacking facilities themselves, the
automobile companies sought to have their parts manufactured; and outside concerns were glad to take their orders. As the date would have it,
the machine and metallurgical industries were well established; and
excess of competitive zeal had created a surplus of capacity that needed
to be turned to account. The parts manufacturer did not have to lay out
money in a reckless investment; he had to take a chance only upon a
single bill of goods. The customary thirty days' credit was extended; the
automobile companies quickly assembled parts into cars and as quickly
disposed of them to customers who had more faith in the new-fangled
vehicle than the financial rectitude of the investment banker could rise
to. The speedy sales for cash supplied funds for paying the bills for parts
before they were due. In like manner the lack of capital denied the
opportunity to establish sales agencies and to indulge the luxury of credit.
The dealer became an independent merchant with whom all dealings
had to be on the lofty plane of ready money.

Such answers of early years became deeply embedded in the structure
of the industry. The business proper, with all excrescences cut off, was
limited to assembly. A shed alone was needed; a few simple machines
supplied the accessories; the process could be broken down into elementary tasks and laid out along a straight line. It was chance that made
the analysis; man's ingenuity did no more than convert an expediency
into the brilliant institution of "the assembly line." A standardization of
parts, of tasks and of processes was carried to such perfection as to be

called "the second industrial revolution." It was quickly apparent that as output increased, the cost per unit could be materially lessened. So, with the bait of ever-lower prices, the automobile magnates set out to tempt the whole American public. As the years passed income class after income class fell before the seduction of better cars and cheaper. At last the industry, in need of fresh bait, went off in quest of style.

As wealth and respectability were attained, the structure of the industry was not revised. Instead the expediencies provoked by poverty became the policies of power. By playing off one manufacturer against another the magnates of the motor-car could secure their parts more cheaply than they could make them in their own shops. The inability to afford their own outlets was turned to a like golden account. The risk of merchandising, the loss on the trade-in, the hazard of left-over stock were all laid on the shoulders of the dealer. Operating at the strategic point of the assembly line, the automobile companies used contract to accomplish what ownership could hardly have been made to yield. Without the investment of real money they made secure their control over the fashioning of materials and the marketing of product. It is the superb example of the grand old American motto, "Let the other fellow's dollars do it for you."

But an ingenuity which turned a liability into an asset was not to stop here. The assembly line—for the time at least—kept the labor problem quiescent. Abroad skilled workmen were needed for parts; but the clash with the union was another man's worry. At home production was reduced to a great ceremonial; laborers were cogs of assorted kinds in a gigantic machine; a worker inefficient, out of tune with the symphony, or tainted with the contumacy of personal rights, could quietly be replaced by his brother automaton. The consumer, a mere amateur, was lured into the role which the investment banker had refused. The price of his car was made to include its cost, a sum towards bonus and profits, and gracious surplus to be ploughed back as investment. Thus the capital on which the industry grew came from the pockets of the motorist. The man-at-the-wheel was too anonymous and too multiple to have his name as owner legally written in the books. But, according to correct accounting procedure, a return upon this investment was set down as a charge against the car, and the motorist was graciously permitted to pay interest upon the funds he himself had contributed.

A brilliant strategy was contrived against the purchasing power of the public. It is an axiom that the sum of the parts is less than the whole;

and the automobile industry, in sale on installments, proceeded to a practical demonstration of a truth which is still beyond the comprehension of mathematics. A small initial outlay is enough to secure possession of the car; the fulfillment of the exactions denominated in the bond—which turned the legend "f.o.b. Detroit" into a sheer fiction—come later. Thus the motor-car was brought within the means of hundreds of thousands who could not afford it; the resulting notes became in time of depression a kind of first mortgage on vanishing income; and the industry took unto itself somewhat more than its proper share of the nation's wealth. Against such incursions other industries were without remedy in equity or at law.

Thus, in the beginning the poverty of the industry forced it to improvise and out of casual answers an industrial pattern was fashioned. From the hub of the assembly line, with a minimum of capital and risk, the magnates of the motor-car lord it over a conquered empire.

### III

Across the frontier lie the principalities of tires and of gasoline. There the topography reveals a different industrial landscape. The tire is gradually being reduced to a state of industrial vassalage. A good fourth of all its product is sold as "original equipment" to automobile manufacturers—on terms quite acceptable to the buyers. The price of raw rubber is beyond the industry's control; a restriction of production half way across the world—to which the consumer is not a party—forces the manufacturer to gamble upon inventories. The tire has not even a market demand of its own; the number wanted is fixed by the mileage of automobiles on-the-go down the concrete highway. In response to pressure the companies which must compete for large orders have been driven to a continuous improvement of their product. As average tire-life has mounted from a bare 3500 to more than 25,000 miles, the pitting of concern against concern has substantially reduced the market for all. In recent years the chain-store and the mail-order house have come from over the border to make a "leader" of automobile tires. It has been possible for them, in accordance with the principles of multiple merchandising, to assess a large share of the costs of distribution against other goods, to ease the marketing expenses charged up against tires, and to execute a brilliant flank movement against the retail outlets of the companies. Thus the automobile tire is hemmed in on all sides by great industrial powers; and, before superior bargaining strength, nominal independence masks a tributary province.

No such fealty to motor-car magnate or national-chain is acknowledged by petroleum. In the good old days when coal-oil kept the home lights of a nation burning, it was the Octopus which public servants went forth to hunt. But as the nation went motor-mad and kerosene gave way to gasoline, a dozen giant companies—each larger than the parent—sprang into life out of the fragments into which the old standard trust had been dissolved. As petty trade gave way to big business, the pattern of the industry was promoted from monopoly to competition. The change brought with it a spirit of militancy now everywhere in evidence. At one end of the productive process "off-set" wells glare at each other across property lines. At the other rival retail outlets lie in wait for "gal-lonage" at the corners of intersecting roads. A truce between "majors" and "independents" permits "the little fellows"—a grand window display —to live within the interstices of the industry. The smouldering rivalry flames now and then into a "price-war"; but, with some thirty million flexible vehicles on the road and any service station a stop en route, price-cutting becomes too dangerous for competition to employ. At every point along the way—oil well, refinery, pipe-line, service station—a number of militant corporate entities confront each other as each attempts to occupy a continent.

It is far across country from gasoline to milk; at the ends of the journey lie distinct industrial cultures. A structure has been created for milk by shrewdly turning an administrative control to account. In a primitive age—which still lingers on—the cow was domiciled in the back-yard and the milky way ran from teat to table. In the next economic era, the cow had migrated to the country and at a godless hour the farmer made his urban round. Then, as the city sprang into being, the periph-ery became too much for his time, capital and capacity to get about— and history really got under way. In ages that followed too fast to be dated, the middleman entered, drove a wedge between producer and consumer, and usurped the strategic place in the industry. The milk from many cows was mingled in the great commune of the pool. The protec-tion of the public health decreed inspection—and later pasteurization. Inspection fell to the lot of the city; it was easier to inspect near-by than far-away farms; the area of supervision, with its urban focus, came to be a "milk-shed." It was easy to convert inspection into a tariff-wall around the local market; and legal measures aimed at health were gradually converted into barriers about vested interests.

Thus the industry was closed; and within so unique a scheme of control many unapostolic things became possible. A separation was made between "fluid" and "surplus" milk; a quantity large enough to meet the demand was measured off for fluid use; the surplus was sold at a lower figure to be processed into butter and cheese. The simple distinction was often resolved into a number of classes; and quarts from the same source were sold at prices differing according to the uses to which they were put. A technique of multiple price for identical units of the same commodity enabled the industry to extract from the market all it had to give. A mighty buttress about vested interest was created out of the liability of municipal regulation.

In the hinterland between milk and gasoline lie many quaint and colorful codes of industrial usage. In steel it is impossible to fix prices without indulging a series of fictions cryptically set down as "Pittsburgh plus." The mystic symbol means that the buyer pays for his ingots and bars "as if" they had been manufactured in, and sent to him direct from, Pittsburgh. In other words, wherever they are fashioned and whatever the point of delivery, the price is the Pittsburgh quotation plus freight to the old home town. . . . Cottonseed is an adventitious by-product of cotton. Useless in itself, it is crushed into oil, meal, hulls and linters and these in turn enter a thousand products from vegetable lard and soap to pillow stuffing and paint. No conscious will this side of the planting of the cotton crop decrees the quantity of any of these raw materials. Demand can only accommodate itself to an output it is impotent to control. Thus a series of judgments about an alien matter, in a rural culture encrusted in custom, fixes the supply of cotton; and its by-product, with *its* joint products, and *their* derivative products once, twice, or thrice removed must take the consequences. . . . In dresses the compulsions of fashion beset a whole industry. Style issues its orders; decrees are revised or repealed without notice; the stage is kept in a constant uproar; concerns must respond in a quick staccato. A firm's policy can have no grounding in statistics; the competitive struggle manages to get along without ethics; business success has to be won freshly each season. The one abiding mandate from fashion is that no pattern shall be imposed upon the affairs of the industry. . . .

A stroll down industrial byways presents a like variety. A trade, be it never so grand or humble, has a colorful identity all its own. . . . A public intolerance of strong drink hangs heavily over the whiskey industry. In the purchase of a fifth of rye or scotch, one lays out a few cents on the original brew, a few more for aging, trade-name, and marketing.

A large part of the rest is a sacrificial tax designed to keep the traffic down. . . . A compact organization among undertakers has been alert to the interest of the mournful brethren. A conscious policy of "upward merchandising" has been made to overcome the jeopardy caused by a tremendous increase in numbers. At the turn of the century the one who had the heroic role at a funeral possessed a poor understanding of his pecuniary duty. Now the average corpse has been taught to carry the average establishment for a week; and the faith of the fraternity in the possibilities of educating the dead still moves triumphantly forward. . . .

An "auction market" lords it over citrus fruit. The producer must accept for his crop—ripened, picked, sorted, boxed and delivered—whatever an urban market years removed from the planting and hundreds of miles away from the harvest decrees. A "contract market" rules bituminous coal which is mined in response to orders. Yet the plight of bituminous coal is more acute than that of citrus fruits. . . . The man-with-the-radio-set may search the ether freely in a price-less pursuit of auditory happiness. He pays for the pleasure, boredom or torture he captures only through the circumlocutious indirection of purchasing commodities whose unproven excellencies are touted over the air. . . . At the very edge of industrial respectability lie "the salvage trades." Wastepaper is an industry in reverse. As, from the home to the mill, bits become bales and so on to paper board, the producer and the consumer swap roles in an unorthodox economic process.

And so it goes. It is impossible to present a panorama of the whole economic landscape. A few cases must in their concretions do such duty as they can for a varied actuality that defies expression. Even the miniatures achieved here are at the expense of an infinitude of striking detail. It is only in the books that the business system is simple and bleak, drab and dull, a lifeless automaton that works—or fails to work—of itself. Things that are real belie the picture plates, and in American culture few institutions can rival in richness of color and intricacy of design the fabric of the usages of trade. A genuine expression of the American spirit, in all its strength and frailty, the web of industry is forever being woven.

## IV

In haste industry has grown up to possess the land. The old has lingered as the new has appeared; the parts have emerged at their several rates of speed; the industrial landscape is all broken up with fault-lines.

In technology we are reaching out toward the unknown—yet the dynamo and the water-wheel exist side by side. In business a corporate structure tries to encompass bigger and better intricacies—yet petty trade in its glorious inefficiency persists. A lingering culture—fiction, drama, music, painting—tried vainly to bring itself alongside current industrial fact. And the captain of industry, who reigns over terra incognita, is not quite sure in what century he lives.

It is inevitably a period of confusion. Inside the shop whatever can be oriented into the service of money-making is trimness and dispatch. But, within and without, where the balance-sheet cannot point the way, direction is uncertain. The man of business is clever at making a go of it within a competitive situation; and as daily the unexpected turns up, he takes difficulty after difficulty in his stride. But he has not mastered the problem of creating jobs for willing workers, smoothing out the curve of employment, or getting from the human and material resources at hand anything like all they have to give. Nor has he even made a promising start at arresting his revolutionary techniques at the frontiers of industry and preventing their overflow into a contiguous culture. Master in his own house, he has signally failed to make the material means of life serve the common good.

A myopia that blurs perspective everywhere persists. A few firms have led the way and high costs are there to prod; yet the general attitude towards the worker is still innocent of considerations of policy. Labor is bought in small increments as needed; the contract between master and man—if so legal an instrument exists—is usually subject to cancellation almost at notice. Nor has industry seriously set about conserving its assets in labor force for future use against the ravages of depression. The right of the laborer to a voice in the conditions of his employment have been generally recognized only where collective bargaining could make it effective. In his naïveté the American employer has let himself in for a gigantic system of labor espionage which has imposed a substantial cost upon his production, created an atmosphere of hostility, and laid a blight upon the morale of the workers. The man of business seems unable to escape the delusion of an archaic notion of property. In a system in which all wealth has been tangled into a gigantic entity he has commuted his privileges into "rights" which he regards as "absolute" and "sacred." In the name of ownership he has extended his control far beyond the bounds of his industrial estate. He has made the habits, the leisure and the ways of life of his workers a tributary province to his business domain.

Industrial relations are easily touched off into industrial conflict. In strategy and tactics alike an attitude prevails not yet accommodated to the modern scene. In the pecuniary calculus the lasting costs of a strike—in impaired morale, in disorganized labor force, in a cataclysmic break in activity—are discounted to almost nothing; and the insistent demands of the workers are exalted almost to treason against the established order. In such matters wages and hours are held of less account than the inroad upon an indefeasible managerial authority. In a world gone relative the business man would maintain a vestigial absolute in its antique purity. In his zeal for dominance he buys a momentary peace at the price of deferred turmoil. As long as the automobile force was a mechanical sum of separate and replaceable units, all was well. Even when the workers were organized into a body, little was lost. They could stage a good old-fashioned walk-out; an equivalent number of raw recruits could be walked in and a couple of months would obliterate their lack of monotonous skill. But the contrivance of a sit-down strike was a shrewd offset to a lack of bargaining power, and with its invention came labor trouble with a bang. It was smart a couple of decades ago to get after trade unions with the federal anti-trust acts; but to pull off the trick their activities had to be brought within "commerce among the several States"—and the constitutional way was thus cleared by employers for national intervention in behalf of the employee. It is an irony stranger than fiction that the concern selected to do judicial battle against the National Labor Relations Act as an invasion of the rights of the State had to be hurriedly withdrawn—and a substitute sent into action—because a little while ago, to serve an anti-union cause, the courts had been persuaded to rule its affairs to be in interstate commerce. In respect to labor the captain of industry has displayed talent for the expediency that will betray him.

In the rivalry for trade the same slavery to the moment is apparent. It is good business for one firm to make cost an irrelevance, to fix a quality price, to buttress a brand behind a trade-name, and to bribe the dealer with a large mark-up to push the goods. But when all the concerns in an industry play, and the contagion runs riot through the industrial system, the game quickly absorbs the consumer's dollar, plays havoc with purchasing power, and chills with its strictures the whole apparatus of production. It pays a single concern to advertise; but the beat of stimulus and symbol must be countered by the defensive moves of competitors. So an indulgence by one becomes an exaction upon all; and corporate entities are compelled to defend their frontiers by extensive appropriations for verbal armament. For the fortunate business unit there is still a competitive advantage; but the industry must maintain at the expense of its members—and their customers—rival troops of salesmen, advertising experts and other technicians whose task it is to make the ordinary appear the superlative good. The baronial establishment of feudal days has reappeared in modern dress; chivalrous steel has been replaced by insidious adjective and frays in armor have given way to an exchange of blasts over the air. One is not permitted to purchase the motor-car of his desire without paying for an inordinate amount of sales-talk he does not want. Against the invasion of privacy and the sumptuary tax for talk the consumer is without representation—and no firm dares call for the reduction of armament.

A man is at his best in his own shop; as he takes an amateur fling at public control the business man does not appear in an heroic role. The bother is the usual one of bringing to an alien task the tricks of one's ordinary calling. A series of measures may serve well enough the competitive fortunes of an enterprise; but, when cut to national scale, fall short of the requirements of public policy. A "floor" is a grand thing to put under one's prices—provided he can sell his goods. And it is common sense that the proviso can be removed if the same floor is forced under the other fellow's prices. So—with no longer look ahead—the industrialist lets himself in for the hubbub of a disillusioning adventure. He discovers that "cost" is a treacherous word, that amid the inordinate variety of mercantile practice he is confronted with a bewildering problem of police, and that even if a price holds, other terms of the bargain may give way. He is let in for a gigantic undertaking along the whole industrial front; and even if it succeeds, defeat may emerge from the very jaws of victory. For the device makes a political matter of cost and price: substitutes administrative discretion for the judgment of the market; appoints standards for pecuniary behavior, and gives their control into the hands of the majority of the industry. The probable result is to inhibit innovation, make the trade safe for inefficiency and freeze the grooves of production and marketing. The swing is towards a high level of prices and the not so far off event towards which the mechanism of industry moves is an economics of scarcity. As the NRA revealed, it takes experience—concrete experiences—to demonstrate to the industrialist that a corporation is one thing, an industry quite another, and the industrial system something else again.

Our culture lies in many ages, and the American man of business is not to be condemned if he misses his century. It is not the industrialist alone who drives ahead and yet tarries in a period that is gone. On many a tongue appear such archaisms as "individual initiative," "free enterprise" and "private property." In general individual initiative must now find its scope within a business organization; free enterprise must make its way in a world of closed trades; and private property is to be discovered within an intricate structure of corporate securities. Think what individual initiative would do to the works in an automobile factory—how free enterprise could blaze its way through the network of agreements among gentlemen in the steel industry—and where private property is to be discovered among the infinitude of claims, rights, and controls which a giant railway system in operation presents.

But obsolescence marks opinion and policy as well as language. It is still respectable to believe that all industries are alike and that the activities of each fall into the same normal pattern. A clean-cut antithesis between competition and monopoly is still embedded in the law of the land. A competitive industry is "an automatic self-regulating mechanism" and against monopoly the mandates of the antitrust acts are to be leveled. There is little consciousness that there is a competition of big business as well as of petty trade and that their ways lie worlds apart. As yet public policy has hardly come to grips with over-competition, with the variety of industrial behavior, with the fact that an industry can no more carry on without its folk-ways than any other savage tribe.

We live within a material culture; yet we have become a nation of nomads. If a man is to seize the main chance or even to maintain the minimum of security, he must retain his freedom to move. Yet with an outworn wisdom, we encourage him to mortgage his opportunity to one spot and to own his own home.

As yet we have hit upon no way towards economic order. We improvise with the dust of the journey in our eyes as hurriedly we are carried down the decades. We have no certain standards by which to measure industrial performance against what our material resources might be made to give. Yet something is lacking when a surplus of productive capacity marks every major industry while millions must accept relief in lieu of work. Matter has properties still unknown; resources possess potentialities still unexploited; human capacities for enjoyment still await a quickening touch. As the means of life are inadequately turned to account, we balk on the very threshold of an economics of abundance.

## V

As larger things wait in the offing, industry is intent upon its immediate task. The world over it must, as the price of survival, take the tumultuous course of events in such a stride as it can command. As depression gives way to recession, as a stark capitalism dispenses with the stage trappings of democracy, as a proletariat denied bread cries for bigger and better circuses, business sits somewhat insecurely in the saddle. Even in America, where only yesterday the captain of industry was the Lord High Pooh Bah of everything else, threats against the sovereignty of business have been uttered—and even action has disturbed a bit the financial tranquility. A proletariat, armed in an unguarded hour with universal suffrage, has refused to obey the voice of its master at the polls. Its strength has become a strategic counter in a political game; and, as "relief" has joined the R. F. D., a dole for capital has been followed by a dole for labor. In the very recent past politics grown bold has tried to wrest the scepter from industry; and once, in sheer audacity, "the administration" attempted to move the national capital from New York to Washington. Even if, with symbol and slogan in mighty array, the usurpers have been put down, and the national plight has for a time been fastened upon "the government," the danger is not past. The balance sheet is an unmerciful tyrant; final entries in black are not securely buttressed against the invasion of red ink; and industry will be hard put to it to keep its own house in order.

Yet, even amid turbulence, industry is not a thing apart. In all its doings it must come to an understanding with the culture of which it is aspect rather than part. In exacting terms it has the upper hand; and between the wishes of men and the urges of the machine there is not yet that "equality of bargaining power in which freedom of contract begins." But even where the time-clock and the crack of the industrial whip are most insistent, flesh and blood set limits to their discipline. It is the wear and tear on human tissue, not fatigue within the precisions of a monotonous process, which decrees the hours of labor. At least half a million people surrender choice to an inanimate assembly line and make their "homes" in the drab suburbs of Detroit because chance once decreed that automobile factories should be located there. The things that lord it over human values have never perfected an adequate system of police; and in the disorder which attends the economic process the instruments of living have never completely subjugated the ends of life.

In industry the little fellow is there to be picked on. A corporate entity sends its shock troops against the helpless consumer and beats down his resistance with every artifice of suggestion and pressure. Its aspirations rise no higher than the earthly lust for gain; yet its compulsions are as unrestrained as the lurid pictures of hell with which the church once maintained its monopoly of the human necessity called salvation. In an industrial system only partially regimented, sellers have not as yet gotten together to divide the spoils; and, in the heat of the competition for his dollar, the buyer manages here and there to get in a choice. All along the line where functions are in bondage to instruments, an uncertain truce has been patched up between a dynamic industry and a rebellious culture.

Between industry and culture it is impossible to catalogue the points of contact, command and conflict; for so pervasive a contagion knows no points. Industry revises to its requirements the common good it serves. Its personnel comes from without—a steady stream of youths, bred in the family, trained in the schools, moulded into distinctive individuals by the social environment. Yet home, college and club, religious creed and talking film have all responded, each in its own unique way, to the allure of business; and the folk of industry—without resort to celibacy, monastic vows, or even the rigamarole of a mystery—are as consecrated to their god of Mammon as any priesthood of old.

A human urge is the ultimate reference for every ware of trade. But the wants of man reach out beyond sheer necessities, through the comforts, to the vanities and frivolities of life. Moreover even a burning lust for food or sex or make-believe has more than one means of satisfaction; and as lesser passions are given their due, endless changes are rung on the multiple properties with which human life is sustained. Thus an opening is created for the intrusion of alien values; the goods which serve wants are compromised by custom; and business, ever alert to the main chance, shapes the proprieties to its profit. Accordingly the precept of old, "Let no one seek his own but every man another's wealth," has been remade. An ingredient as an article of wealth is still a utility that serves a need; its other dominant elements are a vendible in search of a buyer and a stimulus to touch off in response to the consumer's dollar. In every commodity that goes to market the substantial qualities of the ware are insidiously blended with the persuasions of industry and the beliefs of a people.

As a by-product of money-making, industry fabricates a great part of the stuff of a culture. As matters now go industry holds the first mort-gage against the great mass of us; and, unless our dues of toil and time are regularly discharged, it forecloses upon our means of livelihood. The closed club of the recipients of funded income alone escape; and they must atone for exemption with a bigoted slavery to archaic opinion. It is only the quantum of interest and energy which can be sneaked into the job, or the residuum left over from the day's toil which can be turned to a non-industrial account. But as one shifts to creative play, he cannot check at the barrier the habits of work. In the most shopless of under-takings one must people a story, a novel or a play with characters whose response to industrial stimuli have shaped them into what they are. One must exhibit—even if he cannot unravel—the tangles which industrial circumstance has brought into their lives. One must follow the insidious influence of an industrial habitat to its ultimate destination in belief and action, in human triumph and disaster. Or else one must take his art of creation to an alien scene—and that would be interpreted as "an escape from industrial reality."

Man's communion with his fellows has been made over by economic change. The mark of industry is upon the crisp words he uses, the quick staccato of his idiom, the marching style which has driven the leisurely sentence of the Victorians into oblivion. The least material aspects of life have been able to erect no barriers against industrial penetration. As dis-sonance comes into its own, mathematics is invoked to arrange musical notes into new permutations of harmony—and discord. The quality of one's mind is reduced to a single dimension; human talent in all its bewildering variety has found a common denominator; and all that is intelligence is measured along a single linear line. And even the God of Our Fathers—who only yesterday was "the Lord and Proprietor of the Universe" and the day before "the King of Kings and Lord of Hosts" —has been shorn of the last shred of his anthropomorphic being. He has been put through the ideological mill, and in an up-to-date theology has emerged as the spiritual version of the materialistic law of cause and effect. So religion has been squared with science; and the godhead has been brought into accord with the postulates which underlie industrial technology.

As reason recedes before an even more mechanistic behavior, all things to man must be reasonable. All things—science, music, literature, learn-ing, philosophy, even his gods—must fall into harmony with the funda-ments of his ways of thought. The folk-ways of the mind—the ultimate reference in matters of belief—are shaped by the notions of quantity, precision, mechanism and cause which the empire of business persistently drills into the heads of all of its subjects as common sense. The distinctive creation of industry has been the gift of its passing self as a focus for all creative endeavor.

# ADVERTISING

## [*Roy S. Durstine*]

ADVERTISING is as American as apple pie. It reflects most of our national virtues and many of our national faults.

Like our country, it is young, vital, seething, full of inconsistencies and contrasts, often vulgar if you will, intrusive as an insurance salesman, common as a song-hit, vivid as a redheaded debutante.

It stands for power—usually the power of a streamlined locomotive, sometimes the power of a rogue elephant.

It typifies a country that could produce a Huey Long, a Doctor Townsend, a Father Coughlin, cross-word puzzles, miniature golf, and swing music but could also give us a Carter Glass, a Charles Augustus Lindbergh, a Cordell Hull, a Newton Baker and a Mr. Justice Oliver Wendell Holmes.

A superficial glance at advertising would seem to show that some of it derives from P. T. Barnum and some from the Harvard School of Business Administration, some of it from Babbitt and some from Joseph Leyendecker. Actually it comes from something far more fundamental.

It is the inevitable result of the past one hundred and fifty years when, for the first time in the world's history, there have been melted together the peoples of all the world in one comparatively small patch of the earth's surface called these United States.

European and Asiatic civilization started thousands of years ahead of us. Even when George Washington became our first President there were less than four million Americans, for the most part strung along the Atlantic seaboard. In the spans of two men's lives this country has come a long way—far enough to cause an outside observer, *The London Sphere,* to remark in 1937:

The United States contains 6 per cent of the world's area and 7 per cent of its population. It normally consumes 48 per cent of the world's coffee, 53 per cent of its tin, 56 per cent of its rubber, 21 per cent of its sugar, 72 per cent of its silk, 36 per cent of its coal, 42 per cent of its pig iron, 47 per cent of its copper, and 68 per cent of its crude petroleum.

The United States operates 60 per cent of the world's telephone and telegraph facilities, owns 80 per cent of the motor cars in use, operates 33 per cent of the railroads. It produces 70 per cent of the oil, 60 per cent of the wheat and cotton, 50 per cent of the copper and pig iron, and 40 per cent of the lead and coal output of the globe.

The United States possesses almost $11,000,000,000 in gold, or nearly half of the world's monetary metal. It has two-thirds of civilization's banking resources. The purchasing power of the population is greater than that of the 500,000,000 people in Europe and much larger than that of the more than a billion Asiatics.

Responsible leadership which cannot translate such a bulging economy into assured prosperity is destitute of capacity. But pompous statesmen, looking over the estate, solemnly declare that the methods by which it was created are all wrong, ought to be abandoned, must be discarded, that the time has come to substitute political management for individual initiative and supervision.

There is only one way to characterize that proposal—it is just damn foolishness.

Why did one particular spot on the map of the world come so far so quickly?

It is difficult to explain such progress as that in one country except by these four circumstances:

That here has been provided an environment of complete freedom for the individual in action, in worship and in speech.

That here, for the first time in history, large units of people within the boundaries of one nation were able to engage in free trade with one another.

That here were found enormous natural resources, waiting to be turned into wealth.

That here each individual has found opportunity and encouragement to improve the condition into which he was born.

When this liberty has veered toward license, the correction has come clumsily and slowly but inevitably from public opinion. When Theodore Roosevelt started all this social reform by attacking "malefactors of great wealth," he was simply a leader of already crystallized but inarticulate public opinion.

Sometimes you must measure the improvement by intervals of many years to see the change, but it comes inexorably and needs no edict. Over a period, the people of this country assert their common sense. If they are diverted from time to time, if they seem to rush this way and that, it is only part of the phenomenon of a people by no means solidified, an unfinished and far-flung nation, still reaching out to find itself. The United States is a bubbling kettle, not a cup of lukewarm tea.

As a native type developed in the United States, it fought its way against the obstacles of Nature with endurance and enterprise. When immigrants poured into this country from Europe by the millions to join in the struggle for individual survival or even supremacy, they joined with those they found here in a struggle which demanded sacrifice, stamina and resourcefulness.

The Sixty Families emerged because their founders clawed out a living and then a surplus. The pioneers of this country didn't get maxims out of the copybooks; they put them in.

The business tradition of the United States came out of the struggles of the 19th century as naturally as the first beginnings of trade followed the orginal settlers' struggle for a foothold in the wilderness.

As the railroads were built, as faster mails and the telegraph and finally the telephone and the aeroplane brought communities closer together, business reached out beyond the local circle in which the makers of goods originally sold their products from door to door.

The early national habits changed. Households which at first produced everything for the family from shoes to candles and from homespun to farm tools began to buy from travelling peddlers. Then they started trading at village stores supplied by far-away producers of manufactured goods.

As the turn of the century approached, mass production arrived. And as the years have rolled by since then, advertising as we know it now was the natural herald of mass production as inevitably as the town crier followed the arrival of a ship loaded with goods at any early American port.

The whole thing reduces itself to a very simple formula as Daniel C. Roper, Secretary of Commerce, explained in a radio address in April, 1938. It is this:

"Low prices depend upon mass production. Mass production depends upon mass distribution. Mass distribution depends upon mass advertising. Therefore low prices depend upon mass advertising."

The homes of the United States are full of proofs of this equation.

There are more than twelve million automatic refrigerators in use in this country today. A very good one can be bought for about one hundred dollars. It was little more than a dozen years ago when you had to pay six or seven hundred dollars for one which produced service trouble as often as it did ice.

The magazine advertising bill for helping to sell 75,000 automatic refrigerators in 1925 was $427,480. In 1937 it was $2,820,864, and the number sold was 2,365,000. In 1925 the average unit cost to the consumer was $425; in 1937 it was $169.

A really fine automobile can be bought today for six or seven hundred dollars. If only a few of that same kind of car were manufactured today, it is estimated that each one would cost about fifteen thousand dollars. Certainly it is a far better car than the one for which you paid five thousand dollars fifteen years ago.

A dozen years ago you couldn't buy at any price the radio set which you can get today for less than fifty dollars. Ten tubes couldn't do then what five tubes will do today. Even if you had paid five or six hundred dollars you couldn't have had the tone quality which almost any inexpensive set gives you today.

The Eastman Company, a consistent advertiser since 1889, in explaining why it uses about 3½ per cent of the retail price to tell people about taking pictures says:

"Savings to the consumer as a result of consistent advertising are so many times the amount of money devoted to advertising that we think any question of wasteful practice is untenable."

Eastman research and large-scale production, assisted by advertising, has done more than merely give the consumer finer kodaks for less money. The price of professional motion picture film has been reduced from five cents a foot in 1906 to one cent in 1938. Amateur motion pictures in color have been made as easily produced as black and white. Experimenting for sharper images of distant stars led to the manufacture of a type of film for small images, providing in 8-millimeter amateur motion picture photography a less expensive system for those who could not afford 16-millimeter motion pictures.

Today you pay one-third as much for your Mazda electric light bulbs as you did in 1921 and you get 20 per cent more light. You get over 27 times as much light for your lamp dollar as you did in 1908.

Automobile tires furnish a startling example of the social and economic benefits of mass production with advertising's help. Comparing the mileage which the motorist gets in 1937 over 1929, he may say to himself as he looks at the average best quality tire now costing $15.20, "I get $9.57 more value for my money in 1937 than I did in 1929. In addition, through the purchase of this tire, I am giving the workman who made that tire a 36 per cent higher hourly rate and I am giving the Government an additional 70 cents for its expense and my presumable benefit. It appears to be a pretty good bargain so far as I am concerned." These facts come from Goodyear.

Now in all of these examples, and scores of others, advertising has been only one link in a chain of steps between some man's original idea and the final enjoyment of a product at a reasonable price by millions of consumers. The cost of the advertising has been only one item in the final price.

How much does advertising add to the cost?

Put that question to the great mass of people, those who benefit most from it, those who are in the middle and lower income groups, and you will probably find that they have never thought of it. Yet they are the ones who provide the mass buying without which all but a few high-priced luxuries could not exist. More than 90 per cent of this country's incomes are below two thousand dollars a year.

Ask those critics of it who think they know all about advertising and invariably their estimates of its cost will be many times too high.

There has been so much talk about "our million dollar expenditure in advertising" that people forget how many millions of people must be reached.

Consider it two ways:—the cost per reader or listener for magazines, newspapers or radio; and the cost charged against each package or can.

A page in *The Saturday Evening Post* or *Collier's Weekly* or *Life* costs less than half a cent a home—less than a locally mailed blank postcard. So does a full-page advertisement in a metropolitan newspaper. So does a radio program with even the most expensive talent.

The combined expenditures of all food advertisers in a certain leading newspaper amount to only $1.02 per year per family, or 8.5 cents per month.

In this country we have no unit of coinage less than a cent. So to get an actual saving, not one which is merely an academic theory, by eliminating advertising we must find a reduction in price which will actually give the American housewife a piece of change as she does her daily marketing.

The actual fact is that you would have to get the United States mint to shave our penny into a hundred and sometimes a thousand parts before a clerk would be able to drop a coin representing a saving into the housewife's hand.

Bread is now so good and so cheap that hardly any one can afford to bake it in home ovens. The advertising to make it known costs less than the wrapper to keep it clean.

The story of Sunkist oranges is too well known to need repetition. But the low cost of the advertising which has been an indispensable aid in making orange-growing into a well-ordered industry for the producers and in changing this fruit from a holiday luxury into a healthful daily item in millions of homes is significant. At the maximum the cost of this advertising to the housewife per dozen oranges has been one-third of a cent, or one-thirty-sixth of a cent per orange.

The Loose-Wiles Biscuit Company says that on a ten-cent package, the advertising expenditure is less than a tenth of a cent. An executive of a representative packer of vegetables and fruits gives one-tenth of a cent per can as the advertising expense. He believes that this is a pretty standard figure for the canned goods industry.

As you drink a five-cent glass of Coca-Cola perhaps it will help to refresh you to know that only 1576/100,000ths of one of your five pennies went into telling the people of the United States about this product. On a Lord Pepperell shirt 64/100ths of a cent has gone into public information about it. A well-known cake of soap carries an advertising cost of one-fifth of a cent. Campbell Soup has been quoted so many times that it is almost a classic with its 36/1000ths of a cent per can for advertising.

Any one who has had an opportunity to observe American business over the past twenty years can multiply examples of the way that growth in volume has given the consumer either the same value at a lower price or added value at the same price or both.

Without the volume, without the mass production, which advertising has helped to create, the unit cost would be increased far beyond the amount of the advertising.

But because advertising is so much more conspicuous than the other items—research or warehousing or freight rates or retail profit, for example—it usually gets more than its rightful share of blame or credit in the chain of transactions that occur between a manufacturer's research laboratory and the consumer's home. Advertisements are all about us, whereas very few consumers ever see a warehouse receipt or a bill of lading. Yet they, too, represent a share of the final purchase price.

But the biggest item of all is labor. Smoking one cigarette, for instance, gives about forty-five seconds of employment to a worker.

That fact was developed in a study called "Division of Labor in Cigarette Production" made by the Crowell Publishing Company. It learned, also, that about 352,000 farmers were engaged in 1935 in growing the tobacco for the seven leading brands of cigarettes and that 22,000 wage earners were employed in manufacturing cigarettes.

In terms of one package selling at fourteen cents, the government gets six cents in revenue. That leaves eight cents.

One-quarter of a man hour is required to produce one package. This would indicate thirty-two cents an hour for labor. But actually unskilled labor in 1935 received an average of forty-five cents an hour; farm labor ten cents to thirteen cents an hour. If this averages about twenty-seven cents an hour for all cigarette labor, then the difference between twenty-seven and thirty-two cents or five cents an hour or one and one-quarter cents per package is all that is left for advertising—and profit.

In a democracy, run for the people, what could be fairer than that the lion's share of the cost of a package of cigarettes enjoyed by the people should go to the workers and to the government?

Paul Garrett of General Motors recently had something to say about this job-finding result of mass production when he said that eighty-four cents out of every dollar goes to the employee. He continued:

I refer to the fallacy that the way to create buying power is to level down from the top. That the way to spread wealth is divide it, not multiply it. It is a shameful commentary upon our neglect of elementary business interpretation that such a doctrine, based upon the outworn philosophies of Karl Marx and the Socialist school, should ever have gained a foothold in these United States. For does this theory not ignore the fundamental fact that production of goods precedes distribution of goods—that increase in wealth can only come through producing ever more and more things to distribute?

I refer to the fallacy that the machine is driving men into idleness. Does this theory not ignore the fact that jobs for workers increase almost in direct proportion as workers can call upon horsepower to help them? Does it not ignore the fact that during the last fifty years of machine development the population of the nation has doubled but the number of wage earners in factories trebled? Does it not ignore the fact that for every person given a job in manufacturing enterprise four others automatically were given jobs as suppliers and in corollary services thereby created? Does it not overlook industry's use of the machine to build automobiles by which jobs were eventually provided for 6,000,000—jobs that would never have been created under handcraft methods—as against 60,000 jobs furnished through buggy building in its heyday? Does it not ignore the fact that industry must be dynamic, ever-progressing, ready to capitalize upon technology in order to force costs lower and lower!

Do we, in fact, over-produce? Or do we, perhaps, under-consume? Has the American public suddenly stopped wanting things? Is the American standard of living really anything but a measure of how well American wants are being satisfied? Or can the real reason be found in the magnitude of our relief rolls, the fright of investors, the caution of business men who can't hang out the "Men Wanted" signs because they can't risk more red figures?

Business, and advertising, can never thrive on a philosophy of scarcity. They can never progress in an atmosphere of uncertainty, criticism, distrust and public fear.

It is ridiculous to say that business men can turn on prosperity and turn it off like a spigot. It is the customer, millions of him, who says how many days in the week a factory is to run. Business is bad when in millions of homes people say: "We'd better not get that until things get better."

Of course, the complicated pieces of machinery, human and material, which make up present-day business must be regulated. If they cannot regulate themselves—and the noble experiment of the NRA showed how difficult it is to make individual initiative work under wraps—then some form of government regulation must follow. But it must be an umpire, not a prosecutor nor a persecutor.

You remember the story of the Princeton man who sent two sons to Princeton and one to Yale.

"Why did you send your youngest son to Yale?" some one asked.

"Because," he answered, "The government is paying me to plough one under."

The reason you smile at that idea (as you may, unless you went to Yale) is because you are struck by the impossibility of destroying human initiative like hogs or cotton.

Individual business men are just as eager to hire workers and salesmen as they ever were. When plans are curtailed or postponed it is only because common sense tells them to wait.

A generation ago there were men with vision and ambition ready to use advertising to send collars out of Troy, soup out of Camden, pickles and beans out of Pittsburgh, silverware out of Oneida, linoleum out of Lancaster, automobiles out of Detroit, tires out of Akron and kodaks out of Rochester.

There are ten times as many owners of businesses today just as eager to carve out new fortunes for themeselves and their associates and to employ millions as they do it. What if these key men with the brains and capacity to plan enterprises involving millions of workers do get rich rewards for themselves? When you see big salaries printed in the papers, remember this:

The cost to provide a traditional American incentive for these leaders is no more than a few cents per week per worker and without them these undertakings will not be planned and managed. In other words, if these leaders worked for nothing, and their salaries were divided among all the laborers in their plants, each worker would find only a few extra pennies in his envelope each week. And don't forget that the leaders of tomorrow will be the Knudsens and Sarnoffs and Hooks and Fairlesses of today— men who yesterday stood at the foot of the ladder.

Has this country everything it needs?

In 1937 was published a survey by the Bureau of Foreign and Domestic Commerce covering 2,633,135 dwellings in 64 American cities.

It found that almost a quarter of these homes were without bathtubs or showers; 17 per cent without sanitation.

The New York Housing Authority says that of the 1,899,549 homes in metropolitan New York, 409,157 are without bathtubs or showers; 322,065 are without hot water, and 250,000 are without private indoor toilets.

How many owners of these homes, and the millions of others where the sanitary equipment is obsolete, are hoping for the day when they can make their homes cleaner, more convenient and healthier?

Less than 30 per cent of the people of this country ever use a toothbrush. Only those who have faced nights of agony from toothaches can estimate the human value of a wider understanding of oral hygiene.

Only the woman who moves around a modern kitchen, preparing balanced meals for her healthy children, can really appreciate what the editorial and advertising pages of the *Ladies' Home Journal,* the *Woman's Home Companion, McCall's,* and *Good Housekeeping* have done for the 90 per cent of mothers who do all their own housework.

Yet there are still millions of women carrying up from the cellar scuttles of coal, pumping and carrying water.

It is not difficult to find a basis for scoffing at the cultural effects of advertising. But what pulled this country out of the General Grant period of architecture? The advertising of building materials deserves its share of the credit. What let air and peace into living rooms and taste into dining rooms and bedrooms and banished the stuffiness of mid-Victorian interiors? The advertising of makers of floor coverings and wall papers and paint and glass and curtains cannot be ignored.

What has sold millions of copies of the best books of today and has filled libraries with reprints of the classics, changing literature from something to be exhibited to something to be read? Ask the advertising publishers.

What sends 50,000 Americans abroad in the one month of June, 1938, in spite of a war-scare in Europe? Advertising has had its part in filling those liners.

And in spite of all the vulgar witticisms and horror of the radio, which the public is already diminishing by a twist of the dial, what feast of great music was ever laid before a nation so lavishly as the advertisers of this country provide in any given week?

Unless you want more American homes to be happier and more comfortable, you won't like advertising.

The wife of a certain banker, giving a dinner party one evening in her Park Avenue apartment, was explaining her views.

"Advertising," she said, "is the worm eating at the heart of the American pocketbook."

She and her husband with two grown and unmarried children, with a number of servants, occupied sixteen rooms and five baths on the most expensive street in the world.

"Don't you think it would be nice if a few more of the millions in this country could have at least one bathroom in their homes?" she was asked.

Not fifty miles from New York lives the wife of a farmer. She weighs about ninety pounds in her winter clothes. She is not far beyond her twenties but she has never quite recovered from presenting her husband with three children in rather rapid order from eight to a dozen years ago. She does everything about her home and takes care of her family beautifully.

One morning she couldn't get out of bed.

"She's just tired out," the doctor said. "Can't you find some way to lighten her work after she is rested?"

Her husband decided that the family washing was her hardest task. The purchase price of a washing machine was beyond him. But by arranging time payments he had it in the house the next day.

We hear a lot about the pernicious way that manufacturers inveigle people into overloading themselves with time payments. That farmer's wife didn't think it was so very pernicious.

Her husband went even further. He bought a little car on the same arrangement. Perhaps one evening a week when their children were doing their school work, he and his wife drive the five miles into the nearest town to go to the movies, and occasionally he bundles the whole family into his automobile to drive over to his brother-in-law's house for Sunday dinner.

Often through the day, as she goes about her housework, his wife turns on their radio. While he waits for his supper after a long day riding a tractor, he gets his favorite news announcer, and in the evenings, before turning in, he chuckles at his favorite comedian.

Three possessions—washing machine, automobile, radio. All on time payments. All very silly.

The banker's wife in the luxury of her Park Avenue apartment wouldn't have approved at all. The farmer and his family didn't know how uneconomic they were being. They were just enjoying some things which somebody had put within their reach.

Time payments, heralded in the "new era" of the '20's as an unmixed blessing, more recently have come in for a terrific beating. This is not the place to argue the case for or against. But perhaps it may be pointed out that the evil of the plan may lie more in its abuse than in the plan itself. Perhaps a central point of registration, like a local bank, for all of each individual's undertakings might be a check which would keep him from overloading himself beyond his capacity to work out his time payments.

Let's be fair about it, though. Is it true that sometimes advertising assists in foisting fictitious values on the public? The most often-quoted example is the jar of beauty cream at a fantastic price.

There is a very human trait deep down in women, also frequently noted in men, which accounts for a willingness to pay a price for certain things —a price which never in the world can be justified by reason or a careful weighing of intrinsic values.

A Paris dressmaker puts together a few yards of material costing ten or fifteen dollars and sells the resulting gown for three hundred. Why? Because it is so advanced and knowing that it will be wearable for several seasons? Partly. Sometimes. But there is an added reason: the label.

A Fifth Avenue beauty expert combines a few cents' worth of creamy ingredients and sells them for five dollars. Why? Because they contain magical properties which will bring the bloom of youth to fading cheeks?

Partly. The accompanying rituals of massage and cleansing do their share and the lotions are at least the best so far discovered for their purpose. But the woman who pays a high price for the cellophaned and beribboned jar probably does it with the full knowledge that she wouldn't do it unless it bore that certain label. She could concoct her own mixture for a few pennies. Why doesn't she? Because it wouldn't be the same thing at all.

Her husband has his moments, too. Perhaps he buys his clothes from a Fifth Avenue tailor whose added skill in cutting and sewing is hardly worth the added fifty to one hundred dollars. Perhaps a quotable label has its significance here, too. The set of matched irons bearing the autograph of a famous champion may not take quite so many strokes from his average round of golf as he told himself it would when he paid twice as much as the price of the same number of clubs without the label. But the presence of these clubs in his bag, as reflected in the awe of the caddy or the admiration of the locker-room, may explain a lot.

His wife could probably obtain a refillable prescription from any reliable skin specialist and have it made up at any cut-price drug store or make it up herself if she wanted to take the time and trouble.

But there is one thing which she could not put into a plain jar with a plain top. That is the confidence, the assurance, the satisfaction with which the label of the Fifth Avenue beauty expert sends her from her dressing table into the scrutiny of the evening's social competition.

"How well you are looking this evening!" or "I never saw you look so pretty"—those are the rewards, those represent the return she gets for her money.

"Marvellous set of clubs you've got there, Bill."

"Some irons, mister!"

"Did you get that gown in Paris?"

"Who's your tailor, Jim?"

These are the things we pay for when we pay more than the utilitarian minimum. Which proves nothing so much as that the human race has been very human indeed since long before the days of advertising—since, at least, the days when Cleopatra chose her scented lotions or when young Roman dandies were mindful of their togas' cut.

But considerations related to vanity do not account for all the elements of this satisfaction. Reliance on the continuous quality of a product and the maker's integrity is another controlling cause of this peace of mind. Which explains why large department stores can advertise, at the low prices of loss leaders, their equivalents of standard goods without getting all the business from the independent druggist across the street. The public knows who makes what the druggist sells and is willing and glad to pay a few extra pennies for the satisfaction of knowing.

To be able to go into any crossroads store or neighborhood shop and buy a package of cigarettes, a can of soup, a cake of soap, or a box of crackers and know in advance exactly what you are going to get for your money provides a degree of satisfaction of which the public will not deprive itself. When this constant quality is actually obtainable for less money, as in the great preponderance of cases in which mass production and advertising have worked together, the benefit to the public is obvious.

Let's agree that much of advertising is exaggerated or fantastic, much of it vulgar, and not a little ridiculous.

The "continuty strip" technique, so popular at the moment, is only one case in point. Depicting at the start a dejected young man or young woman, describing in succeeding scenes the unfortunate effects of the plight which makes him or her a misfit in this critical world, and finally ending with a moment of triumph and popular acclaim—that is the technique. The formula is as old as the hills; only the serial pictures, borrowed from the comics page, are new. Apparently there are vast numbers of people who will read anything enclosed in a balloon emanating from a person's mouth or who will read a line or two of text under a picture—persons who cannot be persuaded to read a solid paragraph of type. Hence we have this epidemic of young women gaining popularity, husbands, homes and happy firesides or leisure for the movies, shopping, or bridge —all by clearing up their complexions or sweetening their breath or switching their brands of soap.

Absurd? Of course. Exaggerated? Terribly. Vulgar? Naturally. Then why does advertising do it?

For the same reason that a salesman of bonds or insurance or real estate violates good taste by persisting with his telephone calls or written messages or personal visits long after you have explained that you aren't in the market for what he sells. For the same reason that an author keeps calling on or sending things to editors or a society matron importunes for charity.

Because all these approaches are intrusions. Of our own free wills we would open the doors of our minds or homes or offices to none of them. But it is their job, as it is advertising's, to break through our indifference. People often have to be hounded before they will do such a beneficent thing as to provide for their old age.

The world is filled with people trying to earn a living—ministers preaching trial sermons in anticipation of a "call," musicians looking for auditions, doctors joining golf clubs or attending dinner parties, architects widening social circles, lawyers arranging casual introductions, engineers meeting the right people.

Advertising isn't alone with its intrusions.

Yet a disservice is done to advertising every time an advertisement makes some one say, "Oh, that's just advertising."

The testimonial which a prominent woman gives to a product which she never uses is clearly deceitful even when she shrugs off the implication by having the check sent to her pet charity. Let's hope the Federal Trade Commission stops that one under the new law.

What is going to be the future of advertising?

First, it gives every promise of going straight ahead as a force opposed to drudgery, poverty and misery. It will continue to tell the stories of conveniences and labor-saving devices which at lower and lower prices will continue to find their way into the homes of barbers, elevator men, mechanics, stenographers, bus drivers, policemen, train dispatchers, milliners, farmers and laborers just as they have in the past. Refrigerators, vacuum cleaners, radios, hot water heaters, washing machines, electric clocks and dozens of other products which used to be found only in the homes of the privileged few will be in even greater numbers in the houses and apartments where rents are low. Advertising always has been and always will be a benefit to the underprivileged.

Second, it will continue to help in making jobs for the millions. When you see this work in miniature it is easier to grasp. In an Eastern community are about three thousand workers, all in one factory. The problem of the general manager there is intense and simple. It is: when the factory's output is consumed by the rest of the country, his workers are happy and prosperous. When it isn't, they are idle and wretched. Designing, pricing, and advertising are not academic subjects to him. He *must* arrive at the right combination of style, taste, and value and then tell the United States what he has to sell. Multiply that man's problem by thousands and you see the vital part of advertising in creating and maintaining jobs.

Third, advertising will increasingly tell the story of how American industry has put within the grasp of the American people the best way of living in the history of the world. It will clarify misunderstandings and class hatreds by showing that American business has been on the whole a mighty good citizen. If there is distortion of facts in print or on the air, business has a responsibility to correct false impressions. Freedom of the press and of the air can countenance nothing but the truth. As David Sarnoff has said:

It is no coincidence that in an autocracy where freedom of broadcasting does not exist, neither is there a free economy to which it might look for support. It is no coincidence that where freedom of thought and of speech are denied on the air, they are equally denied on the platform, in the university, and in the church. It is no coincidence that where you find broadcasting enslaved, you also find a slavish press.

The people of this country want the facts. Factory workers want the facts. Six thousand of them scattered all over the country were recently asked: "Do you want information from your employer and if so about what?"

More than half wanted facts on taxes affecting business. Seventy-three per cent wanted facts on business conditions.

Is it too much to hope that the common ground of the future will be found when thoughtful labor veers toward the conservative and thoughtful management becomes more liberal—both from a greater knowledge of each other's point of view?

Even in those industries whose products, like steel and lumber and nickel and aluminum, rarely reach the consumer except in refabricated form, there is a responsibility to go about the task of telling their story as seriously as in the past financing, engineering, and production have been approached. Only when the whole public knows the whole truth will the consumers of this country know the real value of their economic liberty which is their heritage under the American method of individual incentive and reward.

Fourth, as new products and services come from the research laboratories of American business, advertising will be the means of telling the news of their services to the country.

Charles R. Hook started at two dollars a week when he went to work for the American Rolling Mill Company of which he is now president. Recently he said:

Incentive is still here. You will have more opportunities than my generation had, simply because we know a lot more about what makes jobs than we did in the old days.

To have jobs, we must have things to manufacture. Today, we are depending on our scientific laboratories to find these new products. Many of you here tonight—many more of you listening in—will find jobs in companies making products that do not even exist today, or that have only recently been perfected in one or another of our great industrial research laboratories.

Even today, infant industries grow like mushrooms before our very eyes. You all can remember, a few years ago, how unnatural the first trailers seemed— how you would turn and point as one went lumbering past.

Well, trailers represent just such another booming industry today. Air conditioning is another example, offering unlimited possibilities. Or—turning more to the future—think of television—or newspapers with sound tracks, to be played every morning on your breakfast table at home—or mail rockets, operated by remote control. Our scientists are finding ways to make roads from cotton, and airplane propellers from sour milk. They can turn wine into a motor fuel, and beans into steering wheels. These scientists are creating the actualities of tomorrow. You will be living your lives in the midst of the things they invent, and they will contribute mightily to the higher standard of living you have the right to enjoy.

Alfred P. Sloan, Jr., in an exciting article, "The Forward View," in *The Atlantic Monthly* said:

Clerics and statesmen alike have decreed at various times a static economic world. As late as 1886 the first United States Commissioner of Labor solemnly reported that the next fifty years would show no such progress as the preceding fifty years. "The nations of the world," said he, "have overstocked themselves with machinery and manufacturing plants far in excess of the wants of production. . . . This full supply . . . is the most important factor of the present (1886) industrial depression. . . . The day of large profits is probably past."

This government official considered that the cycle of progress ended when it was just about to usher in a wider use of the notable inventions and discoveries of a laborious century. . . . The imagination of the race, the creative faculties of our people, have turned into nonsense the gloomy prophecies of that once-eminent pessimist.

And as for advertising hear this opinion:

"The trade of advertising is now so near to perfection that it is not easy to propose any improvement."

The gentleman who expressed this sentiment was Samuel Johnson, and he said it in 1759.

In the quarter of a century just passed, advertising has come into existence in its modern phase as the only economic means of carrying information of industrial progress to the millions. It is far from a perfect instrument.

It not only works; it works better than any substitute to serve the progress of the country just as surely as a broadcasting station is a better distributor of information than a single human voice.

It seems to Mr. Sloan that one great new industry at least is ready to send the country forward again just as the automobile has been the focal point of progress in the last quarter century.

For a long time [says Mr. Sloan] we have been building office, apartment, and factory buildings of pre-fabricated materials, on steel frames of more or less standard designs. The new mass-housing projects, . . . contemplate adapting this thoroughly tested system to home construction, where the broadest of all markets will permit further economies, thereby bringing to the average citizen values and conveniences hitherto beyond his economic grasp.

To appreciate the significance of this impending change, let us remind ourselves that technology to date has brought no such change to unit housing as it has brought to transportation, communications, food production, clothing, or multiple housing. The man who drives a low-priced mass-production car, whose words are carried to his neighbor or across the continent by telephone with the speed of light, and who wears mass-production clothes of a quality not otherwise attainable at equal costs, dwells in a house erected by antiquated means, yet pays a high price for his accommodation.

In thousands of industrial laboratories American business is preparing the surprises of tomorrow.

You have seen the photo-electric cell opening the doors at the Pennsylvania Station in New York, but have you really seen it do its tricks? Do you know that you can get a gadget which contains a photo-electric cell and which you can hold up to the light and on the back see registered just how wide you should open your camera and what the length of your exposure should be?

Do you know that some of the matters which are getting the attention of the General Electric laboratories today as they look forward to the future are air conditioning in homes, stores, offices, schools, hospitals, and other public buildings; light, streamlined, low-center-of-gravity trains for speeds up to two hundred miles per hour; electrification of all railroads; highway lighting, making high-speed night driving safe; high voltage, direct current transmission, reducing power costs and extending economic radius; new materials, such as improved textiles, new synthetic resins replacing wood, metals and other natural materials for many purposes, new alloys, new structural materials giving better heat and sound insulation; ending household drudgery by complete electrification of every home; and the elimination of needless noise. These are only the non-confidential items which may be expected to come out of General Electric to make our lives pleasanter and richer. And the story of every one of them must be told by advertising.

Scientists and manufacturers will continue to create new products. The public wants them. But the public must be told about them. Advertising has been doing its best to spread your information for you in the past. It is a better tool today than it ever was. It is ready to carry the news which will lift this country into a standard of living and a level of prosperity beyond anything that any of us have ever dreamed.

Only a few years ago a woman on a Detroit bridge held up traffic while she got out of her car to crank up a stalled engine. Luckily for mankind, Charles F. Kettering happened to be there that day and in his mind was born the idea of the self-starter.

Remember that story when some one tries to tell you that the United States is finished.

The electric impulses which come into your home tonight through your radio set have been up there in the air since the world began. Only in our generation have they been turned into the miracle of music and the spoken word coming to you through space. What will the scientists give us next?

Mr. Kettering once said:

"Nothing man ever built arose to touch the skies except from some man's wish to see it rise, some man's belief that it could, some man's will that it must."

America will go forward so long as men like that find here a place to think and plan and live and work.

SCIENCE
AND
INVENTION

# SCIENCE

## [Gerald Wendt]

THE FORCES which shape a civilization are not always evident to those who live under them. Indeed, they need not be a part of the intellectual atmosphere of the time. It is now obvious that the frontier was a powerful factor in moulding the American spirit and American institutions, but this was not fully recognized until its influence had all but disappeared. Today science has taken its place as the primary formative influence on American life, yet neither the nature nor the extent of this influence is generally understood. The immediate products of science are highly valued and research to provide more of them is handsomely supported. Yet we fail to understand, on the one hand, the sources of all these miracles, or to appreciate, on the other hand, the deep and pervasive social changes which they bring with them. Surrounded as we are by the products of science in the form of new materials, enormous power, numberless tools and conveniences, the age of science still lies in the future.

Science is a great unknown spirit that controls the destiny of this land but not, as yet, its thinking, builds its institutions but not its ideals, decrees its action but not its theories. Like a primordial Great Spirit science operates inexorably and almost inscrutably through the highly specialized talents of its priests but reveals itself to the populace only through their works. These are accepted gladly, the priests are revered, but the great spirit behind them remains unknown. It is the full revelation of that spirit and the fact that it envisages all of civilization and not merely useful gadgets that will bring us to the age of science. We are, I believe, at its threshold.

The past decade or two have permitted notable advances by science, both in its power and in its public recognition. Thirty years ago the great industries based on science were still infants. Research in the universities was still personal and precarious. Industrial research had not entered the calculations of the bankers and very few men of science were known by name to the public. In the "Civilization" of 1922, Robert

185

Lowie could write, "American science, notwithstanding its notable achievements, is not an organic product of our soil; it is an epiphenomenon, a hothouse growth. It is still the prerogative of a caste, not a treasure in which the nation glories." Since then we have had the Century of Progress Exposition at Chicago with its great Hall of Science. We have had the growth of industrial research laboratories from 400 to 2400 in number. We have the extraordinarily competent National Association of Science Writers, succeeding in the once impossible task of reporting the news of science day by day in papers and magazines. We have had popular and successful interpretations of scientific research in the drama, the radio, and the motion picture. Such efforts have made the work of scientists an accepted part of our culture.

This acceptance, however, is given only to the works of science and not to science itself. And it is given to these works because they are of economic value, not because they represent a powerful social force. There is, in fact, a growing opposition to science when it reveals itself as an uncontrolled power in altering our social structure. Attention therefore needs to be given to the opposite ends of the problem, both to the basic sources of scientific advance and to the inevitable social changes that it induces.

It is well to recognize at the outset that the word "science" has been so broadened that it covers totally different phenomena. "Science says" may refer to a specific fact, such as the wetness of water, or to a principle of nature such as the law of gravitation, or to an individual professor of science displaying his opinions. It may refer to one of the products of science such as the airplane or television. Finally, it may refer to that spirit and method of investigation which lies beneath all the great structure of science. If we are to understand the role of science in American life today it is important to distinguish between these various aspects.

Fundamentally science is a vast body of knowledge, of facts and principles, of organized technical information concerning this universe, recorded in a score of specialized vocabularies, each unintelligible even to scientists of other fields. This is the great treasure house of science, valueless in itself but enormously powerful when intelligently applied. Because of its size and complexity it is also the great obstacle to the understanding of science, since there is no royal road to its mastery.

As every one knows, this knowledge is accumulating at an increasing rate and in all parts of the world. As knowledge, it has no national characteristic. Waldemar Kaempffert has said, "Even now in Japan research is being conducted which will redound to the benefit of the Chinese. Even now the discoveries of scientists in capitalistic countries are freely donated to communistic Russia, which in turn is imparting to us new information about the stars, atoms and genes. Even fascist Italy and Germany are helping the very nations they profess to hate with research in medicine, biology and physics." The facts and principles of science are international and belong to every human being who can comprehend them.

To make them available complete public records are essential. It is characteristic of the unselfishness and international scope of the world of science that publication is the end of almost every research, and facilities for complete publication are available without cost to every scientist no matter how humble, how poor, or how isolated. Furthermore, centralized international records are kept of all new published material. In the single field of chemistry, for instance, *Chemical Abstracts* in 1937 required 3300 pages to publish no less than 44,000 abstracts of scientific articles, and in addition published abstracts of more than 19,000 patents. Every member of the American Chemical Society can have this journal on his desk twice a month, carefully and completely indexed so that any fact discovered anywhere automatically becomes the property of the world in a matter of weeks. The national character of such knowledge as distinguished from the international lies only in the efficiency of the organizations provided for disseminating such information and even here national boundaries are eliminated since *Chemical Abstracts,* though published in the United States, is read in all portions of the globe. The complete internationalism of science is inherent and is often cited as a model for other human activities—though the model is hardly valid, for selfishness is excluded merely because all scientific facts are intrinsically unemotional.

Not even the size of this international activity in fact-finding is generally known. In the field of chemistry the abstracts numbered above were gathered from more than 2800 different research periodicals, published in all parts of the world, and in 31 languages. Comparable figures could be cited for physics and biology. In addition to the research journals there are the review journals, annual reports of progress in various fields, annual tables of scientific data, etc. Following more remotely are innumerable monographs, handbooks and textbooks. The great industry of discovering and recording facts is flourishing and nowhere more so than in the United States.

This growing treasure of information owes its existence to a second factor of what is broadly called science, *i.e.,* to the scientists, to thousands of disinterested, intellectually gifted, highly trained men and women who are organized into hundreds of specialized scientific societies and are for the most part endowed with expensive laboratory facilities and frequently with powerful industrial and financial support. Men of leisure have toyed with science through the ages. The priests of Egypt, the philosophers of Greece, and the alchemists of mediæval times led the way. Since Isaac Newton, two and a half centuries ago, exemplified the scientific method, progress has been more solid but for two centuries was still in the hands of amateurs—noblemen like Lord Cavendish, clergymen like Joseph Priestley, statesmen like Benjamin Franklin. Germany led the way in the late 19th century by promoting scientific research in the universities, and until the time of the World War was far ahead of all other nations in encouraging the devotion of her scholars to this cause and rewarding them with titles and honors.

In the past twenty years, partly as a result of the lessons of the great war, opportunities for research have multiplied. Without resort to statistics, it is evident that a life of science in almost any American university is now not only pleasant but honored and productive. Laboratory facilities have been handsomely provided in both state and endowed institutions and well paid professorships are numerous. The American people are convinced of the ultimate usefulness of apparently useless knowledge and it is no exaggeration to say that in chemistry, physics, biology, medicine, astronomy, and many other sciences not only is the number of specialists greater in this country than in others but the quality is such that more students now travel to America than from America to Europe. The names of Einstein, Millikan, Langmuir, the Comptons, T. H. Morgan, McCollum, Hale, Tolman, G. N. Lewis, Shapley, Conklin, Carlson, Urey are of international distinction, and are comparable with those of any group in the history of science in any country.

Such men follow their individual genius and are organized only as they give stimulus and leadership to the many scientific societies. More immediately potent are the many thousands of scientists who are not personally known to the public and who are organized in efficient industrial laboratories under corporation control. They are specifically employed to investigate puzzling phenomena that stand in the way of industry and to apply new principles and facts to the pursuit of profit. American industrial science is largely a growth of the past fifteen years.

The World War gave rise to the National Research Council, organized in 1916 under the Congressional charter of the National Academy of Sciences. From its palace in Washington it has assisted pure science in all its many branches but its most effective activity has been the Division of Engineering and Industrial Research under a full-time director with offices in New York. Under the chairmanships of Frank B. Jewett, E. A. Sperry, D. C. Jackson, C. F. Kettering, and Vannevar Bush, and under the direction of Maurice Holland, this Division has been tireless in promoting the cause of research in American industry so that now industrial research laboratories spend some three hundred million dollars a year, which is looked upon as an annual insurance premium on industrial life. An average of 1.3 per cent of the capital assets of industry are spent each year upon research. This is an average for 45 industries and for all corporations from the smallest to the largest. Significantly the highest average is in the chemical industry where it amounts to 2.6 per cent of capital assets and this has proved to be almost depression-proof. On the other hand, in the textile industry research expenditures amount to about 0.7 per cent, only one-fourth as much, and this industry is at present in difficulties. Indeed, competition between great industrial corporations and between industries is now based more upon research and patent monopolies than on any other item. Thus there has arisen a great body of unknown scientists whose living depends on successful discovery and invention. Highly organized, and under competent management, they are an outstanding feature of American science. Their prototype is perhaps the group of 142 investigators and 76 assistants who comprise the Mellon Institute for Industrial Research at Pittsburgh, which spent more than a million dollars in 1937-38, and is housed in a Greek temple costing many millions of dollars.

In addition to these primary or producing organizations of science there are innumerable specialized scientific societies—the American Society for Testing Materials may be mentioned for example, or the American Physical Society, the Botanical Society of America, the Technical Association of the Pulp and Paper Industry, etc. All the sciences join in the American Association for the Advancement of Science, with some twenty thousand members, and their interest culminates in the National Academy of Sciences at Washington. There are also related organizations such as "Science Service," which is organized under the National Research Council, and provides the press and the public with reliable news of scientific progress.

Thus the world of science is well organized, self-conscious, and set apart from the current of life. Its eyes are not upon our people but on the universe; not on the present, but on the future. It is worthy of comment that these organizations for the production, application, and dissemination of science pursue their own ends with little reference to the good of society as such. Within the last year there have been protests and efforts to arouse the scientific world to the tremendous social consequences of their achievements. Such voices, however, cry in the wilderness. This is probably inevitable since the scientist could not succeed as such if his outlook were other than purely technical and totally disinterested, while under present conditions an industrial corporation can continue in existence only if it keeps its eye upon the dollar.

This then is the nucleus of the world of science—these many thousands of scientists plus their great store of precise knowledge, to which they add day by day and which they use to fashion those millions of useful products and processes that we meet at every hand. These products form the third general aspect of science and the one which is often confused with science itself. To the casual American science resides in the automobile, the airplane, the electric light, synthetic clothing, and orange juice.

It is neither necessary nor possible to list here the amazing variety of achievements of applied science in the past few years. Every one knows that the flood of useful inventions is still increasing and expects to read of a new miracle with almost every opening of the morning newspaper. Sometimes, as in the case of television, there is even public impatience at the delays in solving technical problems. The standard of living is constantly raised, convenience increases, time and distance are annihilated and costs become steadily less. Ten years ago an automobile cost $17.17 per horsepower; today the cost is only $8.45. In a decade the amount of coal needed to produce a unit of electricity was cut in half, so that today electric generators operating on steam compete successfully with water power. In the same decade the cost of rayon was reduced from $2.00 to 50 cents a pound, and that of cellophane from $2.65 a pound to 41.5 cents. Such a list could be extended almost indefinitely.

It is more important however to note the general appreciation that such progress in applied science depends on the two fundamental factors already mentioned, namely, a tremendous store of information in pure science and efficient laboratory organizations. It is no longer necessary to emphasize that the purely philosophical researches of Faraday, Hertz, J. J. Thomson, and Millikan underlie the inventions of Electrical Research Products, Inc., for instance, and that these in turn are the foundation for the developments of the American Telephone and Telegraph Company, the Westinghouse Electric and Manufacturing Company, the General Electric Company, and the Radio Corporation of America, in such fields as radio broadcasting and reception, television, the electric eye, and the talking motion picture.

There are two strange aspects of the public attitude toward this progress of invention. One is the innate feeling that we have somehow reached an end to these marvels and that we can now anticipate some stability. Yet the flood of invention grows year by year and it is almost certain that the next decade will show more startling changes than the past. The second is the failure to realize that the social consequences of invention do not stop with convenience, reduced cost, and mass production. After these direct consequences come broader ones such as changes in the habits of consumers, which in turn produce wide economic dislocation. Still later, grave changes occur in such social institutions as the family, the home, government, and the church. Finally, these in turn produce basic changes in political philosophy and social views. Such ideas change slowly it is true and this lag is responsible for much of the social turmoil and dislocation ultimately caused by science. If it were possible to realize not only that science will go on but that such fundamental social changes are also inevitable then surely science could become a benign instead of a disturbing force.

An earnest effort to call attention to this situation was made in 1932 by the President's Research Committee on Social Trends, and in 1937 by the Sub-Committee on Technology of the National Resources Committee. In anticipation of serious dislocations of industry and employment it recommends detailed study by planning agencies of such inventions as the mechnical cotton picker, air-conditioning, synthetic fibers and rubber, prefabricated houses, television, steep-flight aircraft, and tray agriculture. A far-sighted report on population problems has recently been issued and a report on the relation of the government to scientific research is now in preparation. The publication of these reports and the inclusion in Congressional appropriations of provision for continuing the study indicate that the time is approaching when the social structure will no longer be at the mercy of science. It may soon attempt to provide in advance for scientific progress, and will perhaps feel it necessary to guide the course of inventions or even to restrict their development until society has taken measures to absorb them with the minimum of unexpected readjustment. Such control, needless to say, will come from government or from social agencies and will have neither the interest in profit which characterizes the corporations nor the total disinterestedness which characterizes science as such. On the other hand, a governmental planning agency may accept inventions as inevitable and uncontrollable, and will then exert wide effort to guide and hasten the social readjustments which must surely follow. In any case foresight and planning are required if social dislocations due to technological advances are to be eliminated.

The three aspects of science now discussed—its facts and principles, its personnel, and its applications—are all superficial and visible from without. In an external sense they constitute science. Yet we do not approach the heart of the problem until we look at two other aspects, namely its spirit and its method. It is only when these are understood and accepted that the age of science will be upon us.

They are so distinct from what is commonly called science that they deserve a separate name—research. The word is inadequate and nondescript as compared with the German *Forschung*. This signifies exploration and penetration into the unknown, and implies too that it is not limited to science alone but has its place in all human affairs. Thus research is a much broader and deeper thing than science. Indeed, what we have defined as science above is the product of research in the study of nature. Civilization is concerned with science as the implement of research but the real source of civilization and its changes is in the research spirit and the research method. In searching for the sources of science and the nature of its power we must therefore give attention to research.

Strangely enough, even among scientists themselves, the research instinct is but vaguely understood. There is a general devotion in principle to the "purity" of research. This assures the disinterestedness of the scientist, and that is essential if his work is to be valid. But what is the appeal of a research career to young men and why do they increasingly aspire to it? There are a number of causes not the least of which is that applied science is well rewarded, and there is always the prospect that success in pure science will lead to a well-paying industrial position. This is nevertheless a minor factor, for more compelling still is the deep instinct to explore, to create, merely for the fun of it. It is fortuitous that American society is now willing to pay reasonably and sometimes handsomely for a life of disinterested service to research, yet for every one who is thus established there are many who lack all rewards except the spiritual satisfaction of having their own hands on nature herself and of creating values out of the unknown.

This is to say that research is essentially a game for amateurs, *i.e.*, for those who love it. It involves such deep human instincts as curiosity, workmanship, love of adventure and the joy of creation. These are present in every human being and are least disguised in childhood. The questions of children, their experiments and explorations are research itself, and, when properly guided, are the essence of a child's education in the world about him. Research achievements of high-school boys and girls in their science clubs, as revealed by the annual Junior Science Fair of the American Institute in New York, are a constant surprise to adults who think of science as dry and technical. The startling success of older amateurs in the field of radio, model aircraft, and motorless gliders in recent years is highly significant as showing increased popularity and respectability of amateurism in science even among those not technically trained. There is every reason to expect that the outright amateur in research will become much more important in the years ahead—not because he will produce more valuable science but because he will add to the richness and content of life by expressing his creative instinct through research.

Thus it is easy to see the kinship between research in science and geographical exploration, between Madame Curie and Columbus, between Pasteur and Magellan. Geography is but one of the sciences and the disappearance of the geographical frontier merely reveals the unlimited frontiers in all the other sciences. Slowly we come to understand that the call of the wild and the call of the unknown are the same and thus come to sanction those adventurous spirits who are irresistibly drawn to a life of research.

Adventure, however, is only a part of the research impulse; there is also the joy of creation. It is a strange misconception that creative art is synonymous with painting, sculpture and music, for it is obvious that there is much painting which is not art. In fact, the difference between art in painting and mere painting is creation, and the difference between research in science and mere science is also creation. Theodore Rousseau said long ago, "the artist does not paint the picture on the canvas, he merely lifts one by one the veils which hide it." It is in this sense that a research scientist is an artist, lifting the veils from the face of nature.

Here then is the ultimate source of science and of social change. Its motive is inherent in the human spirit, from childhood to old age. It has lived since prehistoric days, and once, long ago, lifted man above the apes. Slowly, through a thousand generations, it produced civilization.

Today it is stronger than ever and seems on the verge of more general recognition. In any case, there is no stopping it. Whether professional or amateur, research will go on, science will grow in power and civilization will change. If this is recognized, our intellectual climate may soon be freshened to a degree comparable only with the Renaissance.

Since this instinct to inquire and create is so deep and pervasive it is surprising that science became important only during the last century. The reason is, of course, that throughout history progress was by trial and error and that only recently has the effective technique of research been developed. This, now known as the "scientific method," is actually the research method and is a tool of profound importance to the human race.

The research method consists of four steps. In facing a problem, the first step is to make a guess as to the explanation or the proper solution; the second step is to test that hypothesis by a carefully controlled experiment; the third is to draw the logical conclusion concerning the hypothesis from the results of the experiment; the last is to accept this conclusion whether one likes it or not. Each of these steps involves very real difficulties for the untutored mind. The greatest of these is the exclusion of emotion. The "cold, calculating scientist" evokes little sympathy, but his thinking is successful because he has learned to think unemotionally. If it is easy for any one to offer a guess as to the solution of a cosmic problem, it is not easy to remember that this is only a guess. There is a strong temptation to take it for granted, to become devoted to it, to defend it to the death, or even to elevate it to the status of a religion. The first elementary step in research is to learn that an hypothesis has no value whatever until it is proved.

It is even more difficult to exclude emotion in the final step of the research method, namely the acceptance of logical conclusion. Man in general is still too emotional, too vain, too dominated by likes and dislikes, to venture this step in any matters that concern him deeply. This is the primary reason why science is set apart, why the research method is "scientific" rather than human. The method can be freely used only by those who are disinterested in its outcome. It can be used to explore remote galaxies, or the structure of the atom, but let it be applied to human affairs and at once the pressure of financial investments, of party loyalty, of nationalism, of religious devotion, or merely of established custom, prevent the acceptance of valid conclusions. Hence both at the beginning and at the end of the research method emotions tend to defeat it.

With this understanding of the research spirit and the research method we may now examine the present status of science. Why has progress been so slow in science itself? Why is science still so materialistic? Why has it so little to say about human affairs? The answers lie in the inherent limitations of the research method. Centuries were wasted in the investigation of false hypotheses, for the construction of an hypothesis is in itself not scientific but purely subjective and its nature depends wholly on the mental equipment of the thinker. It is for this reason that progress toward the truth was so slow in the early centuries. The ancient mind and the mediæval mind were unable to free themselves from the obsessions of their time. The correct hypotheses were literally inconceivable to them. This is no discredit to the intelligence of the philosophers. One of the most brilliant minds of all history—that of Sir Isaac Newton, whose accomplishments in mathematics, mechanics and optics opened the modern age—was utterly futile in the studies which occupied most of his eighty-five years, for the religious ideas of his time directed his thoughts toward non-physical problems and his hypotheses were theological rather than scientific. It is for this reason too that the earliest scientific progress came in those subjects which were not bound up with religious teachings. Progress was also easier in all subjects that were remote from man's daily experience. Artists, poets and priests, pondering over the nature of man himself, had so cluttered the scene with subjective and emotional views that objective analysis has only recently become possible. This then is one reason why the sciences of mathematics, astronomy, physics and chemistry were the first to develop. The farther we go from man himself the easier it is to devise hypotheses free from traditional error.

There is, however, another reason why the physical sciences have been the first to develop. This is the requirement of the research method that any hypothesis be tested under precise and rigorously controlled conditions. This too presented insuperable difficulties in the early centuries, for an experiment cannot be carefully controlled until all the pertinent conditions are understood and mastered. Thus, even today, completely controlled experiments in biology are rare. In order to attain full control, it is necessary to build a solid structure of knowledge and this in turn demands that one begin with the simplest possible case. Hence the sequence in which the sciences have developed, *i.e.,* mathematics, astronomy, physics and chemistry. The use of numbers, symbols and logic was needed before the mind could follow the simple motions of the planets. These in turn furnished the laws of motion and of force and thus, in the mind of Isaac Newton, established the basic concepts of physics. Thus, slowly, science progressed until by the end of the 19th century experiment after experiment had made plain a consistent though complicated mechanical universe.

By a similar painful progression through centuries of alchemy, through the establishment of basic chemical concepts by Priestley, Lavoisier and Dalton, to the enormous complexity of present chemical formulas, we now have an understanding of materials and the processes of material change which, quite aside from its usefulness, at last permits the actual control of valid experiments in biology.

That science has been primarily descriptive. Many of its triumphs, such as the isolation of disease germs, have answered no fundamental questions and have not been based on the underlying sciences. It is now evident, however, that the next great chapter in the progress of science will be biochemical. The past decade has already opened it, for such achievements as the synthetic manufacture of the vitamins, and of certain hormones, and the experimental isolation of the viruses of disease would be impossible, yes, inconceivable without using the best and most recent advances in physics and in chemistry. For instance, modern methods of protein chemistry enabled Doctor W. M. Stanley of the Rockefeller Institute for Medical Research, in 1935, to isolate the virus of tobacco mosaic disease as a crystalline protein. Two years later, in collaboration with Doctor R. W. G. Wyckoff, he used a high-speed centrifuge to isolate other less stable viruses, which have thus proved to be very large protein molecules, many times larger than those hitherto known. Although non-living in the usual sense of the word, they possess some properties that are characteristic of living things, for they have the capacity of reproduction and mutation when placed within certain living cells. Here we are at last on the thin border line between living and non-living and have a faint promise that within the next few years the nature of life itself will be revealed. There is probably no question more important to the human race, nor one filled with greater consequences for civilization.

It is because the research method demands controlled experiments and step-wise progress from the known into the unknown that we reach this point only now. It is for the same reason that our civilization is as yet properly called materialistic. We must master physics and chemistry before we can progress in the more complicated sciences. From the research point of view our host of new useful materials and our control of physical forces are quite incidental, yet they have made our age what it is. Materialism and mechanism hold sway because physics and chemistry hold precedence in logic. For the same reason, however, we may expect that this is a passing stage and that in another twenty years biological inventions may dominate our national life.

We need not here be concerned with the future. We live today in a civilization made by science, yet we are uncertain in our appraisal of science. We welcome the wealth it has produced but are not sure that we want more of it. There is some cry for cessation of further progress in science because the social structure seems unable to adjust to it. Has science increased human happiness? Shall we call upon scientists to control our destinies? Shall we insist that governments think scientifically and extend the successes of science to social problems? Such questions and their various replies are characteristic of social thinking in this age in that they do not elicit a scientific answer, *i.e.,* one on which all rational minds can agree. They are perhaps characteristic too in that they convey no meaning, for the word "science" is used as a loose personification and does not actually represent any valid meaning in terms of the analysis of science which we have undertaken here. It will be well to examine the problems of civilization more closely and in the light of the separate aspects of science.

If for the moment we restrict again the meaning of science to the facts, their applications, and to the scientists as such, in other words if we omit research from consideration, then it is apparent that in this restricted sense science is responsible for a myriad blessings and for almost as many evils. For example, improved methods of food production enable millions of human beings to exist who could not have been fed in previous centuries, but they are also responsible for the problems that come with great populations. The machines of transportation have annihilated distance but give us overcrowded cities. The progress of medicine has blessed us with an average life-expectancy of sixty years, perhaps double that of mediæval times, without providing for old age. It would be tedious to enumerate the evils of unemployment, maladjustment, war and ugliness which can well be laid at the doors of science. In that case it would seem to follow that more such science would only increase the difficulties. In fact, since science will certainly advance, we may predict that the difficulties will certainly increase.

What shall we say then of the statement of President Compton of the Massachusetts Institute of Technology: "The progress of our civilization will depend in a large way upon the opportunities which it provides for the advancement of science and the arts and for education in these fields." The apparent contradiction lies in the fact that Doctor Compton is thinking of research rather than of science as we have defined them here. If science is the knowledge and mastery of materials and forces and if scientists are those who control these materials and forces, then there is no need to call upon scientists or their science to solve our social problems. More machines will bring more unemployment; more production will bring more starvation; more speed will bring more confusion; more power will bring more destruction. The human race has not adjusted to present science and it will not more easily adjust to future science.

But if we speak of research instead of science the outlook is far different. If we could apply the spirit and method of research to social problems we should ultimately duplicate in society what has been accomplished in science. Social problems cry for the best use of the human intelligence and that, as science has shown, is the research method.

This is not easy. To study the social environment by the rigorous methods of science does seem hopeless at present. Even if present-day physics and chemistry are adequate to a thorough understanding of biochemistry we are obviously still far from understanding life, consciousness, or social consciousness, *i.e.,* biology, psychology, and sociology. It is impossible at present to conduct a rigorous experiment in psychology, *i.e.,* an experiment under such controlled conditions that every factor is kept constant except one, thus permitting the study of the effect of that one factor. Far more difficult is it thus to control social experiments. Every such experiment today is crude in that we cannot change one condition at a time but must perforce change many and follow our emotional preference in attributing the effect to one of several related causes.

Even if the research attitude could be adopted in its entirety, social processes cannot be accelerated and often there is not time to let an experiment run its course. If Clemenceau and Woodrow Wilson had been research men at heart and had signed the Versailles Treaty purely as an experiment they would not have lived to see the result. Yet if they had listed the assumptions on which they based that experiment, and had designed the experiment to test those assumptions, we might now be able to draw some conclusions with regard to them. Obviously it is not desirable thus to experiment with human beings. It is just as obvious, however, that blind, uncontrolled and meaningless experiments are constantly being performed with millions of human beings.

Nevertheless the situation is far from hopeless. In the development of any science a period of description and analysis precedes the beginning of experimentation. Often it is the precise and impartial description, quite free of tradition or prejudice, that leads to a brilliant new concept and thus to insight and truth. It is interesting to reflect that in the very infancy of biology Charles Darwin on a five-year cruise on the *Beagle* took precise and copious notes on the various forms of animal life which he encountered. From these notes emerged the concept of evolution, which is one of the few great milestones in biology. Such a preliminary and qualitative analysis of human society if it were wholly detached and free from tradition might well provide the basis for valid research, and might work a miracle in our present quandary.

To amplify the challenge without solving the problem, we may note here that one-third of this great nation lives on a standard of misery, that ten to fourteen million men are unemployed, that starvation and suffering bring ominous threats of revolt; and note on the same page that the accepted explanation is overproduction caused by science—too much food, clothing, and goods of every sort, and therefore not enough to go around. By the simplest standards of logic the explanation does not fit. Note then another guess, that means of distribution are lacking; but, note, also, that there are ample trains and trucks, that distances have been annihilated, that if this were war or an earthquake no one would suffer from lack of goods. Again, the explanation does not fit. It is impossible to escape the conclusion that our social theories are in error, being based on past centuries, and assume an economy of scarcity. Our economic machinery seems to work only when demand exceeds the supply and we have not faced the problem of devising machinery that works in the abundance under which we labor. Call, then, for a research mind to face the problem by the research method.

Note then upon another page what people want of life. Shelter and food and clothing, yes; but granted these, security, leisure, the opportunity to live quietly with loved ones, and an outlet for the creative spirit. These man wants, at least; there must be others not yet listed. But what does he do with his income under present conditions? He can buy food and shelter and clothing, but not the others. He can buy comforts, but not happiness. All industry and commerce is geared to sell him material things but not intangible values. Physics and chemistry have so triumphed that things to be bought with money seem eminently desirable, especially to him who sells them with the compelling power of advertising in print and over the ether waves. Yet note in our description that man has asked for bread and we give him a stone, asked for happiness and we give him comfort. Why? Merely, perhaps, because in a material civilization, however passing, money is the medium of exchange and therefore the standard of value. If science progresses beyond materialism and mechanics, science may devise values beyond the monetary. All these are questions, not answers; yet again the call is for more research.

Another page of our notebook we can give to morals. And again we find a welter of contradictions and confusion. The Christian virtues are in this day often contradictory, and simple logic says one or another must be meaningless. Justice and mercy are almost always incompatible. Work, plain labor, is extolled as a gift of God though it is obvious that machines do it better, that it is at best a means to an end and that end is leisure and recreation, both of which we still think of as sinful. Again a great contradiction between the traditions laid down by previous generations, and necessary under their conditions, with circumstances today completely altered by the power of science.

If such is the case with the major factors of civilization any impartial observer can record thousands of absurdities in minor matters. Millions of individual tragedies that reside wholly in the conflict between ancient but untenable social standards in an environment that was undreamt of by Plato, Jesus, Blackstone, or Thomas Jefferson. The ambitions of women, the disintegration of the home, the liberalizing of education, respectability of divorce, the unrestrained dreams of youth, the decline of the church, are all facts not accounted for in our inherited culture.

Viewing civilization thus dispassionately the research man reveals contradictions between fact and theory which should be obvious to all. It would be one of his functions faithfully to give preference to the facts without regard to his own feelings. He would also see emerging, as Darwin did, a few general hypotheses that were not previously recognized. He might, for instance, speculate that the advance of civilization has two major social effects, namely, an increasing dependence of every individual on all others in his economic status, and an increasing independence of each individual from all others in his personal life. He could then examine society from the point of view of the tentative hypothesis that economic freedom tends to disappear as civilization advances while personal freedom expands.

Such an hypothesis would be completely analogous to the basic hypotheses of physical or biological science and would be tested in the light of all available facts. Once thus established as universal, human plans and institutions would be judged in its light. The prospects of dictators and democracies could be reliably evaluated. Ultimately perhaps such social laws would be accepted by the intelligence of mankind even above the protests of their emotions and traditions.

Lest I be accused of proposing a social theory without the slightest right in knowledge or experience to do so I must emphasize that this is purely an hypothetical example. What social concepts will emerge from courageous social research cannot be predicted, nor can the institutions which will be based upon them. It is however certain that science has brought these problems upon us and that research must solve them.

Whether these researches be called science or not is of little moment. The important point is that science as we have defined it, *i.e.,* physical and natural science, can but inflame the crisis by enhancing the conditions which cause it. Scientists at work in their laboratories, like monks in ancient monasteries, cannot possibly attend to the repercussions of their work. To call on present science for help is futile. To call on politicians, lawyers, clergymen, economists, is equally futile until they have learned, from science perhaps, the spirit and method of research.

And so we stand in the midst of the twentieth century with material and mechanical science in our hands as a supremely powerful tool for producing wealth but helpless to give that wealth any meaning in terms of human happiness. There is but one possible solution. The same impartial unprejudiced method of study which has mastered the natural environment can also master our present social environment. Research must be conceived not as the technical study of electrons and atoms, *i.e.,* of nature, but as the best use of the human intelligence to improve the conditions under which we live. It is in science that research has proved its value. If civilization can learn that lesson from science it stands at the threshold of a great new epoch. Thus will science at last be justified when it has revealed its true spirit to humanity.

# CORPORALS OF INDUSTRY

## [*E. D. Kennedy*]

ONCE UPON a time (although not upon any very recent time) it was possible to think of American industry largely in terms of the American industrialist. If we date large-scale industry in this country from about the close of the Civil War and consider the period from 1860 to 1905 as the years in which American industry was growing up, we must admit that it grew up chiefly as a system of individual enterprises, dominated by individual enterprisers. Very often the original impetus for the enterprise was supplied by an individual invention or an individual idea. George Eastman, with his patents on a flexible, non-breakable, foolproof photographic film, was a very good example of the industrial one-man show. So was King Gillette, with his patent on the safety razor and George Westinghouse with his patent on the air brake. It may be argued that patent law was intended to protect inventors and not to promote monopolies but it cannot be denied that Mr. Eastman and Mr. Gillette and Mr. Westinghouse were indispensable items in the creation and the continuance of the concerns they founded.

Not all of the earlier business men had patentable ideas which resulted in legal monoplies. Frank Woolworth could not patent the five-and-ten; the Hartfords could not patent the A. & P. Even Mr. John D. Rockefeller, Sr., had no monopoly on the idea of becoming a monopolist and, at a later date, Mr. Ford's theory that autos were for everybody was not Mr. Ford's uniquely permanent possession. But this very situation made the personality and the ability of the Founder even more important than in the industries which, once established, were legally immune from the competitive theory. Not many of the early industrialists were burdened with any particular social sense. Mr. Rockefeller, in particular, operated with methods that would now be considered illegal although it must be admitted that the Sherman (anti-trust) Act was passed with the particular intention of putting the Standard Oil Trust, among others, on the wrong side of the law. But they were all extremely individualistic. They all started out with very little capital and they were all very good competitors —in fact, Mr. Rockefeller proved to be such a good competitor that it was almost impossible for any one to compete successfully against him. The personal equation was still the dominating factor in the corporation's success.

The pre-1900 period in American industry was also marked by a general shortage of capital, particularly by a shortage of capital for manufacturing concerns. Some of the financing methods of the early industrialists—Mr. Westinghouse is perhaps the most conspicious example—would today be regarded as certain suicide. They all had a weakness for very large and very short-term bank loans, secured primarily on the strength of their personal signatures. Even Mr. Ford got himself badly "extended" (as they call it) as late as 1920 and the bankers tried to take him over in the Panic of 1921. (That is why Mr. Ford still does not like bankers and created something of a sensation when, last April, he paid what appeared to be an innocuous courtesy visit to Mr. J. P. Morgan of 23 Wall Street.) But many of them were reckless by compulsion rather than by choice. Capital (in the sense of the large-scale investment of important money) has always fought shy of competition. Mr. Eastman had faith in the kodak and Mr. Gillette had faith in the safety razor and Mr. Westinghouse had faith in the air brake. But capital, as such, has no ego. It always follows the line of least resistance. And, before the 1900's, that line was the railroads. The railroads, in the earlier days, were considered something in the nature of an investment sure-thing. They were at least semi-monopolies; they had then no Interstate Commerce Commission to regulate them; they exercised a magnetic power upon the investing dollar. And since this country was, comparatively speaking, a poor country (even our railroads were originally financed only with very large contributions from European, particularly British and Dutch funds) by the time that public utilities had been financed, there was not much money left over for the manufacturer to be financed with.

So the manufacturer did his financing on a hand-to-mouth basis and in any period of bad business or hard times his mortality was very great. All the more credit, then, to the successful manufacturer who survived the occupational diseases of the period—all the more glory to American individualism in its most individualistic form. The struggle for existence was, to be sure, ruthless. The captain of industry was commonly an egomaniac and there were a good many self-made men to whose making such impersonal factors as the growth of the country furnished a large but unappreciated contribution. The labor policy of Mr. Carnegie and Mr. Frick was as unenlightened as (for example) the labor policy of Mr. Girdler and Mr. Grace; and if the risks of enterprise were great nevertheless the rewards of enterprise were enormous. Still, the old timer did take his chances and when he lost he did not fall back upon the complaint that the "investor has a right [whatever that may mean] to a return on his investment." And, in the beginning at least, it was largely with his own money that his chances were taken. Finally, he commonly did not indulge in much collaboration with others of his kind because he was determined to achieve a No. 1 position which could not well be reached by coddling his competition.

By about the close of the 19th century, however, the banker was beginning to consider the manufacturing industries as potentially profitable investments, provided of course that certain hazardous aspects of manufacturing could be wholly or even partly removed. There were more capital sources to be tapped and so many railroads had been so badly overcapitalized that epidemics of railroad receiverships were already old stories on financial pages. Besides, purely individual enterprise had produced only one Mr. Rockefeller; in most branches of production there were several more or less equally large and equally able competitors who could not survive an industrial free-for-all in which the ultimate winner would probably not be able to survive his victory. But if the leading competitors could be persuaded to collaborate (as through, for instance, a merger) the situation would be very different indeed. Hence the Consolidation Movement—a movement whose most conspicuous success came when the Carnegie Steel Company merged with the Federal Steel Company and eight other corporations into the United States Steel Corporation. The merged companies owned about two-thirds of the steel-producing facilities of the United States.

The Steel Corporation was, of course, only one of the many mergers that blossomed during this period. Some of the consolidations went a good deal further toward rounding up all the production facilities in their particular fields. The American Can Company, for instance, was organized with more than 90 per cent of the tin-can production of the country. A tin can is a steel can with a very thin tin coating; "tin plate" was and is a basic steel product and the original American Can promoters probably put the company together with the thought of selling it to U. S. Steel. As things worked out, the Steel Corporation never did take over the can company, partly because the Steel Corporation was worried about being prosecuted as a trust[1] and would evidently have been much more monopolistic if it had controlled not only half the steel business but all the can business as well. Still, the Can promoters, what with underwriting commissions, independents bought up by means of giving them not cash but stock in the new company, stock watering, and various other consolidating devices then (and now) common, did very well. The independents signed agreements not to re-enter the tin-can business after the merger was completed, and the promoters took care of any possible over-capacity that they might have accumulated by immediately scrapping more than two-thirds of the newly-acquired factories. Meanwhile the U. S. Rubber Co., the American Tobacco Co. and various other outfits, usually called U. S. This or American That were formed in much the same manner and with the same abhorrence of the competitive principle that the investor (as opposed to the personal industrialist) has always shown.

In most cases, to be sure, the monopolistic companies so organized did not become complete monopolies. After all, the Sherman Act (1890) had already been passed; Mr. Rockefeller had already become extremely unpopular; and a thoroughly Republican President (Theodore Roosevelt) was beginning to grumble about "malefactors of great wealth." So companies like the Steel Corporation did not try to crush their competitors. In fact, they encouraged them and so effectively that today U. S. Steel does, not two-thirds, but hardly more than one-third of the steel business. To encourage competitors was not only good policy. It was also—as long as price competition did not become too acute—good business. And Mr. Morgan was, after all, no fly-by-nighter and did take a keen and permanent interest in the profit possibilities of his ungainly corporate child.

The big company of the Consolidation Era was usually not a very efficient company, which means, essentially, that other producers in the same industry could produce at the same or at lower costs. For in order to get the bulk of the capacity, the Big Company usually had to take over a lot of dubious plant at fancy prices. Furthermore, its production facilities were not centralized; there is a good deal of truth in the proposition that the absentee landlord is never as close to his operations as the owner manager; and the consolidations were usually accompanied by a murderous load of stocks and bonds, on the former of which it was desirable to pay dividends and on the latter of which it was necessary to pay in-

[1]It was prosecuted in 1912 but as it could readily show that since its formation it had not extinguished, or attempted to extinguish, competitive steel companies, the Supreme Court finally decided that bigness, *per se*, was no evil.

terest. Therefore, in order to supply returns on its investment, the monopoly corporation had to allow itself a good healthy profit margin which meant, of course, that it had to price its output high.

According to the classic theory of competition, this handicap should have proved insuperable. But the outstanding characteristic of the classic theory of competition is that—in the fields we are now discussing—its elimination has been practically complete. In the first place, remember that there is no such thing as a really "little" company in the steel industry (or in copper, or lead, or telephones, or electrical equipment or other basic industries which require a large investment of money per dollar of output). Relative to U. S. Steel, National Steel is a "small" company, but its assets nevertheless come to over $200,000,000. And it was much more profitable for the middle-sized company to charge as much as the biggest company and take advantage of its lower cost by making a higher percentage of profit per sale. Suppose that the middle-sized company did decide to undersell the big company. In the first place, it would not have greatly expanded its sales, because it could not add new capacity overnight and you can't sell steel that you haven't the facilities to make. In the second place, it could hold its price advantage only at the pleasure and on the sufferance of the top company. For if its capacity was, or even promised to be, a serious threat to the No. 1 corporation, the No. 1 corporation would have to meet the No. 2 company's price at no matter what cost. The probable result would be a good old-fashioned price war in which the biggest company would certainly suffer, but the other company might very possibly not survive.

But there was not much temptation to indulge in industrial bickerings. For if the smaller company could show a good profit per dollar sale and a sizeable net income, it could grow by reinvesting whatever of its profits it did not pay out as dividends, and its good earnings record would also attract new capital. As long as the total market for the product was increasing (and until 1929 most industries assumed that an expanding market was one of the pleasanter certainties of industrial life) both the big company and the second-flight group increased their business and the big company had no particular complaint. For all hands, therefore, a live-and-let-live policy had obvious advantages. And the modern steel industry in this country today is universally credited with having grown up under what is called the "price umbrella" held over it by U. S. Steel. There is only one trouble with these producers' price umbrellas. They obviously cannot be designed to cover the *customer* too.

I have gone into some detail on this matter of price competition (or rather lack of price-competition) because the principle does not seem to be generally understood. The public still thinks largely of monopolies in the Rockefeller sense, and does not understand that a group of companies, on strictly a "gentleman's agreement" basis, may create what amounts to an *industrial* monoply with all manner of ostensible competition between its members. Furthermore, although companies may not compete on prices, they usually continue to compete on costs. They do not care about selling for less, but they do care about producing for less. Even the Steel Corporation is no longer the unwieldy mastodon that it used to be. Production has become relatively concentrated in the Chicago and Pittsburgh areas; the company has had both the will and the means to be the industry's largest investor in new and modernized plant; the No. 1 steel company is perhaps a better competitor than it has ever been before. But it does not believe in price competition and neither does any other steel company of appreciable size. If steel is quoted at $37 a ton, the figure holds equally for U. S. Steel, Bethlehem, Republic, Youngstown, National, Inland and all the rest.

And the same situation also applies to similar industries—indeed, when production is even more concentrated, prices are even more stiff. The two major sulphur producers have sold sulphur for $18 a ton since 1926. The only nickel producer of any importance (International Nickel) has sold nickel for 35 cents a pound since the same period. The only United States producer of aluminum has held aluminum at between 20 and 24 cents a pound for the past ten years. Copper is an example of a commodity with a price structure which cracks up when times are bad, but leaps up when they are good. Three companies—Kennecott, Anaconda and Phelps Dodge—produce about 80 per cent of the (North American) copper supply. (A 4 cents-a-pound tariff keeps foreign copper out of this country.) Copper costs vary at every copper mine, but most of the copper in this country could profitably be produced to sell for not more than about 9 cents a pound. (During the NRA period and until the autumn of 1936, copper prices were pretty steady at 9 cents to 10 cents a pound.) But in "good" times copper is sold without the slightest relation to its cost. Throughout 1928, for instance, copper was quoted around 15 cents a pound, and the copper companies did very well. But their customers (especially the auto maker, their second biggest customer) were also doing very well and in March, 1929, the copper companies boosted the price to 24 cents a pound—and kept it around 18 cents the rest of the year.

When 1929 prosperity blew up, the price of copper did not long survive it, and in 1933 copper was down to 5 cents a pound. Then the NRA pegged it at 9 cents, where, as I have said, it stayed for over a year.

But the industrialist, like the Bourbons, learns nothing and remembers nothing. In October, 1936, copper was up to 10 cents. But the so-called recovery was well under way and the copper industry thought it might as well get in on it. By March, 1937, the price of copper was up to 16 cents—a 60 per cent increase totally unjustified by increases in wages, taxes or other costs. This time the customers (also the President) protested louder and sooner, but in 1937—even with its bad last quarter—the two largest copper companies made twice what they had made in 1936 and the whole industry was operating on a strictly boom-time basis. Of course, the copper man will explain that he really doesn't make very much on his investment, and that his good years have to balance his bad years, and that his mines are liable to run out at any minute anyhow. Most of his hardluck story is weirdly exaggerated, but the immediate point is that price boosts such as swept the industry in 1929 and again in 1937 could never have occurred in an industry in which the lowest cost producer tried to sell at the lowest prices.

It may be objected that if an entire industry overprices its output, new and more genuinely competitive industrial units will appear. This is another piece of reasoning which dates from Adam Smith and which also retains nothing more than an historical importance. Remember that if you and I decided to go into the copper business, we should have to raise several hundred million dollars to make any impression on existing capacity. But anybody who was interested in putting his money into the copper business would put it into one of the existing large companies, which are always happy to get new capital and which can offer the investor the innumerable advantages connected with long experience in the business, elegant trade and financial connections—everything that we could offer him and much that we could not. When the Du Ponts went into the auto business with some of their war-time profits did they start their own auto company? They certainly did not. They bought a large piece of General Motors. When the Morgans decided to get into the building field, did they start the J. P. Morgan Cellar-to-Garret Corp.? No indeed. They bought control of Johns-Manville, an outfit which dates from 1901 and which the late Thomas F. Manville ran for almost twenty-five years as a strictly one-man show. It takes a large accumulation of capital to get into a big industry in a big way. And capital prefers the safe course of deepening existing channels to the dangerous method of trying to carve out new beds. Nowadays, industry is not a matter of new men starting new businesses. It is a matter of new capital expanding old businesses. You do not meet the American Indian on the warpath any longer. And the American individualist is just as hard to find.

It is true that the Consolidation Era which, as we have said, commenced about 1890, did not make headway in all branches of industry and could only be applied to certain types of industry most favorable to its development. Retailing, for instance, is essentially a local business and the retail chain store—however much it may damage the local "independent"—progresses only to the extent that it sells for *less* than the prevailing prices. Construction too has remained largely a local, small-scale business. Indeed, it is one of the very few major industries in which corporations have not almost entirely supplanted individual proprietors and partnerships. But what perhaps overshadowed the monopoly tendency in the first twenty years of the present century was the development of new industries which for some time persisted in operating on an individualistic basis.

Most important of these industries was, of course, the automobile, upon whose wheels the major portion of our post-war industrial boom is often said to have been carried. It should be noticed, however, that the auto business, which got under way about the time when monopoly was in its fullest flower, tried to start as a respectable, orderly, monopolistic industry. A man named George Selden, who never had manufactured a motor car, nevertheless had gone to the trouble of taking out patents on one; and when the pioneer auto makers began turning out machines, the Selden patents were promptly held over their heads. The result was a patent pool (with royalties for Selden) and close-knit association of auto manufacturers who, through their joint control of the Selden patents, were determined to keep the auto field for themselves. But certain individualistic auto makers, notably Henry Ford, ignored the Selden patents in the field and fought them in the courts, with the result that the monopoly was broken up.

For some time thereafter, the auto field remained wide open, with the result that scores of auto makers went into—and out of—business. Furthermore, large-scale capital kept out of the motor car industry, which it considered to be in the hands of a group of maniacs headed by a freak. Even though the consolidation movement had already appeared in the auto business, that movement (the organization of General Motors by William C. Durant) was largely the work of a brilliant shoestringer, more interested in putting things together than in making them go. It was only after the war when Mr. Durant was succeeded by E. I. du Pont de Nemours that General Motors acquired the size and stability of U. S. Steel and the auto got (largely) into the hands of conservative capital and became a medium in which even the most cautious dollar (and all dollars are cautious) could invest itself. Meanwhile, the survivors of the early free-for-all—Willys, Erskine, Nash, Macauley—emerged as a new group of individual industrialists, representing another triumph of competition, individual enterprise, the American system, and all the rest of it.

The movies went through exactly the same process on a slightly smaller scale. Here, too, an early patent pool was broken up by a group of independents; here too competition was free and capital was not interested; here too a group of survivors—Adolph Zukor, Marcus Loew, Nicholas Schenck, Samuel Goldwyn, Carl Laemmle and William Fox— carried on the tradition of individual big business until a time when even the tradition began to vanish.

The movie industry furnishes an excellent example of the clash between the individualist and the monopolist because the movie industry was changing over from silent to talking pictures in the 1927-29 boom period, when it was very difficult to tell the difference between an investor and a speculator and when capital, for once in its long life (but only once), showed a certain willingness to take a chance. The result was that the individual movie producer was able to get money—but he was not able to get along with it on permanently friendly terms.

Consider, for instance, the case of William Fox. Mr. Fox got into the movies via the nickelodeon. As a producer, his pictures were more popular than distinguished—his leading actress being, for a long time, Theda Bara. Nevertheless (or perhaps therefore) Mr. Fox prospered, and when the movies turned into the talkies Mr. Fox became the biggest show on earth by accumulating movie theatres until at one point he owned nearly 1000 moving picture houses in the United States. In 1929, following the death of Marcus Loew, he bought 660,000 shares of Loew's Inc., thus acquiring control not only of the Loew theatre chain but also of Metro-Goldwyn-Mayer, the Loew's picture-making affiliate. In the spring of '29, he bought control of Gaumont, the greatest British theatre chain. The Loew stock (which the government later claimed was purchased in direct though probably unconscious violation of the Clayton Act) cost about $70,000,000. The Gaumont deal cost another $20,000,000.

Meanwhile, Mr. Fox had not only bought some 700 other theatres but had also been to the expense of wiring them for sound.

During this period, Mr. Fox did not rely entirely upon private financing. He had a banker—Halsey, Stuart & Co., a Chicago and New York house which had been previously connected mostly with public utilities and had been one of the sources of Mr. Insull's capital. But Mr. Fox was expanding so rapidly and needed so much money in a hurry that he went in for personal borrowing, and had run up an indebtedness of about $90,000,000, all in short-term bank loans that were bound to come due before they could be retired out of earnings, no matter how great those earnings might be. The two largest individual creditors were Halsey, Stuart and the American Telephone & Telegraph Co. (which through a subsidiary, was one of the large producers of talking-moving mechanism).

There was nothing necessarily fatal, or even critical, about the position of Mr. Fox in the spring of 1929. Halsey, Stuart had already sold the investing public large quantities of Fox securities (although Mr. Fox, through the device of marketing non-voting stock, kept the control of the business in his own hands) and the obvious procedure was to get out another big block of Fox stock. With the resulting cash, the banks could be paid off. But the obviously necessary financing was never done. Mr. Fox claims that the bankers put off the financing until they could get him in a hole and take over his "great enterprise." The bankers claim that Mr. Fox was hard to get hold of, unwilling to allow examination of his books, and that the Gaumont deal had been undertaken without their knowledge. There was also an auto accident which put Mr. Fox on the shelf during most of the summer of 1929. At any rate, and for whatever reasons, the Fox financing was postponed until the stock market crash in October made it impossible for anybody to do any financing, no matter how sound his proposition or how low his price.

At this point (December, 1929), Mr. Fox rather recklessly signed an agreement whereby three trustees were to be allowed to vote his (controlling) stock. One trustee was a Halsey, Stuart man, another a Telephone man, and the third was Mr. Fox. The arrangement of course left Mr. Fox in a minority and when the other trustees started to do things of which Mr. Fox did not approve, the whole business got into the courts, with everybody calling everybody else a liar and the situation complicated by the United States Government's objections to the Loew deal. Eventually Mr. Fox was paid some $15,000,000 cash to surrender his personal holdings and in the spring of 1930 a group of bankers tried to sell the new securities which should have been marketed in the spring of 1929. The investors did not want the stock; two of the banking houses (Pynchon & Co. of New York and West & Co. of Philadelphia) which tried to market it lost so much money that they permanently shut up shop; and the company (General Theatres Equipment Inc.) which had taken over the Fox shares wound up in a reorganization. Nevertheless, Mr. Fox and his "great enterprise" (as he himself invariably called it) were permanently separated. And since the spring of 1930, Fox films and Fox theatres have been monuments to individual enterprise, American initiative, Adam Smith capitalism, etc., to about the extent that Cleopatra's needle might now be considered a monument to Cleopatra.

The same trend has also marked the motor industry. Here, in the flush period of the good times, one important new factor—Chrysler—added itself to the automotive ranks. But since the Depression the auto Big Three—General Motors, Ford and Chrysler—have sold about 87 per cent of all United States autos and have concentrated their production on three cars—Chevrolet, Ford and Plymouth. Meanwhile the "independents" have practicaly disappeared. It is hard now even to remember when the Studebaker, the Hupmobile, the Hudson and the Nash were important factors in the auto scene; the Packard hung on through the worst of the Depression and in the so-called Recovery period (late 1936 and early 1937) managed to revive sharply through the introduction of two models which, for Packard, were very low-priced cars (one just below, the other just above $1000). The independents were forced out of business by the public rather than by their larger competitors—that is, they were not designed for the mass production of cars in the bottom-price field. The "squeeze" on the medium-priced car was apparent even before the boom ended—General Motors had put Chevrolets out in front as early as 1927 and Mr. Chrysler was ready to push the Plymouth as soon as the Depression set in. Mr. Ford was just where he always had been, except that he had to move over and give his competitors a big part of the bed. But auto makers who could not crash the low-price field either disappeared completely or lost practically their entire markets to G.M., Chrysler and Ford. In 1929, General Motors made about 33 per cent of the United States auto; Chrysler about 9 per cent. Now Motors makes over 40 per cent and Chrysler about 25 per cent. As for profits, Motors turned in a 1936 net of $238,000,000 and a 1937 net of $196,000,000. *Since* 1929 (that is, during the Depression years only), it has made a total profit of a little more than $1,000,000,000; and in both 1936 and 1937 it made more than 30 per cent on its capitalization. This is not a triumph of individual initiative. It is a triumph of protected capital.

It should also be noticed that while auto men and movie men were upholding individualistic tradition during the boom·period, monopolistic practice also was making more rapid and more permanent advances. Woolworth is dead, Gillette is dead, Eastman is dead; their successors— now endowed with ample capital—have been at the most administrators, themselves owning no appreciable interest in their concerns. The new management problem is not to create profits by creating markets but to preserve profits by cutting costs. The current head of Woolworth's, a Mr. Deyo, owes his claim to fame chiefly to the fact that he advocated the principle of putting 20-cent and 25-cent merchandise into the traditionally "five-and-ten" cent stores. This idea sprang from the early days of the recovery, particularly from the NRA period which pegged prices on manufactured products and made it difficult for Woolworth to operate on a 10-cent top. The idea was sound enough, but the fact that competing chains (like Kresge) were already using it was what forced it on Woolworth's (and Deyo's) attention.

In Mr. Gillette's later years, the active operating head of the company was a Mr. Fahey, who had been an office boy, or some such humble employee, back in the days when Mr. Gillette started to make his razor blades, and thus had a kind of seniority right to the top job. Mr. Fahey was irked by the fact that innumerable *blade* manufacturers had sprung up with blades[2] that fitted Gillette razors. Also, these "imitators" had no difficulty in undercutting Gillette prices, which were based on its original monopoly privilege.[3] One day a gentleman named Gaisman, who had invented (and patented) a razor and razor-blade combination· in which perforations in the blade fitted projections in the razor, tried to sell Mr. Fahey his bright idea (which he called the Probak razor). Mr. Fahey turned Mr. Gaisman down, and shortly afterwards Gillette appeared with a blade which was remarkably

---

[2]The money in the razor business lies in the blades, which furnish the "repeat" business on which profits are founded.

[3]The original Gillette patents had run out and a good many "imitators" were not much concerned whether they had or not. Like speakeasy owners in Prohibition days, they made lots of money until the law caught up with them, then disappeared from view to start a new business, under a new name, but with their old customers.

similar to Mr. Gaisman's. Whereupon Mr. Gaisman sued for patent violation, and after a period of wrangling there was a sudden Gillette-Probak merger, in which Mr. Fahey disappeared and Mr. Gaisman became head of the Gillette company.

As for Kodak, Mr. Eastman had practically retired from the company for some years before his death. (He shot himself in 1932.) His successor was a man named Stuber, another old timer who had been with Kodak since before 1900. Mr. Stuber seems to have been a very pleasant gentleman who certainly did not get the Kodak company into any difficulties. To be sure, Kodak had already been the subject of two anti-trust investigations and by 1932 was already selling about 85 per cent of the amateur[4] photographic film in the United States and about 75 per cent of such film throughout the world. Mr. Stuber was himself succeeded by a Mr. Lovejoy, who came up through the accounting and financial side of the business and was born only several years before the establishment of the Kodak company. The identity of the heads of these companies and others like them does not very much matter (unless they are so conspicuously incapable that they cannot make money even with a semi-sure thing). But they shine in the reflected glory of their predecessors, and acquire stature from their office.

While personal management was thus disappearing from some of the older one-man concerns, the epidemic of mergers, holding companies and investment trusts which distinguished the later 1920's further accented the role of capitalism and subordinated the role of management. The most conspicuous "arrivals" of the boom period were financial men, not operating men. The Van Sweringen brothers and Insull were, for example, more akin to Wall Street than to either the railroad business or the electric light and power business. In a sense, they certainly did represent individual initiative, but their efforts were not precisely constructive and their "empires" were extremely ephemeral. Their financial "management" depended too much upon the legerdemain of pulling holding companies out of their hats.

---

[4]The inevitable Du Ponts had broken into the professional (*i.e.*, movie) film industry and very successfully too. Photographic film was a nitrocellulose product chemically not very different from either the "gun cotton" or the rayon on which the Du Ponts had previously specialized; and the Du Ponts were rich enough, tough enough and capable enough to enter the movie-film business and make a big dent in this branch of the Kodak business. Amateur film, however, they have let strictly alone, most of Eastman's small competition coming from an outfit called Agfa Ansco, which is partly owned by I. G. Farbenindustrie, the big German chemical "trust." Germany makes good film, good lenses, good cameras; has prevented Kodak from dominating the German film business and, indirectly, supplies some competition to Eastman even in the U. S. A.

The effect of mergers in reducing competition is obvious enough, although the merger-minded financiers had to be careful not to 'merge competitive companies into organizations which might arouse the government's somewhat out-of-date suspicions of monopoly in the old-fashioned Rockefeller sense. A good example of how even an unsuccessful merger promoted a considerable unity of ownership without any corresponding unity of management is seen in the career of Cyrus Eaton, another Clevelander who, like the Van Sweringens, went empire-building, but never quite attained the emperor's crown.

Mr. Eaton, commonly known as Cyrus the Great, had notions about a combination of Midwestern steel companies which would excel Bethlehem and rival United States Steel. The chief Midwestern steel outfits are Republic, Youngstown, Inland and National. Mr. Eaton got a considerable interest in Republic, which he combined with four other companies, and got Mr. Tom Girdler to run. Then, he got money to buy into Youngstown, and started to promote a Youngstown-Republic merger. He was also commonly supposed to have acquired considerable holdings in Inland, although this company was supposedly controlled by members of the Block family.

The Youngstown-Republic merger did not appeal to Bethlehem. The big companies do not mind having smaller companies get along, but they do mind their getting too big for comfort. So Bethlehem also began to court Youngstown, got the head of Youngstown (a Mr. Campbell) on its side, and initiated a counter-merger proposal. This idea of course upset Mr. Eaton no end and one of the big industrial battles which novelists love and business men avoid took place. The situation came to a head following the 1929 market break, with its consequent reduction in the price of Mr. Eaton's investment holdings. What with trying to get more Youngstown stock (to block the merger) and also with trying to supply more collateral for his loans, Mr. Eaton eventually discovered that the law of gravity sometimes operates disastrously when young men venture out upon the flying trapeze. Eventually Mr. Eaton lost his fight in the company (that is, the majority of the Youngstown stockholders approved the Bethlehem merger) but won it in the courts (which have a great respect for the rights of minorities, particularly of propertied minorities). But in the process, Mr. Eaton encountered financial ruin.

The result was that neither Bethlehem nor Republic got Youngstown. But various banks—particularly the Chase National of New York, the

Cleveland Trust and the Union Trust (Cleveland)—which had been financing Mr. Eaton, took over (at auction prices) blocks of his Republic, his Youngstown and his Inland stock—repaying themselves well for the loans he could not meet. This may account partly for the solid front which the "Little Steel" companies showed last summer against the C. I. O. At any rate, the same banking groups have a large interest in all three companies and would be extremely displeased if any one of them should show any disposition to cut the others' throats. The same tendency was obvious in the railroad industry when, during the period of rail-consolidation rumors so prevalent during the end of the boom, the Pennsylvania bought heavily into the Wabash, the Norfolk & Western and the New Haven. And the Delaware & Hudson has bought so much New York Central stock that Central's dividends would be a basic factor in the D. & H. earnings except that Central has not paid any dividends since the purchase was made.

Here again it is evident that the personalities of the operating executives are not the critical factors in corporate affairs. Mr. Pelley, under whose direction the New Haven ran into a receivership, is now head of the rail operators' association, has become the official voice of railroad capital in its demands for government relief, its protest against federal taxes, its attempt to reduce railroad wages. Mr. Loree, who was head of the Delaware & Hudson during the consolidation era, but whose consolidation ideas never met with ICC approval, recently retired—at the age of eighty—from active management of the road. Offhand, I do not know who succeeded him, or who succeeded Mr. Pelley either. For it never pays to keep track of superfluous information and the identity of the usual corporation executive has long since ceased to be a matter of any importance at all.

It is for this reason that the current concern for individual enterprise, personal initiative, the owner-manager, and the free system of competition so acutely pains the informed observer. It is true that most corporations have remained small corporations. There are about 475,000 corporations in this country. At least 470,000 of them are relatively small, relatively localized, and relatively subject to one-man control. But the other 5000 dominate the mining, fabricating and utility industries, and also the manufacturing industry with respect to manufacturing corporations which turn out their product by mass production and on a national scale.

It is not possible to draw a hard and fast line between competitive companies and monopolistic companies. But it is possible to show that the profits of American industry are becoming more and more concentrated in a few monopolistic hands, and that the deficits of American industry are being almost entirely borne, as a group, by its multitude of small and scattered units.

In 1925, for instance, almost two-thirds of the net profit of all American corporations (of which there were then about 385,000) was made by about 1100 companies which made a minimum of $1,000,000 a year and averaged about $4,500,000. All the other corporations (taken as a whole) had an average profit of about $6900.

In 1929, there were 1350 companies in the million-dollar profit class. That year, they made four-fifths of the net profit of all corporations (which had risen to about 450,000). Their profits were over $5,000,000 each, while the profits of all other companies averaged about $3800.

Since 1929, all except about 1000 of the biggest corporations have shown, as a group, a net deficit which at the end of 1935 totalled over $17,000,000,000. The so-called Recovery period in 1937 was confined almost entirely to a handful of companies in the steel, basic metals, auto, machinery, electrical equipment, petroleum and public utility fields. In the present year, even these companies (except the light and power concerns and perhaps the petroleum producers) will have difficulty in making money; and the run-of-mine company is heading straight back to 1932.

The prosperity of the monopolistic companies has not been accompanied by general prosperity. Concentrated in raw material and manufacturing industries, they keep prices so high that the distributor (*i.e.,* the wholesaler and particularly the retailer) is forced to charge high prices, not on account of his profits but on account of his costs. Some of them are large individual employers of labor, but employment in the manufacturing industry (where some of the most outstanding of the monopolistic companies are concentrated) reached its high spot in 1920. The whole boom of the 1920's was accomplished (through mechanization) with an actual (manufacturing) decline in dollar wages and number of men employed. Smaller companies either cannot afford wholesale mechanization or operate in industries (like department stores) in which the application of machinery is necessarily limited. But they cannot much increase employment because they are not making the profits on which growth depends.

As for the general public, the farmer—who sells in a competitive market but buys in a monopolistic market—was on the edge of insolvency even before the boom ended, and has been totally engulfed by the depression years. The industrial worker has been plagued by unemployment ever since 1929. In 1932, there were 16,000,000 unemployed. At the best part of the 1937 recovery, there were somewhere between 7,000,000 and 9,000,000 unemployed. Since September, 1937, close to 4,000,000 more workers have lost their jobs, bringing the total of unemployed dangerously near to its all-time top. Besides, manufacturers have learned that part-time employment holds down unemployment totals while permitting payrolls to drop almost as rapidly as if complete unemployment were resorted to. In the first quarter of 1938, for instance, the Steel Corporation had 86 per cent as many men working for it as it had in the first quarter of 1937. But its payroll was only 66 per cent as much as it had been in the previous spring.

The professional man—the doctor, lawyer and teacher, for example—knows that while he may still be doing business, he can no longer collect his bills. And the majority of the more dispensable professionals—such as artists and actors—have been practically public charges since the depression set in.

Whether a system of individual enterprise, free competition, and the other classic concepts of the orthodox capitalist theology would have produced a better result, I do not know. Talk about unscrambling the monopolies is obviously foolish, as most of them would have a hard time recalling the elements which originally joined to compose them, and competition is, after all, largely a state of mind. Mr. Rockefeller's oil company was dissolved in 1912, but a whole group of modern oil men were last winter convicted of price-fixing: and the petroleum industry is the outstanding example of a great many very large and very prosperous companies which do not need centralized management to keep them from stepping—in a price way—upon each other's toes. Furthermore, the country was far from prosperous when a multitude of small and medium-sized companies fought for business on a price-cutting basis and in the process cut each other's throats.

But the monopolistic nature of companies like Anaconda Copper, United States Steel, General Motors, Owens Illinois, United States Shoe Machinery, General Electric and many another should be clearly recognized. These companies are the result of great accumulations of capital;

in good times they overproduce to make high profits and in bad times they underemploy to preserve profits which are still very considerable and which smaller and more competitive companies cannot register at any time. They are exactly like the railroads, the light and power companies, and the utilities, and like these so-called "natural" monopolies they should submit to regulation. That regulation might take the form of limitation of income in the shape of maximum prices—just as railroad and other utility "prices" (rates) are regulated in the general good. More effective, however—because less deflationary—would be a stiffly graduated income tax with the rates on corporate profits applied on the same basis as has long been established with rates on personal incomes. The growth of some of our mammoth companies would undoubtedly be somewhat checked, but it is precisely their excessive growth that has made our corporate (let alone our social) structure such a lopsided and one-sided affair.

Meanwhile, the spokesmen of the monopolists have adopted the technique of identifying big business with all business—of pretending that anything which might damage the Aluminum Co. or the present Standard of New Jersey is just as damaging to the neighborhood butcher or the corner druggist. They call upon economic principles which they themselves have made no longer applicable. They appeal to an industrial way of life which began to weaken in 1890 and which was almost entirely destroyed by 1929. They ignore the fact that they were completely in the saddle during the days of Harding, Coolidge, and the first year of Hoover. They forget that they were still "unregimented" during the last three years of the Hoover Administration, but did nothing except watch depression deepen into disaster and then look for a cyclone cellar. They also do not remember that they were glad to have Mr. Roosevelt close the banks and establish the NRA; and that their hostility to the New Deal dates from the time when Mr. Roosevelt's money-spending restored consuming power enough to give them a large measure of restored profits—which they then refused to share, however meagerly, with the unemployed whom they had themselves created. Today they are ranting about "dictatorship," and they are trying to label as the "Roosevelt Depression" a period of acute crisis caused largely by their overproducing and overpricing last winter and last spring. Left to their own devices—which include the election either of a Republican or a reactionary Democrat like Garner as our next President—and they will produce a condition of chronic depression with all the attributes (particularly mass unemployment) which killed the German Republic even before Mr. Hitler started doing business on the corpse.

And they will try to do all these things by appealing to the medium-sized and small businessman as if they were his brothers instead of his oppressors. They will pose as the defenders of American democracy; they will call upon the good old days when the American businessman went out to build up the country in the process of building up himself. There is such a thing as industrial freedom of opportunity in this country as well as personal freedom of opportunity; the little corporation today has about as much chance of ever attracting the unfavorable attention of the Federal Trade Commission as the CCC worker, who has had no private job since leaving school in 1933, has of becoming President.

There is a case to be made out for monopoly, provided it is regulated monopoly. But at least let us not mistake the monopolist for a poor boy trying to get along. In 1929—when the most corporations paid the most dividends to the most people, about 18,000 people got about $2,000,000,000 and less than 40,000 people got over $2,500,000,000, which was over 40 per cent of all the dividends declared. A very small group of very large investors own American industry—no matter how many insignificant stockholders may appear on the corporate books. There are somewhere around 360,000 stockholders in General Motors, but one stockholder —E. I. du Pont de Nemours—owns more than 20 per cent of its 43,000,000 shares of common. In 1931 the late Andrew Mellon submitted evidence in an income-tax evasion case that he and his immediate family had title to one and a third million shares of Gulf Oil, out of 4,500,000 shares outstanding. The big corporation of today is not the product of a big man, it is the product of big money. Capital, not management, determines the important decisions of business today.

From a social standpoint, the oldtimers did not amount to very much. But with all their imperfections, they frequently did start from the bottom, they got to the top, and however unintentionally, they improved the general standard of living while they were on the way up. But do not confuse the captains of industry of yesterday with the corporals of industry of today. The modern corporation executive is interested only in cutting every cost except his own—usually exorbitant—salary. He is not an owner, he is a hired man. The people who appear in the top brackets of our personal income-tax returns derive sometimes as high as 85 per cent of their incomes from corporate dividends, and from dividends which, during the last ten years, less than 1 per cent of American corporations have been consistently able to declare. When it comes to a choice between protecting these dividends—not from elimination, but from reduction—and impoverishing the rest of the country, these people do not hesitate. Neither do the corporate presidents whom they have hired for the job.

# INVENTION

## [Roger Burlingame]

WE HAVE passed, in America, the period of our naïve boasting. We have come into a calmer acceptance of our industrial leadership of the world. We have come to a critical consideration of our technological mastery. That we are economically self-sufficient, that mechanical genius has plotted for us a scheme of industry and transport which reaches beyond our own needs so that we are able to supply much of the world with its substance is no longer a motive for idle flag-waving. Our power among the nations has become the subject not of vaunted pride but of thoughtful speculation and even alarm.

All this means that our period of reflection—of deep backward and forward thought—has already begun. Until recently, we left this exercise to an elder world. Europe had time for it. Europe had finished its building; we were in the midst of ours. We were too busy with our empty spaces to give time to thought. Europe was tormented by social problems; we had none. Our people were absorbed into the emptiness, our society was constructing itself. There was nothing in our physical activity to lead us into philosophical thought; no crowded masses, no encroaching neighbors, no "balance of power" to be maintained. So there was nothing to think about but the immediate physical job of building, from abundant material, a house to live in.

Suddenly, then, the job was finished. The house was built. The material was used. The spaces which had seemed infinite were filled. The frontiers which we supposed capable of perpetual motion had stopped. From their abrupt halt came an astonishing backwash, an unexpected flood of people looking for the interstices that had been overlooked and rapidly filling them. Overnight, as it seemed, the labor was ended. It was at this halt in the march of our history that we began to reflect—as Europe had done centuries before.

Reflection and criticism are corollaries of such a change. But before reflection began, we sat and rested and looked emotionally at our structure. Our house was on the top of the world. It was colossal. It towered over the structures of Europe which had evolved with such slow labor through the centuries. Its turrets and pinnacles, lit by the unobscured western sun of Manifest Destiny, were pure gold. Its masses cast long shadows across the Atlantic and dimmed the glory of the elder world. And, at its doors, stood Europe, begging.

It was a miracle. But the modern mind does not linger long in the static acceptance of miracles. The "wonder-working Providence" of Edward Johnson is no longer part of our scheme. The interval between the reflex of amazement at a trick of magic and the question, "How was it done?" has grown perceptibly shorter.

This question, then, was the first index of our reflective period. It has never quite been answered. We have not yet been able to gather together the material from which an adequate answer can be made. Obviously, the magical quality of our structure derives from the speed of its construction. How was it possible to build such a gigantic edifice in the time that it took? To build what seemed to us an inferior habitation in Western Europe, a building which occupied a fraction of the space, took thousands of years during most of which there was a surplus rather than a shortage of labor. Obviously, then, machinery has turned this trick of ours and machinery is the product of invention.

But how did we acquire this mastery of technology? Are we naturally supermen in the application of science? Were we, from the beginning, from the moment we touched the soil of America, magically inventive, ingenious, resourceful, as if some fluid of originality had flowed into us out of the primeval ground? History shows that we were not. History reveals us as fishermen, sailors, lumbermen, and farmers for two centuries—but mostly farmers and bad farmers at that. History shows the whole industrial revolution of Europe finished before most of us had left the agricultural or the artisan phase. History shows Europe crystallized into a set of compact nations while we were still a loose federation of provinces—anything but a nation and with little better social organization (from the perfection of which invention is supposed to spring) than a tribe of nomads.

History thus shortens the apparent time in which our house was built. It becomes even more miraculous that, having no peculiar inventive flair to start with and being then held back from invention by agriculture for the first two-thirds of our existence, we should have completed our structure from scratch in the remaining hundred years. But history, having deepened the mystery, then refuses us the solution.

What we mean, of course, is that the written history of the United States, as most of us learn it, does not give these answers. We may search for them in vain in the abundant mass of facts and stories which our academic historians have provided for us, in all the details of Pilgrim covenants, Jamestown sufferings, irascible governors, petty rebellions, navigation acts, taxation without representation, stamp acts, revolutions, Louisiana purchases, constitutions, presidencies, Missouri Compromises, wars of aggression and secession, slavery, carpet-bagging, the growth of political parties, Hayes-Tilden jumbles, agrarian revolts, free-silver, trust-busting, popular representation or the income tax. Nor is there an answer in any of the political or economic theories: in Jeffersonian *laissez-faire* or the Jacksonian spoils system, in the Monroe Doctrine, the protective tariff, the gold standard or the federal reserve. Where, here, is the most fleeting glimpse of the genius of invention? In every fifty pages of such history, there will be one vague paragraph on technics. In every fifty pages of wars, political quarrels and governmental theory one will be devoted to industrial development. Such matters as the physical bases of life are apparently beneath the dignity of the historian. Alone from all this ruck of theory rises the fantastic head of the cotton gin, the schoolboy's single symbol of the march of an invented civilization.

Yet until these questions are answered, we shall not understand the house that we have built for ourselves to live in nor shall we be able to accommodate it to the enlarged and changing society of the future. Somehow history must answer them, repugnant as the exercise may be to the academic interpreter. As our reflective phase advances we shall demand this knowledge, for we shall know that only by a study of the steps of our technical procession and the relation of these steps to the parallel march of our society can we overcome that obscuring sense of magic which now bewilders and obstructs us.

We shall return, a little later, to this question. Meanwhile let us follow another activity of the reflective period which is going on all about us: the critical examination of the structure as it stands.

## II

The most obvious fact is the immense cost that the speed of construction has entailed. We cannot judge how far this has exceeded the original estimate because there was no original estimate. We can unearth no plans and no architect. We are aware of an immense waste of material and, day by day, we are aware of the cost of repairing the devastation caused by that waste. As the waste is self-reproducing, it seems impossible that our repairs can ever quite catch up with it. With the ultimate in technology applied to dams and reforestation, for instance, we cannot replace the wood, the water and the soil which we have wasted.

Parts of our palace were so jerry-built that they have already collapsed. Struts, beams, stairways, and floors have broken down, and, while they are being repaired, we must spend many millions every year to give makeshift shelter to the people who were supposed to live in those parts. Between the larder and the kitchen and between the kitchen and the dining room great blocks of masonry have fallen down and obstructed the passages. Certain doors do not open, corridors come to a dead end, rooms are empty because there is no access to them, closets for the storage of valuable property have been forgotten. Almost everywhere there seems to be discomfort: crowding or loneliness, too much heat or too little, blinding light or impenetrable dark and endless restless movement to alter and repair.

In other words, what we seem to see is an infinitely complex scheme of technological invention in which the human unit no longer fits. There is a perfect working of interchangeable machine parts standardized beyond the capacity of the human eye and alongside it a mass of disjointed human parts stubbornly refusing to be interchangeable, and standardized, if at all, in opposition to the mechanical order. The process of invention is eliminating the human factor at every turn, making men inert and valueless to their own society and destroying the consumer of its own production. It is, in short, presenting a paradox to which the only answer appears to be race suicide.

When we have arrived at this point in our reflection we have reached an extremely perilous position. From here it is a short jump to belief in the Frankenstein myth—one of the most dangerous fictions that has ever been fabricated. Once this fancy—that the machine we have created to be our slave has become our master—takes possession of us we are indeed lost.

It is at this point then that, difficult as such an exercise is in America, we must try to explore our social history and its relation to the history of other cultures. In our reflective period this is a reasonable pursuit. It is indeed the next necessary stage. And there is no reflective activity which is so wholesome in the dissipation of chimeras. In a co-ordinated record of human progress, the magic disappears and we are able to see behind the miraculous machine, not an isolated and frightened Frankenstein, but the whole background of mankind.

To do this, we must try a new method of approaching the record. We must forget the academic formula and see if we cannot unravel our fabric in such a way as to reveal its physical, human, and social threads rather than its faint political design.

## III

Unlike the nations of Europe which were carved out of other nations our country was carved out of the rough. To put it in another way, each European nation emerged from the womb of society whereas the United States was born of the wilderness. The men and women who emigrated to America were cut off from all existing civilizations. It was a psychological as well as a physical separation. The will to separate was strong; often it was a religious compulsion or derived from economic pressure in that moment of dead center between the end of the agricultural cycle and the beginning of the industrial revolution. In any case, where there was will at all it was a will to escape from society—a strong anti-inventional factor. The result was a throwback to the primitive.

This was not wholly because these people were physically removed from the instruments of their culture. It was largely because those instruments were useless in the new land. Of what value are printing presses, artisan guilds, the secrets of glass or silk or iron in places where every effort must go to the aboriginal activities of keeping alive?

Thus in the evolution of the United States we see a microcosm of the history of civilization. It is as if a movie were made of the progress of mankind on the earth and its speed greatly increased in the manner of those films which show the growth of plants from seed. In it we see what appear to be primitive men moving from the hunting stage, to agriculture, to handicrafts, to artisanship, to industry. Most of this time there is also migration, moving into new land in which the throwback is repeated.

We must remember, of course, as we watch this movie that these men were not primitive in fact and that the speed of the picture is mainly due to their homesickness for a civilization they have lost. In any case it all militated against invention. Primitive men do not invent especially when they are also nomads. A man may solve the riddle of the universe in his own mind but without a society the secret dies with him.

Invention depends first upon the great body of science which has accumulated through the ages and second upon the needs of society. It began in America only when we established an effective liaison with the past and when our own society took form. It is all very well to blame our non-invention upon the British colonial scheme but we must remember that we fell naturally into that scheme, that we could hardly have begun at all without it and that when finally we broke we immediately established the same scheme on our own continent. It is true, however, that when industrial revolution came in England, English jealousy did operate to keep from us that body of knowledge which is the first essential of invention.

Thus invention was negligible in the Colonial period. At the beginning of the 19th century it was sporadic. There was as yet none of the fine interplay of technology and social needs that we find at that time in Europe. Agriculture, migration and the difficulty of establishing social unity held it back. When it began, it began in the established centers, not on the frontiers. The steamboat, invented to carry on trade with the advancing pioneers—not to transport the pioneers themselves—was a product of organized society. It borrowed its engine from English industry. Its effect was not so much to advance migration as to connect the emigrants with their past—with a civilized rear. So with the canals and the railroad, both borrowed from Europe and Americanized. These did eventually contribute to expansion but their primary function was to induce settlement and the beginning of static societies.

As their acceleration increased, they traced the pattern of empire. They made industry a necessity in the static eastern centers. They transported the farm produce with which the frontier farms paid for their manufactured goods. The cotton gin and the reaper completed the scheme. Thus we find the precise pattern of the British empire reproduced in America: the South and the West became the colonies of the Northeast, supplying its food and the raw materials of its industry. With California gold capital became fluid and money flowed like water through a funnel into the vortex of technology.

But invention, the force which had produced empire, now began at once to destroy it. First it abolished slavery. Lincoln might well have said that a nation cannot endure half-slave and half-machine. Though the post-war reconstruction seemed temporarily to heighten the color of empire, the abolition of slavery paved the way for the industrialization and standardization we see today in the South. The transcontinental railroad which became possible when the Civil War removed the obstruction of Southern jealousy carried industrialization and standardization into the West. From this time on both the technological and the social forces became collective. Every impulse in the second half of the century ended in making a compact, standardized, united nation whose parts became more and more tightly fitting, more precise, more "interchangeable" and more mechanical.

It would be superfluous to go here into the details of the telegraph, the fast presses, the linotype, the improvements in transport of the mass-production formulæ which brought the people together, taught them to think alike and defeated the individualistic tradition. It would be more valuable at this point to stop the machinery of the projector and examine the "still" which shows our condition at the end of the Civil War.

Industrially, we were behind most of Europe. Socially, we were diverse, the individualist tradition was still much alive and for a time lonely frontiers and vast unorganized territory would keep it so. We were building furiously on the vague plan of "manifest destiny." We had tapped the sources of our wealth and were already wasting it prodigiously. Our mistakes in these respects made us, as Kipling said, "the scandal of the elder world." Invention had entered our scheme and had already produced prodigies though from the modern hilltop they look haphazard. But a closer liaison with Europe where the intellectual activity that we had not yet learned was making brilliant discoveries in pure science was strengthening our half-conscious conviction that invention was the genius of our culture. The greatest impetus of all came with the introduction from Europe of the "scientific method" which ended trial-and-error in invention. By it laws were established by experiment in pure science so that the inventor was able to know before he constructed his machine that it would work.

Granted, now, that invention working in the midst of endlessly expendable wealth would initiate a powerful force, we have not yet answered our questions. Except for the factor of wealth, in what way does our progress from this point differ from that of the rest of the world? How has it created any special problems? We have not yet fully explained the phenomenon of our miraculous acceleration. How did we gain such general industrial leadership? What are the origins of our apparent social maladjustment?

## IV

In our simplification it has been necessary to leave aside for the moment the kernel of the difference.

The primary factor is that of labor. In this our dilemma from the beginning has been the reverse of that of England or any industrial country of Europe. The problem in Europe has always been a labor surplus. In America it has been a labor shortage.

In England, from the time of Henry VIII there was an immense surplus population of which only a small proportion was skilled or competent. The evacuation of the monasteries in the Reformation dumped a mass of vagabonds, paupers and unemployables in any trade upon the country. As agriculture waned this mass increased. Therefore, in England, the machine was invented not to replace human labor (though it inevitably did this to some extent) but to eliminate the necessity of skill. This was more or less true throughout Europe depending upon the extent to which each country became industrialized.

In America from the beginning, there were too few men for the job in hand. As population increased it began to move. When industrial centers developed under the scheme of empire, they were constantly depleted by new migrations. Thus, in manufacturing (as indeed even in agriculture itself) there was always a labor shortage. In America, then, the machine was invented not to make use of a surplus of unskilled labor but to replace the human workman entirely.

As a result, there came, early in our history, the greatest of all American inventions and one which was peculiarly American. It was made by Eli Whitney and it was not the cotton gin. It was the "American System" of interchangeable-parts manufacture which is the basis of all modern mass production of machines. Its first application was the poduction of muskets in quantity in a period of extreme labor shortage. It operated over a space of fifty years in every sort of machine manufacture in America before it became known in England. In a word it enabled machine tools working through jigs or patterns to turn out quantities of identical machine parts which could be assembled without special artisan labor. It ended the artisan phase in which each machine was made part by part and fitted as the artisan went along. From it derived most of our automatic machinery.

Another invention in the same epoch was Oliver Evans' flour mill which eliminated the human factor between manufacturing processes.

From it has derived our familiar slogan "untouched by human hands." Evans' mill took in grain from sacks on a cart at one end and turned out barrelled flour at the other with no workmen in the middle.

If these two geniuses had been followed continuously by others as great we might have been spared the problem of our "melting pot," though this would have necessitated a simultaneous advance in the whole of science throughout the world in order to produce such mechanical automaticity as we have today. The fact was, however, that invention by no means compensated the labor shortage. We were not, as yet, an inventive people. Conditions of life still opposed invention. The lure of the land was still too strong. We did not, then, immediately continue the achievements of Whitney and Evans and the importation of labor on a large scale was necessary to our industrial existence.

Nevertheless, these and similar inventions had established the pattern of a mechanical civilization. As new invention came in there were grooves for it to work in: channels which led it inevitably toward automaticity. Thus, even when it became evident that we no longer had a shortage of labor, invention continued to fall into this scheme. In other words, the habit of labor shortage was too strong for us to overcome, even when the fact was no longer there.

In our collective phase other factors multiplied the rate of invention. Any tightening of social organization is bound to have that effect. The single factors of size and distance gave us practice in large-scale enterprises. The strong collective impulse made men impatient of separation, physical or mental. Hence the extraordinary development of our transport and communications.

With all this necessary concentration it was plausible enough for our technology to outrun our sociology and our political science. The habit of social *laissez-faire* persisted in the face of the violent collective convulsion. Society in America had always organized itself according to geography and whim. So we remained unaware of the fact that geography had, so to speak, disappeared and that we had used technology to destroy the whim. Moreover, our political tradition had been dedicated to the glory of the individual and continued to play into the hands of that individual when he undertook to wield the powerful instruments of wealth and technology toward his own aggrandizement—again in the very face of the collective impulse. This brought the concentration of control into a few hands and the corollary financial fictions. Thus there existed one of the most curious phenomena of social history: a highly collectivized society living under highly individualistic forms.

The process, of course, ended by destroying the individual. His destruction was hastened by the fact that the centralized control under a dictator eager for profit made technology more effective, while at the same time the whole trend and result of that technology was irresistibly collective. The economic operation of this trend, however, which involves monopoly, industrial codes, price maintenance and a complexity of other matters lies far beyond our field.

## V

To sum up, then, here are a few of our findings in this brief examination of history through our technological glasses. In the long period of our non-invention, there evolved an individualist society. In this evolution, the sections of this society moved at different paces for with each throwback the cycle began anew at the primitive stage. It was necessary, much of the time, for each man to be a law unto himself and almost economically self-sufficient. As technology caught up with each advance it civilized it by uniting it with a static society behind. Finally, by the time the advances stopped, technology had become primarily a unifying, solidifying, consolidating and standardizing force.

This technology, however, had been applied with so little thought (other than specialized scientific thought)—so little reflection, in short—that the people were not conscious of the change. Thus their forms, their individualist desires and their self-sufficient, law-unto-themselves habits of action remained.

Meanwhile, the inventions at the end of the non-invention period formed a pattern of automaticity based on labor shortage which persisted into the period of labor surplus. Concentrating on this kind of industrial development, we gave no thought to other fields of activity for our people when the surplus should arrive. Finally, we achieved in our rapid period of unreflective building, a *habit of invention* which soon perverted the theoretical inventional basis and produced devices for which there was no social need.

We see, then, that our serious problems today are not due to a mere increase in tempo but rather to an unevenness of tempos. As we look upon the sweep of history we seem to have progressed, not with that smooth interplay of necessity and invention which marks the industrial revolutions of Europe, but rather by jerks—fast in one place, slow in another and with great lapses between technological and social movement. Often they seem quite separate: isolated one from the other. The result is the rambling, inconvenient, jerry-built interior of our magnificent palace. Hence many of the devices designed for comfort produce discomfort, those designed for speed produce slowness, those designed for economy produce waste, those designed for profit produce loss, those designed to be our slaves become our masters and those designed to relieve the burdens of labor cause unemployment, poverty and misery.

It is useless to have a car capable of a hundred miles an hour in traffic conditions which prevent it from going thirty. It is useless to have a telephone to save us time if we have to hire a staff of people to protect us from its constant interruption, its inroads on our working hours. It is valueless to provide leisure for ourselves via machinery if that leisure is used in listening to or turning away salesmen of unconsumable goods either in person or over the radio or in reading the masses of printed matter necessary as a vehicle of advertising. It is profitless to install automatic machinery in our factories if we are obliged to use up the savings this effects in paying for the relief of those persons whom the automatic machinery ejects.

These are a few examples of the effect of inventions which do not seem to supply social needs. Most of them seem to create more social needs than they answer. Some of them, being cultural, like photography, motion pictures, the phonograph, color printing, were always desirable. Others like the airplane, invented years ahead of its time, found their first function a destructive one. Still others like the new gadgets on cars spring from business competition. Some inventions are so utterly lacking in answer to social needs that the whole gigantic fiction of "high-powered" salesmanship is necessary to their consumption.

If all these things and many more like them are true, why, then, is it not a fact that we are in the grip of a Frankenstein monster? The reason is that man has never, in fact, lost control of the machine. On the contrary, he has increased his control. It is only necessary to visit one of the great laboratories of invention—Bell, Westinghouse, the Mellon Institute —or even the central office of some giant industry to be convinced of this. There we shall be conscious of the intensity of the concentration of the naked human mind upon the entire system. There we shall know that if, for a moment, this intensity should relax, the whole scheme might easily collapse. If these men have become gods in relation to the rest of humanity, it does not alter the fact that in their hands lies the permanent control and not in the wheels of an inanimate machine which must remain inert until its creator wills its motion.

It is, then, in the quality of those men that we must look for our answer and not in the Machine or Science or any of the other vague monstrosities which persist in spite of Stuart Chase and the semantic school. Are these men looking towards the security of society in the future? Are they interested primarily in relieving the future burdens of labor or in immediate profit for themselves? Are they working for general social adjustment or merely for the magnification of a particular industry? Are they interested in making goods cheap and therefore accessible to all the people or are they engaged in artifical price maintenance so that their economies will merely stretch the margin of profit? These and other questions must be asked of the human masters, not of their mechanical slaves.

## VI

If our reflection has revealed only this dark aspect of American invention, that is because it has not gone deep enough or because, perhaps, the opposing forces are too recent to be subject to detached study. There is no doubt that they are there.

We have proved the possibility of everything save human adjustment. For the hope of this we must rely on the evidence of the ages in which mankind has rallied from revolutions as profound if less rapid. Otherwise we accept no impossibilities. Our long intolerance of science is ended. If we will go only a little way back into the history of invention we shall see how complete this change has been. It was less than a century ago that innovators in technology were charged with madness. Today our faith and our capital are at the disposal of the inventors.

Invention itself has changed. It has passed from the individual to the group. This was necessary in the new complexities of science. It is no longer possible for the inventor to work without the whole body of science at his command. He must study in concert with many experts, pure scientists and inventors in collateral fields. Inventions today are products of large laboratories.

These laboratories are maintained by industries or by endowments. Sometimes abuses occur. Valuable inventions are shelved, suppressed; certain fields are closed by the filing of patents which are not intended to be developed. These things are done often for commercial reasons, sometimes in cutthroat competition. Though the intent is occasionally dishonest, it is doubtful if the general effect is evil. If there are too many inventions—as we suspected in the review of our history—is not such a check valuable? Does it not create an interval in which social invention may catch up? Is it not time that we think more carefully about the capacity of society to absorb the new devices? Even if this kind of thinking is dictated by questionable motives is not the end desirable?

There is a hue and cry against the trade unions because they have delayed the commercial use of new processes such as offset printing. Offset printing may be immensely valuable to society but do not such delays give us a chance to ask questions?

A striking example of the asking of questions is in the case of television. To the amazement of the general public, thinkers, in the very face of a great technical development, have asked the startling question, "What is it for?" This may be the index of a wholesome change in our headlong habit of thought.

Invention has postulated a check upon itself in making the body of historical knowledge universally accessible. Its operation in libraries is revolutionary. By photographic films, for instance, exact reproductions of unique manuscripts, rare books, inscriptions, hieroglyphs have brought these things out of their hiding places and put them within reach of the whole of society. The new devices for revealing these films have made historical study popular. Understanding of the history of civilization is a long step toward social adjustment in any age.

Other steps in this direction are being made by the careful study of social trends. The great work undertaken by President Hoover which resulted in the volume *Recent Social Trends* has been followed by a survey under Roosevelt of *Technological Trends and National Policy*. In this, the investigators have attempted to predict the inventions of the future so that both industry and society may adjust to them well in advance.

Society itself (if we may use for a moment that abstract and antisemantic term) has often refused inventions under the dictates of fashion or a taste for individuality. Thus the zipper invented in the 1890's remained in obscurity for thirty years. The prefabricated house is meeting that same opposition today. The trailer, tried for a time, may go into the discard as answering no need. This is also a question which is disturbing the promoters of television.

Invention is making great strides in repairing the mistakes of our thoughtless ancestors. The cry against these impulsive builders echoes through the West today though without their waste it is difficult to see quite how our house could have been built at all within the time limit. Their reckless deforestation is certainly causing disastrous floods which destroy our cities, though without it, it is questionable whether there would be any cities to be destroyed. But the dams and irrigation projects which seem, as we look at them, to be almost acts of God in their magnitude and the speed of their construction are not only correcting the mistakes but they are turning waste energy into electric power.

This power, once its economical transmission is mastered, may combine with other forces to produce a new revolution in society. Improvement in transport, communications and power transmission suggest physical decentralization not only of industries but of society. Cities are already stretching far into the country and thinning out as they stretch. It is conceivable that they disappear; that physical grouping of people will become unnecessary. Some one has imagined a director's meeting taking place with the directors a thousand miles apart, each in an isolated country home, talking together via television combined with radiotelephony. Add the new inventions which produce plants from synthetic fertilizer suspended in water and decentralization of food supply may follow, returning families to subsistence farms—each "farm" being a few square feet of roof. These fancies are not altogether consistent; they are still vague indices of a trend.

It is possible, then, that notwithstanding all our moment's troubles, invention may yet fulfill the hope of civilization whatever that hope may be. The technocrats are persistent in their proposals for adjusting unemployment caused by the machine and it is possible that their efforts may be resolved with human nature and education into a workable scheme. The leisure they postulate may be alarming merely because it is new. It is likely that with such a scheme at work, war and revolution could be delayed long enough for invention to show their fallacy. It is almost certain that if the use of invention for destruction can be suspended for a time its use as a preventive of war will become evident. A network of technology over the world will be the strongest possible defense against war. If it is so complete that every strand is dependent on every other no nation can dare to break a single thread.

Meanwhile the calm contemplation of history from the point of view of the basic, physical, human and social needs is probably the most wholesome exercise there is. A good approach is to project ourselves in the

manner of the artist into the mind and skin of some individual of each
epoch. This will better lead us into an understanding of technological
creation than an attempt to understand political fantasies. The proper
study of mankind is man. So is the study of the machine.

POLITICS

# PUBLIC OPINION

## THE CASE OF CITIZEN JONES

*[Bruce Bliven]*

LET US CONSIDER John Jones, plain American, who earns an average salary, lives in an average house, and has the average number of wives (one) and children (about two). John Jones pays his bills, tells the truth (most of the time), belongs to a church and a neighborhood golf club, and visits the second of those more faithfully than the first. He prides himself on being a good citizen; he always votes in Presidential years, and occasionally at other times, if the weather on election day is not so pleasant as to lure him to the golf course.

It is John Jones and people like him who—in theory at any rate—decide the policies of the American Government. By voting for one man or another, one party or another, they say whether this country shall have a high tariff or a low one, visible or invisible taxes, bonuses or pensions—or both—for veterans.

In fact, however, the problems the voters nowadays are supposed to solve are a great deal more complicated than these simple examples would suggest. Let me take a few illustrations from recent history. John Jones is asked to decide, in his capacity as citizen, whether an industrial depression can be cured by large-scale governmental spending for public works, and if so, whether the problem will not return with redoubled force as soon as the expenditures are ended; how much should be spent and whether it should be obtained by borrowing, which increases the national debt, or by taxation. If taxation is preferred, he is supposed to determine whether heavy rates on business enterprise discourage activity, as one school of economists tells him, or are absolutely necessary to start the machinery of business running again, as another faction says.

He is asked to pass upon the merits of an extremely complicated proposal for the reorganization of the executive branch of the Federal Government. It involves scores of individual plans for the abolition or consolidation of bureaus, for the destruction or creation of new posts, for a transfer of power in one direction or another. The plan is so complicated that Mr. Walter Lippmann, a professional student of public affairs who had spent many days in study of its content, complained that after the passage of some time he had forgotten a large part of what the bill was about. Yet John Jones, in such leisure time as he has left over from business, golf, bridge, meetings of the Chamber of Commerce and Rotary, and Sunday drives with his wife and children, is supposed to decide whether this scheme is a sensible proposal in the interest of efficiency, or is in fact the beginning of un-American dictatorship, the first flaw in the dike, through which the waters of fascism may seep.

Citizen Jones is further called upon to decide whether most of the members of the United States Supreme Court are too old to be efficient, whether the Court is behind in its highly complicated maze of duties, at what age exactly the average jurist passes the border-line between competence and incompetence, how many justices constitute the perfect number and whether a proposal to change the number or to set up a retirement age constitutes merely a sensible change in procedure or a profanation of the most sacred aspect of our American democracy.

In foreign affairs John Jones is expected to be equally versatile. He is asked to say whether peace can be preserved by creating an irresistible army and navy, no matter what the cost, and using the threat of this military power to influence the course of action of other nations in all parts of the globe, or by having a comparatively small force with which to defend the continental United States and its near-by territories and let the rest of the world go hang, so far as we are concerned. He is asked to decide the complicated technical question of whether, in case of a naval war which involved the threat of blockade, this country could survive without continuous supplies of imported raw materials such as rubber, manganese, and tin.

Even beyond this, he is requested to say whether we should seek to build up a vast foreign trade, for the employment of our people in time of peace, or avoid it, either because of the danger that it will drag us into war, or because of the dislocation of our economy when foreign customers for any reason stop buying. Assuming that foreign trade is desirable, Mr. Jones must tell whether it is wise to lend our foreign customers the money with which to buy our goods, as we did in the days of Mr. Coolidge and Mr. Hoover, or to conduct our trade on virtually a barter basis, with imports equalling exports, despite the anguished roars of American manufacturers of goods with which these imports compete.

The list of demands on Mr. Jones's omniscience could be continued almost indefinitely. Should electric power be produced entirely from private sources, or entirely from public ones, or from a mixture of the two? If a mixture, should there be just enough public production to check on the prices and services of the private producer or should the public step in wherever, and to whatever extent, it may seem desirable? And if so, who shall be the judge of desirability? When people are unemployed, is it better to let them sit at home in idleness, maintained by the State at a minimum cost, or to spend more money and put them to work creating socially useful goods of whatever type each man is best fitted for? Do unemployment insurance and old age pensions encourage irresponsibility?

As I set down these questions, I marvel that any one should have the audacity to try to reply to any one of them. The simplest would seem to require a lifetime's labor by a distinguished committee of our wisest, most highly trained men. Yet John Jones, oddly enough, answers every one of them, with hardly a moment's hesitation. He knows the answer to everything. One of the marvellous phenomena of this marvellous country is that any newspaper can send an Inquiring Reporter out into the street to button-hole five random passersby and ask them anything under the sun. Each of the five will immediately deliver himself of a firm, thoughtful, well-pondered comment on whether mercy killings are justified, is the climate changing, should we prohibit the export of munitions, and have women's hats Gone Too Far. It is amazing to read the polls of *Fortune* magazine, or of the Institute of Public Opinion, and see how rarely does John Jones profess ignorance or indecision. "Three per cent: Don't know." "Seven per cent: Don't know." "Five per cent: Undecided."

Where does John Jones acquire his omniscience? If all of us collectively could answer that question with the same confidence each of us individually displays, we should have solved many vexing problems of our democracy. We can begin, perhaps, by checking over some possible sources.

In John Jones's town there are three daily newspapers, one morning and two evening (there used to be six, but half of them have been consolidated out of existence). John Jones subscribes to one morning and one evening paper; he does most of the reading of the morning one while his wife and the children are more faithful to the evening edition. Both papers carry a great many comic strips, a large amount of advertising, quantities of local news, especially society, and brief dispatches reporting Washington, New York, and foreign countries—always provided, of course, that these are not crowded out by other demands on the journal's space. The paper carries editorials which are in line with John Jones's own opinions, beliefs, and prejudices. If they weren't, he would not have subscribed; hardly any one ever willingly reads a paper with which he knows in advance he will disagree. The journal also carries several syndicated Washington columns, and insofar as these express an attitude, it is in agreement with the paper's editorial position. If they weren't, they probably wouldn't be there.

Should a scientific investigator call on John Jones and ask him what he reads in the paper every day, the answer would be "national and international news, the financial page, editorials." In point of fact, John Jones spends only a total of fifteen or twenty minutes a day on his paper in toto, distracted during most of this time by the conversation of his family, or by the difficulty of following a connected train of thought in a crowded, jouncing bus. He looks at the front-page headlines, then turns to the financial page for a glance at the stock market. He reads one or two of the comic strips which he happens to be following. He skims the editorial page and the columnists; if any one article starts off in an interesting manner, he may actually read it through.

But even if John Jones did peruse every word in the paper touching on national questions, I am not at all sure how much better off he would be. He would find in the news columns day-to-day accounts of developments in important matters, but invariably these would assume that he already had the fundamental facts in his possession. This assumption is unfortunately erroneous. John Jones couldn't get a grade of sixty in an examination on any of these important matters, if the quiz went below the most superficial aspects.

Where, beside the newspaper, does John Jones get information or opinions on what is happening? He listens three or four nights a week to his favorite radio broadcaster, who tries to cover all the news of the world in fifteen minutes, sometimes coloring it strongly with his own prejudices or those of the sponsor or of the radio network. About one night a week on the average he goes to the movies and sees a newsreel which, by its choice of subject, by the spoken comment, and particularly by the matters of current interest that it leaves out, supplies a surprisingly large amount of colored discussion of public affairs. John Jones and his wife subscribe to half a dozen magazines. Most of them are devoted mainly to amusement or to information on practical subjects—the household, sport, Wall Street, and so on. One or two, however, do discuss public questions, usually from a conservative point of view and with the most bitter controversial subjects generally omitted.

When John Jones goes to church, the sermon quite often deals with "topics of the day." The minister is a good deal of a liberal in his ·hinking, though much less so in his speaking, being inhibited by his rather reactionary Board.

More important than any of these influences is the fact that John Jones talks about public questions with his fellow workers, with the men he meets at the club, in a hundred casual brief colloquies each day—in the men's room, the Pullman smoking compartment, in the course of business calls, on the golf course, before and after a bridge game. Most of his friends think as he does on most subjects; when a new problem comes up, it is amazing how quickly the "party line," so to speak, of every American group is established in regard to it.

John Jones is only dimly aware of it, but he is in fact the object of many and powerful forces in American life, seeking to change his opinion on a remarkable variety of matters. Their purpose is, through John Jones as a citizen, to get legislation passed—or not passed—by the city, state, or federal government. Some of these forces are sinister, some are not. It is regrettable that "power politics" and "pressure groups" have come to be smear words, with an evil connotation. Actually, all politics is power politics; all groups are pressure groups. Those who are concerned about the present situation in this country base their anxiety on the fact that certain groups are heavily over-represented in the battle for public favor while others are just as badly under-represented.

An excellent illustration of how a pressure group operates can be found in the campaign, a few years ago, of the now defunct National Electric Light Association. Its activities were explored in detail by the Federal Trade Commission and the unchallenged facts are set forth in its exhaustive reports.

At that time the private power interests were deeply concerned about the growing movement for government ownership of electric power plants. The industry was not then thinking of anything like the TVA but of coal-steam generating stations in a single city or a small area. A number of these plants already existed, and from time to time reports trickled out, disturbing to the industry, concerning low rates, efficiency of service, and even large profits to the municipalities. The NELA decided to take steps to change the mind of America on this matter, and it instituted a campaign for that purpose.

One of its first activities was to insert tremendous quantities of advertising in the daily and weekly press. No newspaper was too small and obscure for a fat contract, with no haggling over rates. This advertising, to be sure, very rarely or never talked openly about the question of public versus private ownership. It tried to sell appliances, to encourage the use of electricity, to make the reader feel that the industry was a friendly, co-operative institution which did a fine job for very little profit.

Soon, however, the editor began to get press matter also from the NELA, submitted for publication in his news or editorial columns. These articles, prepared with great skill by high-priced publicists, stated the case against government ownership with the utmost persuasiveness. There was no crude suggestion that unless the editor printed this news and these editorials, the advertising would stop, but a great many editors evidently thought so. Some of them, no doubt, agreed with the point of view of this submitted matter and were glad to use it; certain papers reprinted the unsigned editorials from each other, not at all surprised that the struggling editor of *The Podunk Bugle* should have suddenly acquired a mastery of English style and of a complicated subject that should have earned the author $30,000 a year. (As a matter of fact, it did.) The number of column-inches of such material printed in a short time ran into astronomical figures.

Before long, principals of high schools throughout the country began to receive visits from suave and well-dressed gentlemen with a singular proposal to make. They knew, they said, how short of money high schools perennially are. But they also knew how important it is that the rising generation of students should have accurate knowledge of economic matters. Bearing these facts in mind, they were prepared to provide free economics textbooks in any quantity that the school could use. They were good textbooks, too, written by well-known authors, competent professional jobs—in every detail except one. Where any normal, unsubsidized text would give the arguments for and against public ownership and control of such an enterprise, as, for instance, the production of electric power, this one cheerfully assumed that there was no argument except that in favor of private enterprise, and set this forth at length and in glowing terms. Such books were distributed by the million, and similar ones were even passed out to some of the colleges.

Shrewdest of all the devices in this campaign was the approach to college professors of economics, who are not without influence on the attitude and philosophy of the rising generation. To selected men throughout the country went a special representative of the NELA. He explained that the Association (or sometimes it was a near-by electric company, operating in its own name) had heard of Professor So-and-So. His reputation for brilliance had spread afar. The organization wanted to have the right to consult him if any question arose sufficiently serious to warrant an intrusion upon the time of such a busy individual. Would he consider accepting a retaining fee of $500 a year?

Would he! The professor, poor as college teachers almost always are, fell into the trap with painful alacrity. He would be delighted. The agreement was made, the honorarium was handed over. Rarely if ever did the NELA or any of its member companies find occasion to consult an individual thus retained. They simply paid him his money, year after year, and forgot about it, serene in the confidence that in his classroom, at any rate, the power organizations would not be painted as soulless, bloodthirsty corporations taking advantage of the unhappy public.

The most audacious plan was one that has never been traced directly, so far as I know, to the NELA. A gentleman eminent in the paper industry, connected with a company which in turn was a subsidiary of a great power organization, solemnly set out to buy control of twelve or fifteen of the leading newspapers of the United States. It was a large-scale enterprise, involving five or ten million dollars in each of the several cases. One or two papers actually passed to this control, and negotiations for several others were nearly finished, when publication of the facts brought the enterprise to a halt. The gentleman always insisted that he was buying these journals as a paper manufacturer and not as an executive of a vast power company. He was engaged in creating a vertical trust, looking upon a great newspaper merely as an important consumer of wood pulp, which for safety's sake ought to be brought under control. You may draw your own conclusions, however, as to what the attitude of these newspapers would have been on the question of government ownership, if the deal had gone through.

I have told this story in some detail, not because it is unusual but because there is every reason to believe that it is typical. The aspect that is not standard is that the facts were brought out, through the interposition of a great bureau of the Federal Government, which had power to subpœna witnesses and seize records. Throughout the country, every sort of special interest is engaged in trying to change the mind of John Jones and of his representatives in the national Congress, the State legislatures, and other governmental bodies.

Of the two, it is more important in the long run to reach John Jones, since he will finally change the mind of his elected representative—or change the representative. In an emergency, however, work is done directly upon the law-maker, by mail or in person. Every device is employed at one time or another and in varying quantities—skillful presentation of little known facts, equally skillful presentation of plausible half-truths or falsehoods, persuasive sales talks by a high-powered lobbyist, the pressure of old personal friendship (many a former statesman, defeated for re-election, finds a happy hunting ground in working as a lobbyist). Charming but unscrupulous ladies unscrupulously use their charms, though there is less of this than is popularly supposed. As a last resort, plain and simple bribery may be employed. The bribe need not be money; it may be social recognition, flattery, the simulated admiration of "big men."

Sometimes, of course, the propagandist tries to pretend that he *is* John Jones and that unless his wishes are carried out, the public career of the legislator will be brief. It is a standing joke in Washington that no witness volunteers to appear at any public hearing on pending legislation who is not the spokesman for at least 1,000,000 voters. Any one so poor as to represent only 990,000 would be too abashed to present himself. Frequently such witnesses claim to speak for all the manufacturers in the United States, or all the farmers, or the inhabitants of the entire Southwest, or every man and woman past sixty years of age. Such claims are subject to heavy discount, and need not be taken too seriously.

It is an uglier matter when telegrams and letters pour in upon the members of Congress purporting to come from constituents of theirs, but in fact sent under duress or without the individual's knowledge or consent. When the legislation embracing the so-called death sentence for third-degree holding companies was under consideration, petitions were received containing many thousands of signatures. Some of these individuals afterwards communicated privately with the Congressmen saying that they had signed these documents under a strong hint that if they did not, they would lose their jobs. This is blackmail as simple and direct as the familiar practice of hanging a sign outside a factory gate just before a national election saying that "If so-and-so is not elected president, this factory will close for an indefinite period the day after election."

During the same fight on the holding-company bill, large numbers of telegrams were sent, signed by individuals who knew nothing of what was happening. Telegraph-company employees testified that they had been handed local telephone directories with instructions to send a message in the name of every individual on a given page. As a result, messages were sent in the name of dead people, of the very Representative who received the telegram, or in the names of persons who had just sent statements of their own of an exactly contradictory character.

When the proposal for reorganization of the federal bureaus was under consideration, a tremendous number of messages from private citizens were received, nearly all of which opposed the plan. Following a radio appeal by Father Coughlin, something like 200,000 statements were received in one day. Members of Congress who took the trouble to reply (presumably by form letter) to these protestants reported that more than half of the letters came back from the post-office with the statement that no such person was known at the address given, or that no such address existed. The inference seems clear that some one opposed to the bill took the trouble to send in many protests under fictitious names or addresses or both.

It is an open question whether propaganda of this kind is effective, or rather, at what stage the law of diminishing returns begins to work. To be sure, the reorganization bill was defeated by a narrow margin in the House of Representatives (the holding-company bill became law, and the agitation over it has almost been forgotten). When the number of communications sent to members of Congress or the Secretary of State, or the President reaches such vast proportions, no one attempts to read them. Telegrams are put on a scale and weighed, which determines their number with fair accuracy. Letters are tied up in bales, and, presently, destroyed. It is difficult to put on a vast artificial campaign without permitting its fictitious character to become apparent.

When it comes to influencing the citizen himself, the three great media are, obviously, the press, the radio, and the motion picture. How do they perform their jobs? To what extent is their material colored to suit some one's propaganda purpose? In discussing this matter, we are of course concerned with only a small amount of the material presented through each of these vehicles. Ninety per cent of the contents of the newspaper, of the films shown on the screen, and of the programs heard over the air is without political significance one way or the other. It is the limited amount of material that deals with important public questions that is crucial.

In the press there is a continuing conflict between the dual purpose to serve as a public agency of information and as a private enterprise conducted by its owners for profit. Sometimes these two seem to run parallel, at least temporarily; a newspaper campaigning for a new sewer system can do its town a service and at the same time gain readers and prestige. At other times, these interests seem—at least to outsiders—to conflict, as when the newspapers fought an NRA code that would have required them to abandon child labor, bargain collectively with their workers, and so on, under the argument to the public that the proposed code constituted a violation of the freedom of the press.

The typical American newspaper in any big city is a huge business enterprise, with a sale value of millions of dollars, a large payroll, and, in good times, tremendous profits. The owner of such a paper, who nowadays is practically never an active editor, is overwhelmingly likely to be a conservative, extraverted businessman of the energetic and executive type. Other things being equal, he will mirror in his pages the views of the conservative bankers, industrialists, department-store owners of his community, not because they bully him into doing so by threatening to call his loans or to curtail their advertising, but because he is the same kind of person they are, with the same kind of outlook.

The radio is on the whole even more conservative in its point of view than is the press, more timid about frightening the members of its audience, less inclined to fight for its convictions, or even to have any. The radio in its origin was an offshoot of the electric-power industry, and is still strongly affected by this fact. Even more than the press, it is actuated chiefly by the profit motive. It has done many fine things in the public service—sometimes with an anxious eye on the Federal Communications Commission, which can take away its license and wavelength, but these isolated exceptions do not alter the truth of the general statement.

The motion picture, similarly, is big business, and a very big one. Like the newspaper and the radio, its first task is to cater to public taste, and it is assiduous in trying to find out what people want—and to give it to them. Within the boundaries of this general purpose, however, the industry comes to many cross-roads where the direction in which it turns is dictated by the personal views of its top executives—bankers and friends of bankers, money-makers first and last. When the motion-picture industry, most of which is located in California, came to fear that the radical Upton Sinclair might be elected Governor of California and increase its taxes, it did not scruple to use its resources in a vicious campaign of falsehood against him. Actors were dressed as tramps and photographed in railroad yards or along highways, announcing that they had come to California to live off the State after Brother Upton was elected. This photographic falsehood was distributed and shown as genuine newsreel material. It is the newsreels, as I have suggested above, that give the propagandist his great single opportunity. For years William Randolph Hearst has conducted an enthusiastic big-navy campaign by peppering his newsreels with shots of battleships or naval airplanes, accompanied by a far from subtle suggestion that we do not have enough of them. Prohibition has long been attacked on the screen by the simple device of permitting fanatical old women in the temperance movement to pose before the camera and make fools of themselves—and of their cause. Even simpler and more effective is the device of boycotting any individual or crusade you do not like.

The connection between the motion-picture industry and big business in general seems likely to become even closer in the near future. We are on the threshold of a vast proliferation of advertising in the motion-picture theatres. Short advertising films, skilfully made and carrying an unobtrusive message, will soon be shown daily in thousands of theatres, on behalf of great national corporations. Supposedly, the purpose of such films will be to sell goods, but just as Mr. Henry Ford buys time on the air to let Mr. W. J. Cameron utter naïve Tory preachments about the virtues of 18th-century morality, so it seems likely to me that once advertising on the screen has been accepted, it will be used for the dissemination of a philosophy as well as to advise you in your choice of soap or toothpaste or automobile.

The effectiveness of all these channels for the communication of ideas, and particularly the press, has often been challenged of late. The people, so we are told, are in a skeptical mood, and are likely to take an opposite view from the one that is rammed down their throats by the powerful publisher, broadcaster, or motion-picture magnate. The star example usually cited is the national Presidential campaign of 1936, in which a majority of the newspapers of the country were against Mr. Roosevelt while a majority of the citizens were for him. The figure commonly

quoted is that "85 per cent of the press was opposed," although Mr.
Roosevelt received 26,000,000 votes to Mr. Landon's 16,000,000. I do not
know whether this percentage is correct; I suspect it is a guess and may
be too high. I do know that the editors of *The New Republic* found that
in ten leading cities of the United States, widely scattered, papers opposing the New Deal had almost exactly 70 per cent of the total circulation,
and that the President's vote in those cities was almost exactly 70 per
cent of the total. The lesson commonly drawn from this, however, seems
to me much too simple and too easy. Even the newspapers which opposed the President editorially—most of them—printed his speeches, and
other campaign documents, with a fairness that was not known in the
American journalism of fifty or seventy-five years ago. It would be more
accurate to say that the people voted with the news columns and against
the editorials.

It is a truism of newspaper work that the editorial page has been declining for many years. It was of importance in the days when the
editor was also the owner, and you bought *The Sun* or *The Tribune* to
see what Dana or Greeley had to say. But why should any one buy
a newspaper primarily to read and accept the views of an anonymous
individual, hired at slightly more than a reporter's salary, to express the
opinions of some hustling businessman who happened to go into publishing rather than a bond house or a department store?

It is this decay of the editorial page that has brought about the rise
of the columnists. Their articles are in reality signed editorials, and they
have a reputation for integrity and intelligence quite distinct from and
oftentimes superior to that of the publisher in whose pages they appear.
The responsibility they carry is already enormous and it is rapidly growing, especially since they appear in a large number of papers all over the
country. If the evils of journalism are to be solved by licensing somebody, as is occasionally suggested, perhaps we had better begin by
licensing the columnists and requiring a long and arduous preliminary
discipline before permitting them to practice.

The fact that two-thirds of the people in ten great cities wanted Roosevelt while two-thirds of the newspapers wanted Landon may seem to
contradict what I said above, that people are willing to read only a paper
with which they are in agreement. But the contradiction is only on the
surface. The newspaper-buying public—and 25 per cent more papers are
printed every day than we have homes—insists on reading, and if no
paper is available that caters to an individual's prejudice, he will buy and

read a sheet with whose editorial policies he disagrees. In many cities in this country there are only one or two newspapers left, and they are under common or similar ownership. It is also true that many people read popular newspapers, like most of the tabloids for instance, for their sensational pictures, their comic strips, and other entertainment features, and pay little attention to the editorial attitudes these newspapers take. It is often said that many subscribers to Hearst newspapers are in this category.

It should not be assumed, of course, that because people do not read editorials, newspapers are without influence on their thinking. On the contrary. If I wanted to change the mind of the population and had to choose between the news columns alone, and the editorial page alone, I should take the news columns every time. The process is similar to that of the newsreel, mentioned above. You can boycott your enemy, never permitting his name to appear; or you can print attacks upon him without giving any space to his reply. All things considered, it is surprising that the news columns of the American press are as open-minded and as fair as they are—incomparably the best, in these matters, in a world where the rising tide of dictatorship has destroyed the very meaning of journalism for two-thirds of the earth's population.

In my judgment the working press, the reporters and editors who actually handle the news, have standards of fairness and accomplishment substantially higher than those of their publishers. It is to them that the credit must go for the accurate reports, for example, of what the New Deal has accomplished, printed in newspapers editorially opposed to the Democratic administration. (I am not forgetting the few journals which conspicuously failed to live up to this standard, which both falsified their news reports, and launched editorial philippics.) For these higher professional standards among working journalists at least two causes come readily to mind: The advent of schools of journalism, so that a large minority or a majority of the members of the average staff are now college graduates with a professional sense of enthusiasm and responsibility in their calling; and the Newspaper Guild, which has given the individual worker the strength that comes from support of his fellows, increased economic security, and the knowledge that he now has a possible court to which to appeal if he is asked to do something dishonorable.

One of the two or three greatest scientific developments of the 20th century—many persons would say the one greatest achievement—is our new understanding of human motivation. Through the work of many men, among whom Sigmund Freud probably comes first, we have learned how profound is the role of the emotions and of subconscious impulse in determining men's actions, how little "rational" intellectual processes really matter. This new knowledge is available both to the high-minded and to those who are not, with the second group up to now far more prompt, energetic, and successful in its use. You will find an excellent, realistic, and cynical statement of how to regiment opinion in Hitler's *Mein Kampf,* in which he recognizes the value of simple slogans, catchwords, and emotional appeals, and frankly advocates both concealing facts from your followers and misrepresenting them if expediency dictates. The Fascist countries today illustrate the manufacture of public opinion, carried about as far as it can be. It begins with the cradle and ends only with the grave; the dictators overlook no bets; the press, the radio, the motion-picture, the pulpit, the classroom—all are regimented to create a given effect.

If we looked only at the results achieved in the first few years, we should be obliged to despair of the future of civilization as we have known it in the past, with its component elements of freedom for the individual and devotion to the search for pure truth through the scientific approach. But such pessimism would be premature, to say the least. Every dictator must give his people both catchwords and bread. With the right catchwords he can cut down the quantity of bread without too great protests, but there is a lower limit beyond which he cannot go. In the long run too many catchwords and too little bread will produce a revulsion of feeling in the mass of the people. The unanswered question before the world is whether the fabric of civilization can withstand the international strain to which it is being subjected while this process is being carried out.

In the United States the problem for our citizenship is to prevent a process paralleling that by which liberty has already been destroyed in such a great part of the rest of the world. To be sure, we are unlikely to use the European model intact; it has a bad name with us. To the late Huey Long is attributed the remark that if we get Fascism in this country, we shall probably call it anti-Fascism. Huey, the Louisiana dictator, should have known what he was talking about. The United States has always contained powerful elements that are opposed to any freedom of action for individuals or groups with whom they disagree. There can be no doubt that, in recent years, such elements have grown more numerous, more consciously united in a common purpose. These elements may be political, economic, social, racial, or religious, or may combine any of these aspects. Censorship appears in protean forms throughout the country. Mayor Frank Hague of Jersey City refuses to permit trade unionists, liberals, socialists, and others to speak in the community over which he rules. The Roman Catholic Church has a representative in Hollywood who is consulted by the motion-picture producers in advance of "shooting" a script and tells them whether their stories are objectionable to the Church and therefore subject to a possible boycott. Most of the States and some cities maintain motion-picture censorship boards who refuse to permit the exhibition of films, or parts of films, which seem objectionable to the individual members of these boards. Many industrial communities—coal-mining towns in Pennsylvania and West Virginia, textile towns in the Carolinas and Georgia, and many others—permit no stranger to enter the town, or to stay there for more than a few hours, whose errand is or might be obnoxious to the owners of the mine or mill. For millions of Americans, even under the comparatively enlightened national administration of the day, the Bill of Rights remains only a grim joke.

To a certain extent, conditions like these breed their own antidote. For example, the public has by now been thoroughly imbued with the idea that the average successful newspaper is subject to control by "the advertisers" or "the big interests in Wall Street," and professes a degree of skepticism in regard to what it says (the skepticism is usually more apparent than real). The lecture forum, which has experienced a great revival in recent years, undoubtedly owes some of its success to the fact that people feel that a well-informed speaker can and will give them the "inside story" that the daily press does not, and many successful speakers owe their popularity to the skill with which they simulate such an achievement. The daily press, which, as a whole, so heavily over-represents the interests and attitudes of the middle class, of business and finance, has helped to encourage the rise of labor journalism—dailies, weeklies, and other periodicals published by and for trade unions or other working-class groups. I am advised that such papers now have a combined circulation of about 8,000,000, to be compared with a total circulation of standard newspapers which ranges between 40,000,000 and 45,000,000. The liberal press—such papers as *The Christian Century,*

*Common Sense, The Nation,* and *The New Republic*—base their appeal in part on the supposition that they will "print the news the dailies are afraid to touch."

It would be a grave error to put too much reliance upon crumbs of comfort of this sort. In the long run, the means of communication of ideas in any society will be controlled by those who have the chief power in that society. At present the United States is in what seems to be the closing stages of an era predominantly marked by private capitalistic enterprise, and it is natural and inevitable that the spokesmen for such a society should prevail. The danger is, however, that by closing the doors to full and free discussion of alternative philosophies, they will prevent the mobilization of public opinion early enough in regard to the changes that are necessary, or, still more probably, that they will help the country to select the least desirable choice. In simpler words: If some sort of socialized economy is made inevitable by technological progress, both here and throughout the world, it is important that the public mind should be prepared for something other than a sugar-coated regime of Fascism.

Meanwhile, in terms of our present problem, the cure for propaganda is clearly more propaganda. It would be folly for us—even had we the power—to seek to close the door against the pressure groups whose activities I have sketched; any such attempt would be likely to miss its aim and to suppress instead those groups and ideas that are most badly needed. We require for our spiritual health a vast proliferation of the technique of public debate, to the end that a better balance shall be struck between those groups in American life that are now so heavily over-represented and those which struggle ineffectively for the right to be heard. We must build up, beginning in our schools, the strongly emphasized tradition that democracy and freedom of speech go hand in hand, and that no one can be "a good American" who proposes to make himself the judge of what is sound patriotic doctrine and to suppress those who do not conform to his views. I can see no other basis on which democracy, political as well as economic, has any chance to survive.

# RADICALISM

## [*George Soule*]

I N HIS BOOK on Fascism,[1] Wilhelm Reich makes the interesting
point that social psychologists attempting to account for revolutionary movements and personalities have usually asked the wrong questions. They are likely to regard the revolutionist as a deviation from
normal, and inquire what emotional aberrations can produce such a
strange being. But Reich points out that when we have a society which
blocks the instinctual drives of so many persons—one which imposes
hunger, sexual deprivation and lack of opportunity to acquire prestige—
the relevant question is why more persons do not revolt, or why revolutionary impulses become so poorly translated into action that they do
not produce a social order capable of satisfying healthy persons. There
is no more powerful explosive known to science than pent-up hunger for
food and love. When so many millions have been starved for so long,
the phenomenon that requires explanation is not radicalism but its opposite or its perversions.

This comment applies to those who really do suffer important depriva-
tions—to the unemployed or underemployed wage-earners, to the landless or otherwise exploited farmers, to the bankrupt shop-keepers, the
clientless lawyers or doctors, the writers or painters without a market. It
does not apply to the person who has access to security or comfortable
means but who nevertheless invests his emotions in revolutionary thought
and activity. For such a person some intricate psychological explanation
may legitimately be sought. Even in these cases it may be discovered that
the motive force is not an irrational compulsion but rather a realistic and
creative attitude. The effectiveness of intellectual guidance in revolutionary movements will depend largely on the prevalence of the latter
type among both leaders and masses.

These reflections seem to me particularly relevant as I reread the article

[1]Reich, Wilhelm, *Massenpsychologie des Fascismus*. Verlag für Sexualpolitik, 1933, Kopen-
hagen—Prag—Zürich.

on Radicalism which I wrote for *Civilization in the United States* in 1921. At that time, in spite of the revolutionary movements following the war, native radicalism was still a tiny and impotent challenge to the customary order of things. It was largely an affair of confused sects and competing orthodoxies, persecuted and burrowing underground. Its main conscious inspiration was Russian or British. The intellectuals were widely separated from the indigenous labor movement. The trade unions themselves were relatively weak and hesitant. Such ardent spirits as arose within them were channelled off to sects and factions. "The failure of American radicals," I wrote, "to build up a strong movement is in part due, of course, to the natural difficulties of the social and economic situation, but it is also due to the mental traits which accompany remoteness from reality. . . . Too much of American radicalism has been diverted to the easy emotional satisfaction which is substituted for the arduous process of dealing with reality. We suffer a restriction of the personality, we cry out against the oppressor, we invent slogans and doctrines, we fill our minds with day dreams, with intricate mechanisms of some imaginary revolution. At the same time we withdraw from the actual next step."

The spontaneous movement of labor is an effort to grow up, in a social sense. It "arises from a desire to be free, to achieve dignity and independence. . . . The most modest aspects of the labor movement are attempts of the workmen to gain some voice in determining the conditions under which they must work—in other words, to extend democracy into industry. . . . Essentially, this sort of radicalism arises from the instinct of the workman to achieve an adult relationship to the industrial world." But, "If radicalism arises from the instinct for economic maturity, then it can find its place in the world only by expressing its emotion in terms of the actual with which it has to deal." This meant, I pointed out, not just imagining a new world, but improving and extending existing labor organizations, achieving economic and political power in existing society, and exercising that power responsibly.

Has radicalism matured since 1921? If not, why not? The period immediately succeeding the publication of the earlier essay was one of discouragement and retreat for revolutionary and labor movements the world around. Expected overturns in Europe did not occur, and those that had taken place either regressed into impotence or were overcome by reaction. The Russian revolution muddled through, but failed to approach utopia very rapidly. The British Labor Party gained, eventually established partial power with a minority Cabinet, and then failed either to accomplish anything of much value or to sharpen issues so that it could bring about a clear-cut contest with its opponents. In the United States the post-war depression was the signal for a campaign of extermination even against the most non-revolutionary trade unions. It was succeeded by the era of Coolidge prosperity, during which the movement of dissent was able to raise its head only in the unsuccessful LaFollette campaign. One would not have expected, in this period, much revolutionary protest of the more violent sort. But our institutions were still functioning poorly enough, and harbored enough weaknesses visible to rational analysts, so that one might have expected more healthy growth and reform than occurred in the fabric of society. The radicals could not seem to find a way of doing even the jobs that were appropriate to the time, such as a strengthening of unions and collective bargaining, and the passage of moderate social legislation. They could not even capitalize successfully the outrageous political corruptions of the Harding régime.

The economic catastrophe beginning in 1929 brings Reich's question into bold relief. Millions of workers were jobless and hungry for months and even years; millions of farmers lost land and home, or were threatened with that loss. The shock of insecurity spread far up in the income scale. Even when government assumed responsibility, it was estimated that for long periods at a time 20,000,000 persons were receiving public relief. The national income was cut in half; industrial production declined by almost the same amount. At the same time it was clear to every person capable of reflection that all this was not the result of any actual shortage of the means to sustain life or to provide opportunity. "Starvation in the midst of plenty" was the popular cliché. The fault was entirely that of human organization; the way things had been run, the people in power had to shoulder the responsibility. There is therefore no need to account for the surge of unrest. The unemployed leagues, the direct action of farmers against foreclosure, the varied popular movements supporting panaceas, Father Coughlin, Huey Long, Technocracy, Upton Sinclair and his California EPIC, and finally the New Deal itself were merely mild expressions of what might have been expected.

What needs to be explained is why the expression was so mild. Did the majority of the population, as a result of this experience, become confirmed in a position that can truthfully be called radical? Were real and important changes made in the organization and in the personal command of the methods by which we find our livings? Did the consciously revolutionary movements, which all along had looked forward to a crisis of this kind, make the progress that their theories would have led them to expect? Are the frightened reactionaries correct when they speak of Mr. Roosevelt and his lieutenants as Reds who have carried out a revolution? The answer is, on the whole, negative.

Even more striking is the necessary comment when we think of what happened not merely in the United States but in the world at large. The most serious economic crisis that the capitalist régime has ever experienced did not result in a single proletarian revolution anywhere. The movement which gained most was Fascism. This outcome might be called revolutionary in an explosive sense. It used some of the proletarian resentment because its victories could not have been achieved without a certain amount of support from workers. But in effect the Fascists and Nazis are no more revolutionary than a victorious mob of strikebreakers. The outcome in the realm of reality bids fair to be, not a more rational society in which biological and emotional needs may be satisfied and human beings may go on to a higher stage of creativeness, but one in which the primitive hungers are augmented by dangers of maiming and death in war, both civil and foreign, by the murder of defenseless men, women and children from the sky and, what is still more repulsive to responsible and sensitive minds, by the debasement of science and free inquiry, the perversion of art and literature, the destruction of the highest values and the best types of personality that the human race had hitherto been able to achieve. The social trauma of the 1930's seems so far to have induced, not mainly an approach to maturity but, in many instances, regression toward a general psycho-neurosis.

During the darkest days of the last depression I was talking with the leading official spokesman of Communism in the United States and put to him this kind of question. Here was a breakdown of capitalist institutions, a situation that the Communists themselves recognized as potentially revolutionary. Why had they made no more progress with the mind of the masses, why did they have so little influence even in the trade-union movement itself? Did that not imply something wrong with Marx's social theory, or at least with the Communist interpretation of it? The reply was terse. The difficulty, he said, was "inadequate personnel." I do not know how much he intended to imply by this statement: he may merely have been thinking like a factory manager who attributes failures in maintaining scheduled production to frailties of his staff that can soon be remedied by experience, training and better selection. Nevertheless the failure of proletarian revolutionary movements throughout the world so consistently and for so long a period of collapse suggests something more than accidental or easily remediable fault. It suggests a kind and extent of personality inadequacy that has a bearing on the Marxist theory of the process of revolution itself. For, in essence, this theory concerns the way people will behave, fully as much as the way social institutions will operate in bringing pressure to bear on them.

It may throw some light on this crucial problem to trace a little more precisely the course of radicalism in this country since 1929. The details are multifarious and confusing, but the general pattern is obvious enough. There are two main currents—first, the generalized, spontaneous impulse toward social change arising from the experience and background of multitudes of people, and expressing itself in terms of the native culture; second, the organized movements with conscious revolutionary aims, deriving their inspiration from intellectual formulations and their policies from foreign—or perhaps it would be less invidious to say from international—sources.

Of the first component, it is clear that we have had a demonstration hitherto unparalleled in American history. Our former major political overturns, such as the Revolution and the Civil War, moved large masses of people, it is true, but in each case the unrest and the formulation of issues were expressed mainly by the already existing leaders in wealth and prestige. It was the propertied classes, or at least an important section of them, who led the movement for American independence, and it was the struggle between the Southern plantation owners and land speculators on the one hand and the Northern industrialists and capitalists on the other that formed the core of the conflict about slavery. This time, however, the protest that carried so much dead wood out in flood came most insistently from below, and found no solid economic interest among the vested institutions to champion it.

This is not to say that it had no forerunners or that the form of its expression was not determined by traditional forces. It was a little like the democratic uprising under Andrew Jackson. The 19th-century struggles against the railroads and the other big corporations, flowering first in the Populist and later in the Progressive movements, had blazed a rude trail in the same direction. Previous farmers' complaints against low prices for crops, leading to demand for monetary reform (or, in the disparaging terminology, for inflation), had been signposts for part of the program of the New Deal. The agitation for "parity prices" for farmers to be obtained by some offset against the benefits secured by industry under the protective tariff, which had begun under Coolidge and Hoover, was intensified and came to issue in the AAA. The century-old struggle for freedom in labor organization and collective bargaining surged up again and made its mark, first in the NRA and later in the Labor Relations Act. The cry of the underprivileged city workers for more consideration, hitherto expressed mainly through social workers and proponents of social legislation, had its first comprehensive answer in large-scale federal relief, in housing projects and in social security legislation. The protest against the money power and Wall Street, long a political tradition, was the prototype of the new banking legislation and security regulation. Finally, the dead hand of the Supreme Court, concerning which complaints had been lodged for a generation at least, was pushed aside.

The phraseology in which this revolt was clothed, after it had been channelled into political action, was similar to that of a popular revolution. Democracy was supposed to be assuming control of the economic empire in order to use it for the general benefit. The enemies of reforms were identified as "economic royalists." What was done was spoken of as if it were a new social order in some genuine sense. This bombardment of words from the President and his cohorts was returned in good earnest from the other side. The population divided on class lines in its opinions and in its votes more completely than ever before. Above a certain income level it was difficult to find support of the President, difficult at times to find even anything but violent hatred. The press itself went over almost *en masse* to the opposition, while the majority of voters became more loyal to the New Deal, the more vocal the opposition grew.

All the fury, however, marked no fundamental change in the social order itself. The means of production were not expropriated; there was comparatively little advance even in mild socialization of particular industries. Taxes on incomes and profits were somewhat increased, but not so high as they had been after the War. No essential powers were taken from the hands of the traditional rulers of industry; they still decided to as great an extent as before how much to charge for their products, how much to produce, how and when to invest their money. Some policing of the financial markets was undertaken. There was an expansion of public enterprise, chiefly in fields where it involved no competition with private industry. Collective bargaining was made obligatory and union organization gained. But all were things that had occurred in other countries without anything approaching a revolutionary crisis. There was, finally, little permanent alteration in the distribution of income. And the business cycle continued as usual; a sharp depression, with large unemployment, followed the major victories of the New Deal. Radical in its impetus, radical in some of its terminology, but only reformist in its outcome, the popular revolt itself fell far short of its assumed objective.

On the side of the theoretically conscious and organized radicals, there continued the usual divisions and shadings. The Socialists persisted as a political entity without becoming anything more than the agitational minority they had long been. Syndicalists and anarchists, once prominent in revolutionary circles, all but disappeared. The Communists were undoubtedly the greatest beneficiaries on the Left from the economic upheaval. They had behind them the prestige of Soviet Russia, which kept on increasing production and avoiding unemployment while the rest of the world was sinking further and further into the morass. They took their work seriously; to be a party member was more like being in a strict religious order than in a congregation whose religious duty is fulfilled by attending church—or the polls—once in a while. They worked zealously among the unemployed, the tenant farmers, every group where their influence might count. They stimulated the formation of countless committees and councils for all sorts of worthy purposes. Their new tactics emphasized, not so much preaching doctrine or talking revolution as organizing for immediate gains, such as unemployment relief. Nowhere was their advance in influence more striking than among the younger literary men and other intellectuals. The predicted social crisis was at last a reality; Marx and Lenin had the theory that seemed to fit it; the exponents of that theory were in power in one great country and were working lustily toward power in others. At last the lost generations had something solid to believe in, something that was at once unfamiliar enough, adventurous enough and demanding enough to engage their emotional energies.

As soon as the Communists began to take a larger and more active part in the common struggles, however, they faced the problem of doing something to neutralize the doctrinaire quality of their faith that had tended to separate them from the main currents of life and culture. They had long been making enemies of people who were willing to go at least part way with them; their influence had often been disruptive of genuine popular movements wherever it had been felt at all. Whether the failure of their former tactics in this country would have brought a change in policy is uncertain. But at this very moment the unexpected rise of the Nazis in Germany put international Communism on the defensive and led it to look for help. On the field of politics in every country this reorientation led first to the United Front with other groups on the Left, and later to the People's Front, in which the Communists attempted to work on friendly terms with merely democratic and progressive forces which were not revolutionary at all. On the field of diplomacy the new policy led to the effort of Soviet Russia to strengthen the League of Nations as a bulwark against Fascist aggressors and the efforts of Communists everywhere to win converts to the doctrine of "collective security." This program had, for them, the double advantage that if applied in time it might prevent war, and so restrict the growth of Fascism, while if it were unsuccessful in that declared aim it would serve the undeclared aim of ensuring that the Soviet Union, which would presumably be the main object of attack, would have powerful allies in the coming struggle.

So the American party, which had been bitterly attacking the inconsistencies and hesitancies of the New Deal and calling the Socialists social fascists, turned squarely about and became supporters of the Roosevelt administration nationally and of progressive candidates locally. It suppressed, at least for the time being, any hint of revolutionary aim for the sake of broadening its influence.

But in the meantime that influence was becoming undermined from another direction. The factions split off by internal quarrels—the Trotskyites and the Lovestonites—had been small and without importance. But the quarrels in the Soviet Union of which these factions were merely shadows loomed larger and larger through the long series of arrests, trials and executions of prominent revolutionaries which followed the Kiroff assassination. The prestige of the spiritual mother country received incalculable injury as a result of these startling events. Some believed the accused innocent and so either joined or gave vicarious assistance to the dissenting factions. Others, who believed the accused guilty, suffered a shock to their faith in the success, as a desirable form of political and cultural organization, of the Soviet system. The traditional doctrinaire virulence, now withdrawn from its disturbing impact on the external world, seemed to have broken out in an internal malady. All this came to a head at a time when the economic crisis which had given hope of a catastrophic change had been relieved, and when the Communists' domestic program was so watered down that it held promise of nothing more exciting than the New Deal itself. The inevitable result was a widespread loss of élan, especially among the recently converted intellectuals.

So it turned out that the conscious revolutionaries had almost no effect in changing or hastening the course of the native revolt. It went its way almost as if they had not existed. They did, through hard work, help to make it more effective in approaching some of its own goals. Such self-sacrificing zeal might have been sadly missed. But the goals themselves had little connection with the ultimate revolutionary goals of the radicals.

When the social changes occurring as a result of the great depression and the New Deal are assessed, one stands out above all the others—the growth in numbers, power and status of organized labor. The C.I.O., the Wagner Labor Relations Act, the widespread acceptance of collective bargaining, the growing political power of the unions—all this is a real change in the balance of social forces, with implications for the future. Is it radical, however, either in its origin or in its results? Certainly it is not the outcome of the work of conscious revolutionaries, and trade-union movements in other countries, once they have grown strong, have not been noted for their daring. One must regard this development, nevertheless, as a good way of dealing with reality, as a desirable next step. It is the nearest thing we can show to a growing-up of the American radical impulse.

For an effective and rational radicalism, however—that is, for one which can reorganize society so that it will really be worthy of the better human possibilities, offering both economic and emotional satisfaction—we must obviously wait a while longer. We must wait, for one thing, until Reich's question is satisfactorily answered and something is done about the answer. We must find some way to create "adequate personnel" in sufficient quantities. This task is by no means a hopeless one. There are already illuminating hints—such as Reich himself provides. In order to have more creative personalities, capable of dealing with reality in the interest of basic human drives, we shall have to have more people who do not suffer from irrational fear, more who are not dominated in adult life by father-images or mother-images, often well disguised, which forbid them to do rational things or direct their hostility against outside scapegoats. The experience of the past few years indicates that this kind of trouble prevails, not only among those who are not radicals and ought to be, but also among revolutionaries themselves.

# COMMUNIST MENTALITIES

## [*Evelyn Scott*]

BEHIND every developed social movement is an individual rebel —some unhappy man or woman atypically endowed, and driven, by a resultant social maladjustment of one degree or another, to take refuge from the surrounding in the disenvolvement of capacities of intellect and of imagination which men are not impelled to make their resource while it is easier for them to follow, with blind instinct, whatever consoles the senses and primitive egoism. For societies and States originate primarily in practical response to the exigencies of survival, which is an instinctive demand; societies and States represent only secondarily answers to the requirements of a gregariousness with another basis. Intellect and imagination are biologically useful only as their functions are applicable to shrewd calculations of ways to overcome the physical hazards of living. Mental ponderings and the cultivation of imagination for its own sake will not, in themselves, bridge the gap between atypical beings and others. That a man has given genuine proof of clearer thought processes than are average, or of more accurate powers of observation and greater insight than is common, or even of a purer capacity than that of his fellows to demonstrate accepted ethics, will not recommend him to the aggregate of his contemporaries, until he is able to add to such performances those persuasions which alone convince multitudes—*i.e.,* until he has convinced others that acceptance of himself and his works carries the promise of some great utilitarian advantage.

One has only to consult nature to confirm, in the behavior of men with other animals, the conservatism of instinct. Democratic societies (whether their institutions are bourgeois or proletarian), because they are subject to mass domination and can establish judgments and dictate opinions only with a unanimity impossible without the reduction of thought levels to whatever will include the lowest common denominator of represented intelligence—democratic societies, I repeat, tend to judge and act in a character in which the demands of instinct prevail over other demands. The conduct of democratic societies, therefore, inclines to be more conservative than the behavior of exceptional persons. Democracies do not need to undergo effects from machine-regimentation to exhibit consistent intolerance towards nonconformity and atypicalness. The machine, however, is so well adapted to the obliteration of difference, and to the substitution of types for personalities that it inevitably offers itself as congenial to the democratic "soul"—a "soul" always less captivated by the idea that men shall be good, great, or able to perform mighty feats, than by the idea that men are, after all, identical.

The existence of this viewpoint, and the antecedent predilection for banality represented in it, becomes twice understandable when we recognize not only the serviceable stupidity of nature but also the fact that no man alive is really able to grasp as more than mythical the constitution of a fellow-being whose capacities and insights are superior to his own in any manner more fundamental than allows one to excel as a clockmaker and another as a blacksmith. And even in such instances the mutual advantage of an exchange of products of distinguishable talents never eradicates a feeling reserved to the individuals concerned, for example, that clockmaking is, by and large, a little above horse-shoeing—or the reverse. For if egoism were not strong enough to sustain self-righteousness, men would die much sooner than they do.

Yet only powerful egos—able to develop, in defiance of social disapproval and a consequent threat of misfortune, an equivalent compensatory resistance to surrounding influences—can defy and survive general social condemnation: always at some point the fate both of the genius and of the individual whose nonaverage equipment indicates a lag in his physical or mental evolution.

But for the powerful ego, social maladjustment and social criticism never result in anything but a re-enforcement of its conviction that it is superiorly "right." Originally, this "rightness"—which is the same that makes it the "right" of each plant to breathe the air and nourish itself from the soil, or the "right" of one animal species to obliterate from the face of the earth, if it can, all other species that compete with it—is a thing in itself, absolute and independent of vocabularies of extenuation.

But the man who becomes infected with the judgments of others who despise him has already admitted to the core of his being what will sap his will to persist, and what may finally destroy him. It is, initially, the influence on his thoughts from social training, and the tendency of societies to exact self-justificatory arguments from their individual members, which is the first, most moving factor in the attempt of a rebellious individual to search both surroundings and the bedrock of inner resource toward which circumstances have driven him for whatever apparent truths seem best to justify his persistence.

Content, in the beginning, to seem right to himself, the rebel reaction to real or seeming persecution is the gradual extension of the original, specific apology to a theory of "rightness" designed to show that what would solace his own pride and heal his own ego-wounds would inevitably benefit everybody. And the more unhappy individuals are—the more imminent seems a biological defeat they cannot overcome without a complete revision of their natures—the more will they incline to translate self-explanation into cosmic terms. So that, in the end, and more often than not, the individual's interpretation of his biological misfortunes and their consequent penalties becomes tantamount to a statement on the revelation of the character of the Divine.

So did Jesus identify necessities of his own compassionate and nobly outraged temperament with the functions of the Godhead. So have all those rebellious who are intellectually naïve ultimately inclined to assume God embodied in their physical persons. While for a parallel motive, rebels with a more sophisticated awareness of self—and of external "nature" and surroundings—have been at greater real pains to base whatever was self-defensive or self-glorifying in the content of theory on statements capable of support by logic or by physical proof.

For the original instinctive gestures of both small and large souls have their inception in identical needs and impulses. And those who are non-rebellious and conforming are as self-righteous as are protestants, with the single difference that for conformists there is not the same temptation to adventurous dispute and reinvestigation of fact—since for comformists, God is already in the status quo, in His heaven, and all else in its appropriate place! And it is only after the rebel's attempted explanation of himself to the world has begun to demand of his pride, and as an exigency of the situation his own assertions create, that he verify whatever it is he has put forward as admirable—it is only then that he may use his own will power to perform acts and embrace mental or emotional operations which alter even his motives, making of him a creature fundamentally (not merely superficially, in the measure of talents and facilities) unlike others.

This altogether unrepresentative being, tending always to exhibit real capacities not those of the average, and working towards ends too much removed from those which instinct recognizes as advantageous to constitute a usual concern—this being is the true idealist. It should go without saying that such persons are rare, and are not, as a rule, permitted longevity. But idealistic propensities are exemplified in varieties of individuals who exist as a perpetual minority exercising degrees of modifying influence upon the primitive conduct of men in the aggregate, and upon particular men whose motives are not pure in the sense made possible by the rigorous association of feeling with an abstract of intention.

Though it is a fact that, while theories that seem relevant to idealism are untried, their exponents attract to their standards only those with a personal likeness to themselves, which is obviously founded on effects from analogous experiences reacting on similar temperaments, it is also true that, as theories are elaborated and take on the valid impersonality characteristic of all genuine intellectual exercise, such appeals to self-interest as are disguised by doctrine become increasingly beguiling to numbers—even to numbers whose circumstances remove them to a degree from the founders of creeds. Then the belief begins to grow among many that what was at first disparaged as the mere peculiarity of an individual viewpoint does actually represent something capable of producing benefits for the entire race. Then whatever was idiosyncratic in the thinker's outlook—whatever might have been traced to an origin in his specific personal discontent with circumstances—begins to be obliterated from the common recognition.

And it is here that the spectacle of the rebel's incalculable effrontery of self-righteous assertiveness ceases to be an obstacle in accepting him. And his insane bravado, which may previously have marked him as dangerous, begins to fascinate rather than to repel. And all the more because it controverts the biological good sense of average people, who are too unsure of themselves to pass judgments or set up standards of thought without first securing majority confirmation. For their own dependence on the concurrence of opinion is, even at best, only a veiled confession of their subjection to tyrannous necessity, whereas the fool of instinct—the propounder of what seems ideal!—has defied necessity's immediate demands. In doing so, he has flattered humanity as much as could any performer of miracles, since he has invited men to flout "nature" and assert free will. And this popularity of the rebel is the more easily established if he has shown such theoretic foresight as will account for a delayed proof of the reliability of his statements. That a full demonstration in the present of the authenticity in nature of what he asserts to be true should be impossible is requisite for his complete success. For if such a demonstration can conceivably be demanded at once, the illusory identification of a particular doctrine with ultimate knowledge and wisdom—with the perfected realization of good for all mankind!—cannot be brought about. And without this illusion, conversion will not come with the force accompanying the conviction that the proposed application of the specific theory is a guarantee of a future advantage to be inalienably shared by every single human being who accepts it.

This illusion of the unqualified catholicity of the insights embraced in some particular viewpoint is most easily fostered after death has removed the rebel from the sphere of acts, so that he can no more be suspected of any personal design inimical to other individuals. Then, under circumstances which favor sympathy, even those but luke-warmed by idealism may find his memory congenial. Then—when he no longer, even amiably, can compete with his fellows—something æsthetic as well as practically moral may enter into the contemplation of his qualities and attributes. For if appreciation of him is still influenced by self-interest, concern to admire him risks no discouragement from immediate ulterior motives.

It is at this stage that those very talents which first made the defunct rebel abhorred by a majority of men may serve a belated audience as the provocation for moods of gratifying day-dreaming on themes of perfection, exemplified as perfect justice, universal benevolence, and ultimate truth. Or again, the dead man's history may be the useful storehouse of data by which others, also disadvantageously placed with respect to power in society, may demonstrate to their own satisfaction that their apparent shortcomings and seeming failures are, like his, but disguises for victories nobler than those won over flesh. We may safely assume that, while individuals have been discovered who have promulgated doctrines not conducive to their immediate material gain, no one has yet clung to teachings meant to prove him, by his own standards, contemptibly inferior to other men.

For as humble as were the teachings of Christ, and as exacting as Jesus made them when he demanded their strict application, even Christian principles represent originally the inverse glorification of specific material tragedies and discontents. And if we examine philosophers whose teachings have been more mundane, we may trace again—if it is only in the metaphysical poetry of a Nietzsche, the pessimism of a Schopenhauer, or, obliquely but not the less certainly, in the abstractions of a Kant—theories tantamount to absolute sanctions for the requirements of specific temperaments. And surely neither Karl Marx, nor his disciples, who so largely dominate our day, provide any exceptions to this rule.

With respect to those self-delusions which are the mechanisms of happiness for all men temperamentally incapacitated for the achievement of triumphant biological success, Karl Marx was fortunately placed in his era. For he lived while the abhorrence of inductive methods was still so general and so instinctive that his insistence on broad assumptions, preclusive of any examination of the physical, individual subjects who compose classes and societies, was permitted to escape grave challenge. And at the same time he enjoyed enough of the results of the "scientific awakening," which had characterized the 18th century, to be alive to certain implications of science capable of yielding plausible insights. Thus he was able to relieve himself and his followers of all apparent scientific obligation to self-analysis, or to the understanding of specific individuals, or to concern for personally inspired motivations. He has, therefore, with a degree of innocent intention, provided both the instrument and the philosophy best adapted to exploitation by unscrupulous individuals.

For according to the logic of deductions from Marx's dogmatic assumptions in respect to class and class warfare, the study of actual, physical, distinguishable, individual humans is a complete irrelevance in the study of man's nature and of mankind. For Marx, having interpreted history according to laws he assumes to be those of economic determinism, and having expanded the interpretation of these only with class definitions and class references, then proceeds to ascribe every evidence of history that is subversive of ideal justice to the economics of class—the conclusions at which he arrives being, inevitably, those consistent with his own restrictive and exclusive hypothesis.

One would suppose the single illustration provided in cleavages of personalities among members of an average family to be sufficient to point the perilous inaccuracy of such over-simplification as that which proposes to determine all men's characters solely in contexts of class and economics. And even though Marx overlooked anything that could be a direct key to the motivations of Marx himself (a penurious white-collar worker, an intellectual, and a Jew)—anything, for instance, that would serve to distinguish Marx from John Smith, living in the same age and in an analogous position with respect to class and finances—one still marvels to see men of the present day, who are presumably possessed of greater resources in psychological awareness, content to prolong and reassert the original Marxian fallacy.

Yet one would marvel more, were it less apparent that such an original omission of concern for matters involving, among other things, some degree of self-analysis and self-understanding, is a general human tendency, which is sometimes more and sometimes less emphasized in the conduct of rebellious theoreticians than among other people. And if bona fide idealists may, in rare examples, admit self-understanding as the first necessary part of an effort to encompass other knowledge and other wisdom, such an admission is certainly not instinctive. And that average men, finding in self-delusion a last seeming refuge from harsh actuality, are reluctant to yield it up, should, perhaps, be our least cause for wonder. Too much resolute vigilance is required of the man who would clearly examine his own conduct and motives! If he is to do so with any hope of precise and valuable results, he must develop preliminary insights that cannot be machine-made, or be the discoveries of an ensemble.

Therefore nothing short of what is, in terms of sheer instinct, an insane optimism with respect to the attainment of ultimate wisdom and perfect benevolence is ever likely to induce the individual to make the attempt. And if his findings become known to the world, he can scarcely expect to be rewarded for his abandonment of defensive devices, since the first effect of his gesture will be to expose human character in a light unwelcome to those not equivalently inspired to self-renunciatory honesty. And unless the individual is conditioned, through his own unsought experience, to dread self-delusion even more than threats from circumstances and the revenges of society, he will—even if he is idealistic —resist revelations which may jeopardize the strength his self-love gains in his presumed complete identification with universal truth. For though, long ago in our animal history, cunning insidious thought undermined, even for the unthinking, that confidence in unillumined instinct which allows creatures of the wilderness to confront death in every instant of living, and still die unaware of death and unafraid, this same thought has, in an overwhelming majority of cases, only shattered man's resoluteness without altering his purpose. And those hypocrisies imposed in a measure on every man and woman whose survival is contingent on the tolerance of a group have resulted in the dedication of thought to the furtherance of delusion far more often than they have resulted in the substitution of perfectionist aims for the primitive, constant one of preoccupation with survival.

Thus the tendency of all societies to require impossible proof of disinterestedness in every conspicuous personal act has encouraged resort to theories to account for the inevitable postponement in fact of such proof. And while men rush to adopt doctrines formulated as instrumentalities to effect specific changes in surroundings, they persistently omit to investigate that self which is bound to determine *both* theory and the manner of its application.

Rebellion is the product of vicissitudes—either psychological, directly physical, or both. Sufferings and hardships result in psychic lesions which egos clamoring to remain intact feel only as inferiorities. The unconscious and primitive—the most common!—defence of a sensed "inferiority" is its attempted disguise or denial. Except where there is an accompanying superlative degree of self-awareness, it is the individual who has been most gravely wounded in self-esteem who will most often tend to disclaim significance for self.

An easy device for the evasion of self-examination is through the elision of vocabularies, since by merely transcribing the personal mood in a false context, emotions only attributable to vindictiveness or embittered egocentricity are made to seem selfless and fit for the language of benevolent universality. In this way it becomes simple and advantageous to utilize abstraction as the vehicle of personal passions society might otherwise fear and resist. For as long as it is possible to preoccupy the public mind with generalities, a close scrutiny of the individual may be diverted. Then it will seem beside the point to consider what makes men kind or unkind, false or faithful, wise or foolish, in any connection but one which is broadly abstract and apart from individual men. That Marx has given to this common attitude of evasion the sanction of pseudo-science is one of his greatest beguilements. For without having intended it, he has provided, in his account of mechanisms that divorce individuals from their aims, the first completely frank apology for individual relaxation of moral scruple in respect to self. So that gestures once made in the name of institutions like those of the Church—but only successfully under cover of infinite subtlety and deviousness—can now be revealed, without the need for special moral pleading, in the open light of day.

It is in what might be termed the negative phase of revolt, while decisions of preference with respect to instrumentalities for accomplishing millenniums are in abeyance for a remote future, that the inescapable opposition of instinct to idealism remains unemphasized and largely unnoticed. It is in such a period, while the available power-stake is still insignificant, that detailed differences of viewpoint seem unimportant among persons fundamentally united by their single dedication to the fostering of human brotherhood. *Then* the humanitarian descendants of Greeley and Peter Cooper, of Bakunin and Marx, may all dispute amiably. *Then* all sorts of rebels are useful to one another as they disparage the leaders and institutions which contemporaneously hold sway. It is in such a period that the escapist with idealistic proclivities can indulge himself to the full and can sponsor whatever theory of instrumentalities his individual nature favors. For the only test which the propagandist is called upon to give is a test of logic—destructive logic. And since no society has yet existed that has not been, by every *ideal* standard of judgment, almost immeasurably vile, the conscientiously indignant have but to turn honest eyes about them to see brutality and fraud exposed and protest vindicated. Thus it was that, immediately before and after the Great War, the cause of labor in the United States found many supporters among tender-minded Liberals, justly exercised by the spectacle of an enslavement of manual workers and wage-earners as shocking as that of indentured servants brought to our shores in the days of the colonies. So that instantly specific theories plausibly related themselves, if only on the negative side, to perfectionism.

It was the relative triumph of specific revolution in Russia which changed the face, if not the basic character, of the labor movement in this country. This triumph reduced the voluntary advocate of justice to the worker—the only advocate of such justice who might conceivably be regarded as purely disinterested—to his appropriately inept position among instinctive men of affairs, who were leaders according to biological urges in which idealism meant nothing beyond the means it provided for psychological exploitations to affect convenient conversions. It is the concrete example of Russia's strivings—making the power incentive loom large—which has precipitated the present circumstantial division of *révoltés* into sheep and goats; subdividing the goats again into such as are still dominated by the eternal concepts of pure idealism, and such as are obsessed by a fanaticism of idea reserved for a purist view of the implement of reform itself.

For it is in moments of crises that it becomes most apparent that, for all but a few exceptional men, the dictator is Nature—whom the vast majority have obeyed from the first. God help the idealist when he appears about to succeed! If each individual component of a society could be persuaded to confront himself to the end of understanding, and of acknowledging without equivocation, apology, or prepared special pleading, what would account for his motives in the successive concrete circumstances of his life—the result would be either immediate reversion to a barbarism which hypocrisy at present sometimes manages to adorn, or the ushering in of such a millennium of tolerance, love, and general benevolent insight as Christianity has not been able to bring about in twenty centuries. And without this candor as to data, where is science? Truly science itself cannot progress without a background in idealisms which, as religions falter, lack support! Theories of economic determinism go further than all antecedent theories in applying the harsh detachment of the scientific method to an explanation of the cruelties and barbarities of peoples operating in terms that express the will of a class or State: Terms never more brutally exemplified than under Fascist, Nazi, and Soviet régimes. Yet as discouragement for the future—and as an inducement to present confusions—there is still that fatal Marxist omission with respect to individualities.

Instinct cares nothing for universals. These are related to time imaginings and to the depersonalization of feeling, whereas the concern of instinct is with the immediate, its interests inalienably partisan. And movements of masses, together with the conduct of such persons as are best fitted to lead masses into action, symptomize not the protests of idealism, but biological concentrations on ways to survive as advantageously as possible—and in defiance, wherever convenience insists on it, of the tenets of perfectionism! Perfectionism is inescapably individual in its inception; it cannot be demonstrated except in terms of individual functioning.

This description of mass drifts holds equally whether or not these are under feudal, bourgeois, or proletarian ægis. And to strive to realize justice, mercy, or benevolence, in their ideal meanings, is neither within the capacities of most persons nor of societies that are inevitably biologically preoccupied and likely to be satisfied with victories gained by whatever devices seem readiest to hand. And whenever a movement, initially espoused by the rebellious idealist, passes beyond the speculative phase, it is a sign that the rebel is already obsolete. For by then what is actually represented, in changes and social upheavals, is beyond control by any mere exercise of mind. Though the stimulation of emotions in theoretic contexts may have contributed to unleash the forces that are by this time functioning, what is about to occur—and will occur, since circumstances predestine it—is but another capitulation of man to his environment, another victory of the unvarying conservatism of the man without daring who thus deceptively celebrates each recurrent manifestation of nature's tyranny.

The example afforded by Russia of a lapse into compromise is not the unique occasion for disillusion it is sometimes presumed to be. Though a present condition, which is tantamount to that existing in France between 1789 and 1793, has emphasized and thrown into relief discrepancies between ideal anticipations and cold facts, what emerges as obvious is not new anywhere. It is certainly not new in what it indicates of the labor movement in the United States. Actually, from the very beginning, the movements seemingly sanctioned under identical slogans provided by the successive cults of labor advocates have always been two: One, the outcome of the instinctive resistances of hard-pressed persons combating physical misfortunes affecting them directly; the other, only a fresh phase in man's slow, faltering, often bewildered attempted progression through time toward the attainment of perfections, sometimes adumbrated as within human scope, but never yet realized.

The true labor movement, in its restrictive real meaning, since it was initiated in the 1830's (when the guild system had disintegrated, and merchants, employers, and wage-earners were first distinguishable in a light reflected in present categories), has never been anything more or less exalted than the instinctive gesture of people menaced with biological defeat and resolved to wring from nature the best bargain evil circumstances will allow. And with this aim in view, real labor leaders, who are practical men, have presented their constituents and adherents with the whole successive gamut of exploitable theories and programs. These leaders have been free-landers, free-traders, advocates of free-banking, free capital, greenbackism, voluntary co-operation, boycott, syndicalism, and now, finally, Communism—and all for reasons precisely equivalent to those which have encouraged capitalists to the exercise of a parallel eclecticism of hard sense. While physical conditions in America invited to faith in the practicability of sustained individualism, workers, as their own version of a convenience also accepted by the capitalist, tended to support anarchistic philosophies proposing to weaken the powers of the State. But as the frontier shrank and free land ceased to be available—while, with developing industry, came a metropolitan control of politics and finance—capitalists organized trusts and workers organized unions. Until both are now, willy-nilly, prepared for State Socialism, which will logically culminate the chain of events set up during years in which each faction has taken the least resistant, gainful line of accommodation to the machine development of big industry. Labor and capital are now competing for the dictatorial seizure of a centralized government.

But where, in all this, is that which will distinguish one faction from another, in a sense more significant than is represented by a difference between success and defeat, victory and frustration, power domination by one group or by another? For if misfortune were all that were needed to perfect human character—if defeat were an adequate substantiation of virtue!—then we should again seek salvation in orthodox Christianity rather than in State Socialism. And for their own good—and ours—we should keep the poor with us!

Yet for the Marxist the question suggested in the above paragraph will have been answered by his own confounding of absolute virtue with the production of society's tangible wealth. This itself should be sufficient to emphasize the primitivism of Marxist dogmas with respect to cultural values, and to show that Marxism is not in itself, innately, the method of idealism, but only a theory for a dialectic to justify the biological aims of what is now the group handicapped by its biological position. There is no present adequate evidence to support the Marxist presumption that power-ambition, ego-tyranny, and personal revengefulness are but the offshoots of a previous or contemporaneous feudal and bourgeois exploitation of men; whereas justice, wisdom, and mercy are of the original nature of the proletariat—presumptions leading to the conclusion that nothing but the operation of a mechanism to level classes and equalize responsibility for the increase of society's concrete productivity will be needed to release these virtues in the average individual. One does not need to refer to myth to apprehend that the problem of good and evil arose with the existence on earth of two men, rather than one only, and before there was any society at all.

That logical Marxism is able to take so much for granted is due to the Marxist's inferred definition of all virtue as but the negation of class, and to his assumption that virtue is identifiable with elemental productiveness. The validity of positive idealism is contingent on the degree of realistic self-recognition concerning motives present in those persons who invoke idealism and propose to instrument it. But the aims of

Marxism are only as a coincidence—where they embrace the proposal to correct a specific injustice—identical with those of universal benefits. For Marxist aims are power aims—not perfectionist aims. And the instinctual and (in the perfectionist meaning) amoral intention of Marxist-Communism as a movement emerges most pointedly in the general Marxist abhorrence of the Liberal. This Marxist condemnation of the Liberal is based, so Marxist leaders state, on aspects of the character of the Liberal that may be ascribed to his origin outside the class of preference—which is, of course, the proletarian.

And the Marxist is fortified by Marx's own original omission of concern to understand the functions of individuals and the complexities of their conditioning; since the very terms of the Marxist premise altogether deny idealism its individual beginning, which has supplied its universal and permanently persistent interpretation.

Furthermore, the Marxist suspicion of the Liberal—though the basis of it is deliberately misrepresented by the propagandist—is, in its consistency with the Marxist hypothesis, still altogether justified. For whatever the Liberal occasion for embracing the proletarian cause, both the motives and mechanisms ascribable to class and economic determinism are bound to be absent. Hence it becomes clear that the Liberal individual is either, in the purist meaning, of individual genesis and capable of individual demonstration only, an idealist—and therefore, since he is inadequately interested in proletarian partisanship, anomalous by Marxist definitions—or that the liberal is, consciously or unconsciously, a hypocrite and a moral sentimentalist.

Among the supporters of labor's revolt in its speculative phase, which terminated with the early 1920's, were moral sentimentalists in plenty. Some still in that category, as it defines fundamental attributes, continue to offer themselves for the advancement of the Marxist-Communist cause. But their motives are altered. As slogans from Marx have become, not a mere provocation for tepid ethical disputes, but the battle-cry of a group already titillated by the knowledge that the forces of coercion (once used against them) are now almost within their grasp, the breath of the tiger that still lives in humanity has begun to blow, fetid and over-warm, even in polite drawing rooms. The sentimentalists have begun to quake. And, bolstered by quotations from perfectionists long since discarded as useless, such folk frenziedly reassert their rejoicings over the imminent success of a program by which it is proposed to make away with them. (The same kind of sentimentalists were heard in the salons of Paris on the eve of the French Revolution.) And they tremblingly put their heads into nooses proffered them by the practical political leader, who, for so long as they make their money or influence available to him, agrees not to cast too close a scrutiny on the unnaturalness of their acts. Thus they are able to imagine that they have, with shrewd foresight, succeeded in bribing their executioners.

Or there may be, among these deluded beings, some who, having more sincerely committed themselves to the support of the workers, awake to discover themselves involved in sacrifices beyond them, but reject clear-sighted and courageous pessimism, giving way instead to such orgies of unwarrantable optimism as are the surest signals of despair. For it is the rule of human behavior that a general proneness to convert ideologies into vehicles of escapism becomes most noticeable at that very point at which theory ought, rationally, to include an account of self-motivation. And if the deception of others is a frequent resort of the primitive, then self-deception, for men more sophisticated—especially men whose social consciences have been aroused!—is, equally, a major artifice of survival. Among all these types there are, too, persons who, far from feeling discouragement in the defeat of idealism, are refired, by its very refu-tation, to aspire to make the fruits of compromise their personal property.

For the ultimate triumph of democracy, conceived of as the victory of the proletariat, is no more inherently a victory in the ideal meaning of right over might, than were Attila's victories over the Visigoths. That the transference of Divine sanction from one to numbers was in the nature of a biological *coup d'état* for all those not born kings, it would be foolish to dispute. Yet the consequences of a democratic investiture of majorities with the prerogatives of sovereigns—who had unprotested, absolute power—is still good or evil, universally and ideally, only in the degree to which might is modified by influences from conceptions of right which are of individual, subjective origin. For societies are pre-dominantly effects from the circumscribed operations of instincts re-sponding to economic laws, and are never motivated by concern for ultimates. The mass of humans are *not* disciplined to essay truths or realize perfections likely to require a foreseen sacrifice of what consoles instinct most easily.

And even if the mechanical perfection of the proposed new State is better than that of the army for reducing the obstreperous, it might be well to remember that the advice given by Marx and Engels was to slaves who had nothing to lose but their chains, whereas in the future slaves may be amply nourished—for certainly it is the slaves who are most likely to be fed. An unfortunate concomitant of the progression of a "revolution" toward its conclusion in accomplished orthodoxy is the increasing inclusion, in the augmenting ranks of believers, of more and more persons of average—and less than average—mentality and vision: Persons who will not, or cannot, discriminate between the pure motive and its opposite. This, simply because the more persons there are assembled together, the more unavoidable it is that individuals superiorly equipped will be outnumbered by those who are not. Then the perversion of doctrine to disguise motives of ruthless personal ambition and personal retaliation also becomes more frequent. Then the person who has been so victimized by circumstances and heritage that the function of his mind is circumscribed to the articulation of pretexts that will satisfy his individual urge to brutality, ruthlessness, or remorseless contempt for everything not relevant to his personal advantage, comes into his own. Then, too, perhaps, those republican institutions which have been such a trial to the idealist begin to be regretted.

As "revolution" gains ground, and individuals associated under new slogans begin to share the prestige of a diversion of the power to menace and hurt into other hands than those which have grasped it previously, something we have always unwillingly suspected is depressingly confirmed—we see, suddenly, that "Labor" and "Capital"—in their average, individual composition—are, after all, the same. For the behavior and methods of groups bent upon effecting a tangible seizure of force follow an identical pattern, whether the claim to such seizure is referable to the correction of a specific, egregious abuse or not. Revisions of societies, such as are occurring at present, are not brought about as the realization of ideal intentions, but are, instead, expedient adjustments to alterations in physical surroundings. They are acts of necessity which the slow mass judgment has recognized and approved as inevitable only belatedly.

And though Marxism, as it supplies the dialectic for a movement toward proletarian internationalism, carries a just appeal to the emotions of the man who, in the cruel sense of exclusive racial nationalism, is "without a country," while ideally he has every right to claim one, it can be safely assumed that each "Trotskyite" perfectionist of theory, arguing with Rabbinical devoutness for the Marxian version of a means to universal brotherhood, loses something in future realism by his rejection of the discussion of a possible, established effect on himself from personal injuries to his vanity, or to his deeper—maybe less investigated—racial pride. While fear and threat were in abeyance, Jewish racial feeling was submerged in other and more individual interests, and there was not, among Jews, that fervor of clannishness one sometimes meets with now, while Nazi exploitation of shaken racial confidence piles up effects representing one of the most tragic vicious circles history can record. It is the Nazi-erected menace, suggesting to the Jew his final defeat and extermination, that has again reduced Jewish hope to the level of its most primitive ingredients, so that individuals, preaching Marxism in the letter, preach in their hearts only the salvation of the Jew. And this in those same emotional terms Jehovah once sanctioned as applicable to the punishment of offenders, even unto the third and fourth generations of persons not responsible for the original "sin." Thus crass aggressive instinct, expressive in the Nazi, wrings from the Jew in turn that despairing biological challenge it is in the nature of all but idealists to defy ruthlessly! And the Jew who calls himself a laborite recommences the fortification of his beleaguered ghetto which, here in America, exists as yet, thank God, only in his own imaginings. One remembers how Marx ignored as significant the mingling in his own temperament of effects from outraged compassion and longings that confess vehemently to impulses toward blind retributions on sects and races responsible for his personal sufferings and injuries—no public utterances by any man of note were ever more stupid than Marx's commentaries on Christianity. And if Marx did not, like Jesus, identify himself with a God of whom he considered himself the embodied manifestation, yet he may still have been deluded in other terms when he presumed that the specific bent of his theories to explain men owed nothing, either in omissions or commitments, to that overwhelming by hurts and imposed inferiorities which can intermittently warp the clearest insights and the finest thought processes.

For no doctrine and no teaching fails to undergo, as it is passed from lip to lip, some degree of modification that will adapt its meaning to cover such idiosyncratic and personal explanations as the disciple feels impelled to add to the generalized apology and justification he has adopted for his own. Until, in the end, it may well seem to the originator of any popularized creed that his use has been to give names to as many alien gods as there are worshippers.

So, as another instance, the Negro, most of all unwarrantably sacrificed to feast man's lust for cruelties and outrages, is being instructed by the propagandist in the masturbatory process of self-intensifying his hatred of a figure denominated "the boss." This "boss"—whose literal exemplification in real life may be vile enough—is actually, as a symbol for the Negro's violated and tortured emotions, the racial sign of the oppressive White, against whom, the Negro is tempted to believe, efficacious revenge may at last be fomented. For to say that this is not so—inevitably so!—after the long horror of a history of subjugation, is simply to say that the Negro, as an individual, has not suffered; or to insist that he has already, as a majority, achieved the attitude for which Jesus died— an attitude not pure even in such disciplined personalities as Kant and Spinoza. And to admit that, for the Negro, Marxism, in all but exceptional individual instances, is less a vehicle for attaining universal justice, than the feeling implement for the proposed triumph of Black Men over White Men who have long abused them, is to admit of colored people nothing more derogatory than that they are like other folk.

Nor will men cease to confuse ideal aims with those dictated by necessity and obvious physical advantage until somehow, in some manner, it becomes possible to treat frankly—and even publicly—everything involved in the understanding of self. Nor will bald honesty alone guarantee generally beneficial consequences from such public recognition of the individual's imperfections. Men have somehow to be reinspired with conceptions of virtue as a positive individual attainment, and with conceptions of a life wherein daily gestures are the integral part of the progression towards professed ultimate aims. And with all this, they must feel again as Saint Paul did, in another context, that without "charity" they are nothing—and especially that they are nothing without charity while they see, as in the present, but "through a glass darkly," since knowledge is imperfect, and wisdom slow, and must continue to be so for a long while to come. Above all things needed to make a revision of society along effective lines possible, is the discouragement of retaliations and revenges. Strange how the Marxist, attributing to man's physical insecurity so much that is evil, is able to ignore the havoc wrought psychically—the literal invitation to dissemble!—inevitable where the individual's failure to offer the socially correct opinions subjects him at once to the probability of physical threat!

"Between individuals and individuals, the government should put a force that is repressive; between individuals and institutions, a force that is conservative; between individuals and opinions, no force whatever." So wrote Benjamin Constant, with the errors of the French Revolution still fresh in a mind that was the most modern of any in that France of the late 18th century.

And to this writer, Constant seems to have presented the occasions for the exercise of power vested in a temperate state in an appropriately realistic order; and also to have given just examples of the degrees and relations in which force ought to be invoked.

For individuals, in the sense that they tend toward primitive behavior, ought not to be allowed to harm one another. And in the sense in which they represent themselves commonly in their institutions—which are founded on majority agreement only gradually made spontaneous—they ought to undertake changes without that precipitancy which unfailingly brings violence and bloodshed and extreme resorts to coercion.

Whereas, in the matter of public expressions of individual opinion, there ought to be the freedom the anarchist philosopher has long envisaged as ideal. For the public, whatever its individual composition, is, as a mass, intellectually and æsthetically backward—if for no other reason than the clumsiness of the manœuvres required to bring about the articulation of a concerted view. And since from individuals, expressing themselves in art and theoretically, have come all those influences which have modified the culture and conduct of whole peoples with respect to more than instinct sees, it is for ill, not good, that social censorships are set up and official checks put upon philosophers, artists, and speculative scientists. And we shall certainly never progress toward literal perfections without full liberty to explore perfections imagined as we exchange our dreams on canvas and paper. Art, in fact, is a function of life and of the living; it is subject to death, but not to dictation. As for science, its aim is knowledge, and the understanding of life: It is the current version of philosophy. Science differs from earlier philosophies not in ends envisaged, but in its conception of a technique by which to arrive at such ends: The mission the scientist has undertaken is the substitution of objective demonstration of truth for metaphysical insights that anticipate possible external proofs of the philosopher's statements. It would seem that, in Russia, Germany and Italy, those ingredients in Marxist theorizing which were grounded in fact are already being validated. But we are still without adequate data for prognosticating individual behavior. Without such data, we lack the means for implementing virtue, for the socialization of industry alone cannot be said to supply any means superior to that offered by religions exploiting superstitious incentives.

Surely, with our meager wisdom, we cannot, at this juncture, afford to dismiss as "shiboleths" either free speech or those republican institutions guaranteed, by their very imperfections, some measure of elasticity! Perfection in the State is not the realization of the individual's ideal, but is, merely, the crystallization of an instrumentality. It is through the individual that idealism will function, if at all. Surely in America, where we are not yet committed to a totalitarian mechanism, the individual should be re-examined and his significance studied.

# WAR

## [Mauritz A. Hallgren]

AMERICA has an abiding faith in its own moral goodness. It endeavors to give emphasis to this faith by standing haughtily aloof from other nations and particularly from their troubles and quarrels. Europe and Asia seem to most Americans, indeed, to be always getting ready for war, when they are not actually fighting. And America considers itself above all that. It has made it part of its credo that, however much others may be given to war, it is itself devoted to peace. It has persuaded itself that it is, always will be and always has been a peaceful nation.

No one has summed up the country's peace tradition, its belief in its own moral goodness, quite as ably as did Franklin D. Roosevelt in his Chautauqua speech in 1936. He spoke with disparagement of other nations, among whom, he said, "there are many causes that produce war. There are ancient hatreds, turbulent frontiers, the legacy of 'old forgotten, far-off things, and battles long ago.' There are new-born fanaticisms, convictions on the part of certain peoples that they have become the unique depositories of ultimate truth and right. . . . A dark modern world faces wars between conflicting economic and political fanaticisms in which are intertwined race hatreds. . . . The conscience of America revolts against war. . . . Any nation which provokes war forfeits the sympathy of the people of the United States. . . . Of all nations in the world, we are in many ways most singularly blessed. Our closest neighbors are good neighbors. And if there are remoter nations that wish us not good but ill, they know that we are strong; they know that we can and will defend ourselves and defend our neighborhood. They know that we seek to dominate no other nation. That we ask no territorial expansion. That we oppose imperialism and that we desire reduction in world armaments. We believe in democracy; we believe in freedom; and we believe in peace."

Thus have spoken passing Presidents and lesser politicians turned states-men down through the country's history, ever since the republic was founded. In its essentials, indeed, Mr. Roosevelt's Chautauqua speech dif-fered not in the slightest from Washington's Farewell Address. Washing-ton, too, spoke of America as a "free, enlightened" nation, as one that sincerely desired peace, while others were given to fighting. He declared that "Europe has a set of primary interests which to us have none or a very remote relation. Hence she must be engaged in frequent controversies, the causes of which are essentially foreign to our concern. . . . Our de-tached and distant situation invites and enables us to pursue a different course." So he asked: "Why, by interweaving our destiny with that of any part of Europe, entangle our peace and prosperity in the toils of European ambition, rivalship, interest, humor, or caprice?"

This peace tradition is, of course, not entirely without substance. It has been engendered not only by the country's geographic and cultural isolation, but also by that sense of relief which is still subconsciously experienced among the descendants of the millions of Europeans who migrated to this hemisphere to escape the jealousies and confusions of the Old World. It has fed upon the country's century-long fight, now abandoned, for "freedom of the seas," since "freedom" has always been identified with "peace" in the minds of the American people. It has been helped along, too, by the fact that for a few years the United States was, or appeared to be, a warm advocate of arbitration, that is, of the substitution of law for war in the conduct of international affairs.

Unfortunately, there the substance ends. The rest is sentiment and wish-thinking, and in its larger implications does violence to history. For the truth is that in the century and a half of its existence the Ameri-can republic, far from being the peaceful country of its own imagination, has taken part in as many wars as any nation abroad and in more than most. Nor is this all, for in at least three of its major wars, and in most of those of minor historic importance,[1] the United States was, by all reasonable standards of justice, the aggressor and each time enlarged

---

[1]Military men are inclined to boast that, while the average citizen "counts wars on the fingers of one hand, the War Department numbers its actual calls to active service at more than one hundred." The State Department's records show that upon no less than sixty occasions in the history of the country American marines and sailors have been sent on hostile missions into foreign territory. Not all of these "expeditions" and "affairs" can rightly be described as "wars," to be sure. Nevertheless, and with all due apologies to Mr. Roosevelt, the United States did through some of them seek to im-pose its will upon other nations and through even more of them succeeded in adding considerably to its land holdings. That, in fact, was the main result of the seventy-six Indian wars listed by the War Department.

its territory as a result of that aggression. An anything but pacifist writer in *Fortune* has lately put the matter thus:

It is generally supposed that the American military ideal is peace. But unfortunately for this high-school classic, the U. S. army, since 1775, has filched more square miles of the earth by sheer military conquest than any army in the world, except only that of Great Britain. And as between Great Britain and the U. S. it has been a close race. . . . It is all very well for us to study Julius Cæsar as a curiosity and to deplore the modern excursions of Japan into Asia on manufactured pretexts, but our own exploits along those lines, as Mussolini has recently been pointing out, would have stirred Cæsar's Roman heart, and doubtless do elicit the admiration of General Araki of Japan.

Of course, this aggression has always been given a proper moral dress. The army simply *had* to protect the American people from the savage Indians—even though in the process these aboriginal nations were virtually exterminated and their rich lands appropriated by a supposedly more civilized race. In 1845 it was for the avowed purpose of protecting the independence of our new little neighbor, the Republic of Texas, that American troops were sent to the Rio Grande, though the Senate knew and other people suspected at the time that the real purpose was to facilitate the transfer of this territory to the United States—and in the end, as we all know now, this benevolent gesture brought us, not only Texas, but also the immensely valuable lands out of which the States of California, Nevada, New Mexico, and Arizona were formed. And it was to save "the poor Cubans" from "the Spanish butcher" that the great crusade of 1898 was launched—a holy mission that gave the United States the Philippines and Puerto Rico as well as a stranglehold on Cuba itself.

Nor can it have been forgotten that President McKinley sought solace in prayer when he discovered that by defeating the Spaniard the United States had fallen heir to a nice bit of war booty. Nor that the militant Theodore Roosevelt became the soft-spoken moralist and man of peace when he intervened in the Russo-Japanese war to prevent either country from becoming so strong that it could dominate the Chinese market to the possible hurt of American trade. Nor yet that Woodrow Wilson doused us, almost drowned us, with his stratospheric idealism upon taking us into the war with Germany when the credit of the Allies gave out and America was threatened with economic collapse. This habit that American statesmen have of dealing with problems of foreign policy almost exclusively in terms of morals and sentiment has naturally contributed in great measure to the inflation of the national peace tradition.

It is a curious fact, however, that not once has the United States succeeded in safeguarding or strengthening any of the moral principles for which it has from time to time purportedly fought. The War of 1812, for example, was ostensibly waged to establish "the free sea," and it is still almost universally believed that in this the United States was gloriously victorious. Yet the Treaty of Ghent, by which peace was concluded and the issues between America and England settled, neither recognized nor as much as mentioned American neutral rights or the "freedom of the seas." The diplomatic struggle for recognition of "the free sea" was to continue for another century, but with no better results. Although in defending this principle the United States chose to stand on moral grounds and spoke hopefully of "the laws of natural justice" and of "the precepts of Christian charity upon the sea," at bottom it wanted simply to protect what it considered its right to trade freely and unreservedly with all countries at war. It was the lure of bonanza war-trade profits, not peace, that underlay its fight for "freedom of the seas."

Again, if we are to believe Woodrow Wilson and his latter-day apologists, the war with Germany was solely an adventure in morality. America was told only that it was fighting and had to fight because of the inhuman submarine warfare and because it was imperative that the Potsdam gang and militarism in general be destroyed and the world made safe for democracy. To this very day this thesis is ardently defended by the Wilsonians, including especially those who belong to the Seymour school. It might be well to ask, therefore, whether any of these moral objectives were attained. Were the "human rights" for which America fought vindicated by going to war? Is it any safer today to pass through a declared war zone than it was before April 1917? Is the submarine less of a menace? Was militarism destroyed either in Potsdam or elsewhere? Was democracy made more secure? Every one of these questions must be answered with a plain negative.

Mixed up with the peace tradition is the superstition that holds that the American people can be counted upon to spring automatically to the defense of home and country should the need arise. This idea is widely entertained even among pacifists. It is of a piece with the similar theory advanced by certain amateur psychologists that "men like war," that man is by nature a combative animal and that war, therefore, can never be abolished. The theory, whether we take it in its pacifist or its militarist form, is mostly nonsense.

In America, as in other countries, men have never gone willingly to battle. They have had to be cajoled, tricked, bribed and driven into fighting. Hence the bounties that have been paid to "volunteers" in most American wars. Hence the use of conscription as a means of forcing men to fight. Hence the need for extravagant and ceaseless propaganda in time of war. General Washington complained again and again of the difficulty he had in getting soldiers and of keeping them once he had them. His complaint has been repeated by military men ever since, by men like General Upton, who never tired of damning the volunteer and militia system.[2]

Most men prefer to take their fighting, like their other adventures, vicariously instead of directly. They would rather sit in the Yale Bowl or Yankee Stadium and cheer than get down in the field and play. So, too, with their attitude toward war. In April 1917 the country was all but unanimous in its enthusiasm for the war with Germany. Despite this enthusiasm there was no great rush to the recruiting stations. When it came to fighting, the American male was reluctant to move and so had to be drafted for service in the trenches.

Still the theory voiced by William Jennings Bryan that a million Americans would spring to arms overnight in case of need, dubious though it is, has served a useful purpose. It has prevented the military from becoming a powerful or dominant force in the political affairs of the nation. The victorious rebels of 1776–83, having overthrown one military autocracy, made it plain that they did not intend to permit another to gain a foothold in the new republic. So strong was their reaction against the man in uniform, whether king or hireling, that for a while they kept only eighty men under arms. Subsequently, a regular army was created, but even this force was small and was, more or less, under the thumb of the national legislature. No one seemed for a moment to doubt that, if an enemy were to appear, the people themselves would rise spontaneously and *en masse* to the defense of the country. That was how a free democracy was supposed to work. And that was the accepted basis of the military policy of the United States until the early years of the twentieth century.

[2]An example of the reluctance of the common man to share in the dirty work of war may be found in the War of 1812. Washington, the capital of the nation, was threatened by the British. A call was sent out for a force of 93,500 militia and volunteers. General Winder, in command of the Washington military district, was under no illusion as to the number of men who might respond, but he appears to have believed that by asking for 93,500 men he could get together at least 15,000, which he thought might be enough to hold off the British. On the day before Bladensburg, however, he had only 1400 regulars and 1800 militia at his disposal, though on the morning of the battle a brigade of 2200 untrained militia came over from Baltimore to take part in the futile fighting.

About that time, however, the dread of militarism had begun to lose its hold upon the American people. The soldier was still suspect, but by then faith in democracy had become such a matter of fact with the people that they took it for granted that control of the military rested with them. Thus their vigilance relaxed. Simultaneously other forces were at work to relieve the professional soldier of the yoke of democratic control that had been bothering him so much. The nation was increasingly occupied with its domestic economic affairs, with the "American dream," which was to bring everlasting prosperity to every one. The country had grown enormously. It appeared that in consequence the "defense" problem had become far too complex to be dealt with under the simple principles of the 1790 policy. With the growth of the country the "national interest" abroad had expanded and it was supposed that the professional fighting man alone could protect that great and presumably vital interest. War itself and the instruments of war had become infinitely more complicated. The tendency was to leave the military problem in ever larger measure in the hands of the military specialist.

These developments were reflected in the military law of 1903, under which the General Staff was created, and even more so in the National Defense Act of 1916, which for the first time gave the professional soldier the necessary authority to organize the army to suit himself. Further power not only to manage the army but also to formulate defense policy (a power that the Constitution reserves to Congress) was granted the military men under the defense law as rewritten in 1920. At the same time the admirals were extending their control and reaching out for additional power on their own account, though their expanded authority was to rest more upon assumption than upon specific legal sanction.

In a strictly technical sense control of the nation's defense policy still lay, as it still lies, with the national legislature. Yet effective control has now largely passed to the admirals and generals. The former have gone so far as to lay down upon their own initiative and without as much as a by-your-leave to Congress or the people what is today accepted as the "Fundamental Naval Policy of the United States." The generals have not ventured quite that far, but they also are shaping a "defense" policy for America upon their own responsibility and according to their own notion of what America ought to defend, and when and why. In short, the choice between war and peace now lies, not exclusively by any means, but to a dangerous degree, with these professional fighting men.

Congress seems hardly to mind. It is imbued with the spirit of the peace tradition. It feels sure that neither the army nor the navy would ever violate that tradition. It is convinced that the war machine, no matter how big it becomes, will never be used for aggressive or unmoral purpose, but only, if it is used at all, to uphold justice and honor. And since the admirals and generals say the same thing, Congress is doubly assured. It can, of course, keep the fighting services in check through its power to appropriate funds, but in recent years it has used this power solely with the budget in mind and never with the idea of employing it to shape or control military policy.

Naturally the military men have not been slow to take advantage of this state of affairs. While the people continue to rest secure in their belief that defense means defense and nothing else, the army and navy have been preparing a fighting machine far larger and more powerful, in relation to the country's natural security, than that possessed by any other nation on earth. They are using the national defense policy as a cloak behind which they are making extensive preparations for American participation in another mass war on foreign soil.

For instance, if we may judge by the proof the admirals have themselves provided in their writings and in testimony given before Congressional committees over the last twenty years, the United States has today a navy 40 to 70 per cent larger than it actually needs for territorial defense. And the admirals want a still larger fleet. They make no secret of the fact that they hold mere coastal defense in disdain and that all of their war plans call for offensive operations in foreign waters. They do not as much as pretend that their preparations are in any way designed for defense or for anything other than another major war abroad.

The generals, though somewhat more discreet in their public utterances, have the same end in view. They have rebuilt the army upon the "expansible" principle, for the adoption of which Upton had labored so long. As a result, the military establishment today is made up of far more units than will ever be needed for territorial defense, while the available personnel, instead of being concentrated in a small and compact force, complete in itself, has been spread exceedingly thin over these many units. The army is, in brief, a sprawling military skeleton which it is intended in time of war to cover with flesh and blood—in the form of some millions of raw or half-trained recruits. The "defense" program calls for a "covering force" of 600,000 to 1,000,000 men to be immediately mobilized upon the outbreak of war and to be enlarged as rapidly as possible by the addition of anywhere from 2,000,000 to 19,000,000 conscripts.

Not even the generals will argue that such a monster army is or ever will be required to defend the United States against attack or invasion. An army of 50,000 men at the very most would be large enough to give the country complete security against attack. Even such a force might be regarded as a luxury, so slim are the chances of the country's ever being invaded. This army would, of course, have to be complete in itself, not the expansible-collapsible affair the American army of today actually is, and it would have to be highly mobile and thoroughly mechanized. Instead we have a cumbersome skeleton that can hardly move and certainly cannot fight until it has been inflated to Napoleonic proportions. It is not organized for defense and the military men know that it is not. They know that its primary, if not its sole, function is to serve as the nucleus for another expeditionary force to fight in another major war overseas.

The National Defense Act, as rewritten in 1920, is itself based almost entirely upon the principle of the totalitarian war. So, too, is the Industrial Mobilization Plan, which has been prepared under the authority of that act. This plan provides for the automatic establishment upon the beginning of hostilities of a dictatorship more sweeping in scope and rigid in form than any now known to Europe. The dictatorship would be absolute in every detail. Some of the main features of the plan have been embodied in the so-called May bill, which was pending in Congress at the time of writing. While this bill, already greatly modified under pressure of public opinion, might not be enacted, the military men are not disturbed. Their own plan remains intact and they feel confident that Congress will accept it without a single change on the day that war is declared.

It is plain that no such dictatorship would be needed in the event of an attempted invasion, since it would take no more than a handful of troops and a single engagement to beat off any invader who might by some miracle break through the naval and coastal defenses. Only in case America were to fight in another great and protracted war overseas might a dictatorship become necessary. That is unquestionably what is envisaged. For the whole of the current preparedness program turns upon the Industrial Mobilization Plan and upon the War Department's intention to build another mass conscript army to fight in just such a war.

These preparations are the result neither of accident nor of coincidence.

They are indispensable to the defense of the world's richest and strongest imperialist power. If America intends to hold that position, it must be prepared to guard its imperialist interests—or else change itself into some other kind of economic community that would not be dependent upon the fruits of imperialism for its economic welfare. Moreover, since these imperialist interests are virtually certain to be jeopardized, in part at least, in another general imperialist war, America must stand ready to take part in that war.

Prior to 1917 the military men did not see this very clearly. They had no more notion than any one else that the United States would ever, as a matter of "national defense," fight a major war in Europe and under circumstances that did not remotely suggest that the territory or institutions of the country were in danger. Hence they had no plans to move across the Atlantic an army of 2,000,000 men and the ammunition and *matériel* needed to supply them. Now they know better and have made what they consider adequate amends for their previous error in judgment.

The admirals have been more alive to the changes in America's world position. Immediately after the war with Spain, which brought the United States to the fore as an imperialist power, they demanded and came close to getting a navy second only to that of Great Britain. In 1915, the year that saw the United States transformed from a debtor to a creditor nation and that really marked the arrival of the country as the most powerful of the imperialist states, the admirals demanded a navy "second to none." The Wilson Administration hastened to comply and within a year had enacted legislation—the famous 1916 building program—which would actually have given the country the most formidable navy afloat.

Paradox though it may appear, the national peace tradition has been the chief support of the current preparations for another war abroad. America regards itself as a democracy in which the popular will always prevails. The army and navy are a part of this democracy and are controlled by it, *i.e.,* by the popular will. Since this is so, it must follow that whatever the army and navy do is being done in accordance with the popular will, *i.e.,* in accordance with America's belief that it will never fight except in self-defense or, possibly, in defense of some just and noble and wholly moral cause. Indeed, even while the people suppose, on the one hand, that the army and navy are being maintained solely for the sake of guarding the nation and its territory against a foreign foe, they steadfastly refuse, on the other hand, to tolerate any criticism of the motives and purposes of these "defense" forces. Such criticism is looked upon as unpatriotic, even as treason, for it reflects upon the pure and peaceful motives of the American democracy itself.

The soldiers and politicians in Washington seem to prefer it that way. They are forever declaring that "adequate defense" is "the best guarantor of peace." But it may be noted that in this connection they never speak of "territorial defense." To them "national defense" is meant to cover the country's commerce, its economic and other interests abroad, its "national honor"—in short, its position as an imperialist power. Their definition is so broad and flexible that it could be made to cover even a war of aggression without the slightest difficulty. It will be remembered that the Japanese took Manchuria in "self defense" and that it was again in "self defense" that Mussolini swallowed Ethiopia. As a matter of fact, the United States itself has never fought a war in which this notion of "defense" was not put foremost. Of course, the politicians and soldiers never bother to make it clear to the people that "defense" to them means something substantially more than territorial defense. In consequence, when opposition arises in Congress or elsewhere to a "defense" measure, the people are all too apt to believe that the opponents of that measure are not sincere in crying out against militarism or military extravagance, but really want to lay the country open to invasion.

This paradoxical attitude (plus the political illiteracy of the American people, which is itself a product of isolation and the peace tradition, for America considers itself above the necessity of understanding the trials and troubles of other nations) obviously makes the task of the war-makers easier. As things stand now, they would have little difficulty in leading the country into another holy crusade. They would have only to find a sufficiently attractive excuse in keeping with the American credo and the nation would once more go marching off to the plain of Es-draelon—or at least dispatch a mass conscript army in that direction.

And if that happens, we might as well be prepared to bid good-bye to American civilization. For the "next war" will undoubtedly usher in a period, more or less enduring, of military or semi-Fascist dictatorship. The dictatorship would be erected in the first instance for the purpose of carrying on the war. Yet nothing could be more certain than that revolution would sweep Europe and Asia in the event of another great international conflict and that America itself would be confronted with unrest on a scale far exceeding that of 1919. If the war were long drawn out, or if America were to suffer a smashing defeat, revolution might follow here as well. In any case, there would be a psychological upheaval and widespread disturbances, partly as the result of the emotional let-down from the war, partly in consequence of the cessation of the economic effort to carry on the war, and partly in reaction to events abroad. The dictatorship would not do as its relatively feeble predecessor did after the fighting was over in 1919 and voluntarily dissolve itself. It would refuse to give up its power. It would decide at first that its services were needed to maintain "law and order" and later would hold onto its power to "save" the country from revolutionary Europe.

It is not intended here to suggest that this "next war" is inevitable. It can be avoided. But first the people must arrive at a clearer and fuller understanding of the issues at stake. Alas, either the ability or the desire to gain that understanding is sadly lacking. Instead the country remains supremely but blindly confident of its own virtues and intensely sus-picious of other nations. It surely cannot be surprising to find that such a country has no constructive or effective peace policy. It is unwilling to co-operate with others, or to make any sacrifice on its own account, with a view to preserving international peace.

The United States has elected rather to continue to stand haughtily aloof. It is inclined to believe, or at any rate to hope, that if war should come again, it will not be drawn in. Yet even here it has no definite policy, has hit upon no formula that will really serve to "keep us out of war." There are still those, far smaller in number now than they were after 1918, who believe that the only way to keep the country out of war is by keeping the world at peace through some international system of collective peace enforcement. Perhaps, if this were only an ideal world, that would offer the most practical and effective way. Unhappily, the same sort of nationalism and self-pride that is found in America also governs other countries. They are no more willing than is America to yield any of their national sovereignty to the attainment of peace, or to sacrifice any part of their right to have the final say in all matters affecting their "vital interests."

Even the American sponsors of the Geneva idea are now beginning to understand that any effort to apply collective sanctions against a powerful aggressor, real or fancied, would mean war. They talk less and less about the value of the League system as a means of assuring peace and more and more about the desirability of taking a collective stand against "aggression" though that result in war. Some, indeed, quite for-getting 1914–18 and what has happened since, are frankly agitating for another war to save the world for democracy, for another war to end war. It may be fortunate that these agitators are not more numerous, since there is no more chance of "saving" democracy by war today than there was in 1914 or in 1917. Yet the influence of this school, it may be worth noting, extends beyond its numbers, for in the aggregate it represents fairly powerful economic and political interests, while individually its members are rather more literate than the average.

For every one of these neo-Wilsonian propagandists there are at least ten neo-isolationists. The prescription offered by this latter and more popular school is scarcely more promising. Their only solution is still more isolation. They would cut America off from the world in time of war. They would, if they had their way, abolish virtually all economic and political intercourse with belligerent nations. Even those who subscribe to the theory that imminent economic collapse put America into the last war (by all odds the soundest of the theories regarding America's entry into that war) favor this isolationist course, not stopping to realize that that solution would itself invite economic collapse and give rise to a militant war party, as has happened once before in American history.

Though they have an overwhelming majority in Congress, the new isolationists have not been courageous enough (probably because of their unconscious fear of the potential economic consequences) to compel acceptance of their prescription. Instead Congress has, in the Neutrality Act of 1937, approved a weak and contradictory compromise. While this law has been handed down in the name and with the applause of isolationists, it actually offers no barrier whatever to the development of another war-trade boom such as that of 1914–17. It merely provides that the belligerent who controls the sea, has the necessary shipping and can pay cash may buy all the goods, except munitions, that he can possibly haul away from this country. In short, the law literally invites a repetition of the crisis of 1917. What is worse is that, while the Wilson Administration could have adopted a policy to prevent that crisis from breaking had it had sufficient will power or desire, under the 1937 law another Administration would find it next to impossible to adopt any kind of policy to prevent or deal with a similar crisis.

The people could undoubtedly take action on their own direct responsibility to prevent war. They could, independently of the government, organize themselves for peace. Organized mass resistance to war would make war impossible. But mass organization for peace, like criticism of the army and navy, is held to be unpatriotic, even perhaps revolutionary. America prefers to seek refuge in sentiment and in such ineffectual legislation as the Neutrality Act of 1937. It clings doggedly to its belief in its own moral goodness and its democratic virtues, and it has, more or less, entrusted its moral conscience and peace tradition to the safekeeping of its professional warriors. They are the sworn defenders of American democracy and, therefore, can no more do wrong than can that democracy itself—or so the country seems to reason.

For their part the professional warriors envisage defense of the nation in terms of mass warfare and dictatorship, of Napoleonic slaughter and suppression of democracy. They may not have their way in the end, to be sure, but the chances are that they will. It must be conceded that there would be no American civilization today if the army had not by sheer conquest provided the necessary land and material resources. It would be ironic indeed if now, in order to safeguard those gains, the army and navy, with their elaborate and ambitious plans, should turn out to be the means whereby that civilization is turned into something radically different, if not actually destroyed.

# THE LAW

## [Zechariah Chafee, Jr.]

WHAT IS LAW? It is, in one sense, a big slice of life which includes everything that happens while a government is trying to maintain order and settle disputes. So a chapter on Law in the United States since the World War could tell all about the Sacco-Vanzetti case, which failed to account for four of the six payroll robbers (and perhaps for all six of them); the inquest into the sanity of Leopold and Loeb; the conviction of Bruno Hauptmann, which left so much of the mystery forever unsolved; the attempts to free Mooney; the vindication of racial purity at Scottsboro. It would be full of people—corporation lawyers feverishly getting out new bond issues during the boom and picking up the pieces after the crash, studious title searchers and agile ambulance chasers, employers' counsel drawing labor injunctions for judges to sign, law students burning the midnight oil over difficult books in order to graduate and spend years wearing out shoe leather, a witness minutely describing an automobile accident that he saw for five seconds five years before when he was in short pants, jurymen playing pinochle and judges playing golf, young braintrusters upsetting old business practices and aged family lawyers advising widows, deputy sheriffs hunting down elusive debtors, relays of policemen questioning a hungry and sleepless prisoner all night under the glare of searchlights, professors composing profound legal articles for other professors to read, learned judges writing opinions by means of scissors and paste and the brief of the winning counsel, other judges illuminating an obscure doctrine with the flash of one sentence, a government scientist tracing a piece of broken ladder to one lumber yard in all the United States; Clarence Darrow examining Bryan, H. L. Mencken getting arrested on Boston Common for selling a shady short story, Huey Long writing statutes with the speed of a midnight reporter after a big fire, and President Roosevelt and the Senators in the Supreme Court fight; John W. Davis getting introduced to his own client in the midst of arguing the case,

Charles E. Hughes upholding the rights of the people to send Socialists to the New York Assembly, William G. Thompson's last interview with the Italian anarchist whom he could not save from the chair, Mr. Justice Brandeis analyzing the accounts of the Southwestern Bell Telephone Company, Senator Borah urging Cardozo's name upon President Hoover, Mr. Justice Holmes before the microphone on his ninetieth birthday, and Mr. Justice Black also on a nationwide hookup at the opposite end of his judicial career. Then crimes and disorders and lynching are part of law and could not be left out, especially the unforeseen breakdown of Prohibition with all the home brewers, bootleggers, highjackers, speakeasies, coast guards, and bargain-days. The canvas would be crowded with villains and heroes—racketeers and Dewey, forgers and Albert S. Osborn, Dillinger and G-men. It would be a good story, and I cannot write it.

Or law during the last twenty years can be treated very differently, according to the common usage of lawyers and judges, to mean roughly the forms under which order is maintained and disputes are settled. Then this chapter would be much less colorful. It would be like a history of football which did not mention a single breath-taking run or impossible forward pass or long drop-kick, but merely told about the development of the rules, why four downs in ten yards were substituted for three downs and five yards, and how the goal-posts forsook the goal-line. Similar surveys of the growth of various branches of law have lately appeared in the *New York University Law Quarterly Review* and the *Harvard Law Review*. In the predecessor to this volume, I ventured to give a rough aeroplane sketch of the whole domain of American Law, and I undertook the present article expecting just to bring that sketch down to date. But I soon realized that I ought to do more than that, because something else has happened that is much more interesting to citizens at large than changes in the rules. It concerns the very nature and validity of those rules and goes back to the question asked in my first sentence, "What is Law?"

Moreover, not much has occurred in the framework of law since I wrote, which can now be said to possess nationwide and permanent importance. The year 1917 marked a conspicuous slowing down in that rebuilding of governmental and legal institutions which had been actively under way for at least a decade. Ideas for lessening human friction that had long been talked about were rapidly becoming realities. Besides the establishment of a constitutional federal income tax, the popular election of Senators, the organization of banking and money on a much sounder basis, the closer supervision of business, and the other national measures carried out from Theodore Roosevelt's second administration through Wilson's first administration, State after State adopted women's suffrage, executive budgets, initiative and referendum, direct primaries, minimum wage legislation, public utilities commissions, and workmen's compensation, which I still consider the biggest legal event during my lifetime. All at once the tempo changed. The War thrust domestic issues into the background, and long after the Armistice they were overshadowed by international problems. We dreamed about a new world to follow the fighting, and woke up at last to find ourselves on the same old planet, considerably more battered than before. Then, in addition to disillusionment, another obstacle appeared. Law reforms on a grand scale require lawyers with plenty of time to work out thoroughly the detailed provisions by which ideals are harnessed for work on earth. But lawyers were never so busy with clients' affairs as in the years of 1919–29. After adjusting munition contracts and war-risks insurance and straightening out the post-war slump, they got dragged breathlessly along in the expansion of inventions and corporate organizations. The substance of life grew and altered at such accelerated speed that lawyers were too much occupied with the daily grist of the mill to have the desire or ability to make more law. When I review the legal improvements suggested in the predecessor to this volume, I find they are mostly unaccomplished. Ambulance chasers and contingent fees are with us, legal proceedings are still meagerly described in the press except for big criminal trials, a ministry of justice is yet to come, although New York has taken an important step in that direction, judges are chosen in political campaigns wherever this was the practice twenty years ago, minor offenses and automobile accidents overload the courts more than ever, and the problems of a dissolving family stay scattered in most States through several courts instead of being handled as a unit in a Court of Domestic Relations. One reason for the great rush of federal legislation in 1933 was that we were catching up in a few months on tasks that had been accumulating for twenty years. Work that might have been done thoroughly, if it had been spread evenly over the whole period since 1914, was hastily thrown together. It is too soon to say which of the New Deal statutes will last, and which of them will be swept away because they try too much or cost too much. Thus, while part of the law has not advanced conspicuously during the last two decades, another part went ahead so fast at the end that it may have to go back again and make a fresh start.

Nevertheless, a few important developments of legal rules deserve mention here.

First, the law has gradually adjusted itself to practical changes in the relation of a business corporation to the holders of its stocks and bonds. About a hundred years ago, enterprises began to be incorporated, so that those who supplied the capital should risk only the money they put in, whereas partners risked their whole fortunes. However, stockholders went on treating each other almost like partners and did in fact exercise substantial powers over the management of the business. Their legal position as its co-owners corresponded with reality, and this is still true in many small corporations. But the legal conception of ownership by the individual investor became virtually a fiction for corporations with immense capital and thousands of stockholders. Power always tends to go into the hands of a few men. This is as true of the State or other political organizations as it is of business organizations. The insiders on the board of directors of a big business were replicas of the bosses in a political party or the leading officials who can declare "We planned it that way." But political insiders are frequently thrown out by an overturn in the electorate, whereas it became very rare indeed for the board of directors of a large corporation to be ousted by a revolt among the stockholders. The existing management was in an impregnable position, because it could always get enough proxies from its friends and from the considerable number of unthinking stockholders who automatically made use of the printed blanks and stamped envelopes supplied them at the expense of the corporation. Although any stockholder was legally free to choose an independent agent at the annual meeting, this privilege amounted to little because there was no simple and cheap way of getting the small stockholders together to set up their own representation. So the minority stockholders lost all genuine chance of controlling the policies of the enterprise. Whatever their legal position it was plain that economically they were not co-owners of the business but merely claimants to a specified fraction of such portions of the earnings as the directors chose to pay out. During the boom of the '20's this practical situation was legally recognized by statutes in several of the States where large businesses were incorporated, which permitted the issue of stock without any voting power. The investors who bought such stock had no share in the business except the pleasure of receiving dividend checks, which disappeared in its turn after October, 1929. Bondholders also lost ground, though in a different way. Originally they had a powerful grip on the business, although they could not vote at annual meetings, for they were mortgagees who could sell the property of the corporation to the highest bidder just as a bank forecloses on a farm. But when enterprises grew larger and their property became complex, there were no outside bidders. The property of the business was useful only for the business itself as a going concern. Therefore, after a default on the bonds, there was nothing to do but reorganize the business under a slightly different corporate name; and the old bondholders, instead of getting hard cash from the proceeds of a real sale were simply handed new pieces of engraved paper somewhat less safe than their previous investment. The supposed tangible security could not be seized and sold; and its value became even more problematical as bonds were issued that were based, not on land, but on other securities which the insiders could change about almost as if they were their own. In other words, bondholders like stockholders had only a claim to share in the earnings of the business while the insiders should manage it successfully. It was a better claim; the bondholders stood on a higher rung of the corporate ladder; after reorganization they stepped down a few rungs and remained above the stockholders. But they were still on the ladder, and they had to accept what the managers of the reorganization decided to do. Bondholders and stockholders got only what insiders chose to give them, whether they liked it or not.

Nevertheless, as the insiders in a big business got free from control by investors, their powers of management were threatened from a new quarter. When the purchasers of stocks and bonds realized in 1929 that they had acquired only valueless pieces of paper, which had never given them any effective share in determining the policies of great enterprises, they called on the government for help. The Securities and Exchange legislation and the Commission which it set up were designed to give investors protection which was no longer furnished by the internal machinery of the corporation or by the existing methods of selling securities. Some citizens fondly hoped that the government could guarantee them successful investments, just as some bettors at a horse race would be glad to have the government pick out the winner in advance. Of course business will always get into difficulties, whatever the law. But the government can insist on standards of good faith in the issue of securities, and on disinterestedness and a reasonable amount of wisdom on the part of the officers and directors to whom investors necessarily look for returns. The Securities and Exchange legislation seems likely to be the most lasting achievement of the New Deal. But we still have to work out some device which will enable small investors to combine and obtain a fair representation in the management of a large corporation.

Second, the continuing weakness of the administration of criminal justice by states and cities has tended to throw the task of suppressing the most dangerous offenders into the hands of the United States. This was to some extent an unexpected by-product of Prohibition. It created a new kind of crime that was very profitable, especially when organized on a grand scale, with vertical integration uniting under the same management foreign sources of supply, ocean transportation, domestic processing of the raw materials (called "cutting"), wholesaling, and retailing, as well as protection by force and bribery against competitors, highjackers, and government agents. The liquor business became national and international, like so many legitimate businesses during the same decade. And like them it tied up with quite different enterprises. Just as Du Pont combined explosives, paints, and cellophane, so a big liquor business invested its surplus in gambling, prostitution, racketeering, and automobile thefts.

The local authorities, none too efficient before the War, became rapidly more helpless and relied increasingly upon federal aid. In part, this was given directly under existing statutes like the Volstead Act and the White Slave Act, and under new legislation passed to reach offenders who came within the interstate commerce clause by crossing State lines after they had violated local laws against kidnapping or stealing cars. Still more significant was the indirect use of federal powers to suppress numerous old-fashioned evils, which were not themselves within the terms of the United States Constitution. Thus when the State of Illinois was powerless before its most famous criminal, the United States put a stop to extortions and murders by imprisoning him for falsifying his income-tax returns. When State legislators failed to make the participation of corporations in state political campaigns illegal, a federal prosecution could be brought if a Congressman or United States Senator was running at the same election, although the donation had no relation to national affairs. Such methods have stopped a considerable amount of anti-social conduct, but they throw an atmosphere of insincerity about the whole process of punishment and encourage local inefficiency. Instead of improving State legislation or electing better officials or giving them adequate equipment, everybody leaves matters as they are at home and runs to Washington for help. And this habit has extended to many other domestic matters besides crime. Those who complain of the growing centralization of power in the national government have a special duty to make local government strong. The French Revolution and many other great shifts of political power were the results, not so much of tyranny in the previous possessors of power, as of their outright weakness.

Third, it is more agreeable to turn to the real progress we have made in private litigation by simplifying the Rules of Civil Procedure, that is, the machinery by which a party gets his rights determined. This progress is largely the outcome of fruitful co-operation between judges, practitioners, and professors. Thus the recent Illinois Practice Act was drafted by Professor McCaskill of the University of Illinois and Professor Sunderland of the University of Michigan, in collaboration with the bench and bar. And when the Supreme Court made new rules for the lower United States Courts, it had them prepared by a committee of lawyers and law teachers, headed by Dean Charles E. Clark of Yale Law School and aided by extensive criticism from judges and practitioners.

Another important procedural advance since the War is the Declaratory Judgment, also due to Professor Sunderland in association with Professor Borchard of Yale Law School. Laymen should quickly perceive the value of this new device. The older legal remedies, such as damage-suits, were mostly concerned with wrongful acts. Courts were originally established to provide substitutes for violence, and people do not usually fight about disputed rights until one party has done something. So the judges at first stood ready to step in as soon as an act had occurred, and force the parties to settle by money and not by blows. Then courts began to prevent the supposedly wrongful act just before it happened, by an injunction. But they remained reluctant to come in at a still earlier stage and declare the rights of the parties before their differences of opinion threatened to ripen into action. For example, suppose a four-year lease; the monthly rent is to be $100 for the first two years and $150 for the last two; the tenant may if he wishes stay four years more "on the same terms." Early in the fourth year the tenant says this means his rent will drop back to $100 a month for the fifth and sixth years, while the landlord argues it means that the tenant can keep the house for the same rent of $150 that he is now paying. Under American law before the War, the courts would not have done anything to settle this dispute during the first four years. Hence the tenant might move out and leave the landlord with an empty house on his hands. Or he might stay in and refuse to pay more than $100 a month; the landlord would then sue him, and if victorious have the sheriff put his furniture on the sidewalk. In order to settle what the lease means, the tenant would be out of a home, the landlord deprived of any rent, and both parties bitter enemies for the rest of their lives. Contrast what the new law makes possible. Either land-land or tenant can now go to court at any time during the first four years and get a declaratory judgment about the true meaning of "on the same terms." After hearing both sides, the court will tell them whether the rent for the fifth and sixth years is to be $100 or $150 a month. Now the parties know exactly where they stand long before the old lease runs out, and they are much more friendly than if they had to injure each other in order to know their rights. Courts used to be mainly repair shops; now they are also service stations. Or as a Congressman wittily said:

Under the [older] law you take a step in the dark and then turn on the light to see if you stepped into a hole. Under the declaratory judgment law you turn on the light and then take the step.

Fourth, the substantive law, which defines the rights and obligations and defenses of persons, is getting overhauled by the American Law Institute. This is "a permanent organization for the improvement of law," a co-operative enterprise on a grand scale. Its definite conception came from Professor Beale of Harvard Law School, who had urged that the schools should take the lead in "bringing the law into close relation with the needs of contemporary life." In 1921, the Association of American Law Schools enlisted the help of distinguished members of the bench and bar, headed by Elihu Root. Funds were granted by the Carnegie Corporation. Two years of planning followed. Then at Washington in February, 1923, came the first meeting of the Institute, composed of representatives of the various courts and bar associations and other lawyers and law teachers. Similar meetings are held annually. The management of the policies and finances of the Institute is in the hands of a small Council of leaders of the profession. The active Director is William Draper Lewis, formerly Dean of Pennsylvania Law School.

The Institute has been engaged for fifteen years in "restating" important branches of law. Books have already been published on Contracts, Torts (civil wrongs), Property, Agency, Trusts, Restitution, and Conflict of Laws (transactions involving more than one nation or State). These books differ from the usual legal treatise, in which a single writer sets forth his own views on each point in the light of the chief judicial decisions and statutes, besides collecting other cases and legislation in footnotes. A Restatement is self-contained. Since it is hoped that its principles will eventually be accepted in most or all States, its pages make no reference to the doctrines now prevailing in particular States, although such doctrines are carefully studied during the preparation of the book as guides to the formulation of its principles. Each volume follows the form originated by Macaulay a hundred years ago in his draft of a Penal Code for India. Every topic begins with a carefully phrased rule, printed in heavy type (black-letter); under this is an informal explanation; last comes a series of simple illustrations of the rule. Laymen will enjoy these concrete examples and find a Restatement more intelligible than most ordinary law-books.

Each volume is the outcome of a long period of collaboration according to a carefully worked-out method. The Director and the Council select an expert in the particular subject, usually a law professor, who is called the Reporter. Associated with him are the Advisers, a small number of law teachers, practitioners, and judges familiar with the same subject. Compensation is given to the Reporter and the Advisers. After drafting a chapter, the Reporter meets the Advisers and Directors at a conference in some convenient city or pleasant health resort, where his draft is painstakingly discussed sentence by sentence. Then the Reporter redrafts his material, and a new conference is held. This process may be repeated several times. Also, when matters have got beyond the tentative stage, printed drafts are circulated among the members of the Institute and among teachers of the subject, and some of them send valuable suggestions to the Reporter. After all the chapters have thus been accepted by the experts, the volume must be approved by the Council, and finally by the annual meeting of the members of the Institute. The Reporter must either answer the criticisms of these superior bodies or embody them in a revision, before the book can be published and sold. Therefore, each Restatement is the joint product of many of the ablest men in the profession.

What is the value of the work of the American Law Institute to the law? Its successive publications can have no binding effect like statutes. They were not intended to be parts of a new Code Napoléon. But they have already had considerable persuasive influence upon judges, in situations which did not fall within any statute or previous case in the particular State, so that the court was free to seek guiding principles elsewhere. Before the Restatement, a court would then refer to relevant decisions in other States and in England. The Restatement can now serve as a substitute for these out-of-State cases. Indeed, the Supreme Court of Mississippi declares that it will always follow the Restatement whenever no Mississippi statutes or cases apply. Such an attitude seems likely to appear elsewhere, because of the increasing difficulty for judges and lawyers of collecting and reading the decisions on a topic over the whole United States. It is appalling to watch the rapid multiplication of volumes of law reports, indexes to these volumes, and even indexes to the indexes. Hence, courts and counsel may soon turn aside in weariness and disgust from the enormous labor of getting principles out of cases to the easy job of quoting a rule from the Restatement. This publication carries great weight because of the ability of the men who participated in its formulation, the thoroughness with which the material was worked over, the considerable freedom from bias, and the seal of approval from the notable lawyers and judges who make up the Council and the whole membership of the Institute.

Yet doubts have been expressed. These do not go to the methods employed by the Institute so much as to its very purposes. In the first place, it has restated and not created. This does not mean that it has been hidebound. When two or more doctrines appear in the cases in different States, the draftsmen try to select the best rule for the future even though it rests on very little judicial authority. But it must have at least one decision behind it. When all the cases reach an undesirable result, they do not feel free to make a new and better rule out of their own heads, as a legislature could do. Consequently, the Restatement sometimes prolongs the life of a bad doctrine, which judges might otherwise overrule. The Restatement also suffers in a broader way from being so firmly anchored in the past. Its scope is pretty much confined to the selection and rearrangement of the traditional materials found in decided cases. This food lacks some of the vitamins essential to legal growth. For instance, social and economic data which would be presented at a legislative hearing do not lie within the usual training and investigations of the Reporters and their Advisers, nor is the consideration of such data really consistent with "restating." Thus there is a lack of freshness about a Restatement. It is less interesting to read than the best legal treatises, and may even possess less influence. Compare, for example, the greatest lawbook in English during the 20th century, Wigmore's *Treatise on Evidence*. If Wigmore thinks a doctrine bad, he shows the way to get rid of it, and he does not care whether this be done by future judicial action or by legislation. He points out what ought to be substituted, whatever the method; he tests the existing and proposed rules by data from all relevant sources, including statutes, legislative hearings, scientific reports, press discussions, and even novels. And the contrast with Wigmore brings out another weakness in the Restatement—group production squeezes out individuality. Of course, the writing of a single man is more liable to prejudices and errors of judgment, but it has a tang. After all the conferences and compromises that preceded it, the Restatement tastes flat. And a personality like Wigmore's does much to turn ideas into facts. Possibly the Restatement of Contracts, in which Williston was the Reporter, will do less to shape the law than Williston's *Treatise on Contracts*. A final criticism of the Institute cuts even deeper. A Restatement is a collection of general rules. Judges and lawyers have hitherto considered such rules to be the main instruments of their work. But a recent school of thought (soon to be described) has vigorously attacked the significance of legal rules. If it succeeds in undermining them, the whole Restatement falls too.

Finally, no account of law during the last twenty years would be complete without some mention of the great decisions of Benjamin N. Cardozo. He was a national judge long before his appointment to the Supreme Court. As a member of the highest court in New York State, he influenced the growth of the law in all the States. We understand many problems of private law much better than before he wrote, notably the extent of the obligations of good faith and carefulness under modern business conditions. And he has rendered us a service which the great judges of the past neglected to perform. He has explained the way in which his decisions were made. His *Nature of the Judicial Process* guides other judges toward the solution of questions which never happened to come before him. Cardozo, like Wigmore, has proved what one man can do to advance the law.

Here we return to the main theme of this chapter. What a great judge thinks about law is entangled with what he does about law. To a lesser extent this is true of judges and lawyers generally. Their speculations forecast decisions and legislation. And for laymen at least, the changes in legal doctrines during the last twenty years are less interesting than the new ideas concerning the nature and purposes of law, which have been expressed by several able writers in addition to Cardozo. These ideas conflict among themselves, but many of them are so different from traditional views that they are likely to bring about significant alterations in the administration of justice during the next twenty years.

What is Law? Exactly what part do judges play in its development? This problem goes back as far as the year 1345. During a complicated English litigation over church property, one of the lawyers argued to the court, "I think you will do as others have done in the same case, or else we do not know what the law is." "It is the will of the judges," replied Judge Hilary; but Chief Justice Stonore broke in, "No, law is that which is right." Thus these old lawyers and judges made clear-cut the issue which still vexes us. Is law the acts of judges, or does it consist of rules of justice outside the judges, who merely learn about it as best they can and write more or less imperfectly about what they have felt?

Chief Justice Stonore expressed the traditional view. It was made popular in America by Blackstone's *Commentaries*. As Mr. Coolidge remarked with customary brevity: "Men do not make laws. They do but discover them." And Elihu Root observed, "It is not within the judge's function or within his power to enlarge or improve or change the law." According to this view, the law is like a great continent which judges are gradually mapping out by their decisions. A particular judge's personality does play a part, but it does not affect the real rules of the law. It merely influences the accuracy with which his written opinion describes this law outside himself, just as one map-maker may explore farther than another or record what he sees with greater skill. For example, a judge may confuse two legal doctrines that are really distinct, just as early voyagers along the New England Coast confused the summits of Mount Desert with the Camden Hills. But these mountains remained many miles apart, whatever the maps said, and the law that exists somewhere or other stays the same whatever judges do. A wrong decision is simply a mistaken line in the map; a later judge, like a map-maker, can simply rub it out and substitute another line in the correct place. On the other hand, Judge Hilary's view that judges make law treats legal doctrines like the beams of a skyscraper, which judges gradually put up as they wish. If one judge sets a beam wrong, another judge can take it down and build the structure differently, but while it is up that beam is part of the skyscraper.

In short, the problem is whether a judge exercises any choice as to the result of the case before him. According to the traditional view that "Law is that which is right," he has no choice. To vary the metaphor, the judge is a slot-machine, into which the legal rules (either statutes or rules declared by previous judges) are dropped from outside; the wheels of logical syllogisms in his mind revolve, and out comes the decision. And so the judge's main occupation is to discover the pertinent rules. If they are contained in statutes, this task is easy. If they are to be found only in prior judicial decisions, it is somewhat harder. Yet it is believed that any trained man, by studying an existing opinion, can state with certainty the rule which determined who won the case. Then, if the student of the earlier opinion is himself a judge, he can apply its rule to the facts in the new case before him. Of if a lawyer, he can use the opinion to advise a client how to transact his affairs, because he knows that future judges will find the same rule as he does in the old case, and apply that rule whenever a dispute occurs about a client's rights. Thus we have a theory of certain rules existing outside the minds of individual judges and discoverable by lawyers and other judges.

This comfortable theory has undergone severe scrutiny in recent years. Take first a situation involving no statute, where the judge must get the proper rule from prior decisions. A licensed aviator was conducting a flight with the utmost care in his own plane, which had been thoroughly inspected before he started. From no fault of his, something went wrong with the engine and obliged him to glide down at once. As he descended in the dusk, he saw to his horror that he was headed for a large group of greenhouses. Despite all the efforts anybody could make, his plane crashed into the largest, considerably damaging both aviator and greenhouse. The market-gardener is suing the aviator for $500 worth of glass. They agree not to have a jury. How shall the judge decide? Since, we assume, there has never yet been a decision about aviators, the judge must first find a broad rule in the earlier cases and then deduce from it a narrow rule which fits this situation. The traditional view is that, if his examination of the authorities be sufficiently wide and his logic sound, then the judge can determine the proper rule with certainty. He does not make a new law for the new invention, but merely discovers the law about aeroplanes which existed long ago in the days of Darius Green.

But the contemporary thinkers like Professor Morris Cohen (now teaching at Harvard and Chicago) are not satisfied. They ask what really happens while the judge is making up his mind. First comes the aviator's lawyer with a mass of cases about injuries inflicted during other methods of transportation. Back in the horse-and-buggy age, courts refused to make drivers pay damages when they used the care which a reasonable man would exercise under the circumstances. Numberless cases of railroad accidents similarly held that absence of negligence let the company off. The lawyer observes that the judge himself has repeatedly laid down the same rule to juries in automobile trials. From all these prior decisions, the judge can easily formulate a major premise, "Non-negligent operators of vehicles are not liable for injuries caused thereby"; and as the aviator was clearly non-negligent, the natural conclusion follows that the market-gardener must pay his own glass bill. But up walks the gardener's lawyer with a different list of cases. Some hold that injuries done by a wild beast in private hands—a tiger or elephant or monkey—must be borne by the owners, no matter how careful they have been. Others say that those who bring in new and dangerous things like building a TNT factory near dwellings are completely responsible for any subsequent harm, even though it happens beyond their control. They started something, and must take the consequences. And then the lawyer argues that an aeroplane is a new and dangerous thing.

Thus everything turns on which of the major premises the judge uses. If he thinks that the aeroplane is primarily a means of transportation, then he will start with the rule requiring negligence, and decide for the aviator. But if he considers that the aeroplane is more like a tiger or a TNT factory than like a locomotive, then he will apply the rule of liability without fault for dangerous things and give the market-gardener his money. Which of these two general rules is the law here? Apparently, the rule which the judge makes up his mind to select. The prior decisions do not lead to a single sure result, but merely offer two competing analogies. To the extent that the judge has a choice between the two broad rules, the law in this case is "the will of judges," as Judge Hilary declared six hundred years ago. Furthermore, whichever way this case goes will determine the outcome of later aviation accidents in the same State. Then may we not say that this judge, by his choice, does make the law for aeroplanes?

However, it is important to notice that this judge's scope for law-making was not very wide, and also that succeeding judges will have a still narrower scope. As aviation decisions multiply, the rules for the various probable situations will be available for judges to apply, and they will not have much chance for more law-making. This has already happened for automobile accidents.

A statute may seem to leave no opportunity for a judge to make law. This is true if its words exactly cover the case before him, but that does not always happen. For instance, a public land statute of Congress granted land to settlers, a quarter section (160 acres) to "a single man" and a half section (320 acres) to "a married man." Some public land was settled by a widow. Was she outside the generosity of the government; or was she a "single man," or a "married man"? The Land Office refused to give her anything. The Supreme Court sensibly held in 1868 that a widow was a "single man," saying that this was "the intent of the framers" of the statute. They did not find this intention by consulting the men who had been in Congress when the statute was passed. The judges merely looked at the whole statute, and made up their minds what rule for a situation outside its terms would best fit in with the rules it did express. In large measure the intent was the intent of the judges. Congress had left a hole in the statute, and the judges filled the hole. Thus statutory rules are treated in much the same way as judge-made rules. The court often has a choice between various reasonable possibilities of what the statute means, and within those limits they make law that supplements the law made by the legislature. Then part of this statutory law is the will of the legislature and part is the will of the judges.

Is not a constitution, at least, something wholly outside the judges? This supreme law is indeed the will of human beings, but traditionally it is the will of the people, not of the judges. However, the brief phrases of a constitution cannot possibly describe all the fact situations which may conceivably fall within its powers and prohibitions, so that those phrases must be interpreted by court decisions to see whether they do apply. During this interpretation, the court does not merely declare the pre-existing will of the people, because the people probably never thought about the particular state of facts one way or other when they voted for the constitution. Professor Cohen says: "The process of adopting a constitution is frequently spoken of as if it were a magical or supernatural procedure. It is, however, subject to all the frailties of human nature." There is, he points out, no sharp distinction between the capricious will of the people as shown in the election of legislators and the deliberate, solemn will of the people as embodied in constitutions. In fact, election statistics show that the people take much less interest in constitutional provisions than in candidates. How many of those who vote for approval take the trouble or have the opportunity to consider carefully all the possible consequences of every provision? It is absurd to suppose that when the Reconstruction Congresses forced through the Fourteenth Amendment at the point of the bayonet to protect Negroes, the people actually intended that States could fix the rates of fire-insurance companies but could not fix the amounts that New York theatre-ticket agencies might add to the box-office prices. Did not the Supreme Court in some sense make the law on those questions when they construed the general words "due process"?

President Roosevelt's proposal of February, 1937, to increase the size of the Supreme Court and appoint a number of new judges turned these speculations about judicial participation in law-making into a burning political issue. In the controversy that followed, two extreme conceptions of the nature of law found frequent expression. Many opponents of the plan emphasized the United States Constitution as something outside the judges, and tended to treat the Supreme Court like a phonograph which reproduces with high fidelity a record inscribed by the Philadelphia Orchestra in 1787. On the other hand, the President's backers sometimes assumed that each Justice makes law at his own sweet will, and votes for or against the constitutionality of a statute in exactly the same spirit as a Senator votes for or against the statute itself. According to the first view, all the principles declared by the Court since 1933 were plainly discovered on the very parchment of the Constitution, where they would also be found by any other judges (except of course the six new appointees proposed by the President). According to the second view, these principles had no connection with the Constitution; they all came out of the heads of nine human beings (or rather of five or six), who happened to be sitting in the way of Roosevelt's first administration.

The truth lies somewhere in between. It seems correct to say that judges make law while interpreting the Constitution, but the phrase "make law" is itself ambiguous and needs interpretation. *How* do judges make law, in constitutional cases and elsewhere? The right answer to this question requires deep study, but it can take us a long distance toward a reasonable solution of the ultimate problem of the relation of the Court to Congress and the President. Only a few observations will be ventured. Judges do not make law as legislators make law. Their work is limited by the form of a court proceeding and the nature of the material. Recent studies have made plainer some of the differences between judicial law-making and legislative law-making: (1) A legislature almost always formulates rules for future events. In the English-speaking world, it is not considered decent practice for a statute to say that an act already committed and not declared wrongful at the time is nevertheless a crime or the foundation of a damage claim against the doer of the act. But judges deal for the most part with this very situation of acts that have already occurred. Hence, it would not be quite the thing for a judge to say, "I will make a new law for this aeroplane accident that happened five years ago." Instead, he must formulate a rule that can fairly be said to have been applicable at the time of the event. (2) This means that although, as we have seen, the judge sometimes has a choice among two or more major premises from which to derive his rule, he must find such a major premise in the past and cannot make it up out of whole cloth. For example, in the aviation case already discussed, some people would like to apply the major premise that the person with less money should always win, or the one whose politics agree with those of the current administration, or even that victory should follow good looks. The last proposition is said to be popular among jurymen, when unrestrained, especially if a party of the fair sex is really fair. Now, a judge of any ability could never state that either of these broad rules is law, because he could find absolutely no warrant for them in previous decisions. In short, the judge has a choice but it is largely confined to the possibilities he discovers in the past. He makes some law, but not *all* the law for a given case. He only develops what other judges or legislatures or the people have made before him. For example, a particular doctrine of constitutional law was created, not only by the living Supreme Court judges who decided the latest case, but also by a long series of dead judges in earlier cases, which started from the words of the Constitution. So if we reject the map analogy and prefer that of the skyscraper, we have to recognize that a judge has to pay considerable attention to a blueprint already in existence. Indeed, a better image for a legal doctrine than the skyscraper is a Gothic cathedral. A new generation of builders may vary the architectural style but they must lay the new stones on the old walls. Therefore, this judicial law-making is much slower and more limited than legislative law-making. Every judge works within the bounds of traditional methods learned from his studies, his predecessors before whom he practised, and his associates on the bench. These methods have three purposes: first, to decide the dispute between the parties; second, to bring the case within a general rule, logically related to some previously recognized rule or rules (although we shall soon find this disputed); and third, to have this general rule adapted to future disputes. A legislature is not subject to such restrictions.

But legislative law-making is also limited, though less narrowly and by different factors. Careful studies of legislation, like Dicey's *Law and Public Opinion,* show that so far as it changes the substantive law it is not entirely arbitrary but moves somehow in definite directions. The legislator is carried along by currents of contemporary reasoning, and checked by well-recognized obstacles. The fate of the Volstead Act shows that legislation may fail when it goes too far. Therefore, it is not correct to suppose that the work of a legislature is entirely independent of prior law and custom while the work of a court is entirely pre-determined. Both make law in ways conditioned by their methods and materials.

And so the ancient debate between Judge Hilary and Chief Justice Stonore may be reconciled, if we say: "Law is the will of the judges try-ing to do that which is right." We must add, however, that they can do right only so far as the accepted methods of their action permit.

The acts of judges have thus been shown to have much significance in making law, although not so much as is asserted by men who have gone to the opposite extreme from the traditional view. But what acts of judges? So far the controversy has revolved around rules as to rights. The judge in his written opinion states a new rule to explain what he is doing in the particular case, as if that rule had always existed. Many volumes of such opinions line the walls of law-offices, and most of the talk of lawyers and judges is about these rules. Along come Professor Karl N. Llewellyn of Columbia Law School and others to maintain that the rule laid down during a decision may have little or no importance. The real fact is, which way the judge decides the particular dispute. These Realists (as they call themselves, though philosophically they are Nominalists) insist that we ought to concentrate our attention on what the judge and jury do, and not on what the judge says.

For example, we like to say, and the judges encourage us in saying it, that a person has "a right to the performance of a contract." What really happens, so Llewellyn points out, is this:

If the other party does not perform as agreed, you can sue, and *if* you have a fair lawyer, and nothing goes wrong with your witnesses or the jury, *and* you give up four or five days of time and some ten to thirty per cent of the proceeds, and wait two to twenty months, you will *probably* get a judgment for a sum considerably less than what the performance would have been worth—which if the other party is solvent and has not secreted his assets, you can in further due course collect with six per cent interest for delay.

Llewellyn wants to shift the focal point of legal discussion from ab-stract rights and rules to the area of contact between the behavior of judges and the behavior of laymen. The traditional approach is in terms of words. It tacitly assumes that words reflect acts, and influence acts effectively so as to make them conform to the rule, *e.g.,* that the defendant is liable to perform such and such a contract. He admits that accepted rules do sometimes influence the actual behavior of judges, but also the rules and the practice sometimes diverge. "How, and how much, *in each case?*" You cannot generalize on this, *without investigation.* He wants to learn the actual doings of judges and the actual effects of their doings, to compare facts with facts and not words with words. He wants to find how far the paper rule (what the judges say) is mere paper and how far it is real—how far the judges do what the rule tells them to do.

Now we take a very significant step. Most legal discussion centers around the work of appellate courts, whose sayings about rules are readily accessible in official volumes. But if we want to know law-in-action, we must go beyond these upper courts and see how far the rules are followed in the acts of lower court judges. Any disobedience of the rules on their part will perhaps be corrected by the higher court if an appeal is taken, but in the mass of decisions by lower court judges there is no appeal. Yet the acts of the judges in trial courts, even petty courts for small claims and minor offenses, have far more effect on the lives of urban citizens than those of the Supreme Court judges in a much bigger and grander court-house. It often happens that these so-called "inferior" courts do as they desire, regardless of the paper rules issued from on high. Thus the Supreme Judicial Court of Massachusetts has repeatedly laid down the rule that injunctions are not granted unless some property right is to be protected. Yet newspapers tell how one Massachusetts trial judge enjoined Mrs. Tillie Feldman from making any rude or improper faces at her neighbor, Mrs. Minnie Freedman, and how another trial judge enjoined all love affairs between William Beach, of Springfield, and a Mrs. Thompson, whom the judge ordered to go back with her husband to Indianapolis and forget all about Beach. These lower court judges are forbidding interference with the plaintiff's peace of mind although no money is at stake. Which is the law of Massachusetts? Llewellyn says, not the paper rule but what the judges did to the maker of faces and the wandering wife.

Then he goes still further. What influence do the rules have on other officials than judges—sheriffs, policemen, immigration inspectors? Laymen see much more of these officials than of judges. To many a man they are the law. The decision of the official might be set aside by a court, but it never gets to a court. The decision of the $1800 clerk in

Bureau B that travelling expenses to attend a summer session are not deductible from my professor's salary is the law in my case, whatever judges have said to the contrary.

It may well be that the discrepancy is very great between what the statutory or judge-made rule tells an official to do and what the official actually does. Thus the constitution of Illinois says: "No person shall be compelled in any criminal case to give evidence against himself." The Illinois statutes make it a serious crime for two or more persons to commit an assault upon another for the purpose of obtaining a confession or revelation tending to incriminate the man assaulted or anybody else. These are the paper rules. The frequent behavior of the Chicago police, as described by judges of the Illinois Supreme Court, is to question the arrested man for several hours without food or sleep, and then take him to "see the goldfish," which involves his being dragged around by the hair and beaten with a length of rubber hose. Which is the law of Illinois? Llewellyn says what the policemen do. "What these officials do about disputes is, to my mind, the law itself."

One more discrepancy. How far do laymen do what the rules tell them to? We lawyers assume too readily that laymen, especially business men, shape their conduct according to judicial decisions and statutes. For two hundred and fifty years there have been statutes in England and this country making unwritten guarantees of another man's debt worthless. Yet much money is lent and much work done on the faith of the oral promise of some relative or friend that he will take care of the matter if the borrower or customer does not pay up, and probably most such promises are kept. The statute does not seem to be in the picture at all. This sort of thing is worth studying. Obviously, both legislatures and courts will make rules more wisely, the more they know about their probable effect on human conduct. Later, some examples will be given of such investigations about the consequences of what judges and officials do.

Thus the main position of Llewellyn and other Realists like Thurman Arnold is, that law is not a collection of abstract rules but the totality of social behavior, or at least official behavior. The influence of the behaviorist school of psychology is plain, but this theory goes farther back to a remark by Mr. Justice Holmes in 1897: "The prophecies of what the courts will do in fact, and nothing more pretentious, are what I mean by the law."

Yet Holmes's remark has only partial truth, and the point where it falls short is just the trouble with the whole Realist position. At the moment Holmes was describing law as a layman sees it, and the definition gives no help whatever to a judge trying to decide a case. How can he tell whether the plaintiff ought to win or not, by saying to himself that the law is whichever way he decides? If medicine were defined as "what the doctor gives you," this might satisfy a childish patient, but not a physician hesitating what drug to give him. In short, the satisfactory administration of justice necessitates something more than an accurate description of the isolated acts of the men who have recognized powers to put us in jail and seize our property. Any official who takes his job seriously will seek some standard as a guide for his conduct. This means that he must go outside the facts of the particular situation, if only to toss up a nickel. Even a cook does not concoct a succulent dish without using her own past experience and what her teachers said and did; and most cooks read cook-books too to get the rules. Inasmuch as a judge's past experience is not likely to include all the situations that are brought before him, he resorts to law reports to learn how his predecessors handled similar problems. Unless every case is to be regarded as unrelated to every other case, we must formulate links between them, and these links become the legal rules which serve as the standards for action, even though not always lived up to.

Furthermore, we need some way to distinguish between anti-social conduct and social conduct, between lawlessness and what most lawyers call "law." For instance, if we are going to lump together the behavior of all promise-keepers and all promise-breakers and call it "The Law of Contracts," then we shall have to hunt up some other phrase to denote the body of principles by which we think the men who make promises ought to abide. The Realists resemble the people who argue that everybody is selfish, because the man who loses his life to save a little boy from drowning is merely exhibiting his own brand of selfishness. If that be so, we need some word to distinguish that brand of selfishness from the commoner varieties, so that we can encourage it. The trouble is, as Pound has pointed out in his reply to Llewellyn, that "law" like "droit" and "recht" is a very ambiguous word. Llewellyn uses it in one sense, to mean the whole judicial or official process and its practical results—what the outset of this article called a slice of life. But "law" can also mean a collection of rules, of guides to judicial and administrative action. We need maps even though some people do not follow them. We do not have to stop saying that the law forbids murder just because some murderers are not arrested or convicted. Both the rules against murder and the divergence of actual conduct from those rules are worthy of study, but our studies will be more fruitful if we keep the two subjects distinct by not using the word "law" to describe them both. One is a group of "oughts" and the other a group of "ises." It is clearer and more convenient to keep "law" to mean the first group, but Llewellyn has rendered a great service in urging the importance of "is" as well as "ought" and the immense need of measuring the discrepancies between the two. Even if the Realists go too far, they have demonstrated the importance of human beings in the formulation of legal rules. Just as Graham Wallas and Harold Laski have brought into political science problems of the selection, training and thinking of government officials, so legal writers have given increased attention to the mental processes of judges.

Psychology has thus been injected into law, but it makes a good deal of difference what psychology is used. The attitude of the advance guard just described seems to be chiefly influenced by one school, behaviorism, the doctrines of which have been uncritically swallowed as if they possessed the infallibility which the Realists deny in the same breath to rules of law. Quite different legal theories could be produced by an even more famous type of psychology, but the legal scholars were slower to discover Vienna than were the anthropologists and literary critics and poets. As recently as 1928, Professor Scott of Harvard Law School, after outlining some wild ideas about law, remarked:

I thank God that the theories of Freud, which in many quarters were accepted as ultimate psychological truths, were propounded sufficiently long ago, so that their universal validity was generally denied before the teachers of law discovered them. I, for one, would be sorry to be compelled before determining how a question in the law of trusts will be decided, to investigate the love life of the judges who are to make the decision. When Lord Eldon's house caught fire one night, he buried the great seal in his back yard, and Lord Campbell tells us that he became so much absorbed in watching the maids running about in their shifts that he completely forgot where he had buried it. But I doubt whether there is any close connection between this event and one of his important decisions.

Professor Scott's jubilation over the legal repression of Freud was premature. Within two years Mr. Jerome Frank published his *Law and the Modern Mind,* which explains the craving of certainty in law by the desire to regain the uninterrupted serenity we enjoyed in the womb. The child at birth, he tells us, is literally forced from a small world of almost complete and effortless security into a new environment which at once sets up a series of demands. The baby finds himself in what William James called "a big, booming confusion." He longs to find once more peace, comfort, protection from the dangers of the unknown. At first the child satisfies that craving through his confidence in his omnipotent, infallible father. Then repeated experiences erode this fictional over-estimate. There are many things his father does not know and cannot do. Despite advancing years the childish fear of change remains and a grow-ing man attempts to satisfy his longing for serenity through the redis-covery of father, in his employer or a magnetic political leader, or a religious cult, or perhaps in judges and law.

And so according to Frank, the Law, a body of rules purporting to determine infallibly what is right and what is wrong, takes the place of the omnipotent father. Grown men, when they strive to recapture the emotional satisfactions of the pre-natal or childish world, seek in their legal systems the authoritativeness, certainty, and predictability which they once believed they had found in the law laid down by their father. Hence arises the basic legal myth that law is or can be made unwavering, fixed, and settled. In reality, or at least in Mr. Frank's opinion, there is no certainty about law; the judges merely decide as they wish. Why then all these volumes of law reports, full of long judicial opinions? If only what the judges do is important, why do they say anything? Merely because they are in a conspiracy to preserve the Freudian myth of cer-tainty. A former president of the American Bar Association advised Frank at the beginning of his practice, "The way to win a case is to make the judge want to decide in your favor and then, and then only, cite precedents which will justify such a determination. You will find plenty of cases to cite in your favor." Frank also quotes a federal judge, Hutche-son, who has let the cat out of the bag in an article entitled *The Function of the "Hunch" in Judicial Decisions.* Judge Hutcheson says that the judge really decides by feeling and not by judgment, by hunching and not by reasoning. After the astute judge has made up his mind how he will decide on the basis of an intuitive sense of what is right or wrong in the case, he digs up some reasons to justify his hunch to himself, and then sticks these reasons into a written opinion to make the result of the case pass muster with his critics. In other words, the judge is just kidding himself and others by his opinion. This pretense of certainty (as Frank sees it) is desirable to make men obey, just as Plato wanted the rulers of his Republic to use considerable doses of falsehood and deceit for the good of their subjects. But no certainty is really there, none is possible, none is even desirable, for it would prevent law from changing.

Frank's book has two aspects, his psychoanalysis and his doctrine of utter legal uncertainty. His psychoanalysis opens unsuspected chasms before us. He tells us that the judge in learning the facts that are the basis of his hunch is continually subject to minute and distinctly personal biases.

His own past may have created plus or minus reactions to women, or blonde women, or men with beards, or Southerners, or Italians, or Englishmen, or plumbers, or ministers, or college graduates, or Democrats . . . The peculiar traits, dispositions, biases and habits of the particular judge will, then, often determine what he decides to be the law.

So when I once went with Horace Kallen to hear Judge Webster Thayer decide a motion for a new trial for Sacco and Vanzetti on the ground that the jury had got the bullets mixed up, Kallen took one look at Judge Thayer as he sat down in the courtroom and remarked, "That man has something in his past that he is ashamed of and wants to conceal." Professor Mortimer Adler of Chicago turns the tables by suggesting that Frank and his Realist friends are themselves the victims of an inferiority complex. Although they make fun of the awestruck voices with which lawyers mention Marshall, Kent, Story, and Shaw, they themselves are continually citing impressive non-legal names like Freud, Piaget, Dewey, and Malinowski, with implicit confidence. Instead of worshipping law, they worship scientific method. Their myth is that empirical science portrays the real world.

Frank's other doctrine is, that there is no logic or certainty in what judges do, if we disregard as pure bluff what they say. This means that it is as silly to make a system out of decisions as out of the tracks made by fleas whose feet were dipped in ink before they were set free to follow food, fun and flirtation. As to all this, we have first-hand testimony from soberer judges than Hutcheson. Mr. Justice Cardozo, in his *Nature of the Judicial Process* (1922), frankly admits that a judge has choices in developing rules of law, but refuses to deny the existence of genuine rules. He carefully analyzes four factors which have determined his own choices: analogies used logically (as outlined in my aviation illustration); historical forces that have shaped the origins and growth of a legal conception; the customs of the community, such as banking practices in a promissory note case; and considerations of justice, morals, and social welfare. Mr. Justice Cardozo's work lay largely in appellate courts, but the experience of a trial judge is ably described by Judge Ulman of

Maryland in *A Judge Takes the Stand* (1923). He kept a diary of his
trials in which, whenever the jury went out to deliberate, he put down
what he himself would vote if he were on the jury, and afterwards
recorded the jury's verdict in the case; finally, if this verdict was for a
different side or amount than his own view, he wrote out what he believed to be the reasons for the divergence. On one occasion Judge
Ulman, sitting without a jury, had to decide whether the Maryland
Public Service Commission could reduce the fares of Baltimore street
railways, without depriving them of a proper reserve for depreciation.
Since he was much influenced by the dissenting opinions of Mr. Justice
Brandeis, which would justify lower fares, Ulman *wanted* to decide
against the railways. Nevertheless, his study of the majority opinions in
previous cases in the United States Supreme Court made him feel obliged
to decide against the Commission and write an opinion to that effect.
Judge Ulman's decision was sustained by the Supreme Court, with a
dissenting opinion by Mr. Justice Brandeis.

These two judges, Cardozo and Ulman, bring out the point that among
the factors which determine what a judge does are his professional training and experience. His choice among the competing analogies offered by
previous decisions and other sources is not completely arbitrary. Opposing
legal principles do not fit the same set of facts with the same degree of
appropriateness. Thorough consideration of both principles is likely to
show a difference in their respective consequences to society or in their
logical relations to the general body of law. Hard thinking of this sort
affects the judge's final conclusion as much as his initial hunch.

Surely it is better for a judge to examine analytical rules critically than
to act only on intuitive hunches, which are often just a body of prejudices,
illusions, and ancient metaphysics. In so far as trained and open-minded
judges do have such hunches, we cannot assume that the so-called intuition is irrational even when its sources are unconscious. Into the
hunch may go a great deal of previous thinking that is not specifically
remembered. A fruitful illustration is furnished by the workings of a
poet's mind. In *The Road to Xanadu,* Lowes proves that Coleridge unconsciously fused in a particular passage of the *Ancient Mariner* thoughts
drawn from his reading of many different books, doubtless without
specific recollection of his sources. So a judge's long experience in his law
library and on the bench may unconsciously supply the elements which
produce the rapid feeling that the plaintiff ought to recover or ought
to lose.

Although the judicial process as these judges describe it leaves a margin of uncertainty, which is wider than we lawyers customarily admit, still it is far from spreading over the whole law as Mr. Frank contends. One gets a mistaken impression by reading only decisions of the United States Supreme Court, which tends to hear the borderline cases where there is much to be said on both sides. Every lawyer constantly has clients coming in with claims or defenses that fall within clean-cut rules of law, but most of these cases get weeded out long before they reach the Supreme Court or the highest court in a State, and so they do not get printed in the law reports. Some such clients are dissuaded by their lawyers from going to court, and perhaps a settlement is negotiated with the other side. Those who do sue get often discouraged by an adverse judgment, and do not spend more useless money in appealing. It is the uncertain rules that produce the most fighting, up to the last ditch, but whole areas of the law, that were once battlegrounds for judges and lawyers, have long ago become settled and peaceful. For example, a man cannot tie up his property by a will for more than twenty-one years beyond the lives of persons in existence when he dies; a man cannot make a valid gift of a bond by putting it into an envelope in his safe-deposit box and marking on the envelope, "I give this bond to Moll Flanders"; he will not be made to pay damages for libel if he writes with his own hand a letter to his employee saying "I have fired you because you are a thief," and shows this letter to nobody before he mails it; a man cannot collect fire insurance if he burns down his own house, at least if he be sane; a professor's son aged eighteen is not liable on an agreement to purchase a Rolls Royce, but he is liable if he hits a pedestrian with an old Ford driven at the rate of seventy miles an hour. There is no uncertainty about these rules. But just as some people believe in premonitions because they remember only the shivers that were followed by calamities, so it is easy to conclude that the law is highly uncertain by concentrating attention on a few bitterly contested doctrines and overlooking those many rules which are too well settled to get litigated any longer.

The physical sciences constitute another important influence on current legal speculations. Startling glimpses into non-Euclidean space and the inside of the atom have dazzled some writers so much that they can no longer see their own surroundings clearly. Thus Frank thinks that the law must be uncertain because atoms and electrons bounce around by chance. "The physicists," he says, "have just announced the Principle of

Uncertainty or Indeterminacy. If there can be nothing like complete definiteness in the natural sciences, it is surely absurd to expect to realize even approximate certainty and predictability in law, dealing as it does with the vagaries of complicated human adjustments." He might as well argue that the dance of atoms makes it impossible for life insurance companies to build up adequate reserves on the basis of calculations about the probable duration of human life. Other authors like Professor Herman Oliphant (now in the Treasury Department) and Professor Thurman Arnold (now in the Department of Justice) are so enthusiastic over the achievements of the physical sciences and so sure that these results were attained mainly by experiments and the observation of facts, that they want to carry the experimental method over bodily into the social sciences, notably law. At the same time, they propose to junk the abstract phrases used by lawyers and judges on the assumption that words never accomplished anything for physics or chemistry or biology.

The errors of this attitude have been pointed out by Professor Walter Wheeler Cook of Northwestern Law School and Professor Morris Cohen. In the first place, the words of statutes and decisions are "the facts" of law. The proposal to disregard words is just as unwise for the student of law as it would be for the student of philology. Furthermore, scientific analogies cannot be fruitful in law unless we realize the extensive value of hypotheses in the work of an investigator like Pasteur or Darwin. A scientist who sets out to observe facts without first deciding what facts to observe, soon finds himself drifting over the whole sea of the universe. Once he frames an hypothesis, he can direct his search to facts which either support or upset it. Thus Cook considers that the so-called "laws of nature" are not final truths, but only hypotheses that have to be tested. The scientist frames such laws by observing relevant concrete phenomena, and then through trial and error forming generalizations which are merely useful tools to describe in mental shorthand as wide a range of facts as possible and predict future phenomena. He goes on from this position to argue that the rules stated in judicial opinions and legal treatises are the hypotheses of law which are also useful tools to describe its phenomena, namely, the past and future behavior of judges and other officials (including both their external actions and their words). Legal rules, like the generalizations of physics, must from time to time be reformulated to bring them into accord with fresh observations of such new facts as later judicial decisions. The rules of law are certain in the same way that Newton's laws were certain, although they had to be revised in the light of later facts observed by Einstein and Planck. Cook is fully aware of the tendency to uniformity of action, which Frank ignores. Besides having taught mathematics for four years and really knowing something about scientific methods, he is also a legal scholar of the first rank. Finally, such writers as Arnold and Oliphant exaggerate the possibilities of the experimental method in law. The physical sciences furnish interesting suggestions for new approaches to law, but they are not a solution of all our troubles. Cohen has repeatedly emphasized the differences between the natural and social sciences. For example, he says:

The relative backwardness of the social sciences cannot . . . be entirely due to the devotion to theory, but is at least in large part due to the inherent complexity of social facts . . . Hence it is intrinsically more difficult to formulate social relations in accurately stated laws than to do so in physics. Our power to manipulate formulæ or equations wanes when the number of independent variables increases. When we come to social affairs the number of qualifications necessary to make a proposition true is generally more than we can manage. Also, since we cannot subject human beings to experimental conditions as we do hydrogen gas or fruit flies, we cannot always isolate any one factor and study its specific influence.

Elsewhere Cohen states: "The law is a very complicated subject and we need a variety of methods rather than risk everything on what happens to be the latest notion."

Although these hasty attempts to fuse law with physics and chemistry are fallacious, law has entered into valuable and increasingly closer relations with the other social sciences. *The Encyclopædia of Social Sciences,* especially its introductory volume (1930), points out links hitherto unappreciated. For example, the recent ideas about law outlined above are paralleled by many developments in economics, government, ethics, etc., and even literature: general suspicion of theories and standards; attention to emotional and non-rational elements in Wallas's *Human Nature in Politics,* in modernist poems, in Nazi demonstrations, in explanations of the business cycle, and in advertising; the dissolution of a sense of personal responsibility under the influence of psychoanalysis and behaviorism; the tendency of anthropology to emphasize the uniqueness of every tribe and reject the old "successive stages of civilization"; regionalism in geography, which considers all the geological, meteorological, and social forces that have operated in a given area; and a widespread interest in the individual or the single event as the starting-point of study—one sick man in medical or psychiatric monographs, one problem family in social work, one city in *Middletown,* one flaming youth or flare-up husband as the text of ten letters from the readers of a Sunday newspaper, a different prison-term or probation plan for each offender, and a separate curriculum for every school-child. The attack on judicial reasoning recalls debunking biographies. The contempt for legal rules resembles the shift of theology from dogmas and community worship to varieties of religious experience of isolated saints and sinners and cranks, or the eccentricities of Surrealism and Abstract Art, which have abandoned the traditional attempt to represent objects as human beings at large see them, or want them to appear in accordance with some accepted group tradition. Law, conclude the editors of the *Encyclopædia* after their synthetic survey of all the social sciences, shows an amazing and devious carry-over of old ideas to deal with new situations.

No more fertile phase of intellectual history was to be found in any of the social sciences. . . . All along the frontiers of law there was a good deal of stir. . . . One of the oldest of organized studies was passing through a new youthful phase.

From these general discussions, we turn to some recent investigations of the discrepancies between legal rules and their actual operation. The most ambitious of these was by President Hoover's National Commission on Law Observance and Enforcement, commonly called the Wickersham Commission after its chairman (1929–31). This Commission had a distinguished personnel and was assisted by numerous groups of experts. It was granted half a million dollars, and had behind it the power and prestige of the government, which enabled it to obtain information that would not have been disclosed to unofficial investigators. Yet the interest with which the public greeted the formation of this enterprise had dwindled to almost nothing by the time it ended. This was largely due to the fact that its first report was on the highly controversial subject of Prohibition, and was probably the most astonishing official document ever published in the United States. The Commission's excellent summary of admirably collected evidence showing how badly Prohibition had worked led all its members except Monte Lemann of New Orleans to conclude that Prohibition ought to continue. These ten eminent persons then supported their conclusion by ten separate sets of reasons, which agreed neither with the facts nor with each other. The Commission resembled the crew of a racing-shell, in which only one man looks forward while the rest pull one way and face another and are all out of stroke. We shall probably never know how far considerations of political expediency entered into this report, but its failure to appreciate realities deprived the Commission of much further effectiveness. This was very unfortunate, because many of the succeeding reports threw fresh light on such important topics as the best method for assembling nationwide criminal statistics in one place; prosecution and the grand jury; deportation of aliens; more intelligent treatment of child offenders against federal laws; the business of the federal courts; criminal procedure; the third degree; police organization; the cost of crime and of its suppression; and causes of crime with particular reference to the effect of unemployment and the relative shares of immigrants, Negroes, and native-born whites in the commission of crimes.

One of the most important reports was the *Analysis of Criminal Surveys* by Alfred Bettman of Cincinnati. Here he summarizes the lessons to be learned from the numerous local surveys of criminal justice that had lately been made in several States and cities. Particularly significant is his explanation of the "mortality tables" which he originated and applied in the Cleveland Crime Survey, where he was associated with Dean Pound and Professor Frankfurter of Harvard Law School. Before these tables began to be compiled, the attention of the bench and bar was concentrated on the jury trial as supposedly the weakest point in the disposition of criminals and the proper place for improvements. Much was said about the vital need of selecting better juries, simplifying the rules of evidence, and eliminating long hypothetical questions to expert witnesses. This attitude has been completely upset by Mr. Bettman's mortality tables. Such a table resembles the figures gathered by a life insurance company which start with 100,000 persons and show the successive stages at which they die until all are gone. Each of the crime tables starts with a large group of the persons arrested for serious offenses during a year, and shows the number and percentage of such cases which pass out of the hands of justice at the various stages between arrest and conviction. Thereby the table aims to throw some light on the relative responsibility of the various organs of justice for the failure of many offenders to receive adequate punishment. For example, in Chicago, we start with 13,000 prisoners arrested in 1926 for felonies (excluding liquor cases and also prisoners released at once by the police). Out of these 13,000 cases, 6300 or nearly a half were eliminated without even going before the grand jury. (Over 3300 were released by action of the district attorney's office, and about 2400 were discharged by the committing magistrate before whom they were taken soon after arrest, because no sufficient evidence was presented against them.) This left 6700 cases taken before the grand jury, and 1500 of these were eliminated chiefly because they were not indicted. Of the remainder of 5200 who entered the trial court, 1600 more were released by act of the district attorney's office; nearly 500 more pleaded guilty of the offense charged, and over 1600 more pleaded guilty to a lesser offense, so none of these were tried by jury. Out of the original 13,000, 490 were convicted after trial and 580 were acquitted. Thus fewer than 1100 prisoners or 8 per cent of the original group ever came before a trial jury. The number acquitted was less than an eighth of the number released by the district attorney's office, and only a quarter of the number released by the committing magistrate at the preliminary hearing. Perhaps, if the district attorney's office had been more active in prosecuting cases before the magistrate, he would not have released so many prisoners; that office may also be to blame for some of the cases in which the grand jury failed to indict; and it is the district attorney who accepts pleas of lesser offenses. Obviously, the jury trial is a rather unimportant stage, and the proper points for improvement are the district attorney's office and the so-called inferior court which has power to bind prisoners over for trial. How well are these two agencies now fitted to release only the prisoners who are innocent or ought not to be punished? If many who deserve punishment have also been released, this does not necessarily show that the prosecutor and the magistrate are at fault. They may be doing just as well as anybody could with insufficient assistance and equipment to handle such an enormous mass of business that there is very little time for proper preparation of the evidence against a prisoner. Part of the solution may lie in larger appropriations for the staffs of prosecutors and magistrates.

Professor Sheldon Glueck of Harvard and his wife, in their *500 Criminal Careers,* studied 510 men who left the Massachusetts Reformatory at Concord during the years 1911–22. They examined the methods used in the reformatory, but the most important part of their study came after the men left its walls. Through energetic and prolonged investigation, Mr. and Mrs. Glueck ascertained what almost every one of these men did during five years after discharge and tried to learn what effect they showed and felt from the reformatory. One striking fact was that over three-fourths of these men committed crimes during this five-year period. This is diametrically opposed to the estimates in annual reports of reformatories and prisons that 80 per cent of the inmates are "successes" after discharge. It looks as if reformatories do not reform. A similar investigation of 1000 children passing through the Boston Juvenile Court under a judge of great wisdom reveals that within five years after the close of official treatment 88 per cent committed crimes. This need not lead to hopelessness, but it proves that the problem is far more difficult than anybody realized. The Gluecks' later book, *Five Hundred Delinquent Women,* indicates a higher success rate during the five-year period for the graduates of the Massachusetts Reformatory for Women. The strongest cause for reform appeared to be a happy marriage and the responsibility of bringing up children.

Some years ago Everson, formerly on the staff of the Charity Organization Society, studied the sentences in the various magistrates' courts in New York City (1919). Judge A found 97 per cent of his drunkenness cases guilty and Judge B 21 per cent. Judge C discharged 18 per cent in disorderly conduct cases and Judge D 54 per cent. Vagrancy discharges among the judges varied from 5 per cent to 79 per cent. Some judges fined a large proportion of their cases while others ran freely to suspended sentences. The disclosures were "so startling and so disconcerting that it seemed advisable to discontinue the comparative table of the records of justices."

Civil remedies for automobile accidents were investigated by a large group of lawyers and law teachers under the auspices of the Columbia University Council for Research in the Social Sciences (1932). Nearly 9000 cases of actual injury to life or person were studied, in cities of varying size and in rural regions. Legal theories were laid aside in an effort to find what actually happens after an accident. It was shown that the existing policy, which contemplates adequate compensation based upon the defendant's fault, is not carried out. Where this policy would give compensation, recovery is often prevented by the expense, delays, and risks of trial and still more by difficulties of collection. For example, if the defendant was not insured, only a quarter of the injuries were paid for, but 85 per cent if he was insured. In both situations the amount paid was usually too small to cover losses, and anywhere from a quarter to a half went for lawyers and legal expenses. On the other hand, many injured persons recover though not entitled to do so on the common law theory, because the defendant is not negligent. Juries incline to treat the liability insurance of the driver as if it were accident insurance for the victim. The research group wants to scrap the whole machinery, and put automobile accidents under a new statutory scheme like Workmen's Compensation.

In divorce, everybody knows of the wide gulf between law in books and law in action. This subject has been explored by Marshall and May in their study of the records of a large number of divorce cases in Maryland (1932). According to the statutory rules of this state there are only two grounds for divorce—desertion and unfaithfulness, but the facts show that any couple that desire to "split blankets," as the cowboys say, can probably do so by carefully going through motions which they have learned from their lawyers. For example, in a large number of the divorces granted for desertion, the wives gave no explanation of the reasons for their husbands' departure from home except to testify in case after case, "He just packed up and left." In the other type of divorces, the infidelity was usually proved either by the direct evidence of eye-witnesses or by friends of the accused spouse, who eagerly disclosed conversations in which he or she had admitted the breach of marriage vows, although one would naturally suppose that friends would do their best to keep such confidences secret. One gets the impression that adultery must be a very public affair in Maryland. Of course, most of these cases are merely divorces by mutual consent, and the authors maintain that the law ought to recognize this frankly and issue divorce certificates in uncontested cases in much the same way as it issues marriage licenses, instead of forcing the parties to undergo the expensive pretense of a law-suit. The legal formalities would then be reserved for the comparatively few cases where the defendant objects to the divorce. Another interesting point brought out by this book is the contrast between the willingness of both spouses to separate and their bitter disagreements about the so-called subsidiary issues like alimony and the custody of children. Those are evidently the matters which the law ought to investigate with thoroughness, rather than the circumstances which made the marriage break down so that it can no longer benefit either the particular family or society.

In spite of the valuable lessons given by the various investigations described above, we cannot hope to solve all our problems in this way. Such fact-finding researches if done well are very expensive and take an enormous amount of many lawyers' time; if done badly, they are worthless or positively misleading. Fortunately, the discrepancies between legal rules and human conduct can sometimes be studied in other ways, for instance, from books, articles, and reports on social and economic questions. A journal called *Law and Contemporary Problems* has lately been started at Duke University; each issue is devoted to a single problem, *e.g.*, migratory divorce or instalment selling, which is treated by all sorts of experts besides lawyers, so that we shall get more data and opinions about the shortcomings of established legal rules.

At least two good results have come from all this speculation and investigation. We are becoming increasingly aware of the importance of law in action as contrasted with law in books and have worked out new methods for studying the effect of rules on life. We are measuring the human factor in law-making and are getting a better understanding of the mental processes of judges, legislators, and officials.

"So what?" practical men may ask. What tangible changes have come from all this theorizing? So far it has produced few actual improvements in the administration of justice. But it has shown us a good deal about what improvements are needed, and it has helped us to make them wisely when they become practicable. Therefore, it is not unreasonable to expect that after our economic worries have lessened there will be many notable law reforms because of all the thinking that has gone on since the War. We know better where we are going, and we are on the way.

EDUCATION

# EDUCATION

## [Christian Gauss]

THE SITUATION in American higher education was summed up a few years ago by a well-known educator who began an address to a university audience as follows: "There are only three things wrong with higher education in America; first, our students; second, our alumni; and third, our faculties." If, as is likely, this discouraged professor has since read President Hutchins's *The Higher Learning in America* (1936), he would add one further depressing item to his diagnosis. He would include the curriculum or course of study at present being offered by most of our colleges and universities.

## I

It will help us to understand what is happening to education if we consider for a moment what has been happening to our American culture. There is much misunderstanding about many of our present difficulties because of our failure to recognize the forces in our history which are throwing us into confusion. Although we have heard much about the industrial revolution, the power age, "the age of abundance," and how they have brought to the fore new scientific and technological problems, we have failed to perceive why this should have bedevilled American education to a degree which has not been equally evident, for instance, in France, or England, or Denmark. This is probably because one of the most serious complicating factors in the history of American education was that unique American phenomenon, the closing of the frontier, to which Turner called attention many years ago.

Although the importance of this phenomenon has been fully recognized by historians in other fields, we have been unwilling to admit that it lies behind many of the educational problems which are most insistently calling for solution today. There can be little doubt that the beginning of "the rush to the colleges"—which still continues and has brought so many problems in its wake—coincides chronologically with the closing of the frontier. Although accurate statistics are not available, it is generally conceded that in 1890 there were slightly over 70,000 students in our colleges and universities. In 1937 there were about a million and a quarter. The rate of increase, out of all proportion to the increase in population, has been fairly uniform and though it was checked during the depression years, this demand for high school and college education by an ever increasing percentage of our population remains one of the salient aspects of the educational problem in America. For purposes of comparison we may well take 1925. In that year Great Britain with a population of forty-three million had 46,000 enrolled in its institutions of higher learning. Germany with sixty-three million had 68,000. France with forty million had about 54,000. We in the United States with one hundred and seventeen million had 800,000 men and women enrolled. In the ten years from 1925 to 1935 when the increase in our general population was relatively slight, our college population rose from 800,000 to about 1,200,000, showing, in spite of the depression, a climb of nearly 50 per cent.

In fairly typical States the college-going population has over a twenty-five-year period increased from 400 to 500 per cent and a rough computation lends warrant to the statement that where in 1900 from an average community one boy in a hundred went to college, about seven are now going. This problem is complicated further by the fact that this rate of increase varies very markedly from State to State and even within the limits of particular States. In Ohio, for instance, of pupils graduated from high schools in June, 1934, in some counties only 6 per cent proceeded to college, in other counties 43 per cent. Our "racial minorities" also show striking divergences. The percentage of Negroes in high schools and colleges remains far below the average; the percentage of Jewish students runs above. This is the reason given by many colleges and professional schools where enrollment is limited, as it is in most medical schools, for restricting the numbers of Jewish students to a quota basis.

For the present we must confine ourselves to relating this phenomenon to the changes in our American culture during this same period. While the frontier was still open, status and livelihood in America depended, roughly speaking, on native qualities of physical and intellectual energy and individual capacity and skills which could still be effectively exercised alone or in the privately owned establishment. This was true, of course, not only of the pioneer farmer who was willing to take up new lands; it was true also of the blacksmith, the merchant, the builder. Even the lawyer or doctor fresh from college could hang out his shingle from a shack in the newly founded settlements. Until 1890 we were for the most part still actually living in the heyday of "rugged individualism."

In that earlier period the facts prove that it was possible to achieve the highest distinction in virtually all fields without a college education. Our two greatest presidents, Washington and Lincoln, had never been to college. Our two most successful business men, Carnegie and Rockefeller, were in the same case. This was also true of our most successful inventors and technologists, Edison, the Wright brothers, and Henry Ford. It was true even of our two most characteristically American men of letters, Walt Whitman and Mark Twain. These facts which might have been expected to beget an attitude of humility in academic circles have failed to do so. It may still be true that the main forces shaping our lives are even now operating outside of our college campuses, yet the public in general has become convinced that college education provides the easiest, if not the only, way to success.

However this may be, one change in our cultural problems must be noted. Status in our democracy today for the average man (and on the whole, as we shall see, our graduates are only average men and women), depends upon his effectiveness in group or institutional activities. Most men are compelled to make their way in necessarily regimented larger organizations and larger centers of population. The escape from the pressure of the machine age, which an open frontier still provided, has now definitely been closed. Social competence and special training for specialized jobs far more than physical or even intellectual energy have become, for the great majority, prerequisites to a livelihood and status in the white collar class.

These two major aspects of our problem, the increase in enrollment and the insistent demand for specialized vocational training, involve the questions, To whom shall we grant higher education? and What shall we teach them? Until we have reached some rough agreement on these two fundamentals, our educational system must remain chaotic.

## II

In spite of what we have described as a chaotic condition, the general temper of most educational discussion remains optimistic. Since education of any type is still regarded as an asset to democracy, the immense expansion of high school and college enrollments is accepted as that much clear gain. Behind all this we find two contradictory assumptions.

In certain circles it is held that the function of our colleges and universities is to train leaders. This notion was well nigh universal fifteen years ago and though on the decline, is still repeated in any number of college prospectuses and college catalogues. Allied with this view is the belief that the men and women now on our campuses constitute, so far as intellectual capacity is concerned, the elite of the country. In other circles, the egalitarian assumption prevails. This holds that with the exception of a negligible percentage of morons, higher education can be successfully extended to all our young people—with profit to all concerned.

It is no secret that with the rush to the colleges, the standards of accomplishment demanded of the student in any number of our institutions have been considerably relaxed. There is a very general desire to grant A.B. degrees to all those who earnestly desire them. The wastage, even so, is rather staggering. Where State surveys have been made, it seems to be the general rule that about one-half of all entering freshmen fail to proceed to graduation. This is the situation revealed in Ohio and in Minnesota, and by the extensive survey conducted by the Carnegie Foundation, in Pennsylvania. It becomes increasingly evident that the most frequent cause of failure is intellectual incapacity to master the curriculum offered.

This wastage is even more pronounced in those technical schools to which high school graduates are admitted directly, as they are to schools of engineering. In the 1920's the Society for the Promotion of Engineering Education became so much concerned about this situation that with the assistance of the Carnegie Foundation it undertook an exhaustive inquiry into this problem. The assistant director of the investigation reported as follows:

Of each one hundred entering students but sixty-two successfully complete the first year and proceed with their class, and but forty-two complete the first two years. The others drop out of college for one reason or another; the predominant reason being scholastic failure.

It was fair to say that of every five men who matriculated in any given engineering school in America, in all probability at least four would turn out to be relative failures. The report concluded with the statement that it was high time we gave more attention to the quesion of a rational selection of student personnel.

It is of course our high schools that prepare the immense majority of our college students. Do the colleges succeed in attracting the best candidates available? Of 16,600 high school seniors tested in Wisconsin in 1930, 7404 declared their intention of going on to college. The average of the college-going group was found to be only slightly higher than the average of the entire group—61.4 per cent as against 50 per cent for the average. Forty per cent of those planning to go to college were in the lower half of the high school group. Of the relatively small number of seniors in the upper fifth of the scale, which would seem to provide the very best college material, 1198 indicated no intention of going on to college. This does not indicate any high degree of selection on the basis of intellectual aptitude. A study of Ohio high school seniors, reported before the Association of Ohio College Registrars in 1933, gives us much the same result. Dr. Herbert Toops, who had made the study, concluded, "At that time then, the colleges were drawing almost 'run of the mine sampling' of the graduating seniors." Twenty-four thousand or 40 per cent of all the 60,000 high school graduates were better than the median freshman who was enrolling in Ohio colleges. This situation was checked again in 1937 and some improvement was noted, much of which was ascribed to the results of the depression.

Similar results were obtained in a study made by A. M. Jordan, of 19,000 high school seniors in North Carolina. Mr. Jordan found that although on the average students going to college were somewhat superior scholastically to those not going,

Our data show conclusively that literally thousands of students who are scholastically able to do so are *not* continuing their academic training, while other thousands of students with the poorest abilities are attempting to continue their work in academic halls.

When Tyler Dennett, then president of Williams College, announced a few years ago that too many "nice boys" were coming to college and that it was likely that the leaders of the nation twenty years from now would not be drawn from those at present in the colleges, he was voicing a probability which should at least give us pause. It is clear that the prestige enjoyed by college students generally can no longer be explained on the assumption that as a class they are recruited from the prospective intellectual giants of our country.

As a result of all this we are now witnessing on an unprecedented scale an attempt on the part of a good many of the colleges, led by Harvard, to induce the intellectually able candidate to come to college. Large scholarships are offered for this purpose. Excellent as this may be as a means of raising the intellectual level on a particular campus, we can hardly hope that it will do much to correct the situation throughout the country. The Harvard scholarship program for the most part enlists the interest of candidates who are already college-minded and who would go to some college in any case. We have no reason to believe, however, that it will greatly reduce the proportion of the intellectually able high school graduates who are now not being brought into the college fold, or reduce the number of the intellectually incompetent who are now so numerous on our campuses.

In the State of Ohio a few years ago an attempt was made to bring about closer co-operation between high schools and colleges to remedy this situation. A few other States are following this lead, but considering the magnitude of this problem we must admit that very little progress has been made toward its solution. It is of course very largely independent of the innumerable debates upon the question, what should constitute the college or university curriculum, which in the last few years have provoked so much discussion. The colleges will have no right to claim that they are training the leaders of our democracy until they can prove that admission to college is determined, as it now is not, by potential intellectual proficiency.

## III

Whatever opinions we may hold upon the particular solutions proposed, no one deserves more credit for having brought the problem of the curriculum into the foreground than President Hutchins of the University of Chicago. Until recently in America we have divided our educational system roughly into three periods—eight years of schooling in the grades, four years in high school, and four years in college. President Hutchins and many others favor a different division. They would combine the last two years of high school and the first two years of college into a four-year unit devoted to "general education" and at the beginning of what is now the junior year in college would have the abler students begin their more strictly university work. In its allocation of college time this grouping corresponds to the Junior College Plan which has made much headway in our country in the last ten years and which in its essentials was proposed back in the 1890's by President Harper, also of Chicago. It is clear that President Hutchins does not entertain any high hopes of what could be done in this period devoted to general education. He would allow virtually all comers to proceed through what amounts to two years of college and give them a degree.

To many this will seem more like evading than solving a difficulty. The ineffectiveness of freshman and sophomore years in a great many of our colleges results from the fact that the classes are crowded with incompetents who have little native aptitude for the type of instruction offered. This inevitably forces a lowering of the standard of performance required. Frankly stated, we have "watered the soup," thinned the educational gruel that is offered. The type of task assigned makes so little draft upon the abilities of the average or better than average student that he makes very little progress. This is only partially remedied by segregating the dullards in special sections, for the general standard of accomplishment required of the entire class is still too low to make any serious draft upon the intellectual capacity of the potentially abler students.

President Hutchins evidently feels that everybody must be carried through his four-year period of general education. "Democracy," he tells us, "should mean that this curriculum from beginning to end is open to everybody." If this is true, there is no reason why democracy should not also mean that the university course following this unit must also be open to everybody. Once we admit this principle, any attempt to raise the level of higher education is doomed.

Fortunately, there is no reason for admitting it. Many excellent democracies, like the French, do not. Admission to her highest institution of learning, the École Normale Supérieure, is based solely upon the competitive principle. Even in our own country no one is inclined to call West Point or Annapolis or our Civil Service undemocratic in so far as admission to them is based upon competitive examinations. The fault is not with democracy. In the last ten years many colleges and a few State universities have been raising their requirements for admission, and where such selective admission has been resorted to, the wastage has been much reduced and the level of work done in the college has been appreciably raised. Democracy certainly means, or should mean, that the State should give every boy and girl, no matter what the economic status of the family may be, the best training it can possibly provide. Unless democracy is merely another name for inefficiency, this does not mean that it shall be the *same* education.

The remedy here, if good and effective education is our aim, would seem to lie along other lines. There should evidently be a bifurcation of the system and after a set period, but certainly long before the age of our present sophomores, training should be directed toward different ends. Which line a particular child should follow should not in the least be determined by economic status. Where the pupil's previous performance in school and his scholastic aptitude tests indicate clearly that he has very little native capacity along verbal or mathematical lines, he should be directed toward trade schools and the vocations. Such trade schools might very well be allowed to run on through as many years as are now required for the liberal arts course. The "schools of commerce" or "business" which are now a part of our higher educational system could be transferred over to these trade schools. These schools of commerce or business even now grant A.B. degrees. There is no reason why they should not be allowed to continue to do so.

We seem to have progressed far enough with our testing programs to be able to say with confidence that students with low verbal and mathematical scholastic aptitude cannot be successfully trained for the "learned professions" or draw any serious profit from continuing into a liberal arts curriculum. Even under our present system of low standards these low I. Q. students constitute the immense army of our failures. The reason is simple. Any liberal arts curriculum worthy of the name demands that the student make progress along either literary or scientific lines. Where his verbal and mathematical aptitude is slight, he cannot climb to the upper rungs of this particular ladder. This does not mean that he may not possess many other admirable qualities, such as social adaptability, in much higher degree than the liberal arts student. What we call "intelligence tests" do not measure social competence and there is little if any correlation between them.

From this curriculum leading to a "general education," President Hutchins would eliminate as unessential all of the laboratory sciences, all historical studies, all of the languages except English, all of the arts except certain literary classics. The course of study would consist of grammar, rhetoric, logic, and mathematics. For the average American youth this would constitute a dreary curriculum. The type of contradiction in which President Hutchins involves himself becomes apparent when he discusses grammar. It is, he tells us, "the *scientific* analysis of language; it disciplines the mind and develops the logical faculty. It is also good in itself and an aid to reading the classics." No one has ever sung the praises of grammar more eloquently. In going back to the mediæval curriculum President Hutchins seems however to forget that his course of study would be thinner than that pursued by the boy of the Middle Ages. He at least had two languages, his own and Latin, for it was of course Latin grammar that he studied.

Even those who favor linguistic studies for qualified candidates would not recommend them as scientific disciplines designed primarily to develop the logical faculty. The criterion of correctness is not logic but usage. If logical training is what President Hutchins is seeking, we should certainly recommend the grammar of almost any other language—Greek, Latin or French, for instance—rather than English, since they are somewhat more "logical," and if, as he says, grammar is good in itself, why not include at least one of these languages? If English grammar is to be given so large a place, most teachers will feel that it should have been started, perhaps completed, before the student enters the general educational college. Somewhat the same objections could be urged against rhetoric.

With the addition of only logic and mathematics we have, of course, a hopelessly one-sided curriculum, which would be curiously devoid of factual, scientific, historical, linguistic or cultural content. The most interesting suggestion is that which involves the reading of literary classics, though the boy who knows no other language or culture than his own is likely to remain provincial and nationalistic in his attitude toward life.

Mathematics is not a universal solvent of our problems. It cannot help us, for instance, in dealing with significant human relationships. One and one are two in mathematics but a man and his friend, a husband and wife, a father and his son are not, and neither arithmetic nor differential calculus can help us to shape more satisfying human ideals. Something, indeed much, can be learned about the latter in the arts and in humanistic disciplines which find little place in President Hutchins's curriculum. Even in economics and politics the mathematical or statistical method which makes for accuracy becomes effective only in proportion as the problem is dehumanized, depersonalized and is resolved into its purely materialistic aspects, like car loadings, steel production, price indices.

We have dealt more particularly with the curriculum proposed by President Hutchins, not because it provides an adequate remedy but because it recognizes frankly one of the evils, vocationalism, which has been the cause of so much of our confusion. The interest which it has aroused, even among those who oppose it, is a healthy sign, for it may be taken to indicate that we are at least beginning to realize that the helter-skelter system we have been following is leading us nowhere.

Our contemporary life has become too complicated to admit of the simple, mediæval solution which President Hutchins has offered. It should, however, give us pause to remember that the European dictators, like Stalin, Mussolini, and Hitler, have been far more successful in training their youth for life under dictatorship than we have been in training them for life in a liberal democracy. For that reason we may now profitably revert to a consideration of the historic factors which have disorganized our higher education. They will probably be found to be the same factors which are tending to disorganize our culture.

## IV

In the days when Daniel Boone, Kit Carson, and even Buffalo Bill were still the heroes of the American schoolboy, our older American culture could exist upon certain assumptions which have been rapidly wearing out. Those assumptions can no longer provide any sound foundation for the age of Hitler, Mussolini, and Stalin; of Henry Ford and John L. Lewis, or for life in the New York or Chicago of today. The brutal fact seems to be that we have come to believe only in the ECONOMIC MAN and in the NATION. For that reason, our supposedly higher education has become ever more vocational and nationalistic. Even colleges which call themselves colleges of the liberal arts have, as we have seen, added schools of commerce or business, or courses in insurance, banking, marketing, salesmanship, business psychology, or what not. Any one who wishes to study the changes in the curriculum of American colleges need only consult the successive catalogues issued by institutions of higher learning over a period of years. Where the curriculum of fifty or seventy-five years ago was printed in six or eight pages, it now runs to six or eight hundred. Some of this expansion was the result of the developing of new sciences and subjects of study which have won and deserve *droit de cité*. The immense majority of the new courses, however, have come in as a result of our blind acceptance of these beliefs that man is primarily or exclusively an economic entity and that the nation is and should be the ultimate factor in human history. The first belief has resulted in vocationalizing even higher education. The second has resulted in nationalizing it. We are only beginning to realize that as a result the older, humane tradition, with its faith in the humanities, has almost disappeared. It was this humane tradition which gave us the philosophy of liberalism which now seems so hopelessly ineffective.

Vocational schools or courses then have become immensely popular since they are supposed to lead to financial success—which is the supreme aim of our life. This same general tendency has made American business men and Chambers of Commerce believe to a degree that has never been true in any other age or nation, that they are in fact and by prescriptive right the dominant force in our culture. So long as our economic interests are our highest interests, this will continue to be the case. Higher education will not be an end in itself and can do little to further the search for truth and the welfare of mankind. This is only one of the maladies of our time which is reflecting itself in our educational system.

## V

The second malady, the nationalistic, has not yet been recognized and is therefore more insidious. For it the universities themselves are more directly responsible. The vocational trend, in part at least, has been forced upon us. The nationalistic trend is in much larger measure a creation of our schools. We have accepted with too little question the work of the 19th-century patriotic historians and critics, and have based our curriculum upon it. The older curriculum of the liberal arts college, whatever may be urged against it, still possessed at least one advantage. It was humane. It consisted of the classical languages and literary master-pieces of those older peoples and times. The ancient Greeks and Romans and their masterpieces were presented as still possessing general human validity. Mathematics, the sciences, philosophy, and "political economy" were studied in the same spirit. Fathers named their sons Homer or Virgil or Horace with no sense that they were handicapping them with archaic or exotic cognomens. The staples of this training were the same for educated men everywhere—in Russia, Germany, France, England, Italy or Spain. It involved the notion that there was something like a common measure, a possible common denominator for human activities. Where men believed in progress, they realized that this could be achieved only when humanity advanced on a wide front.

Without admitting it to ourselves, we have given up these general conceptions. We no longer believe in humanity. We believe in nations, usually only in our own. It should be borne in mind that Jared Sparks, the first professor of history, was appointed to the Harvard faculty only a hundred years ago. Since then, and especially in the 20th century, nearly all disciplines have been treated from the nationalistic standpoint. We study not history now but *German* history, *English* history, *French* history, above all, *American* history. We have largely ceased studying *belles lettres* or literature. We study *French* literature, *German* literature, *Italian* literature, *Spanish* literature, above all *American* literature. It will sometimes be found that the only course in literature which a student followed in college was a course in American literature, although that literature can boast of very few generally recognized masterpieces, and no single epic poem, no single tragedy, no single comedy, no single novel, satire or lyric, of first-rate importance in the world's literature. In some colleges we have introduced courses in "American philosophy." We do this because we have come to regard the nation as something unique, absolute, ultimate. It can be expected to observe only its own law. Any literature, any philosophy, or any political system is accepted as the product of the "historical process" and is therefore as good, as valid, as any other. We have broken down what was once called "the unity of knowledge" into innumerable, unrelated fragments. The curricula of our colleges show that in following this nationalistic trend we are fully as guilty as any other people.

There was much outcry in American academic circles in 1937 when it became evident that the Germans were attempting to create for themselves an exclusively German science. We who regard American literature, American philosophy, American culture, as unique, finally valid revelations, will do well to recall that we are only a step behind them in this new form of disruptive chauvinism. If we are to look forward to anything like a humanly desirable future, we must give up our blind faith in separatist nationalistic heavens, and deprovincialize, denationalize, our curricula and seek to discover whether there are or can be anything approaching common norms in literature, politics, and life. This problem, if not altogether new, has at present reached the acute stage. One of the most striking contradictions on our contemporary American campuses is that of our undergraduates pledging themselves not to bear arms in any international wars, while our teachers unwittingly propound exclusively nationalistic philosophies which imply that even among civilized men, there can be no human common denominator and that physical force, war, must therefore be the *ultima ratio mundi*.

# JOURNALISM

## The Magazines

### [Robert Cantwell]

EARLY in May, 1906, an extraordinary group of journalists walked
out of the most sensationally successful magazine in American
history. They left in a body. There were two men from the
business department, an associate editor, the managing editor
and his assistant, and three of the most celebrated magazine writers of
the time—Ida Tarbell, Lincoln Steffens, and Ray Stannard Baker. Ida
Tarbell was nearly fifty; she had written her lives of Lincoln and her
famous *History of the Standard Oil Company*. Steffens was celebrating
his fortieth birthday at the time of the walkout; he had published his
*Shame of the Cities* and had been in Colorado, working on an article on
Ben Lindsay, when the break came. Baker had not at that time written
his best sellers under the name of David Grayson, but he was widely
known, and he had been with the magazine through the six years of its
greatest growth. These writers were joined by William Allen White and
Finley Peter Dunne; they raised $200,000, bought *The American Maga-
zine* and set out to rival the magazine they had left.

This was *McClure's*. Founded thirteen years before by the ambitious,
volatile Samuel Sidney McClure, it had swept into an exhilarating financial, political, and literary success so rapidly that no other publication of
its time could be compared to it. When it was founded, American
periodical publishing was dominated by the four great, venerable, distinguished literary magazines—*Harpers, Scribners,* the *Atlantic* and *Century*. Modelled on the English magazines, printing genteel fiction by
some highly skilled practitioners and a good deal of expertly composed
but unexciting literary criticism, they had never been really popular.
*Harpers* led them with a circulation of 130,000. This was, however, as
great a circulation as any American magazine had up to that time, with
the brief exception of *Godey's Lady's Book,* which had reached 150,000 in

345

1850. Indeed, it was commonly believed then that Americans were not magazine readers, just as it is generally believed now that they will not buy books: Poe had increased the circulation of *Gresham's* from 6000 to 30,000, but Henry Adams, despite some distinguished contributors and some timely articles, could not get *The North American Review* above 2000. That had been the tradition when McClure and Munsey launched their cheap magazines. By the time Steffens and Tarbell left in 1906, popular magazines were firmly established in American cultural life: *McClure's* alone had a circulation of 750,000. More importantly, a group of magazines with similar policies had swept up with it: *Hampton's* increased from 13,000 to 440,000; *Everybody's,* which had been the house organ for Wanamaker's department store, climbed to 735,000; *Collier's* had 500,000 by 1909 and one million by 1912; *Cosmopolitan* and *The American Magazine* grew in proportion. Consequently, when Steffens and Tarbell left *McClure's* it was no mere editorial squabble—American popular magazines, and not simply *McClure's* and the muckrakers, had come into existence during their careers. Largely, in fact, as a result of their bold and simultaneous editorial coups—*The History of the Standard Oil Company* and *The Shame of the Cities.* When they began these works there were no popular American magazines; when they left *McClure's,* magazines had something of the popularity, and a good deal of the character, that they have now.

The term muckrakers applied to these people is as misleading now as it was when Ellery Sedgwick, then a young journalist, first tagged them with it—for it was Sedgwick and not Roosevelt who first applied Bunyan's phrase to describe them. Why had they been so sensationally successful? The commonly accepted answer has been that their exposures of the corruption of American political and social life coincided with a great stirring of popular revolt. Theirs was, Parrington says, "a dramatic discovery . . . when the corruption of American politics was laid on the threshold of business—like a bastard on the doorstep of the father—a tremendous disturbance resulted. There was a great fluttering and clamor amongst the bats and the owls. . . ." The political side of the muckrakers' contribution was unquestionably great, but it has been overvalued, and the simple journalistic boldness and effectiveness of their writing has been overlooked. After thirty years the simple bulk of their work is astonishing; in five years' time a handful of gifted writers conducted a searching exploration of American society—industrial, financial, political, and moral. Moreover, they did this with a wealth of local color, with wonderful savory names and places that had never been elevated into prose before. It was not because the muckrakers exposed the corruption of Minneapolis, for example, that they were widely read, but because they wrote about Minneapolis at a time when it had not been written about, without patronizing or boosting it, and with an attempt to explore its life realistically and intelligently.

They wrote, in short, an intimate, anecdotal, behind-the-scenes history of their own times—or, rather, they tried to write it, for they often fell down. They traced the intricate relationship of the police, the underworld, the local political bosses, the secret connections between the new corporations (then consolidating at an unprecedented rate) and the legislatures and the courts. In doing this they drew a new cast of characters for the drama of American society: bosses, professional politicians, reformers, racketeers, captains of industry. Everybody recognized these native types; everybody knew about them; but they had not been characterized before; their social functions had not been analyzed. At the same time, the muckrakers pictured stage settings that everybody recognized but that nobody had written about—oil refineries, slums, the red-light districts, the hotel rooms where political deals were made—the familiar, unadorned, homely stages where the teeming day-to-day dramas of American life were enacted. How could the aloof literary magazines of the East, with their essays and their contributions from distinguished English novelists, tap this rich material?

For literary, and not for political reasons, the muckrakers were successful. Their writing was jagged and hasty, and their moralizing now sounds not only dull but a little phony, yet they charged into situations that were deliberately obscured by the people involved in them; they sized up hundreds of complicated and intense struggles at their moment of greatest intensity; they dealt with material subject to great pressure and about which journalists could easily be misled. In a time of oppressive literary gentility they covered the histories of the great fortunes and the histories of corporations—something that had not been done before and that has scarcely been done well since—the real estate holdings of churches, the ownership of houses of prostitution, insurance scandals, railway scandals, the political set-ups of Ohio, Missouri, Wisconsin, Chicago, Cleveland, San Francisco, New York. The new huge cities of the West had not been explored after their growth through the 70's and 80's (just as, say, Tulsa, Oklahoma, has not been written about after its astonishing growth through the 1920's) and because they wrote of them, the writing of the muckrakers was packed with local color, the names and appearance of hotels and bars, crusading ministers and town bosses and bankers. They told people who owned the factories they worked in, who rigged the votes they cast, who profited from the new bond issue, the new street-railway franchise and the new city hall, who foreclosed the mortgage, tightened credit, and controlled the Irish vote on the other side of the river. Their exposures, as such, were not so sensational. People knew all the scandals, and worse ones. But they liked to read about towns they knew, characters they recognized, and a setting they understood. The old magazines had never given them that.

American popular magazines thus began by making an original contribution to American literature and to American social life. But from the start there had been a split between the people who wrote for the muckraking magazines and the people who owned them, and the break between owner and editors was symbolized by the walkout at *McClure's*. McClure had not wanted a crusading publication. He wanted a cheap one that would appeal to the masses, and he believed that the masses wanted sensational, if not lurid, general informative articles—short, easily digestible material like biographies of Lincoln and Napoleon. If he had to have muckraking, he wanted it to be non-political—an account of the increase in murders, for example. According to Steffens, McClure came to believe that democracy itself was responsible for the evils that the muckrakers exposed, and consequently tried to direct their exposures to attacks on democracy. Some stories had been killed, an attack on the insurance companies was shelved. Why the break came so dramatically was not made clear in either Steffens' or McClure's autobiography; writing to his father a few days after it occurred, Steffens said that McClure was planning to launch a giant stock promotion and organize a string of commercial companies. The significant point is that the direction of *McClure's* changed after the split—and the change was typical of that taking place in popular magazines in general. Willa Cather, who had not joined the insurgents, was made editor of *McClure's*. The type of writing that she did, finished and careful—far better in detail, in fact, than the hasty journalism of her predecessors—set the tone for American popular magazine writing. It bore only an indirect relation to current political and economic struggles; it cried no evils and proposed no remedies. After a brief flyer in what might be called right-wing muckraking (Ellery Sedgwick joined the staff after Steffens and Tarbell left) Mc-

*Clure's* settled down to the printing of more fiction, the stories of the outstanding English romancers—and more advertising.

*McClure's* was only an episode in American periodical publishing history, but it throws a good deal of light on its entire thirty-year course. Popular magazines began by distributing a literature of information and inquiry—even of discontent—a kind of writing which, for all its unevenness, was calculated to inform readers of the life of communities like their own, and to stimulate skeptical discussion of their institutions. Having gained circulation in this way, they insensibly shifted and began to distribute a different kind of reading matter which has grown into the magazine literature we now have. It would be wrong to imply that the owners and advertisers were solely responsible for this; the limitations of the muckrakers, their inability to set any new goal for themselves once their initial survey was completed, was as great a factor. In any event a literature that was, in a studied way, not political and not controversial came into being and became the chief product of the popular magazines. It still is. Their circulation did not fall, but it assumed a different character. The muckraking magazines grew almost without advertising and their income was based on their sales; in the later publications advertising income became at least as important as the income from newsstand sales. People continued to buy magazines, in other words, after magazines ceased to publish the type of material that had made them popular, but readers no longer carried the full cost of them. There are innumerable explanations of the economics of advertising, none of which carry much conviction, but in the history of popular magazines advertising has played a unique role: It has constituted, in effect, a gigantic subsidy placed behind a certain type of literature—a subsidy given by the biggest national corporations, making it possible for the magazines receiving it to be distributed for less than their cost of production. The literature that is thus supported is varied and sometimes it is so skillfully done as to seem brilliant—the magazines that carry it now are so competently edited that beside them the scratchy publications of the muckrakers seem as heavy as a Sears-Roebuck catalogue. But it is essentially a literature, not of inquiry, but of distraction, a literature least of all calculated to provoke questions or excite controversy, and with the strange characteristic of being unsuited for the communication of information or the analysis of ideas.

It has flourished mightily, and is now going stronger than ever before.

There are now about 1200 weekly magazines with a circulation of around 50,000,000, and 2000 monthly magazines with a circulation of approximately 100,000,000. These figures include those for devotional and pious publications given away in Sunday Schools, the two-million-monthly circulation of the comic-strip magazines for children, and other such phenomena, but they suggest what has happened since *McClure's* jumped to the first 750,000 back in 1903. Magazines died like flies during the depression, but the number of magazine readers nevertheless increased during that period, the circulation of the pulp magazines (and of others aimed at the same audience) increasing from about 8,000,000 in 1928 to nearly 14,000,000 monthly in 1938.

The field of periodical publishing is now so vast and so complex, so little charted, so seldom analyzed and criticized, that its value as an index to the level of American culture has not been clearly established. It accounts for as much printed matter *each month* as is included in all the 10,000 books published in the United States *each year*. In view of its great bulk, its monotony is perhaps its outstanding characteristic—it is amazing that the blood-and-thunder pulps can retell the same stories so exactly, that the smug slicks can go on repeating the romances they were running before the war, that the motion-picture magazines with their staggering circulations can continue to print the same pictures of the same stars month after month. A case can certainly be made for the charge that American popular magazines do *not* accurately reflect American taste, any more than *Harpers,* for example, reflected American taste in the days before the muckrakers. But that case must take into account some formidable statistics.

The first of these relate to the pulp magazines. Advertising, with the technical refinements that it makes possible, helps a good deal in explaining away the circulation of magazines like *The Saturday Evening Post* or *The Ladies' Home Journal;* they could not continue in their present form without it. But advertising plays a small part in the pulp magazines. They are supported by their readers, and their readers are primarily drawn from the working-class, especially from working-class youth, and while pulp magazines are notoriously hazardous and unprofitable publishing ventures, they are nevertheless unique in that they keep going without great levies drawn from advertisers. The literature they contain, then, reflects the taste and the intellectual level of the audience without ambiguity. It is almost entirely a literature of violence (in the Western story magazines and the innumerable crime magazines) and of sickly and even morbid sentiment in the romantic publications for women. In simple circulation it dwarfs all branches of American periodical publishing except the most popular slick-paper women's magazines and general magazines. One small wing of it, the Modern Fiction Group, publishing *Spicy Adventure Stories, Spicy Detective Stories, Spicy Mystery Stories* and *Spicy Western Stories,* boasts a circulation of 400,000 which about equals the combined circulation of the intellectual and cultural magazines—*Scribners, Harpers, The Atlantic Monthly, The Nation* and the *New Republic.*

This lowbrow literature for the masses has seen one momentous change in the last few years—the emergence of crime stories, gangster stories, G-man stories so lurid and bloody that the traditional Wild West tales of American boyhood are genteel beside them. They have none of the intricacy or puzzle-solving appeal of mystery stories—the fiction deals primarily with crimes of brutality, and the factual articles, often illustrated with photographs of mutilated bodies, emphasize assaults and crimes of perversion. The pathological quality of this literature, its exploitation of abnormality, its delight in violence for the sake of violence, its lack of humor or even of adventure, make the immense circulation of the pulp magazines disquieting—particularly when it is seen as a depression phenomenon, springing into existence when unemployment became widespread early in 1930. If the literature that reaches the working-class is taken at its lowest level—at the level represented by these magazines, by such publications as the astrology magazines, which reach 100,000 readers, by the confession magazines, which reach almost 4,-000,000—the mixture of insipidity, superstition, and violence found in them gives an appalling picture of working-class culture. The best of them, like *Adventure,* which prints straightforward and often excellent action narratives, are characterized by a complete remoteness from the problems of the class they reach;[1] the worst have a morbid and nightmarish quality of frenzy that seems to imply desperation in the people who read them, and irresponsibility in the people who turn them out.

There is, however, a far healthier side of periodicals that reach predominately working-class audiences. Except for the confession magazines, which are apparently read by both men and women, the magazines with the greatest popularity among the working-class are the scientific and

---

[1] At the lowest point of the depression, *True Story Magazine* (circulation 2,268,000) solicited advertising on the grounds that its reading matter was calculated to quiet the unrest of the unemployed.

handicraft publications. *Popular Mechanics* and *Popular Science* together reach a million readers. Both are informative and detailed; both give an engaging month-to-month account of how a vast section of the American proletariat spends its spare time—tinkering in innumerable backyards with innumerable gadgets, devising automatic doorstops out of old inner tubes, hot water heaters out of second-hand bicycle pumps, or contraptions to open windows, built of washing-machine parts—with a homely practical fertility that is proof of how deeply rooted in American life the inventive implse is. The total circulation of the 12 big movie magazines (3,500,000) surpasses that of the popular science magazines, but only one movie magazine has a higher circulation than *Popular Mechanics* with its 536,000 monthly. And there are probably far more overlapping readers of the crime magazines and the movie magazines than there are of the scientific magazines, which cost more and are as meaty as the movie magazines are thin. The extraordinary popularity of the outdoor and sports magazines with working-class readers is another antidote to the hypnotic and narcotic literature of the crime stories—*Hunting and Fishing* reaches almost half a million readers, and *Field and Stream* and *Outdoor Life* another half-million—revealing the extent to which the natives of the most highly industrialized nation on earth have kept to their disappearing woods.

The slick-paper magazines are to the American middle-class what the pulps are to the working-class; and if in the pulps a literature of distraction degenerates to lurid grotesque, in the slicks it has been raised to a craft, almost, at times, an art. *The Saturday Evening Post* with its 3,000,000 readers, its innumerable smooth stories which by some magic can never be remembered after they are read, its querulous editorials and its ill-tempered, explosive attacks on the Roosevelt administration—attacks that always seem out of place in the midst of good-natured fiction whose point invariably is that everything is going to turn out all right—*The Saturday Evening Post* has refined the formula of popular American magazines to the point where further improvement seems impossible. These middle-class publications—excluding the women's magazines—have a combined circulation of about 13,000,000. They have been growing steadily: the *Post* gained 1,000,000 readers in the past decade; *Liberty,* some 800,000; *Collier's* 1,300,000; *Redbook* 400,000. The women's magazines, with their uninterrupted romances cut as neatly as the dress patterns that often come in the same issue, with their earnest editorials on the desirability of peace and—lately—with their determined and daring discussions of birth control, syphilis, and the prostate gland, also seem to have carried their formula about as far as it can go, and as successfully. *Good Housekeeping's* circulation has increased from 1,442,-174 in 1928 to 2,142,719 in 1938; *McCall's* has jumped 400,000 in the same period, *Pictorial Review* 800,000, *The Woman's Home Companion* 700,-000 and *The Ladies' Home Journal* 500,000—their combined circulation now is also about 13,000,000. With their recurring articles on how to keep a budget, how to make your own clothes, how to conceal the wear in old chairs, restore old pictures, repaint shabby walls, make a tasty meal of left-overs, and glue together furniture that is falling apart—with all this practical and pathetic advice, the women's magazines seem to be run by people who know what shape the middle-class is in. As a result they are far more realistic than the general magazines like the *Post* or *Redbook*. Moreover, in the women's magazines the halting informative articles on sex, birth control, and venereal diseases stand out in startling contrast to the domestic romances that accompany them:—The people in the romances do not go around warming up yesterday's dinner, and they are certainly never troubled about birth control or their husbands' prostate glands, as the readers seem to be.

Within the limits that they set for themselves these magazines are edited with extraordinary technical competence. As a result, the limitation of their aims is terribly apparent in every issue. It is not that they have contributed nothing new—that their staffs have not been set to work on consequential contemporary problems—nor is it that they have not undertaken crusades. With their technical skill and reactionary beliefs, it is probably fortunate that their editors do not go in for crusading. They are depressing because of their extreme aloofness from everything that has been going on; the country has been shaken from top to bottom with panics and riots, and they have kept right on doing business at the same stand, with the same symbols, with the same cast of characters dusted off a little to bring them up-to-date. They have nothing to say, for instance, about the findings of contemporary psychology, and very little to say about modern science; they have not reported on the modern labor movement, except for occasional spiritless sniping, nor on the gigantic migration of industry to the South, the convulsions of the railroads under the impact of the automobile industry, the transformation of American open-shop cities to union towns, the current discoveries in medicine. They are depressing in terms of what they have missed and what they are missing; American life has passed them by so completely that their writing has the air of a dexterous and artificial game, played by experts and of value only as a distraction. Their vast collective indifference is almost as great a barrier to the intellectual exploration of the modern world as censorship itself would be. The news magazines and many of the newspapers are more flexible and receptive, but the limitation of their function to reporting, and the brevity of their reports, prevent them from undertaking the analysis of current affairs that was once a periodical's prime reason for existence.

In the face of the huge circulations and their constant bombardment of irrelevancies of the popular magazines, the cultural periodicals seem feeble. The biggest art magazine in the country reaches 12,000 people; the only magazine of literary criticism, *The Saturday Review of Literature,* reaches about 25,000. *The New Republic* and *The Nation* reach about 100,000, and it appears that when the circulation of one increases, that of the other declines. *The Atlantic Monthly, Harpers,* and *Scribners* each account for 100,000. And except for the university quarterlies of very small circulation, and the little literary magazines which now appear infrequently, these are the publications that attempt objective and extended appraisals of contemporary literature, or generalized discussions of current beliefs.

Their small circulation, however, is not a clear index to their importance, any more than the small circulation of *Oil Weekly* or *Iron Age* indicates their importance in their respective industries. They are the trade papers of the intellectuals, as *Iron Age* is the trade paper of the steel industry. And it is in the trade papers that the history of the modern world is being recorded, insofar as it is being recorded at all—in the graphs and charts of declining and rising production, in the painstaking reports of orders, of drilling in West Texas and Oklahoma, of the opening of textile mills, the erection of chemical plants in Louisiana—the blind moves of industry that drag our social life behind it. The circulation of the trade papers is small—*Iron Age* has 14,000 and *Oil Weekly* 12,000—and their general commentaries are usually wretchedly written. Their editorials are usually explosive with incoherent outrage at some governmental interference with customary liberties or at some labor union advance. But in the flood of publications they alone are keeping the detailed record of industrial production on which employment and unemployment, the fortunes of politicians, the circulation of magazines, ultimately depend. And they picture, however dimly, the huge and smoky stages on which history is being made: the steel mills along the Calumet and the Mahoning, so vast that two or three of them can produce more steel than is made in all of Germany; the chemical plants along the Kill van Kull; the handful of automobile works at Flint and Detroit and Dearborn that produce the world's automobiles; the refineries, electrical works and laboratories that dominate American economy as industry has dominated no other country on earth. The popular magazines are filled with records of the struggles and tribulations of individuals, and usually with very genteel reflections of what contemporary Americans —of whatever class—actually experience. When you read the industrial trade papers you are aware at once of the conflict of corporations against corporations, of industries with other industries, of sectional and international rivalries. The trade papers in the main are so awkwardly assembled that more imagination is required to read them—and get anything out of them—than went into their editing. But in view of the irrelevancies that fill the popular press, their contribution to understanding seems considerable, and it will probably seem greater as time passes. For we are in a period when life has outrun our interpreters—when a new cast of characters, still undefined, has begun to appear on new stages, while the popular press is still discussing performances on which the curtain has descended. We are in a period like that when the muckrakers began their explorations. But where they had a clear field before them there is now heavy artillery laying down a rolling barrage, week by week and month by month, against trenches that were taken long ago.

# THE AMERICAN NEWSPAPERS

## [John Cowles]

T HAT public confidence in the integrity and disinterestedness of American newspapers as a whole has declined in recent years few journalists will deny. Attacks on newspapers have increased both in number and importance. The question as to whether that lessened confidence is deserved may for the moment be set aside. Whether or not a thing is true may in the short run be of less importance than whether people think it is true.

Excerpts from a speech by Arthur Hays Sulzberger, publisher of *The New York Times,* generally regarded as America's most important newspaper, illustrate the existing situation.

Said Mr. Sulzberger: "There is, in my opinion, a growing disposition on the part of the public to view with skepticism that which they read in their newspapers and to distrust newspaper motives. . . . I detect certain doubts as to the accuracy of reporting. . . . There is discernible a feeling among a considerable group of readers that the personal interests of publishers are often put ahead of public service. . . . The failure to keep editorial opinion out of the news columns, and closely akin to it, the failure to present adequately both sides of a moot question, are matters of growing concern. . . ."

In the same vein speaks George Fort Milton of *The Chattanooga News:* "Some enemies of the freedom of the press are in the press itself. These are the men who ignore the public trusteeship of their institutions, who give only one side of the picture, who deal in half-truths or whole lies, whether about government, political parties, labor and capital, or about the poor, helpless individual caught in the hideous glare of some news event."

To understand the present situation more clearly, it may be helpful to trace what has happened to American newspapers during the last generation, particularly from the economic aspect. Believers in the theory of economic interpretation of all events will find much to support their views, but, at the same time, more than a little to refute them.

First of all, the metropolitan American newspapers have become great capitalistic business enterprises, requiring huge investments in plant and equipment, with enormously expensive weekly payrolls and outlays for gathering, processing, printing, and distributing the news.

Two or three generations ago an ambitious printer with a few hundred dollars and a passion to express his opinions could start a little newspaper. If he caught the popular fancy his journal might grow out of its earnings to become influential and successful. Many of our leading dailies were started in just that way. Newspaper publishing was a vocation easy to enter. There was the traditional free play of competition. Cities large and small had many papers. They started and flourished or languished and died. There was a voice for every opinion.

As newspapers, they were poor according to current standards. Few attempted either to print all the news or to print it impartially and objectively, as our more responsible papers try to do today. Almost anybody, however, could start a paper if the spirit moved him, and a reader could choose from the many some one to read that coincided with his own opinions or prejudices.

Then just as the great industrial and banking and transportation corporations were beginning to take form and rise to power in their fields, a similar trend toward concentration, toward fewer and stronger—and better—newspapers, commenced. The thing was inexorable.

Thirty years ago there were scores of different automobile manufacturers—by today's standards all relatively small and weak. Gradually some companies, because of more capital, or better engineering facilities, or more aggressive management, began to draw away from the rest. They could offer the public more for their money than could their weaker competitors, and their volume of business pyramided while the smaller units fell by the way.

Possibly it is socially undesirable for the automobile industry to be concentrated into the relatively few great aggregations that exist today. Possibly it is also socially undesirable that today Detroit, for example, with a million and a half people, should have but one morning newspaper. The same force—that apparently irresistible economic trend toward fewer and larger and stronger units—whether automobile manufacturing or newspaper publishing—is responsible.

During the first three decades of the twentieth century advertising volume grew enormously in America, along with the merchandising of goods on a national scale and the accelerated trend toward larger business units. The increased income that the newspapers received from this development in advertising enabled them greatly to extend their news-gathering facilities and improve their product, provided them with the revenue with which to add "features"—comic strips and serial stories and all the other things that the average person prefers to serious, heavy news.

The newspapers get the greater part of their income from advertising. They could not exist solely on what the reader pays. As results from advertising are in rough proportion to a publication's circulation, the newspapers with the most circulation, broadly speaking, produce the most profitable returns for the advertiser.

Consequently the pressure to get more and more circulation steadily increased. The revenue from the increased advertising patronage enabled those newspapers that received it to enlarge their staffs and services and to print more news and features. This in turn widened still further their circulation leadership over their weaker competitors. The financially weaker papers were thus at a steadily increasing disadvantage in their efforts to win new or hold old readers.

The trend toward fewer newspapers, through mergers and suspensions, became nation-wide until today many fairly sizable cities (Denver, Louisville, Omaha, Toledo, St. Paul, Hartford, Des Moines, Memphis, Grand Rapids, Nashville, and others) have but one morning and one afternoon paper. In several of those cities both papers are owned by the same individual or company.

Many of our largest cities (Detroit, Cleveland, Baltimore, St. Louis, Buffalo, Pittsburgh, Kansas City, Seattle) have only one morning paper and only two afternoon dailies. In three of these cities the single morning paper has common ownership with one of the two afternoon papers.

It would be a serious error, however, for one to assume that this trend toward fewer newspapers indicates that a few big nation-wide newspaper corporations are likely in the near future to own and operate any alarming proportion of the surviving papers.

Experience has proved that "chain papers," controlled and edited at one place, whether New York or San Simeon, are not the menace to alert locally owned and edited papers that some alarmists have believed. There are only two really large newspaper chains—Scripps-Howard and Hearst. The most successful Scripps-Howard papers are apparently those with the largest measure of local management. The "Hearst menace" has steadily receded as a competitive threat to individually owned papers and Hearst's current influence on journalism has shrivelled to but a shadow of what it was. Within a few years the Hearst empire, already shrunk by sales and suspensions, will probably disintegrate into a handful of separate duchies and principalities. Even Scripps-Howard has recently sold or suspended some of the weaker links in its chain.

As the successful operation of a newspaper in a competitive field depends so largely upon the quality of its management and its ability to keep in tune with the town, being neither too far ahead of nor behind the local mores, a newspaper cannot be successfully operated like a branch of a mass-production factory. Intangible factors and the human elements are too important. There is small likelihood that a great newspaper trust could ever successfully operate a hundred papers in a hundred cities against locally owned competitors. The threat of any nation-wide newspaper monopoly is a phantom.

Similarly, distances in America are so great, and the appetite for local and State and regional news is so strong, that no "national daily" in the English sense is conceivable.

The trend toward mergers and suspensions, however, is accelerating. The prospect is for steadily fewer papers, many of them actual, or semi, *local* monopolies.

Immediately the question arises as to whether these actual or semi-monopolistic papers are doing a better or worse job of serving the public interest than are the papers in those cities where there are many competitors rather than few or none.

Eliminating New York City, which is in a class by itself because of its size and importance, the answer seems to be that the newspapers in those cities where there are comparatively few publications are certainly no worse and probably relatively better from both the professional and the public-service standpoint than are the papers in the towns with more dailies.

No list of "best" newspapers, no matter how small, would be complete without including such dailies as *The Baltimore Sunpapers* and *The St. Louis Post-Dispatch*. Both are in cities with limited competition. Conversely, the cities that are the most "over-newspapered," such as Boston, have, on the average, the poorest papers from all standpoints.

The explanation is simple. Those newspapers that are competitively the strongest not only have the financial means to give their readers a superior product, but—*other things being equal*—naturally have the greater editorial independence and are the less susceptible to pressure or venality.

Corruption of newspapers in any open or direct way is less common than critics of the press would have us believe. Pressure from advertisers does affect in greater or less degree many newspapers' policies in handling news, but so does pressure from other sources: pressure from religious bodies, from political machines with favors to dispense, from union labor, from organized groups of various kinds, as, in the '20's, in some sections, the Klan.

That the editorial and news policies of many newspapers are controlled by their business offices no one can deny. On the other hand, the evidence indicates that those newspapers that are financially the strongest and most firmly entrenched are less likely to be venal than are the weaker papers struggling to keep their noses above the water line. Therefore the trend toward fewer and stronger papers seems on the whole to mean a trend toward less corruptible papers.

From the social aspect probably the great danger in the existing newspaper situation is that because the surviving newspapers have on the whole been highly prosperous, or at least have represented large amounts of invested capital even if their current earnings have not been large, their owners as a class have tended to be too conservative, too well satisfied with things as they are.

In the first place, although few of them seem to realize it, newspaper owners as a class were beneficiaries of lavish unearned increment in the form of a huge increase in advertising revenue in the first three decades of this century. The values and earnings of their papers increased enormously. At the same time mechanical improvements and the expansion of news and feature services, which the reading public quickly came to take for granted, increased the costs of starting and operating new papers to a point where as a practical matter no new competing publication could be established.

Persons unfamiliar with newspapering grossly underestimate what it would cost to start a new paper or what the operating losses would be until a new paper, regardless of its management's ability, could conceivably change readers' and advertisers' habits sufficiently to become profitable.

Because the newspaper publishers feel well entrenched, because many of them are rich, because they have powerful organs through which to present their views, as a class they tend to take themselves too seriously. Many unconsciously regard themselves about the way the feudal liege lords of the Middle Ages must have regarded themselves, and, as local potentates, conduct themselves accordingly.

Because their newspapers are great capitalistic enterprises, it is quite understandable why many of the owners have become too conservative, and why most of their papers do not seem accurately to reflect the aspirations of the common run of people or the ideals of those who see visions of a brave new world.

Now all this does not mean that newspaper publishers as a class are intentionally dishonest in handling news, that they purposely color or suppress reports of happenings to suit their social or economic or political prejudices. Some, including several of the most conspicuous and powerful, do.

If one will simply stop to think of the practical difficulties of accurately reporting, say, the causes and developments in a sit-down strike in half a dozen scattered automobile plants, with all of the conflicting charges and counter-charges by employer, by the A. F. of L. and by the C. I. O., one will appreciate what a newspaper, with its inflexible press-times, is up against.

While it is entirely possible that Arthur Sulzberger or Roy Howard may personally be so prosperous that he may fail to become as exercised over the plight of the underprivileged as the flaming idealists wish he did, that is no proof that he does not get more satisfaction, greater professional pride, and deeper ego gratification from seeing that his paper, whether *The New York Times* or *The World-Telegram,* prints the news honestly and fairly than he gets from anything else.

Similarly, such charges as that the Associated Press, for example, is consciously "coloring" the news of the Spanish civil war in behalf of the Loyalists or would intentionally misrepresent the Catholic Church's attitude toward the Japanese invasion of China are ridiculous to any one familiar with the A. P.'s set-up. As a mutual association of some 1300 American papers representing almost every shade of opinion (although the bulk of the member papers are economically conservative) and with many Catholic members, including some on the board of directors, it is childish to believe that the Associated Press would try to do other than transmit what it believed to be facts. That the A. P. makes an occasional mistake is less remarkable than that Kent Cooper has developed the organization to the point where it transmits so much news so rapidly with so few errors.

It is true that the Associated Press gets much of its American news originally from member papers. These members are predominantly conservative. In some cases their local news of, say, a capital-labor controversy may be biased pro-employer. Consequently the Associated Press, in spite of its efforts to transmit an objective news report, may at times carry stories that are not fair and accurate, but such instances are much fewer than the left wing critics assume.

Aside from the criticisms of the newspapers on the grounds that their reporting of the capital-labor controversy is biased, and that the newspapers' own views are those of vested capitalistic interests, the major current criticisms have a political origin.

To understand the background of the Roosevelt administration's frequent attacks on the integrity of the press and the accuracy of its reporting it is necessary to go back into the ancient history of 1933.

When the NRA was established, whether intentionally or not it provided what many or most publishers honestly regarded as the opening wedge toward possible control by the government of the press. That idea may have never originally occurred to President Roosevelt. Nevertheless, a large proportion of the publishers with complete sincerity feared it.

The administration threatened to impose a code—which in effect meant licensing—on the newspapers. The newspapers roared—and properly so —about their constitutional rights and about freedom of the press. Naturally they attacked the administration. The administration professed complete purity of motive but demanded a code and retaliated to the newspapers' attacks, blow for blow. The controversy grew intensely bitter.

Now it so happens that many newspapers, particularly in the smaller cities and towns, employ school boys as carriers to deliver papers to the homes in their neighborhoods, an occupation quite dissimilar from street selling of papers in big cities.

Many of these smaller papers, using boys as home carriers, feared that under the child labor provisions of the NRA, a Washington bureaucracy might wreck their distribution systems. They feared that the government officials, unfamiliar with local conditions and unaware of the fact that many school authorities, particularly in the smaller communities, encourage the carrying of newspapers and regard it as beneficial for school boys from both the health and business training standpoints, might rule that persons under eighteen could not be carriers.

During this controversy many newspapers denounced Roosevelt as a would-be dictator planning to prevent criticism of his administration through possible use of the licensing power. Government spokesmen in turn denounced the newspapers as "exploiters of child labor."

The public—many of whom harbored grudges against their local papers because of any of a dozen reasons, valid or otherwise, revelled at hearing the newspapers "get theirs." Those papers that had not printed the news fairly and impartially over a long period of years, or that had short-sightedly not given expression to all points of view through allowing different groups to blow off steam in their "Letters to the Editor" columns, or newspapers that had been reticent about correcting errors or making deserved retractions, discovered to their surprise that many in their own communities strongly disliked them and enjoyed seeing them squirm.

It was a rude shock to the newspapers—and a good thing for them. The smart ones began to realize that just because they personally understood why it was imperative to have a free press in order to make democracy function, it didn't necessarily follow that the mass of the public shared their view.

It began to dawn on the newspaper owners that they had a big educational job ahead of them in order to make it clear that a free press is not simply a publisher's selfish privilege but a public heritage, and that newspapers should conduct themselves so that the average citizen would realize that freedom of the press was a matter of vital importance to him—not simply license for a publication owner to do with as he wished.

Whether one regards this whole "freedom of the press" controversy as a fake issue, which is the Roosevelt administration's professed attitude, or whether one regards it as most of the publishers in complete sincerity did, as an educational crusade against the imminent possibility of governmental control through licensing, in any event certain phases of the thing reacted adversely on the press as a whole.

Most newspapers endeavor to keep their news and views in separate compartments, plainly labelled so an unsuspecting reader will not imbibe opinion thinking it is fact.

If, in the early days of the NRA, the publisher of some prominent paper that is generally accepted as being objective in its news columns, such as *The New York Times* or *World-Telegram,* had only seized the torch of leadership for all the newspapers and had led the educational crusade explaining what freedom of the press means, and what the implications of press licensing are, the whole idea of democracy would today be more solidly grounded.

It so happened, however, that Colonel R. R. McCormick of *The Chicago Tribune* was chairman of the then relatively dormant "freedom of the press" committee of The American Newspaper Publishers Association.

From not infrequent contacts with Colonel McCormick over a period of years I have come to have not only real admiration for his outspoken courage but also a belief in his basic intellectual honesty according to his own convictions.

While most papers content themselves with printing news in their news columns and confining their views to the editorial page, *The Chicago Tribune,* however, possesses such complete confidence in the rectitude of its own opinions and such assurance in its clairvoyance that it feels it unnecessary to make this—to it superfluous—distinction between news and views. It feels that it is performing a greater public service by jumping ahead a cog and giving its opinions along with the news.

Because this situation is widely realized and because *The Chicago Tribune's* news columns had been anything but free from bias in reporting its detestation of everything connected with Mr. Roosevelt and the New Deal, the effect of Colonel McCormick's otherwise magnificent free press educational crusade was largely vitiated.

If other less partisan publishers had been out in the limelight as spokesmen for the press, the public reaction to and the effectiveness of the whole campaign might have been far different.

But Colonel McCormick and *The Chicago Tribune* did lead the fight, where others either failed to appreciate the significance of the issue or from expediency shrank back. No one can take that credit away from Colonel McCormick.

Next to *The Chicago Tribune,* probably Mr. Hearst's papers are most given to editorializing in their news columns. Mr. Hearst liked Mr. Roosevelt and the New Deal no better than did Colonel McCormick, and did not hesitate to say so in discussing either freedom of the press or anything else, in his news columns as well as on his editorial pages.

As a consequence, probably the two most important out of the extremely small group of metropolitan publishers who do not regard press freedom as an obligation to keep their news columns uncontaminated by their personal convictions or prejudices were put into the spotlight as representatives of the views of all publishers. And all newspapers were put into the same class and spattered with the same mud when the hand grenades were tossed back by the White House troops.

Partly due to this NRA row, partly to the fact that most newspaper owners are economic conservatives, the 1936 presidential campaign found an extraordinarily high proportion of the dailies supporting Landon— or at least not supporting Roosevelt.

The Roosevelt forces, realizing that the newspaper publishers were a popular whipping boy, used the opportunity to attack the newspapers generally and charge them with all sorts of heinous offences, some of them undeniably deserved by some papers. Roosevelt rode triumphantly back into the White House and public confidence in the integrity and influence of the newspapers was reduced to a new low.

Apparently the administration still regards the newspapers as a popular target, for in November, 1937, a year after his re-election, Mr. Roosevelt pointedly omitted any reference to newspapers, although commending the radio and movies for keeping the public informed.

Jim Farley followed the President's lead in praising the radio as a new agency for communication because speeches are "uncontaminated by coincident editorial comment" and the public mind consequently not "confused."

The great stimulus to unionization that the New Deal and Wagner Act produced also had another curious effect on newspapers. Most newspapers had had union contracts with their mechanical department workers for years, and at the highest annual wages paid by any industry for comparable work. Consequently it superficially appeared that newspapers as a class would be relatively little affected by the growth of unions.

As a black mark on the publishers' record, however, was the theoretically indefensible fact that many if not most papers were paying their rank and file news and editorial employees lower wages than they were paying mechanical union employees.

Being a reporter was a job with romance. Half of the college graduates each June wanted to join news staffs, so there was no shortage of labor. Applicants for editorial jobs far outran the number that could be employed. Reporters and editorial desk men, moreover, were naturally individualists and many wanted only a few years of that strenuous life before graduating into lucrative posts as press agents or advertising men. In any event, average newspaper editorial wages were low, too low.

Almost over night a union of editorial department workers—the American Newspaper Guild—was formed. Under the glamorous and energetic leadership of Heywood Broun the guild movement took on the garb of a holy crusade and swept much of the country.

Broun's exceptional ability and flair for phrase-making had carried him from the ranks of the sports writers through a colorful career including an unsuccessful campaign for Congress on the Socialist ticket up to a reputed salary of $40,000 or more a year as a Scripps-Howard columnist. Without his personality, the guild movement would probably have never reached the magnitude or taken the course it did.

Pro-guild articles attacking newspaper publishers as a class filled *The Nation* and *New Republic* and other magazines. News and editorial department wage scales, many of which had been too low, were raised. Meanwhile the steady barrage against the newspapers from the guild still further weakened public confidence in them.

The guild movement, largely controlled by the New Yorkers with extreme left-wing tendencies, did not stop when its original wage, hour, and working condition complaints had been largely satisfied. New demands were imposed. One was for a "guild shop," which meant that every new editorial department employee must be or become a guild member. As the guild had by this time joined the C. I. O. and adopted sweeping resolutions calling on its members to support the Farmer-Labor Party and other highly controversial movements, the publishers, not unnaturally, felt horrified at the idea of agreeing to employ only such new reporters and other editorial men as were or would become members of an organization belligerently committed to a specific side of the subjects on which they would be supposed to write objectively and impartially.

The publishers almost unanimously determined to resist demands for the closed guild shop. Although there have been a few strikes of editorial workers over that question and a few papers have capitulated, there are signs that the guild membership, except in a few cities, is gradually becoming more mature in its attitude and more appreciative of some of the problems the employers face. There is reason to hope that the guild, having largely attained its primary objective of raising salary levels, will ultimately tend to become increasingly a professional society of working journalists, comparable to the American Bar Association or the American Medical Association. If so, the guild movement will have proved highly beneficial, and Mr. Broun will deserve the thanks both of the working news writers and of the publishers for having inspired the crusade that brought that result. For the time being, however, the more radical guild spokesmen are continuing their denunciations of the publishers, and confidence in the press is being still further impaired.

Another intangible factor weakening respect for the integrity of the press has been the growing disillusionment that has resulted from the increasingly widespread realization of the amount and type of Allied propaganda designed to precipitate our entry into the World War that was published in many American newspapers in 1915, '16, and '17.

As the maladjustments in the world came into clearer focus during the miseries of the depression, there also developed a general disintegration of faith in and respect for most of the traditional pillars of civilization, including the press.

These are the principal reasons why newspapers enjoy less confidence than they did a decade ago. There is no need for alarm. As a whole, American newspapers are better than ever before. Most of them are trying harder to print the news objectively, impartially, honestly. Many of them have a deeper sense of their responsibilities. A steadily increasing number recognize an obligation to give their readers *all* points of view. It is no longer considered extraordinary for a newspaper to print, say, Jay Franklin's rather leftish views alongside of, say, David Lawrence's rather rightish views. Or to run Raymond Clapper and Frank Kent in parallel columns. The publishers are beginning to realize that the public wants, and is entitled to have, both sides.

The distinction between news and views, however, is frequently much more difficult to make than a layman might assume. Can a correspondent cabling from China, for example, give his readers a really comprehensive picture of the Japanese invasion with all its complications and implications unless he goes beyond a mere recital of specific happenings and from his knowledge of the whole situation paints in a background that will make that day's small part of the jigsaw puzzle understandable?

How far should a newspaper go in its news columns (excluding the editorial page) in attempting to explain a highly involved piece of proposed federal legislation? Criticisms are made that newspaper reports are frequently unintelligible to the average reader, because they do not explain and interpret.

Assume that the administration introduces in Congress an involved, technical agricultural bill covering crop control. The administration says it is voluntary. The opposition says it is compulsory. Should a newspaper in its news columns attempt to analyze the bill and indicate whether the proposed crop control is voluntary or compulsory? Can it, as a practical matter, do so without expressing opinion as contrasted with summarizing fact?

Democratic government cannot keep functioning unless the newspapers do their part of the job: inform people about what is happening. Sometimes it is impossible to inform without expressing opinions, because there is no proof as to what is fact and what isn't.

This whole field of interpretive news writing lies in the shadows be-tween straight reporting of fact on the one hand and editorial expression of opinion on the other. It is one of the most difficult problems to handle, and one of the most important, that confront editors today.

Many similar questions, some trivial or innocuous and some important, stem from the same basic problem of distinction between news in the news columns and opinions on the editorial page.

Should papers use their news columns, which most everybody reads, to try to reduce the ghastly total of automobile accidents, or should they confine themselves to the editorial page that only a small minority reads?

If gambling or liquor or other laws are being flagrantly violated in its community should a newspaper confine a law enforcement crusade to its editorial page? Or is it proper by emphasis of news handling, by playing up, say, the charges of an obscure preacher, to carry on in the news columns what is in effect a crusade that theoretically belongs on the editorial page alone?

So involved are some of the daily problems of assessing news values, of interpreting news, of emphasizing or minimizing it, that no general standards can be laid down.

It is easy to say that newspapers debase public taste. Most critics fail to realize that except for New York City there are not enough potential readers in any community for a newspaper to try to be a "class medium." A newspaper in most cities must, in a realistic sense, be like a cafeteria, and try to offer something for every reader's taste and appetite, else it cannot, unless it be subsidized, hold enough readers to continue pub-lishing.

A thousand critics have attacked newspapers for debasing the public taste, for printing or emphasizing stories with sex appeal. They might well ponder what Doctor Henry Noble MacCracken, president of Vassar College, recently said on this score:

News values have not varied in the slightest in 500 years. The popular ballads have first sex appeal. They tell of sensational love affairs—amours, abductions, elopements, desertions, revenges. They also tell of uncommon fidelity and con-stancy, of virtue rewarded. They tell of family tragedies, of murders and execu-tions, of raids and robberies, of outlaws and "G" men, of kings and their sweet-hearts.

No one will deny that the newspapers do have many and varied sins to atone for, some serious and some trivial. The broad problems of newspaper invasion of the privacy of individuals and of the reporting of trials both need—and are currently receiving—serious attention. Committees of journalists of the highest professional standards, men like Paul Bellamy of *The Cleveland Plain Dealer* and Stuart Perry of *The Adrian Telegram,* are collaborating with equally distinguished lawyers in attempting to arrive at proper solutions. Probably the newspapers' rights will be somewhat abridged along certain lines either by the adoption of new legal restrictions or by the voluntary acceptance by the press of certain restraints that will reduce or eliminate the evils.

The manner in which the Lindberghs' personal privacy was invaded and the way in which the Hauptmann trial, with the apparent acquiescence of the court, was handled at Flemington are blots upon all newspapers, even though only a few may have had any direct part.

Another almost universal failing is the newspapers' reluctance to print adequate, if any, reports of libel suits, because such publication stimulates the bringing of other suits.

Most newspapers, including some of the best, have been negligent in not adequately reporting certain newspaper strikes. They probably feel that by minimizing such news they will reduce the likelihood of stimulating similar trouble for themselves.

Most of the newspapers' shortcomings are, we must admit, directly traceable to the fact that their private profit motive sometimes conflicts with their public obligation to print all the news, and print it fairly and objectively.

In other words, in the final analysis the only Achilles heel in our present-day newspapers is that they are large capitalistic enterprises. As such some of them, when their own selfish interests are involved, are, in greater or less degree, dishonest. Most of them may be too conservative in their social and economic and political views. They naturally look at things from the capitalistic standpoint. They tend to lack "social consciousness." They are too prone to think all's right in the world.

But conceding all these weaknesses in our present newspapers, serious as they are in some cases, nevertheless our newspapers today are by almost every standard far better than ever before.

And even if they do fall far short of perfection, what's the alternative?

Certainly we want no government-owned and taxpayer-subsidized newspapers. They would inevitably be completely partisan to whatever group of politicians was in the saddle at Washington, and far less honest and trustworthy than is our present press.

Even if at some future time every newspaper in the country should deliberately try to prevent the then current administration from adequately and fairly getting the news of its program to the people, the administration would always have access to the radio. No radio station, since its very existence depends on a short-term government license, could refuse any administration's requests for time. The radio chains are only too prone to give a disproportionate amount of their time to those that are currently in power. They are inevitably subservient to the existing administration, no matter which party it be. Some method should be evolved of guaranteeing that the "outs" have an equal division of radio time with which to answer the "ins." But the "ins" never are anxious to enact a law guaranteeing that, because, being in, they have the advantage.

If government subsidy is not the answer to the newspaper problem, what other alternatives are there?

Nothing prevents any rich person from subsidizing a newspaper to present his views, whatever they may be. The Socialists or Communists will reply that rich persons are almost all in favor of the capitalistic system anyway, and what they want are papers to present the non-capitalistic viewpoint, so that's not much of a solution.

Conceivably—but not probably—a relatively highbrow tabloid morning paper condensing the news could be so brilliantly edited and operated that at five cents or ten cents a copy it could live without advertising and without any capitalistic taint. New York would be the only city large enough for the experiment and its chances for success would about equal those of a candidate opposing Joe Stalin in Russia's new free elections.

Theoretically, some group of flaming reformers might band together and edit a newspaper that could attract as readers enough followers of that cause so that it could live on subscription receipts alone, without benefit of support from capitalistic advertisers. The answer to that seems to be that such publications as *The Nation* and *New Republic,* well edited as they are, have pitifully small circulations. Considering the country's population their relatively minute readership indicates that most of the people, despite their criticisms and complaints, are at least tolerably satisfied with the existing, capitalistic press.

Nor have the Socialists or Communists or Prohibitionists or Townsendites or any other group, with the possible exception of the Christian Scientists with their *Monitor,* ever been able successfully to publish on any large scale or over any long period any organ that compared with the privately owned, capitalistic press. We do have the Communist *Daily Worker,* largely supported by party funds, and a few other relatively weak Communist or Socialist dailies.

The Communists may say, and with some truth, that the Communist viewpoint ought to be presented in our present capitalistic press. That day may come.

The widely syndicated signed columnists of today have far more power than the personal editors of a generation that is gone. Walter Lippmann's influence far transcends what Horace Greeley or Marse Henry Watterson ever had. Conceivably a Communist columnist may arise who is a sufficiently interesting writer so that capitalistic publishers will be glad to present his daily views. And if he is a persuasive enough propagandist, conceivably he may, through the columns of the capitalistic papers, do what no Communist organ could hope to do.

Since there seems to be no preferable and workable alternative to our capitalistic press, probably we shall continue to have about our present kind of newspapers so long as individualistic democracy survives in America. On the whole our papers are pretty honest and getting better each year. For the most part, they're feeling an increasing sense of obligation to the public.

Probably, when the collectivist ideas that have temporarily seized the minds of our otherwise enlightened liberals begin to lose their hypnotic charms, attacks on the press will diminish. Newspaper publishing will then gradually regain some of its former prestige, and public confidence in newspapers will slowly return.

But the next few years, while we are waiting for the happy days to come again, don't look any too bright from the financial standpoint to the publishers. Faced with staggering increases in newsprint costs and pay-rolls and other operating expenses, the newspapers see shrinking advertising revenues with which to try to meet the bills. Many papers that were highly profitable only a few years ago are now operating in red ink. Many more mergers and suspensions are inevitable.

Radio broadcasting continues to take a steadily larger part of the national advertisers' dollars. Radio stations are natural complements of newspapers. They should be allies, not enemies. Other things being equal, those broadcasting stations that are affiliated with newspapers can and do render a greater public service than do independent stations.

Unfortunately for the newspapers, most publishers were too short-sighted to apply for radio stations when the wave lengths were available. Instead of embracing radio as a new and in some ways superior method of transmitting information and entertainment, many publishers stupidly attacked radio's right to broadcast news as if it were an infringement on an exclusive prerogative of their own.

Now the spectre of television and of news broadcasting by facsimile grins down mawkishly on the publishers in their nightmares. That there will be no unearned increment for the newspapers in the next few years is certain.

But because this analysis of the current newspaper situation has stressed the economic interpretation viewpoint, let none get the impression that newspapering is a money-making capitalistic enterprise and nothing else. Newspapering is actually a little of everything, with probably more pure idealism and high adventure thrown in, with more of a mixture of professional and commercial contradictions, than any other occupation.

On almost every newspaper throughout the country there is a steady flow of romance, of crusades against corruption. Whether the crusade be against Tammany Hall in New York or against a crooked sheriff or mayor in a small community makes no difference in the thrill that the newspaper editor or reporter gets from the job. The satisfaction that comes to a working newspaperman out of a good story well written, out of the endless sacrifice and labor to get beats against one's rival, whether it be a competitor across the street or a paper in a near-by town or a distant city—that satisfaction is as great in Emporia, Kansas, as it is in New York.

When you hear a critic charge that the journalist as a professional man in an honorable craft is nonexistent, tell him his statement is bunk! There are embryonic Arthur Krocks and Harold Dennys throughout the land, thrilling at their local jobs with just as much zest as if they were heading a bureau in Washington or Moscow, willing to run any risk to get and print the news.

There's nothing much wrong with American newspapers today except us publishers.

# THE INTELLECTUAL LIFE

*[Harold E. Stearns]*

WHEN we speak of somebody leading a "philosophic" life, we may mean somebody whose normal, every-day activities are infused and informed with a general "philosophy." In fact, however, we are much more likely to mean somebody leading a life of acceptance of one's condition—almost a "resigned" life. Certainly the popular expression, to take a thing philosophically, means to take it without grumbling: As something inevitable, something in nature stronger than any of our desires or our powers of alteration. We do not mean that we interpret this thing—say sudden death, or disaster, or accident, or unexpected happiness—in terms of a wide yet specific outlook and a definite point of view. Rather we mean that we interpret it as "the will of God," or as something that couldn't be helped, something that, in the popular expression, was "just on the cards."

Our own personal will did not enter into this thing, any more than into summer rain; it just happened *to* us. If a civilized man is on a Pacific isle when an earthquake hits it, he does not hypostasize an evil spirit who is responsible for the disaster, and curse that spirit. Again to use the popular expression, he "takes" it: There is nothing else to do.

For convenience, we often call this civilized attitude "philosophic," which adjective by usage has come practically to mean "grown-up"—or, simply, mature. We smile, even when sympathetically, at our small sons and daughters who burst into tears when it rains on picnic-days. That is non-philosophic, which by usage has come in the same way practically to mean "childish." Thus whether the abstract noun itself—philosophy—has much or little clear meaning to us, both the adjective and the adverb derived from that noun do have considerable meaning. They are descriptive terms we understand; they point to a certain recognizable way or manner of action. They have living references. Few of us, for example, would have the temerity to attempt even a brief definition of the noun, religion, but most of us would not flinch at giving at least some explanation of the adjective, religious.

I indulge in this little verbal preamble because the very title of my essay (dutifully repeated from the first *Civilization*) refers to something which does not, strictly speaking, exist at all. Neither in the United States, nor anywhere else, is there any such thing as the "intellectual" life—at all events, not in the same way in which we speak of the "sporting" life, the "business" life, or the "social" life. About a generation ago, to be sure, there was in fairly common use the expression, "the young intellectuals," which I myself did far too much to make a kind of *cliché* for exasperated conservative newspaper editors, who were trying to bewail the excesses (mostly alcoholic and sexual) of the younger generation, though a social historian today, drawing his conclusions from, say, F. Scott Fitzgerald's *This Side of Paradise* and *The Great Gatsby,* would say that these excesses were not confined to the younger or any other generation, but pretty generally spread throughout the world—a kind of amoral by-product of the cynicism and brutality and meaninglessness of the Great War. In popular opinion, I believe, the "intellectual" life, insofar as it was thought about or mentioned at all, was vaguely identified with the life supposedly led by these "young intellectuals," that is to say, the life of a new and sophisticated mental and moral Bohemianism, or, in a word, irresponsibility. As the post-war pressure of disappointed and disillusioned idealists became sharper, it was inevitable that the phrase would be extended to cover also the so-called "Bolsheviks," and by this time both the people who exemplified it and the phrase itself were in thorough disrepute.

But all was forgiven (or, more accurately, forgotten) while the strange era of the post-war "boom" lasted: This was the time of what Mr. Westbrook Pegler has wittily called "the era of beautiful nonsense." The "intellectuals" were quietly passed by on the other side, no matter how loudly they proclaimed their superior insight into our difficulties, the plain truth simply being that everybody either was, or expected soon to be, making so much money that nothing else mattered. This mood of popular indifference had a rather pathetically comic side, too, for this was the period when the "intellectuals"—exasperated, probably, at being neglected, and determined to recapture the well-known and better-loved spotlight—put on almost as good a show as any old-time vaudeville artist. They not only called each other bad names, they staged verbal fights in the newspapers and magazines—indeed, sometimes went to the extreme of fisticuffs in semi-public brawls. Even the most casual newspaper reader heard of the famous Sinclair Lewis *versus* Theodore Dreiser match, as later on he was to hear of the equally famous Ernest Hemingway *versus* Max Eastman match. A few people mistook these encounters for a sign of healthy convictions and of new life in intellectual interests among the members of the literary and artistic "sets." Most people, however, merely smiled and thought them rather absurd.

But a little reflection led a few observers to note that this phenomenon was more than just a case of bad manners and poor taste—it was a sign of some deep inner conflict and maladjustment, of something sadly portentous. In brief, it was a sign of the times, this coupling of belligerency and intellectuality, this curious identification of personal and subjective irritation with impersonal and objective thought. We can see its perfect example in the dogmas of fascism, which psychologically is just communism turned upside down, that is to say, the same thing. Like Mussolini, Hitler, Stalin, and the other homicidal clowns of today, the "intellectuals" became less interesting as advocates of ideas than as test cases for neurologists, psychopathologists, and physicians. Like the talking dog mentioned by Doctor Sam Johnson, what they said was not remarkable—it was remarkable that they said anything at all.

What was happening was an infection from Europe, particularly from Germany. It was a new and exciting germ of infantilism and obscurantism falling on American intellectual soil, already weakened by the mythologies and compulsions of the Great War and soon to be made fertile with bitterness by the widespread economic collapse. There has always been, unfortunately, a powerful strain of violence and intolerance in the American tradition—a kind of hang-over from pioneer times—and this strain obtained a new lease of life by dramatic examples from over the seas. But it went far further than a recrudescence of lynching psychology in the South and a new and more drastic form of anti-Semitism in the North: It extended into labor disputes also. Not, of course, that there hadn't been traditional violence here, too, but this was a new accent and a new methodology. It now, if you please, had an *intellectual* apologetic.

Or what some people mistook for one—as almost every form of violence and unreason always finds sophistical defenders. History is littered with movements and "ideologies" (to use the current Marxian cant) which not only justify killing your opponent but pin a glowing term of approbation upon you for doing so. (Any war furnishes a good example; you have only to read your daily newspaper and see what is happening today and now in China and Spain, for instance, to wonder just why we have the hardihood to regard the religious persecutions of the Middle Ages with any superior horror or to regard ourselves as any more "civilized" than the peasants of the 13th century.) When you begin to "think with your blood," as Hitler's famous aphorism puts it, you might just as well say you had ceased to think at all. The low-grade white moron of Georgia or Mississippi is thinking with his blood—enough to please the most exacting Hitler—when he applies the torch to the execution-pyre of a Negro suspected of rape; the faultlessly attired secretary of an exclusive New York club is thinking no less with his blood when an application for membership is rejected because the applicant is a Jew. Though I didn't know it at the time, I was encouraged to think with my blood, too, in my New England boyhood, when it was impressed upon me as an indisputable truth that all the Irish, living "on the other side of the railroad tracks," were "Micks" and "rough-necks."

But after all an apologetic for *racial* intolerance is fairly respectable and is based at least on recognizable differences—even, perhaps, deep biological antipathies—in color, stature, speech, and the like. What, however, shall be said of the kind of *class* intolerance, based on economic differences, which underlies the Marxian philosophy? If the first is to a certain degree natural, then the second is to an equally certain degree artificial. If the first arises from ignorance and primitive fear before the unknown, then the second arises from sophistication and a false bravado before the known. It is a passionate, if unconscious, carrying-over of primitive fear and intolerance into a realm where such impulses and instincts are irrelevant and absurd: It is like speaking of mathematics as "charming" and astronomy as "disturbing."

Very likely my communist friends would cite the above paragraph as a classic example of intellectual naïveté—in exactly the same way, and with the same curious assumption of superior insight, that the believers in Christian Science, among whom I happen also to have a few friends, regard my (and every other dissident's) failure to "see the light." The convinced believer in a narrow economic interpretation of history employs the same strained, artificial, and unrealistic dialectic with which any student, say of 19th-century German philosophic idealism, is only too painfully familiar—language which is unreal, remote from experience, and enwrapped in a vague penumbra of personal bitterness. Masquerading as "scientific," such language is, in reality, merely sophistical; pretending to be "realistic" in a welter of sentimentalism, it ends up by being more miasmatic and equivocal than ordinary "common sense" discourse. And more inhuman—by which I mean very simply that all sacrosanct dialectical jargons, such as most communist theorists employ, are sure psychopathological symptoms; they reveal a feeling of inferiority trying to find compensation in a patterned orthodoxy, reserved only for the initiate few, who have the magic pass-word, a feeling of inferiority, too, coupled with a subtle appeal to those sadistic impulses to destroy your opponent which conventional civilization at least attempts to aerate and bring into the open in order to render them relatively harmless. We see the old paradox of the French Revolution repeated in a new form— "Be my brother, or I'll chop your head off." No wonder a person with any sense of history sometimes—particularly in Soviet Russia—cannot avoid the impression that he is in a kind of psychiatric Alice-in-Wonderland.

Thus in the last sixteen years the two clusters of ideas we have imported from Europe have been the philosophies represented by what we call communism and fascism—nobody would, I should suppose, attempt to deny this. And both sets of ideas are definitely anti-intellectual in trend; they have that much in common, which is perhaps a more important similarity than their avowed disparities and divergencies of economic outlook and theory. The heart of both doctrines is bitter in the same way; both doctrines believe, too, in the same sanction of force as against persuasion; both doctrines are contemptuous of democracy, insofar as democracy means tolerance and reasonableness. It is this basic anti-intellectualism which gives both doctrines their homogeneity, their irrational driving-force, their power over weak minds and dissatisfied characters. They apotheosize the hatred of the ordinary man for culture —or perhaps a better phrase would be, since "culture" has come to have overtones of a false snobbishness—the hatred of the ordinary man for *disinterestedness*. Indeed, not only his hatred, but his incomprehension of it; his cheap conviction that all thought, like most men, has its price.

As this infiltration of anti-intellectual viewpoints from Europe has increased, we have become more and more nationalistic—Dean Gauss in his chapter on "Education" in this book[1] shows pretty clearly the way this comes about in too many of our universities. But "when," writes Howard Mumford Jones, "nations become fanatically nationalistic, they are out of a right relation with the rest of the human race. Now the ideal

[1] See chapter on "Education," p. 331.

of humane scholarship has not been to demonstrate the superiority of the Aryan race or Roman militarism or dialectic materialism or even the Declaration of Independence. The ideal of humane scholarship has been, and still ought to be, to demonstrate the unity of history. For its purposes the world is one. The republic of letters is an international republic. It rests in the faith that humanity is more than a nation, a race, a religious creed, or a system of economics. That is why nations which have become zealots in advocating a theory of racial superiority, a particular economic organization, or a militant imperialism have universally been the nations to stifle humane scholarship as we at Harvard understand humane scholarship. German laboratories continue to function; it is the scholar in the lecture hall who is watched by the police. He deals with ideas."[2]

It is a curious irony of our times that a communistic philosophy, which pretends to be international, ends up by being as provincial as any of the most absurd and intense nationalism of the pre-1914 Balkan States. Similarly, fascism, which pretends to be a binding together of forces into a common discipline, ends up likewise by being not only nationalistic—and a nationalism sharpened by the drug of racial arrogance—but also with dreams of imperialism on the side. You may enter through the door of theoretical brotherhood, but you somehow emerge through the same old familiar gateway of terror at home and attempted conquest abroad. Your fine talk about human solidarity terminates unromantically and tragically in domestic executions and air-raids over innocent foreign civilian populations. And, of course, the more intense become these terrors, the louder are the protestations of the highest ethical ends: Blood finally crowns your idealism, and the sons of men are crucified on the cross of doctrine. About the only difference thus far discernible to an outsider between communism and fascism is that the first does exactly this with its own people; the second appears a bit more ambitious and does it with (preferably) helpless and defenseless outsiders, like Ethiopian children and Barcelona women.

From 1914—when the famous defense of Germany's course by its intellectuals shocked other nations in the outside world, although, to be sure, their own intellectuals shortly thereafter began to do precisely the same thing—until about 1924 one of the saddest phenomena of that sad decade was the almost universal breakdown of that international "republic of letters" of which Professor Jones speaks. It was severe enough in France, Italy, England, and even in America, but it was severest of

[2]*Harvard Alumni Bulletin*, June 3, 1938, p. 1024.

all in Germany and Austria, where to the humiliations of defeat on the field were added the strains, dislocations, and hysterias of actual war-time. Russia, of course, was busy "consolidating" the Revolution, which also meant "liquidating" a large section of the old professional and intellectual class, many of whom migrated to Paris and to the United States. As I happen to know from living there then myself, not all the Russians in Paris in 1925, for example, were émigrés of the old aristocracy, living either from the sale of "crown" jewels, or—when these went—from driving taxicabs: Quite a few were former students and professors in universities of Moscow, Leningrad, and the other cities which had once been centers of Russian learning. And the same was true even here in the United States, where not *all* the Russian émigrés of that period were charming but indigent adventurers and exploiters of dubious or non-existent titles for marital—and some financial—advantage. In fact, these were the publicized and noisy minority, who haunted the so-called "café society" of New York; the majority were not only decent people, they were in many instances members of the intellectually superior class of their unhappy country.

Though, as I have said above, our own intellectual soil had been weakened by the fact that it had been used as a testing-ground for so many propagandas during the war (including our own), and though since the war it has also been a kind of neutral duelling place for the post-war ideologies,[3] the merciful fact remained that, as contrasted with European countries, we suffered neither identical nor similarly extensive injuries to our basic social system. To be sure, we had an economic merry-go-round sufficiently fast to make even our college professors of economics quite dizzy, and in the whirligig we invented as glittering an array of panaceas as ever crossed the mind of a modern Bellamy—among which one of the most spectacular was the now forgotten technocracy, and one of the most sensible, I think, was what was then called "planned economy." But there had not been—there has not yet been, however close we may now and then seem to be to it—the kind of general overturn of an entire type of civilization, or of the intellectual life which goes with it, which we have seen take place in other parts of the world. We have remained pretty steady in an upset international chaos—even if to the disgust of the large crop of Americans who have the sure and only

[3]And not merely for political ideologies, either. An entire chapter could be written on the literary and artistic ideologies that have had a sort of field-day of laboratory experiment on the sometimes all-too-receptive American public. Only the other evening I listened to a "surrealist" drama over the radio, appropriately with "surrealist" music.

one-way ticket to perfection. (Like the poor, we have always had these, so to speak, sporadic Brook Farm revivals and revivalists; they seem to be a temperamental necessity with us.)

"Pretty steady," I said above, and I still maintain that. But one highly interesting reaction in our American intellectual world to the mythologies and "blah" (using a popular expressive term) of the war and post-war periods has been a characteristic revolt against what is often termed—mistakenly, I believe—the intellectualism of language itself. This revolt is in the old American tradition of appeal to the facts: William James voiced it first in his pragmatic method; John Dewey expanded upon it and refined it; the so-called behaviorists tried to wring the fabulous and imaginative water out of psychological terms, ending up by disposing of consciousness altogether; the psychoanalysts for a time seemed to have turned the tables merely to show, on closer examination and further exposition of their theories, that they were really neurologists at heart, only regretting that they couldn't put dreams and poetry on a scale in the laboratory. Latest of all came the advocates of "semantics," like Stuart Chase—and you might say the full cycle had been completed.

For the real trouble with semantics lies in the fact that the center of intellectual gravity is off balance—the interest is in the contradictions and evasions of structure in language rather than in the discrete and differentiated realities toward which that structure points and calls attention. Because language is an inadequate—sometimes even a self-destructive—tool for turning up the variegated soil of experience we ought to devise a new tool. Perhaps we ought, *provided the new tool really does a better job of digging.* But the very minute we say this we begin to suspect the mare's nest. We are like children who won't play in the garden unless their shovels are new, shiny, and streamlined; that is to say, we are primarily interested in the shovels and not in digging up worms. It is not surprising that grammarians—who are only semantic enthusiasts *a rebours,* so to speak—have throughout literature been the butt of humorous writers. They chase the shadow for the substance, and in reaching for perfection, like the foolish crow in the fable, let what they have drop out of their mouths.

Yet the intellectual life in America, like everything else, exists in a particular stage-setting; and I believe it is this, rather than any spread or diminution of these new winds of doctrine, which will in the long run pull us back to that old integrity of thought and belief, where one can speak of intellectual interests without being regarded with suspicion, as if he were a sort of æsthetic and moral weakling. Perhaps the soundest and most native aspect, too, of the American stage-setting is a keen sense of the ludicrous and absurd. This is our much maligned sense of humor, which also happens to be our surest disinfectant against doctrinaires, language-wreckers, ideologists, and all the rest of the motley crew who carry over into manhood the nursery habit of playing with alphabetical blocks. It is not our American habit to be inhospitable to new ideas, even when these ideas are fantastic; but it is our habit to dispose of the fantasy in them with great speed. In five minutes Will Rogers, for instance, could do more to deflate a rabble of doctrine-mongers than could the most astute college professor or literary lion of the moment— and Will Rogers, if anybody ever did, spoke that authentic American language which all Americans understand.

Nor is it irrelevant to speak of the enormous effect our geography and temperature and soil situations have upon our intellectual climate. For there is not the pressure of any immediate fear of semi-starvation, or of invasion by a foreign foe, which stultifies life for so many European states. To a certain extent we may even be wasting our natural resources much too fast, as the conservationists tell us, but we still have a sufficient margin of abundance for the life of inquiry and research to be carried on naturally. The frontier may be closed but the utilization of our leisure is still limitless. We still have an intellectual horizon. Without forgetting Florida hurricanes, California earthquakes, and natural floods, we do not, speaking generally, live under the shadow of a fear of some great natural catastrophe: Most of our troubles in this respect, like soil erosion and Mississippi floods, are of our own careless making, and can be remedied by intelligent foresight and co-operation. Our medical and hygienic science has practically abolished the ancient fears of God's wrath in the form of pestilence and disease. Most of these ancient terrors —in the shadow of which no intellectual life can exist—have been exorcised from America. We have almost forgotten how relatively free we are to make something of our intellectual life—if we choose to do so.

Proof that we already *have* so chosen seems to me abundant. Every reader of this book will think of different exemplifications of this desire of ours to learn more and to think a bit straighter: How many more examples there are than one can recall offhand, like the New School for Social Research; the Town Hall; the radio programs devoted to science; adult education, as it is called; unions organizing workers' classes; civic centers and the like; vocational training camps; university "extension" classes; even correspondence schools. And when natural skepticism assails you, think merely of our public, private, and "lending" libraries—recalling Carlyle's words that, in our day, a true university is a collection of books.

This book itself is one of the best exemplifications of a willingness on the part of most Americans to undertake the great adventure of intellectual co-operation. If it had no other justification, I think that alone would be sufficient.

TYPES
OF
LIVING

# THE SMALL TOWN

## [*R. L. Duffus*]

IN EVERY American's mind there is undoubtedly a concept labelled "The Small Town." If these concepts could be tabulated and compared I think we should find some amazing discrepancies, for some would be based on hazy boyhood memories of a thing that is gone, some on casual adult observation and some on a shifting and vague tradition of what a small town is or ought to be. A real and living experience with a small town is, of course, another thing, but the resulting impressions would vary according to the location of the community. But however we define our small town or whatever mental picture we have of it, colored by no matter what emotional attitude, we can safely say that the actuality has changed more during the past decade and a half than any other feature of American life.

What is this actuality? A precise answer to this question is difficult to make. At what point does small town merge into big town or small city? The federal census takers, being obliged to draw a line somewhere, consider communities of 2500 population or more as urban, yet it is clear that a community of that size is more likely to seem urban in a sparsely settled State like Montana than it does, say, in Southern New England. I think we shall get closer to our subject if we dispense with statistics, beyond a reminder that towns of between 2500 and 5000 population increased steadily in number down to 1920 but very little betwen 1920 and 1930, and that cities of 8000 or more population have gone on increasing in number and in the percentage of the total population which lives in them. We shall not know quite what has happened until the census of 1940 has been taken, but there is not much doubt that as far as population goes the small towns are comparatively static and that the cities of moderate size are doing most of the growing.

Not being a statistician I am inclined to forget the census figures and to describe the small town as a combination of a physical entity and a state of mind. It is, in short, a community in which every one knows every one else. A year or so ago William Allen White told me with some regret that when he first went to Emporia he soon knew every one he met on the street, but that in later years he could not call more than half of them by name. What had happened was that Emporia had ceased to be a small town and had become a city. Yet I am sure that Mr. White is still associated in most people's minds with the genial and lovable qualities of the small town.

Before going very deeply into the subject of small communities in general it is expedient to make note of the wide variations which are historical, racial, economic or climatic, and which have nothing to do with size. The New England town, with its elms and maples, its general store, its white church, its village green, the rude democracy of its town meetings, is as neat a picture as Washington crossing the Delaware. Moreover, it exists. But it is not universal, even in New England. I can think of a farming town in Vermont that is just that, in a simple way, and of other towns in Connecticut and Massachusetts that are like it in a more sophisticated way, with city visitors coming in the summer to admire. I can also think of a small village in Connecticut which centers about a little metalworking factory and I believe I could find an industrial town on the Kennebec, with a large ingredient of French-Canadians in its population —both of them utterly different from what we mean by New England village.

Go further afield and we find even wider variations. Small-town life has flourished, at least during times past, in Kansas, Nebraska, Ohio, Indiana, and Iowa. It has a New England flavor because many of its first settlers came from New England, but it has been conditioned by its prairie environment, has mellowed somewhat, has grown more co-operative, is more given to mass movements of various sorts. The Ku Klux Klan once flourished like the green bay tree in Indiana. Try to imagine it taking root in the shadow of one of those white church spires in the New Hampshire hills. Drop into a hill town in Tennessee or Georgia—its life is perhaps conditioned by two things, a worn-out soil and a race problem. Visit Southern Louisiana—you can find villages where a French patois is still spoken by descendants of Evangeline's people. In New Mexico a whole town may be speaking archaic Spanish, and thinking in the same terms. In California a new small town may just have been laid out by a realtor; it may be so tightly dominated by a packing company or a growers' association that no one dare call his soul his own; it may not be a community at all in the old-fashioned New England sense.

In short, our small towns are of many origins and types; they are rich and poor, Nordic and otherwise, free and unfree, dependent sometimes on industry, sometimes on agriculture, tied to coal or copper mines, impoverished by the absentee ownership of land, dying because the land has been worn out, surviving strangely after most visible means of support have been withdrawn, sometimes independent and democratic in their texture, sometimes not. If we generalize about them we must do so with these facts in mind. I think we shall find that we are generalizing about small towns that are or have been trading centers. We shall tend to overlook small towns that are merely fragments of industrial cities which happen to have been detached and set down in the open country. For essentially the small town as it has been conceived in the United States is an intersection of highways which lead to and from farms. It is a ganglion in a commercial nervous system. It is not merely a grouping of stores, houses and shops—it is those structures, plus the people who live and work in them, plus the people from an outlying area who come to them to buy and sell, to amuse themselves, to meet their friends, to find schooling for their children, to go to church.

The classic country town in America may be regarded as the fruit of a mutually beneficial exchange of goods and services between its immediate residents and these others who come to town for various reasons. Or we may look at it as Thorstein Veblen did.[1] Veblen's comments were devastating, as was customary with him. "The country town," he conceded, "is one of the great American institutions; perhaps the greatest, in the sense that it has had and continues to have a greater part than any other in shaping public sentiment and giving character to American culture." He saw it, however, mainly as a conspiracy of traders who "as a body direct their collective efforts to getting what can be got out of the underlying farm population." He added, writing in 1923: "However natural and legitimate it all undoubtedly may be, the arrangement as it runs today imposes on the country's farm industry an annual overhead charge which runs into ten or twelve figures, and all to the benefit of no one." The trends he noticed have since gone forward at a great rate, though the depression may have slowed them down or even diverted them. What he saw was "grocers, hardware dealers, meat-markets, druggists, shoe-shops, more and more extensively falling into the position of local distributors for jobbing houses and manufacturers,"

[1]See his *Absentee Ownership and Business Enterprise in Recent Times: The Case of America,* pp. 142 ff. B. W. Huebsch, Inc., New York, 1923.

the general result of which was that the country town was "falling into the position of a way-station in the distributive system."

We may, if we like, accept part of this diagnosis and not all of it. We may not see quite the brutality and hypocrisy that Veblen did in the relationships between the small-town merchant and his country customers. We may recall that the farmer's son used to come in to clerk in the general store and in time to become himself a store-owner. We may remember merchants and bankers who knew the people of a scattered rural community almost as well as the country doctor did, who showed a neighborly interest in their welfare and who often extended credit, to their own disaster, on intangible collateral. But whatever may have been the interaction of social forces the economic forces were always there. The small town, which was also the country town, was the scene of the farmer's first encounter with the economic system. Economically, in the long run, he got the worst of the bargain. If his invisible profits were added in—the cultural and social advantages of the village—perhaps he came out even.

The country town, at times and in places, certainly had its gentle and genial side. I can illustrate what it sometimes was and what it has sometimes become by describing one which I knew well in boyhood and have since occasionally revisited. It was a Vermont village of a few hundred population, and part of a township which may have had as many as fifteen hundred inhabitants. It had been settled for about a hundred years when I knew it. There were three churches, a Methodist, a Universalist (presided over by a woman minister) and, of course, a Congregationalist. Its schools carried a student through the grammar grades, after which, if he sought further education, he must go elsewhere to a high school or to one of the surviving "Academies" in larger neighboring towns. It had a small library, which "auctioned off" books at regular intervals. It had a surprisingly good brass band. It had a general store, a clothing store, a drugstore and a town hall where lectures and concerts were occasionally given.

Its older industries were a creamery, a cheese factory, a box factory, a grist-mill and a saw-mill. During my boyhood it must have enjoyed a brief prosperity when granite-sheds were established there, new houses were jerry-built on Construction Hill, and a considerable number of Scotch and Italian granite-cutters and French-Canadian teamsters and "muckers" were brought in. It was all rather jolly and cosmopolitan when all four of our racial stocks were represented in and around the general store on Saturday night; or foregathered for meals at the Monument House. As I look back at it through mature eyes, clearing away the golden mists as much as possible, the town seems to me to have had coherence and integrity, even though a fairly large city (for Vermont) lay only six miles away and the State capital was only twelve miles away. Gossip flourished, there were ructions in the churches and wild youth expressed itself in the primeval way, then as now. On the other hand, you could count on a neighbor to come in and help if any one in your family were seriously ill. Church affairs, "sociables," singing classes, band practice, and gatherings at the store made up a simple but tolerable social life. Few were shut out. You had a warm sensation of "belonging"—a homesickness for that sensation is, I believe, behind the swift growth and multiplication of fraternal orders among small-towners and especially among former small-towners.

I passed through that town a few weeks ago. The granite industry had departed, merging itself with enterprises in the neighboring small cities; the grist-mill, saw-mill, hotel and general store had all burned down; a chain-store had appeared in the ashes; many of the houses, including the one in which our richest man, the proprietor of the general store, had lived, were badly in need of paint; and only the white Congregational Church on the little hill, spick and span and at that moment opening its doors for some sort of festival, was as my boyhood remembered it. I stopped to speak to an old friend. He was just starting for the near-by city to bring back some ice cream for the church supper. In the pre-automobile days this trip would have taken him about half a day, and he would not have dreamed of making it for that purpose. The ice cream would have been manufactured at home, probably with some boy turning the freezer in the hope of being allowed to lick the dasher afterwards.

I am certain that the people living in the little town have a richer life than their parents did. They can reach a motion-picture theatre by a twenty-minute drive, they have radios, and they think nothing of jaunts to Boston, New York or Canada that many of the old residents never made in an entire life-time. The point is not that life is better or worse. It is different. The town is no longer self-contained. Invention and change have let the inhabitants out, the outer world in. As a community, economic or social, my old home has lost much of its significance. It is no longer sequestered and snug; it is on one of the world's corridors and the wind blows right through, sweeping away the old atmosphere; even the most casual visitor used to arrive on the morning train over the branch line and spend the day, or on the evening train and spend the night, or drive up with horse and buggy from the neighboring city, but now he is usually in and out in the space of ten or fifteen minutes. A pretty little hamlet, he thinks, and is gone.

All of us who have motored about the country have seen such hamlets, though they may be more numerous in New England than elsewhere. I have felt at times a certain indecency in the surfaced roads and traffic which pass through them, as though something which ought to have been kept intimate was being exposed to an uncomprehending and vulgar scrutiny. They were never meant to be seen in that fashion. The parade of speeding strangers cannot understand what was built into those houses, planted with those trees which now are often cut down to widen the road.

Clear across the continent, in California, is another small town of newer growth, which suffered a different fate. It sprung up forty-odd years ago in a field of oaks and wild mustard because a new university needed a railroad station. When I first saw it, about thirty years ago, it was an intimate community of modest size, with two paved streets. One pastured cows on vacant lots. Once, in process of working my way through college, I led a cow down its main street and for several miles along one of the main highways outside, on a Sunday morning. The place was just developing small-town consciousness, including, as was the case in most Western communities, a lively sense of land values. Had it been frozen for a generation or so at that point it might have become a California version of my Vermont town. But the new university prospered and the railroad cut the running time to the metropolis thirty miles away. The small town of thirty years ago is a little city, and I doubt that the small-town mind feels much at home there any more.

Somewhere between the extremes indicated in my illustrations there lie, I believe, the majority of America's small towns. Many have been killed as trading centers by the automobile and the good road. We do not need as many trading centers as we did; we can go thirty miles to a really well-stocked town, with commercial amusements thrown in, during the time it used to take for a farmer to drive down from the East Hill to the church or general store. Competition decides which small town shall go ahead, perhaps to become a small city, while many more become static or retrogress. Many a filling-station, where casual motorists halt momentarily, is a monument to what was once a lively commerce. What is this burg, asks the traveller? But by the time an answer can be formulated he is somewhere else. For an answer that would tell the whole story would be long—it would deal with pioneers struggling through forests and over mountains or across prairies; it would tell of rural statesmanship organizing to provide the necessary primitive services; it would deal with lives lived slowly, lonesomely, yet always under the close scrutiny of neighbors; it would concern itself with the boom that followed the coming of the branch railway line; it would record the dispersion of youth to the cities; it would somehow have to explain what happened when the space barriers were removed and the whole countryside, in a decade or two, became liquid. We are a nation of nomads, it is true. But the people of the small town did not use to be nomadic. They liked it where they were, were afraid to go elsewhere, were accustomed to a mode of life. They were the people who stayed put.

It was doubtless the small-town people who went away who made the small town seem romantic. One can never know just how much romance was intrinsic to it. The truth is that, romance or no romance, it is a completed episode. Completed, that is, in the sense that the thing that made it what it was, its isolation, is now in most cases a thing of the past. To the visitor from the city it may, indeed, seem isolated, but in fact almost every village lane is now a tributary to America's great Main Street. It hears the President speak from Washington, sees him on the films and hears his voice again, studies the latest Hollywood styles in clothes, love, adventure and vulgarity, gets into its car and goes touring when it has time and the urge. It plays more, even on its own heath.

If we lump it with the rest of the rural population—and that is what we had better do if we want to understand it—we can draw forth certain contrasts between it and the city-dwelling population. It continues to produce more children per capita; it commits suicide less often but dies in infancy a little oftener; it is more subject to influenza, smallpox, malaria and dysentery, but less subject to venereal disease, tuberculosis, epidemic diseases, alcoholism, drug addiction, general paralysis, heart disease and cancer; it commits from one-third to two-thirds as many murders as its city cousins and goes to jail about one-third as often; it has fewer telephones, fewer books, fewer newspapers, sees fewer motion pictures and gets its mail less often; it has about half as many radios as are found in cities; it has fewer automobiles per capita than people in medium-sized cities but more than those in large cities; it has more representatives per capita in Congress; strangest of all, it seems to be a little less pious, since only half its people are church members, as compared with 60 per cent in cities.[2] Racially, of course, it is likely to be relatively homogeneous, and except when it has a common grievance—say, a decline in the proportion of the national income that goes to farmers and small-townspeople—it is politically and economically conservative. It can be stirred up to progressive political action—witness the success of two generations of La Follettes in rural Wisconsin. It may be turning to co-operation as one way out of its economic difficulties. But these trends take a long time.

There is an apparent but not real inconsistency in saying that the small town as we used to know it is disappearing, and then proceeding to discuss its contemporary characteristics. The small town has merely had to adapt itself to a present-day technology. Sometimes it does this by freezing and becoming a kind of museum piece, sometimes by growing, occasionally by disappearing. It is not so likely to disappear, however, as to become a suburb—or perhaps I should say sub-town. The automobile makes the larger trading center easily accessible, but by the same token it makes it easier to get away from. One may shop there, even work there, and still live in one's old small-town home. The California town I mentioned has already developed suburbs of its own, although it is itself a suburb of the metropolis.

I suspect that the American small town will continue to exist, though stripped of many of its old economic functions, because it meets a spiritual, a cultural, or, if one likes, a psychological need. In a profound book which received less attention than it deserved[3] Harvey Fergusson comments discerningly on this phase of our subject. He is speaking of degrees of social freedom in modern societies. "If the communities of the United States were studied from this viewpoint," he believes, "it would surely be found that, from the rural village, which is almost as completely ruled by group compulsion and taboo as a savage tribe, to the city of New York, where the individual is subject only to a few absolute necessities, there exists a graded series of types, and it would surely also be apparent that this graded environment is the necessary growth-form of a society so diverse and mutable as ours." Some of us cannot endure what Mr. Fergusson regards as the "terrifying" freedom of a large and impersonal urban community. For such persons the small town or its equivalent may be an absolute necessity—in short, if the small town did not exist it would be incumbent upon us to invent it. We cannot, indeed, restore

<hr />

[2]These facts are summarized from the report of the Urbanism Committee of the National Resources Committee, Government Printing Office, Washington, September, 1937.
[3]*Modern Man. His Belief and Behavior.* Alfred A. Knopf, New York, 1936. P. 97 and after.

its old serenity and security, but we can preserve them in a comparative degree.

A decade and a half ago I think we worried more about the cultural significance, or lack of significance, of the small town than we do now. Culturally it may seem dead, yet how many writers, born in its bosom, have arisen with astonishing vigor to sing its deadness, its monotony! At the worst, and barring such extremes as are celebrated in works of art of the genre of *Tobacco Road,* I would regard it as being less a cultural death than a refreshing and ultimately fruitful sleep. The small town is not swept by winds of doctrine. It is natural, human, petty, mean, poetic, friendly, jealous—anything but impersonal, anything but inhuman. It will not easily be swung out of its anchorage by either of the great extremes that seem so frightfully close to the city dweller. It will submit to vague and remote tyrannies, of which it is not fully conscious, but it will not march with the dictators. I am not idealizing it, for it is flesh and weak. Simply in self-preservation it will not shift far and abruptly, for in so doing it would be destroying itself. It has the tenacity of any human institution, of any organism. It can be—it has been—greatly changed, but in its essence it will persist.

In saying this I do not mean to predict that it will persist in exactly its present physical form. That form is already archaic, though it may be preserved for sentimental reasons. The classic small town is an aggregation of stores, shops, churches, schools and houses grouped for the convenience of persons going from one to another on foot. No one building is more than a few minutes' walk from another. Preserve the time interval but translate it into automotive terms and we might have a small town of the same characteristics dispersed for many miles over a countryside. Already the farmer is an integral part of many small towns as he could not possibly be a generation or less ago. By bringing him into closer touch the small town may retain many of its social characteristics even in the face of economic disadvantages.

The general effect of what is going on is, of course, to blur many of the old differences between town and country, between big town and little town. But one small-town quality—intimacy—cannot be blurred. It exists or it does not exist. I see no reason to believe that it will not continue to exist. I think the desire for intimacy, for personal relationships having a stability not attainable in cities, is more responsible for the exodus toward the rims of metropolitan regions than is any love for trees, grass, birds or flowers. This movement represents a genuine revolt against the impersonal and mechanized character of urban civilization. It is more likely to grow than diminish. Widely diffused, it helps to preserve the essence of the small-town idea. It may be strengthened by technological changes which will decentralize industry, but at this point the picture begins to grow hazy. The semi-self-sustaining small town may be technologically possible, but it does not fit into the prevailing economy. At present such communities must be either very primitive or to a certain extent parasitic. The adjective, I hasten to add, is not intended to be disparaging. The small town simply cannot get its living out of its own creative efforts. It must survive because society as a whole wants what it gives and is willing to pay what it costs.

What, then, has it to contribute? A stabilizing influence, perhaps. A tendency to reduce abstractions to human terms. A reservoir from which creative energy can be drawn, though in itself it will tend to be passive. It will be a place of relative quietness. It will encourage thought rather than action. It may help to break the great waves of passion which otherwise might sweep an urbanized nation.

I should hate to visualize what our literature, our music, our art, our science might become if it were not for the small town. But I look for these movements to gather their forces there, not to discharge them there. The small town is the reserve battalion in the eternal battle. The city will remain the firing line.

# SPORTS

## [John Kieran]

OF THE earlier essays in civilization the glory that was Greece often has been held aloft as a model by admiring antiquarians. That sports held a high place in the Greek design for living is documented by the odes of Pindar and attested by the chisel of Phidias. The ancient Olympic Games were great events in that day when the federated cities of the Hellenic peninsula held sway over the Mediterranean "world" and the phalanx carried the cultural advance into the barbarous regions of the interior. In that era the Greeks were leaders not only in culture and conquest but also in sport and organized athletics. Whether or not there were interlocking causes for this joint leadership is debatable. But for all its leadership and supremacy in athletics, as a power among nations Greece fell. The United States of America is today the world leader in sports and organized athletics. *Absit omen!*

There is little doubt that sport can be and has been a cultural or civilizing influence in many ways. This has been discovered by missionaries who went out among the heathens with something quite different in mind. It may seem odd to discover or admit this uplifting quality in sports when the original—or aboriginal—urge toward the sport field is dissected. Thoreau somewhere set it down in his writings that the sports of the civilized were the pursuits of the savage. In a broad sense this is true. The hunting and fishing, the sailing and swimming, the running and jumping that the savage undertook to obtain meat and drink, clothing and lodging or personal safety from nasty neighbors, have become in the civilized State either individual or organized sorties by groups for the purpose of relaxation, exercise or amusement.

Fundamentally, then, a turning toward sports is a reversion to type and, in type, Man is not a poet or painter or lexicographer or astronomer but a biped of the mammalian order, an animal. And an animal must have exercise. With this definite and fundamental background of an animal nature, it would be useless to seek on the sports field for signs of the furthest advance in what is more or less loosely known as civilization. But if civilization is the advancement and .improvement in intelligence and culture of persons and pursuits, it may be fairly maintained that the contestants and the games of today represent a long gain over the Stone Age subtleties in sports, the Greek and Roman diversions, the mediæval riotous rompings, and even the mid-Victorian amusements.

There is little argument on that score. Some of our common contests for individuals in tests of speed or strength remain as simple now as they were "in the dim dusk of dolorous years" when the Cro-Magnons sprinted along the banks of the Dordogne or wrestled for dear life on the cliffs above, but most of the popular team games of today were unknown to the ancients and some are not yet a century old. It's true that most modern team games are developments or offshoots of older stock but the changes are so great in many cases that only a sporting anthropologist could find the missing links.

Many of the great changes on the sports field are due to great changes in the economic or political condition of the contestants. The spread of democracy brought a sweeping revision along the whole sports front. Where the ancient inhabitants of countries were divided into masters and slaves, what we call sports were exclusively game for the master's table. Even the ancient Olympic Games, supposedly open to any freeborn Greek citizen without a crime record, called upon the contestant for leisure and training expenses that only the richer class could afford. Down the ages the helots, the serfs, and the peasants had their low-class diversions but, historically, modern sport as the world knows it today is largely of English heritage, and the document that ultimately brought about a great measure of democracy in sports around the world was the Magna Charta sullenly signed by King John and wrenched from his quivering hands by the barons of England in 1215 A.D.

The progressive breakdowns of class barriers as the tide of democracy rose had their repercussions on the sports field. The lists were open to master and man. Better wages and higher standards of living brought added hours of leisure to the workingman. Added hours of leisure meant more hours spent at sports. Millions of added contestants joined in the games with the natural result of producing better games and better players. Compulsory education, scientific training methods, improved equipment, and governmental interest in national health problems have contributed to the growth and improvement in all lines of popular athletics. But this is academic, if not superfluous, and leaps to the mind of any one who gives the matter a few moments of thought. There are other points to consider, of which some are distinctly debatable.

One that is debated, if not debatable, is that the athletes of today are not the equal of the hardy heroes of yesteryear. The cry of the complainants is that our young men of today have been softened by the luxuries of modern life. They have been done in by autos and movies and swing orchestras and night clubs. They no longer tramp the hills, run the roads, and wrestle with the elements. Wherefore the strength has gone out of them and they are a sissy lot whom their forbears would have smitten hip and thigh and laid low in the dust of defeat at any game a man of spirit and muscle might play.

To the revered but stubborn and doddering gaffers who insist that fighters or football players of the old school would have broken our modern champions like sticks, there can be but the brief, irreverent, and Shakespearean answer: "Go shake your ears!" The athletes and standards of play of today, on the average, are so far ahead of the athletes and standards of play of older days that any comparison verges on the ridiculous. Where there is any factual basis of comparison, such as the stopwatch or steel tape, the advance of the moderns over their predecessors is demonstrated with considerable clarity.

And why not? There are a hundred young fellows on our sports fields today for one who was competing there fifty years ago. Modern equipment is better. The modern sprinter runs on a better cinderpath. The modern pole vaulter has a lighter and better pole with which to haul himself over the lofty crossbar. Bats and balls, shoes, gloves, racquets, and assorted accessories for all games have been improved, thus lifting the level of the play in the contests. The modern training table furnishes a better balanced diet for athletes, based on scientific studies of that particular problem. The training quarters at many clubs and colleges are equipped with electric thermal appliances of costly and astonishing variety for the treatment of the ills the human flesh is heir to, especially in rough-and-ready contact games like intercollegiate football.

It might be urged, then, that this improvement in equipment is the reason for improvement over old records, the setting of new high marks in tests of skill and strength, and new low marks in the time-tests of speed over standard distances. But that is only a part of the explanation. The best man of ten may not be the best man of a hundred. The incomparably greater number in the field today produces better champions if only through the process of wider selectivity. That is, on the average. It is readily admitted that there are exceptional athletes today as there were exceptional athletes fifty or five hundred years ago. But the mass movement on the athletic field is forward through the means and for the reasons just stated.

One added bit of evidence should come close to clinching the argument. Vast charts of vital statistics gathered by government agencies and life insurance companies show definitely that the race is growing bigger. The average inhabitant of the United States today is an inch or so taller and some pounds heavier than the average inhabitant of fifty years ago, the exact figures depending upon who did the weighing and measuring to strike the balances. Though the estimates may vary slightly, the general report is unanimous. A striking example of the upward trend may be found by perusing a thin volume entitled *Yale Athletics,* written by Richard M. Hurd, Yale '88, and published just about a half-century ago. In it the reader will find that the average weight of the men in Yale and Harvard crews for the decade of 1878–87 was a fraction under 168 pounds and the average height was 5 feet 10½ inches. The Harvard and Yale crews of modern races on the Thames above New London have averaged nearly two inches taller and fifteen pounds heavier. To carry this argument to a *reductio ad absurdum,* all that an investigator has to do is to visit the Metropolitan Museum of Art in New York City or some similar resting-place for museum pieces and look at the suits of mediæval armor mounting a hollow guard on pedestals in those educational halls. Remember the stirring stories of the huge heroes of the romantic mêlées when knighthood was in flower? *Va bene!* "Romantic" is right! There wouldn't be one man in ten on the Stanford, Notre Dame, or Yale football squads of today who could cramp or squeeze himself into the hardware trappings of those "gigantic" heroes of mediæval history.

Then we have better athletes, better games, and better playing fields today, and more of them in every direction. But it isn't time to sound the loud timbrel and proclaim that sports have reached the highest peak of perfection possible in this comparatively civilized age. There remain many ancient evils, and some modern additions vary between the sinister and the ridiculous. One of the greatest industries and, at the same time, one of the broadest farces in the United States is horse racing, the turf, the "Sport of Kings." Kings? What kings? *Les grands rois sont morts!* Presidents are elected, dictators rise from the ranks to seize nations or unwashed comrades come to power over millions. The turf? There isn't a square foot of turf on the main racing strip of any big track between New York and California, between Florida and the Canadian border. As for the horse in horse racing, the solemn declaration is made that the fundamental purpose of horse racing is "for the improvement of the breed." Of what? The horse? For any useful purpose in any really civilized area in this age, the horse is as dead as the dodo.

No! The remaining aristocrats and the arriving nouveaux riches who maintain racing stables and support the game as a real sport are swamped by the hordes that make modern racing in this country nothing but common gambling on a stupendous scale. It is on this basis that it prospers and, though the judicious may grieve and the hypocritical may attempt to ignore or conceal it, there is no doubt that one of the great industries of the United States today is horse racing. A single race track like Belmont Park on Long Island represents a standing investment of millions. A single owner like John Hay Whitney has racing strings and breeding establishments valued at well over a million. Less than half the States have legalized racing and not all those States allow betting in mutuel machines or totalisators, but in seventeen States that permitted betting machines in 1937 the total "handle," or money wagered through the machines, was $284,017,996 for the calendar year. Since this is only part of the total wagered at race tracks in this country during that period and since the money wagered at the tracks is only a minor fraction of the money wagered away from the tracks through "handbooks" and "poolrooms," the extent of the wagering on horse racing in this country in a single year must run to an awe-inspiring total. Only an astronomer would be competent to juggle such big figures and, anyway, as the old vaudeville comedian put it: "Such a sum should only be mentioned kneeling."

Here, then, is an allegedly civilized country unofficially condoning in some sections and officially encouraging in other sections the series of operations known as horse racing, which is nothing more than common gambling on a gigantic scale. A sport? To the Wideners and Whitneys and Vanderbilts and their aristocratic ilk it is, and a quite expensive sport, too. But to the overwhelming majority of racegoers it is strictly a gambling game *et praeterea nihil*. Every day in the United States there are bets placed on horses by thousands of men and women who never in their lives were inside a race track or saw a thoroughbred horse pounding along the rail in a stretch drive.

An even more ludicrous sidelight on our civilization is the low-class relative of the lofty turf, or dog racing. Here the sponsors didn't bother to propound any sham slogan to the effect that it was for "the improvement of the breed." They simply set the greyhounds out in chase of a mechanical "rabbit" in an oval enclosure and invited the public to step in and wager on which dogs would come in first, second and third at odds to be determined by the tide of betting. To show how far a thing of that kind may go, it might be mentioned that at one dog track in the vicinity of Boston the mutuel "handle" was approximately $250,000 in a single night!

The question of morals doesn't enter into this argument. What is maintained here is that this method of gambling is not civilized. It is barbaric in its trappings and its stupidity. For ninety-nine out of a hundred of its followers, why the horses or the dogs? Why the journeys by day or night to the tracks? It would be much more civilized, more efficient, more convenient and more comfortable to set up roulette wheels in sufficient quantities in convenient localities at a great saving of time and energy and staggering investments in practically wasted accessories. It isn't the common gambling that is condemned here; it's the lack of common sense in the program as now conducted.

But that's only one item in the relationship of sports to contemporary civilization. There are others of interest. Have we reached a high stage of civilization when the public spectacle that draws the record-breaking receipts of $2,600,000 for a single performance is a prizefight in the open at night? That was the "gate" at the Tunney-Dempsey fight in Chicago. Gene Tunney received $990,000 for exactly thirty minutes of work, not much of it wasted, in beating Dempsey about the head. When the yearly income of many learned scientists is set against that, the comparison is enough to make a thoughtful person look back and agree with the decision of Benjamin Robert Haydon, the great British painter of vast canvases. Haydon killed himself in a fit of despondency because the public, when he hired a hall for an exhibition of his magnificent paintings, left him alone in his glory and rushed past his door in throngs to see General Tom Thumb at a shilling a head. In some ways it does not appear that we have made much progress along the road to culture since that time.

Many of our colleges and universities are best known for what? For the prowess of their football teams. Beyond the town limits of New Haven, how many men halted on the streets of any city could give the name of the president of Yale? Eheu, too few! But most of those interrogated could give the name of the football coach in a jiffy. At a Texas institution of learning the football coach receives a yearly salary twice as large as that paid to the president of the university. In the field of sport it would be natural to look to the conduct of college athletics for uplift and enlightenment, but that there is much hypocrisy and some skullduggery in the annual production of powerful college football teams about the country is beyond sensible question. One team of recent years selected to play in the Rose Bowl game in Pasadena, the *summa cum laude* award of the football field, included five married men in the line-up of the starting eleven! It would strain the credulity to believe that this was a representative array of student material in athletics. There is little doubt that some of our colleges and universities, or departments thereof, are definitely engaged in professional football ventures under the cover of an amateur and educational banner. The aims are not wicked. The purpose is to gain local or national advertising for the college or university as a whole and to obtain through football gate receipts the money to finance a wide variety of sports that are far from self-supporting. But even if it were granted that the aims were lofty, the means are too often stultifying.

Still, the situation in college football is far better than it was, and is steadily improving. The gridiron sport, rising to such tremendous heights of popularity, got a little out of hand. But the educators are beginning to catch up with it, and sooner or later it is hopefully believed that, like almost all other college activities, it will come under reasonable faculty control. This will be a small but distinct advance in the process of civilization of this country.

While there may be no great harm in it, any common custom that insults the intelligence is a petty blot on the 'scutcheon of civilization, and the sham of allegedly amateur tennis falls within that field. Most of those players who, of recent years, have gone over frankly to the professional ranks have admitted the hilarious mockery of their "amateur" careers. There was Ellsworth Vines, a young Californian who dropped out of the freshman class of a university located in his home area because he didn't have enough money to continue his college course. But within the next year and a half he toured this country, Europe, and Australia. He stopped at the best hotels and travelled on the best trains and ships. He had all the luxuries of the rich and he even considered himself sufficiently affluent to take unto himself a wife, wherefore he married a charming and beautiful young lady. And how had he done all this, the young fellow who had to leave college because he couldn't afford to remain in class? He had done it by playing "amateur" tennis.

"Yes," said Ellsworth with a chuckle, when talking it over later. "It was a bit of a joke, at that."

It is still a joke, if that's the right word. Polo and golf are conducted along more enlightened and consequently more civilized standards. In polo there is no distinction made between amateurs and professionals on horseback. A man is either a good polo player or he is not and his amateurism doesn't enter into it. This leaves no room for hypocrisy on the subject. In golf, except for a team financed once every four years for international competition in Great Britain, no amateur golf player is allowed to receive expense money of any kind from any source but his own pocket. This abolishes the chance of making a professional career of an amateur game. It's a civilized attitude to have and to hold and possibly the example on the golf links, in time, will have a cultural effect on the neighboring tennis courts, a consummation devoutly to be wished.

In wider fields and on a broader basis it is sometimes maintained that the modern Olympic Games breed more enmity than amity among nations. If so, the Olympic Games certainly should be halted as a menace to contemporary civilization.

But upon any slight investigation or sober reflection, this adverse opinion is not tenable. There have been squabbles among officials, spectators and contestants at modern Olympic Games and in some of these bickerings there was race as well as personal prejudice displayed. What sways popular opinion in the wrong direction in this field is that attention is directed to the few fellows who are fighting and not to the many men who are making friends. The Olympic Games provide a fine opportunity for enlightening contact among the husky, upstanding young men of the nations of the world. At the revival of the ancient games at Athens in 1896, only eight nations were represented in Olympic competition. At Berlin in 1936 there were gathered approximately 5000 individual athletes representing 53 nations. Unless the human race is inherently vicious, such meetings in athletic rivalry should tend toward a better understanding among the representatives of the various nations and provide young men in the formative and receptive period of their intellectual development with a broader view of international problems that should be of benefit to the world as they grow older. This was the aim of the late Baron Pierre de Coubertin, founder of the modern games. That such results are being obtained is the testimony of the athletes themselves by an overwhelming majority. The Olympic Games, despite petty quarrels at home or abroad over the details, should be supported and encouraged as sport's greatest contribution toward the civilization of the world.

# FAMILY

## [*Elsie Clews Parsons*]

WHAT'S the matter with that young couple?" said the man at the wheel, the boy's uncle. The boy and girl were out on the bowsprit and our yawl was running into the wind, as we made for the Thoroughfare, in Penobscot Bay. "Oh, they just like getting wet."—"That's just it! Instead of going back to college this autumn, they're both in the Sophomore class in a Western college, they're going to get married and earn their living in New York, somehow."—"Why didn't you at least suggest trying it out without getting married?"—"I did. They said they wouldn't like that, and talked about something else." The man at the wheel was a Baltimorean, a conservative, middle-aged professional man quite unaware he had been advocating something once called trial marriage.

Not long after, in western Massachusetts, I listened to a middle-aged couple from Greenwich Village tell a girl from Park Avenue how they had finally decided to have the ceremony after being kept out of a hotel in Paris, of all places! "What old stuff!" the girl said to me afterwards, "why talk about it?" The mood of rebellious talk has passed completely. Do what you like, marry or "live in sin" in the Baltimorean cliché, but don't talk about it; nobody is interested. Unless you produce a baby, as in a recent notorious case, two months after graduation and marriage, and the class has to vote on whether or not to recognize the baby as the class baby. Whatever its reasons, the class voted conservatively.

If there has been any change in attitude in the last two decades toward mating and childbearing—statistically the age at marriage appears slightly older,[1] the divorce rate has gone up somewhat, the birthrate has dropped —the change has not proceeded through ideological clarification. Although knowledge about contraception has increased and spread, I find no clearer

[1]The trend since 1890 toward more youthful marriage slackened from 1920 to 1930, the decline in numbers marrying young being greater in city than in country. William F. Ogburn, "Recent Changes in Marriage," *American Journal of Sociology*, XLI (1935), pp. 287, 288.

thinking in distinguishing between mating as a private function and child-bearing as a public or social one than in the days when Mrs. Sanger was not an international figure and the medical profession was content to be supine on any social relationship. Pictures of childbirth are still condemned as private obscenities and the Catholic clergy can still talk about controlled parenthood, the new tag for birth control, as breaking the dam against lust or to use *their* new tag, totalitarian sex, and still find an audience, perhaps even one that doesn't laugh. One more case of social lag for the rationalists to stomach!

So let us turn from old views rationally undigested, from youth and sex, to later age classes and to various aspects of family life. As Katharine Anthony pointed out in our volume of 1922, the extended family, grandma, the spinster aunt, the orphaned cousin, all that was left of the family of more than two generations, is disappearing and even the single family is shrinking, as the number of children lowers and the children marry earlier or, for other and increasing reasons, leave home. What then do the old people do? Some of them close or sell the homestead, if they have one and if they can, and, like philosophic Hindus in the final stage of life, take to the road, carrying their rice bowl by trailer or in that priceless invention for the aging, especially aging women, the cruise boat.

There are more aging women than aging men. One night recently in the Massachusetts resort already referred to I listened to a distinguished novelist become a serio-comic enumerator of vital statistics and list from village to village the husbands who have died in the past decade as against the wives, about 15 to 1. Had he realized that something similar was occurring not only in New England but throughout rural non-farming America, he might have been personally less disturbed, at least he was not living in a district peculiarly unlucky for his own marital age class. For the country at large there are twice as many widows as widowers.

One effect of this disproportion is that wealth tends to increase in the hands of aging females; a nucleus of rich old ladies is forming. (For the popular category of Haves and Have-nots, I suggest substituting in this connection Havers and Doers, as more penetrating, women and the aged constituting the Havers, broadly speaking, and men and the young constituting the Doers.) What are these old women going to do with themselves and their riches? The vicarious satisfaction they once got from an active husband they would like to go on getting from sons, but sons may be elusive, irked by the maternal need or preferring young Havers to old ones. More clash in the family, between generations, and between mothers and sons at that! Let ideologists of the Oedipus complex school take notice! Indeed too long has been neglected the theme of vicarious satisfaction in general in family life. Here may be one of the secrets, if only a lesser one, why fathers (Doers) and daughters (Havers) get on together better than mothers (Havers) and daughters (Havers) or why mothers and sons are sympathetic, for a time.

The concentration of wealth in female hands has had an effect upon its distribution. Women disburse 85 per cent of retail expenditure but to welfare or educational groups they give only one half as much as men. To remedy this situation, Doctor Townsend, if not the Administration, might consider placing a cumulative income tax on old ladies who have for the benefit of old ladies who have not. If this check or balance were considered to be unconstitutional, the nucleus of niggardly old ladies might be reduced in other ways, by men deciding to let up and live longer or by women deciding to do more and die younger. At least girls might be taught to look ahead to middle age or even to old age, and diversify their interests.

Outside of classes in the higher income brackets, women *are* doing more; the increase of women in gainful occupations has long been familiar among economic changes and recently was rendered even more conspicuous by the Depression, at least in the early part of it. As the Depression continued and during the recovery the advantage in holding or getting jobs that women had over men was diminished. There may have been a tendency to discriminate against the long-time flow of married women into gainful occupations.[2] In 1930–31, 77 per cent of 1500 city school systems were refusing to hire married women as teachers and 63 per cent discharged single women teachers who married; an old-time attitude of conservatives on school boards was reviving. The same conservative attitude was expressed in a new Federal rule providing for the dismissal of a married person in the United States Government service in the case of a reduction of personnel if the spouse also was employed by Government. In industry no report on comparable attitudes or practices is available. We know in general that one out of every four women at work is married.

Knowledge of the effects of the Depression upon the family is in general meagre or contradictory. Marriages of course diminished. Between 1930 and 1935 a deficit of 750,000 marriages is estimated. In 1932 the marriage rate dropped to the lowest point on record. But nothing is known about what happened to mating outside of marriage. There may have been

[2] In 1920 one out of every eleven married women worked for pay as against one out of every twenty-two in 1890. William F. Ogburn, "The Changing Family," *Publications of the American Sociological Society*, XXIII (1929), p. 129.

thousands of unofficial "trial marriages," but there is of course no record of them. (There is no nationwide record of annual official marriages.) The birthrate fell with the marriage rate; but not as low as was expected, given increasing knowledge of contraception. (Medically directed birth control clinics increased from 40 in 1930 to 288 in 1936, in 40 States and the District of Columbia.) Divorces as well as marriages diminished. It has been estimated that between 1930 and 1935 there was a loss in divorces of 170,000 from the number which would have been expected from the preceding divorce trend. But whether or not desertions or separations decreased or increased is not known. Nor is anything known about changes in the general temper of family life, in parental control, in proportionate influence of father or mother; or of effects from family doubling up which was very extensive, furnishing a curious simulacrum of the vanishing type of extended family with its larger functions, economic, educational, recreational, and protective. In short, the interesting report from which I have been quoting, "Research Memorandum on the Family in the Depression," prepared for the Social Science Research Council, is a report not on what we know but on what we would like to know.

Out of the Depression developed fresh interest in extending from the rich to the poor two social policies bearing importantly on family life and on each other; insurance in old age and prolonging education or, specifically for the poor, prohibiting child labor in industry. As children or young people cease to contribute to the family purse or welfare, they may also cease to develop a sense of responsibility in caring for aging parents or relatives, and the burden will fall on the Government. In turn, offspring who make little or no returns for the care given them become less desirable and the birthrate may be expected to go down. Diminishing parental control or satisfaction means a diminishing birthrate in any economic class. Appreciation of all these relationships is clear to the Catholic Church, if not always to others, and is, I think, the real ground of the Church's opposition to child labor legislation. That quaint journalistic term, youth control, was convenient camouflage for Church as well as newspaper. Actually the Church opposes child labor legislation for the same reason it opposes legalization of contraception, both threaten to reduce the size of its constituency. As the Church may foresee a time when the United States will be its chief stronghold or refuge, American population figures are peculiarly important.

But sociological prediction, in or out of the Church, is a rash pursuit, so many unexpected things can happen. In a world where whole populations may be annihilated by sterilization, disease germ or lethal gas, or reproduced through test tubes, and where toleration or enjoyment of divergencies, never very vigorous in any form of life, are vanishing attitudes, church, family, age-classes, any of the terms we have been using in a particularized sense may appear quaint or archaic, and incredibly soon too, once they who play God or the White Queen become a little more imaginative.

A changing world, and so why not prepare for it, each man for himself, and, as he or particularly she deals with juniors, by encouraging them to take pleasure in the unexpected and to live in the day, enjoying time and place without sense of crisis or of bondage to their nest, familial or national, spiritual or material, every day or hour to be prized as good or valuable in itself, the whole world a workshop or a playground and all the people in it playmates or fellow workers? In time our civilization might conceive of new values, head away from suicide and begin to bloom.

HEALTH

# GENERAL MEDICINE

## [*Logan Clendening, M.D.*[1]]

MEDICINE in the United States today is the leader of the world. This is a simple statement of fact, not an opinion— a statement with which I believe fair-minded physicians in all countries would agree. What the "leader of the world" means is, I take it, that the United States sets the pace in research, practice, physical equipment and organization; it attracts students; it occupies the same position that Vienna did before the war; that Paris did before Vienna; that Dublin, Edinburgh and Leyden have occupied at various times in history.

The causes which have brought about this situation are many, but it may be largely ascribed to the demoralization of Europe after the war and the comparative material prosperity in the United States. Science, unlike the arts, tends to flourish in tranquil soil.

The socialization of medicine in foreign countries has been a factor in placing American medicine in a dominant position, according to many, including outstanding physicians who reside and practise in Europe.

The aspects of American medicine pertinent to this volume can be taken up under these headings:

(1) THE GENERAL STATE OF PRACTICE. If you were sick in Peru or Poland or Czecho-Slovakia—anywhere you were unacquainted—your natural first thought would be "What kind of a doctor am I likely to get if I pick at random?" That seems to me the fundamental test of any medical civilization.

In the United States, I think it can be said quite sincerely that if you pick out in any city a member of the regular profession you are more than likely to get extremely efficient service, comfort, courtesy, and sound, disinterested advice. How you will fare economically is not part of my subject here, and will be discussed below.

[1]The opinions herein expressed are entirely individual to me and do not commit any medical organization to which I may belong.

411

Since 1910 when the Flexner report, by the sheer force of its cool statement of facts, swept away the old privately owned medical colleges, the standard of medical education has been universally high. Today any physician you are likely to encounter, even in the most remote and sparsely populated villages, has been well grounded in the fundamental sciences of anatomy, physiology, pathology, bacteriology and pharmacology, trained for over two years in the clinical branches of medicine, obstetrics, surgery, eye, ear, nose and throat, children, women, skin, nervous and mental diseases, hygiene and other specialties, has served at least a year in a general hospital, and has passed a state board examination. That condition has existed for more than a generation, so that the products of the loose training and licensure of the 19th century have largely been antiquated.

(2) HYGIENE. Of equal, if not of more importance than practice, is the control of public health. The United States Public Health Service is one of the most efficient on earth, and the health departments of cities and states are worthy adjuncts. Pure water, good food, safe occupation, are almost universally assured. The infectious diseases and occupational diseases have been, for many decades, the focus of attack. Typhoid fever, smallpox and diphtheria are now diminishing to the vanishing point, and tuberculosis is rapidly declining. The latest diseases to be included in the attack by the United States Public Health Service are the so-called social diseases—syphilis and gonorrhœa.[2]

(3) EDUCATION. Medical education in the United States is very evenly efficient. The mountainous differences which used to exist between such outstanding schools as Harvard, Johns Hopkins, Pennsylvania and Columbia and the commercial colleges have been swept away. The great majority of medical departments of a state university or of a well-endowed university and the standards for teaching and equipment are very exacting. The student is required to complete two years of study in the general

[2]A very well-informed physician, to whom I submitted this manuscript, commented as follows on this paragraph:

"I am inclined to doubt that the statement made to the effect that pure water, good food and safe occupation are almost universally assured is altogether justified. That word, 'universally,' takes in a lot of territory. When I call to mind the conditions that existed in most parts of the country when I began my own work in the field of public health and mentally compare those conditions with existing conditions, I wonder that so much progress has been made toward insuring the comparative purity of water and food supplies and in safeguarding workers against occupational diseases and accidents. Even so, I know that there is yet much to be done in these fields, though I am very sure that the efforts now being made to improve the general situation are more intensively and intelligently applied than ever before in so far as medicine is concerned, even though there still exist some hampering influences of a most important nature."

college before entering the medical department and is expected to be well grounded in mathematics, physics, chemistry, biology and, of course, English and a living foreign language. His training in medical school is indicated in the paragraph above. The hospitals which accept internes are well equipped and well staffed and alert to the necessity for post-graduate training of the young physician. There are many opportunities for residencies (prolonged hospital training) and assistantships and other means of post-graduate education.

LIBRARIES. The medical libraries of the United States have rapidly developed to rival the great collections of the Old World.

The Surgeon General's Library in Washington, that monument to the industry and scholarship of John Shaw Billings, is the greatest accumulation of its kind in the world today. Not the British Museum, not the Bodleian, not the Bibliothèque Nationale can rival it. The Catalogue of the Surgeon General's Library is a recognized standard among bibliographers everywhere.

In naming distinguished libraries, I refer particularly to the historical collections. There are innumerable libraries that contain competent and practically complete files of current literature back to 1890.

Other great libraries in the United States housing this precious historical material are: The Library of the College of Physicians, Philadelphia; of the Institute of Medicine at Baltimore; of the Academy of Medicine, New York; the Boston Medical Library; the Crerar Library, Chicago; of the University of Michigan, Ann Arbor; of The Denver Medical Society; and just across our border, the Osler Library at McGill University, Montreal.

The Huntington Library at San Marino, California, contains a few almost unique volumes.

The great private collections of Harvey Cushing and John F. Fulton at New Haven, of James Waring of Denver, and of Herbert Evans at Berkeley, California, will eventually, it is believed, go to public institutions.

(4) HOSPITALS. There are 6189 hospitals in the United States registered with the Council on Hospitals and Medical Education of the American Medical Association. Of these, 584 are for patients with mental disease or the feeble-minded. Nine hundred and sixty-nine of the remaining are denominational institutions controlled by some religious body. Most of the large hospitals are of the last type.

In all the larger cities—of over 100,000 population—a general hospital is established for patients who are unable to pay the ordinary medical costs. These hospitals are well staffed and well equipped and often make valuable contributions to medical science.

The denominational hospitals are mostly for private patients—patients able to afford adequate fees—with a certain amount of charity work. How much of this latter service is given varies widely with different hospitals. The staff of physicians and surgeons is carefully selected and controlled, although naturally men with the largest practices are given preferment.

The system differs considerably, in spite of surface resemblances, from the English and Continental system of general hospitals and nursing homes. A London consultant of eminence, to make the example specific, is on the staff of St. Bartholomew's Hospital. Here he makes his original investigations and gains wide clinical experience. For his private patients he conducts his own nursing home, either exclusive to him and his assistants or in association with one or more other consultants of the same rank.

The advantages of the nursing home are that it is far more comfortable for the patient and conducted with far more regard to the amenities than the American private hospital. It is probably, on the average, more expensive. It is decidedly for the upper classes.

The American private hospital is a convenience for the physician because it saves time and effort to have all his bed patients under one roof, but it is simple torture for the patient. Most patients in a hospital are convalescent, not suffering acutely, and perfectly alert to the comforts of existence. For them, American hospitals, with rare exceptions of which I have heard but never experienced, provide food of a quality and cooked in a way suitable only for a rustic laborer. This is offered to the flighty palate of the invalid, and served at hours that fit the routine of a three-year-old baby. The convalescent is awakened from a refreshing sleep in the middle of the night to behold a breakfast that would make a strong man shudder. At four or four-thirty in the afternoon he is faced with the last meal of the day.

Noise in American hospitals is continuous day and night, and rises to a crescendo at about 11 A.M. Discipline among attendants is sloppy and consideration for the feelings of patients hardly taught at all.

In 1913 the American College of Surgeons began to rate and standardize American hospitals. Particular emphasis was put on available laboratory and X-ray facilities and complete records of the patients. The procedure was doubtless needed at the time, but it has resulted in much unnecessary laboratory work and entailed expense to the patient. One gets impatient at the rigid standardization—as if a competent physician were not capable of determining what laboratory examination his patient needed—but the good result has been that in regard to surgical operating rooms, obstetric delivery rooms, laboratory and X-ray facilities, the American hospital maintains a high order of excellence.

One of the curses of the American hospital system is that it has eliminated the home as a place to be sick. "Be born at home, die at home," was a rule of our grandfathers and is still a good one. In many communities and in many social circles no mother would think nowadays of having her baby at home. Yet it is, in most instances, considerably safer, infinitely more comfortable and indubitably cheaper.

Hospitals grew into prominence when modern surgery developed: and for surgical operations they are still best designed.

Efficiency the American hospital has achieved, but, as is usual in such cases, at the expense of the humanities.

(5) MEDICAL ORGANIZATION AND MEDICAL SOCIETIES. The American Medical Association is the official organization of the American medical profession. It has about 106,000 members, and it admits any ethical physician of good or reasonably good education in the country. As affiliates it has the organized societies of every State, which, in turn, are made up of the integral county societies. The American Medical Association has a Board of Trustees elected nominally at large, but really selected to represent the different sections of the country, and a House of Delegates elected by each State society in numerical proportion.

All of these units have regular meetings—the county societies, weekly or monthly; the State and national society, annually. At these meetings the chief interest is in the presentation and discussion of scientific and clinical research, discovery and experience, but probably more important are the discussions and determination of the policy of the profession as to political, economic and social problems.

Frequently denounced by the outsiders and its enemies as a trust, the American Medical Association is, in fact, an extremely sensible, democratic, enlightened and public-spirited professional organization, without which the public would be in hazardous condition indeed.

Any profession, since it has no trade secrets, obviously should meet together to discuss recent discoveries, to exchange and pool experiences. For this purpose learned societies were established. If the numerical strength of such societies were an indication of progress the United States would, indeed, without argument, be the leader of the world. The American is a natural joiner and the mere list of all the medical societies in the United States would fill two pages of this book in small type.

Among the most important are the two colleges—The American College of Surgeons and The American College of Physicians. Modelled after the English Royal Colleges, they were meant to set an ideal and to honor only men of marked distinction in the two great branches of clinical practice.

Unfortunately, they have fallen far short of such an ideal. The older, the College of Surgeons, was founded in 1913. The original roster showed largely men of real accomplishment. But as soon as the average surgeon found that his superior colleagues were setting up an aristocracy which might discriminate against him, there was a scramble to get on the band wagon. Patients were left to recover by the processes of nature, while all the wires were pulled, and pressure of every kind was brought to bear on admitting the bourgeoisie to fellowship. The pressure proved too strong—every great man has a little friend, every great man has ambitions and votes are necessary, even great men must eat and consultations and good will are never amiss—and the fellowships multiplied until now there are 12,166—12,000 surgeons of extraordinary distinction in the United States?—Or a mob of mediocrities?

The American College of Physicians has suffered much the same fate. It has 3405 fellows! It is true both colleges attempt an examination of candidates. But this has not resulted in any discrimination in their election. The candidates, instead of being chosen for eminence, in most instances propose themselves.

The two colleges are simply two more large, cumbersome, expensive medical societies. The real distinction in the two fields belongs to those who are members of the American Surgical Association and the Association of American Physicians. It is far more of an honor to be asked to read a paper before any section of the American Medical Association at its annual meeting than at the convocation of either college.

It was not really the fault of the governing boards of the colleges that they thus descended into bathos. It is a typical American spectacle. In England, with its sense of caste and the advantage of historical tradition, the royal colleges stand for something. But democracy, whatever its other benefits, does not make for the recognition of excellence.

Nearly every specialty in practice has a special society, and here the membership is far more representative of the best type of American practitioner.

Beyond all this there are several societies of a sort of popular brand. The Southern Medical Society has an enormous roster.

The International Post-Graduate Medical Assembly, among its other activities, arranges rather Babbitt-like junketings to Europe for groups of doctors and their families.

In many cities, annual conferences are held for the profession of the surrounding territory.

All of these drain the importance of the national and State meetings, and, in my opinion, are to be deplored. The reports made at these meetings are almost never of original research, but second-rate rehashings of second-hand materials. A thick air of commercialism hangs about them—back-slappings and forced good fellowship—in short, bids for consultations.

(6) RESEARCH. American medical research is as distinguished as any in the world. Of medical Nobel Prize winners, the United States has had six. And certainly in point of importance, such achievements as the discovery of the specific hormone for the cure of pernicious anemia take precedence over any other in our time save the discovery of the specific hormone for the treatment of diabetes, and the latter we can claim for North America, if not for the United States.

It would be impossible in the space at my disposal to list all the examples of successful American research. But mention must be made of such brilliant studies as Flexner's isolation of the meningococcus and his experimental work in poliomyelitis; the classification by Cole and his associates of the pneumococci; Harvey Cushing's series of studies on the pituitary gland and his pioneer work in the surgery of the nervous system, which latter inspired the investigations of Walter Dandy; the work of Blake, Dochez and the Dicks on scarlet fever; Sauer's whooping-cough vaccine; Francis' isolation of the cause of tularemia; Herrick's clinical observations on coronary thrombosis; and Atwater's invention of the respiration calorimeter.

All these belong to a recent period and form a worthy succession to the great tradition of American medicine, which includes the introduction of anesthesia; the declaration of the contagiousness of puerperal fever; the foundation of the physiology of digestion; the separation of typhoid and typhus fevers; the work of Theobald Smith and of Reed and Carroll on insect vectors in contagious diseases; Fitz's clinical description of appendicitis; O'Dwyer's invention of intubation; and the groundwork of Sims in gynecology, of Sayre in orthopedic surgery, and of Halstead in local anesthesia.

There are a number of institutions or endowments in the United States especially devoted to medical research. The largest is the Rockefeller Institute in New York. The Simpson Memorial in Ann Arbor is dedicated to research on blood disease. The Memorial Hospital for Cancer in New York is practically a research institution. As is the entire Mayo Clinic in Rochester, Minnesota, besides having a special research foundation.

(7) THE ALLIED PROFESSIONS. Dentistry, nursing and pharmacy in the United States—our allies and our friends—maintain the same high standard of training and efficiency as medicine itself.

(8) THE SECTS. America has always been the butt of European, especially English, laughter as the home and fount of quackery and sectarianism in medicine. If one can judge from street signs and newspaper advertisements, however, the British Isles are quite as gullible and quite as plagued as we are in this respect. The only living churches in England today are the Church of Rome and the Church of Christ Scientist, and the latter blossoms quite as vigorously as its more ancient sister.

Still we have to take the rap on the "fount" accusation. Homeopathy we are not responsible for. But Eclecticism, Osteopathy, Chiropractic and Christian Science are our very own.

It is unnecessary to describe here these systems in detail. That has been done, to the Queen's taste, by Doctor Morris Fishbein in his book *Fads and Quackery in Healing*. Homeopathy and Eclecticism have abode their destined hour and passed away. Osteopathy gives every indication of following that historical tradition and joining the company of the lion and the lizard in the courts where Jamshýd gloried and drank deep. The doom of Osteopathy was sounded when the standards of education of osteopathic schools were raised. No man who has been exposed to even a partial medical education is so lost to all sense of decency as to be able to practice such nonsense for long. The osteopath tends to seek a regular M.D. degree and to practice regular medicine. There are only 8000 osteopaths practicing in the United States today.

Between Christian Science and Osteopathy, as well as its bastard offspring, Chiropractic, a distinction must be made. Christian Science is a ritual, a religious system; if any one accepts the tenets of this system —which, as every one knows, is fundamentally that there is no such thing as disease in the world—it explains all external phenomena in its own way and there is no basis for an argument, because if you believe that disease processes follow natural laws, you and the Christian Scientist start at different places.

But Osteopathy-Chiropractic claim to be based on science. And science is demonstrable by experiment and observation. And experiment and observation wreck Osteopathy-Chiropractic.

To be fair to all concerned, including the public, sick people do not usually go to a chiropractor until they have been disappointed in the medical profession. Or else if they go, primarily they go for some obvious "bone" condition. They go because they will try anything for relief. There is a large group of floating patients who have nothing tangible the matter with them, who would be dissatisfied with any kind of medical advice, who find in the vague atmosphere of the chiropractic's explanation a logic which fits their crude mentalities. For all the pother, Osteopathy or Chiropractic or Christian Science does not really interfere, even financially, with regular medicine. The irritation that doctors display towards them is intellectual—like the irritation one displays towards divorce, or the New Deal, or an abhorrent religious doctrine. If any one dies in their hands, that is manifest destiny.

Three other classes of practitioners deserve comment.

*Midwives.* There are 47,000 midwives in the United States. This is an estimate. More than 80 per cent of all midwives are in the South; they are mostly colored women, their education is limited, their superstitions unlimited, and their methods dirty. In such cities as New York and Philadelphia, they are carefully supervised and licensed and capable of giving a highly efficient type of maternity care. Such supervision will have to be extended to all communities where midwives flourish. In the South the scarcity of physicians in rural districts and the poverty of the population make midwives indispensable. They will probably persist for a long time in the South, but elsewhere the number of births they attend is decreasing annually.

*Optometrists.* An *oculist* is a graduate physician who has spent extra time in post-graduate work on a study of the eye. Oculists are well aware that many eye diseases are dependent upon general bodily disease and they are perfectly familiar with those diseases. An *optician* is a manufacturer of eyeglasses: he simply grinds lenses to the oculist's prescription.

An *optometrist* is one of a profession who claims to measure ocular defects. They prescribe glasses and supply them.

There are 20,200 optometrists in the United States. They are not graduates of a medical school. They are trained by a three years' course given in several optometry schools. They pass an examination by a State board and are licensed in most States. But they are not licensed to use medicine (*i.e.,* drugs) of any kind. This is a serious disadvantage because in measuring optical defects accurately the lens of the eye must be put at rest with a drug such as atropine or homatropine. Otherwise it is like trying to measure the length of the inside of an accordion while it is being played.

Oculists are antagonistic to optometry. But the Committee on the Costs of Medical Care stated that there are not enough oculists in the United States to care for all the people who need glasses and that, therefore, optometrists are needed.

Optometrists claim that their training is sufficiently comprehensive that they are able to recognize usual defects that are due to organic disease of the eye and send such patients to a physician. They are very belligerent about it: in my career as a medical journalist I never make even so mild a remark as that a child with a squint should be treated by a trained oculist but that I receive a dozen or more letters of indignant protest from optometrists, over half of them written in bad English and displaying an elementary lack of reasoning power.

I have even been chided by members of my profession in good standing who say that oculists are not interested in glasses or fitting them, do not know much about them, that the optometrists do a better job. It is because of such apologists that I take up so much space with the subject.

The answers to these claims of the optometrists came with a set of investigations reported by Roger William Riis and set down in the *Reader's Digest* for August, 1937.[3] One example was of a Mr. D., an attorney of established reputation, who consented to take part in the investigation. He suffers from major ocular troubles—glaucoma in an arrested state and iritis, and, furthermore, cross eyes. He visited 41 optometrists, in various parts of the country, and got not one single correct diagnosis of his eye trouble. To the patient's exposition of his symptoms of glaucoma and iritis, 12 optometrists made no response at all. Explanations were advanced such as that his troubles were due to the sun and to driving, to shadows on his present lenses, that the cranial nerve got tired, immoral thinking, or the need of eye drops.

In prescribing glasses for him, eight urged the need of expensive frames.

[3]Abstracted by permission without quotes.

Optometrists charge nothing for examination and therefore sell as many and as high-priced spectacles as possible. Of the glasses prescribed by the 41 optometrists, 24 were wrong, 17 could charitably be considered passable.

So much for the optometrists' claims that they recognize organic disease of the eye that cannot be helped by glasses and refer the patient to an oculist.

Another case, reported by Mr. Riis, was of Bessie, aged thirteen, declared by competent oculists to have as nearly perfect eyesight as it is possible to discover. She visited optometrists from Boston to the Rockies; some said she was farsighted, some nearsighted, some that she had astigmatism. One said her eyes were all right. It was evident that most of the optometrists were bent more on selling glasses in expensive frames than in determining the true condition of Bessie's eyes.

So much for the optometrists' claims that they are better fitted to prescribe glasses than the oculist.

Optometry dumps a difficult problem on our hands. If the report of the Committee on the Costs of Medical Care is to be believed, we need some such organization. The question of finances also arises: although in the long run going to an optometrist and buying his expensive frames is probably costlier than going to an oculist, the public doesn't realize it, and they can always, if pressed, select cheaper frames. But it is a typical American scene, with the preference for shoddy, and the astonishing thing is that people will trust of all structures, the most delicate, most sensitive and most cherished organ in the body to a group of inadequately trained spectacle venders. But in this article I am not concerned with remedies.

*Podiatry* is another profession of the same sort, dealing with the feet. Originally, I suppose, chiropody; its practitioners now resent that name.

There are schools of podiatry with a course three years in length, and like the optometrist, the graduates are licensed in most States. They treat all conditions of the feet, not only corns, and prescribe shoes, etc. I regard podiatry with more favor than optometry, partly because the structure they deal with is neither so delicate nor complicated, nor important as the eye, and partly because, especially in the matter of corns, the practicing physician or surgeon is, on the average, far more ignorant than the podiatrist.

(9) SOCIAL ASPECTS OF MEDICINE. The United States has more physicians per capita population than any other country in the world—about

1 to 750. It has been estimated that about 2 per cent of the population is sick at any given hour (not always the same people, of course), so that if distribution were even every doctor would have fifteen patients on his hands every day. Theoretically, if half these patients were treated in charitable institutions, and if the physician collected on the average of three dollars a visit on the rest, his income would be about $7500 a year—a good living wage. The actual figures, as estimated in *The Economic Aspects of Medical Services* (University of Chicago Press, 1933), gives the average gross income at $9000 (net income $5300). The range is between less than enough to meet running expenses to amounts in excess of $100,000 annually. Seventy thousand practitioners, according to the report of the Committee on the Costs of Medical Care, have a net income of less than $4000.

It has been estimated that there are 1500 graduates thrown into the practice of medicine per year, *over and above* the decrement by death or retirement. So it is at least a crowded, even if not an overcrowded, profession.

With such competition it might be thought that the cost of medical service would be low. But it is probably higher than in any other country.

This high cost of medical care presents a real problem. As has been emphasized to the point of surfeitude the poor and the well-to-do get adequate medical care. The middle class in the financial sense suffers the burden of costs they cannot easily afford. At the same time the expense is inevitable: the improvements in medical science—X-ray, laboratory work, surgery, hospitals, trained nurses—are all an immense advance in caring for the sick, but they are costly.

Socialized, or state medicine, has been suggested as a remedy, but the medical profession is very suspicious of it: they honestly believe that the public's interests will not be protected in that way. The personal physician is still the keystone of the public's confidence in scientific medicine. Sick-benefit insurance clubs, which have been tried (with only indifferent success) in Europe, have made little headway here.

The question has been discussed to the point of ennui and I intend to make only a brief personal comment. The real difficulty is that the medical profession has overcapitalized. A good three-quarters of the sickness in the United States is of a simple kind—colds, measles, whooping cough, sprains, infant feeding, pregnancy, etc.—which do not require elaborate tests or apparatus to care for. But the graduates of our medical schools have become so dazzled with the length, intricacy and expense of their education that they scorn to be general practitioners: they all want to be specialists. They set up in elaborate offices with a large overhead, and have to charge high prices to keep going.

The situation is best expressed as Morris Markey did it, in concrete terms. A girl goes to a strange city and is earning $125 a month: she is not an object of charity; she can pay her ordinary expenses. She falls ill. She knows no doctor. Where shall she go? On the other hand, there is available a young doctor, well trained, capable of taking care of her at a fee within her means, who would be glad to get the fee. How are we going to bring those two together?

That is the question the organized medical profession has to solve. As yet they have proposed no adequate answer. I admit I do not know the answer, but I suggest that, slow and painful as it is, the proper one is education. When the young doctor learns that the best way to antagonize people and to starve is to charge high fees, the solution is at hand.

It will not do to say that the problem doesn't exist. I know better. Every day in my mail I receive from one to five requests for me to recommend a good physician in some city with which I am unfamiliar—usually a specialist in some department. Let us say the city is Montgomery, Alabama. Now I can look up in my directory a specialist in that line in Montgomery, but it so happens I am not acquainted with the profession there and my fear is not that I will not name a competent man but that I will name one whose ideas of charges are out of all proportion to the ability of my correspondent to pay. There isn't any use telling me that such a condition doesn't exist because I have had experience. I know men in my own community—competent, but who have no delusions of grandeur about what they should charge: there should be a guarantee that if I select one in the strange city the same principle will obtain, but there is no such guarantee.

Nor can it be said that the profession charges, as they claim to do, in proportion to the ability of the patients to pay. As an instance, I know of two brothers in business together, with about equal and quite adequate means. It happened that within six months' time each had to consult a specialist, one in Los Angeles and one in New York, for the very same thing. Essentially it was a cystoscopic examination: they consulted specialists of comparatively equal eminence. One charged one brother $1500 for service; the other, $150. The circumstances were exactly equal except for the fees. It is by no means an isolated instance.

My prediction is that there will develop a system comparable to our public-school system—a public, State-controlled medical organization open to all, and because that State organization will be inadequate and incompetent for those who can afford something better, there will be private practitioners—just as there are private schools, and for the same reason.

The attitude of the medical profession towards population control is not entirely settled. Legalized abortion they disapprove for the simple reason that it kills people. Contraceptive devices were the subject of a resolution at the 1937 session of the American Medical Association. The conclusions are too complicated to be reviewed here in detail: briefly, following the decision of the United States Circuit Court of Appeals (November 30, 1936), which recognized the legitimate activities of the physician in the teaching of contraception, the teaching of contraceptive technique in medical schools was recommended, as well as that the management of dispensaries and clinics for the purpose of birth control should be in professional hands. There is no legal reason why any physician should not give out information of this kind.[4] Sterilization of unfit males by section of the *vas* and of unfit females by *salpingectomy* is generally approved.

*To summarize:* The practice of medicine in the United States is, at best, in the hands of men of real culture—with enlightened, advanced, humanitarian minds. If in some respects, as indicated above, some vulgarisms and commercialisms have made a place for themselves, that is only to be expected and is not beyond the hope of reform.

[4] I think a question mark should be put in the margin here. The statutes of the different States are not unified and I confess I have not been able to examine them all. The report of the Committee to Study Contraceptive Practices and Related Problems dealt almost entirely with contraception and not with birth control: that is, with the scientific considerations of contraception and the duties of physicians to their individual patients.

# PSYCHIATRY

## [*Karl A. Menninger, M.D.*]

T HE VERY fact that this volume contains a discussion of psychiatry is an indication of the change which has taken place in its content and meaning since the appearance of the previous similar collection of essays describing aspects of civilization in the United States. A thousand years from now some research student seeking for dates that mark transitions may discover this pair of books[1] along with hundreds that have preceded them and will follow them, and he will make a note that "in 1938 there appeared for the first time, in a study of contemporary civilization, a formal representation of psychiatry."

This will seem interesting to him and worthy of note because perhaps by then or long before then what was until 1938 the small esoteric interest in a tabooed and ostracized group of society on the part of a few may have become the mother science of all systematic investigations of interpersonal human relationships.

If such ambitious, if not presumptuous, dreams about the future of psychiatry seem to the reader improbable of fulfillment, let him not forget that even in 1938, psychiatry has been expanded in its scope by discoveries as revolutionary and far reaching as the basic discoveries which have recently revolutionized transportation and sound transmission.

I shall shortly indicate what these discoveries are, but I should point out before discussing them that there is a vast difference in the extent to which they have been assimilated into the life of the man of the street as compared with the mechanical discoveries referred to. In fact, this is probably the most striking characteristic of modern psychiatry. Assume for the moment that my belief is correct that recent progress in uncovering fundamental principles of psychology has been as rapid as the progress in physics and mechanics of the last century, and compare the knowledge of the average citizen with respect to the automobile or the radio with his knowledge concerning psychiatry or psychoanalysis.

It is no objection that the man of the street knows very little of the scientific principles of the radio; the fact is that he knows that radios

[1]The present volume, and Mr. Stearns' earlier symposium, *Civilization in the United States*, Harcourt, Brace & Co., 1922.

exist, that they are available to him, and that they are capable of performing certain functions which make life more endurable for him, and these things the man of the street does not know about psychiatry. The words *psychiatry* and *psychiatrist* are not mentioned in those extraordinary studies of the average American community, *Middletown* and *Middletown in Transition*,[2] not because the authors were unfamiliar with their existence but presumably because they found no evidence of any such familiarity among the people of this community, a community well equipped with radios, automobiles, factories, airplanes, hospitals, and other items of American civilization. And if the authors were to demur to this, insisting that they had not mentioned surgery or obstetrics, either, subjects which the citizens of Middletown undoubtedly know about and utilize as needed, I would reply that this would imply that psychiatry is only a medical specialty whereas, as I hope to demonstrate, the discoveries of psychiatry operate in many fields of human endeavor and show their influence there even if anonymously.

I propose to review the development of psychiatry and then to show how and to what extent it has influenced the content of literature, drama and art, the theory and practice of education, the practice of law and the functioning of industry, the concepts and techniques of sociology and psychology. Finally, I shall indicate its present relation to medicine and its influence upon the science and art of that profession. And I shall return in the end to the paradox that a scientific discipline of such relatively recent development which has already made its mark upon all these phases of civilization remains as yet an enigma or a nonentity or perhaps even a joke to the average citizen.

The art of observing and of seeking to influence the course of mental disorders is not new; it appears as a medical discipline in the writings of Hippocrates (400 B.C.) and competent clinical observations and practical therapeutic techniques had been worked out by the Greeks and were preserved and expanded by the Arabians. In Europe, to be sure, demonology and witchcraft swallowed up the achievements of the early physicians and for many centuries the scientific study of the personality was non-existent.[3]

Slowly, then, and more the result of sentiment and sympathy than of scientific curiosity a new interest was awakened in those long tabooed and persecuted members of society who obeyed inner demands and

[2]Lynd, R. S., and Lynd, H. M. New York, Harcourt, Brace & Co., 1929 and 1937, respectively.
[3]See the excellent historical resumé by Sullivan, H. S.: "Psychiatry." *Encyclopædia of the Social Sciences*. New York, The Macmillan Co., 1937. Volume 6, pp. 578–580.

impulses of a nature inexplicable to their associates, and hence regarded by them as irrational or "insane." These victims differed from those other victims of society, the criminals, in that the immediate objectives of their behavior were less transparent. Society, therefore, took a slightly less hostile attitude toward them but they were left without the pale of scientific study.

When the humanitarians, Dorothea Dix in the United States and comparable figures in each of the European countries, finally succeeded in extending a small measure of the protection and decencies of civilization to these sufferers, the scientists once more turned their attention to a systematic description of the peculiar reactions which characterized their patients' behavior[4] who thus fared far better than the supposedly better understood criminals who remained (and still remain) the scapegoats of society without benefit of science.

These 19th-century physicians worked away patiently with their material and systematically, accurately described what was extremely visible in the patients for whom they cared. They established some fairly dependable designations for certain clinical syndromes. They learned something of the technique of describing behavior and the personality as a whole. They detected some correlation between certain physical and chemical symptoms and certain pictures of gross psychological pathology. They learned some very practical methods of sedation and some important principles of custodial care and they learned to know what to expect in the way of improvement or recession in the development of certain syndromes. And they discovered the relationship of one type of acute mental illness to syphilitic infection and because it was possible to attack syphilis chemically it became possible to cure a few of these forms of "insanity" by chemical means.

As we look back on it there seems to have been a prodigious amount of waste effort in certain directions, but that is bound to be the case on

---

[4]It is quite natural that the earlier affiliations of psychiatry with medicine should have been with neurology on the assumption that mental pathology was the expression of more or less obscure neuropathology. This was the strictly physical viewpoint characteristic of the medical thought of the day. The chemical viewpoint that mental pathology was essentially humoral in origin was represented later by the endocrinological approach. In this we see a new epitomization of an old cycle. For although the earliest conceptions of the personality (Empedocles) were essentially *psychological,* Galen elaborated the *chemical* theory of personality ascribing it even then (170 A.D.) to various internal secretions and chemistry continued to dominate medical concepts of personality for nearly 1700 years. Philosophers (*e. g.,* Kant, 1798) returned to an emphasis upon the psychological aspect of personality but this was not reflected in medicine until much later. Later the *physical* elements seemed more important to the experimentalists and led to such *tours de forces* as the theories of Galton, Lombroso and, more recently, Kretschmer.

any scientific research frontier. A standardized nomenclature developed and, for all the fallacies that naming things introduces, it had the merit of giving us a tentative vocabulary with which to discuss the large masses of data such as were now accumulating. Much of the psychiatry of the early 1900's consisted in efforts to correctly apply these names and establish some basis for a statistical psychiatry.[5]

In the midst of all this effort to correctly name, describe and recognize different forms of the extreme stages of maladjustment, the psychiatrists in the early years of this century were suddenly called upon in a very practical way by the exigencies of the World War. The army medical corps of all countries were well provided with surgeons, but army psychiatrists were unheard of. Such specialists had been left at home to continue to preside over their mediæval castles, the hospitals for the insane. Imagine the astonishment and dismay of the military, therefore, when the psychiatric casualties of many engagements far outnumbered the surgical casualties and it became immediately necessary to obtain some psychiatric facilities and to train a large number of medical men in the elements of psychiatry in order to enable them to handle intelligently these cases developing on the European front. In this way the attention not only of the public but of medical men themselves was directed to the great practical importance of psychiatry. This, in turn, led to a greater interest in psychiatric theory. This interest continued and expanded. Even those medical men who did not themselves engage in psychiatry or limit their professional attention to it began to see in it something other than the mere caring for incompetents and began to think of it as a scientific discipline relative to the study and correction of maladjustment of the individual to his environment.

It is difficult to say just how much of this change in attitude was due to the practical experience of these hastily recruited psychiatrists in dealing with these so-called shell-shocked soldiers. The very designation "shell-shocked" indicates to what extent these cases were at first misunderstood; there were lengthy academic arguments in those days as

[5]Emil Kraepelin deserves the credit for pioneering in this business of naming and describing psychiatric entities in such a way as to afford some points of international agreement. He made many mistakes and in our present mood we should regard him as extremely limited in his depth of vision, but no one can deny his breadth. He saw in a large number of patients certain similarities of onset, course, and duration which led him to define a precocious dementia in contrast to a senile dementia. It took Bleuler to recognize the essential descriptive characteristic of these cases and give them a better name (schizophrenia) and it took Jung, another psychiatrist who had some psychoanalytic training in his earlier days, to understand the forces determining this split-mindedness.

to whether *all* or only *some* of the acute mental illnesses developed in the war were due to minute hemorrhages caused by the shock of expanding gas.[6] That the ego could be so repelled by the horror of the war situation as to repudiate all loyalty to reality seems scarcely to have entered medical consciousness. This seems a little strange in view of the fact that novelists have assumed it to be common knowledge for centuries. The issue was clouded by the fact that in many instances it was not "fair reason" that deserted the afflicted soldier but the use of his legs or arms or voice. These physical expressions of unendurable psychic conflict puzzled the doctors no end and were treated and interpreted in all sorts of ways. The organic explanation to which most of them were committed has already been mentioned; a considerable minority held to an opposite view, that they were all malingerers. This is the conception to which many industrial surgeons had clung doggedly for years but its plausibility declined with great rapidity as experience with the war cases increased. In spite of the fact that these patients would frequently recover suddenly and spontaneously when removed from the danger zone, long continued contact and observation ultimately convinced all but the most obdurate and obtuse that if this were malingering it was unconscious malingering.

After the war ended, the treatment of these cases continued in psychiatric clinics and hospitals and the conviction gradually gained ground that it was actually possible for such a paradoxical phenomenon to occur as unconscious malingering. In this way medical men discovered for themselves what one of them—Sigmund Freud—had been talking about for nearly thirty years, namely, the existence of an unconscious portion of the personality, a reservoir of powers and determining forces of which the individual was only faintly if at all aware.

Recognition of this fact had already revolutionized the conception and treatment of the neuroses on the part of a negligibly small group of physicians who had caught the spark of Freud's brilliant discoveries. This group had already learned from experience and from the mouth of their teacher that human beings do not accept without great resistance the suggestion that a part of oneself is unknown to him. But the experience of the war did much to pave the way for a rapid extension of the corollary implications of the discoveries of Freud including that of the active participation of emotion in disease.

For in their zeal, the doctors who had so carefully examined in vain

[6]We know, now, that none of them were.

the brains and the reflexes and the blood chemistry of innumerable sick patients had forgotten to consider the feelings of these patients, the experiences they had undergone, the strivings in which they were thwarted. They had attempted, in a curious dualistic way, to separate structure and function. One sees this reflected even today in the way in which some colleagues seek to find physical and chemical "causes" for the increased blood pressure of a woman who is struggling against the temptation to kill her huband. Body weight and blood chlorides can be measured in units lodged in the Bureau of Standards at Washington, but temptation cannot. Yet it is as absurd to discard it from consideration as it would be for an engineer to eliminate from consideration the weight of the traffic which a bridge is to bear simply because he cannot measure it but can only estimate it in terms of probability.

The usefulness of the new concepts of psychiatry were increasingly recognized and sought after. For these practical men know that psychiatry is no longer a science of calling strange and incurable diseases by strange and unpronounceable names. The discovery of the unconscious led to the understanding of many previously obscure matters relating to the symptoms of disease and their alleviation. Later as the result of Freud's patient, inspired labors psychoanalysis was born, and this psychoanalysis grew up and married the old, sterile psychiatry and brought forth a new child, who has grown so fast that some of her neighbors—other medical specialties—scarcely recognize her. For the new psychiatry, the psychiatry resulting from the infusion of psychoanalytic knowledge, is no longer a specialty limited to asylums, to hopeless or freakish sufferers from strange or "imaginary" diseases. It has become a specialty in which the motives of human behavior so largely neglected in other branches of medicine have been given the wide recognition as participants in illness, not only mental illness, but all forms of illness.

The war experience had another effect upon American psychiatry.[7] This was a wave of expanded provision for the proper housing of psychiatric patients. State medicine had its first great inning in this field and institutions for the care of as many as ten thousand patients were planned, constructed, staffed and almost immediately filled. Some of the credit for the high plane on which this planning was done should go to the mental hygiene movement, a popular interest in the better care of the insane

[7]Perhaps this is the best place to remark that European psychiatry, that of England excepted, died with the war. Psychiatry in Germany, France, and Italy today is as dead as a dodo, as sterile and mediæval as in 1900. It is too long a story and one beyond our province to outline the reasons for this.

stimulated in the first place by the personal efforts of a single individual, Clifford Beers, who had been disturbed, not by what he saw happening to others as had been the case with Dorothea Dix so much as by what he himself experienced and which he described in his autobiographical book *A Mind That Found Itself.*[8]

The increase of interest in the phenomena of mental disease, the use of the expression *mental hygiene* in various senses apart from its original connotations, the experiences of the doctors in the war—these things all combined to extend the frontiers of psychiatry. The difference between the psychotic, on the one hand, and the eccentric, the disagreeable, the unhappy and the wicked began to be looked upon as one of degree rather than of kind.

"Is it possible," pointedly asked the professor of psychiatry[9] of Harvard Medical School, "that our intense devotion to a philanthropic cause may in some instances be a disorder, rather than an indication of a healthy moral superiority? Is it possible that suspicion of employers and accusations of social injustice may be a disorder, and not the expression of an enlightened and impersonal grasp of economic and social relations? Can raucous patriotism and so-called pacifism be scrutinized in the same way? Is antivivisectionism not altogether to be explained by a surplus of the milk of human kindness in those who level virulent and illfounded accusations at men, working earnestly in the interests even of those who revile them? Is intense intellectual activity, in apparent devotion to the pursuit of abstract truth, sometimes the expression of a disorder, rather than the wholesome activity of a well-balanced personality? Can the blameless and model individual, following smugly in the parental footsteps, be the victim of a disorder consisting essentially in the repression of the most productive elements in the individual's nature? Can the emancipated and unconventional individual, who is expressing his personality to the amazement of his social circle, be the victim of illusion and be really in the throes of a mild mental disorder? Is it possible that many of our beliefs, attitudes, emotions, habits, standards, are not as valid as we have assumed them to be, but are of the same stuff of which mental disorder is made?"

The implied answers to such questions came more and more to be regarded as self-evident and the whole scope of psychiatry began to change as the field of study broadened. Instead of a few miserable quarantined outcasts, the subject matter of psychiatry began to include persons all

[8]New York, Doubleday, Doran. First published, 1908.
[9]Campbell, C. Macfie: *A Present-day Conception of Mental Disorders.* Cambridge, Harvard University Press, 1924, pp. 14–16.

about us. Not only the criminal, the delinquent, and the maladjusted child, but the unhappy housewife, the inefficient business manager, the religious and political enthusiasts became the subject of psychiatric study. Psychiatrists developed the courage to think of themselves as scientific students of personality. It is as if a group of workers in an automobile repair shop from long experience in mending the results of various accidents and breakdowns gradually acquired the audacity to think in terms of the evaluation and improvement of the less obviously damaged car. This led inevitably to a more accurate estimation of the environment with which serious conflict was sometimes encountered. Almost without knowing it psychiatrists began to think in terms of the concept so eloquently cast by a non-psychiatric, non-medical predecessor:

"All of our lives long, every day and every hour, we are engaged in the process of accommodating our changed and unchanged selves to changed and unchanged surroundings; living, in fact, is nothing else than this process of accommodation; when we fail in it a little we are stupid, when we fail flagrantly we are mad, when we suspend it temporarily we sleep, when we give up the attempt altogether we die. In quiet, uneventful lives the changes internal and external are so small that there is little or no strain in the process of fusion and accommodation; in other lives there is great strain, but there is also great fusing and accommodating power; in others great strain with little accommodating power. A life will be successful or not, according as the power of accommodation is equal to or unequal to the strain of fusing and adjusting internal and external changes." (Samuel Butler in *The Way of All Flesh*.)

Such a concept of psychiatry then requires, on the one hand, a scientific methodology for describing the human personality—physically, chemically, and psychologically—and describing it not only in terms of its present state but in terms of its development, its encounters with and readjustments to the more or less unyielding elements of environmental reality. It implies, too, that a careful survey and evaluation of the environment are necessary.

These indeed are the pre-eminent tasks of psychiatry and sociology today. That they are in a state of incompletion, scientists from both groups would be quick to acknowledge. For it is one thing to collect data in large quantities, but it is quite another to put them together in a form that will convey accurately to others something about a personality which careful study has elicited. To say that a man is six feet tall, has sugar in his urine and is afraid to ascend to high places does not describe his personality, nor would his personality be fully described if similar traits were elaborated in great detail, or if so-called diagnostic designations were appended, such as diabetes or acrophobia. For without gainsaying the practical benefits deriving from the introduction of such terms as schizophrenia and manic depressive psychosis (if we confine ourselves to psychiatric nomenclature), it must be admitted that much harm has also been done by these words. I do not refer now to their mistaken application to patients who might have been more successfully treated had they been more correctly classified. I refer rather to the fact that a patient who has been assigned to this or that diagnostic category is so frequently treated as if the category, rather than the patient, determined the treatment.

If our psychiatric designations were something very definite and precise as in the case of syphilis of the eye, for example, advantages might accrue from this. But as yet we have no basis for such a rigid conception of schizophrenia and other psychiatric syndromes and yet the attitude of physicians and the attitudes which they help to build up in the relatives of their patients are often based upon pessimistic conclusions based on the reputation of the named disease as they conceive of it rather than to the actual patient as they discover him to be.

In the sense that it is a summary of the historical and examinational data pertinent to the description of the personality, a diagnosis should certainly embrace decisions or indicate generic relationships with respect to five items: (1) a personality type or structure for which static crystallized terms are as yet, fortunately, lacking; (2) the physical status, expressed in terms established by long experience and usage in medicine; (3) the characteristic psychological reactions, especially to frustration (the psychiatric syndrome); (4) an estimate of the social situation in which the patient lives and of which he is a part—a social diagnosis; (5) symptomatic diagnoses of various kinds which cannot be implied in any of these generic designations.

Such a complex diagnostic summary is far too unwieldy and implies too great a knowledge of the individual for it to be rapidly adopted into scientific medicine, or even into psychiatry. Nevertheless in some such direction our present efforts are heading, for it is certain that now we have learned how to accumulate data concerning personality structure, psychological reactions, and social interaction, we come into possession of more data than we are able to assimilate or to organize and yet without such organization a genuine comprehension of the personality is impossible and hence the communication of a sufficiently accurate picture to others is rendered difficult.

It would be easy to stop at this point, assuming that we had brought the matter to its point of contemporary emphasis with justice to the more important trends. The reader will assume correctly that additional physical and chemical improvements have been made in the therapeutic devices applicable to the more extreme treatment of mental illness. He will have heard of the metrazol and insulin shock treatments for schizophrenia, of more specific endocrine treatments for some depressions, of improved methods of sedation therapy, hydrotherapy, and physiotherapy, of more skillfully applied occupational and recreational therapies. But all these things pale in significance, both as practical agents and as indicators of underlying theory, in comparison with another discovery of Freud's which is the dynamic essence of modern psychiatry. I refer to the scientific study of the emotional linkage determining interpersonal relationships.

It will be recalled that Freud, observing the readiness with which hypnotized subjects responded to suggestion, asked himself why such patients would accept the suggestion of the hypnotist to abandon his symptoms when all the influences of everyday life and of the patient's own wish to get well had been unavailing. He worked for a time in complete ignorance of a satisfactory explanation for this and that only gradually and as a result of many observations did he become aware of what seems obvious and elementary to us now, namely, that the patient accepts such suggestions to get well because he wants to please the physician. To this we should add quickly what Freud discovered only slowly and what his predecessors had never discovered at all, that it is not the physician as such whom the patient wishes to please but some one else whom, for the moment, the physician in some mysterious way seems to replace and to represent. For the genius of Freud showed itself in that, unlike almost every other human being that has ever lived and treated patients and seen this same thing happen, he was not egotistic enough (or else he was too scientific) to allow himself to conclude that there was anything in his own personality which so captivated and compelled the unwilling patient. "Not I, the doctor" (he thought), "but something the patient reads into me is the effective agency." Having already discovered the existence of the unconscious and of repressed memories, it was possible for him to see that the patient was reliving with him an interpersonal relationship which had been incompletely gratified in its original setting. That which had only flattered or frightened other physicians became to him the most important subject of his investigations. The understanding of this principle and of the subsequent discoveries relative to the proper handling of this transference of affect now forms the basis of all effective scientific psychotherapy.

If one looks back to the psychiatry of 1900, or for that matter of 1920, one is aware of this vast difference, that, whereas then the patient and his symptoms were treated as if unrelated to the physician as a symbol of society, today in the evaluation of the personality and its attempted adjustments with society, psychiatry gives primary attention to the nature of the interpersonal relationship, the extent to which it is determined by irrational unconscious elements, the extent to which it is susceptible to modification by interpretation, the way in which it is formed and modified by the prevailing social structure in which the patient lives or has lived.

### The Influence of Psychiatry Upon General Medicine

I have already indicated that psychiatry is in the anomalous stepchild position of belonging to medicine and yet until recently not accepted by medicine. It is one thing to say that psychiatric principles are receiving more consideration by the medical profession than formerly, but quite another thing to demonstrate that the general practice of medicine has been in any perceptible way influenced by this process. Chemistry remains far more important in the theory and practice of medicine than does psychology.

It sounds so glib to describe the earlier orientations and the age-long preoccupations of medical science as chemical that I am tempted to give an illustration to make it more vivid. It is particularly striking when one encounters a case, such as we psychiatrists frequently do, let us say, an intelligent and attractive woman who presents herself with a history of intermittent vomiting of many years duration. Such a patient will have been treated by hundreds of drugs, hypodermics, diets, and repeated abdominal operations. As I am dictating, the names and faces of three or four recent examples of this come to my mind; in one instance four operations had been performed, in another three, in another the patient had acquired a morphine habit. In spite of all these procedures, the symptoms had persisted. Subjected to psychological treatment, such symptoms will sometimes disappear permanently in twenty-four hours. Such sudden, astonishing, "miraculous" cures, when offered by charlatans or ignorant persons, have several times in the past formed the bases of new religions because of their dramatic qualities, but the scientific psychological treatment of such cases is scarcely yet an established method. I was very much impressed by my own father's comments, a man who had practiced medicine with what I am sure was an unusual degree of intelligence and good judgment for many years. He said, "As I look back upon my medical practice before my association with psychiatry, I can think of how many such cases I worried over for months and even years, giving them all sorts of treatments which did them no good and which only made them seem incurable and ungrateful. For many years our only recourse was some kind of drugs; as surgery increased in popularity we turned to that, but with no better results. I cannot quite understand how it was that we did not ever consider the possible psychological factors and the possibility of psychological therapy. But we never did."

That energies can be directed and redirected by physical agencies, we know. That energies can be directed and redirected by chemical agencies, we also know. That energies can be directed by psychological agencies, some of us know and some are still skeptical about. The misdirected energy of a toxic goiter may be corrected by the physical manipulations of the surgeon; it may also be cured by the chemical rearrangements effected by the ministrations of the internist; it may also be corrected (and I mean cured) by the manipulation of psychological forces at the hands of a psychiatrist. These things are so well known to some that it may seem as if I were laboring the point and yet one must reflect that the organization of the American medical teaching at the present time, fine as it is in so many ways, takes very little cognizance of them. There are probably a thousand demonstrations in progress at this moment in the various medical schools, hospitals and clinics of this country, serious and earnest efforts on the part of devoted and high minded medical men to set forth to medical students the physical and chemical facts about— let us say—goiter. Does the reader seriously believe that the methods of observing and manipulating the psychological factors involved in goiter are being systematically presented by as many as a dozen of this thousand?

That psychiatry has come to occupy a much larger part of the teaching time in the medical schools is a matter of statistical record. In at least one of the leading medical schools more actual hours are devoted to instruction in psychiatry than to instruction in surgery. The psychiatric departments of several schools have active co-operation not only with all the other hospital services but with the law school, business school and numerous other departments of the University. In many institutions psychiatrists are now called to the medical and surgical wards for consultations on cases which in previous days would have been regarded as strictly medical or surgical, the psychological aspects entirely disregarded. It is conceivable that by such gradual absorption into medicine, psychiatry will ultimately eliminate itself, and that in the future every doctor will be to some extent a psychiatrist. It would be painting too rosy a picture, however, to say that such a state of affairs appears to be coming to pass immediately. The old physical and chemical concepts still prevail in medicine and dominate it to a degree far greater than psychiatrists like to believe. The chances of the average patient with a mild depression reaching a psychiatrist as a result of medical advice may be, let us say, perhaps one in twenty. The chances of a patient with a psychologically determined physical disease, such as gastric hyperacidity or mucous colitis, reaching a psychiatrist are surely not much better than one in five hundred, if ineed they are that great. This is not because the physicians wish in some way to thwart the psychiatrists or that they do not feel that psychiatrists would be able to help the patients. It is in some instances due to ignorance and in some to prejudice and in still others to practical difficulties such as the relative scarcity of psychiatrists; but in the vast majority of instances, it is because the doctors do not think in psychological terms—it simply does not enter the mind of the average physician that the psychological approach might be as effective as an operation or a dose of medicine or a change of environment. The doctor knows from experience that sometimes these latter devices effect a cure and it usually does not occur to him that it is possible either to discover or eliminate that inner psychological weakness within the patient that makes him susceptible to the peculiar environmental problem, chemical disorder, or physical agent immediately responsible for the symptoms which he calls the disease.

Furthermore, even when it does occur to him, the doctor is almost helpless in the face of prevalent popular prejudices. It requires the utmost tact to introduce to a patient the idea that he himself may be contributing to his present condition, that his illness has some purpose. He would much prefer to believe that fate, circumstance, bacteria, or some mysterious influence present at birth or absorbed from the atmosphere are responsible for his suffering and to believe steadfastly in the magic principles of exorcism as represented for him by the paraphernalia and procedures in the doctor's office. This is not to gainsay the fact that quinine, for example, does kill malarial organisms, but for every dose of specific medicament like quinine there are a thousand doses of medicine consumed in the belief that they will combat these internal afflictions of fate and any attempt on the part of the doctor to substitute something for this kind of magic or for the more spectacular achievements of surgical operations is certain to be met with powerful resistance. Patients want to be dosed and rubbed and cut into. They welcome any evidence that such methods may relieve them and fight valiantly against the surrender of secret fears, prejudices and hates. The development of the psychological concept in medicine cannot proceed very far beyond the slowly changing philosophies and protective ignorance of the general public. Hence for some time to come medicine will be obliged to partake of psychiatry sparingly, perhaps hopefully, but with an understandable conservatism.

### The Influence of Psychiatry Upon Literature, Art and Music

It was Freud himself who pointed out that the poets and philosophers understood the laws of unconscious mental functioning long before they were known to the scientists. Indeed, the works of Freud are best described as a reduction to scientific order of the knowledge about the inner motives of human beings which had previously been vouchsafed only to those gifted with deep intuition, and then in an unsystematized, disconnected and un-teachable form. The masterful psychological studies which comprise the works of Dostoyevsky, Balzac, Poe, Thackeray, and many others were written long before Freud had formulated the principles which they illustrate. It was to some of the early Greek plays that Freud turned for some of the titles which he used to describe characteristic psychic constellations and interpersonal relationships. The plays of Shakespeare and even the musical dramas of Wagner have, along with many other compositions, lent themselves to illuminating psychoanalytic expositions.

Early in the 20th century, however, the first reports of Freud's work having become available, alert authors showed a more prompt response to the implications of these findings than did the scientists. It can safely be said that in 1915, and even more so in 1920, the influences of psychoanalysis were much more apparent in literature and drama than in medicine, the realm of their origin. The plays of Eugene O'Neill alone probably introduced psychoanalysis to more people in the United States than all of the scientific books put together. To be sure, the theory was not always correctly stated or convincingly represented, but the fundamental ideas of conflict, repression, unconscious motives, etc. were vividly portrayed. The same could be said of numerous novels and poems of this period, to list all of which would be difficult as well as tiresome.

Still another tendency in the literature which bore the stamp of direct influence of psychoanalytic methods and discoveries was the style of writing classically represented by Joyce's *Ulysses*. Heralded as a masterpiece by many, and denounced as meaningless and indecent by many others, this large mass of words, phrases, sentences, ideas is written down as if each thought of the speaker or writer had been recorded without any modification arising from a consideration of the listener or reader. This corresponds closely with the material to which the psychoanalyst listens daily in response to his instructions to the patient that every thought be uttered just as it occurs without modification or suppression from any motives whatsoever. Indeed, I have heard many psychiatrists say of *Ulysses,* and similar compositions, that they cannot enjoy it because it is identical with the material to which they must devote all of their working hours. More recently the effects of psychiatry and particularly psychoanalysis upon literature have been less conspicuous and more subtle and appear most definitely in the interpretative biography, fictional or real. Once it was sufficient merely to describe the events in a man's life, the peculiarities of his behavior and environment. Now such descriptive accounts would be considered dull and pointless, and the modern author would attempt to make some connection between the childhood experiences and the adult product. The whole "debunking" tendency which was so popular for a while was a protest against naïve hypocritical representations of people and events without reference to the malignant trends and satisfactions which accompanied them.

Similar stylistic effects have appeared in poetry (for example, that of E. E. Cummings, who attempts to produce a certain effect not only by a certain word and sentence arrangement but by his unconventional punctuation and capitalization). This same principle of a greater freedom has also found its expression in plastic and pictorial art and music. Here, however, it is very much more difficult to relate either the product or the technique to the influence of psychiatry. Its analogy to similar freedom in literature is obvious enough, but it may well be that this is an evolution taking place in art and music depending in part upon intrinsic principles of change and acceptance of symbolic representations and in part upon social attitudes, which, in turn, are dependent upon economic and political as well as psychological factors.

### The Influence of Psychiatry Upon Educational Theory and Practice

In theory, the influence of psychiatry upon education depends upon this —that we now know what was absolutely unknown before, namely, why any child wants to learn anything. Trite as this may sound, search of all the pedagogical treatises prior to 1910 will give the reader no definite information on this point. It was not until Freud pointed out that the child accepts as true statements about reality given him by some one—*i.e.,* by the teacher, only because he wishes to please that teacher—that we gained some insight into the basic psychological principles upon which every school room operates. This is the more curious in view of the fact that in practice the emotional relations of the pupils to the teacher are considered unimportant by-products, sometimes interesting, sometimes annoying, but never worth any consideration. In the light of modern psychological theory, the child turns to the teacher for emotional satisfaction *in loco parentis* and goes about to win such affection in the way prescribed by that teacher. When one reflects that in the primary grades at least the personality of the teacher is of the utmost importance in serving as a model for perfecting the ideal love object of the child, one must be the more disturbed to realize how many unattractive, unlovely, inexperienced and often neurotic men and women are placed in strategic positions. The general custom is to promote teachers to the higher grades and secondary schools and here increase their salaries. It would be more intelligent to reverse the direction of progress from the upper grades to the lower, since the elementary teachers have so much greater responsibility for the formation of the child's personality. Not only should such teachers be the most nearly normal individuals that could be obtained but they should be the best trained and such training should certainly include instruction in those aspects of dynamic psychology which relate to the interaction of human beings upon one another. Such psychological principles, although basic, have no currency at present except in psychiatry, which is another way of saying that the tendency is to wait until the child becomes impossible before any effort is made to find out how he thinks and feels about his teacher, his parents, his siblings and others. Such an investigation the average teacher is incapable of making or even of understanding. I owe to the professor of education at one of our universities the suggestion that this training in mental hygiene or psychiatry or the psychological understanding of children or whatever it be called should be one of the fundamental studies of primary teachers instead of one of the subjects of which they are usually completely ignorant.

The use of professional psychiatrists or clinically trained psychologists in the solution of emotional difficulties and behavior disorders suffers from this same fault, the fault of concentrating upon the older children to the neglect of the younger ones. As we shall see presently, many college students have available to them at least some professional psychiatric counsel, but this is true of very few school children.

The behavior problems of the average school child are still treated in most places with a mixture of political expediency, conventional hypocrisy and so-called "common sense." This prevails generally, but there are many exceptions. In several large cities there are psychiatrists attached to the board of education, or psychiatric clinics available to school children which provide for handling such cases upon a more scientific basis. In some cities psychologists function in a somewhat similar capacity. The net result of this is that the *poor* children in the schools of the *larger cities* whose capacity for adjustment is exceeded by unfortunate environmental requirements to the extent of developing various kinds of emotional or behavior problems are likely to receive intelligent scientific treatment. The well-to-do children, however, attending private schools receive, as a rule, no such help and the same is to be said of children in the average middle-sized towns of the country. It is difficult to render this in any statistically accurate way but let us take two very representative middle western states, Kansas and Missouri, situated in the center of the United States, one containing some of the most literate rural population of the country, and the other two of the large, wealthy and in many ways progressive cities of the country. In some of the towns and cities of this large and populous area the boards of education have employed visiting teachers to investigate the home situations of problem children, psychologists to study the peculiar learning disabilities of certain children, and in one or two instances, psychiatrically trained social workers for similar purposes. There are very few of these but they do exist and the nature of their work is essentially psychiatric in the generic sense. But in not a single town or city in either Kansas or Missouri is there any actual professional *psychiatric* supervision of this work or any consultation service for the problem children in the schools. This is through no lack of facilities; within the borders of these two States there are three child guidance clinics, two schools for maladjusted children, several schools for feeble-minded children, forty or fifty psychiatrists in private practice and a larger number in state practice, and a number of psychiatric clinics, to say nothing of three medical schools, five or six universities and a half a hundred colleges, in most of which abnormal psychology and psychological principles relating to adjustment problems of childhood are studied and taught. And lest anyone suppose that this is some peculiar backwardness of Kansas and Missouri, I can assure them that with the exception of New York and Massachusetts, the names of almost any other two states in the Union could be substituted for these two.

I seem to have veered around to a demonstration not so much of the application of psychiatry to education as to a lack of application. The situation in colleges and universities is quite different. In perhaps a hundred schools in the United States there are now well established counselors in mental hygiene, devoting their energies to special problems of college students. Many other colleges have expressed an interest in obtaining similar services, but here a practical difficulty is encountered in that the supply of men properly trained for this function is yet small. Eleven years ago the dean of one of the oldest and most famous institutions in the country said "The advance of mental hygiene in colleges and universities has come with such rapidity in the last five or ten years that it is no longer progressive to have an expert in mental hygiene on the staff, and to give as respectable a place in the curriculum to mental as to physical hygiene. It is reactionary *not* to do these things."

An intangible effect of psychiatry upon education which cannot be estimated but is probably more widespread and more influential than more obvious expressions mentioned is the insidious change in teachers' attitudes derived not so much from any formal psychiatric experience or from exposure to any particular psychiatric institutions but rather from the combination of the psychiatric influences of literature, the mental hygiene movement, the writings of numerous popular psychologists, the implications of speakers on political and economic topics, etc. Some years ago a psychologist (Wickman) compared the attitudes of a group of teachers and a group of psychiatrically trained persons—psychologists and others—toward certain characteristic schoolroom behavior, and the teachers were shown, in general, to attach great significance to behavior which psychiatrists regarded as less serious, and to put less value on behavior which psychiatrists considered most serious. I think if such a test were conducted today in the average school, there would be much less discrepancy. Teachers have come to learn that unuttered hostility, seclusiveness and extreme quietness, convenient as they may be from the standpoint of schoolroom administration, are not evidences of the greatest mental health. The severe discipline has almost entirely disappeared from the schools. (I submitted this statement to Professor Bert Nash of the department of education of the University of Kansas. "I believe," he commented, "that you are a little optimistic here. There has been some improvement but psychiatry has not affected the teachers in rural areas and smaller towns much. The larger areas usually have better qualified teachers and more supervision by supervisors trained in the mental hygiene aspects of these problems. The superintendents and principals in many small towns are not up with many of the teachers.")

## The Influence of Psychiatry Upon Legal and Criminal Procedures

Psychiatry has a natural interest in aberrant behavior, whether the aggressiveness is directed upon society or directed upon the individual himself. The law is particularly interested in the former. The law aims at a proper protection of society from certain individuals; but traditionally it has based its procedure upon so-called "common-sense" principles, many of which run counter to modern scientific findings. Logically, the law should revise its attitude, borrowing from psychiatry such knowledge and techniques as will increase the protection afforded the public. In theory, law, criminology and penology have made these revisions. The American Bar Association (with the American Psychiatric Association and the American Medical Association) formulated and unanimously adopted resolutions to the effect that every judge hearing a criminal case should have at his disposal a psychiatric opinion concerning the accused and that this person's subsequent disposition should depend upon such a psychiatric examination; they even went further and indicated that the detention of such a prisoner in a prison and his subsequent discharge should be determined by scientific personality studies instead of by statute book prescriptions, political expediency, etc. But in practice very few of these principles have been followed. The contrast between the new-fashioned theories and the old-fashioned practices in criminal administration is astounding. The practical application of psychiatry is used in a few places, such as at Sing Sing prison in New York and in a number of courts and prisons in the State of Massachusetts, to a greater or lesser extent; but in 99 per cent of the courts of the United States psychiatry still remains something to be invoked by an occasional prisoner as a means of obtaining mitigation or suspension of sentence on the grounds that his behavior was based upon sickness and not upon normal human instinctual expression. A respectable married merchant of forty-two eminently successful in his business suddenly comes before the court charged with having sexually molested several twelve-year-old girls. He is arraigned for trial. The judge becomes involved with such technical questions as whether rape or only attempted rape is the charge to be entertained, whom to admit to the courtroom, whether certain witnesses are competent, etc. An occasional judge will wish to protect the subsequent proceedings of the court by obtaining a preliminary "sanity" hearing. A commission of local medical men is appointed and these gentlemen are called from the surgical operating rooms, from the rounds of general practice and from the halls of the nearest state hospital to pass upon the question of whether or not the accused man is "sane." The question of why a man of forty-two should wish to derive his sexual satisfaction in this strange way, the question of how this man's life has gone awry to produce this result, the likelihood or rather unlikelihood of the court proceedings and the penitentiary sentence affecting this proclivity favorably or unfavorably, never seem to enter any one's mind, least of all the judge's. If a psychiatrist is called he is not allowed to say how such an affliction might be successfully treated; he is condemned to attempt to swear that the man's condition does or does not conform to something which seventy-five years ago was called insanity.

Psychiatry has touched the law to this extent—that if the offender is young enough, the offense not too flagrant and if the family has money, the case can probably be settled out of court and the offender placed under psychiatric treatment. Psychiatrists deplore this abominable situation as much as any one, but it is not something they can change.

### THE INFLUENCE OF PSYCHIATRY UPON INDUSTRY

Twenty years ago when psychiatry was first recognized popularly as a science of evaluating and correcting personality disorders, Ernest Southard proposed that no one should be able to make more practical use of it than those industrialists whose labor turnover was a source of large expense. "Why are men discharged?" he asked. Examination of typical records shows that the same behavior disorders for which we treat people in the clinic serve to bring them into disfavor with their employers. Would it not be logical, he said, to apply our methods to these problem employees just as we apply them to problem children in the schools or problem housewives in the home?

The suggestion was promptly taken up by a number of large organizations and put to some fruitful use. Various books were written reporting the good results of the experiment but the practice has not spread. On the contrary, there has been a recession. All the factors determining this I could not attempt to list but among them one would certainly include the changed attitude of labor and capital toward one another, a decrease in the paternalistic attitude of employers. Another reason, I think, lies in the greater adaptability of various quantitative psychological tests to the selection of employees. The selection of ten good employees by appropriate psychological tests can be made at less expense than the psychiatric examination or rehabilitation of one employee about to be discharged. This is one of the reproaches of the capitalistic system which is interested in the product and not the producer. But it should be added that this lack of scientific treatment of the worker is furthered by the attitude of labor itself, which suspects all psychiatry and applied psychology of being devices for further exploiting the worker.

A reason even more fundamental than these is to be inferred I think from an experience I had many years ago. The president of a manufacturing corporation who had received some personal benefit from my services became so enthusiastic over the application of psychiatry that he went with me to New York to study its application to industry with the avowed purpose of introducing it into his plant. Upon our return he had me spend several days surveying his plant in operation and getting acquainted with numerous key employees. Then he called a meeting of the board of directors and outlined what he had in mind. I, properly assisted, was to examine every employee from the president to the janitor, noting such evidence of maladjustment as might require some special management. Most of the directors agreed wholeheartedly. One of them, however, protested violently. The president was somewhat crestfallen to meet with this opposition and action was deferred until he could ascertain the special reasons back of the opposition and win over the dissenter. In this he was totally unsuccessful, for reasons which he did not fully understand until long afterwards. The dissenting officer was at that very moment carrying on an intense feud with another man in the corporation whom he was ultimately successful in ousting. Scores of the employees were involved in this, and while discretion prevents the citation of details, I may give it as my opinion that enormous losses of money and of efficiency in this company were due to the psychopathology of this official who blocked the plan of psychiatric service in an industry rather than have his remissness detected.

### The Influence of Psychiatry Upon Sociology

Between the fields of sociology and psychiatry, both of them relatively new sciences, there has always been a close practical affiliation with a wide theoretical separation. This is precisely the opposite situation of that which exists between psychiatry and criminology. Psychiatric and criminological theories overlap hugely, but in actual practice, as I have indicated, psychiatry and psychiatrists are but little used in court and prison. Sociology however, until recently, considered the psychological vagaries of the individual to be factors of relative unimportance, negligible errors so to speak. Its chief attention was upon the accurate description of mass phenomena, of large social movements, conditions, attitudes, and preoccupations. There was, to be sure, a counter movement in the direction of the Carlylean theory of hero leadership, a theory that had more popular than scientific support. Hitler, for example, was the clever psychopath who happened to achieve a position of power where he could then inflict his psychopathic notions and ambitions upon a helpless and pliable German people. Napoleon was another such a moulder of men and events.

Lasswell of Chicago helped to destroy this idea by giving it further scientific scrutiny. He demonstrated[10] by a psychological analysis of numerous major and minor politicians how the careers, the methods, the ideology of political "leaders" had been determined by their own pathological childhood experiences. In so doing he guided sociological thinking toward the recognition that similar and reciprocal psychopathological trends exist in those whom these men "chose" to lead.

The increasing trend of sociology seems, therefore, to lean toward the old subject matter viewed from a new angle. If I, who am not a sociologist and not in intimate contact with the thought of that profession, can estimate it, the trend of sociological thinking is toward a study of the way in which accumulated, reinforced thinking and feeling of the community interact with the thinking and feeling of the individual. Just as the psychiatrist has realized that he cannot study any patient irrespective of the social environment to which that patient has had to adjust himself, so the sociologist has come to realize that he cannot study that mass without some idea of the individual units which comprise it. Individual problems reflect themselves in the social structure, and in turn are affected by the community mores.

[10]Lasswell, Harold D.: *Psychopathology and Politics.* Chicago, The University of Chicago Press, 1930.

One might say that the rise of social psychology is a reflection of these tendencies. It is an indication of the dissatisfaction of psychology with the assumption that human reactions are determined entirely within the individual and a dissatisfaction on the part of sociology with the assumption that mass acts without any individual psychic determinants. Up until 1908 there was only one modern textbook on social psychology; today texts and treatises appear almost as frequently as do those on sociology and psychology themselves. Two journals devote themselves exclusively to this field.

If this summary seems incomplete, let me assure the reader that the present relations of psychiatry and sociology are as awkward and groping as the first meetings of a brother and sister who have not seen each other for twenty years. Psychiatrists write articles and caution fellow psychiatrists not to psychoanalyze society, but to remember that society is not the same as an individual. Sociologists write articles and caution their fellows not to ignore the importance of the psychology of the unconscious since the efforts of every individual must to some extent influence the whole mass. Writers of serious articles make brave statements like this, "It has been demonstrated that there is a relation between social and personal disorganization." The recent appearance of a number of the *American Journal of Sociology* devoted entirely to articles by psychiatrists and sociologists dealing with the problem of the relationship of the two sciences shows the present tendencies of rapprochement.

In general, the present impression seems to be that we should regard psychiatry as the microscopic and sociology the macroscopic study of the gregarious life of the human being. Exactly how much the nature of the relationship between its constituent elements, the interpersonal relations, is determined by internal needs of individuals, and how much by certain external conditions which have been in part determined by previous expressions of individual psychology is at the present time a matter of conjecture.

### The Influence of Psychiatry Upon Psychology

Psychology means so many things that one must begin by defining the sense in which it is used in this caption. Psychiatry is, after all, according to my lights, a medical science with a proper inclusion of the psychological factor in our concepts and techniques. It is, in short, the result of the influence of psychology upon medicine. When we speak, therefore, of the influence of this clinical science upon one of its mother disciplines, the basic science of formal psychology, what we really do is to measure to what extent the concepts of mind and mental processes have been modified by clinical observations. The union of psychology with the rest of medical science was a fruitful one and brought forth many new ideas, new discoveries, new points of view, which in turn have fructified academic or formal psychology. The older psychology devoted itself largely to the study of how we become aware of the world about us, the faculties of perception and cognition as they were called. These bore a well-established relationship to anatomical facts, to nerve trunks and brain areas, and it was possible to introduce experimental and quantitative methods, not only in regard to the rapidity of the processes of recognition and association but as to capacities of memory and grasp. This gave rise to two important developments in psychology, the experimental projects in the laboratory, and quantitative clinical applications in the form of intelligence tests and performance tests.

Increasingly, however, under the influence of psychiatry and particularly of psychoanalysis, the trend in psychology has been away from these quantitative estimations and perceptions, away from the experimental laboratory and the "brass instrument psychology" of the early part of the century in the direction of more qualitative studies of the emotional processes. Interest and intelligence tests have given way to a greater interest in tests which show not so much static achievement as dynamic striving, *e.g.,* the Rorschach rather than the Binet has been the instrument of examination. This in turn has influenced the former concepts of perception and cognition; we no longer assume, as was formerly believed, that the Intelligence Quotient remains fixed and invariable throughout life, independent of the external conditions. In addition, experimental procedures relating to the particular way in which intelligence determines emotions and behavior have been developed at Harvard (Murray), Yale (Homburger), Topeka (Brown), and elsewhere.

In other words, psychologists, partly under the influence of psychiatry, became interested thirty years ago (1905) in measuring certain capacities in the individual which we call intelligence. Under the further influence of their contacts with psychiatry, the clinical interest extended to the investigation of the emotional processes which lay behind this intelligence.

If one looks at a representative psychological textbook of twenty-five years ago, that of William James, for example, and compares it with a modern text on psychology, one will see that the whole problem of the emotional factor and motivation which formerly received scant attention, perhaps a brief discussion at the end of the book, has now become the basic portion of the modern textbook. Encouraged by co-operation with psychiatry and by utilizations in psychiatry of different discoveries, psychology has paid increasing attention to what was formerly called abnormal psychology. The very title shows under what difficulties the subject matter formerly labored; of course there can be no such thing as abnormal psychology any more than there is an abnormal physics or an abnormal chemistry. There are, rather, phenomena which are unusual and which do not seem to conform to the rules which ordinarily determine human reactions, and these have been called abnormal. If psychology is a science, however, it cannot be a thing apart from the laws that determine all psychological processes, but it must be the product of certain less usual or less advantageous combinations of forces.

With an eye to reducing behavior and psychological reactions to general principles capable of more adequate scientific formulation, the school of Gestalt psychology has recently developed. Frustration and disappointment are important factors in human behavior and empirically it is possible to estimate roughly some greater or lesser disappointments, and certain types of deviation in the response to such disappointments. But theoretically it ought to be possible to measure the amount of frustration more exactly and to introduce the various factors which determine the peculiar individual response to frustration that one observes in any particular type of situation. It requires the erection of a defined field of operation and a description both in terms of direction and in terms of quantity of the modifying forces of inhibition, stimulation, deflection, exaggeration, disguise, etc. The great difficulties and complications of this task have so discouraged some as to make them intolerant of the method; others, however, have hopes that this is the beginning of a more accurate statement of the basic principles of psychology. Brown has shown that Gestalt psychology has many aims and methods in common with psychoanalysis and it is certain that they have been of reciprocal value to one another.[11]

In summary, psychology, one of the parents of modern psychiatry, has been reciprocally enriched and reanimated by the developments of its child. It continues to be the basic science related to the investigation of certain aspects of biological phenomena we call mental with an increasing scope of activity, and an increasing interest in the dynamic forces back of behavior.

[11]Brown, J. F., *Psychology and the Social Order*. New York, McGraw-Hill, 1937.

### The Influence of Psychiatry Upon Religion

As in so many of the previously discussed fields of activity, the influence of psychiatry upon religion has been both direct and indirect, manifest and subtle. Of its subtle influences and those derived from the increasing popularity of science generally I shall not speak because to do so would involve an elaborate discussion of the function of religion and the relation of religious theory to religious practice for which I am not qualified.

On the other hand, it is not difficult to observe many direct and undisguised influences of psychiatry upon religious conceptions and activities and of these I may speak briefly. It was under the religious influences of a church that certain very definite and helpful experiments in psychotherapy were begun very early in the 20th century. These progressively minded ministers and physicians had the impression that there was a wide border area between medical science and formal religion which could be approached through some co-operation to the benefit of persons suffering from diseases of the soul manifested by illness of the body. These experiments met with prejudice from two standpoints: first, from the standpoint that psychiatry properly conceived should include a consideration of so-called disease of the soul and should do so without theories about the supernatural; secondly, from the influence of the charlatanry and intellectual dishonesty of some of the adherents of Mary Baker Eddy. It is perfectly true that some of the prejudice which medical men have against Christian Science has arisen from the fact that this over-reaction against the materialism of medicine and of civilization in general resulted in the disappearance of many neurotic symptoms in some of its believers and this success reflected upon the physicians and their abilities. However, the most fair-minded physician could not but have misgivings about the empirical and pragmatic benefits to be derived from fooling people, even if such deceptions led to an appearance of health. To put it in another way, conscientious medical men, entirely aside from their professional prejudices, might well have their doubts about the desirability of substituting an artificial psychosis for a naturally acquired neurosis, even though the latter may have been the more painful.

Psychiatry struggled valiantly against confusion with Christian Science for many years and there are still some reputable medical men who refer patients to Christian Science practitioners rather than to psychiatrists, not because they prefer the former, but because they are more numerous and more available and better known to the public.

Gradually the distinction between psychiatric principles utilized in religious work, and the distortion of psychological principles under the guise of a religion became more definitely differentiated in the public mind. It seems to me that now neither the scientists nor the religionists (I do not mean the Christian Scientists) are quite so proud of their authority or quite so certain of their absolutism. There seem to be increasing evidences of *rapprochement* between them. The most conspicuous evidences have been the appearance of numerous books,[12] some of them by ministers and some of them by psychiatrists, dealing with the problems of the minister from the psychiatric standpoint. If one assumes that the avowed purpose of both religion and psychiatry is to make men more comfortable, then it is natural that the leaders of those professions should exchange views. And since the views of the ministers have been for so many centuries more or less common knowledge and the views of the psychiatrists relatively unknown it is natural that the didactic information should now come more largely from the psychiatrists.

In addition to what might be called manuals of instruction which purport to give the minister some scientific information about the nature of the personality as psychiatrically conceived, the characteristic forms of adjustment aberrancies, and some conception of the technique of effecting changes in individuals as the result of personal contacts, there has been some scientific research with respect to the precise nature of the function of religion as it can be discovered in the lives of individuals obliged for therapeutic purposes to submit themselves to thorough analysis.[13] Furthermore, there has been an increasing number of books written by ministers giving the results of their own efforts to absorb psychiatric principles and apply them to the tasks of ministerial functions.

It is true that some ministers have regarded the psychiatrists as anti-Christs, but this cannot be said to be the attitude of the majority; rather it can fairly be said that the ministers have been more open-minded toward psychiatry than have the lawyers. This open-mindedness has led to certain complications, especially that of lay therapy which has also been a problem with the psychologists. If anything, the ministers have a rather stronger position here than have the psychologists, since they can logically invoke the authority and assistance of divine forces. In short, the minister can say, "It is my duty and my pleasure to counsel my parishioners, happy

[12]See, for example, Oliver, John Rathbone: *Psychiatry and Mental Health: the Hale Lectures at Western Theological Seminary,* 1932 (New York, Charles Scribner's Sons, 1932).

[13]See, for example, Boisen, Anton T., *The Exploration of the Newer World: A Study of Mental Disorder and Religious Experience.* Chicago and New York, Willett, Clark & Co., 1936.

or unhappy, sick or well. If my faith and the faith of my parishioner in God means anything at all, it should mean something from which to draw comfort and reassurance. Such comfort and reassurance should not be denied to those who suffer from fears of unreal menaces, nor from those who suffer from pains ascribed to nonexistent organic diseases. And, if, as the psychiatrists say, transference is an instrument of highest therapeutic efficacy, surely a minister in whom a parishioner puts his trust and in whose integrity he believes and with whom he shares a common faith should be one most likely to be psychotherapeutically helpful to him. If, as scientists have declared, relieving oneself of certain hate and other undesirable mental attitudes serves to relieve one of depressions and even of physical illnesses, is it not logical that the minister or priest whose ideal it is to dispel hatred applies this gospel in a therapeutic way?"

Some ministers have bravely accepted this challenge and have set themselves up more or less definitely as ministers to the minds of their parishioners no less than to their souls. Others have preferred to organize within the church mental hygiene clinics or institutions of similar intention presided over by a psychiatrist under the auspices of the church and with the blessings and often the active participation of the minister.

At first it might seem very narrow indeed for psychiatrists to make objections to such worthy purposes, carried out in the main by such high-minded, intelligent and conscientious men. It is only fair to say, however, that the objections of psychiatrists have a validity which commends itself to many other ministers. In the first place, it should be remembered that while it is true that transference is a powerful therapeutic instrument, it is also true that the use of it requires long training and expert skill and that its mismanagement is apt to cause much distress to all parties concerned. Many an embarrassing situation has arisen through ignorance of the basic principles involved in the correct management of transference; in plain language, many a minister who has begun by wishing to help a parishioner has ended by being dismissed from his church for complications over which he ultimately found that he had no control whatever. Again, it should be remembered that a minister is without training adequate to enable him to make a differential diagnosis. Relinquishing one's envy of a sister under the inspiration of a minister may indeed cure a neurotic headache, but it will not cure a headache arising from an incipient uremia or brain tumor and may postpone the recommendation of a proper treatment until too late. And, finally, there is the objection that most ministers have too many other things to do. Therapeutic treatment

·of individuals is a time-consuming task of vast proportions, and a minister who turns psychiatrist in function would best turn psychiatrist in training and in profession.[14]

Nevertheless, what I have cited is sufficient to indicate how increasingly formal religion has become interested in the application of the scientific principles of human personality and to those functions which it performs by virtue of inspiration and faith. To what extent psychiatry will replace religion is problematical; the writer's own opinion is that religion will long continue to supply the healing of the nations to a far greater extent than will psychiatry. One might say that psychiatry will continue to do for the individual what religion has endeavored to do and to some extent succeeded in doing for the masses.

## CONCLUSION

We return at last to the question as to why the theories, principles and discoveries that are massed under the general term *psychiatry,* the healing of the mind, should have so profoundly affected these diverse expressions of human thinking and human activity with so little awareness on the part of the majority of American citizens. The discoveries of Einstein, immensely more difficult of comprehension and of practical application, were such as to make his name familiar to every literate American citizen within a few years. The acclaim with which his discoveries were met is in startling contrast to the blankness, sneers or suspicion which still greet the name of Sigmund Freud in many quarters, and the general ignorance about him and his work which prevails generally.[15] Both have been classed with Aristotle, Plato, Leonardo, Columbus, and Newton but such a classification does not linger in the public mind so far as Freud or any other psychiatrist is concerned. Why should there be this enormous contrast? Why should the man in the street struggle to understand the principle of relativity which in no way concerns him and revere the man who discovered or emphasized it, but shut his eyes to material which concerns his own life, the structure of his own personality, his failures and successes, his strengths and weaknesses? Clearly there is a resistance to the acceptance of such unpleasant information and unpleasant it would seem to be to the average person. Freud himself first showed us why

[14]See Chapter VI, Religious Applications of Psychiatry in the writer's *The Human Mind.* Revised edition. New York, A. A. Knopf, 1937.

[15]I realize of course that intelligent people the world over know about Freud, know something of the nature and importance of his work and in many instances regard him very highly. The fact remains, however, that he has never even been considered for a Nobel prize, he holds no professorship, he has had nothing like the popular acclaim that has met Einstein and Madame Curie.

psychiatry would always be unpopular although he also reminded us that the formulations of Galileo and of Darwin met with a similar resistance, traces of which are still observable.

It would not be accurate to fail to mention the fact that psychiatry has not always had the best of representatives, that it has not been possible to separate it in practice from the cloying restrictions and adulterations of politics, economics and human inertia. Psychiatry has suffered as have all rapidly developing modern sciences from an archaic and often terrifying vocabulary, partly for the reason that we are tied by tradition to the misconceptions of the earlier workers and partly because the structure of our language is inadequate to cast in verbal form the subtle configurations and interrelationships of our data. Again, the over-enthusiasm of a few whose hopes had been stimulated to new heights by the startling discoveries of psychiatry likewise brought about some disappointments and, perhaps, occasional confusion. The proverbial conflict of opinion within the ranks of psychiatrists and psychoanalysts has weakened the interest and the faith of some who felt that those best acquainted with the human instincts and patterns of behavior should be the most successful in avoiding their untoward expression.

The fact remains, however, that psychiatry in the modern sense has already definitely and in some ways prodigiously affected the life of every American citizen, whether he knows it or not. It is to be expected that it will continue to exert its effect in two directions: first, in its therapeutic application to those who suffer or cause their environment to suffer unduly; and, second, in the molding of our conceptions of the purposes and methods of living and of influencing those with whom we must live.

The psychiatry of 1938 is an organized science, art, and profession linked in a three-way combination with medicine, psychology, and sociology. It is a branch of medicine, a branch in which the psychological factors in human characterology are given more recognition and consideration both in diagnosis and in treatment than is the case in the routine practice of the internist, obstetrician, or surgeon. Such psychological emphasis, however, cannot ignore the psychology of the rest of the human environment, since no patient lives in a vacuum or on a desert island. In this way psychiatry is, very naturally, and properly, bringing sociologists, psychologists, and physicians closer together and from this there would appear to be evolving at the present time a new concept of human beings. The essence of this new concept in its broadest sense is that human beings possess a physical and chemical and psychological structure partly self-determined, partly socially determined. This is most apparent in the psychological factor but it, in turn, modifies the physical and chemical reactions of each individual. It is not a question of whether we should think of society as being made up of individuals or of individuals as making up society. It is imperative that we be able to think both ways simultaneously. In doing so we realize that we have much to learn as to the exact nature of the interpersonal relationships linking the parts of the whole, concerning which we have only begun to think scientifically. But that we have begun to think of this is characteristic of psychiatry in 1938.

# BIRTH CONTROL AND POPULATION

*[Hannah M. Stone]*

THE SMALL family system is rapidly becoming an accepted
social pattern in the United States. The parents of today are
having fewer children than their parents or grandparents. According to the 1930 census report, the average present American family totals only 3.81 persons. The rapidity with which the family
size has decreased, the causes which have brought it about, and the influence which it is bound to exert upon the future of our social and cultural
development constitute a most interesting chapter in the story of contemporary American civilization.

The American birth rate began to fall over a century ago and some
concern over the decreasing size of the family found expression as early
as the middle of the 19th century.[1] In 1868, for instance, Allen,[2] a New
England obstetrician who was much interested in the problem of population, pointed out that while the early settlers of New England averaged
eight to ten children per family, the second and fourth generations averaged seven to nine, the fifth and sixth only four to five, and the current
(1868) generation averaged only three children. Similarly, an editorial
in *The Medical Record* (March 1, 1872) observed that "practitioners in
New York and vicinity tell us that they found not more than an average
of three children in a family." The concern at that time, however, centered more around the fact that the "native stock" was being outnumbered by the foreign-born than around the general birth decline
in the country.

The fall in the birth rate did not of course imply an actual decline in
the population. On the contrary, due to a concomitant marked reduction in the death rate and to immigration from other lands, the American
population continued to increase rapidly. From some five and a half

[1]Spengler, Joseph J., "Notes on Abortion, Birth Control, and Medical and Sociological Interpretations of the Decline of the Birth Rate in Nineteenth Century America." *Marriage Hygiene*, August,
1935.

[2]Allen, Nathan, "The Law of Human Increase." *Quarterly Journal of Psychological Medicine*,
April, 1868.

million in 1800 it grew to 76 million in 1900 and to 123 million in 1930. Calculations showed that if the American population were to continue increasing at the rate which prevailed in the '20's, it would double within a period of some 60 years. Hence it was that a decade or so ago economists and sociologists expressed much more anxiety over the dangers of overpopulation than over the decline of the birth rate. The Malthusian viewpoint that man tends to increase faster than the means of subsistence was re-emphasized at that time by a number of writers, and calamitous results were predicted for mankind unless the rate of reproduction were reduced by voluntary control.

But the birth rate in the United States, as well as in all western European countries, continued to fall. From 23.7 births per thousand of population in 1920 it declined to 18.9 in 1930 and to 16.6 in 1936. As the death rate during this period remained practically stationary at about 11 per thousand, and as immigration was materially curtailed, the rate of population growth slowed down very markedly during the last decade. Some population authorities now claim that with the present trend our national growth will cease altogether within 20 to 40 years and that instead of increasing, the population will then become stationary or even decline in numbers. As a consequence, instead of concern about overpopulation, considerable anxiety is today being expressed over the possibilities of underpopulation. First in western Europe, where the problem is much more acute because of its political and military implications, and more recently in America, articles and books have been appearing in increasing numbers dealing with the dangers of the declining rate of reproduction and the "menace of depopulation." The population question of today is quite different from what it was a decade ago, and we may now be on the verge of a new orientation in our population policies.

The possibilities inherent in the declining natality will be given some consideration later on. For the present we shall inquire briefly into the causes that have brought about the decrease in the size of the family and the factors that have been responsible for the rapid fall in the American birth rate.

Some have maintained that the present small family is due in part at least to an actual decrease in the capacity for reproduction. Men and women of today, it is claimed, are physiologically incapable of reproducing at the rate of their parents, and the declining birth rate is partly the result of involuntary sterility. There are few data, however, to support this viewpoint. Although it is quite likely that emotionally, and perhaps also physically, American women are now less capable of bring-ing up large families, there is little evidence that the woman of today is on an average less fertile than the woman of a century ago. "I am frankly skeptical about the assertion," says Meaker,[3] in his study of human sterility, "that the total proportion of sterile matings has notably in-creased during the past hundred years." Involuntary sterility has prob-ably played but a minor role in the diminution of the birth rate.

Nor does it seem that the postponement of marriage has been a serious factor in this respect. It is quite true that the fertility of a woman reaches an optimum at a certain age of her life, probably in the mid-twenties, and gradually diminishes thereafter. Obviously if marriage is postponed much beyond a woman's most fertile period, the time element may lessen her marital fecundity. Nevertheless, it is the opinion of population authorities[4] that neither the decline in marriage nor the rise in the age at marriage has had any considerable influence in curtailing the reproduction rate.

The decrease in the size of the American family is, it would seem then, not due to any biological loss of procreative capacity. If the Ameri-can birth rate is decreasing it must be ascribed almost entirely to the fact that American parents are voluntarily limiting the size of their families. This has been and is being accomplished either through a resort to abortion or through the employment of contraception.

The practice of abortion has been traced back to primitive peoples, and has probably been resorted to in America ever since the country was first settled. Even during the last century much was written about the extent and prevalence of artificial interruptions of pregnancy, and the claim was made then that abortions were largely responsible for the diminishing rate of reproduction. As early as 1857 abortions became so frequent that the American Medical Association appointed a committee to investigate the practice. In 1881 the estimate was made that in Michi-gan there were 17 abortions for each 100 pregnancies, and the compiler of the statistics thought that the actual rate may have been double that amount. Whatever the extent of the practice may have been at that time, however, there is much evidence that the resort to abortion has very greatly increased during the last decades. While official figures are of course not available, it has been fairly reliably estimated[5] that from three-

[3]Meaker, Samuel R., *Human Sterility*. Williams & Wilkins Co., 1934.

[4]Kuczynski, Robert R., "Future Trends in Population." *Eugenics Review*, July, 1937.

[5]Taussig, Frederick J., *Abortion, Spontaneous and Induced*. C. V. Moshy Co., 1936.

quarters of a million to one million abortions are now performed annually in the United States. As the total number of live births in this country is only a little over two million, this implies that nearly one-third of the potential birth rate is lost through abortion.

Contraception, too, was not unknown to primitive peoples, and Himes devotes an entire chapter to the subject in his *Medical History of Contraception.*[6] Although preliterate peoples relied for the regulation of family size more upon abortion, infanticide and prolonged periods of abstinence which were enforced by tribal taboos, they also made use of diverse measures for the avoidance of conception. Even the North American Indians are said to have possessed several kinds of magical formulæ for preventing childbirth. One method of preventing conception, furthermore, a method which is widely utilized even today, is mentioned in the Bible in connection with the story of Onan.[7] Undoubtedly, then, contraceptive measures have been employed by the American settlers since colonial days. Advertisements of contraceptives are said to have been published in American newspapers in the early days of the Republic. Later during the 19th century the resort to contraceptive measures became more widespread. "Stress upon the social and economic desirability of birth control," says Himes, "is a characteristic of the 19th century." In 1830, Robert Dale Owen published his *Moral Physiology,* the first book on the subject of prevention of conception to be issued in this country, and in 1832 Doctor Charles Knowlton of Boston published the *Fruits of Philosophy,* the first American medical treatise on the subject. Knowlton spent several months in jail for publishing this little volume, but his and Owen's book were widely distributed and probably had considerable influence on the diffusion of contraceptive knowledge.

It was not, however, until the second decade of the present century, when Margaret Sanger[8] initiated, in 1914, her epochal campaign for voluntary parenthood, that family limitation assumed a true social significance in this country. It was at that time that Margaret Sanger coined the term "birth control," a phrase which in its implications and applications has had a revolutionary effect upon social trends. When she first launched her educational program the whole subject of prevention of conception was still under a cloud of social taboos and legal prohibitions. The Comstock laws, enacted in 1873, had classified contraception with obscenity and made the dissemination of con-

[6]Himes, Norman E., *Medical History of Contraception.* Williams & Wilkins Co., 1936.
[7]Genesis 38:7–10.     [8]Sanger, Margaret, *My Fight for Birth Control.* Farrar & Rinehart, 1931.

traceptive knowledge a Federal offense. Margaret Sanger was indicted for merely publishing a paper on the sociological aspects of the prevention of conception in *The Woman Rebel*. There were few people at that time willing openly to support her ideas and her work. The church opposed her, the law was against her, the doctors and scientists were apathetic, if not hostile, and there was little organized public opinion.

The change in attitude that has taken place since then is indeed one of the striking phenomena in our social history. Within less than twenty-five years the practice of birth control has become an accepted and integral part of our family mores. The church with hardly an exception has by now fully approved the main principles of voluntary parenthood. The law has on a number of occasions been redefined and reinterpreted so as to recognize officially the medical and legal justification for the use of contraceptives. And only last year the medical profession, as expressed by the resolution adopted by the American Medical Association at its annual session in 1937,[9] officially acknowledged that contraception is an important therapeutic and public-health measure and a legitimate branch of medical practice.

Public opinion, too, has within the last decade definitely crystallized and is today accepting family planning and family regulation as an essential element in modern life. In a poll, for instance, conducted by *The Country Home* in 1930 among its rural subscribers, 67 per cent voted affirmatively on the question whether physicians should be permitted to impart contraceptive knowledge to married couples. More recently in a nationwide survey conducted by *The Ladies' Home Journal* (March, 1938), 79 per cent of the American women expressed themselves openly and positively in favor of birth control. From farms and villages and cities, and from every geographical section of the country came a very decided vote for family planning. The ideas and practices of birth control are now evidently penetrating into every section of American life.

The development and extension of clinical facilities for contraception is further evidence of the increasing demand for birth-control knowledge. Less than fifteen years ago there was not a single birth-control clinic in this country. It was not until 1923 that the first birth-control center in America, the Birth Control Clinical Research Bureau, was organized by Margaret Sanger. Today, there are more than 400 centers in this country and they are found in nearly every State of the Union. In several states

[9]"Report of the Committee to Study Contraceptive Practices and Related Problems." *Journal of the American Medical Association* (p. 2217), June 26, 1937.

contraceptive services have now even been officially organized by public health authorities.[10]

A decade ago, furthermore, there was no medical literature on contraception and not a single medical text on the subject. No instruction in contraceptive technique was given to the students in any of the medical colleges and very little scientific research was carried on in this field. Today not only are there several authoritative medical texts on contraception available, including one by Doctor Robert L. Dickinson, the distinguished gynecologist and obstetrician, but a special scientific journal devoted to the medical aspects of human fertility and its control, *The Journal of Contraception,* is now being published. Instruction in contraceptive technique is given in over a third of the medical colleges in this country and scientific investigations for the development of newer and simpler techniques are being carried on in a number of clinics and laboratories.

Clearly, then, birth-control practices have been extended widely within a remarkably short period of time. What has been responsible for this extension? What forces have brought about this rapidly increasing acceptance and diffusion of birth control in this country?

The major factor in the spread of contraception has no doubt been the industrialization and urbanization of the American people. "Abundant data show," say Lorimer and Osborn,[11] in their elaborate study of population trends, "that size of family decreases in any given area progressively from open country to village, from villages to towns, from towns to cities of moderate size, and from small cities to large cities." Large families which may be an asset in an agricultural society are not compatible with a mechanized civilization, while life in the city is inimical to the bearing of many children. The financial and physical difficulties of child-rearing in a city atmosphere, the rising standards of life, the multiplication of wants—these serve as deterrents to unrestricted procreation. On the farm the child is often an economic asset, since he is able to perform a variety of tasks even in his younger years. In the city a child is generally an economic liability and is in competition with many other satisfactions. The extension of child labor laws prevent him from contributing to the family income until late in life, nor do parents any longer regard large families as a form of old-age insurance. The changing standards of life and the increasing urbanization of the popu-

[10]"Twelve Months of State Contraception." *Journal of Contraception,* June–July, 1937.
[11]Lorimer, Frank, and Osborn, Frederick: *Dynamics of Population.* The Macmillan Co., 1934.

lation have therefore been responsible to a very large degree for the extension of family restriction.

The emancipation of woman has also played a dominant role in the rapid extension of birth control. Having become economically independent and politically emancipated, women readily grasped at the opportunity to become sexually liberated as well. This process was hastened by their entry into the industrial life of the nation. Between 1870 and 1930 the number of gainfully employed women gradually increased. Of late there has also been an increase in the percentage of *married* women engaged in gainful occupations. These economic and cultural pressures have broken down the bonds of the old patriarchal system, and new attitudes toward sex morals and sex behaviors have developed.

This change in attitude has in itself contributed to the readier adoption of contraception. Today sex is no longer looked upon as merely a means of procreation. In increasing numbers American parents have come to accept the fact that it is possible and feasible to dissociate sex from reproduction. Even the Catholic Church, by its tacit and official approval of the "safe period" and the consequent sanction of marital relations on days when the woman presumably cannot conceive, has furthered the basic idea that the sex function need not necessarily be restricted to procreation. Hence the control of conception is no longer looked upon as "immoral" or "sinful" by the majority of American men and women, and birth control has become an accepted norm of social behavior.

These, then, are probably the main factors that have contributed towards the wide dissemination and acceptance of contraception. The development of the industrial system in a machine age, the increasing urbanization of the population, the higher standards of living, the economic and cultural emancipation of woman, the passing of moral taboos, and the weakening of former social restrictions and controls, all have acted and interacted to create new social patterns leading to the small family system.

But how will the spread of contraceptive knowledge affect our civilization? Will it improve it or will it destroy it? That in one way or another birth control is bound to have a profound influence upon the future of our nation is obvious. "I regard birth control," writes Thompson,[12] "as one of the great discoveries of mankind. It will have an influence on human affairs as great as the discovery of fire, the invention of printing, or the application of electricity to communication and indus-

[12]Thompson, Warren S., *Danger Spots in World Population.* Alfred A. Knopf, 1930.

try. . . . In time it will change the entire course of history." What direction will this change take?

In this discussion we are concerned primarily with the problem of population and we must limit our inquiry to the possible effects of birth control upon the composition and size of our population. How will birth control influence the quality and the quantity of the American people?

The claim is frequently made that the spread of contraceptive knowledge tends to produce a dysgenic social balance. It is almost axiomatic that new techniques and new inventions are adopted first by the more advanced, the more progressive and the more intelligent portions of the population. The same holds true of the use of birth control. The more able, the more prudent and the more foresighted are among the first to make use of this knowledge and limit the size of the families, while the incompetent, the careless, the "unfit" continue to breed without any comparable restriction. It has been shown, for instance, that the highest fertility is at present found in the rural groups with the lowest economic and cultural levels. In the cities, too, the people in the lower grades of occupational and cultural development are more fertile than those who are economically better placed. "The liberals," Will Durant once wrote, figuratively, "are reproducing too conservatively, while the conservatives reproduce too liberally." We are in danger then, it is claimed, of being overrun by the socially inadequate and by the "legions of the ill-born."

When we attempt, however, to stratify society into desirable and undesirable groups we are apt to be misled by preconceived notions and prejudices. We must be careful to distinguish between real genetic endowments and mere social qualities. It is often very difficult to tell whether an individual or group of individuals are inferior because they are actually biologically unsound or whether the apparent inadequacy is merely the result of environmental, social and economic factors which have kept them from realizing their full native potentialities. Of late, as a matter of fact, greater stress has been laid by the American eugenists on the personal qualities of the individual and on his home environment than on the class of society in which he is found. They rightly point out that people with good hereditary qualities and suitable home conditions are apt to be found among all the occupational and racial groups, just as people with bad heredity and bad homes may be found in every social class.

Aside from these considerations, however, there are increasing signs that a better balanced birth rate is even now in the process of developing.

On the one hand, there is evidence that family limitation practices are rapidly spreading to the rural areas and to the groups of population that had hitherto retained a high birth rate. During the last few years, for instance, the decline in reproductivity has been sharpest in those States where the birth rate had formerly been comparatively high.[13] Declines have been greatest in the Southern section of the country, as in South Carolina, Florida, North Carolina, Georgia, Alabama, etc., and least in the New England and Northern States where the birth rate had already declined considerably during past decades. The present social and sectional differences in the birth rate are thus gradually being levelled off.

On the other hand, figures have of late become available which indicate an increasing fertility among the economically better situated portions of the community. This was first observed in Sweden more than ten years ago by Karl Edin[14] who found that, contrary to the usual expectations, marital fertility in Stockholm was about 25 per cent higher among the well-to-do groups than among the industrial workers, and that fertility increased in direct ratio with the family income. More recently, Notestein,[15] in a study of fertility in certain areas of the United States found that while generally fertility and economic status were inversely associated, exceptions were found among the highest "value-of-home" groups, that is, among those who were economically privileged. The average number of children was larger in families living in the more costly homes. He tentatively interprets this phenomenon as the beginning of a reversal in the standard inverse association of fertility and economic status. It is not at all improbable, then, that when contraceptive information will become equally available to all social strata those with the greatest intellectual and social endowments will assume the leadership in the differential fertility and bear the larger number of children.

This, of course, is the goal of the eugenists. Their program is "to encourage large families where children are likely to be well trained and to have good inheritance, and to discourage large families in homes of the opposite sort."[16] This presupposes the ability to control conception. When all parents understand how to limit their children to such num-

[13]*Statistical Bulletin.* Metropolitan Life Insurance Company, March, 1938.

[14]Edin, Karl Arvid, *Proceedings of the World Population Conference* (p. 205). (Edited by Margaret Sanger.) Edward Arnold Co., London, 1927.

[15]Notestein, Frank W., "Differential Fertility in the East North Central States." *Milbank Memorial Fund Quarterly,* April, 1938.

[16]Huntington, Ellsworth, *Tomorrow's Children, The Goal of Eugenics.* John Wiley and Sons, Inc., 1935.

bers as they can bear and rear, when birth control methods are so simple that even the most ignorant and weak-willed can use them, and when sufficient incentives and motivations are provided for genetically well-endowed parents to bear more children, the current dysgenic population trend will no longer prevail.

To produce a better equilibrium in the differential fertility, efforts must therefore first be directed towards insuring an even wider social diffusion, or, what Himes calls "democratization," of contraceptive information. The demand is present, but the knowledge is lacking. The clinical facilities available now can reach only a small percentage of the population. The task then is, as Margaret Sanger[17] has recently pointed out, "to supply the demand of the submerged sections . . . the women on homesteads, on farms and in the mining districts, and the millions of women in outlying rural districts where medical help is not available." This can be realized when simplified and inexpensive techniques are developed and when birth control services are included in the program of the national and local public health authorities. Incidentally, the wider diffusion of birth control will serve as the best and surest means of combatting the evils of abortion.

But if birth control becomes universally available and birth control methods sufficiently simplified, will it not seriously affect the quantity of the population? Is there not a danger that its widespread use will eventually lead to national depopulation and decadence?

It is quite true, as has been pointed out before, that the birth rate in the United States has been declining consistently since about 1820 and that in recent decades the decline has been even more precipitous than formerly. To understand the situation more clearly, however, we should view it in the perspective of the history of the general world population. In the middle of the 17th century the total population of the world, according to an estimate made by Pearl and Gould, was about 445 million; by 1931, it had reached 2,073 million. Carr-Saunders,[18] using different sources for his calculations, estimates the population of the world to have been 545 million in 1650, 728 million in 1750, 1,171 million in 1850, and 2,057 million in 1933. Considering the general statistical uncertainties about the world population, the two figures are not very far apart.

What do they show? They show first of all that in 1650 the total

[17]Sanger, Margaret, "The Future of Contraception." *Journal of Contraception*, January, 1937.
[18]Carr-Saunders, A. M., *World Population*. Oxford University Press, 1936.

world population was only about 500 million. Man had emerged on the face of the earth several hundred thousand years ago, yet during all this lengthy period of his existence his total population up to 1650 had not reached beyond 500 million. Like the population of all other animals, the human population, too, had remained quite stationary. A high death rate, the widespread practice of infanticide and abortion, tribal customs which tabooed intercourse during the lactation period and at other times, had kept the family of primitive man down to a rather low size and had limited the population to the means of subsistence. Then, rather suddenly, from 1650 on, the human race began to increase and multiply at an enormous rate. Within a period of less than three hundred years the total world population increased more than fourfold, from 500 million to over 2000 million. The discovery of new lands, technological and industrial progress, improvements in communications which facilitated migration, these provided new and unexpected sources of subsistence for mankind and favored a high birth rate and a rapid extension of its numbers. At the same time, advances in sanitation, in hygiene, and in the medical sciences operated to reduce very markedly the human death rate. More people were born, fewer people died, and the human world population expanded tremendously.

But this could not go on indefinitely. Towards the latter part of the 19th century the birth rate in northwestern Europe began to decline, even while the total populations were still rising. In France, in England, in the Scandinavian countries, and later in Germany, in Italy and other southeastern European countries, people began voluntarily to curtail the number of their offspring and restrict the size of their families. Here and there voices began to arise urging familiy limitation and demanding the extension of contraceptive knowledge. The Bradlaugh-Besant trial in 1877 gave a strong impetus to the entire movement and the birth rate curve began its descent. In spite of the measures which have been promulgated in recent years in several European countries to artificially stimulate natality, the birth rate still continues to decline.

In the United States, too, the population rose rapidly during the past century, and it has continued to rise in spite of the declining birth rate. From five and a half million in 1800 it grew to over 128 million in 1936. But the decline in the birth rate has become more precipitous of late, from 55 births per 1000 population in 1800 it diminished to 30 in 1900, to 23.7 in 1920, and to 16.6 in 1936. Gradually, therefore, the population growth is slowing down. Should the birth rate continue to fall and the death

rate remain stationary, as it is likely to do, we shall, within a comparatively few decades, enter an era of a stationary, if not an actually declining, population. Lorimer and Osborn calculate that the population in
the United States will reach a maximum of some 150 millions within a
few decades and then probably remain stationary or else decline for
several decades thereafter. "There are so many uncertain elements in the
picture," they add, however, "that it is idle to speculate far into the
future."

There are many political economists and sociologists who regard the
possibility of a stationary population with serious misgivings. They feel
that it would endanger national stability and would lead to racial decadence and deterioration. Other competent students of the problem,
however, look upon the decline in the rate of the population growth as
a necessary and welcome human adaptation. "There is no doubt," writes
Professor Fairchild,[19] in a keen and lucid analysis of the present situation,
"that a century or two of stationary population the world over would
be a boon to mankind, at least equalling the material blessings of the
19th century." Not only is there no cause for alarm in his opinion over
the slowing up of the population growth, but it should be welcomed
as an intelligent human adaptation to changing needs and conditions.

Similarly, the Committtee on Population Problems of the National
Resources Committee, in an exhaustive and thoughtful study of our population problems recently submitted to the President, points out that the
transition to a stationary population may indeed be a salutary phenomenon. "It may," reads the report, "on the whole be beneficial rather than
injurious to the life of the nation. It insures the continuance of a favorable
ration of population to natural resources in the United States. Each citizen
of this country will continue to have, on the average, a larger amount of
arable land, minerals and other natural resources at his disposal than the
citizen of any of the countries of the Old World. This supplies the material basis for a high level of living, if these resources are used wisely and
if cultural conditions are stimulating to initiative and cooperative endeavor." It is the considered opinion of this Committee, furthermore, that
"there is no reason for the hasty adoption of any measures to stimulate
population growth in this country."

The fact is that once people have acquired techniques of family limitation they will not revert to unrestricted procreation. The fecundity of
mankind cannot be influenced materially by political exhortations, legal

[19]Fairchild, Henry Pratt, "When the Population Levels Off." *Harpers*, May, 1938.

restrictions on the dissemination of birth control knowledge, or minor economic inducements to larger families. The birth rate can be increased only when social conditions become favorable towards an increasing fertility. "No society," says Fairchild, "can expect socially conscious families to bring large numbers of children into a world that threatens them with economic hardship, political tyranny and spiritual starvation. Procreation waits upon the assurance of liberty, security and abundance."

In this connection it might also be pointed out that the voluntary control of procreation is not the ultimate *cause* of the declining birth rate. Birth control is merely a tool or a technique utilized for the purpose. People use birth control measures not simply because they have acquired the necessary knowledge, but because there are numerous social and cultural reasons for their use, reasons which spring from the complexities of modern life. A fundamental change in the birth rate can therefore result only from a fundamental change in our social order and from the development of new social attitudes and cultural patterns. When it becomes possible for the average parents to have both a large family and a reasonably decent standard of life, our national birth rate will most probably soon adapt itself to the newer conditions.

Birth control here has, in a sense, been one of the main forces in the evolution of life. The lower animals are very prolific, but their death rate, especially that of the young, is also tremendous, and their survival rate is therefore comparatively low. Among the higher animals parental care effectively combats the destructive agencies in the world. The death rate falls and there is consequently no need for a high fertility in order to maintain the species. As we go up the scale of evolution both fertility and mortality decline. In the human world, too, as civilization rises, both the birth rate and the death rate decrease, and man's energies are released for the development of his potentialities and faculties and for the manifold social and cultural pursuits of modern life.

RACE

# RACE-PREJUDICE

## [*Jacques Barzun*]

AT THE present moment a wave of anti-Japanese feeling is sweeping over the United States. Everywhere, in high circles and low, condemnation of the Japanese for their war on China is to be heard, and practical effect is given to it in the form of a buyers' boycott of articles made or originating in Japan, from silk stockings to ten-cent-store cigarette boxes. The Japanese living in this country are put on the defensive and must perforce be apologetic or defiant. They must either uphold the policies of their mother-country or explain them away as the doings of a military clique with which they, the Japanese-Americans, are not in sympathy.

In this contemporary example can be found most characteristics of American race-prejudice as it affects an important minority of the population. The principal of these characteristics is what may be called "tribal identification." During the World War it applied to the German-Americans, and almost every one knows of some person of German descent whose career, prospects or individual happiness was marred, perhaps permanently, through the operation on a large scale of this process of tribal identification let loose in a land of "liberty and justice for all." More recently, Italian imperialism in Abyssinia had its repercussions in Chicago and New York in the form of clashes between Italians and Negroes on the same basis of identification with the two groups warring in the Ethiopian mountains.

It is easily seen how slight the real bond between the two pairs of opponents in such a racial situation can be. Even on the basis of color the Abyssinians and the American Negroes hardly form a homogeneous group, and on a political or economic or cultural or geographical basis, there is no discoverable similarity between the population of Harlem and that of Addis Ababa.

The first factor in race-prejudice, therefore, is that of lumping together what is essentially different for the sake of releasing animus or unspent aggressiveness. To return to the Japanese, let us look for a moment not at the red-hot prejudice of indignation meetings but at the factual situation of the Japanese in California. Let us imagine ourselves walking in some byway of Los Angeles and coming upon two Japanese men walking together, the one aged fifty, the other twenty, each showing enough likeness to the other to make the pair presumably father and son. Here, we say, are two of those crafty Orientals who would soon over-run the white man's California if we let them, plotting some mischief or perhaps gloating over *their* murdering of women and children in Shanghai. Thus do we assume by mere inspection on the basis of color, features and social contiguity a number of profound and important similarities. But what are the facts? These two Japanese, united by the bond of generation, are separated from each other by a personal and cultural chasm that it would be hard to exaggerate. The father, born in Japan, belongs to the *issei* or old generation. The son, born in Los Angeles, is of the *nissei,* that is, Americans of Japanese extraction. The father views life as a scene of duty and sacrifice to the family interests. He expects obedience and reverence from his wife and children, cherishes the formality and ceremonial of old Japanese ways, the segregation of the sexes, the insistence on work, on hierarchy, on polite manners and on religion. The culture to which the father belongs is that of Japan as it was thirty years ago and it is in truth a culture that no longer exists anywhere except in his mind and in that of other Japanese of his generation in America. Unlike them, their sons, without becoming complete Americans, have lost their belief in almost everything that makes the Japanese what we conceive them to be. Such a youth as we have imagined has "democratic" ideas of freedom and equality; he wishes to marry a girl of his own choice and not of the family's; he enjoys American ways of recreation and social intercourse; his speech is standard American, as are his manners: nothing but the superficial appearance of color and hair and eyes stands in the way of his being accepted as an American. But that physical difference, unimportant in the eyes of science, is all-important in the eyes of society, with the result that he is excluded from the social group he wishes to belong to and is fitted to belong to, at the same time as he is a riddle and a source of dismay to the group that he genetically springs from.

Viewed once again from the average American standpoint, that twenty-year-old Japanese is both an alien and a potential menace. To be sure, he was born on United States territory, so he is *ipso facto* an American;

but this fact is probably taken advantage of by his family to get around the provisions of the California Alien Land Act, and thus a motive of economic rivalry is introduced into a situation already complicated on the social and cultural sides. The labor unions of the West Coast have from the beginning stood in the forefront of anti-Oriental agitation, particularly in San Francisco and the State of Washington, and the political expression of that well-grounded economic fear has taken the familiar form of *prejudicial* slanders: The Orientals—for the Japanese have inherited all the prejudices created in California by the earlier Chinese immigration —are "unassimilable," "criminal," "clannish," "crafty and secretive," "dishonest," "inscrutable," "inferior from a moral and mental point of view"; their towns and settlements are "filthy dens of prostitution and gambling"; they make the "neighborhood unsanitary and uninhabitable"— in a word, "the opposition to Oriental immigration is justified upon the simple ground of race" and exclusion is "the only alternative of race degeneration or race war."

The anti-Japanese prejudice—aroused anew in the United States by the war in China—is thus a typical prejudice comprising all the emotions behind all prejudices against the so-called "racial" minorities. Tribal identification, the first step, is a mental lumping together of the foreigners, whoever they may be and without much regard for the facts. At one time the "yellow peril" is Chinese, later it is Chinese *and* Japanese, now it tends to be exclusively Japanese with a new-born love of the Chinese based upon their "ancient civilization" and "wonderful philosophy."[1] At a much earlier time, when there were railroads to be built across the continent and "dirt cheap labor" was also wanted on the farms of the Far West, the Chinese immigrants were held to be universally "sober, thrifty, tractable, inoffensive and law-abiding." The process of tribal identification works both ways.

The second factor in race prejudice is economic, as can be seen in the last comment on tribal identification. When the "coolies" were no longer useful and began to offer real competition to white labor they turned from "sober and thrifty workers of all-round ability" to "moon-eyed lepers." Economic status in America is closely allied to social position, and the distinctions, although not embodied in rigid terms or titles, are keenly felt, often with surprising alterations in the form of the local race-prejudice. For example, it is generally true that the recent or un-

[1] A well-known publisher reports that the works of Confucius, included in a set of popularly priced volumes on philosophy, ousted 2 to 1 every other volume in the series during the fall of 1937.

assimilated immigrant in this country is felt by the "older stock" to belong to an inferior social and racial group. The "hunky," "Cannuck," "Mick," or "Wop" is a lower sort of animal in comparison with the alleged "Anglo-Saxon." But observe the effect of economics upon this pattern of thought and feeling: In Fresno, the Armenian population is well established, well-to-do, and thoroughly respectable. When, therefore, during the last depression, Fresno was invaded by homeless immigrants from poverty-stricken regions of the South, these dispossessed "Anglo-Saxons," whose family trees in some cases had struck roots on this continent before the Revolution, were considered by the Armenians an undesirable alien lot, and the usual batch of contemptuous adjectives rained down upon them in spite of their great past and pedigree. Dirty, shiftless, crooked and criminal were among the milder of the terms applied to the new "race" huddling across the railroad tracks in improvised shanties and un-American squalor.

From the combination of these factors—tribal identification, economic and social grouping, and culture patterns—can be drawn the general conclusion that race prejudices are always local in origin and variable in content, within the general form of all race-thinking. This in turn must be defined as the attribution to a whole group of certain undesirable qualities perceived or assumed in a few individuals, and the belief that these traits are inherited "with the blood." Occasionally the whole nation execrates another whole nation. The Germans *were* Huns, down to the last man; the Japanese *are* Huns in exactly the same way. But the feeling dies relatively quickly, dependent as it is on a stretching of the entire national imagination by means of newspapers and movies to a point that cannot be long sustained without discomfort. Boredom sets in and novelty is demanded, as in the nationality of movie villains.[2] But with local prejudices no effort of the imagination is required. The facts seem to speak for themselves, and whatever propaganda there may be from interested quarters plays, in Mr. Schrieke's apt words, "on attitudes that already exist and is primarily the expression of prevailing public opinion."[3] The "facts" are indeed often true, in the sense that any sizable group newly settled in a community is likely to be poor, to have low standards of living and "different" standards of conduct, and is sure to be discriminated against by the "old families" who may have got there

[2]One can observe this cycle in the career of that excellent movie actor, Mr. Warner Oland. In his Pearl White days he was always an Oriental mischief-maker whose eyes slanted dangerously and who invariably came to a bad end. Now he is the beloved Charlie Chan.

[3]*Alien Americans,* 1936, p. 22.

only a decade previously. It is an exaggerated form of the feeling the Seniors have for the Freshmen, together with the desire to haze them, and it is naturally complicated in the big world by a social and economic competition that never ceases to operate and so to maintain the original social and economic grounds of friction. It is these perfectly real grounds that confirm our generalization that race-prejudices are always "local." The seeming exceptions relating to the Jews, the "Latins," and the colored races generally will be dealt with in a moment. At this point it is only necessary to suggest that there is no prejudice in America against the Eskimos or the inhabitants of Tierra del Fuego, for the simple reason that we never see either of them. We can, it is true, come into psychological contact with distant peoples, as when some South Sea Islanders commit an outrage upon an American woman, and immediately we discover from conversation with our friends that they are in possession of all the "racial facts" needed to account for its incident. But apart from these isolated cases that flare up and die out, we find that the normal American race prejudices involve almost exclusively the minority peoples residing on the continent and are strongest at the points of contact. They occur in fact wherever an unassimilated alien group, marked off by class, occupation, or manners, is found in the midst of the population that is called by courtesy "native American." Thus the United States has not only a Negro problem, a Japanese problem, an Indian problem, but it has the problems and the prejudices arising from the presence of Chinese, Mexican, Filipinos, Poles, Swedes, Hungarians, and other so-called nationalities recognized as separate "races" by the Naturalization Service of the Department of Labor. In addition to the color groups and the nation groups the "race" problem is oddly complicated by the inclusion of two religious groups—the Catholics and the Jews.

The renewed activity of the Ku Klux Klan in the 1920's beautifully demonstrates the localized diversity of race-prejudice, for on behalf of the Protestant Anglo-Saxon white, the Klan was by turns and in different places anti-Negro, anti-Catholic, anti-Jewish, anti-Japanese and anti-Irish, and everywhere anti-foreign. In the population at large all these prejudices are based upon "facts" and are themselves facts that influence the course of national and individual life so profoundly and persistently that the exhortation to be "broadminded" will no more abolish them than the injunction to be internationally-minded will abolish war. Nor can any one boast of an existence free from the feelings or effects of such prejudices. As Professor Donald Young put it: ". . . The Southerner who walks out of a Northern restaurant because a Negro is being served is giving expression to a racial attitude, while the white patrons who remain may be free from this particular tendency. . . . The employer who refuses to hire Negroes, Jews, Orientals, Mexicans, or aliens also demonstrates the possession of racial attitudes, as does the Negro who refuses to work for a Jew, the Oriental who will not accept employment from a Negro or a Mexican, or the Irishman who would rather go hungry than obey the orders of a French Canadian foreman."[4] The criss-crossings of social, economic, national, cultural, and color factors are infinite, and they infect the minorities themselves by social imitation so that we find Negroes despising "niggers," Jews despising "kikes," and second-generation Americans of all nationalities looking down on the latest batch of arrivals from the mother-country. The United States has no monopoly on race-prejudice, but as in other matters, the size of the country and the recency of its settlement provide opportunities for the study of the phenomenon on a liberal scale and in a great variety of manifestations.

In this welter of entities, real or imaginary, what is the intelligent layman to think? What "problems" should alarm him, and what should leave him unconcerned? How can he fight his own irrational prejudices and yet retain a sense of the realities which are going to be fought out mainly in the heat of prejudice? Among the current propaganda for or against the Negro, the Jew, and the Japanese, what is fact, and what is fiction that ought to be rejected as confusing an already complicated question? It would take more than a chapter, more than a volume, to answer these queries, and the reader must be referred to two recent books—both quoted from here[5]—for an introduction to the details of the many-sided subject. What can and must be done in the remaining pages of this essay is to tackle the question of race *per se,* and to show what part the idea, the mere notion, plays in the situations that we approached first in empirical fashion when we described the present anti-Japanese feeling and the actual economic and cultural situation in California. Dealing with race as such will also enable us to answer the question raised a few paragraphs back about the status of the Jewish, "Latin," and colored "races" in public opinion.

Race, which is a word of uncertain origin probably meaning "family"

---

[4] *American Minority Peoples,* 1932, p. 3.

[5] Donald Young, *American Minority Peoples,* New York, 1932, Harpers; B. Schrieke, *Alien Americans,* New York, 1936, Viking Press.

or "line," definitely implies in modern usage the idea of heredity or transmission of human characteristics by the ordinary course of generation, and it is upon this implied transmission that "tribal identification" rests for its every-day likelihood of truth. That is the common understanding of the matter, and that is why, in this discussion, I have spoken indifferently of Japanese, Irish, Hungarians, Mexicans, and French Canadians as "races" and of the prejudices centering around these groups as "racial prejudices." The feeling is strong in our Western European culture that not only physical, but mental and moral, traits are, as well, handed down from father to son—a faith that leads one consciously or unconsciously to formulate the typical race-syllogism:

> All Orientals are crafty—
> This man is an Oriental;
> This man is crafty.

How the major premise is derived, very few bother to think about; indeed, very few bother to state the major premise at all, though it is quite possible that its elevation to the dignity of a truth runs something like this:

> Slanting eyes indicate slyness—
> All Orientals have slanting eyes;
> All Orientals are sly.

The physical fact that the Orientals' eyes are *not* slanting does not come into logical play at all, so that the racial warning—"This man is crafty"—rests upon two unwarranted propositions themselves, based upon an incorrectly observed physical fact. By the same process we come to feel that all Swedes are stupid, all Mexicans lazy, all foreign women scheming, all Jews and Armenians obtrusive, all Catholics superstitious, all Hungarians unclean, all Irish liars, and all American Indians noble. Two things are taken for granted—the initial fact and its predictable presence in all the members of the "race." Now the "fact" is generally an error. The lazy Mexican is only the Mexican who works just enough to keep body and soul together and refuses to work more because he values his leisure. If he could write a book, he would be called a philosopher and be given degrees by universities for his fidelity to the contemplative life in spite of the temptations of wealth, but since he is only a "damned dago," he is put down as lazy, his brothers and sisters are lazy, the whole tribe is lazy: It is their race; they have it in the blood. The fact that the Mexicans are "always in revolt," "incapable of self-government," "restless," tormented by their "hot Southern blood"—those facts of equal standing do not invalidate, for the believer in race, his earlier generalization. Accuracy of observation, consistency in theorizing, and a desire to verify his results by comparisons or experience—these do not exist for the race-thinker. True, he appeals now to common sense, now to science, but without ever using either, or without ever learning the verdicts of either. And the reason for his willful blindness is usually not far to seek: He has perfectly sound resentments, grounded in economic, social, or personal realities which must find an outlet. Race-prejudice is such an outlet, and woe to him who tries to plug it up with a few facts held together by a little logic. Race-prejudice of this kind is therefore emotionally on a par with hating one's neighbor on t'other side of fence, being "ag'in" the government, and cursing the sun-spots when the stock market takes a dip. Race-hatred of this kind may be a relief to jangled nerves as well as excellent material for political campaigns, but it is blind, deaf, and infantile, and it can only produce new conflicts, more prejudices, and more violence in the situations where it is given undisputed sway.

Side by side with it, however, in the educated classes and in areas where no group conflicts obtain, there flourishes another form of belief in race which is supposedly based on scientific truth. This form of belief generally distinguishes between nations and races. The colored groups, the Jews, the Mediterraneans, the Nordics are "races." The French, the Mexicans, the Japanese, the Americans are "peoples," or "nations." Whereas nations can be made up of several races and so imply no intellectual or social characteristics, the races themselves are indestructible units which do carry the fatal "traits" that are either prized or despised by the observer. A distinguished and learned expounder of this doctrine is Mr. Lothrop Stoddard, who, after warning us of the Yellow Peril in the early 1920's, still finds cause, in 1936, for urging precautions against racial admixture. And he is but one of many racialist "authorities" in this country who carry on a well-established European tradition. Indeed, it is safe to say that our whole Western Culture and educational practice since the beginning of the 19th century has been permeated by race-thinking of this sort,[6] sometimes with harmless and sometimes with harmful intent. In the United States Emerson, Bronson Alcott, John Lothrop Motley, James Russell Lowell, and many others of the leading 19th cen-

[6]For a full account see Jacques Barzun, *Race: A Study in Modern Superstition*, New York, 1937, Harcourt, Brace.

tury spirits harbored race notions which they thought scientifically and historically sound. Lowell, for one, was persuaded that he was descended from the Rousseau stock—hence Russell—who were, in his mind, gifted, red-headed Jews, the destined leaders of the world. He saw Jews everywhere just as Bronson Alcott saw Greeks at every turn, and for much the same reason, namely, for discovering an infallible connection between race and mental ability.

After John Fiske, Asa Grey, and others on these shores had popularized Spencer and Darwin's theory of evolution, the racial attitude flourished in this country with the added renown of science. The French racialist, Gobineau, was translated in garbled form in the 1850's, and the high-class polemical literature about the Abolitionist and Emancipation question teemed with supposedly scientific references to prove both sides of the issue. Between the Civil War and the turn of the century, the immigration of Chinese and Japanese, the change in the geographical origins of the European immigrants, the gradual settlement of the continent, and the increasing participation of the United States in world imperialism—especially in South America and the Far East—created more and more occasions for race-thinking to come to the fore as an explanation of the present, and a guide to future policy. And it must be confessed that with the highly developed methods of the then modern anthropology —particularly the refined measurements of skulls and the microscopic examination of hair and tissues—it looked as if science were in a fair way to distinguishing with complete accuracy the "several races of Man" whose existence had hitherto been assumed or crudely defined. Delivering one of "Eight Lectures on Race Power" at the Lowell Institute in 1905, a notable of the non-scientific world could therefore utter the following words and have them easily understood by his audience:

It belongs to a highly developed race to become, in a true sense, aristocratic—a treasury of the best in practical and spiritual types, and then to disappear in the surrounding types of men. So Athens dissolved like a pearl in the cup of the Mediterranean, and Rome in the cup of Europe, and Judea in the cup of Universal Communion . . . Nay, if the aristocracy of the whole white race is so to melt in a world of the colored races of the earth, I for one should only rejoice in such a divine triumph of the sacrificial idea in history.[7]

Although most Americans would nowadays decline to rejoice at the prospect of dissolving like a pearl in anybody's cup, very likely the words

[7] G. E. Woodberry, *The Torch*, New York, 1905, pp. 3, 6.

still carry a meaning, just as they did thirty years ago. "Types of men," "race," "race-mixture," "colored races" are all real things to the average man, at the very time when science, which helped to create these entities, is beginning to disown them. For it is a fact that skull-anthropology is discredited, that the division of races into the five color groups that we learned in our school geographies no longer holds; that pigmentation and the transmission of characteristics are being re-studied from the ground up; that the formation of individual and group minds is being viewed as much more complex phenomena than was first believed—in short, that the whole science of man, from genetics to psychology and sociology, has undergone a wholesale scrapping, and that modern investigators are proceeding very cautiously with the least possible number of assumptions, names, and theories. In place of the "Nordic," the "dolichocephalic," and the dozens of other "races" of the 19th century, we have nothing but the statement that "characters are not inherited at all; certain material which will produce a particular character under certain conditions is inherited."[8] Anthropologists like Boas and Lowie speak of "culture-groups" on one hand, and of "families" which seem to carry certain physical traits like black hair and blue eyes, on the other; but no correlation has as yet been found between a set of physical features and a set of mental habits. The latter depend so completely upon the individual's conditions within the culture group that tribal identification becomes impossible. One *can* call a man a Jap or a "Wop": It places him vaguely in our culture and perhaps definitely in our estimation. But his behavior, his opinions, the agglutinative type of his blood, and the color of his liver remain outside our power of inspection. We cannot predict them from our hasty classification within the purely arbitrary racial group which we formerly supposed to have a real existence in the world of things and a compelling influence in the world of mental and moral values.

Seen in the light of these facts and the negative conclusions based upon them, the modern problem of Nordicism and anti-Semitism shrinks to its proper proportions. It is but one of the many similar race-problems—so-called—and it must be broken up into its two constituent parts, economic and psychological, before any sane attitude can be taken towards it. The same procedure must be applied to the Nordic-Latin question. Mediterranean immigrants who "infest our shores" and who, according to

8H. S. Jennings, quoted in Beard's *Whither Mankind*, p. 242.

a crude reading of statistics, "provide all our criminals," are a proper subject for political and social action. But science has nothing to offer about their "race," for that is a fiction—and a fiction of the kind that breeds not practical measures but prejudice. Economically it may be very desirable to push all the Latins into the Atlantic ocean and thus to make more jobs: That is a question for economists to thrash out. Politically, it may be very useful to have the Jews as scapegoats to persecute in order that some of us may pose as saviors of the nation: That is a matter for a political democracy such as ours to decide. In the intellectual battle it may be fitting and proper to assume that the Catholics are all Irish Celts, all superstitious and "mediæval":—Those who make personal capital out of being "Anglo-Saxon," "scientific," and "modern" know best where their interests lie. All these are issues to be fought out, no doubt, and the experience of history suggests that quarter will neither be given nor taken. But "Let them be fought out in the open!" is what the sincere man of science, or the careful student of history, must insist upon. Race, they both assert, is a mere cloak superimposed upon reality in order to give a knock-down, drag-out affair the appearance of a justifiable homicide or a disinterested crusade.

It has been shown over and over again that the Jews are not a race, but a heterogeneous mass of people held together by a religious and cultural tradition as well as by long discrimination and persecution. Similarly, the "Latins" or "Mediterraneans" are no more a race than are taxicab drivers or poets, and as for the Irish Catholics, their belief is due—not to some hidden racial propensity, but, like every other belief—to individual circumstance and cultural opportunity. When we accuse any group of "clannishness" or "conspiracy" we are only recording the effects of our own ostracism upon certain people that we disapprove of for theoretical or practical reasons. "The Jews have got hold of all important posts," and "those Catholics are united in a vast enterprise to seize the Government," are two ways of indicating our childish notions of how the world is run, and our legitimate fears that our lumping people together out of contempt is going to meet with an equal and opposite reaction in the form of banding together on the basis of common minority feelings and forming an effective—indeed, often savage—resistance to majority oppression.

This examination of the nature of racial prejudice in America has obviously led us to conclusions very different from those ordinarily to be anticipated from a discussion of the subject. Race-prejudices are not matters for indignant splutterings or appeals to broad-mindedness. An outburst of anti-Japanese or anti-Semitic feeling in the United States is no going to be quenched by calling the fanatics hard names or by pointing out that the Japanese are a fine people who paint very cleverly on silk and that some Jews have charming manners and repudiate Communism. Nor can the problem be solved by a Live-and-Let-Live resolution, since it is quite obvious that the last thing anybody wants to do is to let live somebody else whom he fears and therefore dislikes. We are thrown back on two courses, one practical and the other theoretical, though with practical implications.

The first is already in effect wherever social agencies are at work reducing poverty, ignorance, insanitation, and all the other social-economic ills which we have seen to be at the basis of all persistent race-prejudices. The Christian injunction to love our neighbor as ourselves is not, as the world tends to think, a piece of high altruism impossible to achieve. It is practical advice to keep fear and violence down to a minimum. But obviously we cannot love our neighbor until he is human, like ourselves, and being human means having as many habits, manners, standards, and ways of speech in common as possible—all of which can only be achieved after decent economic and social conditions obtain among the previously despised groups.

So much for the practical side. On the theoretical—or, better, the psychological—the task is no less huge, but it has the advantage of being open to any one to begin, with his own mind as the site of operations. Mr. Punch reports the conversation of British hod-carriers as follows: "Bill, there goes a furriner." . . . " 'Eave 'arf a brick at 'im!" That, no doubt, is the normal response for the fine flower of Western civilization educated at public expense in the elements of nationalistic and racialist philosophy, and the intellectual classes have only themselves to blame if it is so. To correct the situation they must begin by correcting themselves. They must discard resolutely the pseudo-scientific anthropolgy of the late 19th century, however congenial a habit it may be to think with its *clichés*. They must give up tribal identification, and cease to think of their Japanese butler in East 72d Street as personally responsible for bombing civilians at Shanghai, for even the Common Law has given up making the entire family responsible when a member of it commits murder.

Moreover, belief in scientific method must mean a willingness to uproot old fallacies and to suspend judgment in the presence of verified facts and explicit warnings against jumping to conclusions. Finally, a belief in American democracy, if it is to engender something better than hysterical fears and aggressiveness among separate amorphous lumps of the population—the Catholics fearing the Protestants, the whites fearing the Negroes, the Orientals hating the whites, and all of them finding a convenient scapegoat in the Jews—must mean a willingness to judge individuals by their works instead of by the label they happen to have inherited from a superstitious age. Groups exist, to be sure, and when they act as groups must be judged as such. But the failure to recognize the endless variety of human character under the national, social, economic, and racial label is the key-fallacy in all so-called race-prejudices. Whence it follows that our daily judgments upon our neighbors living across the railroad tracks constitute perhaps the only realm where a little rugged individualism of the Jeffersonian type would be both patriotic in the best sense and productive of social peace.

# THE NEGRO

## [V. F. Calverton]

THE AMERICAN NEGRO represents the most interesting and the most difficult, the most provocative and the most perplexing, race problem in the world today. Transplanted from Africa to America early in the 17th century, bound as a slave to a soil to which he was a stranger, that Negro succeeded in adapting himself to the new country which was to become his home with an expedition and an agility which were scarcely short of miraculous. Today he has become as much at home in his new environment as the men who brought him to it. He has not only become part of his new environment; he has flourished under it. At the present time, for example, there are more Negroes in America than there are Irish in Ireland or Jews in the entire world; what is more pertinent, if not more astonishing, is that the Negro represents one-tenth of the total population of the United States, which is a greater minority than that of any other people.

The fact that the Negro has multiplied in America with such fecundity is proof in itself that he has found his new environment conducive to more than mere survival. Inferior though his status has been, after as well as before manumission, he has managed to preserve a cultural independence in the midst of a *milieu* which discouraged every semblance whatsoever of independence. Whatever he adopted from the white man's way of life he gave his own cultural stamp, converting it, however ancient, into something emphatically and ineluctably new. His religion, his folklore, his music, his dances, all attest his cultural genius. Like the Jew, he has succeeded in being himself, despite an environment which has tried to coerce him into being anything but himself. Neither slavery nor poverty, nor an environment which has cornered and harassed him, has been able to destroy his hedonistic attitude toward life. Unlike the Jew, whose cultural interests have been more erudite, the Negro has developed his best powers in the more popular forms of culture, wherein his supremacy has been indisputable.

Being a Negro in the United States today is like being a prisoner in a jail which has several corridors and squares, in which it is possible occasionally to see the sun and walk amid the flowers and fields that belong to the unimprisoned elements of humanity. Beyond the contours of that circumscribed world there is little territory, economic or physical, in which he can have that freedom necessary for individual advance and social progress. Today, for instance, generations after bond-slavery has disappeared, and centuries after the New England Puritans first transported the blacks to the Colonies because it was "God's work," since it brought the Negro within the influence of the "gospel dispensation," the Negro is faced with laws prohibiting him from living in Syracuse, Ohio, Lawrenceburg, Ellwood, and Salem, Indiana, and Canton, Haywood County, Mitchell and Madison Counties, North Carolina. In other Southern localities the Negro is bound to the land by laws designed to hinder his freedom of locomotion, *viz.,* the contract law, the chain-gang system, and those numerous criminal laws which permit the hiring of Negro convicts to private individuals. In communities where he *can* live he is segregated, persecuted, suppressed.

All through the South, for example, he finds life possible and tolerable only if he adopts the Booker T. Washington psychology, which is that of Uncle Tom; if he dares assert himself—if he dares to insist on his rights, privileges, and liberties as guaranteed by the 13th, 14th and 15th Amendments to the Constitution—he is considered a "bad nigger" and immediately becomes suspect in the community and subject to the persecutions and oppressions which are common under such circumstances. He is not allowed to vote. His education is supervised by white men or by Negroes who represent the Uncle Tom psychology approved by white men. His labor is exploited as ruthlessly as if he were a slave. In the courts, as instanced by the Scottsboro case and many others, he is faced with a prejudice as violent and insane as that confronting a Jew or a Communist in Germany today. In fact, when lynching is included in the picture, his plight is far worse than that of the German Jew or Communist.

In the North, it is true, his situation is less tragic, but that is all. He can move with more freedom within his segregated circle; he can vote; he can in some States attend white schools; he can even attend colleges, if he can find the necessary money—but beyond that his association with white people ends, that is, with the exception of radicals and bohemians who may readily enough become his friends but who are in no position to aid him immediately in his struggle for recognition as a human being on the basis of merit, quality, or distinction. Walter White, in one of his most interesting essays, tells about an experience with Paul Robeson which illuminates the nature of that difficulty. Paul Robeson had just finished singing at one of his best concerts; the audience had been thrilled by his vocal eloquence; the applause rang throughout the house for over ten minutes. Robeson bowed and rebowed dozens of times; people rushed up to him congratulating him on the magnificence of his performance. Fifteen minutes later White and Robeson went out to a restaurant to dine but found that they couldn't dine in any of the restaurants they preferred—because Walter White and Paul Robeson, over whom the whites had been so enthusiastic such a short time before, were Negroes, and Negroes could not eat in any of those restaurants. They were reserved only for whites. Countless episodes of similar character could be described about ever so many distinguished Negroes in ever so many places all through the North and East—in fact, through all the country.

The same situation holds for Negroes in every walk of life. Negro physicians, lawyers, teachers, painters, sculptors, writers, dancers are all equally circumscribed as to their whereabouts and whithers, as to their associations and aspirations. I recall very well, in that connection, a conversation with Abram L. Harris, who is not only the best Negro economist in the United States but also one of the very best of the younger economists in the country, when he complained of the fact that he was never able to come into contact with the leading white economists except in a most academic and exterior sense, the result of which was he lost so much of what white economists were able to gain by more intimate and continued contacts with such personalities.

Abram L. Harris, who is now professor of economics in Howard University, is—in his field—as important as Paul Robeson is in his art; both, however, are balked by the environment. Paul Robeson decided to become an inhabitant of, if not an official citizen in, the Soviet Union, because that was one place where he did not find his Negro heritage a handicap and an encumbrance. Abram L. Harris, despite the difficulties and handicaps of the environment, has decided to stay in the United States.

I could go on indefinitely describing what Negro intellectuals have to endure in order to achieve any kind of recognition at all in this country. L. D. Reddick, an associate professor of history at Dillard University in New Orleans, has described the situation better than any one I know, and because of the excellence of his account I take the liberty of quoting a section of it at this point:

The inadequacy of buildings, books, and apparatus is so patent that the Negro deans and registrars in convention this year advised against the attempt to give graduate training in the publicly-supported institutions of several States. As for salaries, the general condition may be suggested in the observation that the income of the presidents of these colleges is far above that of their faculties. Yet when the president of the State college for Negroes in Florida raised his pay in the budget, it is reported that the Governor vetoed the increase with the words, "No Negro is worth $4000." In the government-supported Howard University and the three leading "privately endowed" schools—Fisk, Atlanta, and Dillard—the *average* income of the assistant, associate, and full professors is $2600.

Obviously, a research man cannot work without data. Here special obstructions are met. It goes without saying that the doors to most private papers and collections are closed to black men. The same is largely true when it comes to public records. The State libraries follow a mixed policy. In Kentucky, for example, there is no interference. The more general practice is, as the Editor of the *Journal of Negro History* puts it, to seat the Negro "somewhere in the building" and to bring to this place the materials he may wish. In other tax-supported libraries and those provided by philanthropy, the Negro is usually excluded. Sometimes use of the books, but not the building, is granted.

A stirring chapter could be written on the ingenious devices employed to gain access to the necessary books and documents. Ties of kinship are always useful. Often the old classmate in Harvard's "History 400," who may be teaching in the neighboring university, is helpful. The trick may be turned by a chain of letters to someone who knows someone who knows someone who knows the custodian. A good practice is to denounce a pro-Northern history book on the Civil War. The prize, no doubt, should go to the passionate devotee who entered into conspiracy with the Negro janitor (who alone knew the place of every book in the building). Every evening the required books were removed and returned early the next morning before the arrival of the political appointee, the librarian.

## SPECIAL FORMS OF DISCRIMINATION

There is, too, the outrage of downright vandalism. Any number of cases of the mysterious disappearance of source materials may be cited. In one of the largest cities of the South, the files of the Superintendent of Public Instruction during Reconstruction days were removed when it became known that a study was to be made of that administration. Doctor W. E. B. DuBois reports a similar experience when a Negro professor planned to write an account of that highly efficient Jonathan C. Gibbs (Negro), Secretary of the State of Florida and Superintendent of Public Instruction, 1872–74.

When it comes to the historical associations and other scientific or semi-scientific conclaves, their programs are arranged and executed without thought of the colored brother. This is not only true of the local or regional societies, but of important national associations which happen to convene in the South. Last February the Department of Superintendents of the National Education Association meeting in New Orleans (where there is, perhaps, less agonizing over the incidence of color than in any other Southern city) was so indifferent to deliberate discourtesy to Negro members that the Julius Rosenwald Fund in a vigorous letter of protest withdrew. Some were sufficiently interested to go through the back door of the freight entrance to attend the sessions in the hotel. The American Historical Association has on occasion allowed such men as Professor Munroe Work, of Tuskegee, to appear. On the other hand, when one member of the committee on programs and arrangements suggested the names of Doctor Carter G. Woodson and Doctor Charles S. Wesley (both Harvard Ph.D.'s and authors of several volumes), who happen to stem from a more aggressive tradition, the committee was immediately reshuffled and this member was promptly dropped.

The effects of these impediments to the intellectual life are manifest. Here may be found one reason, at least, for the interminable round of faculty members wives' bridge parties and the absorption in campus politics. One man came to a Southern Negro college well known as the author of two highly creditable monographs. Today he is better known as the auction bridge champion of the region. Another was known to babble in his sleep of the French Revolution; now his nocturnal murmurings are more related to the last fraternity initiation.

All of this is but additional proof of how difficult it is for a Negro to carve out a career for himself in the United States today. His chances of success are about as unhappy as those of a runner who has one leg tied at the beginning of a race. Underlying all these difficulties, of course, is the attitude of the ruling class which considers the Negro an inferior being and believes that he should be denied liberties and equalities possessed by the white man. This attitude is not confined only to the upper classes but is unfortunately shared also by the lower classes who find a psychological compensation in viewing the Negro as their inferior. The labor movement, for example, has been notoriously hostile to the Negro, and the American Federation of Labor in most of its unions excludes the Negro from membership. As late as 1924 the National Association for the Advancement of Colored People addressed an open letter to the American Federation of Labor urging it to revise its statutes so as to admit Negroes to all its unions, pointing out the advantages which white labor as well as black labor stood to gain from such unity. The coming of the Committee on Industrial Organization has remedied the situation to a considerable extent, and, as George Schuyler writes in *The Pittsburgh Courier,* the Negroes have responded with alacrity to the opportunity the C. I. O. has offered them to become members of its industrial unions. In most of the A. F. of L. unions, however, the Negro still remains an outcast. The provision in the union constitution of the Brotherhood of Railway Clerks—that the doors of the organization are open only to "White workers of good moral character"—is typical of other union constitutions in the A. F. of L.

## II

It is a common belief that the Negro in Africa was an uncultured savage, a wild man of the jungle, who was disciplined to civilized ways by his white masters in the South. "If I could find a Negro who knew Greek syntax," Calhoun declared, "I should believe that the Negro was a human being and ought to be treated as a man." Calhoun's conception of the Negro was characteristic of his day. As a matter of fact, it continues to be characteristic of the South even today, despite the fact that not only have Negroes learned Greek syntax but some of them have succeeded in becoming reputable and distinguished Greek scholars. Such achievements are invariably explained away by the assertion that successful Negroes succeed because they have white blood in their veins. That this is not the case is proven by the fact that many of the most successful Negroes have had no trace of white blood in them at all.

But the blood hypothesis is only one of the many ways in which white men, scholars as well as laymen, have striven to establish the biological inferiority of the Negro. The evolutionary argument is one of the most conspicuous for its absurdity. That the Negro is the lowest in the evolutionary scale between man and the anthropoid ape cannot be argued from any consistent array of anatomical facts. If certain physical characteristics of the Negro seem closely connected with more primitive forms, others reveal him further removed from these evolutionary stocks than the so-called white peoples. One of the characteristics that "delimit man from the apes . . . is the acquisition of an external lip,"[1] and in this respect the thick lip of the Negro is an advance over the thin, simian-

[1]Langdon-Davies, *New Age of Faith,* p. 240; Fino, *Race Prejudice,* and Arthur Keith, *Antiquity of Man.*

resembling lip of the white man. In type of hair and form of head again the Negro is far removed from the straight-haired, brachycephalic apes. In mental tests the endeavor to establish the inferiority of the Negro also has been negative. The work of Peterson and Ferguson, and the general interpretations of the army intelligence tests in the matter of race-inferiority have been criticized so sharply and so successfully by Kroeber that we shall not discuss them here, except to quote Woodworth, whose statement in reference to race-difference, as studied in relationship to the application of intelligence tests to backward people, is at once pertinent and significant:

We are probably justified in inferring that the sensory and motor processes and the elementary brain activities, though differing in degree from one individual to another, are about the same from one race to another.

It is interesting to observe how strictly this statement is in line with that of Finot, who declared many years ago that "there are no inferior and superior races living outside or within the influence of outline. The appearance of civilization and the evolution among certain white peoples within a certain geographical latitude is only the effect of circumstances."

The following testimony of Woodworth is instructive in pointing out the tendency and its manifestations:

Our inveterate love for types and sharp distinctions is apt to stay with us even after we have become scientific, and vitiate our use of statistics to such an extent that the average becomes a stumbling-block rather than an aid to knowledge. We desire, for example, to compare the brain weights of whites and Negroes. We weigh the brains of a sufficient number of each race—let us assume the number to be sufficient. When our measurements are all obtained and spread before us, they convey to the unaided eye no clear idea of a racial difference, so much do they overlap. If they should become jumbled together, we should never be able to separate the Negroes from the whites by aid of brain weight. But now we cast up the average of each group and find them to differ, and though the difference is small, we straightway seize on it as the important result, and announce that the Negro has a smaller brain than the whites. We go a step further, and class the white as a large brained man, the Negro as small brained. Such transforming of differences of degree into differences of kind, and making antitheses between overlapping groups, partakes not a little of the ludicrous.

In brief, the more the attitudes and arguments of the racialists are studied, particularly in reference to the Negro, the more apparent does it become that beneath them all is the argument of race-supremacy and color-mania. Professor Hankins also detects this tendency to racial rationalization, as the following words indicate:

Illusions, especially of superiority and power, are primary elements in the faiths that men live by. It is unusual for even the scholar to pursue truth unalloyed in the fields of religion, history, and the social sciences.

If the Negro's past were better known, there would be fewer attempts to prove his biological inferiority. The discoveries of archæologists, dating from the explorations of over a century ago, have disclosed the remnants of an African culture that hitherto was almost completely unknown. Tennyson's youthful apostrophe to Timbuctoo has a deeper meaning and import today. Timbuctoo stands now as but a single reminder of an ancient civilization that was, perhaps, as rare in diversity and as advanced in ways of life as any civilization, however adjacent or remote, of its time. The products of this civilization, or if we wish to include the civilizations of Ethiopia, Ghana, Melle, and the Songhay in separate categories, then of these civilizations, are an eloquent testimony to their progress.

In the Songhay empire, for example, education was advanced to such a point that people from all over the Islamic world came to teach in its schools; and the savants of the Songhay were active also in the Mohammedan countries to the North and East. In fact, throughout the Sudan, university life was fairly extensive. Ahmed Baba, one of the strongly arresting figures of his period, stands out as a brilliant example of the sweep of Sudanese erudition. An author of more than forty books upon such diverse themes as theology, astronomy, ethnography, and biography, Baba was a scholar of great depth and inspiration. With his expatriation from Timbuctoo—he was in the city at the time that it was invaded by the Moroccans in 1592 and protested against their occupation of it—he lost, in his collection of 1600 books, one of the richest libraries of his day. Ahmed Baba, of course, although the most conspicuous, was only one scholar among many. All through West Africa the Negroes had established many centers of learning. In their schools and universities, courses were given in rhetoric, logic, eloquence, diction, the principles of arithmetic, hygiene, medicine, prosody, philosophy, ethnography, music, and astronomy. The Negro scholars in many instances surpassed the Arabian. In Ethiopia their contribution to culture streamed far beyond the borders of their own nation in influence and power. Every exploration and excavation of African materials adds to this historical revelation.

We see rising before us, in the form of obscure manuscript, relics of apparel, and architectural remains, the lives of peoples and the movements of civilizations, once buried in the sands of a dead world. In this Negro ancestry there were discovered rulers who expanded their kingdoms into empires, generals who advanced the technique of military science, and scholars who brought with their wisdom an advancing vision of life.

The Negro, it is obvious, was *not* an unenlightened primitive, brought to America in order to be Christianized and enslaved. He was *not* of a people without a tradition. In fact, Emile Torday declared, in the light of the Negro's contribution to ancient culture, that "we are indebted to the Negro for the very keystone of our modern civilization and we owe to him the discovery of iron."

Leo Africanus, who travelled through parts of Africa when life in many of the African cities still hummed with activity, has described these early Negro civilizations in a most vivid manner:

I my-selfe saw fifteene kingdoms of the Negroes; howbeit there are many more, which although I saw not with mine owne eues, yet are they by the Negroes sufficiently knowen and frequented. Their names therefore (beginning from the West, and so proceeding Eastward and Southward) are these following: Gualeta, Ghinea, Milli, Tombuto, Gago, Guber, Agadez, Cano, Cafena, Zegzeg, Zanfora, Guangara, Burno, Gaogo, Mibe. These fifteen kingdoms are for the most part situate upon the river Niger, through the which merchants usually travell from Gualate to the cities of Alcoir in Egypt. The iourney indeede is very long, but yet secure and voide of danger. All the said kingdomes adjoine one upon another; ten whereof are separated wither by the river Niger, or by some sandie desert; and in times past each one of the fifteene had a general king, but now at this present, they are all in a manner subicht unto three kings onely; namely, to the king of Borno, who governeth the least part, and the residue is in subiection unto the king of Gaogo; howbeit he that possesseth the wise these kingdomes have many other kingdomes bordering upon the South frontiers of them; to wit, Biro, Temism, Dauma, Medra, and Gorhan; the governors and inhabitants whereof are most rich and industrious people, great lovers of justice and equitie, albeit some lead a brutish kinde of life.[2]

More important still is Africanus' comment upon the learning and culture that prevailed in Timbuctoo:

Here are doctors, judges, priests, and other learned men that are bountifully maintained at the king's cost and charges. And hither are brought divers manu-

[2]Leo Africanus, *Description of Africa.* First Book, p. 128.

scripts or written books out of Barbarie, which are sold for more money than any other merchandise.

From what evidence has been garnered there can be little doubt that the Sudanese University of Sankore at Timbuctoo was practically equal in ambitiousness of undertaking and attainment of culture to the leading European universities of the time. Nor do the universities at Jenna, Aiwalatin, Khago, or Tinderma, although not so portentous in size or design, suffer by comparison with the European institutions of the era. What had happened to those civilizations is like asking what has happened to the Greeks, who once the greatest people in the world are now one of the lowliest. Invasion is the first explanation. The defenselessness of the Africans before gunpowder made them a quick prey to the invaders from the North. Internecine warfare also helped weaken the conflicting kingdoms. The drying up of the Sahara likewise contributed its share in the destruction. The slave raids too, carried on by the natives as well as by the Europeans, were scarcely less disastrous.

For a combination of reasons, then, what had been one of the most interesting civilizations of its day crumbled and collapsed and was buried in the sands of the Sahara—not to be rediscovered until centuries afterwards.

### III

When we realize that the Negro is not without a cultural past, we can readily understand his achievements in American art and literature in terms of environmental evolution.

The contributions of the Negro to American culture are as indigenous to our soil as the legendary cowboy or the gold-seeking frontiersman. And in addition, it is no exaggeration whatsoever to contend that they are more striking and singular in substance and structure than any contributions that have been made by the white man to American culture. In fact, they constitute America's chief claim to originality in its cultural history. In song, the Negro spirituals and to a less extent the blues; in tradition, Negro folk-lore; and in music, Nego jazz—these three constitute the Negro contribution to American culture. In fact it can be said that they constitute all that is unique in our cultural life. Since Indian remains have been largely exterminated, Indian culture, with its native originality, has been mainly lost. At least, enough does not remain to challenge the contributions of the Negro. When Dvořák sought to find an inspiration in the American environment for his New World Symphony, inevitably he turned to the Negro. After all, the Negro, in his simple, unsophisticated way, has developed out of the American *milieu* a form of expression, a mood, a literary *genre,* a folk-tradition, that are distinctly and undeniably American. This is more than the white man has done. The white man in America has continued, and in an inferior manner, a culture of European origin. He has not developed a culture that is definitely and unequivocally American. In respect of originality, then, the Negro is more important in the growth of an American culture than has been the white man. His art is richer, more spontaneous, and more captivating and convincing in its appeal.

The social background of Negro life in itself was sufficient to inspire an art of no ordinary character. Indeed, the very fact that the Negro, by the nature of his environment, was deprived of education, prevented his art from ever becoming purely imitative. Even where he adopted the white man's substance, as in the case of religion, he never adopted his forms. He gave to whatever he took a new style and a new interpretation. In truth, he made it practically into a new thing. There were no ancient conventions that he, in his untutored zeal, felt duty-bound to respect, and no age-old traditions that instructed him, perforce, as to what was art and what was not. He could express his soul, as it were, without concern for grammar or the eye of the carping critic. As a result, his art is, as is all art that springs from the people, an artless art, and in that sense is the most genuine art of the world. While the white man has gone to Europe for his models, and is still seeking an European approval of his artistic endeavor, the Negro in his art forms has never gone beyond America for his background and has never sought the acclaim of any culture other than his own. This is particularly true of those forms of Negro art that come directly from the people. It is, of course, not so true of a poet such as Phyllis Wheatley or of the numerous Negro poets and artists of today, who in more ways than one have followed the traditions of their white contemporaries rather than have extended and perfected the original art forms of their own race. Of course, in the 18th century, when Phyllis Wheatley wrote, those Negro art forms were scarcely more than embryonic. Today, on the other hand, their existence has become a commonplace to the white writer as well as to the black.

In a subtle way Negro art and literature in America have had an economic origin. All that is original in Negro folk-lore, or singular in Negro spirituals and blues, can be traced to the economic institution of slavery and its influence upon the Negro soul. The Negro lived in America as a slave for over two hundred and forty years. He was forced by the system of slavery into habits of life and forms of behavior that inevitably drove him in the direction of emotional escape and religious delirium. Existence offered nothing to hope for but endless labor and pain. Life was a continuous crucifixion. The earth became a place of evil. As a downtrodden and suppressed race he had nothing to discover within himself that insured emancipation or escape. His revolts had all proved ineffectual. Inevitably he turned toward the white man for the materials of his "under-dog" logic. He accepted and absorbed the ideas of the ruling class, as do most subordinate groups and classes, until they became a part of his reaction. The white man's paradise suddenly became a consuming aspiration. He became enamored of it as a holy vision. His belief in it became a ferocious faith. Its other-worldly aspect only lent it a richer enchantment. There were no realistic categories to thwart or limit its undimensioned beauty and magnificence. The scarcities of this world had no meaning in the infinite plenitudes of the next. Gold could be had for the asking, and everything was as dream would have it if in a land beyond the sun.

It was as an expression of this consecrated other-worldly ardor that the Negro spirituals came into being and grew into form. There is more, far more than the ordinary Christian zeal embodied in them. These spirituals are not mere religious hymns written or recited to sweeten the service or improve the ritual. They are the aching, poignant cry of an entire people. Jesus to the Negro is no simple religious savior, worshipped on Sundays and forgotten during the week. He is the incarnation of the suffering soul of a race.

When we turn to the blues and the labor songs, the economic connection is more obvious. Here we have folklore in poetic form, springing spontaneously from the simple everyday life of an oppressed people. The Blues have a primitive kinship with the old ballads that is strikingly curious upon close comparison. While the rhyme-scheme employed in the blues is often less clever and arresting than that found in the ballads, the incremental repetitions are not less effective, and the simple, quick descriptions are often as fine in this form as in the other. The labor songs, growing up as part of the workaday rhythms of daily toil, have a swing about them that is irresistibly infectious. The musical swing of the hammer, its sweeping rise and fall, is communicated for instance with rhythmic power in the song entitled "John Henry":

> Dis is de hammer
> Killed John Henry,
> Killed him dead, killed him dead,
> Busted de brains all outer my pardner
> In his head, yes, in his head.

And in the familiar levee song we meet with another but not less enticing rhythm:

> Where wuz your sweet mamma
> When de boat went down?
> On de deck, Babe,
> Hollerin' Alabama Bound.

Unquestionably the Negro has retained in his art a certain primitivism that is wonderfully refreshing in contrast to the stilted affectations of the more cultured styles and conceptions. We come closer to life with these primitivisms, feel beauty in its more genuine and intimate, and less artificial and cerebral, forms.

These primitivisms of the Negro are a singular evolution of our American environment. In describing them as primitive we do not mean that they are savage in origin, or that the instincts of savagery linger in them, but that they are untutored in form and unsophisticated in content, and in these aspects are more primitive than civilized in character. The art of primitive peoples is often the very opposite in spirit to that of the American Negro. The art of the African Negro, for instance, is entirely without that exuberance which is so emphatically dominant in the art-expression of the American Negro. African art is rigid, economical of energy, and almost classic in its discipline. The exuberance of sentiment, the spirited denial of discipline, and the contempt for the conventional that are so conspicuous in the art of the American Negro are direct out-growths of the nature of his life in this country.

In jazz this vital and overwhelming exuberance of the American Negro reaches its apex in physical dynamics. If the origin of jazz is not entirely Negroid—for, that its fundamental form is derivative of Negro rhythms no longer can be disputed—its development of attitude and expression in America has certainly been chiefly advanced by the Negro. While the spirituals represent the religious escape of the Negro, the jazz rhythms vivify his mundane abandon.

Jazz reflects something of the essential irresponsibility—or rather, the irresponsible enthusiasms and ecstasies—that underlies Negro life here in America; and it is these enthusiasms and ecstasies which give to Negro art such singular distinction in verve and spontaneity. While jazz in its inferior forms is a vulgar removal from the idea of the exquisite which prevailed in music before our day, it nevertheless has the virtue of great originality and the vigor of deep challenge. In one very significant sense, indeed, it remains as the only original contribution to music that has been made in America.

If the recent developments in Negro literature cannot be characterized as a renaissance, certainly they must be noted as marking off a new stage in the literary history of a people. Without question the work of Jean Toomer, Rudolph Fisher, W. Burghardt Du Bois, Walter White, and Zora Neale Hurston in fiction; James Langston Hughes, Countee Cullen, Claude McKay, and M. B. Tolson in verse; and Alain Locke, Franklin Frazier, James Weldon Johnson, Charles S. Johnson, Abram L. Harris, and George Schuyler in the essay—all this has been distinguished by fine intelligence and advancing artistic vision. Surely at no other period, and certainly never in so short a time, have so many Negro writers of genuine talent appeared. If, among these writers, no great artist nor great thinker has thus far evolved, there is no reason for despair. The great achievement of Roland Hayes on the concert stage, and of Paul Robeson in the theatre, gives promise at least of similar success in the literary art of the future. The appearance of these and numerous similar artists, and the growth of this newer spirit on the part of the Negro, are really not so much a rebirth in the sense of a renaissance as they constitute the hastening of an old birth which had formerly been retarded in its growth and evolution.

Steadily in this New Negro literature the trend has developed in favor of the vigorous instead of the exquisite. Challenge has become more significant than charm. The submissive acquiescences of the Booker T. Washington attitude and era have now become contemptuously anachronistic. The sentimental cry of a 19th-century poet such as Corrothers—

> To be a Negro in a day like this—
> Alas! Lord God, what ill have we done

has been superseded by the charging defiance of a 20th-century poet such as McKay:

### IF WE MUST DIE

If we must die—let it not be like hogs
Hunted and penned in an inglorious spot,
While round us bark the mad and hungry dogs,
Making their mock at our accursed lot.

If we must die—oh, let us nobly die,
So that our precious blood may not be shed
In vain; then even the monsters we defy
Shall be constrained to honor us though dead!

Oh, Kinsmen! We must meet the common foe;
Though far outnumbered, let us still be brave,
And for their thousand blows deal one death-blow!
What though before us lies the open grave?
Like men we'll face the murderous, cowardly pack,
Pressed to the wall, dying, but—fighting back!

The admission of inferiority which was implicit in so much of the earlier verse, the supplicatory note which ran like a lugubrious echo through so many of its stanzas, has been supplanted by an attitude of superiority and independence on the part of such poets as Countee Cullen, James Langston Hughes, and Gwendolyn Bennett.

In Cullen's lines:

My love is dark as yours is fair,
Yet lovelier I hold her
Than listless maids with pallid hair,
And blood that's thin and colder . . .

one discovers this attitude expressed with exquisite conviction. In Gwendolyn Bennett's stanza:

I love you for your brownness
And the rounded darkness of your breast;
I love you for the breaking sadness in your voice
And shadows where your wayward eye-lids rest . . .

we are confronted with it again in definite form. Hughes gives to this same attitude a touch of African aspiration:

We should have a land of trees
Bowed down with chattering parrots
Brilliant as the day,
And not this land where birds are grey . . .

George Schuyler in prose has given this same attitude a sharp, ironic turn. His clean-cut, biting style—inevitably in keeping with his theme and purpose—is at times superb. He meets his materials with a directness that compels by its vigor. His writing is never sentimental; it has, rather, a hard, metallic brilliance that convinces without endeavoring to caress. In *Our Greatest Gift to America,* which deals in satiric form with the Negro's position in this country, Schuyler's criticism is acute and devastating:

It is fairly well established, I think, that our presence in the Great Republic has been of incalculable psychological value to the masses of which we are citizens. Descendants of convicts, serfs, and half-wits, with the rest they have been buoyed up and greatly exalted by being constantly assured of their superiority to all other races and their equality with each other. On the stages of a thousand music-halls, they have their vanity tickled by black-face performers parading the idiocies of mythical black roustabouts and rustics. Between belly-cracking guffaws they have secretly congratulated themselves on the fact that they are not like these buffoons. Their books and magazines have told them, or insinuated, that morality, beauty, refinement and culture are restricted to Caucasians. On every hand they have seen smokes endeavoring to change from black to white, and from kinky hair to straight by means of deleterious chemicals, and constantly they hear the Negroes urging each other to do this and that like white folks. Nor do the crackers fail to observe either—that pink epidermis is as highly treasured among blacks as in Nordic America, and that the most devastating charge that one Negro can make against another is that he acts "just like a nigger." Anything excellent they hear labelled by the race-conscious Negroes as "like white folks," nor is it unusual for them while loitering in the Negro ghetto, to hear black women compared to Fords, mulatto women to Cadillacs and white women to Packards. With so much flattery it is no wonder that the Caucasians have a very high opinion of themselves and attempt to live up to the lofty niche in which the Negroes have placed them. We should not marvel that every white elevator operator, school teacher and bricklayer identifies himself with Shakespeare, Julius Cæsar, Napoleon, Newton, Edison, Wagner, Tennyson, and Rembrandt as creators of this great civilization. As a result we have our American society, where everybody who sports a pink color believes himself to be the equal of all other whites by virtue of his lack of skin pigmentation, and his classic Caucasian features.

It is not surprising, then, that democracy has worked better in this country than elsewhere. This belief in the equality of all white folks—making skin color the gauge of worth and the measure of citizenship rights—has caused the lowest to strive to become among the highest. Because of this great ferment, America has become the Utopia of the material world; the land of hope and opportunity. Without the transplanted African in their midst to bolster up the illusion, America would have unquestionably been a much different place; but instead the shine has served as a mud-sill upon which all white people alike can stand and reach toward the stars. I submit that here is the gift par excellence of the Negro to America. To spur ten times our number on to great heights of achievement; to spare the nation the enervating presence of a destructive social caste system, such as exists elsewhere, by substituting a colored caste system that roused the hope and pride of teeming millions of ofays—this indeed is a gift of which we can well be proud.

As the racialism of the Negro has become more assertive and radical, a new attitude has begun to reveal itself in his fiction. There has been a marked tendency in the past—except in stories of dialect—for Negro writers to center their attention upon the more enlightened and prosperous members of the race. In *Fire in the Flint,* for instance, Walter White has chosen a doctor for his protagonist; in *There Is Confusion* Jessie Fauset has featured a dancer as her star; in *Quicksand* Nella Larsen has selected a school teacher for her main character; and in *The Dark Princess* Du Bois has made an aristocratic woman into his heroine. Since that time in the novels of Rudolph Fisher and Claude McKay the class of characters has shifted. In *The Walls of Jericho* and *Home to Harlem* the main characters are proletarian types, piano-movers and stevedores, who are endowed with little education and less culture. The lives of these lower types are seen to be as fascinating and dramatic as those of the upper.

In Zora Neale Hurston's work we meet these types in even more striking form. In her latest novel, *Their Eyes Are Watching God,* the character of Teacake is an exceptionally effective portrayal of a type of Negro that has never been captured in fiction before. In M. B. Tolson's *Harlem Gallery,* which is an urbanized Negro "Spoon River Anthology," still other and even more various types come to life in a most direct and intimate fashion. Tolson promises to be one of the richest talents produced by Negro literature in America. The latest Negro writer, following in this same simple, proletarian tradition, is Richard Wright, whose collection of short stories, *Uncle Tom's Children,* has about it the unquestioned stamp of genius.

In fact, a certain native drama is revealed in the lives of these colored folk that is absent in the lives of most white people in the same class of society. This added drama flows from the freer and more irresponsibly spontaneous way in which these black men live. No doubt in time these proletarian types—since the Negro, dating from his vast migrations from Southern to Northern latitudes during and immediately following the war, is becoming rapidly proletarianized—will occupy an increasingly large part in the entire literary scene.

This new challenge on the part of the contemporary Negro was first expressed in 1912 by W. Burghardt Du Bois in his famous Atlanta speech, which was dynamic in its various provocations. This speech in its statement of purpose chalked off the beginning of a new era in the intellectual life of the American Negro:

We plan an organization so effective and so powerful that when discrimination and injustice touched one Negro, it would touch 12,000,000. We have not got this yet, but we have taken a great step toward it. We have dreamed, too, of an organization that would work ceaselessly to make Americans know that the so-called "Negro-Problem" is simply one phase of the vaster problem of democracy in America, and that those who wish freedom and justice for their country must wish it for every black citizen. This is the great and insistent message of the National Association of Colored People.

This meant that the Booker T. Washington philosophy, which had prevailed for over a generation, had been at last criticized and condemned. The intellectual acquiescence which Washington had encouraged and endorsed was supplanted by a doctrine of resistance. Henceforth the American Negro, through the establishment of this and other organizations, would fight rather than surrender. The World War, of course, was enormously instrumental in strengthening this change of attitude on the part of the Negro.

As we have seen, this change in intellectual conviction, this shifting from an attitude of compromise to one of challenge, is reflected in the literature of the Negro during the recent decade.

Today, Negro leadership can be divided into three groups: right, center, and left. The right is led by those Negroes who still believe that the Uncle Tom psychology advocated by Booker T. Washington is best for the race; the center, derived from Burghardt Du Bois, believes in fighting for Negro rights upon every occasion but at the same time fighting for them within the framework of our present economic system; the left believes that the real fight must be waged against the capitalist system because so long as capitalism survives the Negro will be downtrodden and oppressed. The first type is still dominant, although its influence has waned since the World War. In large part it is little more than a pawn of white philanthropy, accepting the gratuities of the Rosenwald, Rockefeller, and other foundations, backing segregation and all the various forms of race separation which encourage a most reprehensible and regrettable docility and obsequiousness on the part of the race. Most Negro institutions are still headed by Negroes of that caliber; most departments in Negro universities are in charge of Negroes of that stripe; most Negro organizations—business, social, fraternal—are controlled by Negroes who adopt that attitude. The forces of the center and the left, however, have grown in recent years, and though they may not hold many positions of power and influence in the Negro world, they have become instrumental in changing the attitude of the Negro populace, infusing it with a determination to stand up for its rights, to fight for its freedom, and to direct its energies in progressive instead of retrogressive channels.

With the advent of the C. I. O., the Negro's position in the labor movement has been revolutionized; it is impossible to build industrial unions without the support and inclusion of Negro labor, and it is that inclusion which is undermining the separatist argument of the conservative Negro leaders. There is no other force in America which is so powerful in breaking down race lines as the labor movement, and already the C. I. O. has taken the first steps in that direction. In the past, as we have seen, white labor has been hostile to the Negro. Under such conditions the future of the great masses of Negroes was bound to be a hopeless one. Under these changed conditions, however, the Negro has a new future to look forward to, because when the unity of white and black labor is finally established the greatest step to date will have been taken toward the destruction of those prejudices, antagonisms, and hostilities which have rendered the relationship between the races so unhappy and so inhuman in the past.

RELIGION

# RELIGION

## THE PROTESTANT FAITHS

### [*H. Paul Douglass*]

THE MOST obvious objective warrant for treating as a unity the one hundred and fifty, more or less, American Protestant groups which call themselves churches, is that more than nine-tenths of all Protestants are found in about forty denominations —which, with a few exceptions, are actually united in membership and active participation in significant inter-church organizations. These collective agencies of the Protestant faiths exist for mutual counsel and practical co-operative service, for religious education, for missionary extension, and for relations with other church bodies throughout the world. The connective structure which they have developed is of the same kind as the separate denominational structures into which they are divided, though less authoritative.

Moreover, their unity is cumulative. Churches representing 70 per cent of American Protestants are nationally united in four or five inter-church organizations. The broadest evidence of their substantial unity is their agreement upon the outlines of a common culture, which they attempt to hand down to the next generation through religious education. This indicates a profoundly realistic core of agreement.

The total situation is as if the skeleton of an over-arching cathedral had been erected over many denominational churches, which remain as separate chapels within the one cathedral. Speaking literally, in spite of the varied circumstances and different lands in which it originated, American Protestantism is organized about a very large common center of belief and attitude which endows it with distinct internal unity. Attached to this center are minor denominations which, in the main, are only normal variations. Their characteristics are still more largely those of the central group than divergences from it. The total situation is an expression of strongly integrative tendencies in Protestantism, and affords an adequate justification for treating it as one phenomenon.

In equating this topic with those of the other essays of the present volume the Protestant faiths are treated as an aspect of American society —one of its many significant activities and interests. Their churches are part of the national culture, and their life belongs to our times.

Inclined as it is to distinguish between the essence and the mechanics of religion, Protestantism is relatively prepared to be rated as merely one interest among many, and—as far at least as its external and institutional expressions go—to take the same sort of treatment as is meted out to all the rest. One would be well advised to leave the matter here but for two facts: First, though accustomed to being bracketed with other interests of the contemporary world, Protestantism—along with all other versions of Christianity—implicitly holds to the assumption that it has corporate relationships which extend into a second world; second, the church—Protestant quite as much as Catholic—presumes to be a society, one of the functions of which is to judge the culture of which it is a part from a standpoint somehow higher than that culture, and ultimately derived from, relationships outside of it.

Now to admit such conceptions as these into the universe of scientific description not only adds to the factors demanding to be discussed, but also distinctly changes their balance. Yet in so far as the pressure of these assumptions inevitably works out into the behavior of the members of the Protestant faiths, their existence has to be registered, if this behavior is to be properly described and evaluated.

Any organized religion has to be recognized and accounted for in two phases and on two levels, which, taken together, constitute the single movement: First, the popular; second, the ecclesiastical.

Popular Protestantism is much the same thing as ecclesiastical Protestantism, except that the former occupies a sub-church level. The main difference is not located in the realm of faith, but relates merely to a more or less definite and fixed expression in institutional form.

Ecclesiastical Protestantism, accordingly, is the churches with the organization and formulation of doctrine; their regular practices, organized officials; their enterprises, and their property. To be ecclesiastically organized is, moreover, to have a definite membership—the pragmatic test of participation in the activities of the church supplementing the test of formal membership.

Both popular and ecclesiastical Protestantism have their more static and more dynamic phases. However, no dangerous tension can be developed in an unconfined area. Within popular Protestantism leachings away of meaning and of sanction are quite possible, but since it is under no authoritative control, it generates no resistance which could produce an explosion.

The contrast between the more static and the more dynamic phases of the situation applies, therefore, only within ecclesiastical Protestantism. Within its boundaries, however, one may first distinguish the merely normal tensions between the opposing forces of inertia and change. The balance shifts back and forth, but its general movement is controlled by a strong tendency toward equilibrium in a mediating position. There is generally enough elasticity in the situation to absorb any resulting pressures.

But in addition—as will appear later—Protestantism shows certain signs of extreme tensions which threaten to disrupt the boundaries themselves.

This analysis supplies structure to the further consideration of the theme. This discussion will deal, first with popular Protestantism, second, with ecclesiastical Protestantism under normal tension, and third, with points of most acute stress which hold possibilities for its disruption.

## POPULAR PROTESTANTISM

Popular Protestantism corresponds substantially to the total American population of Protestant antecedents which is not already in the churches. Little though the church itself may admit religious value in nebulous ties, subjectively felt but not publicly acknowledged, it is most pertinent to an understanding of such modern societies as the United States and Canada to know that virtually every non-church member acknowledges a certain attachment to some religious faith. This is well established both by official census questions and by representative house-to-house surveys.

Moreover, nearly every one who is Protestant by antecedent also identifies himself as having some inner attachment to a particular sect or denomination.

All this means that popular Protestantism is not a mere aggregate of non-church individuals. In the strict sociological sense there *is* a Protestant community existing on the level of inherited traditions. It is marked by what can be called limited institutionalization; but in general terms its forms can be described, its ideology stated, and its characteristics indicated.

Popular Protestantism appears under the forms of national custom and legal enactment. It is the sort of "religion" which the Northwestern Ordinance declared to be necesary for good government, and is publicly recognized by ritual observances in courts and legislatures as well as by religious rites observed by a very large fraction of non-church Protestants in connection with marriages and funerals. In his *American Road to Culture*[1] Counts points out that the American people are steeped in an intensely religious tradition, which finds its way into the public schools, whenever it is not definitely prevented, in the form of prayer, hymn-singing, and Scripture-reading. And the virtues which the public schools attempt to inculcate are Christian virtues, conceived in conventional Protestant forms.

On the theory of giving the public what it wants—and quite apart from broadcasting by the churches themselves—an immense amount of "religion" is put on the air by radio operators and advertisers. Most of it is definitely Protestant in tone and antecedent—for example, the Negro spirituals. The essential Protestant quality of such forms and expressions lies in the further fact that these broadcast religious talks dissociate religion from the church in a way contrary to Catholic instinct. (Perhaps feeling the competition, there has recently been some definitely Catholic broadcasting, with one or two spectacular features, such as the broad-casting of the bells from Rome on Easter.)

As a privately held religion, popular Protestantism cherishes attitudes highly critical of the church, yet it informally accepts and perpetuates a creed and a code closely resembling the church's own. First-hand inves-tigation of cross-sectional sample of America's population, obtained chiefly from persons outside the churches (along with more limited question-naires and surveys), reveals that the masses generally maintain an in-articulate religious faith. They believe—in a shadowy way, to be sure—in God and in immortality. They respect and admire the good—though, as generally viewed, the impractical—Jesus. Of actual historical facts about him they are ignorant. About the theological Christ they know little and care less. In extreme emergencies they pray, almost to the last man; but the concept of salvation from sin, or the sense of participation in the cosmic drama of redemption, is either shockingly crude or else lacking altogether.

Sharing, though in vaguer terms than its own, the basic faith of the church, privately held Protestantism, nevertheless, is usually denunciatory of the church, which it blames for falsifying its ideals by its practices, for trivial and external requirements, and for the irrelevance of its thinking to the actual living problems of humantiy. The majority of

[1] *The American Road to Culture.*

the church's critics were under some sort of religious influence in childhood, and they generally still regard themselves as entitled to claim the services of priest or clergyman in connection with a wedding or a death. In brief, while essential significance in the realm of religion has been denied the church, its vogue continues as popular Protestantism's whipping-boy, on whom all resentments over the failures of private religion are visited.

On the sub-church level, Protestantism tends to merge with the widespread secular idealism of the nation, which wishes to be good but does not claim to be religious. Indeed, the difference between the church and the "world" has largely disappeared. Rotarians and Kiwanians are interchangeable with the priesthood. Radical humanism undertakes to rationalize this position.

The general characteristics of popular Protestantism are those of the American people. It is enterprising and melioristic. The rough-and-ready distinctions between essentials and non-essentials strip religious requirements to the smallest common denominator. Because they do *some* good, the churches are supported even when they are criticized.

Europeans generally interpret the American slogan—"Deed rather than creed"—as identifying Protestantism with a vicious form of "activism," the tendency always to be running around "doing" something without any clear or ultimate sanction. (H. G. Wells once called these people the "Forgawdsakers.")

Popular Protestantism is conservative. This is because it is uncritical. Compared with the Protestantism of the churches it lacks recognized norms which it may use as a point of departure in evaluating change. Popular Protestantism has no institutional framework to call in question, no mechanism through which to work adaptations. It can only drift.

Lacking alike external standards and tested inner sanction, popular Protestantism varies with the strength of childhood impressions, with later acquired philosophies, with the vicissitudes of individual fortunes, and with the unequally distributed natural piety of men. Yet in some crude fashion popular Protestantism works and contrives to keep alive the sense of constituting a distinct community within the forms and ideas of our wider culture and with the folk-characteristics just enumerated.

It would be quite possible to organize a church on this level and—with efficient management and renewal from such genuine faith and devotion as undoubtedly exists outside the church—to operate it indefinitely. But this Protestantism has not done. Nor are the churches primarily the development of popular Protestantism on the institutional level. They express, rather, the distinctive inner genius of the Protestant movement and the modifications of that genius by their peculiar evolution in America.

To this aspect of the theme consideration now turns.

### Ecclesiastical Protestantism

The Protestant church inevitably takes over all the elemental characteristics of its constituency, now a major fraction of the American people. In some measure it refines and improves the quality of diluted popular Christianity, and it transmutes the whole according to its peculiar genius, which is far more than a mere form of organization.

On one hand, though not without a sense of inconsistency, the church accepts and uses the backing of popular traits. Americans believe in progress by gradual stages and are not greatly concerned about ultimate goals providing they have the comforting sense of being faced in the right direction. This is the church's working creed as well. Americans distrust experts. Widespread doubt prevails in the church with respect to theological issues so sharply drawn by intellectuals. The common man—in the church as well as out of it—suspects that differences between abstract notions are largely artificial. All along the line ecclesiastical characteristics turn out to be popular traits.

On the other hand, the genius of Protestantism puts a peculiar stamp upon all the traditionally recognized basic qualities of the American people—their individualism, their democracy, their love of freedom. This is best expressed by saying that the Protestant church raises religion from the communal to the associative level and puts its stress upon the less inevitable and the more variable traits of society which differentiate association from community.

In contrast with community—which implies a common focus for all of life—modern Western society consists of a large number of associations, each standing for a single interest within life. Except the State, no association is coextensive with the total population of the community. Association arises when a fraction of the population directs its attention to this or to that aspect of the previously shared life of the communal group—and isolates this particular aspect as an object of special concern. This means that each aspect selected for attention has to be separately evaluated as more or as less important than the others. It secures continuity of attention—not according to its accidental rating within the common tradition, but increasingly according to the contemporary strength of its proved value.

As a result of this evaluation any one of these aspects may be dropped out entirely from the scheme of life. All of the functions of the primitive community are taken for granted and have to be; *no* function of the Western association is merely taken for granted—and most of the structure of modern society is created in behalf of particular interests.

As organized about such special interest, the life of modern society is controlled by more specific standards and by more inward standards, ethically speaking, than those of the original community. Association is selective in the sense that there are ways of getting out of it, but also in the sense that one can stay inside and criticize. Its arrangements are not so fixed as those of communal society. The association marks the more plastic phase of social organization and potentially the more progressive. Finally, in contrast to the passivity of communal society, association is purposive; it is more or less clearly conscious of some limited interest which it serves. And to that interest it renders a different and a far more complex type of loyalty than that of habitual response to communal situations. In brief, the loyalties arising from association are always compatible with questioning and with change.

Now, within a society of the sort that has just been described, the Protestant church has selected religion from among the shared communal interests, has directed special attention toward it, and has given it differentiated development. Within the social processes in their associative phases the ends of religion thus come to be served more conclusively and directly, and with more particular loyalty, than ever they were in primitive society.

Within such a society the church, at any given time, appears simply as one associate among many. Measured by bulk—its vast numbers of adherents, its colossal institutional structure, its prestige—the Protestant church is one of the great associations. But in spite of its magnitude—and its high private self-evaluation—its essential social character within the mundane sphere is not different from that of others.

Yet a still more profound result is that the identification of ecclesiastical Protestantism with society on the associative level injects new qualities into its historic emphases. Its insistence on voluntary decision on the part of its adherents whether to accept or to reject the religious tradition, upon religion as something to be possessed personally, upon the unique supremacy of inwardly-apprehended values against the claims of secular community or State—all this is endowed with the meanings of the new social principle. It is in this new freedom that Protestantism asserts the compatibility of religion with questioning and change, and stresses flexible loyalty. These affirmations—in which the peculiar dynamics of Protestantism have always been found—get fresh flavor within a culture organized as a group of special interests.

Apart from this question of its inner character, the current status of ecclesiastical Protestantism in the United States need not greatly concern one. For what they may be worth, however, certain facts about its size and numerical growth should be noted. In formal church membership it enrolls about 33,500,000 Americans above thirteen years of age.[2] It is impossible to tell even approximately how much of the population of the United States is Protestant by antecedents. Total church membership, however, has reached higher proportions during the first one-third of the 20th century than ever before. Proportionately, tenfold more of the population of this country belongs to the church by formal enrollment than at the time of the adoption of our Constitution. And during the last three decades the church has somewhat more than kept up with the growth of the population. Protestants commonly believe—especially since the virtual stoppage of foreign immigration—that their membership is growing faster than is that of the non-Protestant branches of the Christian church.

In a seconday sense membership is augmented by Sunday School pupils, persons enrolled in subsidiary societies and groups, and pledged financial supporters. Beyond these is the unidentified group "under pastoral care," including the church's clients and dependents as well as sponsored groups such as the Boy Scouts and the various other clubs, which are in the church rather than of it.

All these go to make up the determinate constituency of the church at a given time. Moreover, birth, marriage, and the last extremity of death return multitudes of remote adherents to the church's sacraments. From the sociological standpoint—which concerns the associative process as such, whatever its alleged grounds—the church's definition of formal membership is less important than these more inclusive relationships.

The test of participation in the church's activities both adds to and subtracts from the numerical account as given in terms of formal mem-

[2]This equals about 64 per cent of the total membership of the nation above this age.

bership. Attendance at conventional public services and Sunday School enrollment has doubtless diminished on the week-to-week basis, but the much more varied programs of many churches, the more intensified use of church property for semi-secular activities, and the massing of attendance at special seasons and holidays make it more than probable that Protestant Americans "darken the church door" today more often than ever they have before.

While Protestants constitute less than two-thirds of the church membership of the United States, about four-fifths of the some 2,500,000 organized in local congregations are Protestant. This means that Protestantism runs to small local churches—the number of which has been greatly overdone by sectarian zeal.

It is not necessary to pursue in detail the story of the Protestant ministry —the majority of its members being drawn from humble rural antecedents and not well educated professionally. Nor is it necessary to count the church's wealth—though, up to the time of the depression, it was increasing faster, proportionately, than the national wealth; nor to describe the vast area of Protestant organization and activity beyond its local parishes—its schools and colleges, its charities and missions, its publications and cultural activities. Space does not permit the tracing, for example, of its significant ties with the arts of music, architecture, and public discourse. Magnitude and activity in all these fields is, however, less significant than the trends which they represent.

The Protestant church of today is partly the product of long-continued trends, partly of their recent sharp reversal. Its general historical lineage is well known. Its main source was British Puritanism, chiefly in its nonconformist version, the Church of England contributing only a minor element. Dutch and Swedish religious minorities also existed from early Colonial times. Considering the Colonial period as a whole, the transplanted churches—whether as the legal establishments of the incipient States, or as dissenting sects—were not numerically successful. At the end of the Colonial period, in fact, religion was in an exceedingly low state.

Our early national period released tremendous new energies under the stimulus of fresh opportunity for the common man. Religion shared in this new dynamic. The churches—mainly Protestant, of course, and built by individual recruiting of membership and supported on a purely voluntary basis—tripled their enrolled membership, relative to the population, in the next fifty years. Church extension and church building took their places as characteristic features of national enterprise. Home, school, and church became the cultural foci of the new civilization which rapidly formed behind succeeding frontiers.

This same period, however, registered great cultural losses for the church. In its frontier expression religion was terribly crude. Standards of ministerial education were debased to a point from which they have never entirely recovered. Revivalism triumphed over the more churchly religion of the Colonial Protestant tradition and flourished as the emotional spring of religious progress for a century. Despite multiplying sectarian differences, Protestantism's prevalence tended to create a Protestant cultural type. All this signified the preservation and re-establishment of the traditional faith and morality of the earlier period. It was a triumph of religion still on the communal level.

During the succeeding half-century the church successfully kept up its momentum. Avoiding the bare-handed struggle with the wilderness, later-coming immigrant populations of all races found it comparatively easy to build on foundations laid by the pioneers. These tardier religious cultures were transplanted with less change and impoverishment. New sources of immigration rapidly reinforced the total large resources of the nation, but reduced the numerical ascendency of Protestantism.

As the urbanization of the nation now came rapidly on, religious enterprise continued more than to keep up with national growth. It became— and continued—easier to conserve gains. Energies once absorbed in foundation-building were now released to improve the quality of church life. Technically, the church became more adequate to its task than ever before.

It has remained for urbanization, both in its rural and in its city phase, to give the church the greatest inner revolution it has ever known, and really to establish it on the associative level—as well as to stretch the associative principle well-nigh to the breaking point.

To understand the significance of what has suddenly happened one must consider that within the last twenty-five years—by means of improved communication and transportation, and the re-grouping of the rural population about town centers—the typical rural person has had opened to him a wider association than his kind ever had in America— and probably wider than any rural population ever had before since society became human.

From the earliest beginnings of society the relations of rural and village communities had concerned the same people, over and over again. Throughout the re-groupings the personnel of the community remained substantially the same. Marriage, occupation, and economic opportunity, for the great majority, had to be achieved within the limits of a few-score families, composed of a hundred or two hundred persons. A common working philosophy, and a religious outlook, had to be derived primarily from the experiences and outlooks of these petty groups.

The consequences of this re-grouping of rural populations in town- or city-centered units are epochal because of the inner changes which they have impelled. For both country and city they have involved new principles of association, while in the town they have greatly complicated the old principles. The decisive quality of the changes just described has not yet been adequately sensed, either in their rural or urban setting. But it is the city, of course, which shows urbanization in its most extreme form.

Full-blown urbanization tends to give the adult city or suburban dweller a different set of fellows for every major relationship. He does not live near the people with whom he works, and, when he plays, it is with a still different group. The trade, the profession, the informal groupings of fellow-workers bring newly rewarding and compelling ties, different from the rest. Special cultural interests or avocations place one in the literary, the artistic, or the musical crowd. Thus the urban man has manifold ties in many directions—but all relatively feeble. His associations are based on selective affinity rather than on contiguity in a self-contained neighborhood—or on the deeper ties of the racial group or family clan which originally explained the cohesion of all social groups.

Corresponding to these changes in the underlying terms of secular socialization, the church tends to get reduced merely to one of the many groups in which persons, detached from locality, associate together with segments of their personalities.

Moreover, each segment of personality, expressing itself in a different context and as a response to a different set of people, tends to project a separate set of moral standards. In this segmentation of culture we find the essence of urbanization, and, as well, the substitution of multiple moral standards for a single communal standard. This fact confronts organized religion with the task of integrating and disciplining its components—a task, the like of which it never had before.

Certain to be radical was the effect of so momentous a shift of principle upon the church's institutional stability. In the present instance it has been greatly exaggerated by the rapidity with which corresponding secular changes have taken place. The hurried pace of environmental change has given the experiences of the church a high dramatic quality. In typical cities a fourth of all Protestant churches which ever existed have died; a third of the survivors are essentially stranded institutions, living on a poor dying rate. Three out of four city churches have moved at least once during their history. Colonies of churches—often leaders of their respective denominations—have been neighbors and rivals in three or four different locations—each moving to the "best" new territory every time its old territory went bad. Many of these removals were institutionally for the better. In brief, the Protestant church is on wheels and moves in response to environmental change.

Similar evidence of environmental conditioning is found on a still larger scale. The seven least religious States—measured by church membership—have enrolled only 30 per cent of their adult population in the church; the seven most religious States, 73 per cent. Why should one group show nearly two-and-one-half times more church membership than another? No sane person would argue for any corresponding difference in ethical conduct or in subjective difference of Christian belief. But between the years 1900 and 1930 the seven least religious States had increased their populations three times as fast as the most religious ones— and a half of their total population was born outside their borders, whereas the slow-growing and stay-at-home States were the most religious.

The success of Protestantism as an institutional religion, then, is a matter of degree and rapidity of social change and the resulting composition of the population. When change is unusually rapid, the church cannot keep up, and a temporary lag exists between the population and institutional effectiveness. With the present slowing down of the rate of growth of the American population, the churches are able to conserve a larger proportion of their members. Fewer sheep are lost between folds.

The small villages and towns of the United States are its most static communities. They are almost twice as well evangelized as is the farming population about them. Their some 20,000,000 people retain more of the communal identification of the church and local society, and are least shaken of any group in their traditional loyalty to the Protestant church.

Now the more specific features of the Protestant church, as one objectively knows it in the United States, are the product of these more massive factors—its deep foundation in the inherited folk-ways and characteristics, and its historical religious emphasis raised to tottery heights by the sudden urbanization of the nation and swaying under direct environmental pressure. Its primordial impulses and convictions—as a religion and as historically Christian—to some degree inform this complex of more external factors. But in no significant direction is it possible fully to disentangle the skein of operative influences, so as to say, "This marks the survival of popular communal religion: That shows the incursion of a new principle." One can only trace the intricacies of a highly complicated situation.

As a result of these varied pressures Protestantism is much less immediately responsive to the changed outlooks of secular culture than it is to direct environmental forces. The shifting of religious positions to match changes in science and philosophy is relatively slow. The "new climate"—which so strongly affects many other areas of human interest— touches the churches more remotely than it does most of the other phases of culture.

Sanderson secured a theological self-classification from about 1000 urban churches. Sixteen per cent called themselves fundamentalist; 48 per cent, conservative; 32 per cent, liberal; and 2 per cent, radical. More than one-half of the fundamentalist churches—and relatively few liberal churches—were found in areas dominated by the underprivileged and poorer populations.

From the viewpoint of the country as a whole, modernity is very unequally distributed. Regionalism dominates the religious climate, and the "Bible Belt" is more than an ungracious figure of speech.

In studies embodied in the 1934 report on *Recent Social Trends* minor shifts of religious position over a relatively brief period have been interestingly measured at numerous points. Thus, in American periodicals, while approving references to traditional Christianity still outnumber disapproving ones by nearly two to one, the ratio of approval has declined since the first of the century. In the so-called "intellectual" magazines about two-thirds of the references are disapproving, while in the "mass circulation" and the women's magazines about the same proportion of references are approving. The sensational periodicals, however, are the best supporters of conventional religion. A magazine's orthodoxy is about in proportion to its unworthiness to exist at all!

There appears to be more mention of God in periodical literature than formerly—but more skepticism about Him. A less personal conception of Deity prevails. Interest in life after death appears to have declined, though 70 per cent of New York Methodists, questioned in a recent study, still asserted they believed in it "strongly." Attitude toward "open-minded" religion, which approves of science as an ally to the religious quest, has become more frequent, along with decreased liking for creed, dogma, and authority. Even in the intellectual magazines religion of this liberal type is approved in two-thirds of the references. Thus the essential conservatism and practicality of the American masses greatly retard changes in the intellectual and religious climate, and make their progress less certain and clear-cut.

The slowness of the church in responding to external influences is matched by its leisurely response to its own new internal situations. Nevertheless, the accentuation of the associative principle has begun to add a distinctive touch to Protestant cultural methods. Much of the church's institutional expression is in terms of specialized interest. There are separate agencies and occasions for worship, evangelism, education, social action, and missions. This departmentalizing of religious fields is, in turn, crossed by additional differentiations according to age, sex, and status of constituents.

Subsidiary organizations arise in behalf of almost every interest and for every age group, which organizations duplicate the general organization of the church. Often these subordinate interests are essentially independent bits of the church, giving their primary loyalties to attenuated, secondary interests rather than parts of a closely knit whole. One is attached to the church as Boy Scout, as member of the Aid Society, or as a member of one of the men's groups rather than to the church as a church. Yet all this subdivision may not merely signify that the church is being over-organized; it may likewise mean that religion, so to speak, is being more effectively aerated—the breaking up of its particles giving them the maximum exposure to the atmosphere of reality and of relevancy. As a consequence—in spite of the notorious lack of cohesion in which it results—Protestantism is increasingly committed to a thorough-going differentiation in religious processes.

However, the leaven of associative processes is working in certain more constructive ways: For example, in forums, discussion groups, and the like, in which traditional religion is subjected to free examination and a co-operative attempt is made to work out its implications, especially with reference to the current needs of the community; in the increasing number of intimate groups in the contemporary church, who, by personal confession and discipline, seek to associate their members in terms of the deeper unities of their total personalities; and, finally, in attempts to raise worship above the communal level, dramatically supplying a nobler frame of reference for religious imagination to build upon, but also aiming to criticize life as well as to celebrate it, and to develop a more searching quality within the ideals and symbols of the church.

All told, ecclesiastical Protestantism's multitude of limited objectives in the larger sense represent its effort to make religion applicable to contemporary life. A continuous decentralization of religious interest is going on. The totality of religious reality, originally suspended in the communal solution, gets precipitated in more intelligible and ethically challenging forms in the manifold separate concerns of the modern church.

The most directly traceable consequence of the transfer of Protestantism to the associative level has been its increasing tendency to reach a normal distribution of attitudes and positions about a center. Conflict has softened into accommodations. On most issues a working equilibrium has emerged out of the free play of selective energies. This vital balancing of right, middle, and left positions constitutes the unity both of the Protestant whole and most of its denominational parts.

In fact the tendency to take the middle ground is illustrated throughout practically the whole range of the current internal issues. The old intransigeance is missing.

Consequently, whether the issue be that of the contribution of the social inheritance to religion, relative to that of individual experience; of revelation as over against science as the way of knowledge; or of the significance of the ancient creeds as standards of belief as over against authentic present insights; whether the issue is between fixed and informal worship or the hierarchical principle as over against democratic organization—whatever it may be, the tensions and conflicts within current Protestantism incline to be relatively moderate. Ability to compromise and to find a common working basis is very great. On all these positions right and left wing points of view appear in the guise of parties in most denominational bodies.

In spite of their tensions, however, there is little tendency to schism. All the parties remain within the church. The result is less obviously due to the grace of God than to the church's participation in the secular traits of the American people.

All in all, currently the integrative tendency has the upper hand. This is manifest in the numerous interchurch structures for common activity (which my introductory section offered in evidence); in numerous organic unions of separate denominations which have steadily reduced the number of separate churches relative to population; and, finally, in vast world-wide "ecumenical" movements seeking to bring about the unity of Christendom.

With the cultural methods described, and under the prevailing mood of accommodation and compromise, what success has ecclesiastical Protestantism in establishing and maintaining a clearly recognizable and distinctly higher type of humanity? What is its version of the Christian type?

First-hand studies have produced amusing results concerning the difference between the professed, or official, attitudes of church members and their private attitudes expressed in confidence, and, in turn, between *their* private attitudes and those of the non-church-going public in the same communities. Private attitudes, generally, were found to be less orthodox and less exacting than the publicly professed ones. Indeed, the church member's private attitudes tended to approximate closely to those of the non-church-going group. This was true of 81 per cent of the comparisons covered by the study in question. The public and private attitudes of church members more nearly coincided in the realm of Christian rites and symbolism than in that of ethical conduct. Conversely, the greatest difference between church and non-church members lay precisely in the realm of rites and symbols. Finally, it was in matters of conduct that private views of church members departed farthest from their church views and compared most closely with those of the secular community.

Such near-identification of the church with the "world" obviously challenges the church's sources of moral authority. What happens when the salt has lost its savor?

But as has often been pointed out, some such outcome has always followed, apparently inevitably, whenever a church comes to include a considerable majority of the population of any nation. As sect, the church may successfully strive for inner purity, and—so long as it is small—it may exercise intimate discipline in a way to secure at least the purity of outward conformity. Yet as an inclusive major human association the church always actually receives within herself the moral standards of the population which she comes to include.

Here in the United States is a voluntary group rallying to its standard more than half the population and receiving at least a nominal adherence from most of the remainder. Yet from the standpoint of New Testament Christianity—or even as compared with the best ethical sensitiveness of the secular world itself—the average moral level is unquestionably and shockingly low. In all its sober moments the church regretfully confesses this.

However, the extension of religious association to include so much of the population of the nation necessarily disposes of the charge that the church is separated from the masses. It is not true that the socially privileged attach themselves to the church on the associative level, leaving the poor to adhere to it only on the communal level. In actual fact Protestant churches are well and proportionately distributed among *all* social classes, and occur with due frequency on *all* economic levels. Of course this does not mean there are not class churches among them, but an inventory of nearly 2000 churches—painstakingly studied in geographical cross-sections of sixteen major cities, found the churches of all major denominations located with about the same frequency in the poorest, the average, and the best territory. Again, tracing the sources of church attendance, about an equal proportion of Protestants will be found coming from the poor, the middle-class, and the wealthy sections of the cities. This fairly creditable showing has been considerably improved by the northern migration of Negroes—mostly Protestant—in recent decades.

Protestantism has undoubtedly inherited a cultural frame of reference that assumes the existence of private property, individual initiative, industry and thrift. These elements in the national tradition have not, in the main, been abandoned. At this point there is a lag in the church's response to change—as there is in all other areas of acute change. In this sense Protestantism is capitalistic. However, positions still branded as economic radicalism have been widely advocated in the leading denominations for several decades and have had conspicuous place in official social pronouncements.

Moreover, the innumerable local units of Protestantism—its scores of thousands of little self-sufficing churches—present a situation far too decentralized for any capitalistic control. Local offices doubtless are frequently held by local capitalists, but in a much more significant sense women run the church, while, from a realistic standpoint, the need to attract and placate youth gives young people the upper hand.

Turning to the contour and texture of the inner life as it exists within the Protestant church, one must consider first that determinative and indelible experiences go on, generation after generation, within hundreds of thousands of face-to-face social groups. Here, as nowhere else except in the family, the essential social tradition of the larger cultural groups is actually communicated. All the more meaningful and powerful significances of religion are present in the bosom of such groups. Here are familiar hands known as forever grasping the axe, the spade, the reins, the car; hands which sowed, reaped, washed, mended, weeded, kneaded, knitted, but which lie passive in church, relaxed, quiet. Faces are smoothed and voices made gentle. What is this strange other-dimension of adult life, belonging to the high, still, white meeting house, which puts tense and knotted hands at rest? What is this mystery of the neighborhood's other self, the church? No other experience of early life poses so impressive and intriguing a question.

To sum up: Sociologically speaking, neighborhoods are the essence of community, while religiously speaking the hordes of insignificant churches are the church, and will continue to be, no matter what type of overhead organization they may develop.

In the strength of such profoundly authentic and personality-creating origins the religious inner life even of modern people often shows highly durable qualities. Anything approaching a large-scale scientific exploration of the quality and course of the mature religious life of persons now in the Protestant church is manifestly difficult and has rarely been undertaken. Consequently it cannot be well documented. Fragmentary evidence, chiefly from liberal sources, does, however, justify some such statement as the following: Somewhere along the road, a more or less rationalized personal version of creed and code has been arrived at, but as a scheme or system has largely dropped out of sight. Of the formal and external practices of religion—such as Bible reading and church attendance —some acquire an increasing significance while others dwindle or are abandoned. But formal observance, as such, shows no tendency to disappear from religion. Its changes are more of fashion than of essence.

There is much shifting of religious and supposedly related ethical values. Some turn out to be more firmly and rewardingly held than formerly; others, less so. The ethical aspects of religion appear, on the whole, to survive better than its theological formulations. With the group just observed, "God" and "Jesus Christ" were responded to as symbolizing the highest values, but were less frequently said to represent growing values than were terms expressing humane aspiration and service.

However, the most enduring and dynamic factors of the inner life of these moderns are what may be called the religious appreciations—that is to say, attitudes not fixed as custom nor hardened into dogma. Frequently they are little talked about, but they are still capable of being rated on a rather vague scale of religious evaluation. They center upon the meaning of life and often permit the affirmation of some more or less attenuated feeling of relationship between God and man.

If these appreciations were to be characterized in philosophic terms some would have to be labelled rationalistic, others mystical; some humanistic, others theistic; some extrovert, some introvert; some traditionally Christian, others common to all faiths. In short, all the primary apprehensions of religion, as they have come to light in the history of humanity, tend to be perpetuated in the modern man's working attitudes and are represented in most of the individual cases reported.

Thus the religious stream draws on all manner of sources and finds a variety of sanctions. Few persons embody distinctive, clear-cut types of piety, such as the mystical, the humanistic, or the legalistic.

From time to time, moreover, the inner life is invaded by crucial experiences. One person in five, in the sample taken, recorded that at some time he had undergone a revolutionary reversal or renewal of his inner values. Perhaps because one who cannot keep his illusions ceases to be actively religious the great majority said that they increasingly responded to what they regard as the more important values of the inner life.

All told, then, the Protestant church—institutionally speaking—is by no means down and out. Its striking numerical growth and the fact that its strength as a social enterprise is now at the peak reflect a situation in which both the stability and changes of contemporary American culture are at least partly on the church's side. In other words, the church continues to utilize both communal and associative principles of social organization. The sway of popular religion with its robust vulgar acceptance of suprahuman postulates, and the general acceptance of a quasi-Christian ethics, constitute a dependable foundation on which to build.

Ever surer is the permanent manifoldness of contemporary social processes. Evolution itself is never entirely consistent. It never merely moves in one direction. If this mixture of tendencies can keep on co-existing in the community itself, it can also do so in the church, which might go on indefinitely on its present lines.

It is certain that the church cannot go back to the primitive level. The social process has gone too far in dislodging men from their communal ties to make such an idea practically tenable. Social interpretation is inclined to envisage democratic society as consisting primarily of loosely federated units. There is no actual entity corresponding to the words "American people," and no nation so lacking in homogeneity as ours can dream of incarnating itself in a national church.

On the whole, therefore, Protestantism is committed to the method of perpetually bringing additional differentiated aspects and segments of life under the interpretative sway of religion—and stakes the future on the capacity of the process to reach universality. It manifestly cannot go on indefinitely as a mere process of differentiation. This would be to press the Protestant principle quite beyond the mark. Emancipation from the bondage of communal tradition was one thing; an actual share in the acceleration of disintegrating processes, quite another. Yet in serious respects this is what Protestantism has come to be, for lack of application of its own inner correctives. In order to complete its own logic voluntary association must be balanced by voluntary reintegration. The effort to make religion relevant to life in its parts must first find a religion capable of manifesting life in its wholeness.

Protestantism, accordingly, is now making fresh effort to achieve the Catholic mind and temper. If the modern world is to find unity, some agency must offer a viewpoint focal enough to synthesize contemporary life. This, many think, is the supreme intellectual, æsthetic, ethical, and technical task of our age. Protestantism cherishes a newly kindled hope of accomplishing this on the religious level, and of expressing it in compellingly, in genuinely religious terms. Its problem, then, is to recover the universalistic note, and to find inner energy sufficient to reintegrate the organized life of the world without coercing its variants into conformity.

But, obviously, the American Protestant church is no longer a collection of sects, essentially separated from and at war with the "world," attempting to develop a completely separate culture and ethical outlook. In fact—as I have reiterated—it has become a segment of society, quite like the rest. Still less in the persons of its individual members is the church a collection of saints—that is, of individuals inwardly distinguishable from the mass by a unique faith, or by the peculiar graces of Christian character.

How, then, can the church hope to find inner energies sufficient to motivate its universalistic dream? The issue is not whether, and for how long, traditionalism will support ecclesiasticism, or whether matters might not be worse for the church than they are. The issue has come to this: Has the church enough energy to save the demoralized world from falling back into chaos? Can she reinstate religion as the central integrating force in society—something which has never yet been done on the large scale of modern society and under conditions of intellectual and political freedom? This—and no less an issue—is now forcing Protestantism in America towards its first really major crisis since the dawn of the urban era.

## DYNAMIC ASPECTS OF CONTEMPORARY PROTESTANTISM

Within its habitual boundaries Protestantism finds its adherents normally distributed in middle, right, and left wing positions; and over most issues, whether internal, or instigated from below or above, it experiences only moderate tensions. On its left wing, popular Protestantism completely merges into secularism, while ecclesiastical Protestantism has extensive contacts with secularism as its neighbor. On its right wing lies the field of more extreme supernaturalism—which is just now receiving strong reinforcements.

Now the general *instinct* of Protestantism is to extend itself in both directions at once and to try to keep both its right-wing and left-wing extremes in general contact with its central position, according to the familiar formula of compromise. But—apart from its own inner tensions —the likelihood that Protestantism can make this policy succeed is diminished by the increasingly violent attacks it is suffering from both sides.

Modern secularism hitherto had been unorganized, and had consisted in the main of people who are already religiously associated as Protestants but who also grouped themselves in behalf of other separate cultural interests. The "worlds" of politics or education or art were simply the principle of specialization, as it works out into all aspects of contemporary life. They were in no conscious antagonism to religion, broadly defined, and the moral sense of Christianity had largely ceased to set the "world" over against the church. Neither, indeed, had much reason for drawing any line against the other, because both were actually very much alike.

More recently, however, organized secularism has increasingly become aggressive in the two forms of Utopianism—politically expressed by Communism and Totalitarianism. The temper of Utopianism inclines it to try to compel the church to take sides in the supposedly inevitable class struggle and ultimately to come over on its specific side, on penalty otherwise of being opposed or suppressed. Meanwhile the modern State increasingly assumes the previous functions of the church, and other voluntary societies, and also shows disquieting signs of wanting to assume exclusive control of the education of youth—and even of the symbols of the inner life. Fear of this new aggressiveness of these movements now joins with the inner revulsion from its own worldliness and with disillusionment over the tendency of the principle of voluntary association to fritter itself away in a multiplicity of unrelated interests and petty loyalties— fear, revulsion, and disillusion all, in a word, join to impel Protestantism to an amazing venture: The venture of itself attempting the reorganization of our disintegrating civilization about a religiously motivated society. This would involve greater distinctiveness of doctrinal and ethical positions and stronger inner discipline than Protestantism has ever previously attempted in the United States. This is one meaning of the recent interest in the so-called "ecumenical" movement.

Whether such an attempt will seriously be made, and whether Protestantism will try the actual measures necessary to implement it, depend partly on the vigor of the external attack, partly on the vigor of its internal tensions. It appears obvious, however, that any hope for successfully rallying society about organized religion would require the united energies of the entire church, Catholic as well as Protestant. The unbridged gulf between these two great divisions of Christendom makes such a union doubtful, at least at any early date.

Meanwhile, what is happening on the right? This is largely being determined by what has just been described as happening on the left. Logically it is quite possible that a revival of ancient tendencies in Protestantism will force a decisive break between the church and the "world" at a point which would leave most of the church on the "world's" side and would reduce the surviving Protestantism to a bare remnant. For one of the deepest instincts of Protestantism is its sectarianism. All along the path of its history multitudinous little sects have remained nonconformist with respect to contemporary culture—have defied the "world" and sought to keep themselves unspotted from it.

Sectarian possibilities remain in American Protestantism which might conceivably emerge into a dominant position. Just now they are greatly encouraged by a philosophical doctrine which ascribes a "demoniac" quality to certain elements in the universe—this involving the hopelessness of human moral effort and the probability of a catastrophic doom for Western society. In the more outspoken theological version the "world" (including nature, man, history, and the mysterious cosmic forces) is placed in complete antagonism to God. As recently as December, 1937, a national interchurch gathering of students attested to the current vogue of this type of thinking by declaring:

"If any trend can be said to be taking place in the thinking of theological students, it is one which moves away from humanism and superficial optimism toward either a more realistic empiricism or some form of supernaturalism or orthodoxy. This trend, if it may be called that, is generally recognized as the result of the great complexity (the post-war disillusionment, economic collapse and inadequacy of liberalism) of the social order in which we live and the seeming inability of man to do anything about it."

From this viewpoint all attempts to rectify the situation by the liberal technic of self-criticism are futile, because of the irrelevance of mere science, the superficiality of all "activism," and the certainty that deceitful pride is at the bottom of every effort of the human mind and will.

Such views are currently reinforced by the spread in America of a theology and philosophy of history identified with the name of Karl Barth, with its arresting slogan, "Man is nothing; God is all." Apocalypticism has always been the prophet of social catastrophe, and any crushing blow to the civilization of the United States as we know it today—like a dictatorship or a defeat in war—might very plausibly and possibly hinge the resulting central religious conflict on the question of whether or not the church should literally secede from the world and await passively for the coming of its Lord in the clouds.

For the moment it is sufficient to locate possible breaking-points. Tension is not yet acute enough to make the actual breaking-up of the existing situation an early possibility. Ecclesiastical Protestantism is still attempting to maintain its middle-of-the-road compromising position; and this it may successfully hold for an indefinite time. As for the future, much depends on the degree of sanity of which America is capable in the face of world-wide disintegrating tendencies, distress, and fear of external disaster. The more ultimate question is whether growing ethical consciousness within the church will compel it to draw a sharper and more subtle line between itself and the "world," and whether the essential religious postulates and demands of the inner life can be satisfied by the present indiscriminate alliance between the church and the national culture.

# CATHOLICISM IN AMERICA

## [Reverend Francis X. Talbot, S.J.]

WHEN one sees a cross above a church, one may quite safely infer that the church belongs to those Catholics. Protestant houses of worship, among other differentiating styles of architecture, mark the apex with a needle steeple, a weather-vane or some other decorative gewgaw. But the Catholic edifices, whether of marble or granite, whether of drab brick or painted planks, raise the symbol of salvation above their humbleness or their magnificence.

These cross-topped churches have been erected in nearly 11,000 American villages, towns and cities. They are to be found in almost every neighborhood of the larger population centers. At the present time, there are exactly 18,428 Catholic churches in continental United States, as against 15,520 in 1917. Set in a geographical area called a parish, they are administered by a pastor, assisted by curates. All the Catholics living within the specified limits of the parish belong automatically, by virtue of their residence, to the parish church and are under the spiritual authority of the pastor. These parish units are included in a larger geographical area known as a diocese, or an archdiocese, and all the faithful, clerical or lay, within the boundaries owe spiritual obedience to the bishop or archbishop or cardinal. Of dioceses in the United States, there are ninety-four; and of archdioceses, nineteen.

Continuing with statistics, the latest records reveal that 21,451,460 Catholics inhabit the United States. Twenty years ago, there were 17,022,879. They are ministered to by 32,668 priests, a substantial increase over the 19,983 listed in 1917. The hierarchy is composed of 4 cardinals, 16 archbishops and 112 bishops. As can be seen from the mere presentation of the figures, Catholics constitute the largest religious group in the country, about one-sixth of the entire population.

They form, likewise, the most cohesive group. In all essential matters of doctrine and morals, they are indissolubly united. In all other matters, social, economic, ethical, moral, cultural (but not political), they think in almost identical patterns. When they act, clergy and laity together, they merge into one tremendous national force. Not many decades ago, Catholics were a small religious minority, mostly poor and largely unschooled. They were without influence and prestige, but, having courage and patience, they militantly fought to defend themselves and their rights against an overwhelming Protestant population. They are vocal now, in this year of grace, they have attended high school and college, they have prospered in the goods of this world, and they are conscious of their united strength.

Whatever opinions and benighted prejudices may be held about them, Catholics do not consider themselves an American problem. Nor can they conceive of themselves as an alien segment in the national life. Three-fourths of them, at least, are native-born, and the others are almost all naturalized citizens. They like the United States. They have fought for it in the just, and even unjust, wars it waged. They have helped to draw up its legislation in Washington and the State capitals. They have dispensed justice to all alike, from the Supreme Court rostrum down to the magistrate's bench. They have been raised to the highest executive offices, with the exception of one which has been withheld from them by undemocratic bigotry. They have been pre-eminent in the professions and at the top in industry, finance and commerce. These statements are made, not in boast but in evidence, to show that the Catholics are and judge themselves an historical and integral part of the American people.

When the Catholic of 1938 reads the chronicles of Anglo-Saxondom for the past four centuries, he pities his poor ancestors. They endured outrageous Christian hate with Catholic courage and stubbornness. They were fulminated against by pulpiteers and patriots for their Romanism, dual allegiances, treachery, Popery, toe-kissing, nunneries, for being apocalyptic scarlet whores, for having horned and cloven-footed priests. They were penalized for their religious beliefs, persecuted by Know Nothings, A. P. A.'s and Ku Klux Klans. Even yet, a Marshall or a Rutherford or a worried editor of a liberal periodical will brand the stamp of the beast on them, or will solemnly warn them that unless they behave more sheepishly, they will become offensive, and therefore will have to be handled roughly.

This American insanity of the Christian and the Liberal is, I repeat, difficult for the Catholic to comprehend. Testifying as a reputedly intelligent and honest man, I have always entertained the notion that my Americanism was as strong as that of President Roosevelt, and that my Catholicism was as undefiled as that of Pope Pius. Thus would testify the four cardinals and every fervent Catholic who has reached the age of reason. Americanism and Catholicism are both natural, both normal professions, with never a hyphen to separate them. The Catholic holds the theory, proved in practice, that the better Catholic he is, the better American he must be. Within the past few years, he has been inclined to believe that the Catholics are the largest bloc in the dwindling number of Americans who hold fast to the Constitutional and traditional Americanism that made the country what it was before 1914. And if he indulges in a bit of prophecy, he might submit the proposition that, when the inevitable crisis is reached in the United States some few years hence, he and his fellow-Catholics will be the strongest force upholding democracy, the American institutions, the Constitution and, in the world sphere, Western civilization.

There is no blinking the fact that the non-Catholic American has as much difficulty in understanding the Catholic soul and spirit as the Catholic American has in plumbing the intricacies of the minds and emotions of the non-Catholic citizen. The Catholic church is forever being misunderstood and misjudged; and it is continually asserting itself in such ways that it gives cause for new misjudgments.

It is unique among American institutions, as it is unique in every country in which it exists. It cannot be bracketed with Protestant Christianity nor with religious Judaism. It is a religion, a society, a culture in itself. It is integrated in every nation and race, and yet it is supra-racial and supra-national. It offers civil allegiance to emperor, king, president, or dictator, and spiritual allegiance to its local bishops and the universal Pope. The simplest explanation of the mystery of Catholicism is this: the Catholic church claims that it is the only completely revealed religion and the single religion instituted by Jesus Christ. When a Catholic has such a belief, he regards the world about him as one which needs enlightenment. When he attempts to manifest his belief, he is regarded by his non-Catholic neighbor with suspicion, not unmixed with alarm.

It would be arrogance, if it were based on human proofs, for the Catholic to make the claim that his church is the only possible church divinely intended and instituted, that his church possesses, alone, the complete divine truth. But, originating from God, its assertion is not arrogance but the compulsion of truth. It is an irritating assertion, however, to the American mind which holds one religion as good as another, which sees no need for organization in God-relations, which holds all truth to be relative, which wobbles between tolerance, expedience and compromise. For the Catholic the claim means religious security and infallible certitude. Personally, if I did not believe that God appointed a single way of religious life, that Jesus Christ was divine and originated a divinely guided church, and only one, I could not believe in a God of any sort.

Catholicism is not merely an affirmation, or acceptance, of a set of religious principles bound up into a creed; it is not a membership corporation for community worship. In germ, it is a divine revelation that permeates all human society and in its ultimate expansion is a culture in itself. The kernel of it is the wisdom revealed by God before and at the coming of Christ. This deposit of Faith, partly written and partly tradition, was irrevocably closed when those teachers died who knew Christ in the flesh. No truth could be added to it, none deleted or neglected or forgotten. Out of this closed depositary of faith, the teachers, preachers, writers of succeeding generations drew deductions and conclusions, and these were eventually co-ordinated in the science of theology. There is possible no falsity, no error, in the official church doctrine, since Christ had promised infallibility in respect to faith and morals to the successor of Saint Peter.

From purely natural reasoning guided by revelation and tradition developed the Catholic system of philosophy. From these combined, came an intellectual evaluation of human existence, then a way of life for the individual, then a co-ordinated form of society, then a distinctive approach toward the arts, the sciences and all the activities of mankind. For perpetuation, in accordance with the design of Christ, there grew naturally the hierarchical organization of an institutional church. Catholicism in its entirety civilized Europe and stamped the Catholic culture upon the races and nations of Europe. It remains essentially the same in the United States as it has been for twenty centuries in the old countries of the world.

Though a culture and a fully constituted society, Catholicism is not in opposition to any form of civil government, legitimately established. Taking the words of Christ: "Render, therefore, unto Cæsar the things that are Cæsar's, and unto God the things that are God's," it reasons that there are two governing powers: one civil and one spiritual. Civil society and the government established is supreme in its own function, that of caring for the material, human welfare of mankind. Spiritual society, likewise, is supreme in all that affects the welfare of the soul and its relation to God. In the ideal structure of society, these two powers should co-exist in peace and mutual co-operation for the good of the people. Civil government should not invade the realm of the spiritual, nor may the spiritual authority meddle with or attempt to control the civil, unless the rights of God are menaced.

Now the Catholic church makes another affirmation, arrogant perhaps to you but reasonable to me, namely, that it alone is this supreme and single spiritual society. Asserting its equal and superior rights, it has engaged in conflict with emperors, kings, princes, oligarchies, dictators and directors of totalitarian regimes. But, and this must be well noted, it has never clashed with American democracy or the government constitutionally established in the United States. When differences arose between the American civil power and the Catholic spiritual authority, they were settled by American courts.

Observing him candidly, the Catholic does not seem to be much different from his fellow-American. He takes his drinks, his smokes, his sports, his clubs, his business, his politics as seriously as the next man. He enjoys the new inventions and indulges in the latest caprices and hobbies. He lives in the American environment as he finds it, or makes it. But he does differ in his soul. For religious reasons he does not eat meat on Friday, should go to confession on Saturday, is obliged to attend Mass on Sunday, is expected to live a moral life and say his prayers every day of the week. On the one side he has an obligation of avoiding every sin included in the ramifications of the Ten Commandments, and on the other side he must pursue a positive sanctity through the Sacraments and the other means of attaining a union with God. In the strictest sense, he is a member of the mystical body of Christ.

There is more than this to a Catholic, however. If he wishes to remain a Catholic, he must accept Catholic dogmatic and moral certainties in their entirety; otherwise he is rejected as heretical. He is not expected to gulp these down, intellectually, as mysterious pellets; he is urged to examine them and freely to adopt them. Then, he is required, but not with absolute compulsion, to agree with the accepted Catholic interpretations of ethical, social, economic and other domestic questions. He submits, though not without occasional grumbling, to the disciplinary regulations imposed by Pope, bishop, or priest. Through such processes, he finds himself, when he thinks it over, with a Catholic instinct toward everything, and with a well-defined Catholic attitude. He is, thus, a product of the Catholic culture. He is but one of millions in the United

States, all similarly endowed with almost identical instincts and attitudes.

From his own vantage point, the Catholic examines the United States and the civilization that characterizes the American people. One of the strongest Catholic instincts is that of propagating itself. Every one of the eleven first Catholics, together with Paul and Matthias, spread out from Jerusalem to some foreign land as propagandists. Their example was followed by apostolic missioners through all the centuries since. Today hundreds of American priests and thousands of American nuns are making Catholics out of Chinese, Indians, Africans, Esquimaux and the pagan peoples of all the continents. Here in the domestic fields, likewise, both lay and clerical Catholics labor and pray to make all Americans Catholic, for an inherent element in Catholicism is that of bringing all people, of all degrees, within the fold. They are not supremely successful in convert-making in the United States, principally because of the American heritage of bigotry and the agnostic mentality that now exists. Their method, of course, is persuasion not force, and their appeal is to the spiritual aspirations not to the material considerations.

As Catholics have an energizing desire to convert Americans to their church, so they strive also to propagate their Catholic ideas even among those who will never accept Catholicism. They have a persuasion that American civilization needs their ideas, dreadfully, and that this civilization can be saved only by the infiltration of the Catholic theory of human and divine relations. They are convinced that they can furnish the answer to every national question, and prescribe the spiritual medicine to cure each national ill. The Catholic church, they will tell you, does not need to seek new answers and strange medicines; it needs only to adapt to contemporary conditions the remedies which it has preserved for nineteen hundred years. Human nature does not change, nor do human instincts, nor do human needs; neither do answers of the Catholic church change in essentials. Hence, the church remains traditional; it flits not with the upstart reformer or philosopher of the century, it wavers not with the fads of the times, it wriggles not with the pressure of the extremes. The church is set firmly in the middle of a straight road that does not vary with the stretch of time. What it taught to the people of the time of Augustus, Constantine, Charlemagne and Napoleon, it teaches to those in our world of Roosevelt, George VI, Hitler, Mussolini, and Stalin. Though frankly conservative, it is dynamically progressive; though traditional it is not reactionary; it is much concerned with the life after death, but also with the throbbing life before death.

Catholic efforts to make contact with American civilization, and t produce an effect on it, follow two rather undefined policies. The ex ponents of these approaches do not constitute groups or parties; the represent attitudes which might be designated as Positivist and Concilia tionist. The former stresses American Catholicism, the latter accent Catholic Americanism.

The Positivists propound an unmitigated, unblushing presentation o a full, militant Catholicism to the American people. They propose th Catholic doctrine in all its hardness with a take-it-or-leave-it gesture They are neither unreasonable people nor intentionally crude; rathe they would be unwilling to offend Protestant and agnostic sensibilities But they are eminently honest and they refuse to whittle away the rough edges or enclose their thoughts in honeyed words. They are considered the soundest, the more orthodox and the more ecclesiastical, as they are the most numerous.

The Conciliationists, though equally orthodox and loyal and pious favor a more ingratiating approach. They are usually worldly-wise and intelligent. They would point out to non-Catholics the similaritie rather than the differences between Catholic and non-Catholic; they would create a spirit of fellowship and sympathy and tolerance; they would join with Protestant and Jew and Liberal in social, charitable, religious movements; they would level hills and valleys, build bridges over chasms, hoe the soil along the juncture of the adjoining fields. They apologize for their belligerent brethren and lament their narrow-minded rigidity. They propose a more liberal view in facing the contemporary panorama.

More and more in later years, the rugged hundred-per-cent Positivists are shrugging their shoulders nonchalantly about what non-Catholics think of them. Utilizing their rights of free-speech and the free exercise of their religion, they offer their religion undiluted, and boldly condemn the Americanism which offends them. They have, it is true, a tendency toward isolationism, but they are not ostriches. Rather they are keenly, pathetically aware of the devastating changes coming over American civilization. They are in open conflict with many current intellectual and moral Americanisms. Without being pessimists, they sense decadence in the American air, detect clouds gathering on the national horizons, await the storm that will endanger the traditional American spirit. By being outspoken, they have the sublime audacity to think that the people of the United States must heed their sound moral, ethical, philosophical and theological proposals.

Endless pages would be consumed if I attempted to illustrate such assertions comprehensively or by detailed argument. A sampling of surface issues, proferred but not proved, must suffice. For example, there is a God, and the Catholic church has a divine command to bring the knowledge of this God to all men. The surest way is that of inducting the child into Catholicism. From this proposition are derived many corollaries with practical sequences. One of these is sometimes interpreted as an affront to the non-Catholic. At a marriage between a Catholic and a non-Catholic, the latter party is required to sign a written guarantee that all children born of the union be reared as Catholics. Should the non-Catholic party refuse, the church refuses to sanction the marriage. The reason for this procedure is, simply, the dogma founded on divine law that the child has a right to the graces of baptism and the aids to salvation instituted by Christ. Most non-Catholics, acting on the general American assumption that one religion is as good as another, or as no religion, and holding few principles as certain, are not too much bothered about the Catholic insistence.

Another instance is the Catholic educational system. Mr. Mann inaugurated our present public-school system in a revolutionary change from the colonial and early American concept of education in denominational schools. The American people in some inexplicable way, mostly through Protestant idealists, embraced Mr. Mann's exclusion of all religious teaching from the public-supported schools. Catholics were not content with teaching their children the three r's; they wanted to give their children the additional r of religion. Since the American government would not permit them, or anyone else, to instruct students about God and morality founded on religious beliefs, in government or State schools, they invoked their constitutional rights to build a school system of their own. They paid their taxes as American citizens for the support of the public schools which they would not use. In addition, out of their limited, and often meager, wages, they paid magnificently to erect their own school buildings and to maintain a high standard of education, including the Catholic religion.

By gathering their children into their own parish schools, the Catholics have saved the State the costs of erecting 7885 grammar schools, the annual payment of the salaries of 58,183 teachers, and the annual sup-

port of 2,571,894 children. Likewise, in higher education, the Catholi
church conducts 2544 high schools, academies, colleges, seminaries anc
universities which educate about 500,000 students. Every hope is enter
tained that some day every Catholic American child will be placed ii
a Catholic school. Until this hope is fulfilled, the church authoritie
strive to gather Catholic students of public and secular institutions to
gether for Sunday schools, catechism classes, study groups and in New
man Clubs. The Catholic church is tender to the souls of its little ones
If it should abandon them it would suffer the fate of the Protestan
denominations, the loss of faith and the disappearance of congregations

American civilization and the Catholic church are in open conflict or
practically every phase of sex. The Catholic ideal recognizes the sexua
instinct as normal, good and God-given, and as a powerful motivating
force. It holds, however, that this instinct should be co-ordinated with
and subject to the spiritual instincts and to the moral code. Sex may
rebel against soul; sex must then be controlled. The American view has
tended in more recent years to liberate sex from the traditional controls.
The old discipline over adolescents, the former safeguards and decencies,
the estimation of guilt, the teaching of reverence for the human body,
and like considerations, have faded out of the national conscience. The
general view is that sex should get what sex demands; that wrong is not
in the doing but in being discovered; that all grandmas were prudes
when they were young; that senseless taboos kill fun. Briefly, the Catholic
view holds sex and its manifestations as sacred; the American view regards it as somewhat more serious than a sneeze.

Catholicism strives to protect its adolescents and also its maturer members from contamination. It preaches vehemently against the much-
talked-of growing laxity of the times. In the classroom and in the church
and in the confessional it cries out against the all-enveloping moral loose-
ness. The case against American decadence is strong, as every sane
person will admit. But the decadence is becoming more widespread
and, what is dangerous, more subtle and respectable. The Catholic
moralists, therefore, priest and parent and teacher, redouble their efforts
to apply a prophylaxis. They watch minds being tarnished through the
various mediums of communication, and raise the signals of warning.

They listen to radio programs that are vulgar and indecent, and they
rouse a mighty tempest, as recently, that was not confined to a coffee pot.
They note the intended nudity of the cheap art magazines, the seductive
posings in the higher-class periodicals; they read the inflaming patter in

he pulps, the beautifully phrased enticements to unmarried passion in
he sophisticated monthlies. These are the panderings that the people
of America seem to like; these are the poisons that Catholics, without
being Puritans, detest and denounce so loudly that they are considered
a nuisance. There is published no official index of American prohibited
books; but a bad book, even though our American courts pronounce it
art, brings a national Catholic ban on it.

The legitimate stage has thus far warded off effective Catholic action
when it portrayed unchastity and blasphemy. But the motion-picture
industry is a salutary example of what Catholics do when they are exasperated. The screen was, a few years back, undoubtedly syphilitic. It
was corrupting imaginations and minds. Under the united leadership
of the bishops, the Catholic Legion of Decency was put into operation.
The motion-picture producers had a choice between a code and suicide.
They chose the code, medicalized the movies, and raised the level of
American civilization. The issue is not that of censorship nor that of
irrational taboos. It is merely this: Catholics do not like and will not tolerate smut, human animality, sexual sin and enticements to unregulated
passion; they will protect themselves and their children against the
prevalent decadence of language, pictures and people. And so, they are
liable to break out any time into a tirade or a campaign on visual or
actual immorality.

In two other matters, at least, the Catholic church is waging an un-
remitting warfare. The first of these is divorce, with remarriage. When
a Catholic marries, he contracts "until death do us part." The church
may judge that the marriage contract, for specified reasons, was defec-
tive, and therefore null and void; after searching investigation it may
declare an annulment. But, granting the validity of the marriage contract and the matrimonial Sacrament, together with the actual consummation, the church affirms that the man and woman are indissolubly
bound to one another until death, that neither the contracting parties
themselves, nor the State, nor the church has the power to sunder the
bond between them and permit them to bind themselves to new matrimonial spouses.

The American concept of marriage is purely human and materialistic.
If it works, it continues; if it breaks down through incompatibility or
more serious reasons, it is abandoned. It is sacred only so long as the
couple loves or lives together with an adequate degree of amicability.
The American way yields the harvest of more than 200,000 divorces a

year, about 16 per cent of the marriages, with the number increasing annually, the grounds becoming laxer, the courts proceeding more expeditiously and hypocritically. The Catholic church is alarmed about the national trend toward marital promiscuity, about the disruption of the family as a social institution, about the weakening of the fiber of the citizenry, individually and as a whole, but most of all about the violation of the divine command that governs human society.

The second deadly conflict between Americanism and Catholicism is waged about the conception of children. The Catholic church, as in divorce, takes a definite and, to the non-Catholic, disagreeable and illiberal stand. It teaches that intercourse, even within marriage, must be stemmed by no artificial mechanical or chemical, interference. Prevention of the natural juncture of seed and ovum is classified as a sin in the moral order and as an abuse of a bodily function in the physical order. The American view disregards the spiritual and the supernatural phases and purposes of intercourse, and considers the emissions as waste. The propaganda in favor of birth control is one of the most militantly destructive tendencies in American life. The evil effects of it are already evident in our increased neuroticism, and the consequences of its practice will be a weakened society. In the matter of spreading birth-limitation information, in the sale of devices, in the lobbying of legislatures to lift the present embargo, the Catholic church will be ranged on the opposite side. It will conduct, as it has, an increasing warfare against this decivilizing movement.

Dating from the World War, world civilization entered upon a new era. During the '20's, Europe and the United States grew conscious of strange forces at work. At the turn into the '30's, our worst economic depression struck us. Then came President Roosevelt with his reputed cures. Now we are trying to fend off another critical recession. The problems are economic, societal and governmental. Upon the solutions now effected, depend the cast and color of American civilization during the latter half of this century. In this transitional period, the Catholic church, as a teaching body and as a firmly knit union of Americans, dedicates itself to the duty of swaying American opinion through all legitimate methods.

Capitalism is not Catholic. It is a development of the Protestant Reformation. The Catholic attitude has been to make the best of it, since it existed, and to mitigate its evils. From the system of capitalism have germinated the injustices that plague society in our explosive times.

In the economic plane, there must be equity, there must be probity, there must not be exploitation of the weaker element, there must not be ruthlessness in the dominating groups. The rights and duties of employer and employee must be recognized, the profits and the wages must be mediatized, and economic clashes must be averted. The theory of the Catholic church is expressed for the world to read in an immortal document that was issued by Peope Leo XIII in 1891, the Encyclical *On the Condition of the Working Classes.* This was followed forty years later by the equally important *Encyclical* of Pope Pius XI, in 1931, on *The Reconstruction of the Social Order.* These Papal statements are applicable in every detail to American economic problems, even though the United States is not a Christian nation. They proclaim hard doctrines and presuppose that men are just and God-fearing. Hence, they have little chance for adoption in our country. Nevertheless, these Encyclicals are the texts of the American Catholic doctrine on the economic and social order, and they furnish the planks in the Catholic platform.

A Papal document, likewise, gives the Catholic theory on the ideal government. In his *Christian Constitution of States,* dated 1885, and in *Christian Democracy,* 1901, Leo XIII lays down the principles that should actuate civil and religious societies. Here, again, there is an ideological dissension between Americanism and Catholicism. There is, however, no practical conflict, and no danger of an expressed opposition as long as the United States remains what it has been. The Catholic church has an ideal of a Christian, Catholic state: that ideal, perhaps, will never be fully expressed in a modern nation, and obviously, never in America. The church, therefore, in its immemorial practice, adjusting itself to the existing order so long as its divine and human rights are not molested, co-operates in peace with that non-religious, secular order.

In the United States, then, the Catholic church recognizes the government established by the will of the people as wholly and undeniably legitimate; demands that the Catholic communicants give free and unreserved allegiance to that government; and pledges itself to uphold that government in every exigency, to the best of its ability. Nevertheless, the American Catholic, enthusiastically affirming that the American constitutional system of government is the best non-Catholic form yet devised, claiming, furthermore, that the American Declaration of Independence and Constitution were derived from Catholic sources, can declare in utter good faith that a government erected on the Leonine principles would be a more perfect instrument.

That American democracy stands in more danger at the present time than in any period during the 19th century is an observation self-evident. The Roosevelt program, whether one lauds or laments it, has introduced new concepts of social and governmental relations that are influencing American civilization. The future commentator, having seen the future consequences, will apportion the praise or blame. We judge but blindly. This I see: the dictator and the totalitarian state have returned to Europe in a modernized dress; the ideologies of Communism, Fascism, Nazism are leaping the ocean and spreading in the United States; the so-called American Liberals, who have always been as sentimental as they are mutable, are being infected with un-American ideas, and the American proletariat is being mobilized for social redress. Now a virile, vigilant and clear-eyed American citizenry must defend our traditional American democracy from these northern, middle and lower European influences. That is the Catholic view. American Catholics find Communism, Fascism, Nazism repugnant. But American Catholics are not supported in their contentions by official Protestantism and Judaism. These other religious leaders are so hysterically combating Fascism and Nazism that they are being encircled by Communism. The grave issue is not which ism is a more immediate threat; it is that all are to be repelled as undemocratic and un-American.

When I repeat once more that the Catholic American likes the United States, and that the Catholic church feels comfortable within the American framework, I have no intention of being condescending. Nor do I wish to be lacking in graciousness when I suggest that the Catholic and Catholicism are adversely affected by the current civilization in the United States. The disabilities are not to be attributed to popular persecution or to constitutional limitations. They well from the American society itself which, dropping to lower levels, draws Catholic society with it. Being materialistic, naturalistic, agnostic, turning rapidly to a neo-paganism, it creates an environment that tends to stifle the Catholic spirituality and supernaturalism. Being capitalistic, idolizing wealth, it distorts the Catholic doctrine of poverty of spirit and social justice. Being rationalistic and liberalistic, it weakens the Catholic insistence on authority and absolute truth. Animated by a flair for license of behavior, it vitiates the Catholic concept of chastity and control. Truly, the Catholic church must struggle in America to keep itself true to its traditions and ideals.

Reducing generalizations such as these to facts, the story is somewhat distressing. The Catholic church has lost large numbers of its children. There are no data available, or possible, as to the extent of the leakage. But those who observe believe that it is far too great. To preserve one's Catholicism in modern America requires strength of conviction and soundness of spirit. The causes for defection are many. A few may be instanced: attendance at the public schools, with a consequent lack of religious instruction and training; attendance at secular institutions of higher learning, with the inculcation of liberalism and agnosticism; marriage with non-Catholics; failure of parents in these mixed marriages to rear their children as Catholics; divorce and remarriage; ambition to climb the social ladder; ambition to reach the top in business; reading matter, whether books or periodicals; and visual matter, whether the stage or the screen; the quest for luxury, personal comfort, material ease, self-expression; the deadening of the spiritual ideal through many combined processes. The above listing is partial, but the items bring a toll of spiritual deaths.

An immediate reflection, however, must be added; many of these enjoy, through God's grace, a resurrection before their actual death. In mature years, in sickness, they return to the fold. If their minds have remained Catholic but the flesh was weak, they die Catholics. These are the joy of the priest, and his secret with God. If their minds have been weaned from Catholicism, they are lost. But this is a note to be added to American civilization; if these Catholics cease to be Catholic intellectually, they cease, likewise, to be religious. Only in the very rarest cases, does a Catholic become a Jew or a Protestant. He lapses usually into a typical American.

As against these defections from the Catholic church must be mentioned the accretions. More and more, in my experience, intelligent Americans are seeking the spiritual, the certain, the ultimate in life. They are looking at the Catholic church, mostly from afar, and deciding, as they often express it, that if they wanted or needed any religion they would adopt the Catholic. They cannot, however, take Catholicism in its entirety. Being true Americans, they would like to make it over, add amendments or delete doctrines. They are restrained, also, by material considerations of varying degrees of importance. But each year, some 40,000 Americans who have been reared as Protestants or nothing, step in or back into the Catholic church. Some of these enter because they are marrying Catholics. Others because they see a light burning, and they feel themselves to be in darkness. These converts so often shame the born Catholic by their piety, their zeal, their crusading spirit. In a very large percentage, they have written the best Catholic literature.

Apart from the losses and gains, both largely a mystery of Divine Grace, the Catholic body is a throbbing, pulsating unit of national life. The people respect the priests, and the priests are the spiritual leavening of the laity. They form a compact whole, one in doctrine, one in discipline, one in every type of Catholic action. In a brief survey such as this, it is impossible to outline the far-flung organization of Catholicism in its wider meanings. It is not possible to speak of the most heroic among the Catholics, and the most loved and revered, the nuns and Sisters with their strange garbs and their vows of poverty, chastity and obedience. A book would be needed, adequately to describe their labors in schools, hospitals, orphanages, and other social endeavors, as well as their prayers and sacrifices within the cloister walls. Within these limited pages, it is not possible even to mention the hundreds of lay societies and sodalities, dedicated to the sanctification of the individual, and including in many instances hundreds of thousands of members. Nor is it permitted to me to do more than note the existence of the Catholic press, with the splendid news Service of the National Catholic Welfare Conference, with a local weekly in almost every diocese, with two national intellectual weeklies, with hundreds of weeklies, monthlies and other periodicals that cover every Catholic need.

It is possible only to end as I have begun, and to return to the churches. Any one who seeks to understand the Catholic church in the United States and to comprehend its relation to American civilization will find an answer on any Sunday morning, from about two-thirty o'clock, in certain metropolitan churches, and from six o'clock in other places, until about twelve noon or a little later. Catholics must attend Mass on Sunday, under pain of mortal sin. They flock to Mass in millions, every Sunday of the year. Those Masses participated in by those millions are a symbol of the Catholic contribution to America.

# SUPPLEMENT

*American Civilization*
*from the Foreign Point of View*

# ORIENTAL

## A Chinese–American Evening

### [Lin Yutang]

CHRISTOPHER: Now, I have arranged the fire as you exactly want it. Will you be quite frank with me tonight and tell me what you think of this so-called American civilization?

*Taierchang:*[1] You are asking a disturbing question. American civilization is a disturbing thing. It worries you, doesn't it? Just as Chinese civilization worries me.

*C.:* Never mind, it worries only the civilized part of any nation. But tell me quite frankly what is in your mind.

*T.:* It is such a vast topic. Perhaps, after an hour's talk, we shall have reached no conclusions, but shall only have opened up certain suggestions for further thought on the subject. I really have no opinions.

*C.:* You are being a Chinese gentleman.

*T.:* That's an easy way of being a gentleman. Now, I'll be quite frank. You may think that there is something high and fine in Oriental civilization. But that is only because you are a civilized American. Civilized Chinese, too, think there is something high and fine in Western, or American, civilization. And they are both right.

Anyway, here we are, you and I, talking about civilization in the English language. Isn't that already a compliment? My education is English, my point of view is often quite English—or American; it doesn't make any difference—and my thinking is at present in English. I could not have learned to think and discuss problems of civilization in the English language, unless there were something high and fine in that language. It is intellectually a fully adequate language. When you ask me about American civilization I at once ask whether you mean "civilization," or "culture." And these are English words.

[1]Pronounced "tie-er-jwahng."

545

*C.*: What is your word for "culture" in Chinese?

*T.*: There are several words. There are modern equivalents for "culture" and "civilization" in Chinese—which shows the influence of Western thought in China. But in ancient Chinese the word was *chiao*. It meant both "culture" and "religion": We had no specific word for "religion" apart from culture, just as in Judaism you could not find any secular activity that was not a part of religion. The word meant "teaching" and referred to a current of accepted teachings or ideas, or spiritual values, as you say. It is only as certain ideas prevail that we may speak of them as that nation's culture.

*C.*: That was a beautiful thought. If we could abolish the distinction between secular and religious ideas and include them all in one homogeneous lot, and such ideas could prevail as the workingman's daily religion or attitude toward life! But evidently we cannot. Our ideas shift too fast.

*T.*: That's exactly it. The modern world shall forever flounder in a constant stream of shifting ideas, which will never get into shape.

*C.*: That's also the beauty of modern life. We don't know where we are drifting, and because of that, we can forever hope and dream. Or "adventure nonchalantly in the realm of no affairs," as your Taoist poet has put it.

*T.*: You agree, don't you, that civilization, in its narrower sense, refers to the things seen and the comforts of life, while culture refers to the things unseen?

*C.*: In the narrower sense, of course. In the broader sense civilization also refers to the unseen values, as when we speak of a "civilized" warfare in a different sense from "mechanical" warfare. In the narrower sense, civilization simply means the increased comforts of living. Or civilization is comfort. In the everyday sense, we do mean just those things—better housing conditions, for instance.

*T.*: That is quite true. When you take a bath in a white-enamelled tub, you are civilized, and when you don't take a bath, you are uncivilized. But there is also danger in this line of thinking. We had a philosopher who died a decade ago. A marvelous old fellow, an Edinburgh A.M., who kept his queue under the Republic, and a wit. Ku Hungming was his name. He said: When you take a bath, you are civilized; when you don't take a bath, you are cultured.

*C.*: Did he really say that?

*T.*: No, but he might have. What he said was, the fact that the old

Chinese scholar was often so dirty was proof of his spirituality, of his obliviousness to his physical surroundings. He made Chinese civilization depend on the dirt.

*C*.: How charming!

*T*.: Charming, but unreal. That man went so far in his rage against Western civilization that he denounced it as a police civilization. But you have to have police—and baths. You don't become less spiritual for taking a good, hot bath, with nice clean towels. We mustn't fool ourselves. Even a cultured man can dislike unclean towels, you admit, don't you?

*C*.: I do, most heartedly. Now what do you think of American civilization *and* culture?

*T*.: I think your towels are fine. I think we agree so far that a material civilization is a proper *basis* for culture, but not culture itself. Well, then, American civilization is a definite, a fine, basis for culture. Clean towels are better than unclean towels, and unclean towels are better than no towels. I'd rather build a civilization on clean than upon unclean towels. American civilization is an achievement. Two million Ford cars. As an achievement, it is amazing. We won't go into those things. Most imposing. But American culture is an unknown quantity—yet.

*C*.: You are forthright. You mean we have made a most imposing achievement as basis for an unknown quantity?

*T*.: I don't make my meaning quite clear. I love occasional ambiguities, so that people will think I am wickeder than I really am. What I mean is, what we can see in the modern American world are only certain trends, and we are not quite certain what those trends are taking us to. Which trend will win out in the end? Many of the trends are decidedly conflicting in character. And you've got the freedom to fight it out. The old frontier spirit is still within you.

*C*.: We've heard enough of that frontier spirit. It doesn't explain everything.

*T*.: Symbolically, it means something very definite to me—a new world to conquer and men with tremendous energy to conquer it—and the freedom to fight it out. Isn't that the essence of American civilization, just as energy is the most characteristic thing about American life? That is what I mean by the frontier spirit. American civilzation is young, terribly young. You haven't yet even defined your spiritual frontiers. James Truslow Adams says both his grandparents were living as children when Jefferson died. Imagine! And you call that ancient history, as you call Thomas Jefferson an ancient figure! Your spiritual frontiers are changing incredibly fast, and who shall be able to say what American culture will be like even fifty years from now, not to say a hundred years? That is why it is an unknown quantity yet.

*C.*: What are those conflicting trends you spoke about?

*T.*: First, the conflict between the old American strong individualism and this modern collectivism, economic and moral. Funny thing, the way matter and spirit are tied up like that. Living in a materially collectivistic age, you also get spiritually collectivistic. I hate to think of it —it is the most ugly scar on modern American civilization. I mean *conformity,* the spiritual conformity of persons and things. You can't be an individualist and a conformist at the same time. Rebel—rebel! Why don't you Americans rebel? Rebel against this crushing, overwhelming conformity of things and standards! That is the most important task in American literature and criticism today. You are really in a quandary. Don't you feel spiritually wounded?

*C.*: I hardly know what to think. The matter is really so complicated. I have often thought about it—how matter affects the spirit. You agreed that it was good to have clean towels and enamelled bathtubs and refrigerators. You would agree also, I am sure, that it is a better civilization which provides more clean towels and enamelled bathtubs and refrigerators for a great number of people. In order to have that you must have mass production, if only to make those refrigerators cheaper and more available to the common man. Civilization must mean that— increased comforts of, or a higher standard of, living for the common man. Or it is not worth having at all. And then, with mass-production methods, out you come with standardization.

*T.*: That is the modern dilemma. For civilization is not worth having, either, if human beings get standardized in their ways of living and in their ideas. For me, civilization simply means the development of personality. The more you standardize, the less chance you have to develop personality. The philosophic dilemma lies in this: You can spread civilization by mass-production methods, while you can't spread culture by the same methods. The spirit of the log cabin! Why doesn't one shut himself up in his own log cabin and stake out his own spiritual fences? One might develop into something. You can spread culture only by the log-cabin method, not by the factory method. Make yourself lord of the universe—at least of what your eyes survey. Allow no poachers into your territory. Thus and only thus shall you have your culture. But having left the log cabin physically, you have also left the log cabin spiritually.

I am not trying to romanticize the log cabin: We can't go back. A thousand influences are playing upon our daily life. The other day I read what William Allen White said about the changes in life in a Middle-western town in the last two or three decades. By all material standards, the American nation is making some amazingly swift progress. There is no use decrying progress; man has got to be big enough to take it. It is all a matter of intelligent adjustment to the new situation, and nothing more. Always the inner man remains the center of things. William Allen White, for instance. White in Emporia is making him-self the center of things changing and developing around him—and always standing his ground. That is the log-cabin spirit I mean. I under-stand that some of that log-cabin spirit still remains in Kansas. When I see how happily they live out there, I can even forgive them for being die-hard isolationists. They don't want to be bothered with the outside world, and they don't care. Do you know that the Chinese were the greatest isolationists on earth, because we had—or thought we had—found a way of life that satisfied? That is, until we were beaten out of it about fifty years ago. When you attain the goal of human existence, you feel you can hang the means. But that is because Kansas is prin-cipally agricultural—as China was, and in fact still is. You get a little more space that way, and you become simpler, kinder, and more con-tented. Freedom comes from contentment.

This America that we see before us is a sea of changing, complex cur-rents. First you felled the forests, then you fought off the English, and killed off the Indians—yes, you did. Then you rushed for gold, and built railroads. Then you stopped the people who built the railroads, like Harriman and Hill, and you had your antitrust laws. Then you de-veloped a dual personality: John D. Rockefeller amassing a fortune, and John D. Rockefeller spending it. That is the present stage. That dual personality is now in you—a heightened conflict of materialism and ideal-ism, so comical to me. Andrew Mellon founding a National Museum, for instance. That is the second conflict, really a gigantic conflict between materialism and idealism. Some people like Ford try to avoid a split personality by apothesizing Money, attempting to make materialism and idealism live together as good bed-fellows. So sentimental idealism be-comes material idealism. Ford against Rousseau, or Ford against Thomas Jefferson.

*C*.: Ford is not a person, but an idea. I believe Ford is inevitable. The Jeffersonian lost and the Hamiltonian won. America stands for two ideas, the power of money and service to the country; and only the Ford idea has combined them into one. Sell more cars and serve the people. And thus "I sell" and "I serve" become identical. It is nearer to the American way of thinking, and it sounds like a good program.

*T*.: Of course it sounds good to the man who is serving the people and amassing a billion-dollar fortune for himself. (Not that I don't have great admiration for Ford; it is the system.) It sounds good also to hundreds of thousands of lesser Fords—people selling rubber tires, or mouth washes, or tooth pastes, or ladies' undies. What I am thinking of is what this doctrine of material prosperity as an end in itself is doing to man himself. Confucius said, "The true man develops his personality by means of his wealth, and the unworthy man develops his wealth at the expense of his personality." And it may be true with nations also.

Do you know what has happened in the last hundred and fifty years of swift material developments to the ideal of American democracy? From the ideal of the greatest *good* of the greatest number, it has become that of the greatest quantity of *goods* sold to the greatest number of customers. That—undefined—is your present-day political ideal. What has happened in America is that the democratic citizen is now chiefly conceived of as an actual or prospective consumer whose Buying Potentialities it is the sacred duty of Big Business to bring out and properly develop. If he does not want an article, you create that want in him —and if he can't be made to buy, by definition he becomes a bad citizen. In America it is immoral for a person not to want to buy anything. The man who does not want anything is ashamed of himself—the fellow with the 1927 Buick, for instance, which has a perfectly first-class engine. Pretty soon you have a nation of persons who want the same things and who do the same things. It is amazing how the "hi-li" game conquered America and was played in every street and every alley—in July, 1937. After my return from Havana in September everybody had forgotten about it. It came like a locust pest and blew over like a locust pest.

That is merely an outward illustration of American uniformity of action and desire. I want variety in life, and I see very little of it. It makes it painful to me. Where is the queer, the eccentric, the unconventional personality in America? I won't change it for anything else on earth. Variety is the very breath of life. It is what you call Personality in philosophy or metaphysics. But you are aware, of course, that personality hurts Big Business.

*C.*: That is because we are really living in a corporate State—economically, though not politically, corporate. Perhaps "collectivism" is a better word. You don't want undisciplined individuals in a collectivistic economic society any more than in a collectivistic political State, like a Fascist country. The problem is how you are going to salvage the individual. Don't you think that is the most vital problem in modern philosophy, having regard to the actual tendencies in the modern world?

*T.*: I agree perfectly. I see the sinister influence of Big Business, how it dominates our dress, food, amusements, colleges, newspapers and magazines, personal habits and ideas—and levels them all to the lowest common denominator of the Citizen-Buyer. The Citizen-Buyer is your great god. But, poor fellow, he is given no rest. You whip him and mould him into a common pattern, and the pattern changes every year.

Between you and me, you know that you don't know what the Citizen-Buyer of 1948 is going to be like—what he is going to eat and how he is going to dress. By George you don't! You are all rolling stones that gather no moss. It is essential to the beauty of life that you gather some moss, or life becomes unbearable. The beauty of stones is that they have moss; the beauty of human life is that it has tradition. The spirit of man in America is distracted because it is given no repose. What hurries him? Big Business. To keep or not to keep the 1927 Buick— that is the great problem for the American Hamlet.

*C.*: You know sometimes I think America is the grandest country in the world where everybody has the freest opportunity to grow alike. But coming back to the conflict between materialism and idealism, and its effect on man himself, what do you think of the American man as such?

*T.*: You mean how he lives and enjoys himself?

*C.*: Well, I suppose so. Go ahead with your line of thought.

*T.*: What else is there in life? How a man lives—that is the essential, the central problem of a practical philosophy, the basis of all values. Here we must make a distinction between the best product of American civilization and culture—the flower of American manhood—and the common or average man. Culture, in every country and age, is attained only by a few. I have seen some of the best, most cultured types of American manhood—learned, cultured, keen-minded, a little sad, idealistic, loving his home, and truly religious with a keen social consciousness, and liberal and at home in ideas. You've got that—people with gray hair and a lot of sense, people you meet in some of the men's clubs in New York. How different they look from the men you meet on Broadway, those hustlers! Their intellectual life is also keen, critical, and active. I mustn't forget to mention their delightful sense of humor. I think lots of American young men have got wonderful parents to worship, and I suspect some of them do worship their parents. Still, I don't know— I've got an impression that these men—the best of American humanity —are not in sympathy with the whole damn go-getterism of contemporary America, and that they suppress those antipathies. Some of the best are the best of all humanity. Will Rogers, for instance, who liberated himself through a sense of humor that is completely and genuinely American. You see how difficult it is to characterize a whole nation in a few words—there are so many types. But I must say that this best is characterized on the whole by a sense of humor, an ease of manners, and a simplicity and kindness of heart. It is the product of American soil. My impression of American Quakers is extremely good, though I have heard contrary opinions.

Then there is your average American. I find it hard to make a composite picture in spite of your conformity. There is Janet Gaynor, for instance, and there is Mayor Hague. How can I possibly put their spiritual profiles together? It is an impossible job. Tell your zoologist to make a composite picture of all the animals in the zoo, and you get a nonentity. There is as much difference between one American and another as there is between the head of a dove and that of a rhinoceros. But, allowing for the risk of all generalization, I shall try. Since in matters of culture the majority in any nation falls below the average, so the average must be below the average—if you understand what I mean.

Now, the average American is light-headed. He doesn't know life and sorrow, and his laughter is the laughter of youth. He is an optimist, and eats pork and beans, or hot-dogs and sauerkraut, hastily—without knowing or caring how it tastes. He lives principally on milk, and his wife principally on orange juice and vegetables. He loves what is big; what is bigger and what is better become synonymous for him; he has imagination for the big, but no imagination for the small; his sense of humor is often merely the humor of exaggeration. He loves struggle for its own sake, because he has great bodily vitality. He believes in the present world and in success, and wants to keep up with the Joneses. When he is successful, he feels like "a million dollars," but he does not take failure and sorrow so well. I don't think I can say he is "brave in sorrow"—not in the Oriental sense—because, living in a lucky, young nation, he does not know what sorrow means. His optimism, therefore, tends to be bumptious. At bottom he is not very religious, but he is extremely good-hearted and helpful toward people in distress. His idealism, however, is often sentimental.

Politically and geographically he is too well situated to care much about international politics. His taste for music is—not so good. But inherently he is a good dancer. He makes a very good soldier, but dislikes war. On the whole, as a human type, he is too much of an individualist for me—particularly in his home life. The mother is an individualist mother and the daughter is an individualist daughter; and they are afraid to interfere with each other. Nor would they stand for interference.

In spite of that, he always loves his mother—and quite often loves his wife. But his quick emotionality and light-headedness make him a bad lover.

At whatever age he tries to appear ten years younger than he really is.

He is a bad law-maker, and his legislation is often sentimental and hasty and ill-considered; it is conceivable he might pass a perfectly senseless law by an overwhelming majority, and then regret it afterwards.

He is an extremely efficient business man—in that he exceeds any other nationality.

He believes in God, but cares very little for immortality.

He likes plenty of action in life and literature.

His reasoning is fairly sound, usually though not always. Practicalness is the chief characteristic of his thought-life and of his academic life. He is always getting educated—for what, he doesn't know. On the whole he respects correspondence schools more than universities. He makes a better engineer than a philosopher.

He has a great sense of realism, an idealistically tinged imagination, and a good originality—but on the whole, little depth. He is not very mystical. By and large he is certainly happy, or doesn't know that he is unhappy, which is the same thing whether in China, Soviet Russia, or America. Lucky he isn't too sensitive about this, or he might be less happy.

Like all human beings, a curious animal.

*C.*: Have you no worse criticism than that?

*T.*: Nothing beyond the serious charge that he is light-headed. The worst criticism is that you haven't got enough sorrow in your country. I'm blowed if I can make my meaning clear to you. You see I come from a poor family, and from a poor nation. I don't think I am envious of other people being rich, because I like to see people happy. But there is something in poverty that gives a man backbone and soberness and determination, something that steadies his character and tempers his idealism. That is good.

But as a lucky, young, and rich people you really haven't known sorrow and danger—nationally speaking. Light-headedness is the characteristic of youth. There is so much bounce and go in you. You live very much for the moment and don't take long views of things. There is, of course, a gay bravado in it, which is extremely charming. How you say "Okay." Note the tone in which you say it, and also the tone in which you say, "You bet." It seems to say you are going to beat the next man to it, and that you are going to trip your way lightly from one difficulty to another and come out on top of the world. Your world is an Okay world, but you've got to learn to take things when they are *not* Okay. This much at least explains what failures there are in your marriages, and it explains it completely for me. Take life as you take a wife, expecting she is going to fail you, and you usually come out better that way. American humor is usually the humor of success, but seldom the humor of failure or resignation.

*C.*: Tell me, then, what you think of the American woman and of American home life.

*T.*: Ah, at last you are asking the important question, the question that really matters in life. Well, I'll say your average American girl is worth a lot more than your average American man. Why? Very simple. She is more sober and more realistic. That is so in almost all nations. I have, of course, seen a few foolish girls, who think life is all gay parties and that they can eat it all. You know what I mean, the "café society" men and women who want to kick night into day. But they cannot represent normal people. She—I mean the average American girl—she, too, has the same enormous vitality that is the characteristic of American men. Also I cannot get over the feeling of her efficiency. Certainly if a man wants to marry a wife for his secretary, he must marry an American one. But if he wants a good cook, he has to exercise great discrimination. I also like a touch of femininity in the office—then the office becomes personal and humanly alive. You feel more and think less then; you yield more to your unsound judgments and you make more errors through righteous sympathies and antipathies—and thus life becomes worth living again.

But I want to say a last word about American home life. The only important thing to note about it is that it is breaking up. It terrifies me. In the first place, there are too few children; in the second place, you don't see enough of your children; and in the third place, you don't discipline your children—not at all. That is the most amazing thing about American life: How Youth sits on its throne, defiant of experience and wisdom and old age. Now I am not in sympathy with the father of the Barretts of Wimpole Street. But one can go too far in the other direction.

It all comes from that psychological nonsense about inhibitions. I don't believe a word of it. You've got to learn inhibitions in life. The whole Freud stuff has been played up until it becomes exaggerated nonsense. Do you suppose we can go through life having everything our own way and not without knocking our will against all sorts of repressions and inhibitions and frustrations in life? Life is full of frustrations. Ask a man over fifty, and see if he does not agree. How then can you prepare yourself for a life of hard knocks without having some hard knocks first in the formative years of your life? Why then let a young child have it all his own way, and then learn not to have it all his own way first when he enters an office and works with his boss? Is his boss going to let him have it all his own way? It simply does not make sense. Some day, I am sure—or I hope—there will come a revolt of the parents.

*C.*: You seem to talk like a Roman Catholic.

*T.*: Perhaps, or like a fustian old Confucianist. But I believe in the home and I believe that it is the bedrock of all human life and the cornerstone of all human civilization. There is nothing more important, philosophically, than the question of maintaining the integrity of the American home. When the home is changed, all human life is changed. This is the last and the most significant conflict, the tendency of modern industrial life to tear apart the old and beautiful American home.

Who is doing that? Ford—this time not the Ford idea, but the Ford car. Something must be done about that tin flivver.

But it isn't all that car alone. It is the city life. In a few decades I suppose city life will be so patterned by wise human thought and planning that the city will become a good, healthy, and enjoyable place in which to live again—morally and physically healthy, combining the beauties of rural health and urban culture, giving at the same time repose to man's spirit and stimulation to man's mind. Your active American minds are already tackling this problem—probably your most important and all-embracing concrete problem. Lewis Mumford's book, *The Culture of Cities*,[2] is truly important philosophically. Out of the solution of such problems of the home and the city will come a type of culture that will be full, rich, and satisfying—and American. A type of culture about which we at present know nothing.

*C.*: The unknown quantity again?

*T.*: Yes, the unknown quantity again—even yet. When that new and beautiful American city arises, New York of 1938 will appear hopelessly and ludicrously antiquated.

[2] Harcourt, Brace & Co., New York, 1937.

# CIVILIZATION IN THE UNITED STATES
# FROM THE MEXICAN POINT OF VIEW

[*H. Valle*]

Translated from the Spanish by Henriette Romeike Van de Velde

AFTER there have been serious conflicts between them in the past, and while old prejudices, which prevent a complete understanding, have not even yet disappeared, it is not an easy task to interpret the feelings and opinions of one country with respect to another. The temptations to generalize, the dangers of pronouncing judgments—these are obvious to a keen observer. And there is a special and further difficulty: It is not possible for a writer to assume full responsibility for the opinions of other people, especially when these opinions, due to conflicting ideologies, are dissimilar.

Perhaps the time I have spent in the United States enables me to rise above prejudice and to express myself with sincerity. It may be that these notes, which do not pretend to be an essay (for I am but a journalist), will be of some use to those who desire that Mexico and the United States succeed in cementing honestly their friendship and becoming truly good neighbors.

Daily the desire for mutual understanding is increasing. This of itself is a good deal, for it is only through such a desire that mistrust can be banished and the way prepared for the advent of a new era when both countries may further progress, not merely one. And it is only by telling the truth that the two countries may come to a clearer understanding of each other.

As a kind of preliminary to my discussion, I should like first to present the opinions of three representative Mexican authors on the subject of the United States.

In his book, *Viaje a los Estados Unidos del Norte de America* (Paris, 1834), Don Lorenzo de Zavala said the following:

There [in the United States] will be found a true description of the nation that our legislators have wished to imitate. A nation that is hard-working, active, given to reflection, circumspect, religious in the midst of a multiplicity of sects, tolerant, miserly, free, proud and persevering. The Mexican is flighty, lazy, intolerant, generous and almost a spendthrift, vain, belligerent, superstitious, ignorant, and opposed to any sort of yoke. The North American works; the Mexican amuses himself. The first spends the least possible, the second spends even what he has not; the one carries the most arduous undertakings to a successful conclusion, the other abandons them at the very beginning. One lives in his house, decorates it, furnishes it, and protects it from the elements; the other passes his time in the streets; he flees from his habitation and, in a land where there are no seasons, he gives but little care to the place where he takes his rest. In the Northern States every one owns something and is working to augment his holdings; in Mexico the few who possess anything are careless of it and some let it go to ruin.

Jose Vasconcelos, former Minister of Public Education, has written, in his *Bolivarismo y Monroismo*[1] volume, one of the strongest attacks on the United States:

For many years common opinion was led to believe that the North American millionaire was the personification of modern activity, the torch-bearer of progress, that benevolent element which transforms the wastes of the desert into abundance. There have been times when the primary school in North America was consecrated to this new creed: The worship of daring enterprise and of success. And the Carnegies and Rockefellers have come almost to be saints of the new religion, and if not exactly patrons of the new school, at least living Garyites. Even Dewey, the philosopher, points out as a model among schools those of a certain Mr. Wirt who accused the advisers of Mr. Roosevelt of being Communists because they dared to regulate North American economics without consulting the barons of Wall Street, portrayed in Josephson's book.[2] And not only the pedagogues, but even poets of the importance of Ibsen have gone so far as to take as models [Peer Gynt] the suppositive heroes of industrial adventure and get-rich-quickness.

Speaking of the paintings patronized by the money of Ambassador Morrow, and expressing his opinion that the painter was unjust to Cortes, the Spaniards, and the Indians, Don Rafael Garcia Granados, of the faculty of the University of Mexico, says the following:

And to this artist, Diego Rivera, the Ambassador gave the commission to paint—in the same spirit and using the same themes as in his previous work— great frescos on the wall of the old palace of Cortes, today the Government Palace, in Cuernavaca.

[1] Ed. Ercilla, Santiago de Chile, 1934.
[2] *The Robber Barons,* by Matthew Josephson. New York, 1933.

That the Government of Mexico must of necessity maintain harmonious relations with that of the United States is hidden from no one. But this harmony can be of no possible advantage to Mexico if, in order to conserve it, we must pretend not to see when North American functionaries attempt to undermine the bases of our nationalism.

No one in Mexico today is trying to inculcate in the minds of our youth hatred and rancor against our neighbors in the North because they once, with extreme perfidy, dispossessed us of half of our territory. Is it too much to ask in exchange —since we are not an enemy to be feared—that their officials abstain from stirring up our discords?[3]

From the Mexican point of view the people of the United States have one special interest in life: To work to make money—but considering money as the source of material well-being, as that which provides all the comforts whereby life is made agreeable. True, many Mexicans who have lived in the United States have come to change this opinion when they realized that, to the North Americans, money is not only the source of individual welfare but the means for bringing about collaboration for the general well-being. Especially by establishing foundations—such as those bearing the names of Carnegie, Guggenheim, and Rockefeller—and by financing great cultural enterprises, money is made to produce real benefits which are not only at the service of North Americans but also at the disposal of any and all who may need help in case of some collective catastrophe, such as an earthquake, an epidemic, or a war.

For some time in Mexico it was believed that, as a general thing, American business men were actuated by bad faith when they ventured into this country, and that the swindler was an exceptional type in Mexico while a common one in the United States. This belief was expressed by a daily paper, *La Voz de Mexico* (January 18, 1898), in commenting upon a swindle perpetrated on Fred H. Franke, a German citizen, by Christen, Whitney, McKey, and other Americans. Protesting against "the protection that Americans find here," the newspaper had this to say:

The adventurer[4] does exist in Mexico, but as a type that is so uncommon that he is immediately recognized as such. The contrary is the case in the United States of the North, and their contact with Mexico will be more lamentable every day. Over there bad faith is an endemic disease, a substantial condition of character.

[3]*Filias y Fobias*, 1937.　　　　[4]Spanish: *Caballero de industria.*

Even in the smallest towns the swindler abounds, and will be found in great numbers in all classes, companies, and social categories.

This is one of the first things observed by a foreigner.

For this reason, while confidence in business matters is the rule in Mexico, in the United States a profound and colossal lack of confidence dominates personal, family, social, and economic relations. Nobody has any faith, not even in the strongest firms. Bad faith is the essence of business. Even the authorities themselves will advise travellers not to listen to any Yankee offering any sort of a business proposition, be it radical or such as might interest any traveller.

Nothing is more dangerous than to allow oneself to be guided to a hotel, theatre, commercial establishment, or rooming-house by a person who has not been vouched for either by old acquaintances or by the police.

In business, the swindling is colossal. The Yankee adventurer is a real professor, whose science consists, above all, in two important studies—a knowledge of the human heart, and an exquisite delicacy in social usage, which goes so far in politeness as to be almost feminine.

Every Yankee swindler, one might say, is "a perfect lady."

One of the things that strikes the attention of a foreigner when visiting the United States, or when reading the American newspapers, is the fact that they are always claiming to have "the best in the world"— the best aviators, the finest railroads, the greatest millionaires, the highest skyscrapers, the fattest woman, the World's Champion. It is possible that, to the American, this is nothing more than an act of ingenuousness, and it may even be a system of commercial propaganda—assuming that in business a lie is not a lie. In Spanish America we have adopted a word, when speaking of exaggeration, to express this state of mind: "Bluff."

It is believed here that the morals of our Mexican women are very superior, in many ways, to those of the women in the United States, and that the moving-picture stories are largely responsible for the fact that, in the United States, the contrary is believed. It all started by the United States offending Mexico by presenting, as a typical Mexican, the "villain" of the film, who was invariably knocked out by a healthy, simple-minded youth playing the role of cowboy—with the face of a child and the muscles of an athlete. And this should not have been shown on the screen. For the type invented by the moving pictures was but a reflection of hypocrisy.

Lately, many customs have made their appearance in Mexico and Mexican homes—customs which are slowly breaking down the tradition of the home as founded by the Spaniards. This is attributed to an imitation of the feministic customs of the United States. A great many people think that the moving pictures are to blame for what has happened, especially in the matter of certain liberties that our women are taking unto themselves. Among these are the changes that—in the name of emancipation—have been brought about with respect to certain juridical standards, of which that of matrimony is one. At this point one ought to remember that Catholic morality, as taught by the priests, has always opposed divorce.

Here in Mexico we believe that the North Americans are not aware of many things which other nations know. For example, there is the matter of culinary art—an art which we think they do not understand, since in the United States everything is standardized. And after all, this opinion is not without certain justification to those who know the cities, the suburbs, the theatres, the restaurants, the capitals of each State, for they all look—if not exactly alike—certainly very similar and even monotonously the same. What is lacking is personality. (Punctuality in keeping engagements, and strict adherence to time-tables are also considered "standard.") For this reason, when we order "ham-and-eggs," or "hot dogs," whether in San Francisco, Boston, New Orleans, or Chicago, we are exasperated to find that each dish seems to have been prepared by the same cook, all being identical in flavor, size, and price. This is not the case in Mexico, where everything—the songs, the liquors, the meals, the likes and dislikes of the people—are very diverse. For Mexico is a country of contrasts, not of similarities. In Mexico, too, we are struck by the different colors of ice-cream, made in imitation of that of the United States. But gourmets of Spanish tradition, or those with French tastes, know that the sum of these flavors is a minimum of gastronomic pleasure.

In general, American tourists do not come to Mexico for the purpose of increasing their knowledge of the country. They come rather in search of agreeable pastimes, while taking advantage of the cheapness of Mexican money. Many of them come simply to have a good time. And it should be noted, too, that they come for only a short visit. Hence it is not possible for them really to understand Mexico—not even those who, having some intellectual preparation, later say very foolish things in the books they write about this country, after having only glimpsed the surface.

A North American citizen who lives in Taxco, William Spratling, has written a most interesting book, entitled *Little Mexico,* which gives a good picture of a certain class of tourist. The Summer Courses, of six weeks, at the University of Mexico, have made it possible for many students and professors to form different ideas of what Mexico actually is like. Yet sometimes, in the beginning, they ask questions that seem almost infantile. To which the guides answer: "This building cost 200,000 pesos; the construction took one year and nine days; the total weight of the building material is 500 tons. . . ." It is a case of repetition of the Babbitt type that has made the American tourist a world-wide personality. Today in Mexico, however, Babbitt is no longer the extravagant spender who used to buy things at the price asked for them—now he knows how to bargain.

Nevertheless there are many Americans who are so charmed with Mexico that they come here to live. Among them, fortunately, are not a few writers who make true observations and who write books that even Mexicans can consult with profit: Such are, among others, Carleton Beals, Ernest Gruening, Frank Tannenbaum, William Spratling, Earl N. Simpson, and Stuart Chase.

Many Mexican students of contemporary realities affirm that in the United States there is no democracy—only a plutocracy. Even the elections, they say, are controlled by the capitalist class, and if the public goes to the polls, it is only to obey orders. However, the course now being traced by President Roosevelt has caused this opinion to be modified, for many of us are judging him as a revolutionary who is endeavoring to save capital from a revolution—a revolution that might well take place in the United States, if a drastic change is not made in the present condition of the proletariat there.

When prohibition went into effect in 1919, we called it a hypocritical law. And now that Mexico herself is starting her own anti-alcoholic campaign, we recall the comments made upon the American law at that time. And we still think that prohibiton's failure was due to the fact that is was not possible to bring about a popular conviction solely by means of an educational campaign.

There are those who affirm that if, among us Latins, the weakness is women, that of the Americans is alcohol. One might cite cases of North Americans who have visited Mexico and have become passionately fond of *tequila,* one of the most dangerous of liquors.

The majority of our people believe that the North Americans are lacking in artistic appreciation, even although it is granted that they take great pains to educate themselves by travel, by enriching museums and libraries, and by bringing to the United States great conductors of symphonies, singers, and actors, to all of whom they pay enviable salaries.

Some of us believe, for instance, that even after becoming a rich country —well organized and with many millionaires—all the money in the United States has not enabled our northern neighbor to make a single original contribution to the history of art, as have, of course, several European countries. It is conceded that in architecture our neighbors have produced the skyscraper—this style being, in New York and Chicago at least, undoubtedly a product of urban economics—and that in music they have produced "jazz," even though the latter be of Negro origin. Some students of contemporary creative impulses, nevertheless, point out that there is one art being created—that of photography. Due to the extraordinary progress along this line we do in fact consider it a really new art, and one that has no rival in the world.[5]

However, few Spanish-Americans will admit that there have been poets in the United States whom Spanish-American literature has not been able to rival: Whitman and Poe are, perhaps, the exceptions, to whom only Rubén Darío may be compared.

On the part of many who attend moving pictures as well as those who take trips to the United States there is a marked tendency in our country: That of a continuous imitation of all that is bad. This tendency has even invaded the Spanish language, and we are adopting English words—such as "close-up," "standard," "okay," "bye-bye," and so on, particularly in the jargon of sport, such as football. Moreover, this tendency is responsible for a word—a term of reproach and disapproval—*Pochismo*. First it was the Mexican-Texans who were called *Pochos,* and later Jose Vasconcelos dedicated the word in a book censuring the attitude of those Mexicans who, after a short stay on the other side of the Rio Bravo, return to their native country speaking Spanish with an English accent. There is an excellent book by Victoriano Salado Alvarez[6] compiling all the words of Spanish origin now commonly used in those States which, previous to 1847, belonged to Mexico. This book proves that Spanish

[5]See Chapter, p. 82ff., on "Art."
[6]*El Mexico Peregrino.*

is capable of exercising an influence on English, and, further, that there is no reason why the contrary should necessarily take place.

Measures have been taken which make an attempt to stem the increasing influence of English over Spanish in Mexico. One of these was the official prohibition by the municipal authorities of the Mexican capital of street signs in a foreign language, and the name of one of the residential sections of the capital (Chapultepec Heights) was changed.

In spite of everything, however, one cannot deny the tendency to imitate the United States—not only in that which is worthy of imitation but in much that should not serve as a model. This is especially true among people of scant culture, and it is curious to note that many Mexicans who consider themselves nationalistic are the first to imitate North American dances, drinks, and—especially—sports. Some of these imitations may be due to certain organizations, which, although of Mexican membership, are basically of North American origin: the Rotary Club, the Y. M. C. A., the Pan-American Round Table, the Country Club, and the Auto Club.

When it concerns our better class journalism, no one can deny that the Mexican press follows the principal outlines of that of the United States, especially in the matter of format and in the scandalous, or yellow, note.

When it concerns city planning and urban architecture, many Mexicans who are desirous of preserving the artistic tradition left to us by the Indians and the Spaniards deplore what is just one more imitation of what is being done in the United States. They think that the City of Mexico, due to the appearance of tall buildings, apartment houses, and bungalows, is losing its distinctive quality.

Eduardo Noguera, the archæologist, is among those who have expressed themselves on this subject.[7] He says:

Saddest of all is the fact that not all that is good is imitated, nor do we understand all that is worthy of being taken into consideration. Rather it is the contrary that is happening. First thousands and then millions of Mexicans, desirous of making high salaries, cross the border and the contact of the two nations produces—first at the boundaries, and later well within our national territory—a hybridism of two strong civilizations, the Latin and the Anglo-Saxon. The Mexican corrupts his Spanish and changes his manner of dress from that which is national and to which he is accustomed to the cheap garments of the other side. Even his mental attitude becomes ridiculous and in bad taste. Sometimes he denies everything Mexican, pretending to have become 100 per cent Ameri-

[7]"La Influencia Americana y el Pochismo," published in *Mexicoal Dia*, December 1, 1937.

can, and in the end he only makes himself ridiculous and disliked by his coun-trymen as well as despised by those he is trying to imitate. From this comes the word "Pocho." Much has been written about this lamentable state of affairs, which can only harm everything that is ours. But the danger is not only there (on the other side of the border); it tends to advance over the entire country and to influence all those Mexicans who aspire to become imitations of the American in his lowest aspects.

The moving picture, the radio, and the innumerable tourists who visit us daily, all are carriers of this slow but disastrous germ of transformation. A short stroll through Mexico City will suffice to observe to what point this influence is to be feared.

In the first place, our architecture has suffered lamentable changes by follow-ing the evolution of the new art while losing the old beauty. This is producing regular "hen houses," in the construction of which the practical is the first con-sideration; cheapness and profit come next, and then, if there is anything left over, perhaps some thought is given to the æsthetic. A great deal has already been said about what Mexico will look like in a few years, thanks to the invasion of this new architecture. It will be a servile copy of any nondescript town in the United States.

Constantly the Mexican press makes mention of attacks and humilia-tions suffered by Mexicans in certain parts of the United States, and, it is insisted, there are places where the Mexicans are classed among the "colored people." Many Mexicans who have worked there as laborers, or on the cotton plantations, say that these humiliations are a fact, and that—even in American schools on the border, attended by Mexican children—incidents of this nature may be witnessed. There is a widely-read novel depicting the plight of the Mexicans who have been cast up on the other side of the "Bravo," and who, in spite of the long term of their exile, still preserve their Mexicanism and sigh to return to their "home."[8]

The word "greaser," applied by the man in the street to Mexicans, is still being used with crude disdain. We are also assured that there are many cases of Mexicans in straitened circumstances who, when applying for work at a factory, are urged to become American citizens. If they do not accept the invitation, they will not be given work. Or, if already employed, they are dismissed in order to make room for Americans.

Shortly after the Great War the problem of unemployment became acute in the United States, and thousands of Mexicans were replaced by Americans. Commenting upon this, the Mexican press used terms of

[8] The novel is *La Patria Perdida*, by Teodoro Torres.

profound disagreement. Here we may recall the popular demonstrations that took place in the City of Mexico in 1908, when news was received of the lynching of one Antonio Rodriguez in Texas. One has to add, of course, that these riots, during which some American business houses were damaged, were directed as well against the dictator, Porfirio Diaz, who was considered the champion of North American capitalism in Mexico.

The enthusiasms with which, since 1920, North American scholars, art critics, and journalists have sung the praises of our artists and those of us who dedicate ourselves to the industrial arts has somewhat abated our belief in this hostility towards the sons of Mexico. It has been further abated since the Guggenheim Foundation has bestowed scholarships on some of our Mexican University students. Among these scholars particularly there is a grateful acknowledgment of the co-operation and help in scientific investigation given in the past and still extended by the Carnegie and Rockefeller Institutes, the Middle America Department of the University of Tulane, and other institutions.

In Mexico it is not forgotten—not even by the cultured class, and still less by any other social stratum—that the war of 1847 was a great injustice. Yet, since the United States at that time needed a field for further development and hoped to find it by expansion to the south, which had to be done at any cost, it is an injustice that North American historians— particularly those who write textbooks—attempt to excuse as an entirely natural biological phenomenon. In a series of lectures delivered at the Summer School in the City of Mexico several years ago, Doctor J. Fred Rippy, the American historian, expressed himself in this sense, and his opinions were adversely commented upon by the Mexican press.

This resentment—which, I repeat, is common to all Mexicans, and which only a long work of common understanding will ever destroy— was also expressed at the Pan-American Conference in Buenos Aires. One of the resolutions passed called for a full revision of all the historical textbooks used in American countries, with the object of deleting those opinions and facts which tended to perpetuate the memory of events that are obstacles in the path of true comprehension. The Mexican historians present, as well as the delegates from the Department of Public Education, were not in favor of this resolution, alleging that, if it were passed, it would be necessary to delete all mention of the invasion of 1847, as well as the interventions of Spain and France.

Anything that happens in the United States is news in Mexico. This is shown by our daily press, which interested itself to an extraordinary degree in the result of the last Presidential election in the United States. Besides, our public is always interested in the smallest details of the cable news of the international policies of the United States. This is particularly true when there is news of a difference of opinion with Japan—a country which, we think, the United States will sooner or later have to fight. In this connection, it will suffice to note that a high representative of the Mexican Army, General J. Andrew Almazan, publicly declared—and it appeared in the press—that, in the event of a war with a rival power, it was the duty of Mexico to side with the United States.

On less serious topics, I might add that the Mexican sporting public gets very much exercised over reports of the baseball and boxing world championship contests, while the public in general is avid for news of your moving picture stars.

Since the epoch of Juarez nobody can deny that the United States has exercised a political influence on Mexico—an influence that at times has tended to become undisguised interference, as when Mr. P. C. Knox announced what we call the "Policy of the Dollar." We also believe that the Monroe Doctrine is an excuse for the exercise of this influence: This, while granting that nobody knows the exact meaning of the Doctrine, which has had so many interpretations. One of these—the one formulated by Under-Secretary of State, Mr. J. Reuben Clark, former Ambassador to Mexico—appears to be definite.

Some Liberals, defending and explaining the conduct of Benito Juarez at the time of what is called the McLean-Ocampo Treaty (although it was not ratified by the American Senate), admit that Juarez sought moral support, and even material aid, from the government of the United States in his struggle against the French invaders. But in defense of Juarez they point out that the influence of the United States has been beneficial, whenever Mexico has tried to progress politically.

They cite the banding together of the Liberals against the Conservative Party from the time of the Federal Wars (Gomez Farias and Santa Ana) up to the Constitutional Revolution headed by Carranza. In the meanwhile ever since the Texas War the Conservative Party has professed to believe that what was necessary for Mexico's salvation was the influence of some European power—which faith they proved by invoking the aid of Napoleon III. The attitude of President Wilson in refusing to recognize the Huerta government—and to understand this one ought to read the memoirs of Mr. John Lind—is believed by the enemies of the Mexican Revolution to be still another proof of the fact that Wilson was trying to give effective aid to those who were fighting Huerta, if only to bring about an ousting of English interests—primarily in the oil business—so as to leave Mexico open to American capital. The historians say practically the same thing regarding the diplomatic activities of Joel R. Poinsett, who was strongly opposed to the Conservative group. They claim that Poinsett endeavored to keep Mexico in a constant state of civil strife so that the country would become debilitated and easily dominated by the United States.

These historians have affirmed that Poinsett's aim, obeying instructions, was to foment hatred of the Spaniards, who, their property rights being well protected, had remained in Mexico after the Independence of 1821. By removing Spanish capital, and by preventing the growth of English interests, they say, Poinsett hoped to make Americans masters of the Mexican economic situation. Along this line, one should read *Alaman, Estadista e Historiador,* by José C. Valadez, who, in Chapter V, speaks of the struggles between Alaman and Poinsett and his Mexican allies, the York Rite Masons.

The Mexicans who aspire to see Mexico absolutely liberated from foreign influence blame American interests for many of the civil wars in the country. They believe that American capital has lent moral and financial support to Mexican uprisings in the hope that, in return, it would receive oil and mining concessions; they believe also that it planned to use for this purpose the wealth of the United States (although without the consent of the American public). This public—being well disciplined and only recently interested in events taking place beyond their own boundaries—did not protest against the use of the naval and military forces of the United States in the several invasions of Mexico. That is to say, the Texas War and the invasions of 1847 and of 1914 did not have the popular support of the American people; they were promoted in the interests of slave-holding capitalists in the first instance, and, in the second, by those of Wall Street. The aggressive activities of these interests in their effort to take possession of raw materials, trade-routes, and markets constitute what we call "American Imperialism."

That is why the activities of the Pan-American Union of Washington, and the manifestations of a desire to erase past differences and create "good will" have not received popular sympathy and support in Mexico.

These activities are judged as poorly disguised evidences of a real, even if a non-military, policy of penetration.

Even as late as last year we knew the case of a distinguished American teacher, Doctor Julius L. Spivak, who, when arranging for the Spanish edition of his book with a publishing house in Mexico, could not believe that the edition would compare with the original. He was very much surprised to find that it not only equalled the first edition, but surpassed it.

To what is due this lack of comprehension between the two countries? Difficult as it is to put one's finger on all the contributing factors, it would seem that, fundamentally, its origin lies in the following:

1. The serious conflicts and the aggressions of which Mexico has been the victim.

2. The affirmation that Anglo-Saxon culture is superior to Latin-American.

3. The economic inequality of the two countries.

4. The difference in language.

5. The bad faith of certain writers who have specialized in discrediting Mexico in books and in articles for the American press. Outstanding among them is John K. Turner, who, in 1909, published in *The American Magazine* a series of articles which later were incorporated in his book, *Barbarous Mexico*.

In all fairness it must be said that Mexicans who have visited or resided in the United States recognize that Americans possess the following qualities:

1. A formidable capacity for hard work. This is strengthened by organization and a sensible preparation for life, an ability to face facts (thereby acquiring a virtue that Spanish-America could well emulate), and punctuality even in small matters.

2. A respect for the property rights of others. This seems to be common to Americans, with the exception of professional thieves.

3. The generosity of the rich. Although we, too, produced philanthropists during the Spanish domination, we have not yet been able to equal the example of those in the United States who have established charitable and benevolent foundations and institutions for social service.

4. Personal cleanliness, and a devotion to the principles of hygiene.

5. Admirable public utilities. In this respect the United States undoubtedly leads the world.

6. The American faith in the possibilities of human achievement, as expressed in the fight against disease and the work in favor of world peace. Most Spanish-Americans believe that God made the poor and the rich, that disease is a punishment for sin, and that it is useless to struggle against the will of God, who evidently did not wish the world to be perfect.

7. An almost fanatical respect for children, in each of whom Americans visualize a possible Lincoln. This feeling is an intelligent and reasonable affection—yet Americans are not so effusive with their children as are we.

8. The way in which children are brought up to earn their own living —even the children of millionaires.

9. The chivalrous protection accorded their women. This protection, it seems to us Mexicans, American women put to poor use, while every day exercising a greater influence in both private and public life in the United States. This American attitude is championed by Mexican feminists, who are working for full political equality for women.

10. The American press, which has a large reading public in Mexico. We grant it first place in world journalism.

11. The American desire to learn, to ask questions, to increase knowledge, and above all, the American ability to take advantage of universal values, giving no thought to the fact that Toscanini is an Italian; Noguchi, a Japanese; Doctor Spivak, a Russian; or Sandoval Vallarta, a Mexican. This is a great quality. It explains the strength of the United States: You have learned to utilize different intellectual resources, promoting and fostering them, and later giving them back to the service of the world.

12. Your great progress in the realm of applied science.

13. Your tolerance for all ideas and towards all creeds. Would that we in Spanish-America could imitate the United States in this respect— despite the justification that our intolerance has historical backgrounds! A Spanish thinker, Salvador de Madariaga, once said that America is divided into the United States of America, and the Dis-United States of America. Numerous racial factors are to be taken into consideration on both the Northern and Southern banks of the Rio Bravo, but we in Spanish-America have not been able to achieve any sort of unity within the borders of one country, and still less to establish any real confederation. This, in spite of the lyric attempts of such men of vision as Bolivar, Morazan, and José Marti.

One more thing greatly impresses us: The "team-work" of the Americans. In the United States a book is very often written (like this one) by several authors: In Mexico we are individualists, and we do not comprehend the miracles of co-operation.

But in Mexico we are likewise well aware of the following:

1. The early settlers of the United States arrived at a very opportune moment for colonization. They were, moreover, greatly favored by gifts of nature, such as harbors and navigable rivers, which was not the case in Mexico. The English arrived at the very moment that the world was afire with the idea of industrial progress. They did not encounter such an organized nucleus of Indians, such as the Aztecs and the Peruvians. They adopted a policy that, in its large outlines, had unity and also had an eye to the future. This was not the case in Spanish-America, where each king and governor followed a different policy from that of his predecessor. While the English colonists were working, praying, founding workshops and industries, and cultivating the soil, the Creoles and the Meztizos were amusing themselves, and the Indians remained as much enslaved as before the coming of Cortes. From the very beginning the English colonists had liberty. Also, they were fortunate in having to struggle for their existence, while in Mexico there are regions where nature is so prodigal that, besides the climate, "fruit is one of the worst enemies of man," according to Agustin Rivera. It is a curious fact that apples, grapes, and oranges—which today form a big part of the wealth of California—were first brought to Mexico. Today, we import them from Californian orchards. And long before Henry Hudson was born— as early as the first quarter of the 16th century—we already had in Mexico our first printing press, our first University, and our first city. That press, that University, that city were the first on this continent.

2. We do not understand the treatment accorded to Negroes by Americans. It is, of course, quite true that the Spaniard and the Creole treated the conquered Indians in much the same fashion. But the practice of lynching we consider abominable—even while admitting that certain Indians in Mexico have this custom, although it is exceptional. We also believe that sooner or later the United States will have to contend with the problem of an increasing colored population. And we think, too, that you still treat your Indians with disdain, considering them incapable of self-betterment in spite of the opportunities given them on the reservations.

Some there are who, with marked skepticism, maintain that it will never be possible for Mexico to arrive at a sincere understanding with the United States. On the other hand, some of our thinkers maintain a contrary opinion and affirm that in time there will be a real friendship, if only because geography influences destinies. (Though Europe of today hardly supports this contention.) The first group invokes the fact that the strong cannot truly befriend the weak. They say, too, that in spite of education it is impossible to wipe out racial prejudice.

The second group maintains that, in spite of the injustices committed against Mexico, there have always been men in the United States who, with brave sincerity, have protested against the invasion of Mexico—as did Walt Whitman during the war of 1847 (and as did Favre and Hugo in France at the time of the Napoleonic invasion). During the past twenty years a growing number of Americans have become convinced of the advisability of a change of tactics with respect to the countries to the south of the Rio Bravo, and are desirous of bringing about a better understanding between them—not entirely with disinterested enthusiasm, to be sure, but because there is a near future when the United States (and this was seen during the Great War) might need friends and allies in Spanish-America.

Perhaps the Good Neighbor policy, proclaimed by President Roosevelt, has its origin in the thoughts expressed by certain American diplomats, among them Mr. Thomas Corwin, who—in 1862—signed the Corwin-Doblado Treaty with Mexico. When sending the draft of this Treaty to the Secretary of State, he said: "Let it be remembered that Mexico is *our neighbor* and enlightened self-interest requires that we should not be indifferent to the welfare of such."

However, it must be admitted that in the United States there is a greater knowledge of Mexico than that which we possess of the United States. This is because of greater opportunities and resources which make possible such studies. Besides, the American investments in Mexico are much more important than those which a few Mexicans may have in the United States.

# AN ENGLISHMAN LOOKS AT AMERICA

*[Sir Willmott Lewis]*

<small>WASHINGTON CORRESPONDENT OF "THE LONDON TIMES"</small>

A MAN is in a desperate business when he writes of any country not his own, and of its civilization. He must go delicately, for even a native who displays any independence of judgment nowadays invites resentment rather than temperate rejoinder. The only utterance which seems to find favor anywhere is crowd-language, aimed at the lowest prejudice of the greatest number. What may be called public thinking has taken the place of private thinking. The real danger in the field of opinion is not Marxism, but mass-ism. Thinker's cramp is a disease of our day, as it has been of so many yesterdays.

Certainly you cannot distill the story of the United States into any drop of truth; the country is too vast for the uses of any alembic. No observer's mind has pigeon-holes enough for the sorting and containment of its diversity. You may pile Bryce on Tocqueville, and both on Ostrogorski, but their height will not give you the 360-degree horizon you need. These admirable men were not parodic like Dickens, nor atrabilious like Mrs. Trollope, but, for all that, they were observers only, not a living part of what they observed. The mere journalist like myself should remember this with humility. Long residence and constant workaday immersion in the American stream, much travel and reading, are all I can claim—unless I add a grateful awareness that America has changed me for the better, and a lively sense of the unvarying kindness which has been meted out to me for more than thirty years. George Santayana said somewhere that if he were to meet a man of whom he knew nothing, and were to find that he was not a kindly man, he would know at least that the stranger was not an American.

You cannot talk of the Old World and the New World as though the experience of mankind could be sliced into sections, and these sections represented by lines upon a globe. Truth, I think, would not suffer too severely, if we adapted to the United States Bacon's saying about Rome: "It was not the Romans that spread upon the world, but the world that spread upon the Romans; and that was the sure way of greatness." Twentieth-century Europe, to be sure, could not have been what it is without the discovery of America, and without the deep changes wrought upon the face of America by the birth and growth, the political, economic and cultural development of the American people; but, more by token, there is a sense in which the United States is every European's "second country." Something of the genius, the native energy, and the modes of thought and being of every European people has been woven into the texture of American life; and always this "something," subtly modified, Americanized, has returned across the Atlantic to work its alchemy of change upon the pattern of living of the older world.

More than twenty years ago a French writer—R. Johannet, in his *Principe des Nationalités*—considered Germany as "a race"; Great Britain, "an island"; France, "a territory"; Italy, "a language"; Austria-Hungary, "a policy"; Egypt, "a river"; Judæa, "a religion." There is enough leaven of truth in these little epigrams to leaven some of the history of the lands he wrote of, but less, I think, than we find in this addition to the list: the United States, "a continent." How much of the history of the American nation can be found in the implications of that word! The story has no parallel. Never before had a civilized people been transplanted to a territory at once so vast and so incomparably rich in untouched natural wealth, for its surface had not even been scratched by the early nomadic dwellers. This civilized people did not bring political democracy with them to Jamestown or to Plymouth Rock. Their descendants have not fully achieved it yet. As with England, with France, and with Switzerland, the United States is a political democracy in the making. When the old colonial establishments became the sovereign States of a narrow strip between the Atlantic coast and the Alleghenies, they were ruled by their "gentry," their landed, professional and merchant classes, and it was these who made the Constitution in 1787. By as much as political democracy exists today, it came to life and grew at the frontier, most sturdily in the once empty empire of the Ohio and Mississippi valleys, where the institutions of an older society were worked over and tested, where equalitarianism spread. And since 1890 there has been no frontier.

It was one of Emerson's articles of faith that a man's thoughts spring from his actions, rather than his actions from his thoughts. The belief has a wider and more "scientific" acceptance today than it had a century ago, and its application to society at large is no longer altogether fanciful. Let us, by way of applying it, begin with a quotation from Arthur Twining Hadley:

The whole American political and social system is based on industrial property right, far more completely than has ever been the case in any European country. In every nation of Europe there has been a certain amount of traditional opposition between the government and the industrial classes. In the United States no such tradition exists. In the public law of European communities industrial freeholding is a comparatively recent development. In the United States, on the contrary, industrial freeholding is the foundation on which the whole social order has been established and built up.[1]

This statement will be accepted, by the historical student at least, without moral qualms. Society must be ordered on some basis which appeals with sufficient strength to fundamental instincts, and the United States of 1789 resembled, as H. C. Emery said, "a great ship undermanned and poorly equipped." The problem here was not, as elsewhere in that day, that of administering a territory so as to fulfill the needs of its population, but—urgently and imperatively, while empty lands and untouched wealth bred fears of foreign invasion—that of finding a population which should settle upon and develop the soil, and of providing capital to put the settlers effectively to work. It was not, therefore, the desire for power —as in feudal Europe or Japan—which determined the form of the social order, but the desire for possession. From the beginning of the American Commonwealth, from the day when General Washington took the oath of office and the genius of Alexander Hamilton found a theatre of activity, American society has been erected on an economic basis. The result, let us remember, was the greatest material achievement of the white race in the modern world—the development and exploitation, in 150 years, of the immense natural wealth of a continental area more than 3,000,000 square miles in extent.

Something should here be said, moreover, of Puritan New England, whose share in all this is not often or enough recalled. The sons of the Puritans moved westward, carrying more than thew and sinew, taking

[1]*Undercurrents in American Politics.* By Arthur Twining Hadley. New Haven: Yale University Press.

with them a state of mind which was long to be determinant of the national mood, and is still a factor of importance. This, on its good side, was self-reliance, joined to a conviction of personal responsibility. But, like all good things when pushed to excess, qualities breed defects. Self-reliance may come near to selfishness; and personal responsibility, when set on a plane too high above the claims of the community, may turn to the blind worship of individual rights, its devotees may too narrowly assume that character always, and not circumstance, is the parent of poverty and failure. There are moments when the Puritan resembles Thwackem, who was for doing justice, and leaving mercy to Heaven. His theory of individual rights, as R. H. Tawney said, once "secularized and generalized, was to be among the most potent explosives that the world has known." His influence upon his times, for good or evil, was immense, and it persists. Himself the incarnation of nonconformity in matters of religion, he became the instrument, in the moral—which is the social—sphere, of a veritable tyranny of conformity. While free cultivable land remained, the opportunities, even for the weak, which abounded at the frontier disguised the poverty of his thought. He was a conservative to the nth power, believing that the terrestrial order of things was as good as human frailty would permit. And "the conservative," as Emerson said in an unforgettable passage, "assumes sickness as a necessity," with the result that "sickness gets organized as well as health, the vice as well as the virtue."

But Emerson was ahead of his time. How should he or any like him prevail, when things were what they were, and the brilliance of the material results obscured all else? An amazing economic development had been possible without any preconceived idea or determining will. The initiative of individuals, seeking independently their own interest, had secured a wide diffusion of property, and the beliefs regarding property which this encouraged had been uncritically accepted by the popular mind. The idea of democracy became strangely mingled with that of *laissez-faire;* the "rugged individual" was exalted; industry advanced steadily to a position of predominance among American interests which no single interest (and industry least of all) is fit to occupy; and over it all was a luxuriant growth of that mistletoe of society, Finance, whose roots are not in the soil, but in the tree. This was so, of course, wherever the Industrial Revolution had worked its physical wonders, but overwhelmingly so in a land whose natural wealth was so vast as to give new methods and new non-human dexterities an unexampled field of operation, and whose social and political system had, as Hadley said, been based on the concept of industrial property right.

It was this which moved John Jay Chapman to say that "misgovernment in the United States is an incident in the history of commerce . . . part of the triumph of industrial progress." In no other land could the generalization be sharpened to so narrow an edge. Misgovernment in England, for instance, was successively the accompaniment of "divine right," of feudal and quasi-feudal oligarchy, of religious strife, and only when a millennium had run its course did "industrial progress" demand its share of privilege. Here Chapman's saying can stand without gloss; but here also we can thankfully recall that he saw salvation in the American form of government—"a great educational machine which no one can stop," enlisting "the power of light on the side of order"—and in the American people, visibly to his eyes sane and healthy creatures, the masses of them "the most promising people extant."

The Pasha in Kinglake's "Eothen" summed up the 19th century as "Whirr-whirr—all by wheels; whizz-whizz—all by steam." Wheels and steam are good things, as may be all the innumerable gadgets we have added unto them, but they are not good in themselves. Civilization never has been, is not, and cannot be a product. It is a process. It is visible when men have dealings one with another at a high level of experience, it is not even perceptible when men are uplifted or downcast by the record of car-loadings or the jerking of a stock-market ticker. I was taught in my youth to accept as true the saying of John Richard Green that here, in America and not in Europe, lies "the hope of the world," and I believe it still. Here, I was told, was a Europe from which the past had been stripped away, able to run unencumbered into a better future; here, in a land of plenty, free men could not help but build a glorious pattern of social behavior. I have known the United States for thirty-three years, it is part of my duty as it has been my pleasure to travel about the country, and it is my delight to speak with many men. I say now, and I say it with sadness but by no means without hope, that when there is no prosperity American life seems to have lost its meaning for the great mass of the American people. Is it by bread alone that men live? I do not believe it. Has long dependence upon material advantages alone destroyed the qualities which created the advantages—the self-reliance, the sense of responsibility, the unquenchable faith, the abiding hope which moved and upheld the men of an earlier time? I do not believe this either. The older institutions and moralities have been corrupted by industry—any man not stricken into a blind complacency can see that. The American people, with all the riches available to them, have not yet learned how little money can buy, that "man's life consisteth not in the abundance of the things which he possesseth"—that is as painfully evident here as elsewhere. But there are signs that the day when social well-being could be acceptably identified with the volume of business is over, that at last, and of deliberate purpose, the usufruct of material achievement can be applied to the enrichment of the spiritual life of the nation.

No man, and least of all a foreigner, should criticise or arraign American things by any but an American standard. If I have misunderstood the American standard the fault is in me, but I certainly do not undervalue it. An older standard has been set aside for something newer and less worthy, but this new thing cannot endure because it has bred inequality. The country which was to be, and still may be, a pattern for the world, shows a dangerous inequality of economic advantage as among its great regional subdivisions, and as between industry and agriculture; an inequality of contractual status as between industry highly integrated and labor still unorganized; and finally, though in what seems a diminishing degree, an inequality of power as between the Federal and the State governments on the one hand, and certain groups of private citizens on the other. Inequity and iniquity, let us remember, once meant the same thing, and still come from the same root.

There are Americans known to me, and they are many, who truly perceive and unhesitatingly declare that the nation to which they owe allegiance is not a material thing, but a spiritual principle in which past and present have a place. From the past comes a rich bequest of memories and traditions, which should arouse and strengthen in the present a will to make effective for all the heritage received as an undivided unity. This truth is not diluted by the fact that the American people come of many and differing racial elements, that they are mixed of varying kins, or breeds, or stocks. The conception of the nation as "an ideal unit founded on the race," was long since decried by Lord Acton, who wrote prophetically of what we see today—how a sovereign people, professing to be a race as well as a people, might become a dangerous instrument of centralizing tyranny, defying both the history of the past and the local feelings and religious associations of the present, subverting traditional rights and the liberty of worship. What is there in heterogeneity that should dismay us, when we reflect that the world's civilizations have arisen only in areas of mixed population? The only homogeneity worth desiring or striving for is not an accident of blood, but a guarantee of equality of opportunity and of equality under the law. To be the citizen of a nation homogeneous in this sense is the produest of boasts, and it rests with Americans to keep their pride beyond the fear of challenge.

The "democracy" which this and my own and other nations are so fond of vaunting, is not a system of government, for politics does not make democracy—it expresses it. Democracy is in its essence a state of mind; that state of mind in each individual which recognizes and pays scrupulous honor to the essential dignity of the other human being, no matter what his status or condition, his "race, color, or previous condition of servitude." The social and political institutions which we establish are worth nothing unless they make a body wherein that state of mind may fitly dwell. Have we anywhere—here or elsewhere—yet built such an habitation for the spirit of democracy? Not yet. Nor shall we build it if we think of democracy as a freedom granted to each man to set his own interest first rather than an obligation to set above personal interest something higher: the interest of the community. There is no place in our time, there is no longer any place in the United States, for the "rugged individual," considered as a lonely embodiment of ruthless will and physical strength. It is not upon these qualities, any more than upon material possessions, that the history of civilized man and of his civilization must depend. It is upon the primary quality of man, which is his social quality—his capacity for living and working adequately with other men, adjusting his mind to theirs, maintaining certain faith and unbroken loyalty, despising cruelty and ensuing justice. In service to others individuality has its finest flowering. "If you love and serve men," said Ralph Waldo Emerson in one of the noblest of his utterances, "you can never, by any hiding or stratagem, escape the remuneration."

Here is a faith in which every American should live, and the more fully he lives for it the less chance there will be that he should have to die for it. I cannot say that I learned this faith wholly in the United States, but my life here has enriched it, out of something rare and indestructible in the American tradition which is the hope of the future. The world would be a sorry place indeed if this hope could find a breathing-place only in the United States, but true it is that there are few lands in which the possibility of economic freedom is so bright. "Without economic freedom," said a writer in *The Freeman,* which is unhappily no longer published for our delight, "no other freedom is significant or lasting . . . if economic freedom be attained, no other freedom can be withheld." This truth is winning to acceptance, however slowly. We walk, as Vaihinger said, by a series of regulated errors, a perpetual succession of falls to one and the other side, and so it is with the march of the truth that economic freedom is the very life-blood of social justice, and that morality and social justice are one and indivisible.

# WHO'S WHO OF THE CONTRIBUTORS

BARZUN, JACQUES, was born in 1907 at Creteil, France, in the literary colony known as the Abbaye de Creteil, associated in modern French literature with the names of Duhamel, Jules Romains, and the author's father, H. Martin-Barzun. Barzun attended the Lycee Janson de Sailly in Paris through 1920, when he came to this country to rejoin his father, sent here on a government mission in 1918. He went to Columbia and took three degrees, A.B., M.A., and a Ph.D. in 1932. Besides reviewing books for *The Herald Tribune* and *The Nation,* he has had lectureships at Bennington, Sarah Lawrence, and Briarcliffe. He has been a member of the History Department at Columbia since 1928. He is the author of *The French Race—Theories of Its Origins* (1932).

BLIVEN, BRUCE, was born July 17, 1889, at Emmetsburg, Iowa. He was graduated from Stanford University in 1911. He was on the editorial staff of *The San Francisco Bulletin* from 1909–12. From 1912–14 he was an advertising writer and wrote many magazine articles. From 1914–16 he was a director of the Department of Journalism at the University of Southern California. He was on the editorial staff of *Printer's Ink* from 1916–18. He then became successively chief editorial writer, magazine editor, and associate editor of *The New York Globe* until 1923. From 1923–30 he was managing editor of *The New Republic* and has been president and editor since 1930. He has been New York correspondent for *The Manchester Guardian* since 1927. He is a director of the Twentieth Century Fund and of the Foreign Policy Association of the United States. He is a lecturer, belongs to the Town Hall Club, and lives in New York City.

BOGAN, LOUISE, was born August 11, 1897, at Livermore Falls, Maine. She was educated in New England schools, including the Girls' Latin School in Boston, and one year of study at Boston University. Her first book of poetry, *Body of This Death,* was published in 1923; she began to do reviewing in the same year. She has published two later books of verse: *Dark Summer* (1929) and *The Sleeping Fury* (1937). She won *Poetry's* John Reed Memorial Prize in 1920, and the Helen Haire Levinson Prize, given by the same magazine, in 1937. She was awarded a Guggenheim Fellowship in 1935. She has contributed verse and prose to *The New Republic,*

*Poetry, Scribner's, The Nation,* and *The Atlantic Monthly.* She has reviewed books of verse for *The New Yorker* since 1931. She lives in New York.

BURLINGAME, ROGER, was born in 1889, in New York City. He prepared for college at the Morristown, N. J., School, 1905–9, and was graduated from Harvard, where he specialized in scientific and engineering courses, in 1913. He worked on the editorial staff of *The Independent* during the editorship of Hamilton Holt, and joined the staff of Charles Scribner's Sons, publishers, in 1914, as advertising manager. He served through the World War as first lieutenant, 308th Machine Gun Battallion, A. E. F. After the war he rejoined the staff of Charles Scribner's Sons, acting as an editor until 1926. He is the author of *March of the Iron Men: A Social History of Union through Invention; Peace Veterans;* and of the novels, *You Too, Susan Shane, High Thursday, The Heir, Cartwheels,* and *Three Bags Full,* and of numerous magazine articles.

CALVERTON, VICTOR F., was born in 1900, at Baltimore, Md. He studied at Baltimore City College and was graduated from Johns Hopkins in 1921. In 1923 he founded, and has since been the editor of *The Modern Quarterly* (now *The Modern Monthly*), and he also edits the book review department of *Book League Monthly.* He is a lecturer on sociology and history. He is the author of *The Newer Spirit, Sex Expression in Literature, The Bankruptcy of Marriage, Three Strange Lovers, The New Ground of Criticism, American Literature at the Crossroads, The Liberation of American Literature, For Revolution, The Passing of the Gods, The Man Inside, The Making of Man,* and editor of *An Anthology of American Negro Literature.*

CANTWELL, ROBERT, was born January 31, 1908, at Little Falls, Washington. He attended the University of Washington for one year. He worked at various jobs throughout the West after 1924: in a veneer factory; in a wholesale house in San Francisco; and on a pipe-line construction crew in Texas. His first story was published in *The American Caravan* in 1929. Thereafter he contributed to several publications, including *The Nation, The New Republic, Vanity Fair, The New Outlook, Scribner's,* etc., and worked on the staffs of *The New Republic* and *Fortune.* His first novel, *Laugh and Sit Down,* in 1931, was followed by *The Land of Plenty,* in 1934. His third novel, *The Enchanted City,* is soon to be published. He is married, has two children, lives in New York City. At present he is an associate editor of *Time.*

CHAFEE, ZECHARIAH, Jr., was born December 7, 1885, in Providence, R. I. He prepared for college at Hope Street High School, Providence, was graduated from Brown University, A.B. (1907), LL.D. (1937); Harvard University, LL.B. (1913); St. John's University, Brooklyn, LL.D. (1936). He is the author of *Freedom of Speech* (1920); *The Inquiring Mind* (1928); Chapter on Law in *Civilization in the United States* (1922); Legal Introduction to *Suffolk County Court Records 1671-1680* (1933); *State House versus Pent House: Legal Problems of the Rhode Island Racetrack Row* (1937); *The Constitutional Convention That Never Met* (1938). He has also edited several casebooks on Equity and the Fourth Edition of Brennan's *Negotiable Instruments Law, Annotated.* He has written numerous technical articles in legal periodicals, and several articles explaining legal problems in *The New Republic, The Nation, Harpers, The Atlantic,* and other magazines and is the author of several articles in the *Encyclopedia of Social Sciences* and the *Dictionary of American Biography.* He was the draftsman of the Federal Interpleader Act, of 1936. He was a member of the Committee on Lawless Enforcement of Law, reporting to the Wickersham Commission on the third degree, etc. He is the author of a verse translation of *Pervigilium Veneris,* of a letter to Secretary Morgenthau on Savings Bonds and he was the principal draftsman of a statement of Harvard professors on behalf of Alfred E. Smith (1928). He is interested in carefully worked-out law reforms. In politics, he writes: "I value thorough workmanship as well as vision. Therefore, I detest Republican policies and Democratic methods." He has been a member of the Rhode Island Bar since 1914. He was associated with Tillinghast & Collins, attorneys, Providence (1913-16 and 1922-25). He was Assistant Professor, Harvard Law School (1916-19) and Professor of Law since 1919. He became Langdell Professor of Law in 1938. He is a lecturer at summer sessions at Columbia and Chicago and a director of Builders Iron Foundry, Providence. He married Bess Searle Chafee in 1912 and has four children.

CHAMBERLAIN, JOHN, was born October 28, 1903, in New Haven, Conn. He was graduated from Yale in 1925, Ph.B. He was a daily book columnist on *The New York Times* from 1933-36, and is now a staff writer on *Fortune,* and a monthly contributor to *Scribner's* for which he writes the Book Review section. He has lectured on modern fiction at the New School for Social Research, and on book reviewing at the Columbia School of Journalism. He is the author of *Farewell to Reform, Critique of Humanism,* and an essay, "Drift and Mastery in our Novelists." He also wrote the essay on Theodore Dreiser for Malcolm Cowley's symposium, "After the Genteel Tradition."

CHENEY, SHELDON, was born in 1886, in Berkeley, California. He was graduated from the University of California, B.A., took a brief post-graduate course at Harvard University, and was an Honorary Fellow in Art at

Union College, 1938–39. He was the founder and first editor of *Theatre Arts Magazine,* and has been a contributor to many art and general periodicals, encyclopedias, etc. He collected and edited Isadora Duncan's essays, under the title, *The Art of the Dance.* He is a lecturer and is the author of *A World History of Art, A Primer of Modern Art, Expressionism in Art, The Theatre: 3000 Years of Drama, Acting, and Stagecraft, The New World Architecture,* and co-author with Martha Chandler Cheney of *Art and the Machine.*

CLENDENING, LOGAN, was born May 25, 1884, in Kansas City, Missouri. He was a student at the University of Michigan, 1902–05; M.D., University of Kansas, 1907. He was an instructor in internal medicine, Medical Department, University of Kansas, 1910–17, associate professor of medicine, 1920–28, and has been professor of clinical medicine since 1928. He was president, St. Luke's Hospital Staff, 1922–23, major, Medical Corps, chief of medical service, base hospital, Fort Sam Houston, 1917–19, fellow, American College of Physicians (board of governors, 1926–30; board of regents, 1931), American Therapeutic Society; American Climatol. and Clin. Association. He is the author of *Modern Methods of Treatment, The Human Body, The Care and Feeding of Adults,* and *Behind the Doctor.* He lives in Kansas City.

COWLES, JOHN, was born December 14, 1898, in Algona, Iowa. He is a graduate of Phillips Exeter Academy, Exeter, New Hampshire (1917), of which school he is now a trustee. Graduated from Harvard College (A.B. *cum laude*) in 1920, as of 1921. He is president of *The Minneapolis Star,* vice-president of *The Des Moines Register and Tribune,* vice-president of the picture magazine, *Look,* and vice-president of several newspaper-affiliated radio stations. He is also a director of The Associated Press, and has been active in other newspaper organizations. He currently maintains homes in both Minneapolis and Des Moines, and commutes frequently between them and New York.

DOUGLASS, H. PAUL, was born January 4, 1871, in Osage, Iowa. He was graduated from Grinnell College, Grinnell, Iowa, A.B. and M.A.; Andover Theological Seminary; Harvard University (post-graduate year). He is secretary of the Commission for the Study of Christian Unity of the Federal Council of Churches, 297 Fourth Avenue, New York City, and was formerly professor of philosophy, Drury College; secretary, American Missionary Association; research director of the Institute of Social and Religious Research; director, China Fact-Finding Staff, Laymen's Foreign Missionary Inquiry. He was a member of the Commission on The Church's Unity in Life and Worship, of the World Conference of Faith and Order. He participated in the Oxford and Edinburgh World Conferences, 1937, and prepared a report, "A Decade of Objective Progress in Church Unity, 1927–1937," for the Edinburgh Conference. He is the author of *Christian Reconstruction in the South, The New Home Missions, The Little Town, The St. Louis Church Survey, The Suburban Trend, How Shall Country Youth Be Served? The Church in the Changing City, How to Study the City Church, Church Comity, The City's Church, Protestent Cooperation in American Cities, Church Unity Movements in the United States* and co-author with E. de S. Brunner of *The Protestant Church as a Social Institution.*

DUFFUS, R. L., was born July 10, 1888, in Waterbury, Vermont. His mother was a New Englander and his father, a Scotch granite cutter. He was educated in the grade and grammar schools, Williamstown, Vermont; high school, Waterbury, Vermont; worked his way through Stanford University: A.B., 1910; M.A., in history, 1911. He is the author of a number of novels and other books. His acquaintance with small towns was acquired by personal experience in Vermont and California; also by working as a newspaper reporter and editorial writer in California and New York. He has given special attention to American history, economics, education, and sociology, and has visited every State in the Union except Florida. He is at present a member of the editorial staff, *New York Times* and writes also for *Times* "Book Review" and *Times* "Sunday Magazine." In 1938 he received an LL.D. from Middlebury College.

DURSTINE, ROY S., was born December 13, 1889, in Jamestown, North Dakota (when the State was still part of Dakota Territory). He was educated at Lawrenceville School and Princeton University (1908). He is the author of two advertising books, *Making Advertisements,* and *This Advertising Business,* and of *Red Thunder,* an account of a trip in the winter of 1933 to Russia, Germany, and Austria. He has been president of the advertising firm of Batten, Barton, Durstine & Osborn since 1928. In 1925–26 he was president of the American Association of Advertising Agencies— the youngest man who had ever held that office. In 1936 he received the first individual award for radio given by the jury of the Annual Advertising Awards, "for recognition of his distinguished contribution to the knowledge and technique of radio advertising." At Princeton Mr. Durstine wrote and played in the annual shows of the Triangle Club, and was editor of *The Princeton Tiger.* In those days it was the ambition of every youngster with newspaper leanings to get on the staff of *The New York Sun.* To *The Sun* went Durstine in 1908. For that famous newspaper in his very first summer he won the enviable assignment of "covering" President Taft at his summer home in Beverly, Massachusetts. He left

*The Sun* in 1912 to do publicity work for Theodore Roosevelt's "Bull Moose" campaign—and that led him into advertising. He was with Calkins & Holden until, in 1914, he and the late James G. Berrien went into partnership as Berrien & Durstine. In 1919 he and two other young men—Bruce Barton and Alex F. Osborn—organized the firm of Barton, Durstine & Osborn, which merged with the George Batten Company under the name of Batten, Barton, Durstine & Osborn.

FLYNN, JOHN T., was born in 1882, at Bladensburgh, Maryland. He was educated in the parochial schools in New York City and Georgetown University, Washington, D. C. He was reporter and city editor of *The New Haven Register* from 1916 to 1918, city editor of *The New York Globe* in 1920, and managing editor of *The New York Globe* from 1920 to 1923. He has been a columnist for *The New Republic* since 1931. He was an adviser to the U. S. Senate Committee on Banking and Currency in the investigation of the Stock Exchange in 1933, 1934, and economic adviser to U. S. Senate Committee investigating munitions, 1934-35. He is a member of the Board of Higher Education in the City of New York, and lectured in contemporary economics at the New School of Social Research in 1935. He is the author of many magazine articles, and of *Investment Trusts Gone Wrong, Graft in Business, God's Gold,* and *Security Speculation—Its Economic Effects.*

GAUSS, CHRISTIAN, was born February 2, 1878, in Ann Arbor, Michigan. He was educated in the public schools and the University of Michigan, A.B. 1898; A.M. (1899). Later studied in Paris. He has received honorary degrees from several institutions, including Lehigh and Michigan. He is the author of *Through College on Nothing a Year, Life in College,* and *A Primer for Tomorrow* and many magazine articles on educational subjects. In addition to academic duties (especially in the Department of Modern Languages) he has been dean of the College of Princeton University since 1925. Since 1934 he has also had general supervision of Princeton athletics. He has lectured at the University of Cincinnati, Columbia University, New York University, and other colleges. He is a member of the editorial board of *The American Scholar,* and a Senator of Phi Beta Kappa. He is now working on a study of the historians and the part they have played in developing chauvinistic nationalism. He feels that the time has come when we must take more seriously to heart the old Aristotelian statement, "Great poetry is truer than history."

HALLGREN, MAURITZ A., was born June 18, 1899, in Chicago, Illinois. He was educated in the Chicago public schools and the University of Chicago. He is the author of *Seeds of Revolt, The Gay Reformer,* and *The Tragic*

*Fallacy*. He is a newspaperman, writer, and dairy farmer. He has served as a Washington and European correspondent, as associate editor of *The Nation* from 1930 to 1933, and as associate editor of *The Baltimore Sun* from 1933 to 1938. Besides his longer works, he has written extensively on politics and economics for the reviews both in this country and abroad. He is now engaged in farming and occasional writing, and is taking an active part in Democratic Party politics in Maryland. The study of war and peace policies has been a specialty with him ever since he was first assigned to cover the State Department and the War Department for the United Press a few years after the last war. His most recent book, *The Tragic Fallacy,* is the product of fifteen years of research and study in this field.

HAMILTON, WALTON H., was born in Tennessee in 1881. He was graduated from the University of Texas in 1907, and received the degree of Ph.D. from the University of Michigan in 1913. After teaching at the Universities of Michigan and Chicago, he became Olds Professor of Economics in Amherst College in 1915. He was formerly associate editor of *The Journal of Political Economy,* and is associate editor of the series, "Materials for the Study of Economics," published by the University of Chicago Press. During the World War he was on the staff of the War Labor Policies Board. He is co-editor with J. M. Clark and H. G. Moulton of *Readings in the Economics of War,* and the author of *Current Economic Problems* and of various articles in economic journals.

HASKELL, DOUGLAS, turned in 1924 to the study of modern architecture when the Gothic of the Harkness Memorial Buildings at Yale, seen on the return from a trip to Europe, struck him as absurd. He pursued his study of modern architecture and modern architects as assistant editor of *Creative Art* and later *The Architectural Record*. He is a frequent contributor to the magazines on architectural subjects. In 1930, when architectural editors were afraid to publish criticism because sporadic attempts had brought about the libel suits possible in this art field alone, Mr. Haskell persuaded the editors of *The Nation* to assign him a monthly column on architecture, which thus dissipated the bugaboo and established the precedent for regular architectural criticism in the magazines. Not being a registered architect, Mr. Haskell is modest about his "amateur standing" but thinks that it has positive value in freeing the judgment from considerations of professional interest.

KENNEDY, E. D., was born January 5, 1901, in Springfield, Mass. He was graduated from Boston Latin School, 1901, and the University of Cincinnati, 1922. For six years—1922 to 1928—he wrote advertising copy in

Cincinnati, Cleveland, and New York. He joined the staff of the magazine, *Time,* in 1928, when until December, 1929, he wrote the Business and Financial section. At present he is working on a book to be published this fall which is a general study of American Industry. He belongs to the Newspaper Guild and the League of American Writers. He has published articles in *Fortune* running to over 100,000 words a year.

KIERAN, JOHN, was born August 2, 1892, in New York City. He was graduated from Fordham University, 1912, Bachelor of Science, *cum laude.* He is the author of *The Story of the Olympic Games,* and numerous articles on sports and natural history. He is much interested in art, music, and natural history (twenty-five years a member of the Linnæa Society, American Museum of Natural History). He is sports columnist (NOT sports editor), *New York Times.* He states that all other facts are irrelevant. Such as, that he has forgotten a vast amount of German, remembers a little Latin, plays the piano by ear, and can read French at sight. He also pleads guilty to having committed much light verse.

KRUTCH, JOSEPH WOOD, was born in 1893, in Knoxville, Tennessee. He graduated from University of Tennessee in 1915; M.A. and Ph.D. degrees from Columbia University. He was an instructor in English at Columbia 1917–18, a travelling fellow in 1919–20, and associate professor in the School of Journalism from 1925–31. From 1920–23 he was associate professor of English at the Polytechnic Institute of Brooklyn. From 1924 to 1932 he was dramatic critic and associate editor of *The Nation,* and has been a member of the board of editors since 1932. He was a special lecturer with the rank of professor at Vassar College in 1924–25, and since 1932 has been a lecturer at the New School for Social Research. He is the author of *Comedy and Conscience after the Restoration, Edgar Allan Poe—A Study in Genius, The Modern Temper, Five Masters, Experience and Art,* and *Was Europe a Success?*

LEWIS, SIR WILLMOTT, K.B.E. cr. 1931, was born June 18, 1877, at Cardiff, S.E. Wales. He was educated at Eastbourne, and on the Continent of Europe. He worked as journalist in England, France, China, Japan, Korea, Philippine Islands, and the United States. He was in the Far East through the period which included abolition of exterritoriality in Japan, the Boxer Rebellion, the announcement of Anglo-Japanese Alliance, and the Russo-Japanese War. He served in the World War in France, 1917–19. He has been correspondent of *The Times* in Washington since 1920.

MENNINGER, KARL A., M.D., was born in 1893, at Topeka, Kansas. He received his A.B. degree from the University of Wisconsin, 1914; his M.S. degree from the University of Wisconsin, 1915; and his M.D. degree from the Harvard Medical School, 1917. He is the author of *The Human Mind*, which is a book that sums up the views of modern psychiatry about the human personality. In 1930, he and Nelson Antrim Crawford edited *The Healthy-Minded Child*, a symposium for parents and educators. Other writings by Doctor Menninger include a contribution to the book, *Why Men Fail*, and the more technical volume, *Schizophrenia*. Also fifty or more papers published in scientific and medical journals. His latest work is *Man Against Himself*. This book deals with the destructive urges of mankind. For fifteen years Doctor Menninger has been professor of mental hygiene, abnormal psychology, and criminology at Washburn College, in Topeka. He organized the Kansas State Mental Hygiene Society, and is a member of the board of directors of this organization. Doctor Menninger is at present associated with his father, Doctor Charles F. Menninger; his brother, Doctor William C. Menninger, and eleven other physicians in the Menninger Clinic, Topeka, Kansas, where he serves as chief-of-staff. In connection with this clinic these men, assisted by a large staff of clinical assistants and therapists, administer the Menninger Sanitarium for nervous and mental diseases, and the Southard School. Doctor Menninger's professional organizations include the American Medical Association, the American Psychiatric Association, the American Psychoanalytic Association, the Topeka Psychoanalytic Society, the Central Neuropsychiatric Association, and the American Orthopsychiatric Association. The last three named he helped to organize, and he is a charter member. His hobbies are horticulture and music.

PARSONS, ELSIE CLEWS, was graduated from Barnard College in 1896, and received the degree of Ph.D. from Columbia University in 1899. She has been Fellow and Lecturer in Sociology at Barnard College, Lecturer in Anthropology in the New School of Social Research, assistant editor of *The Journal of American Folk-Lore*, treasurer of the American Ethnological Society, and president of the American Folk-Lore Society. She is married and the mother of four children. Among her books are *The Family; The Old-Fashioned Woman; Fear and Conventionality; Social Freedom*, and *Social Rule*.

REID, LOUIS R., was born in Warsaw, N. Y. He was educated at Phillips-Exeter and Rutgers University and has been engaged in newspaper and magazine work since graduation. He was editor for three years of the *Dramatic Mirror*, a famous theatre periodical which was founded by Harrison Grey Fiske. Next came a three years period of publicity work for Messrs. Shubert enterprises. For the last twelve years he has been associated with the Hearst organization. He conducted a column, "The Loudspeaker" for several years on *The New York American,* and is a frequent contributor to magazines. At present he is advertising and publicity manager of Cosmopolitan Productions and News of the Day. He is co-author of *Civilization in the United States,* contributing chapter "The Small Town."

Scott, Evelyn, was born January 17, 1893, in Clarksville, Tennessee. She went to Newcomb College, Tulane University, and also attended Newcomb College of Art. She has contributed criticisms and poetry to a variety of magazines and anthologies, beginning with *The London Outlook* and the old *Dial,* in 1920. She is the author of a three-act play, "Love," produced by the Provincetown Players, 1921 season, and of a mystery novel called *Blue Rum* published under a pseudonym—Ernest Souza—which was popular in France as well as in America. She has published two books of poetry, *Precipitations* and *The Winter Alone,* two autobiographical volumes, *Escapade* and *Background in Tennessee,* and the following novels: *The Narrow House, Narcissus, The Golden Door, Migrations, Ideals, The Wave, A Calendar of Sin, Eva Gay, Breathe upon These Slain,* and *Bread and a Sword.* She is also the author of three juveniles: *In the Endless Sands, Witch Perkins,* and *Billy, the Maverick.* She is a Southerner by birth and upbringing, and lived from 1913 to the end of 1919 in Brazil, from which she returned for a year and a half in New York. Between then and 1936 she lived in Bermuda, France, Algeria, Portugal, and England, with the interlude of a year in New Mexico. She was the recipient of a Guggenheim award in 1932. She began a study both of Karl Marx and of Socialism as early as 1910.

Soule, George, was born June 11, 1887, in Stamford, Connecticut. He was graduated from Yale, A.B., 1908. Since 1923 he has been an editor of *The New Republic.* He is the author of *A Planned Society, The Useful Art of Economics, The Coming American Revolution,* and *The Future of Liberty.* He taught economics in the Columbia University Summer School, 1932 and 1934. He was formerly director of the Labor Bureau, Inc.; a worker in economic research; a member of the staff investigating the steel strike of 1919, of the Interchurch World Movement; a member of the special commission investigating the possibilities of better rural organization of the South, for the Reclamation Bureau of the Department of the Interior. He is now chairman of the Board of the National Bureau of Economic Research, and a trustee of the National Economic and Social Planning Association. He is lecturer of the Sterling Foundation at the Yale Law School.

Stark, Louis, was born May 1, 1888, in Austria-Hungary. He was educated in the New York public schools, New York Training School for Teachers

(1909), Reed College, Portland, Oregon, LL.D. (Honorary, 1937). He is a contributor to many magazines on subjects allied with organized labor and labor relations, and is interested in making available to laymen news of progress in the field of the social sciences. In 1931 he made a study for *The New York Times* of conditions in Harlan County, now being exposed again in the London, Kentucky, trials. Since 1923 he has covered most of the important strikes and labor disputes in the country and has attended most of the A. F. of L. conventions in the last fifteen years. He is acquainted with most of the leading labor leaders and industrialists. From 1923 to 1933 he studied and reported economic labor, and social problems—and the conferences concerning them. When the NIRA was enacted in 1933 he was sent to Washington by *The New York Times* to cover the bituminous coal code negotiations. He was sent for three weeks—but is still there. He is trained to understand the trade, economic, and labor viewpoints rather than the purely political one.

STEARNS, HAROLD E., was born May 7, 1891, in Barre, Massachusetts. He prepared for college at Attleboro and Malden High Schools (Massachusetts) and was graduated from Harvard, A.B. (1913) *cum laude* in philosophy. Publications: *Liberalism in America* (New York: Liveright, 1919); *America and the Young Intellectual* (New York: Doran, 1920); editor, *Civilization in the United States* (New York: Harcourt, Brace, 1922; London, Jonathan Cape); *Rediscovering America* (New York: Liveright, 1934); *The Street I Know,* autobiography (New York: Lee Furman, 1935); *America—A Re-appraisal* (New York: Hillman-Curl, Inc., 1937). Special interests, outside regular work of writing, editing, and reporting, are trotting racing, gardening, the poetry of Walt Whitman (who was born not far from where Stearns now lives on Long Island), statistical studies in gambling (particularly on horse-races), television, French politics and literature (for I lived thirteen years in Paris), and American history. Has a morbid interest in baseball and murder trials. Present interest: Preparing a book on American foibles—from trick gadgets and zippers to self-help and religious revivals. Doing so perhaps as an antidote, or comic backdrop, to the long and serious work demanded in getting out this volume.

STONE, DOCTOR HANNAH M., was born in New York in 1893, and received both her formal and professional education in that city. She received a degree in Pharmacy in 1912, took premedical work at Columbia University, and obtained her medical degree from the New York Medical College and Flower Hospital in 1920. Doctor Stone has taken an active part in the birth-control movement and is one of its pioneers in this country. For the past fifteen years she has been associated with Margaret Sanger as the medical director of the Birth Control Clinical Research Bureau. She has lectured widely on sex education, marriage hygiene and contraception, and her articles on these subjects have appeared both in medical and in lay journals. With Margaret Sanger, Doctor Stone was the editor of a volume on *The Practice of Contraception,* and she is the co-author of *A Marriage Manual,* a standard textbook on sex and marriage. She is also medical director of the Marriage Consultation Center of the Community Church, New York.

TALBOT, FRANCIS X., S. J. Because of the topic treated, the Catholic emphasis may be pardoned in this biographical note. Francis X. Talbot was born in Philadelphia, a little more than forty-nine years before he wrote the chapter in this book. He came to the home of parents who were more pious Catholics than he has ever been, though they never knew as much—intellectually—about Catholicism as he has learned. He was given his early culture in a parish school by gentle and clever nuns belonging to the Society of the Holy Child Jesus. They paved the way of his progress to the Jesuits who conducted St. Joseph's College. Eventually, in a few years, he decided to renounce the world for the spirit, and entered the Society of Jesus. During twelve years of training, his brain was stocked with the ancient and modern classic literature, with good philosophy and science, and with all the results of twenty centuries' conclusions on matters theological. Some of his knowledge he manifested in teaching at Loyola School, New York, and at Boston College. In 1923 he became the literary editor of *America,* the National Catholic Review of the Week. In 1936 he was named editor-in-chief, and continues as such. At the same time he became editor-in-chief of *Thought,* a quarterly of the arts and sciences. In the course of years he has written innumerable (to him) articles, stories, and what-not for his own and other periodicals. He has also issued anthologies of poetry and collections of prose. He has written a few books, the most ambitious being *Saint Among Savages* (New York: Harper's), a biography of the American martyr, Isaac Jogues. He contributed to the *Encyclopedia Britannica* (1936) and to the *Encyclopedia Britannica Year Book* (1938). He spends his leisure lecturing and preaching in widespread areas. Besides writing and talking, he has been an active promoter of Catholic progress. For many years he was the chaplain of the Motion Picture Bureau of the I. F. C. A. (now Legion of Decency), and trustee of the United States Catholic Historical Society. Under his inspiration was founded the Catholic Book Club, the Spiritual Book Associates, and the Pro Parvulis Book Club—all book-of-the-month organizations. He was also a co-founder of the Catholic Poetry Society of America, the largest collection of poets in the country. As for degrees, he has those which precede the Ph.D., and some which follow, such as honorary degree of Doctor of Literature, first from his Alma Mater, St. Joseph's College, and—last

June—from Boston College. In all his works and words, no matter what the subject may be, he concerns himself with the inherent or the correlated Catholicism that may be found in it.

TAYLOR, DEEMS, was born December 22, 1885, in New York. He was educated in the New York Public Schools, Ethical Culture School, New York University. Degrees: B.A., N. Y. U. (1906); Mus.D., *ibid.* (1927); Litt.D., Juniata College (1930). He published critical articles in *The New York World,* 1921–25; *McCall's,* 1926–31; *The New York American,* 1931–32; *Stage,* 1932–38; *Vanity Fair,* 1926–35. He is the author of *Of Men and Music* and of a chapter on Music in the first *Civilization.* He is consultant on music to Columbia Broadcasting System, and intermission commentator, broadcast concerts of the New York Philharmonic Symphony Orchestra since 1936. He has composed songs, choral pieces and arrangements, and orchestral works, including "Through the Looking-Glass," "Jurgen," "Circus Day," chamber music, incidental music for nine plays, including "Beggar on Horseback," "Liliom," and "Casanova"; grand operas—"The King's Henchman," "Peter Ibbetson" (both commissioned by the Metropolitan Opera Association), and "Ramuntcho" (now nearing completion).

VALLE, RAFAEL HELIODORO, was born July 3, 1891, at Tegucigalpa. He was educated at the National School for Teachers of Mexico City, and graduated in 1911. He was Honduran consul in Belize, 1915–16; secretary of the special Honduran missions to Washington (on the boundary question with Guatamala), 1918, 1920, 1931; of the special Honduran mission in Mexico, 1921. He was head of the Department of Publications of the National Museum, and head of the Section on Bibliography of the Secretariat of Public Education, Mexico City, 1921–25. He worked on the editorial staff of *El Universal* of Mexico City, 1922; and of *Excelsior* of Mexico City, since 1923. He is associate editor of *The Hispanic American Historical Review* of Durham, North Carolina; contributor to *La Prensce* of Buenos Aires, *La Prenza* of San Antonio, Texas, *La Opinion* of Los Angeles, California, *Diario de la Marina,* and *Social* of Havana, *El Impurcial* of Guatemala, *El Cronista* of Tegucigalpa, *El Commercio* of Quito, and *La Bibliografia* of Mexico City. He was formerly director of *El Libro y el Pueblo* of Mexico City. He is professor in the National Preparatory School of Mexico City, and technical director of the Editorial González Porto of Mexico City. He is a member of *Sociedad de Geografia e Historia* of Honduras, *Sociedad de Geografia e Historia* of Guatemala, *Sociedad Mexicana de Geografia y Estadistica, Academica Nacional de Ciencias* "Antonio Alzate" of Mexico City, *Sociedad Cientifica Argentina, Junita de Historia y Numismatica Americana* of Buenos Aires, Bibliographical Society of America, Quivira Society, Geographical Societies of Lima, La Paz, and Quito. He was decorated by the Order of the Sun of Peru. He is the author of: *El risal del erimtano,* 1911; *Como la luz del dia,* 1913; *Corno era Iturbide,* 1921; *El convento de Tepozotian,* 1924; *San Bartolone de las Casas, La anexión de Centro America a Mexico* (1921–27), *Diplomático Mexicano, Mexico* (1921–27); *Hubiera sedienta* (poems) (1922), *Indice de escritores* (1928) with E. Velázquez; Co-editor of the *Enciclopedia illustrada hispano-americana.*

WENDT, GERALD, was born March 3, 1891, in Davenport, Iowa. He was graduated from Harvard University, degrees of A.B. (1913), of A.M. (1914), and of Ph.D. (1916). He is the author of *Matter and Energy* (a college textbook), which was one of the first attempts at a survey of this field for nontechnical students. He has reviewed books on science for the book section of *The New York Herald Tribune* since 1925. He has also written a large number of technical research papers for scientific journals and a large number of popular articles for numerous magazines. His present work is that of Director of the Department of Science of the New York World's Fair. Until recently he was Director of The American Institute of the City of New York, an organization founded in 1828 and devoted to the integration of science with social progress. He does a considerable amount of professional lecturing and his topics for 1939 will include: "The Science Revue, 1939," "Life in the Age of Science," and "Science Behind the News."

YUTANG, LIN, was born in 1895, in Changchow, Fukien Province, China. He was educated in mission schools and went to St. John's College, Shanghai. After being graduated from St. John's, he became a teacher of English at Tsinghua, the American Boxer Indemnity College. He then married and came to America, where he studied at Harvard for a year, and then went to Germany, where he studied at Jena and Leipzig. He returned to China and was at once appointed a professor at the Peking National University, where he served from 1923 to 1926. He was counted among the radical professors, took part in student demonstrations and fought the police with poles and bricks, which he says gave him a good opportunity for practicing baseball throws which he had missed in his American college life. His name was finally put on a black list of radical professors and he had to spend a month in hiding, at first in the French Hospital in the legation quarters, and then in the home of a friend. His ardor for the rebellion, which was then stirring China, led him, under the inspiration of Eugene Chen, to join the new Wuham Government as secretary in the Ministry of Foreign Affairs. Lin Yutang is the author of *My Country and My People* and is one of the best-known scholars and writers of China, being notable particularly for his complete grasp of the English language. He is the author of a number of textbooks on English which are used in the Chinese schools and is the editor or a member of the editorial staff of five magazines, two in the English language, and three in Chinese.

# INDEX